*Princes Under the Volcano*

By the same author

THE FORTRESS
A HERMIT DISCLOSED
THE BIG TOMATO

# PRINCES UNDER THE VOLCANO

## RALEIGH TREVELYAN

WILLIAM MORROW & COMPANY, INC.
NEW YORK
1973

Published in the United States in 1973
Copyright © 1972 by Raleigh Trevelyan
Published in Great Britain in 1972

Library of Congress Catalog Card Number 78-182871

Printed in Great Britain
by W & J Mackay Limited, Chatham

# Contents

### PART FIVE: LIVING AS PRINCES

### PART SIX: PRINCES OF FASCISM

### PART SEVEN: IN RETIREMENT

# Illustrations

## ILLUSTRATIONS IN THE TEXT

## MAPS

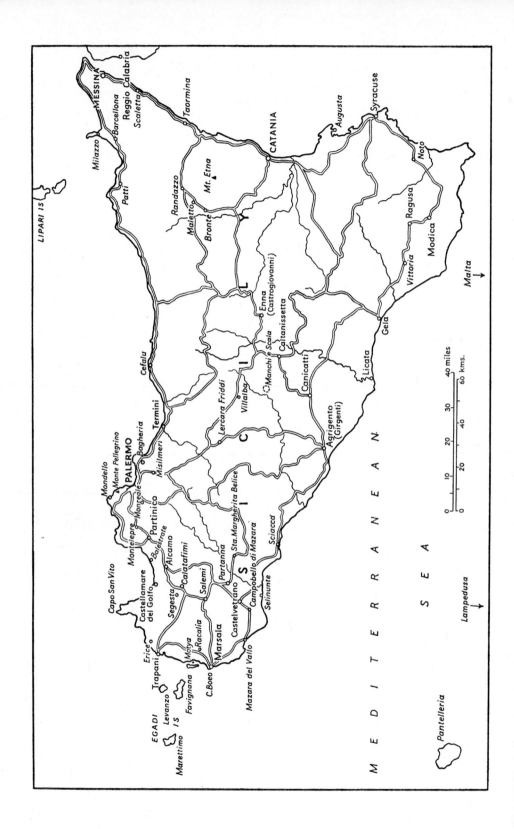

# *Prologue*

I FIRST heard of Tina Whitaker when I was in Rome as a young subaltern in the winter of 1944. Although I remained in Italy for two more years, and although I had known members of the Whitaker family practically all my life, I never actually met her. To me she was a sort of legend, a grand and formidable old lady living up in Monti Parioli, where I would never dare go without a summons. In any case, being just twenty-one when I first arrived, I was probably too busy enjoying my first sight of Rome and going about with Romans of my own age.

I did know that Mrs Whitaker was well into her eighties, and that she had an 'extraordinary' past of some sort. I also knew that she and her two daughters, Norina and Delia, both in late middle age, were living in a state of relative luxury. This last fact was in itself odd. How was it that they, bearing an English name, should have remained unmolested under enemy rule? Gradually, as the years went by, I picked up stories about these Whitakers: their eccentricities, their great wealth originally based on marsala wine, their associations with people such as Garibaldi, Wagner, Empress Eugénie and Queen Mary. Then in 1960 I had a book published about a recluse, Jimmy Mason, who kept a diary and had died at Great Canfield in Essex nearly twenty years before. In the writing of it I found myself taken up with problems of human loneliness and such things as whether any person's life, however quiet and apparently obscure, even tormented, should hold a purpose here on earth. I also became interested in the effect of heredity and environment on an individual. Thus I went to some pains to recreate the atmosphere of the village in Jimmy's most active days. It happened that Mrs Gwen Charlton, born a Whitaker, lived in Great Canfield, and it was she who urged me to consider tackling her aunt Tina's diaries and papers, and to turn them into a book that could be the opposite side of Jimmy's coin: an examination of a very rich and social woman, a published writer, an ambitious mother, with a retiring, scholarly husband, and a person who possessed talent (as a singer) and lived in an exotic setting (Palermo). Tina, moreover, had been born in 1858, the year after the Hermit. Another point was that *The Leopard* had just been published. The Whitakers in Sicily had known the Lampedusa family fairly well, so Tina's diaries would surely illuminate the background to that book.

I was tempted, but declined the suggestion, even though I discussed it with Delia Whitaker. I was too busy then, and – although I knew the Italian mainland – had scarcely visited Sicily. I mentioned that my friend Archibald Colquhoun, the translator of *The Leopard*, would be the ideal person to write about what he called 'the lush international setting of Palermo at the turn of the century'. Indeed Archie was about to start the book when suddenly he died. In May 1964 I had a telegram from Delia Whitaker inviting me to her island of Motya, between Marsala and Trapani. I went there for the day, at the end of which I had agreed to take over from Archie.

This book, or the part of it dealing with Tina, is not quite the antithesis to the one about Jimmy Mason. For instance I have not written the story as a quest. It is much harder to get to grips with the private self of someone like Tina Whitaker, even if one wanted to do so. Jimmy's horizon was limited, his papers were few and the village people I interviewed were mostly unsophisticated, willing to unburden themselves with embarrassing frankness. Sophisticated people are less willing to treat a stranger as a father confessor. In any case what right had I to delve too deeply? Tina's life in a curious way had fewer mysteries to solve than Jimmy's, though at the very end their plights had some parallels. Psychiatrists no doubt will nod their heads over Norina's long, miserable illness; bronchial asthma is often known to start during a period of mental stress, such as when a child is separated from its mother (as in the case of Proust), and Norina's first main attack came when she left home, after her marriage to an ambitious and energetic Sicilian from a different social background.

Tina, although almost brought up as English, was born of Italian and Sicilian parents. I discovered a mass of her papers dealing with her im-mediate ancestors, and this at once involved me in their exploits during the Risorgimento, long before the turn of the century. I also found material on the Italian patriot exiles in London before 1860. Then, more important, there was – for me – the major discovery of some of Benjamin Ingham's business letter-books from 1816 to 1860 that had mercifully been placed in safety at the beginning of the last war. In these letters were first-hand, and therefore perhaps important historically, comments on political and economic news under the Bourbons. So my book has virtually been turned into a two-decker, a kind of saga covering two hundred years, with the first section mostly about the people who made the money and the second about those who spent it. The first is more diffuse and concerned with national and international events, in relation to the Anglo-American community, the second more personal and racy. For the former I have consulted contemporary travellers' descriptions and papers belonging to other British or American families once associated with Marsala, Palermo and Messina, my aim being to recreate as far as possible what it was like to live as an Anglo-Saxon expatriate in Sicily, particularly in the years of revolution and epidemic. Here at least there is some parallel to what I set out to do in my book about Jimmy Mason.

Benjamin Ingham was a participator in events, Tina more of an observer; her comments on politics, though voluminous, are therefore of less value and I have mostly cut them out. He was a leader, she had some capacity as such but underestimated herself, because she knew she was bad at detail. She was fortunate in that she managed to live within her, or rather her husband's, means, unlike some other more reckless beneficiaries of Benjamin Ingham's estate. Both Benjamin Ingham and Tina Whitaker became reactionary in their old age, when before they had been liberal-minded.

The Ingham letter-books form a vast pile. I have only attempted to extract items of general interest, during the most dramatic years up to 1849, just before his retirement. The Garibaldi period has been dealt with as something separate. One day I hope to write a book on the Anglo-American merchants who traded in the Two Sicilies, with Benjamin Ingham as the pivot. For the present I have deliberately avoided too much comment on his commercial affairs, and I have scarcely concerned myself at all with the actual marketing and growing of marsala wine. In any case, because of the Allied bombing of Marsala and Palermo in 1943, a lot of the vital records, particularly about the wine trade and exports to Britain and the United States, are in limbo. The fact that relatively little is known about the day-to-day activities of Ingham's intimate life, except through family word of mouth tradition, does, I realise make for a contrast between the two halves of the book; but that is also my intention.

As an amateur I have stepped with some trepidation into a specialist historian's world. What is more, the history of Sicily can arouse angry emotions. To some it is just a 'sundrenched nightmare', its past and present miseries the direct result of social exploitation, stupidity and waste. Others vehemently refute the 'trotting out of the old saw about absentee landlords'. I have tried to stay impartial in this bloody battlefield of experts. Meekly I point out that my book is mostly about expatriate merchants, some of whom were considerable philanthropists, *nouveaux riches* at first, but *riches* enough to seek friends among the aristocratic families of Palermo. I hope nevertheless that in passing I have given some substance to Lampedusa's famous phrase about the Sicilians, high and low: 'a terrifying insularity of mind'. My aim in this has been to concentrate on the point of view of the observer, or outsider. I would have liked to have had an excuse for writing about baroque churches and Greek temples, the Spanish occupation, the Inquisition, the 1693 earthquake, the Normans and past links with England, slave revolts and so on; but these are outside my main scope. I have had to assume on the part of the reader at least an instinctive knowledge of such things.

Sicily possesses some places of sublime loveliness. It also contains squalor. It can be violent and sinister, or sentimental and soft-hued. Many ghastly acts of cruelty, many disasters have happened there, some quite recently. The island has attracted predators who have come to love and beautify it. It has been described as a cross-roads, a gateway, non-European. Yet it has produced some great Europeans, both in art and politics. In a way it is the most typically Italian part of Italy, with faults and virtues magnified.

At the Colli and Bagheria the crumbling villas of the nobility, with their delicate balustrades and lichened statuary, go far to prove that their eighteenth- and nineteenth-century owners – many of Spanish ancestry as family names such as Valguarnera, Moncada and Monroy show – preferred the delights of the Conca d'Oro to their dusty, sun-parched Donnafugatas. How much though, one asks, of this absenteeism was the fault of sheer neglect by governments in centuries past, and due to the utter lack of roads and to an aversion to the grim, eroded landscapes made barren by the destruction of forests in Roman and Arab times? Meanwhile the wretched peasantry eked out their generations, nurtured in superstition and fear, hardly knowing anything about the world outside.

Etna is on the other side of the island to Palermo, and in a sense plays a small part in this book. Huge, beautiful yet grim, magnificent, proud, treacherous, eternal, it is however a part of every Sicilian's life, the very symbol of sudden death, of unpremeditated violence.

In many ways Sicily is Italy's Ireland, with her separate civilisation, her enigmas, her half-mythologised Christianity, her cussedness, her internal hatreds, her desperate emigrations that stemmed from a monstrous economic system. Again I have had to take it that the reader knows something about, or has access to, the literature on earlier historical and ethnic influences, responsible still for a national way of crime and for so much cruelty, illiteracy and poverty. Enough to say that western Sicilians are of mostly Saracen descent; the eastern, or rather south-eastern, Sicilians have

Greek blood, which somehow means that the *Mafia* has no hold over them.

The book drifts away from Sicily in Tina's time, but that is her doing not mine. Her position in Rome during the last war, as a British subject, was on the face of it more dangerous than that of Inghams or Whitakers in 1848–9 or 1860. In the nineteenth century the British Government always had warships to hand, ready to snatch its nationals on board at the slightest whiff of danger. Ostensibly neutral then, Britain – like America and France – made no secret of the side she favoured. Mercenaries were not only encouraged but sometimes secretly equipped with arms. Thus in 1860 we have the spectacle of expatriate residents in Palermo rushing for safety, while expatriate belligerents pour into the city, only too ready to die for another country's liberty.

If one lives abroad, one can imagine oneself wholly identified with one's hosts' politics, fears, dramas and national rejoicings. But when war comes, one suddenly realises how little one really belongs.

I wish I could have found space for a dissertation on other British wine families, in Bordeaux, Oporto, Jerez, the Canaries and elsewhere. The Empress Eugénie's mother's family, the Kirkpatricks, for example, were wine shippers at Malaga. Some of the port dynasties, such as the Cockburns and the Grahams, dating from 1815 and 1820 respectively, still reign at Oporto. The origin of the British taste for madeira goes back to Catherine of Braganza. Because of foolish import laws, madeira was virtually the only wine shipped to the American colonies in the eighteenth century, and for this reason even now it is considered that there is more appreciation of good madeiras in, say, Boston than anywhere in Britain. In 1793 there were thirty-nine firms of wine shippers in Madeira, twenty-six being British; the garrisons of 1801–2 and 1807–14 also greatly helped the wine's popularity, as did the island's subsequent fame as a winter resort. Names such as Blandy, Reid, Leacock, Cossart and Rutherford are still to be conjured with on the island, and until recently there was a Mrs Blandy who was considered the 'uncrowned queen' and a Noel Cossart the 'king'.

Inghams and Whitakers are of course remembered at Marsala, if only because some brands of wine (now under the aegis of Cinzano) continue to bear their name. Shabby black jalopies hang around the railway station, just as they must have done a hundred years ago. Some streets are cobbled, and there is a strong impression of stepping back in time, of isolation and laxness under a fierce African sun. Yet you have to search hard to find much association with the nineteenth-century British. Unlike Madeira, or Malaga, or Jerez, Marsala is not the sort of place in which an Anglo-Saxon

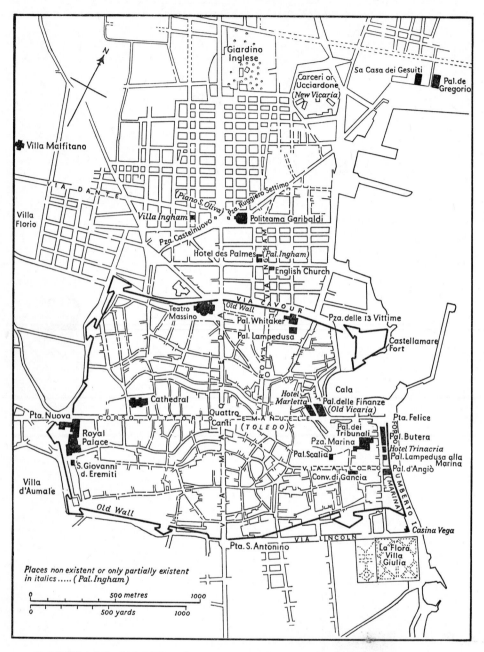

PALERMO AT THE OUTBREAK OF THE FIRST WORLD
WAR

# I

## *The English Croesus of These Parts*

'WE are happy to inform you that His Majesty's troops took quiet possession of the forts in this city yesterday, so that we shall now return to peace and tranquillity after sixteen months of revolutionary misrule with all its evils.'

A bland summing up after a harrowing fortnight, and typical of the unemotional Joseph Whitaker, a British merchant living in Palermo. For him the whole experience could now be neatly bundled up and placed on the filing shelf. In the absence of his 'Senior', Benjamin Ingham, he was writing to his father-in-law and colleague, William Sanderson of Messina, on 19 May 1849. Sicily's brief independence was over. For the past days most Anglo-American families had been sweltering on board warships in Palermo bay, while anarchy gripped the city and 20,000 Neapolitans advanced across the island. Joseph Whitaker had managed to send his wife Sophia and the children to safety in Malta. During the previous year both Palermo and Messina had suffered terrible batterings from King Bomba's men, and both Neapolitans and Sicilians had shown themselves capable of extreme cruelty. As the British were not popular with either side at present, looting and destruction of their property were the least of the dangers that could have been expected.

The anticlimax was in fact almost ridiculous. To show loyalty to the conquerors, the white flag of the Bourbons was paraded along the sea-front by a set of dirty, drunken people, who danced round it as though they were mad. 'The whole scene,' wrote the British Vice-Consul,[1] 'seems more of a bacchanalian feast than one of loyalty.' There was a search for arms, though not a very successful one. Only the 'better class of people' responded, but their faces looked anything but happy. General Filangieri, the commander of the Neapolitan troops, at least seemed disposed to be lenient, and he was known to be a statesmanlike and humane individual. However, the riff-raff of the slums was sullen, and reports poured in of the countryside being overrun with thieves and bandits. A bad earthquake on the nineteenth did not soothe matters. Two blocks of small houses collapsed and sixty people were killed. Not surprisingly Joseph Whitaker decided that the atmosphere in Palermo was far too unsettled for his wife to return.

Sophia was one of those sweet, ringleted Early Victorian women whose main job in married life seems to have been to acquiesce. Her husband usually stayed late in the office, which was next to the Palazzo Lampedusa. He expected dinner to be ready the moment he returned home, and he preferred eating in silence. Undeniably potent-looking in his pictures, over a period of twenty-three years he made her bear him a child on an average every twenty-one months. On 19 June she was allowed back to Palermo. On 19 March 1850 she gave birth to her fourth son, Pip – later to be one of the chief characters in this book, and very different from either of his parents. Although Joseph died a millionaire, it is said that after his death she wistfully remarked that she had always longed to own a brooch.

She herself had been born in Malta in 1816. Her family came from Durham and was possibly related to the Whitakers, who were from Yorkshire. Her father had been a naval captain with a fine war record; in 1817 he had moved to Messina, as much for commercial reasons as for its splendid harbour, the loveliness of its setting and the nobility of its buildings. The town followed the curve of the shore and was at the foot of a range of mountains, part wooded, part covered with vines and olive groves. Across the straits was the incomparable view of the Italian mainland, three miles away. After the 1783 earthquake there had been some ambitious rebuilding. In many ways the harbour was superior to Palermo's, and it was certainly better suited geographically for commerce. William Sanderson traded in essential oils: perfume oils from lemons and bergamot. Other British merchants there dealt mostly in silk and citrus fruit.

Alas, in 1849 all was different and Messina was in a sorry condition. It was reckoned that, as a result of the bombardment the previous September, there had been at least a million pounds' worth of damage, £300,000 of which was to British property. William Sanderson's claim for compensation had been one of the largest. The sanitation of the city was in a disgusting state. Hardly any effort had been made to repair the damage.

Palermo had not suffered nearly as much devastation. Its setting, in the famed Conca d'Oro, or Golden Shell, had a different kind of beauty. Encircled like an amphitheatre by high mountains and dominated by the dramatic bare crag of Monte Pellegrino, the valley in which the domes and towers of the walled city lay was full of delicious gardens, well-watered orange and lemon groves, prickly pear plantations and vineyards. Here were remnants of Arab, Norman and Spanish civilisations, while in front was the vast, blue stretch of the Tyrrhenian Sea. The back streets were narrow and often squalid – the mean houses an extraordinary contrast to the nobles' palaces – but the inhabitants were colourful and vital. Although Messina was traditionally jealous of Palermo as the capital, there was no doubt that Palermo had the aura of a metropolis. The large foreign community, in more peaceful times, was happy here. Many of the British merchants had originally come during the Napoleonic Wars, and had stayed on. The Americans were somewhat fewer and, necessarily because of the 1812 war, had been rather later in arriving.

Palermo and Messina were the two main trading centres. Other, but small, groups of foreigners were to be found at places on the coast such as Syracuse, Catania, Licata and Marsala. 'Few Sicilians', an observer had written as late as 1839, 'carry on commerce with much energy, the major part of the profits springing from this activity goes into the hands of the foreigners.'[2] Only after 1849 did the situation very gradually come to be reversed.

Joseph Whitaker had reached Palermo in about 1820, when he would have been eighteen. He had been summoned there by Benjamin Ingham, who was his uncle, a man of commercial genius and already then heading towards being the richest individual on the island. Ingham employed a series of nephews as underlings in his business, which was founded originally on marsala wine. The story is that when Joseph's elder brother died, Ingham wrote to their mother, his sister: 'Your son is dead. Send me another.' Joseph was so dour, with rather hooded eyes and a sardonic mouth, that even his mighty uncle eventually seemed rather afraid of him. He was a perfect desk man and ran the 'Concern' so well that in June 1851 Ingham was able to announce to his customers and clients that he had retired from active management of 'all commercial affairs', and that his nephew would henceforward be in charge.

Ingham had been safely in Marsala during the early part of May 1849 and his presumed wife, the Duchess of Santa Rosalia, a Sicilian, had taken refuge in a monastery. Like Sophia Whitaker, he did not return to Palermo until mid-June. For at least a decade he had been a multi-millionaire, though mostly in American investments, and during 1848 the revolutionary Government had managed to extract a decent loan from him. Filangieri now approached him, among others, for money but was sternly refused. The feeling of unease in Palermo was not something to encourage Ingham to risk his cash. In any case the political situation elsewhere in Italy was still highly uncertain, to say the least. Although in July Rome was restored to the Pope's temporal power, at this moment of the Risorgimento it was obvious that the forces of revolution were not going to be suppressed for ever, least of all in King Bomba's domains. There was a flicker of a revolt in Sicily in January, as a result of which there were six executions. An ominous beginning to the new régime. In the end it was the Rothschilds who came to Filangieri's rescue.

Benjamin Ingham's retirement was in name only. Like all very successful tycoons he had the art of delegating work, and in Joseph Whitaker he had found a lieutenant only too prepared to beaver away at every smallest detail of the very varied business. Ingham could afford to live almost as well as the Neapolitan Viceroy. He had been created a baron. Through the Duchess he was on familiar terms with the highest families in the island (many indeed owed him money). Yet he could not bear to dissociate himself entirely from something that he had created from the humblest start. He also enjoyed the sense of competition with other merchants in Southern Italy and Sicily. Or, rather, he enjoyed being the first in the race.

The banking side of the business had started before the end of the Napoleonic Wars, and it was over this that he mainly kept control in the 1850s. He had actually arrived in Sicily in 1806, as a representative of his family firm in Leeds, in order to sell cloth and woollens. It was then that he had spotted the potentialities of marsala wine, which tasted very like madeira and was already being marketed with much success by one John Woodhouse, a friend of Nelson. Ingham was not an innovator but he was a wizard at exploiting other people's initiatives and turning them into something far better. This technique he proceeded to apply to John Woodhouse, though with some struggle. He bought a warehouse or *baglio*[3] at Marsala, then set about introducing new methods of marketing and improving the substance of the wine that he had picked up from Spain. Soon he was exporting not only to Britain but, after 1812, in even greater quantities to America; and later still to Brazil and Australia. Sulphur was used as ballast on his ships, so it was natural that he should become one of the island's largest traders in sulphur. He also became one of the main exporters of citrus fruit, olive oil, sumac (used in tanning) and barilla (an alkali) with side-lines in almonds, filberts, manna (a laxative), liquorice paste, pumice, brimstone, currants and, more prosaically, rags.

At first the goods for America were sent 'on consignment' mainly to Boston, New York, Philadelphia, Baltimore and New Orleans, in ships owned by American sea-captains who made their livings out of Ingham, Woodhouse and other merchants who had stayed behind in Sicily after the war. Some of these sea-captains fell under the spell of Palermo and decided to settle there. Such a one was Benjamin Gardner, a Bostonian, whose handsome and suave adopted son, Edward, was a descendant of Paul Revere, hero of the American Revolution.

Later Ingham had his own fleet built. He made a fortune out of sending ships on regular trips to the East Indies. Then, with some leading Palermitans, he acquired the first steamship in Sicily. For here was another secret of success. In the early days, and eventually because of his liaison with the Duchess, he was almost the only member of the foreign merchant community prepared to mingle with the Sicilians socially and to trust them in business; the British, as usual abroad, kept their distance from the natives, intermarrying among themselves and keeping rigidly to their roast-beef-on-Sundays traditions. It also cut the other way. Again because of the Duchess, aristocratic Sicilians were prepared to accept the bourgeois Ingham on equal terms. Needless to say, Ingham took the trouble to learn their very difficult language, quite different from standard Italian – *lingua toscana in bocca romana* (Tuscan tongue in Roman mouth).

Ingham's fabulous wealth in America was basically due to the fact that he had quantities of capital to invest at a time that coincided not only with the canal and railway boom but with a period of great industrial development, especially in New England. The flood of immigration into America had opened up all sorts of markets for speculators;[4] it had also provided cheap labour, mostly Irish, for digging the canals and laying the railways. Imports from America to Sicily, in comparison with exports from Sicily to America, were necessarily small; indeed from Ingham's point of view barrel staves of white oak were among the only feasible items. He found that, in order to get his money from America, he had to route it through London, thereby losing up to twenty per cent in commissions to middlemen. Very naturally, therefore, he preferred to leave it where it was. Unfortunately most of the records of such transactions were among those destroyed in the bombings of the last war. Even so, the few mentions that we come across of the gigantic sums, for those days, being bandied about for investment are mysterious and tantalising. Where *did* they all come from? We read, as a sample, in a letter of June 1850 how £10,000 is being made available from London to the New York office, and shortly afterwards another £5000.[5] From this at any rate one concludes that he was finding America so extraordinarily profitable for investment that he was transferring there any spare money he could possibly accumulate. Ten years later income from dividends seemed to be pouring in at the rate of $10,000 a month. A startling communication from the Michigan Central Railroad Company, in December 1859, suggested that Ingham might care to lend the company $500,000 for three years at a 'rather high rate of interest'. In 1860 he was registered as owning forty per cent of the New York Central Railroad stock. He also owned land in Manhattan: now part of what is known as Fifth Avenue, and bought at 'agricultural prices'.

Thus money earned in Sicily helped to develop the American economy, whilst Sicily herself suffered and sank into worse poverty, creating a fruity breeding ground for the *Mafia* which in future generations was to permeate America. One presumes that Ingham was able to live so comfortably in Sicily and to pay farmers for their wine by means of his banking business, rents from property on the island and, latterly, income from his steamship and imports of spices from the East Indies.

To most Inghams and Whitakers Benjamin Ingham was a thoroughly alarming person, and his temper was supposed only to be equalled by that of his paramour, the Duchess of Santa Rosalia, nearly six years his elder. No doubt he treated his family harshly because, being childless, he knew they were after his money. He therefore indulged in the will game: cutting people out, raising hopes and dropping hints about heirs, encouraging interested parties to dance attendance in humiliating ways. He hated bores, humbugs and procrastinators. He did not mind rivals in business, provided he was satisfied they were playing straight. With simple, guileless people he could be charming. A single glance at any portrait is enough to show that he was a man of exceptional intelligence and vigour, without a vestige of pomposity and completely sure of himself. His features were regular, his mouth and jaw firm, his eyes and hair dark. His build was heavy, his fingers thick and stub-ended. In middle age he seems to have had a liking for horizontally striped waistcoats. But for his clothes his pictures might be those of any modern boardroom giant the world over.

The Duchess of Santa Rosalia had four sons of her own, one married to an heiress and three at that time unmarried and penniless. Ingham's relatives in Palermo considered her a tartar because, with her own children's future in mind, she was quick to make the most of their failings to the crusty old fellow. Sophia Whitaker, whose offspring were Ingham's most likely heirs, had most reason to fear and dislike her. The Duchess's first name was Alessandra, her patronymic Spadafora; she was also the owner of a mighty string of titles – Princess of Venetico, Princess of Maletto, Marchesa of San Martino, Marchesa of Roccella, Baroness of Mazara.[6] A little withdrawn, she had a typically southern face, with black eyes and, in younger days, black hair. A late portrait shows that she was proud of her shoulders. In this picture she is wearing black lace, with a black ribbon under her chin; long heavy gloves conceal her arms – rather surprising in that hot climate, but no doubt, being vain, she considered her arms her worst feature.

The Duke of Santa Rosalia had died in 1821 in a fight at sea against the

Turks. Previously a baron, he had bought his dukedom in 1812, at the height of the British occupation of Sicily, and had been married first to the sister of the Prince of Palagonia, creator of the famous villa of the monsters at Bagheria. Alessandra had probably begun living with Benjamin Ingham soon after the Duke's death. There had been some talk of an impending marriage in 1837, but no records exist of such a ceremony and the name Ingham does not appear on her death certificate. Ingham was obviously fond of her sons, however extravagant and unbusinesslike they might have been: an ominous situation for his potential British heirs. As the Duchess hated being at Marsala, he in due course left that part of the business almost entirely in the hands of one of his other nephews employed in the Concern.

When Joseph Whitaker married, he and his wife took over Ingham's houses on the Vias Bara and Lampedusa,[7] and Ingham and the Duchess moved to a pleasant eighteenth-century villa in the Piano Sant'Oliva and overlooking what is now known as the Piazza Castelnuovo, then just outside the main city walls. We have a description of a party spent in that house in January 1852, providing incidentally a useful summary of Ingham's position in the island. It was written by a young Englishwoman, Mrs Tidman, to her sister. She was the wife of the Rev. Arthur Tidman, who had come to Palermo that winter because of his health and was acting as chaplain to the Protestant community, by whom he was much liked.

*Palermo, 24 and 31 January 1852*

My dearest Ellen,

We have been rather gay this week for us. On Tuesday we were at a large evening party by Mr Ingham, the English Croesus of these parts and the Duchess of Santa Rosalia, his wife. He is the greatest grower of marsala wine in the Island, which he asserts furnishes the greater part of the wine drunk in England as madeira. He has resided in Sicily about forty years and by energy and capital has introduced immense improvements both in the growing and the making of the wine for which he has been rewarded by the title of Cavaliere of the Order of St Ferdinand and another – I forget what. He accordingly always wears a blue and red ribband in his buttonhole. He is also a *Barone* of Sicily. Most of his life he lived at Marsala [sic], and for some years he has entirely retired from active business and settled in Palermo, where he has married the widow of a certain Duke of Santa Rosalia. . . . In consequence of this connection he has associated much more with Sicilians and much less with English society than any other of what we call the colony. Still he is a very stout Protestant and he professes great attachment to the Church, subscribes 60 ounces[8] a year, and has presented the silver communion plate. He treated us with great courtesy, hoped soon to see us to dinner, and made an offer for which all Arthur's friends owe him great gratitude. We have been very anxious ever since we have been here, to prevail upon someone to read the lessons, which would be a great relief to Arthur. We have nearly once or twice prevailed upon the Consul but could not. On Tuesday Mr Ingham, with many expressions of concern for Arthur's health, most kindly volunteered to undertake the office. He is very kind in his manners and rather more scrupulously polite than is customary in England. I won't describe to you the party. It was very like an English one – about eighty or ninety people nearly half English, the rest all Dukes and Princesses, Marquesses and so on, whom we thought rather better than we expected. There was some singing and some dancing and an excellent supper, and only one thing (except the Dukes) to which we are not accustomed, and no amount of custom will induce me to like – one room was set apart for cards and full of gentlemen playing whist all the evening. The room by the way was the Duchess's bedroom. Altogether we spent a very pleasant evening. The Duchess cannot speak a word of English or French but was very polite and showed us all sorts of nooks and crannies in her house. And I was especially overawed by the magnificent array of essence bottles, and all sorts of aids to attraction marshalled upon her toilet table.

The party must have been all the more astonishing because of Sicily's financial crisis at the time. Ingham and the Duchess were then aged sixty-seven and seventy-two respectively. Many leading lights in Palermo society were in fact in exile, voluntary or otherwise. At least two of the Duchess's sons had deemed it sensible, just before the entry of the Neapolitans into the city, to make their escape to Malta, where Ingham naturally had arranged for suitable credits to be available. A curious and dangerous period had begun in Palermo: a real police state atmosphere. Parliament had been abolished and letters arriving by steamer had to be read by the censor. Prisons were overcrowded and people were shot for mere possession of arms. Travelling to and from Naples was made as difficult as possible. British subjects took the precaution of having *sudditi inglesi* (English subjects) placarded over their doorways, whilst Edward Gardner had *casa americana* over his. The situation if anything was worse in Messina, still in ruins and in a state of apathy, moral and political. Gradually, however, as a new generation of liberal Sicilians emerged, one heard stories in

Palermo of plots hatching, bombs being manufactured and secret meetings being held, under the auspices of revolutionary exiles in London, Paris and Turin. Not that Ingham had any sympathy left for those 'cussed young hot-bloods'. He might once have favoured freedom from Naples, but he was heartily tired now of revolutions. When May 1860 arrived he welcomed Garibaldi with even less enthusiasm than did the Prince of Salina in *The Leopard*.

# II

## *Any Gentleman's Table Might Receive It*

Benjamin Ingham had been born on 24 October 1784. His forebears came from Ossett in Yorkshire and had later established themselves as merchants and cloth manufacturers in Leeds. The name was not uncommon in the county, most Inghams being Nonconformists. His great-uncle and namesake had been fairly famous as an associate of the Wesleys and founder of a sect, which still exists and is known as the Inghamites.[1] We are told that young Benjamin accepted the challenge of a trip to Sicily in 1806, in the wake of the British expeditionary force, because a ship, in which all his money had been invested, had been lost and he had consequently been jilted by a mercenary-minded Huddersfield lady.[2] Apparently he determined never to return to Yorkshire until he was rich enough to buy up the whole of his native Ossett. Within a couple of decades he would easily have been able to fulfil this ambition had he so wished.

By 1811 the British troops in Sicily numbered some 17,000. Ingham and his fellow merchants were there not only to satisfy the needs of the army and the Mediterranean fleet, but because the geographical position of Sicily was suitable for shipping goods secretly to the western coastline of the Italian mainland and even to southern France.[3] Soon no less than thirty British Consuls or Vice-consuls were on the island. American traders, until 1812, were also to be seen. The traveller John Galt remarked how the 'general foreign trade is in the hands of the British, while colonial produce is brought by the Americans'.

The Neapolitan royal family in 1806 had been forced for the second time to flee to Palermo. Although King Ferdinand, Bomba's grandfather, had only reluctantly invited the British to send military help (not realising that they had decided to occupy Sicily in any case), the majority of the more liberal-minded Sicilians were in favour of this foreign army. His menopausal Queen, Maria Carolina, addicted to opium as a result of bearing seventeen children, loathed the British – in contrast to those happy days during her first sojourn in Palermo with her beloved Lady Hamilton;

if she also made no secret of her disdain for the Sicilians, they certainly reciprocated the sentiment, and not only towards her but towards Bourbons and Neapolitans in general, the British providing a useful buffer. Employment, too, benefited from the presence of troops, and the Barbary pirates became less of a menace.[4] Sicilians also cherished a vague sense of kinship with England, as that other embattled island, not truly European in the continental sense, but once also ruled by Normans – a period regarded as something of a golden age, compared to 400 years of Spanish and Bourbon domination.

Ingham had acquired his taste for foreign parts when very young and already self-assured, with a fashionable First Consulate haircut, he had gone to Paris in 1802 after the Peace of Amiens. Perhaps his subsequent interest in America was connected with his great-uncle's reputation there; perhaps it was because of the enthusiasm of his brother Joshua, who actually visited Rome in 1804 with a forged American passport.[5] When Ingham arrived in Palermo, as a representative of his family firm, he found a city about the size of Dublin. It delighted him at once, and he wrote in astonishment about the view of the Conca d'Oro, more beautiful than the Garden of the Hesperides, and the fact that he was sure he could see, from Monte Pellegrino, the smoke rising from Etna. Though had he foreseen in what direction the people's smouldering hatred for the Neapolitans would lead, so soon after the departure of the British in 1815, he might have been deterred from making his home there. Eventually, in his will, he gave 1812 as the year in which he definitely took up his domicile in Palermo. That was the year of the Constitution, a key date in Sicilian history and a rallying-point in future upheavals, though at the time seeming to symbolise security and a settled government.

It is possible that, during his busy life, Benjamin Ingham may have met an English officer of exactly his own age, Ensign Edward Charlton,[6] who came to Palermo in 1807 in search of native recruits. Ensign Charlton was in the 61st Regiment; his capabilities had been noticed by Sir John Moore, and he was a friend of a man who was to become one of the greatest of Sicilian patriots, Ruggiero Settimo. Since Charlton's grandson married into the Whitaker family, there is all the more reason to quote from his impressions:

Palermo exhibits a very noble spectacle. The city is walled round almost in a circular form and is divided by two streets which intersect one another. The principal street is called Il Cassero and the other La Nuova.[7] The Marina is a handsome Quay, a fashionable promenade for its inhabitants. The Favorita and the Flora [the Villa Giulia] are also much frequented, and many beautiful women are often to be seen in the walks. I visited the King's Palace, and saw the Neapolitan Guards under arms; these troops appeared well appointed and not indifferently disciplined, their bands were excellent. The Opera also provides scenes of great attractions and always proves a gratifying resource to the lovers of music. I paid my respects to the British Chargé d'Affaires Mr Drummond, from whom I met with great civility and every assistance in his power for procuring recruits. The Sicilian noblesse in Palermo maintain great state in their mansions and equipages, but there is little of that comfort and arrangement to be met with in those of the upper classes in England.

No comment though on the crammed, pullulating back-streets. As Ruggiero Settimo belonged to a princely family, the Fitalias, Ensign Charlton had an enjoyable time of it. One would have been glad to have been able to discover some reference to meeting the Santa Rosalias, which undoubtedly he would have done. The most flamboyant state was kept by the Prince of Butera, whose title for generations had been one of the most important in Sicily. This prince's income was reputed to be no less than £60,000 per annum; he had his palace on the Marina open every night for company, and a supper-table was always laid for twenty. A considerable contrast to the lot of less fortunate Palermitans. As John Galt said, 'poverty really seems to be the ordinary condition of the people', as indeed it was in most of the rest of the island, including the countryside.[8]

The Prince of Butera's income was an exception. Most of the nobility and gentry were weighed down by debts. As the virtual owners of nearly all agricultural Sicily they had neither the means nor the inclination to visit their estates. Villages inland were clusters of 'dark and filthy hovels',[9] plastered with mud. The dress of the peasants was usually black or brown, as dismal as their dwellings. Often the man in the family would have to travel great distances to his work, across a roadless, stark landscape, and might spend the whole week sleeping in a cave or straw hut. On the coast other main groups of labourers were employed in sulphur mines, fisheries and silk and cotton factories. But the people of the vast stretches of the interior – considered as good as inaccessible by the *notabili* of Palermo – were a law unto themselves, primitive, savage when aroused, superstitious.

Marsala, the ancient Lilybaeum founded by the Carthaginians, was among the less depressed parts of western Sicily, though no place of beauty. Sun-baked and Moorish in character, with massive walls, in a flat dull landscape apparently overrun with lizards, it was near Cape Boeo, one of the three points of the Trinacria, and its relative affluence was thanks to the efforts of that worthy English family the Woodhouses.[10] As the Wood-houses were the first to realise that Marsala's white wine had lucrative possibilities, and were thus unwittingly the founders of Ingham's millions, it is necessary to take a step even further back in time.

The original Woodhouse, from Liverpool, had arrived in 1770 ostensibly in search of barilla, made from burning a plant that flourished among the salt pans of Trapani, famed also for its coral-work and tunny fisheries. It was his son John, a dry, energetic bachelor, who was in charge of the business when Ingham first visited the town. The elder Woodhouse's first shipment of wine had in fact been in 1773, when he had sent 8000 gallons to Liverpool. In order to conserve the wine better on its month-long journey, he had added alcohol – two litres per hundred of wine: a fact which shows that he may possibly have had some personal knowledge of the trade. It was an experiment, but the heady beverage sold quickly. He sent some more, and then more. John Woodhouse came out in 1787, on board a brig called *The Big Grampus*. The soil and temperature conditions at Marsala were very like those at Madeira, and for that matter at Jerez and Malaga. The Woodhouses set about what was in effect the beginnings of a complete agrarian revolution. They provided loans to farmers so that they could clear their wheat fields and olive groves, and replace them with vineyards. They repaved the main street and eventually built a long jetty in order to form a harbour for shallow draught sailing ships, the very jetty on which Garibaldi and his Thousand landed in 1860.[11]

Ingham's headquarters were always at Palermo, but the Woodhouses kept sternly to the western coast. The journey to Marsala had necessarily to be by sea, since there were scarcely any roads, and until the building of the jetty wine had to be transported by mule to Trapani along a lonely boulder-strewn track, enlivened by an occasional shrine, windmill, salt-pan or carob tree, that had once been the Roman road between Lilybaeum and Drepanum. John Woodhouse at first lived at the sickle-shaped Trapani, bigger than Marsala but even less picturesque, its great scenic merit being that it was directly below Mount Eryx, the Hill of Venus, 2000 feet high, on the summit of which was the small medieval town of San Giuliano, somewhat Umbrian in character.[12] When he was joined by his brother Will, he bought an old *tonnara*, or shed used by tunny fishers, outside the walls of Marsala and converted it into a *baglio*, with high walls like a fortress's round the surrounding seven acres as a protection against Arab marauders. Inside this little kingdom he built a charming country house in semi-Palladian style, white-plastered with brown points and green jalousies. He also had gardens, poultry-runs, kennels, vines, plots of wheat and even a cemetery, in which the first grave was that of his young friend John Christian, a cooper from the Isle of Man who died in Marsala in October 1793. Woodhouse's *baglio* was the model for many such establishments, including that of Benjamin Ingham, who naturally saw to it that his was far bigger and more impressive.

They were risky days. *The Big Grampus* was wrecked in the Ashley River near Charleston, South Carolina. John was even once captured by pirates. French and Spanish warships lurked near the Straits of Gibraltar. Then, on land, there was always the risk from bandits, who were notorious in that part of Sicily.[13]

The Woodhouses' real success began when Nelson placed a large order for his fleet in 1798, after the Battle of the Nile. It seems possible that he met John in Naples and took him on his flagship, the *Vanguard*, to Marsala via Marettimo, the dramatically beautiful and furthermost island in the Aegadean group, a favourite rendezvous for the Admiral. Nelson seems to have taken a real liking to the earnest bachelor, so very different in temperament from himself. He records in his log-book that, before returning to Malta, he took on board thirty-six pipes and twenty-eight hogsheads of wine 'part of two hundred pipes ordered'.[14]

As in 1806, Sicily was important to Britain as the chief link in her attempt to blockade Europe and keep open the sea routes of the Mediterranean. British warships called frequently at Palermo, Messina, Syracuse and Trapani. Since it was becoming difficult for the fleet to obtain madeira and rum, Nelson's appreciation of marsala set a fashion at once, and the Woodhouses found themselves hardly able to keep up with the demand.[15]

In the last days of 1798 the Neapolitan royal family, with Sir William and Lady Hamilton, made that much romanticised escape from Naples on board the *Vanguard*, and the Hamiltons and Nelson began their strange *ménage à trois*.[16] Nelson was honoured by the King with the title of the Duke of Bronte, and given an estate on the slopes of Mount Etna, with the castle of Maniace as its main feature and an estimated income of £3000 a year.[17] The next year was very festive. John Woodhouse unwillingly had to visit Palermo fairly often, but he kept away from frivolities as much as possible. Not for him the balls and concerts, the masquerades and dazzling fêtes, all-night sessions at faro, fashionable sightseeing on board Nelson's new flagship, the *Foudroyant*. He had to stay on the Marina at Madame de Montagne's hotel, where Lady Hamilton's companion Cornelia Knight and other British refugees had suffered on their arrival

1. Palermo from the sea, gouache by Francesco Zerilli (*d.* 1837 of cholera).

*Left to right:* Casina Vega, in trees; Palazzo Cattolica, next to gateway (Porta dei Greci); churches of S. Teresa and the Crociferi, with Palazzo Torremuzza in front; church of the Pietà, with Palazzo Angiò in front; Palazzo Lampedusa (ten windows); theatre, later Hotel Trinacria; Palazzo Butera (13 windows); Porta Felice; Fort of La Garitta.

2. Palermo and Monte Pellegrino, from S. Maria di Gesù, burial place of the Duchess of Santa Rosalia and General Alfonso Scalia (*artist unknown, in the possession of W. I. Whitaker of Pylewell*).

3. John Woodhouse, a bust in the present *Baglio* Florio.

An Agreement made and entered into by the Right Honble
Rear Admiral Horatio Lord Nelson K. B. Duke of Bronte in
Sicily &c &c with John and William Woodhouse Merchts of Marsala
at Palermo the Nineteenth day of March 1800 to furnish His
Majesty's Ships off Malta with five hundred Pipes of the best
Marsala Wine to be delivered there free of freight and all other
Charges without loss of time at One Shilling and five pence
Sterling per Gallon Wine measure and to be paid for in Bills
upon the Commissioners for Victualing His Majestys Navy
at the usual date by the respective Pursers of His Majestys Ships
to whom the Wine is delivered and should any of the Casks be
wanted with the Wine an additional Charge is to be added of One
pound Sterling each pipe   The Wine to be delivered
as expeditiously as possible and all to be delivered
within the space of five weeks from this date, a
Convoy will be wanted for the Vessel from Marsala but all risks are to run by Mr. Woodhouse

Bronte Nelson

for Brother Juli
John Woodhouse

4. The contract between Nelson and John Woodhouse, 19 March 1800. Nelson's script is remarkably clear, though written with his left hand.

from Naples, as indeed had his father and the renowned travel-writer Patrick Brydone in 1770.[18] The Marina itself was offensive to him, because of all the immorality that took place there.[19]

He must have been aware of the rumblings of disapproval in England at Nelson's execution of Caracciolo. And he could not have failed to have heard some of the scandalous rumours circulating about the conduct of the Admiral and his portly Emma, in appearance by no means the Vivien Leigh of film and legend.[20] Early in the New Year came the bombshell. Nelson was informed by the Admiralty that his command in the Mediterranean had come to an end. Not only this, but Sir William Hamilton was suddenly recalled, after thirty-six years as British envoy to the Bourbon court.

It looked for a while as though the Woodhouses were going to lose the patronage of the navy. Nelson left almost at once for the waters off Malta; he was determined to take the island before he left, as a culmination to his career in the Mediterranean – an ambition he was not in fact able to fulfil. After a fairly unsuccessful time with the blockading squadron, in very dirty weather, he returned to Palermo in March. John Woodhouse was there too, not perhaps entirely fortuitously. At any rate he met with a wonderful piece of luck. On 20 March Nelson wrote this letter to Lord Keith, his Commander-in-chief:

> I have agreed with Mr Woodhouse, at Marsala, for 500 pipes of wine, to be delivered to our Ships at Malta, at 1s 5d per gallon; and as Mr Woodhouse runs all risks, pays all freight etc, I don't think it is a bad bargain. The wine is so good that any gentleman's table might receive it, and it will be of real use to our seamen.

The contract between Nelson and Woodhouse had been signed the day before.[21] Nelson in his own hand wrote that a convoy would be provided, 'but all risks are to be run from Mr Woodhouse.' He signed himself 'Bronte Nelson',[22] and John signed 'for brother Will – John Woodhouse'. It was suggested by the Admiral that the particular brand of marsala that he preferred should henceforward be known as Bronte Madeira. This name stuck, and in time all white Marsala wine came to be known as such (or as Sicily Madeira, even plain Sicily) in the trade, at least until the 1920s. John was so delighted that he even went so far as to give the name Bronte to one of his houses in Liverpool.

In April the *Foudroyant* set sail once more, with a party of guests on board including the Hamiltons and Cornelia Knight. Though the ultimate destination was again the squadron off Malta, Nelson and his friends dallied a while at Syracuse in order to visit the Greek ruins. They were not back until 31 May, in time, not only for the somewhat scandalous wedding of the sixty-three year old Prime Minister of the Two Sicilies, an Englishman, Sir John Acton, to his fourteen-year-old niece, Mary Anne,[23] but for the royal farewell banquet in honour of Nelson, the Hamiltons and the Queen, who was leaving with them on a visit to Austria. The *Foudroyant* departed for Genoa on 10 June after hectic festivities.

Very wisely John Woodhouse had made sure that he was in Palermo during the last week. For he had an urgent problem to communicate to Nelson, who willingly found time to help:

Lord Nelson to His Highness the Dey of Algiers

*'Foudroyant'*, *Palermo, 7 June 1800*

Sir,

I have been informed that one of your Highness's cruisers hath captured a Neapolitan vessel called *San Francisco de Paula*, laden with oak pipe staves from the Port d'Anze [Anzio], in the Roman state, bound to Marsala, in Sicily; and that the said staves are the property of Mr John Woodhouse, a respectable British merchant, as appears by the bill of lading, and the said staves were intended to make casks for the use of his Britannic Majesty's Navy, and the Ships forming the blockade of Malta; I must, therefore, request of your Highness, that you will be pleased to order the restitution of the said cargo of staves, otherwise to pay the amount of the value thereof, at the invoice price, to the Consul General of Great Britain resident at Algiers, which from the well known justice and humanity of your Highness, I can entertain no doubt will be done.

I have the honour to be, etc.

Bronte Nelson of the Nile

We do not know whether the Woodhouses received their staves or their money from the Dey. They certainly continued to have a great deal of trouble with pirates from the Barbary Coast, and in 1805 there was much alarm at the news of the capture of the American warship *Philadelphia* and the enslavement of its officers and men. Cannons were placed on the massive walls of the *baglio* and were still to be seen there a hundred years later.

Nelson, before his departure, ordered some marsala for his personal use. Alas, in the last frenzied moments, he forgot to take it with him. For sentimental reasons John Woodhouse kept this consignment to one side, even though it had not been paid for, long after the Battle of Trafalgar and Nelson's death.

The wine continued to gain popularity with the navy. In the Wood-house *baglio* in later years there was a picture of French prisoners of war obviously enjoying their tots of marsala on board a British warship after Trafalgar. When Malta fell, it was decided by the Woodhouses to set up a depot at Valetta. They took a ninety-nine year lease of the old prisons on the bluff overlooking the entrance to the Grand Harbour. A large *palazzo* was built, and for the period of the lease it served as a temporary residence for visiting members of the family.

It is hardly surprising that Benjamin Ingham, on his first visit to Marsala in 1806, should have felt that he had lighted on a gold-mine. In 1807 he arranged for his brother Joshua, fresh from America, to visit some leading wine firms in Spain and Portugal, in order to study methods employed there in 'fortifying' wines. Then in 1809 he himself visited Boston with a view to taking on Messrs Greenough, father and son, as his agents in New England; they had already proved their worth by disposing successfully of a modest shipment of oranges and lemons that Ingham had sent across the Atlantic two years previously. Soon, in 1812, he had impertinently erected his *baglio*, nearly a mile from John Woodhouse's, and before the war had ended he had acquired other *bagli* as far afield as Castelvetrano, Campobello di Mazara, Balestrate and Vittoria. His work for the family firm in Leeds became secondary. By 1811 it is clear that he had a partner, for 'B. Ingham and Co.' was one of thirteen firms petitioning Robert Fagan, the British Consul in Palermo, against a recently imposed tax of one per cent.

The Woodhouses never owned vineyards and Benjamin Ingham only acquired his in later years. The system was for the rival firms to 'obligate' the farmers in advance and to send their brokers round at intervals during the winter and spring to make sure the vines were being properly pruned and cultivated. In a few instances the grapes were bought by weight, but usually at that time, in the early days, *mosto* or fresh grape-juice was obtained from the farmer's own *palmenti* or treading vats. The basic unfortified wine, indeed, tasted very much like the famous *malvasia* or Malmsey, imported by England in medieval times from Crete.[24]

Ingham's wine, some of which was later known as *Colli*, the better quality being 'London Particular', 'Inghilterra', or 'Bandiera', was usually a shade sweeter than Woodhouse's, which could have been rather like today's *oloroso* sherry, somewhat nutty flavoured, in the parlance of the wine trade. Another basic element in the making of marsala was *passito*, the juice of slightly dried grapes. This was mixed with brandy, in the ratio of three to one, and then mixed with *mosto*, previously heated up to lose about sixty per cent of its liquid, thus becoming denser and sweeter, the colour of caramel. The wine would then be put in casks and left to age, a process which was supposed to last a year but normally now takes three to four years. It was reckoned that the result could be anything between seventeen and thirty-two per cent proof spirit, usually about twenty. The *solera* system was borrowed from Spain: a cask of 'mother wine', never more than half emptied, being topped up by the next youngest wine every time a quantity of the original was drawn off. Wines were always 'in the wood', never bottled on the premises, and casks were made in the owner's own cooperage yard out of oak staves, either Calabrian or, more usually, American.

It was at a *flambeaux* procession along the Marina at Palermo, one luminous June evening in 1808, that Benjamin Ingham caught sight of Estina, the beautiful daughter of Robert Fagan and his Roman wife. He at once forgot the attractions of that earlier love in more prosaic Huddersfield. There were trips with the Fagan family through heavily scented orange-groves to Monreale, and to Bagheria where, under enormous palms, the party ate sorbets made from snow-water brought from Etna. It was even suggested that they might make an expedition to the volcano. Unfortunately, though, Estina did not reciprocate Ingham's love, and Fagan did not encourage it. They were awaiting the return of a bigger fish, Estina's fiancé William Baker, grandson of a Governor of the Hudson Bay and East India Companies, as well as heir to Bayfordbury, an eighteenth-century mansion north of London. A year later Estina and William Baker were married. Ingham was disgusted, and probably for this reason he decided to escape to Boston.[25] It was thanks to Baker's father that Fagan obtained his appointment as Consul.

Actually the Baker marriage was short-lived, for William died in 1813. Estina went to Naples, where she met and married a member of Sir John Acton's family: no doubt another good match paved for her by her father.

Fagan was a mysterious and extremely cultivated man, with a shady background in art-dealing from which he had made a fortune.[26] His good looks must have attracted Queen Maria Carolina, as he became about the only Englishman (or Irishman) whom she really trusted, as a result of which he was inundated with screed after neurotic screed. Preposterous now and hysterical, the Queen – with her minions – did everything she could to make life difficult for British merchants. In the autumn of 1809 Fagan wrote to Lord Amherst, the new Chargé d'Affaires, saying that he could not help observing that 'the conduct in general of most of the Ministers appears to be studiously directed to give disgust to the British'. Sir John Moore,[27] as second-in-command in Sicily, had long been urging, before departing for the Peninsula, that the Queen should be expelled.

Maria Carolina had become ever more paranoid since the guillotining of her sister Marie-Antoinette. Now her life had been made more complicated by the marriage of Napoleon to her grand-daughter, Marie-Louise, and of her daughter to the Duke of Orleans, the future King Louis-Philippe. The fact that the British had made it clear in 1800 that they meant to keep Malta to the exclusion of the Neapolitans, had never been forgotten. Amherst even had reason to believe that she was intriguing with Murat in Naples. Disgust was certainly what he felt for her, and he was thankful to return to England in 1811.

1811 was also the year in which the Queen had ordered the 'despoiling' of a large British merchant vessel. In March 1813, to the mighty relief of all, including her husband, and not least the twice-jilted Benjamin Ingham, the unhappy woman was finally thrown out of the country.

Amherst had recommended to London that a constitution should be imposed on Sicily, and that the Bourbon army should be put under a British commander. Thus his successor, Lord William Bentinck, an ex-Governor of Madras, came not as ambassador but 'Commander-in-chief of the British forces in Sicily and Plenipotentiary and Envoy Extraordinary' – which, again to the relief of many people, particularly the merchants, meant virtual dictator.

The brilliant new Envoy, a considerable contrast to the mild Amherst, arrived two days after five liberal noblemen, including Belmonte and Castelnuovo, had been imprisoned. He at once arranged their release, and soon afterwards the new Constitution, drafted on the British model by the Abbate Balsamo, came into being, to much enthusiasm. Such a rigid imitation (which also meant the abolition of feudalism and torture) would obviously never work for a people with such a very different temperament and Bentinck had warned Balsamo of this. Nevertheless it was a time of hope, both for Sicilians and foreign merchants.[28] Unfortunately Bentinck began to involve himself in domestic affaires. An avowed dream was to make British rule permanent; Sicily would become 'after Ireland, the brightest jewel in the British Crown'. His reckless behaviour as commander of an expeditionary force to Tuscany led to another abrupt dismissal; he was replaced by Sir William A'Court, deliberately chosen once more by London for his contrasting character. A'Court was cynical and ultra-conservative, and did not like Sicilians. Meanwhile the King reinstated all the men whom Bentinck had previously dismissed in 1811. A'Court tried, fruitlessly, to persuade the Government to revise the Constitution on more logical lines. Thus, by the time the Napoleonic Wars had ended, and the British forces had been withdrawn, the way had been well and truly prepared for a reversion to tyranny and the total abolition of the Constitution – as well as of the freedom of the Press and of several Sicilian national institutions dating back as far as Norman times. It was made clear that Parliament would not be recalled. The bitterness and frustration that remained led directly to the riots of 1820 and 1837, and were to be perpetuated in the far greater upheavals of 1848–9 and 1860. In 1817 a Sicilian delegation was actually sent to London to beg for help, but to no avail.[29] Indeed, such was the feeling of general despair that when Castelnuovo died in 1822 he left £25,000 to anyone who would induce the King to bring back the Constitution.

For the rest of his life Benjamin Ingham had to contend with this background of simmering revolt. He died in 1861, the year after Garibaldi had removed the Bourbons finally from the island. Several of his colleagues had decided that it would be wisest to return home after the Great Powers' Settlement of 1815. Ingham, the Woodhouses and various leading merchants in Messina were among those in particular who decided to brave the frustrations, red tape, money crises and very real physical dangers. Indeed, after a year or two, some merchants even came back, while veterans from the forces, such as William Sanderson, returned to start up their own businesses. 1815 was a vintage year at Marsala, for the Woodhouses one of the best in their entire history – so much so that when John heard of the victory at Waterloo, he set aside one *solera*, which he christened the 'Waterloo', for the pleasure of distinguished visitors.[30] Bronte Madeira was now reasonably well-known to connoisseurs both in England and North America.

# III

## The Fleas With Which Your House
## is Pestered

THE Anglo-American war of 1812 had been a nasty setback to Benjamin
Ingham's efforts. As soon as the fighting was over, his representatives
went posting off to New York and Boston, where Greenough was reinstated as agent. Trade with America prospered, but at home in Sicily there
were to be some exceedingly anxious – not to say precarious – moments.

On 25 June 1816 Ingham wrote gloomily to the British Consul at
Messina:

> If you were to return to Palermo, you would be astonished. Never
> place was so much changed in so short a time. All the money is going
> out of the Kingdom for the purchase of grain. There is no trade in the
> shops as they sell nothing.

A few days later he was writing to a client in Nottingham:

> We are truly sorry we cannot communicate to you any amelioration
> in the state of the market here. In fact the very limited sales which have
> been made this winter have been with enormous sacrifice. The removal of
> the Court to Naples has resulted in 20 to 30,000 emigrants, and with the
> vacuation of the whole island by our Army the consumption of foreign
> manufactures is diminished. There is also the competition from articles
> made by the French troops [a reference to prisoners of war] and from
> German manufactures. To add to our misery the harvest of last year
> completely failed, and money is sent out of the island to purchase our
> daily bread.

The situation indeed looked disastrous. Ferdinand had left Sicily for the
last time in May 1815. As he had married a lady from Syracuse, the
Duchess of Floridia (just two months after the death of Maria Carolina in
Vienna), various Sicilian noblemen had felt it wise to follow her with their
entourages, and this had partly accounted for the loss of trade for Palermo
shopkeepers. Ingham repeated to his partner in Marsala, John Lee-Brown:

'I never knew money so scarce as at present. The shops sell nothing and cannot consequently pay us.' His mention of a grain shortage showed more than anything else the bad straits into which Sicily had now fallen; since Roman times she had been regarded as the granary of the Mediterranean.

As for the legacy of the British, this was summed up by the excellent travel-writer Simond – not entirely favourably, but then he was a Frenchman who had spent twenty years in America:

> The English, it must be acknowledged, have left here no honourable monument of a power paramount to sovereignty . . . the roads,[1] the prisons, the hospitals, the corrupt and barbarous administration of justice, remained just in as wretched a state as before they interfered. It is true they saved the island from French dominion; from the violence and plunder which attended it at Naples and in Calabria; they kept strict discipline; they paid honestly and liberally for all they had; but they did not mix cordially with the people. They continued meddling, teaching, ruling, with a high hand and a supercilious pride, till all classes were tired out; and yet all classes regret them, simply because they saved them from Naples for a while.

Ingham was now dealing in a great assortment of goods, besides marsala and olive oil. With Smithson of Messina, a relative, he held the agency for woollens sent out by Ingham Brothers of Leeds, and he imported velvets, printed cottons and suchlike, for which there was a traditional market. He also ran a lively business in bill broking, in addition to his other activities as a general banker. Then he acted as a 'commission merchant' for a number of British firms, several of whom were experiencing a great deal of trouble with bad debts. Indeed the years 1816–17 were made even more alarming by the great rash of bankruptcies among traders in Sicily, both native and foreign.

His letters reveal that John Woodhouse, usually referred to as 'Old John', although only aged forty-eight in 1816, was still very much the giant of the wine trade in the island. Two other rival Englishmen, Wood and Corlett, had also settled in Marsala. As it happened, many years later scions of the families of both married Ingham's relatives; but he, naturally enough, was not to know this and for the present they had no sympathy or assistance when they found themselves in financial straits. John Lee-Brown was not a success, to put it mildly. His presence at Marsala had grown more and more irksome, and Ingham was not one to hide his feelings.

Many of the first letters are to Lee-Brown, or about him, and trace an almost inevitable path to the great breakup, in other words a lawsuit. Ingham's forthright and impatient nature is revealed almost at once. His early letters also show the anxious time he was having in trying to establish a firm demand for his wine in the United States. This anxiety was to continue well into 1818, though by the end of that year he was obviously far more confident.

Lee-Brown, a Cockney, was permanently based at Marsala. He would ship the wine to Palermo, where Ingham would find some sea-captain willing to risk the investment of taking it on board (along with other commodities such as barilla and sumac), usually for resale in North America or England. Ingham also had similar arrangements with other merchants, like his special friend, the grizzled old Joseph Payne of Mazara, and on occasion, when things were not going so well, he might pass on his wine to Messina in the hope that some colleague there, Smithson perhaps or (eventually) Sanderson, might ensnare a more obliging sea-captain.

The struggle against the magic charm of Woodhouse's name could be very annoying to Ingham. On 1 February 1816 he told Lee-Brown that an American captain had arrived in Palermo wanting fifty pipes of wine, but 'as usual will only have Woodhouse's'. He was irritated by Lee-Brown's complacency and his blind, time-wasting and money-wasting ideas about alternative markets. 'This captain,' he wrote, 'went from Halifax in Nova Scotia last summer to the West Indies and took with him twenty pipes of marsala wine, but he says that he was obliged to take it back to Halifax as they would not give fifty dollars a pipe for it. Your quaint idea of finding a market with the West Indies is therefore exploded.'

Lee-Brown just would not listen to advice. For instance, in spite of everything Ingham had said previously, he continued to make the wine far too dark – 'it must be the colour of madeira, as the buyers will have it that colour'. He was also extravagant. Indeed there was very little at all that could be found in his favour.

Finally Ingham could bear the situation no more, and wrote:

*To John Lee-Brown, Marsala*                                  *25 April 1816*
I have received your several letters. I give no reply whatever to the first. Your drafts have been paid, but you must not draw for any more as I have advanced already more than I engaged to do, and your conduct is not such as to induce me to go in deeper, even if I had all the money in Palermo at my command. I will endeavour to be in Marsala in eight or ten days' time, but I request that you will procure a lodging for me in the town, as I cannot stand the fleas with which your house is pestered.

The visit took place, and does not appear to have made relations between the two men any easier. For instance Ingham found that wine was being shipped to Boston before it was even properly matured. The Concern's reputation in that city would be wrecked for ever. He had quite enough trouble with captains being subverted in Palermo itself: 'You may rely that Gibbs [Abraham Gibbs, another great rival, this time in banking] does everything to prejudice the Americans against everybody's wine but Woodhouse's.[2] Act with judgement and reason, and we shall have them in want of our wines very soon.'

'Judgement and reason'. Vain words. The ranting letters continued at the least provocation.

Marsala wine was now selling in Boston at $1¼ a gallon, duty being an extra half dollar – pure robbery. Ingham was aghast. Then consternation, a bombshell from Thomas Kettlewell, Ingham's agent for wine in London. 'Our wine judges found your product to leave a disagreeable sweat upon the palate.' Orders would have to be halved.

This bit of news was, however, soon counter-balanced by another that was more satisfactory: Abraham Gibbs had gone bankrupt. 'Old John will lose near 10,000 *onze* by Gibbs' failure, as scarcely anything will ever be paid,' wrote Ingham, not without a sort of pleasure.

Lee-Brown had been grumbling about overwork and lack of staff at Marsala. Ingham, needless to say, was not impressed. He had nobody to send, as he only had his nephew to help him in Palermo. This was the elder Whitaker boy, William, aged twenty and, one would guess, a rather more endearing character than his brother Joseph. He had only just arrived from England, mainly to help over Ingham Brothers' affairs and was very much on approval. Like the Inghams, the Whitakers were of yeoman stock, their name – originally White Acre – also being quite a frequent one in Yorkshire. Such fragments as exist of William's brief apprenticeship add up to something rather sad; some are worth chronicling here as a further illumination of Benjamin Ingham's character. Almost immediately he was put to the test by Uncle Benjamin and sent to Naples on the delicate task of investigating the rumours that two firms, Leydings and Vallin,[3] were in financial trouble. Soon he too was to be bombarded with complicated letters, all to do with remissions of tolls and rates of exhange.

There were other duties too. The poor boy must have felt overwhelmed.

*20 September 1816*

And I request you will buy for me two hats. Enclosed you will find a card to show the circumference of my head, and let them be larger rather than smaller, as by padding they can easily be made to fit if even rather too large. Pray not to forget this, but above all remember to get every penny possible from Leydings and their debtors before you leave.

On 31 October Ingham told Lee-Brown: 'I am expecting daily Mr Whitaker from Naples.' But a fortnight later William still had not arrived. Ingham wrote angrily to the boy. No reply.

Thirteen days later there was an explosion:

*23 November 1816*

Dear William,

. . . I have been looking out for you on every vessel from Naples, the more so as you were acquainted with the accident I met with by the fall of my horse, and were besides aware that your presence was absolutely necessary here. Imagine therefore of my surprise and disappointment at your not coming all through this week. There have been three eligible English vessels arriving from Naples. I am frantic in consequence. . . . Really William, such conduct can neither conciliate my affection as a relative nor inspire me with regard to your attention to business. You ought to recollect that you are in the commencement of life and must do something to put yourself forward, for if you show no exertion, you cannot expect that my brother Joseph [i.e. in Leeds] will ever consent to giving you an interest in our business.

Although so much displeased with your inattention, and although my mind labours under the severest agony in consequence, I subscribe myself as usual

Yours affectionately

Meanwhile in Palermo the usual parrot-talk was going on from American captains who had 'positive orders from Baltimore and New York only to take Old John's wine'. Ingham also heard that 'in Italy the vintage has completely failed, as in France'. Very depressing.

December came, and then at last some news from William, which completely mollified Ingham. Apparently Leydings had been giving William a vast amount of 'trouble and vexation', so much so that he had been compelled to break with them completely and give power of attorney to Ascione, to enable him to return. He had felt that he would only worry his uncle unduly if he told him the truth earlier on. Of course the truth would have been what Ingham wanted. Nevertheless he forgave him.

*9 December 1816*

Dear William,

. . . Had I known the real cause of your delay in Naples, I should have been much less agitated than I was from the uncertainty in which you left me. I am very glad to find that you have been attentive and thank you for the motive, although false, which induced you to keep me in the dark. You will understand that the mind suffers more in agitation from apprehension than from reality.

So all ended happily. Uncle Benjamin was never to know that the *actual* reason for William's delay (confided to a younger brother) was that he had succumbed to a black-eyed, black-haired Neapolitan *baronessa*, married one assumes, called Clotilde. At any rate the affaire soon was ended, and William seems to have acquitted himself fairly well in Palermo during the crucial year of 1817, so worrying financially not only for his uncle but for nearly anyone trading in Sicily. Unfortunately his career was destined to be cut short all too soon by death. The following correspondence – which involves a temporary leap forward in the story – shows that Benjamin Ingham could never have been such an icy-hearted brute as to write that letter, much quoted in the Whitaker family: 'Your son is dead . . .'

We move to the winter of 1818. The first letter is actually written by young William and shows the state of his distress:

*To Thomas Kettlewell, London*　　　　　　　　　　*2 November 1818*
Our Mr Benjamin Ingham is at Naples and will reply to your notes [some severe letters of complaint]. The writer begs you will excuse the writing as well as the brevity, as he is confined to his bed with sickness. My head turns and I hope to be restored to health in a few days.

Joseph Payne of Mazara obviously felt a sense of responsibility towards the boy during Ingham's absence. Replies to a letter of inquiry about his health, as well as to other correspondence, were written by a Sicilian clerk, who rather comically retained the phrase 'our nephew' which Ingham himself was accustomed to use:

*To Joseph Payne, Mazara*　　　　　　　　　　　*7 November 1818*
Our nephew is very touched by the interest you are taking in his health, and has begged us to let you know that the fever that troubles him is a daily fever of fourteen degrees and is much diminished.

There was a brief recovery. Then:

*To Joseph Payne, Mazara* (in Italian)　　　　　　*19 November 1818*
Our nephew goes from bad to worse and we have no other hope than his youth and to commit ourselves to the wishes of Heaven.

*To Joseph Payne, Mazara* (in Italian)               *23 November 1818*
We have received yours of the 18th, and we must at once inform you that to our utmost grief God Almighty has taken our nephew Mr W. I. Whitaker to heaven in the flower of his youth and mourned by all his family and friends. In the meantime we hope any day to see the arrival of our Mr Benjamin. Consider the prospect of our grief at seeing him arrive and not being greeted by his dear and precious nephew.

By the time the news had reached Benjamin Ingham and he had been able to get a passage back to Palermo, ten days had passed. He wrote these letters soon afterwards:

*To Thomas Kettlewell, London*                 *7 December 1818*
You will readily conceive how disturbed the writer must be at so un-expected an event, but he consoles himself with the conviction that his late dear nephew is gone to a better world and to endless bliss. In the state of agony in which our minds are placed by this deplorable event, we feel little disposed to resume the disagreeable subject of our correspon-dence, as we trust that what has been written to you will convince you that the ill-natured observations in which you so liberally indulged were unnecessary. We consequently pass them over in silence.

*To Joseph Ascione, Naples*                 *10 December 1818*
The writer arrived in Sicily during the night of Wednesday 3rd after a short but rough passage of 27 hours. He found that every measure had been taken for his interest, which the truly deplorable and melancholy death of his nephew had rendered necessary. . . . On the 12th November William was so far recovered that the physician gave him hopes that he would be able to get up and sit in a chair in order to give orders relative to business. But on the 14th he was again seized by a violent fever of the most malignant kind, which baffled the skill of the most eminent doctors of Palermo, and he expired early on Saturday morning the 21st, universally regretted by all who knew him. You will be aware how great a loss it is to me and what a chasm it makes in my little society here, but the *Lord's Will* be done. It gives me no little consolation to find that every attention and care possible was rendered to my poor nephew during his illness and every honour rendered at his obsequies, both by the British Consul and all the British residents here.

Joseph Payne accompanied his condolences with a present of two fine turkeys and six capons, which were much appreciated. Further attentions, however, proved almost embarrassing.

*To Joseph Payne, Mazara*                                    *21 December 1818*
I feel much obliged for your promise of yet more capons and a fish,[4]
but I very much hope the present letter will arrive in time to prevent
your sending them. I wish not to seem ungrateful but would prefer you
to reserve them for the last day of the year, when the consul and other
gentlemen dine with me. We dine at Le Mesurier's [a Swiss banker] on
the 25th, and with the Consul on the 1st January. Be assured that nobody
would be happier than myself if you could be with us.

To return to the beginning of 1817. Ingham's suspicions that Leydings
were in a rocky state had soon been justified. When he withdrew his
custom, they threatened to sue him, but he took no notice. Other firms
collapsed throughout the Two Sicilies, as Ferdinand had announced that
the Kingdom was now to be called.[5] Ingham often had bad news to break;
for example:

*To Churchill and Price, Nottingham*                          *24 March 1817*
The subject of the present is as disagreeable to us as no doubt it will be
to you also, and we would very gladly have refrained from being the
bearers of such unpleasant tidings. Last week your debtor Signor
Martinez, finding that he could not possibly carry on any longer,
stopped payment. . . . In truth, dear Sirs, the times at the present moment are critical. Our Customs House is shut and all the books away in
consequence of a denunciation against all the foreign officers and merchants for malpractices and fraud [a somewhat pathetic attempt at
discrimination].

Only Old John seemed to be flourishing. Oates's bankruptcy was
expected to be a 'particularly bad affair'.[6] 'As for the failure of Samuel
Millot and others', wrote Ingham to Ascione, 'we say nothing further
than that our property has been sacrificed through trusting rascals.' The
shame of ruin had been too much for Abraham Gibbs. In July 1816 he had
committed suicide, within an hour of playing an apparently happy game
of backgammon. Immediately a major scandal broke out, Gibbs' son-in-
law, Colonel A'Court, claimed that he had a right to the first £30,000 out
of the estate before any credit was paid. This was the sum that Gibbs had
promised as a dowry, all too hastily, when the Colonel married his only
daughter Mary.[7] As the Colonel was the brother of Sir William A'Court,
the British Minister in Naples, unfair strings were being pulled at Court.
By June it is clear that all was virtually up between Lee-Brown and
Ingham. The portly *Abate* (Abbot) of Marsala was called in temporarily

to supervise matters. No doubt he was the distributor of the local *beni della chiesa* (goods of the church), and as the local people obviously held him in much awe he must have been the equivalent of a good plain *Capo Mafia*. A useful ally indeed, especially when it came to influencing judges and lawyers, and Ingham was always careful to flatter him. It was he who eventually drew Ingham's attention to the fact that there was at the *Baglio* a young English clerk, by name Richard Stephens, who was perfectly worthy of trust.

Stephens, an earnest young man, though with some fire in his veins, of the type that Ingham seemed fated to attract towards himself, had been a *casus belli* the previous spring when Lee-Brown, complaining of staff shortage, had hired him without Ingham's permission. Letters now sped to both him and the Abbot by *felucca*, sometimes two or three at a time. So the complicated whirl, in which Ingham thrived, continued. New characters bobbed up and down as in a marionette show.

There was one peaceful interlude: some sightseeing. Ingham went to look at Selinunte in the company of his good friend Payne. He was amazed to see those columns 'hurled confusedly together, as though in a battle of giants'. But trouble was always lurking. They must have been followed by a spy in the pay of Lee-Brown, for it was reported immediately afterwards in Palermo that Ingham whilst bathing had been observed to be covered in tattoos. The ensuing rumour, fostered by his enemy, was that he was an escaped convict. Not so wild as it might seem today, for tattooing was 'a fashion very much in vogue then in England, but little known in Sicily except as a forced branding [for smuggling].'[8] Everyone knew that Ingham must have indulged in smuggling occasionally, because nearly every one did it as a matter of course. The story took quite a bit of scotching, but whispers of it lingered among his detractors right until his death.

Lee-Brown's behaviour was altogether peculiar nowadays. One day he happened to meet Ingham in the Maqueda and started braying like a donkey. On another occasion he danced a Highland fling in Via Bara outside Ingham's counting house; he adorned his hat with peacocks' feathers, 'torn from the tails of the unfortunate birds owned by the Princess of Palagonia'. Very distasteful.

At last Woodhouse agreed to deal with the Marsala inventory, the main serious disagreement left. The sly Abbot, knowing Old John's penchant for fresh and youthful Englishmen, had been responsible for sending round Stephens to inquire after his gout. The ruse had worked miraculously, so much so that there were fears that Stephens might be lured to work for the Woodhouse *baglio*. All would have gone well with the inventory had not proof been discovered of Lee-Brown slipping a bribe to the Abbot's magistrate. Ingham immediately retaliated by 'winning over' the judge of the high court in Palermo. Then everything was turned upside down once more by the Government deciding to abolish commercial tribunals.

The following February it was the turn of Stephens to be rude.

*To Richard Stephens, Marsala*                    *18 February 1819*
You must have very extraordinary notions of the relative situation between employers and employees. I shall send your letter to Mr Payne to show him what a high bred fellow you are. In the meantime I request you will not write to me again in such fulsome language.

This was due to Stephens, in desperation no doubt, and possibly egged on by his admirer Old John, having applied to the Civil judge for payment of his salary. He too had been a victim of Sicilian legal procrastination. Ingham also wrote to the Abbot asking him to 'tell Stephens not to be so cheeky when he writes to me.'

The correspondence of this period is interesting for its references to Gardner, the foremost name in expatriate American society in western Sicily for most of the rest of the nineteenth century. In March 1817 a Captain Gardner's brig, the *Prudent*, had arrived from Boston with a shipment including twenty bags of pepper, forty barrels of salmon and a quantity of grass rope, addressed to the American Consul. This captain might well have been the same as the Benjamin Gardner mentioned on 8 February 1819 as a trader just arrived from Boston. Two months later Ingham wrote to Boston to say that Benjamin Gardner had definitely decided to establish himself in Sicily.

Gardner eventually himself became American Consul. It was his sister-in-law who was married to a grandson of Paul Revere, and her son whom he eventually adopted – being childless – and who took on the name of Gardner. Indeed the appearance of Gardner, connected as it was with another brig, the *Francis*, could not have had pleasant memories for Ingham. The American offered him a lift in the *Francis* to Marsala, but at Cape San Vito, on the wild and beautiful north-west corner of Sicily, they were caught by contrary winds. It was impossible either to proceed or to return to Palermo, so for a full week they were kept tossing at sea on a mere ninety-mile journey. No wonder Ingham swore that he would rather do the journey across the mountains by *lettiga* (litter), and risk the bandits near Segesta, than attempt it again by sea.[9]

By June 1819 the inventory was at long last complete, and an auction was to be held at the *Baglio*. Daylight at last? Not a bit of it. For instance the Marsala judge had now 'joined forces with the other thief Genna', one of Lee-Brown's many lawyers.[10] The inference becomes clear: Ingham had, through the Abbot, again bribed the judge, to fake the auction in his favour, but now the judge was turning sour. As Ingham said, by way of explanation: 'The salary of a judge of commerce is very miserable, viz. three ducats.' Then the Abbot wanted his commission too. All very Sicilian.

Ingham never missed an opportunity of making an ironic reference to the Bourbons, whom he obviously hated as much as any good islander. In a letter to Payne he wrote: 'The Prince [the Duke of Calabria, the future King Francis I] does not see fit to take his departure from Naples as early as was expected, since the lily-livers there are fearful on his account, in consequence of *leva forzosa* [conscription] in Sicily. His horses and baggage nevertheless continue to arrive, together with troops in ever-increasing and altogether ludicrous numbers.'

Shortly afterwards, there was an unexpected twist in Ingham's favour. Lee-Brown's chief lawyer, Professor Scagliosa, was heard to be dying of galloping consumption.

*To Joseph Payne, Mazara*         *1 July 1819*

May the Lord have mercy on his soul, for he has been a great sinner. . . . I hear that Stephens spends much time in the *taverne* of Marsala, getting tipsy with the farmers. That young man is too warm and hasty, and not without a considerable portion of pride. I do not in the least object to the form of his friendship with John Woodhouse. The weather may excuse an edgy mood, but a proud man is despised by all. . . . We this morning heard the flying reports of war between Britain and the Emperor of Austria, confirmed from totally respectable authority. I have asked Ascione in Naples for his opinion of the truth of this matter. . . . My hens and cocks begin to cry out for the arrival of the *frumentoni* [grain], which you were so kind as to promise them.

Scagliosa at last defunct, troubles with Lee-Brown were now more or less settled. Then a new row began, this time with Old John, who accused Ingham of trying to impinge on his preserves in Philadelphia. Ingham was of course perfectly prepared to do battle, but suddenly the whole matter of the American market was put in jeopardy by international politics.

*To Richard Stephens, Marsala*                                    *5 August 1819*
I beg that you will not purchase any more wine for the present as there
is some talk of an American war. Americans here are all of the opinion
that there will be a war between their country and Spain.

*To Joseph Payne, Mazara*                                         *5 August 1819*
Do not buy too much linseed and barilla, as the news from England
continues to get worse and worse. The report on an American war gains
ground, and the last letters from Leghorn and Naples mention that the
prices of both sugar and coffee have taken a start under this impression.
The two Americans here say that they fully expect that the United
States will declare war against Spain, in which case England will interfere, as there is no doubt that it was at their instigation that the King of
Spain refused to ratify the cession of the Floridas. The Americans do not
like the cession which it is said has been made of Havana by Spain to
England, as it will not only destroy all their West India trade, but in case
of a war might cut off all communication by sea with New Orleans,
being the key of the Gulf of Mexico.

*To Richard Stephens, Marsala*                                   *25 August 1819*
I must fear that this American war will take place. Indeed it is said that
the American squadron has left the Mediterranean for home.

War was not in the end declared on Spain, but the threat was enough for
her formally to cede West and East Florida on Washington's birthday that
year, for a sum of $5,000,000.
During this anxious time the fat old Abbot had paid a visit to Palermo.
Ingham wrote politely to ask if he had arrived back safely at Marsala. The
letter contains a sarcastic reference to the royal visit, which had at last
materialised.

*To Abate Canale, Marsala*                                       *12 August 1819*
The honey and the hens have arrived, for which thanks. The honey I
have given to the Prince of Cutò, who was highly surprised to hear that
you had already left without having the patience to wait for the long
awaited arrival of our lord and master the Duke of Calabria, who
appeared last night at 11 p.m. with all the ceremonial due to his station
and acclaimed by all the population. The illuminations were all over the
city, and even I must admit that those opposite the royal palace were
really something quite majestic.

During the autumn and winter of 1819 there were frequent visitors from England, many of whom had come to spend the season in fashionable Naples and had dared to make the sea excursion to Palermo, in spite of rumours of unrest there. Lady Morgan was one of those who arrived in Naples early in 1820. She wrote: 'The approach of spring, as we arrived in Naples, was marked by the first flittings of "Les Hirondelles". The multitudinous English, who had very literally occupied Naples during the winter, were now "ready furnished for their flight". Many were gone, others were going; some to niche themselves in Rome, while yet a pigeon-hole was left them to roost in, others to embark for Greece, Turkey or the Ionian Islands.' She went on to remark on the extraordinary number of dinners and evening parties, given by English people, following the example set by their ambassador – 'the weekly assemblies of Sir William and Lady A'Court were brilliant and crowded, and we have to acknowledge their polite and hospitable attentions.'

'The English merchants, established at Naples,' she observed, 'do not mingle with the society of the upper classes: some of them complained to us bitterly of their position, and of the annoyances to which they were subjected, from the government of Naples and the neglect of their own. Ships from England were obliged to perform quarantine . . .' Presumably Benjamin Ingham never suffered from this ostracism when he visited Naples – thanks to the Duchess of Santa Rosalia, by now his mistress.

'Les Hirondelles' had done well to escape from Naples, for an insurrection occurred there, 'bloodless and decorous'[11] but nevertheless alarming. The King was induced to sign a more liberal Constitution based on that of Spain, for the whole of the Two Sicilies. In Europe this was an important event; not only was it the first of the Italian revolutions but the first to test the strength of Metternich's system.

For Palermo it was the signal for trouble that was by no means bloodless. By the end of July 1820 a full-scale revolution had spread across Sicily.

# IV

## Scissors into Swords

THE Sicilians were not pleased with the new Constitution, as it meant
the continuance of centralised government in the hated Naples. Messina
and Trapani were on the whole in favour of the Spanish model, provided
Sicily could have her autonomy. Palermo, and more especially the faction
headed by the nobles, wanted a return to the Constitution of 1812. As
Messina was jealous of Palermo's position and considered itself more
suited to be the capital, there was a lack of unity among would-be revolutionaries from the start.

Poverty had increased greatly since 1815. The slum-dwellers of the bigger
cities cared little of course about constitutions. They just knew that the
Bourbons must be to blame for their troubles – the Bourbons and those
princes and *baroni* who kow-towed to them.

Some mild rioting had taken place around Palermo during the early
part of 1820, but the news of unrest in Naples reached the city at an explosive moment: during the *festa* of Santa Rosalia (the patron saint of
Palermo whose name Ingham's Duchess also bore), when the streets were
packed with over-excited crowds.[1] Ingham soon had to write soothing
letters to his many anxious clients in Britain and America.

*To Thomas Kettlewell, London*                                       *24 July 1820*
You will be in possession of the details of the revolution in Naples long
before this reaches you. Since the report of the one here may create
anxiety in your minds as to the fate of your goods, we send you a hasty
sketch of the events which have recently taken place.

On Friday the 14th we received intelligence of the King having signed
the Constitution. This of course created a very considerable fermentation
in the minds of the people, the more so in consequence of it coming at
the feast of Santa Rosalia, a time of mirth and festivity, occupying a week
during which time nothing is thought of but amusement, from prince to
beggar.

On Saturday the 15th, the last day of the feast, we received intelligence that the inhabitants of Messina had declared themselves deter-

mined to have a different constitution, and that they had burnt the King's statue, the stamps and such things as were considered tyrannical. This in Palermo had an effect similar to throwing oil upon fire. The national cockade was instantly hoisted, and in the evening some soldiers were even parading arm-in-arm with the citizens. The next day the mob took possession of the Castle and armed themselves. The Viceroy became alarmed and ordered the main troops to put down the people. The result was a most sanguinary conflict. . . . After a few days these troops were obliged to yield unconditionally and have now to a man been imprisoned in the town's different prisons, which at the beginning of the fracas had been emptied of all felons, galley slaves and prisoners of every description, deliberately let loose on the world to join the people against the soldiers.

Upon conquering the troops a provisional government was formed, at the head of which is the Archbishop of Palermo. What the form of government will eventually be is unknown. Good order is however restored, and we begin to sleep a little more peaceably in our beds. No one who was not an actual spectator can have any idea of the horror and confusion. We were for some days uncertain which way the popular fury might turn. However up to this moment they seem well disposed towards us English . . . We regret to mention that the mob, falling short of shot, went to the Custom House and helped themselves to what lead they wanted. We understand that amongst the rest they have taken about fifty pigs of your lead . . .

The Viceroy and all the members of the late Government, are imprisoned. Many who were attached to the Royal Family of Naples have escaped, and the people have vented their spleen towards them by burning furniture, and papers of every kind in most of the public offices.

Commerce is, as you may easily conceive, at a complete stand. The intense heat we have endured the past week has not made things any easier.

Ingham's letter to his friend Payne was a good deal more alarming and explicit.

*To Joseph Payne, Mazara*                              *24 July 1820*
A provisional Government is now established, at the head of which is the Archbishop, aided by a council of the first men in the place, viz. Pantelleria, Raddusa, Bonanno and others, and everything seems gaining its wonted quiet. A military force of six regiments is to be organised forthwith, and everyone seems desirous of being amongst the first to be enrolled. We know little of the politics more than that they seem deter-

mined to have nothing to do with Naples. Our prayer is that we English may escape unhurt. . . . On the night of the 18th the Prince of Aci was caught disguised in the Crucivia. He was shot in an instant, and being beheaded was dragged round the town with every ignominy. This happened at the back of our house and under our eyes as it were.

The end of the Prince of Aci, Praetor of Palermo and Minister of War under Lord William Bentinck, had indeed been gruesome. A man called Picciuno 'cut off his head and hands and stuck them on a bayonet; then he tied up the body and dragged it round the town, inviting everybody to pay their fines to it.'[2] Then at midnight the body was burnt in front of the Monte di Pietà, while the head was displayed at the Quattro Canti. The Prince of Cattolica later (on the twenty-third) suffered an almost similar fate in Bagheria and his body was exposed for several days; his palace and its *casina*, in which Nelson and the Hamiltons had stayed, were burnt to the ground.[3]

The Viceroy, General Naselli, had in fact fled to Naples, on 17 July. Perhaps Ingham had not wanted to sound too alarmist. What was more, the Royal Palace had been entered by the mob.

An Irishman, or rather an Anglo-Irishman, Lieutenant-General Richard Church,[4] one of those odd expatriates who found their way into the service of the Bourbons, had been as responsible as anyone for exasperating popular feeling on the fifteenth. The story is a bit confused and some details are contradictory – it was certainly one of the most inglorious episodes in the career of the man who became known as the 'Liberator of Greece'. He had been sent from Naples as *comandante generale* of the troops in Sicily. This was a foolish move, as he was already unpopular for his reputation for having been a persecutor of the *Carbonari* in Apulia, the *Carbonari* being a mostly upper-class and bourgeois secret society, very loosely organised and vaguely against all forms of tyranny.[5] There was also a rumour that he intended to impose conscription.

It was thus Church's job to order the fraternising soldiers to return to barracks. The soldiers were drunk and refused. This was the very signal for revolt. He was hit by a stone and chased in his open carriage by a mob brandishing daggers. In the nick of time he was smuggled to Trapani. An aide-de-camp (some say a coachman, some a general accompanying him) was wounded. Meanwhile the mob, not realising that he had escaped, made a rush for the Hotel d'Angleterre, where he had been staying. In their rage at finding that he was not there, the people sacked the whole building and burnt the furniture (another version says it was his own furniture) in the Piano della Marina. Another Irishman, Marshal O'Farris, who was Chief of Staff, was not so fortunate as Church and flung into a murderer's prison with other *marescialli*, naked and bleeding.[6]

Church 'found no welcome at Trapani', so he and his followers sailed on to Marsala – 'where they were most hospitably received by Mr Woodhouse. . . . He [Mr Woodhouse] ordered wine, and food: and ammunition to be got ready for provisioning their boat, and brought them all home to dine with him, assuring them they need fear nothing either for themselves or for him: for, in the first place, the people of Marsala owed him too much to wish to offend him; and in the second, he had workmen enough to defend his house against the whole population.'[7] Woodhouse who, unlike Ingham, sided with the Bourbons, as representing law and order, wanted him to remain a day or two; but Church returned to Naples, after a chase by sea and carrying some of 'Mr Woodhouse's excellent wine'. Disgraced, he was promptly clapped into prison in the Castel dell'Ovo.

In Palermo the *Giunta* or provisional Government, headed by Archbishop Gravina, was joined by the Prince of Villafranca, Ruggiero Settimo and other leading citizens. For a while the prospects seemed encouraging, and some sort of order returned to Palermo. The appearance of Neapolitan warships caused certain alarm, but 'they did not fire a gun'. A local Palermitan regiment was formed. Ingham wrote: 'What we have as yet seen of them resembles more the awkward squad than soldiers.' The *Giunta* prepared to take over the rest of Sicily, now that tempers seemed to be calming a little. Luckily all was at present quiet in Marsala. Woodhouse who kept more money to hand than Stephens would probably have been in the worse danger.

Meanwhile Ingham continued to keep his various clients informed of developments.

*To Alexander & John Haddon, Nottingham*          *31 July 1820*
It is said that a deputation of the *Giunta* has followed the Neapolitan squadron to Naples, offering to put the crown of Sicily on the head of Don Carlo – second son of the hereditary prince. Don Carlo is as yet a child of seven or eight years, and consequently it is intended that he shall reign under a regency. We are at present in some anxiety as to the fate of this mission and whether there is to be war with Naples or not. . . . The *Tamar* has been chartered by the merchants of Palermo to go to Malta to request that the Governor would send an English frigate here forthwith. Everything in fact wears the appearance of tranquillity. Our greatest comfort is the prevailing spirit of amity towards English and American persons.

As usual Payne received more realistic news:

*To Joseph Payne, Mazara*                              *3 August 1820*
An army is organizing here with the greatest rapidity. Many a tailor has
turned his scissors into a sword, and even the priests in one or two
instances have changed their cassocks into regimentals.

*To Joseph Payne, Mazara*                            *10 August 1820*
We are all thrown into complete alarm by the report that the Government of Naples have refused Independence. This news was brought by
Marquis Tortorici in a boat of thirty oars. It is as yet kept secret. In the
meantime the spirit which reigns in the blood of Palermitans, great and
small, gentle, noble and beggar, may be judged by all having hoisted a
yellow piece of ribbon [the symbol of Sicilian autonomy] on their hats
with this inscription, *Indipendenza o Morte* [Independence or Death], and
in the middle of this a death's head and bones. For my part I feel anything but comfortable.

The nobles on the mission from Palermo were arrested. A general lawlessness was beginning to spread through Sicily. Peasants made use of the
situation to settle private vendettas. Houses were burnt or sacked; at
Bronte, where the people were reputed to be descended from Albanians
and therefore of a blood-thirsty disposition, a private civil war broke out
against the neighbouring village of Maletto. Worse, it became obvious
that the other main towns of Sicily were not supporting Palermo. Marsala
now took the opportunity not only of declaring herself free from Trapani,
the capital of the province, but the *Capo Vallo*, i.e. capital itself.

*To Thomas Kettlewell, London*                      *14 August 1820*
The inhabitants of Messina are in great confusion, in consequence of
there being two parties, one for and one against the independence of
Sicily. The latter is composed of the military, who still have possession
of the citadel. All communications with Messina are at an end. We hear
from Naples that the troops when ordered to march against Sicily
refused to do this. . . . Austria, it is reported, has despatched an army of
observation against Naples.

Ingham was soon alarmed by reports of 'thieves and robbers devastating
the *campagna* under the plea of going against Trapani', especially as there
had been no news from Stephens for quite a while. Then the Prince of
San Cataldo led an army against Caltanissetta, which 'fell with a terrible
slaughter and has been reduced to obedience'. This was supposed to be a
lesson to 'those two accursed cities Trapani and Messina', but to no avail.
Six regiments had now been formed by the Palermo *Giunta*.

It was becoming obvious that the Neapolitans were doing everything they could to 'fan civil war in Sicily into a flame'. 'Lawless brigands from Trapani' were now attacking Mazara. Now there were fears for Payne's safety. A subversive group was caught on its way to Syracuse – 'every fifth man is to suffer death'.

*To Joseph Ascione, Naples*            *30 August 1820*
We cannot but consider the conduct of your ministers to be infamous in the highest degree, in their endeavour to excite civil war, brother against brother, father against son. British lives are now seriously in danger. . . . We take the liberty of sending you a letter for the Prince of Belmonte,[8] one of the deputies from here to Messina whence he has been carried off prisoner. We request you to ask your ministers to let him send an answer merely announcing his state of health for the consolation of his afflicted wife and mother.

*To Jameson Hunter, Malta*            *30 August 1820*
We solicit your kindest civilities and attentions to the bearer, our very particular friend the Countess Lucchesi, a lady who having felt considerable alarm of the late events in Sicily visits your island as a place of security. We request that you will advance such sums as she may require, taking in reimbursement the drafts of the Prince of Maletto.

Foreign property, to everybody's relief, now looked like being respected, judging from slightly reassuring letters from both Stephens and Payne. Later Ingham arranged for money to be sent to Belmonte in prison. The mention of the Prince of Maletto in his letter is the first reference in the letters to the family, in this case the brother, of the Duchess of Santa Rosalia. The Prince's title came from that same village which was warring with Bronte, where the situation had become tangled and desperate, leading to several violent deaths.[9]

Then Catania joined Messina against Palermo, which promptly sent 'a large force' against the rebels. As Ingham told a worried Richard Stephens: 'The regiments of soldiers are forming very rapidly, since the old troops have been released from the prisons and incorporated in the Sicilian regiments under Sicilian officers; as they are better paid, fed and clothed than before they are well satisfied.' There was, however, no reason for optimism.

*To Richard Stephens, Marsala*            *11 September 1820*
Since my last letter our quietness has been very much disturbed. We were on Saturday morning thrown into some alarm by the news that

Orlando[10] had been attacked most shamefully by Costa, the Messinese General, and his guerrillas. He has been obliged to abandon Caltanissetta and has lost four pieces of artillery and all the baggage. . . . On Sunday morning there arrived a Palermitan vessel from Naples, bringing back four of our deputies. . . . We are in an insufferable state of suspense.

*To Richard Stephens, Marsala*                    *18 September 1820*
A deputation has been despatched by the *Giunta* to treat with General Pepe [Neapolitan] and to accept with some little modification the terms offered by the Court of Naples. . . . The Austrians are still pouring into Italy, and the Emperor has published an edict against the *Carbonari*, making it high treason either to be one of them or to know anything about them. What Mr Payne mentions of the Trapanese plundering in his neighbourhood is far from pleasant.

The terms accepted by the *Giunta* were not at all what the general population of Palermo wanted.

*To Thomas Kettlewell, London*                    *9 October 1820*
We had up to the 25th entertained very sanguine hopes that everything would be conducted in the most peaceable and pleasant way. Indeed, all preliminaries were so far concluded that, on the evening of the 25th, the Neapolitan troops were to have entered under the escort of the civic guard, composed of the nobility and gentry, and to have taken posses-sion of the forts, castle etc. and to have been encamped outside the town. However, on that morning the rabble commenced an attack on the civic guard and on the newly formed regiments, and seized possession of their arms, forts etc. As soon as the Neapolitan troops advanced near the town, they were in like manner attacked and kept at bay for a week, during which time we suffered all the horrors of a siege in conjunction with the fear of being plundered, or even murdered, by the rabble. Peace has, however, at length been signed and tranquillity is restored to the city . . . The horror of our situation is scarce to be described and far outdid the momentous day of the 17th July. The fear of the shots and bombs, which were consequently flying over our heads, was not in any way to be compared to that which we felt at a populace who were hourly showing us that they were capable of any crime of which murder was the least.

Palermo had lost 5000 men, whereas the Neapolitans only suffered 200 casualties.[11]

*To Joseph Ascione, Naples*                                    *9 October 1820*
Bombarded by land and sea, without any police, nothing but rape, robbery and murder going on in the town, we really know not how we escaped. Peace and tranquillity are however restored by the treaty, which has been signed on board His Britannic Majesty's cutter *Racer* between General Pepe and Prince Paternò, as head of the *Giunta*. Ten thousand men have possession of the forts, castle and different batteries and are encamped outside the town. . . . We understand that the system of things in vigour previous to the 15th July 1820 is to be put in force.

*To Thomas Kettlewell, London*                              *16 October 1820*
The Government is restoring everything upon the very same footing as it was previous to the 15th July last, so that the only result of so much bloodshed and of this revolution in general has been the half ruining of the nobility and gentry and giving us three months of misery, anarchy and confusion. The lower classes and soldiery, who have made hay while the sun shone, are the only classes who have money to make purchases.

These last words were only too true. The nobles had lost much prestige during the past month and several, including the Prince of Villafranca, had had their houses burnt down. Indeed the rebellion of 1820 marked the end of the *mito di baronaggio*, the myth of the divine right of the aristocracy to rule.[12] Palermo itself was generally in disgrace, and Messina took the opportunity to demand again that she should be capital of Sicily. The occupying force meant, of course, an increase in taxes. Sullenly, the Palermitan poor retreated to their narrow alleys.

The families of the foreign merchants had on the whole been lucky, nightmarish though the experience had been. None of them had been in *really* grave danger, which was not to be the case in later outbursts in Sicily's convulsive history.

It was hardly an auspicious time for Mrs Whitaker, Benjamin Ingham's sister, to allow her younger son to go to Sicily. Nevertheless she gamely agreed; and Joseph was just at the age that would look forward to danger. The Austrians marched into Naples in March 1821 and shortly afterwards occupied Sicily. John Woodhouse was convinced that there would be a war and shipped 3000 pipes of wine to Malta for safety. Yet Joseph's presence in the Concern was badly needed, for business was at last beginning to stride forward. What was more, the vintage of 1821 was prodigal. It is indeed a pity we have so few details of the growth of Ingham's wealth just at this time, let alone of the stir that he must have created by living openly with the Duchess.

The *Baglio* buildings were greatly enlarged, work continuing on them until 1826, by which time they included a large cooperage shop employing on occasions sixty men and boys, a smithy, a carpenter's shop, a refectory for workers and two distilleries for making brandy. Coal was imported from England. A special *palmento* had been built for treading out grapes, and new rotary machinery had been acquired for washing casks. There were twenty-seven wine stores, not underground as in Spain: long, up to 150 yards, and lofty, with picturesque vaulted ceilings, Gothic in style. Nearly eighty people were on the regular payroll. In the Whitaker archives there is a fragment of a letter describing the blue-tunicked workers filing into the courtyard, while a guard with a gun paced the walls above. The writer also speaks of the 'ghastly' din of the wine casks rolling on the cobbles. Much later in date, another description is given of a typical *vendemmia*, or vintage, on one of the vineyards supplying the Ingham *baglio*. Brilliantly coloured carts, painted in traditional manner with battle scenes between mythological heroes, were trundled behind mules with bells and scarlet head-dresses. In the carts were brown-faced girls, with slanting eyes and Phoenician features, among piles of golden grapes. Then came the climax when the grapes were put in the *palmento*, and bare-legged boys with special boots leapt inside, to the accompaniment of clarinets and bagpipes made of goat bladders. . . .

The storehouses are in use to this day. The central building, in which Stephens presumably lived, and where Ingham would have stayed on his visits to Marsala, is now derelict, and more's the pity, for it is a handsome place. Almost on the scale of a colonial mansion in Virginia, it is flat-roofed with two storeys. A portico runs the length of the building down-stairs, to provide shade, while the first floor has seven French windows leading on to a balustraded balcony with eight pairs of columns. In front is a large courtyard, which used to have arcades along each side. Naturally all very much grander than the house in the *Baglio* Woodhouse.

Stephens had an eye for landscape. He planted oleanders and fig trees in strategic places and made pergolas of vines. He also built a summer-house, to catch the breezes from the sea. In the centre of the garden there was a large white *gebbia* or Saracenic cistern, filled from a well by a chain of buckets worked by a blindfolded mule.

All the lavish expenditure that went into the extending of the *Baglio* seemed spectacular in view of the financial troubles that were once more afflicting businessmen in Sicily. The trouble now was not inflation but a drastic drop in the prices of all commodities, including wine. As a result Ingham was able to sell his marsala very cheaply in both America and Britain. One also realises that he did not find the presence of the Austrians too much of an inconvenience.

> *To Richard Stephens, Marsala*                                    *2 June 1823*
> I wish you to make up a pipe of excellent old wine for the Austrian general Reitskzi, and send it in the course of a month to Palermo. At dinner last week he was particularly appreciative of our wine, and was so kind as to place an order. . . . I am now making my preparations for setting out for England and expect to be off in a week or ten days at latest. I enclose certain instructions for the management of the Concern during my absence, which I beg your particular care and attention.

Was this to be the great triumphal return to Ossett? Stephens was now virtually in the position of partner; indeed he became so in 1826, and the name of the Marsala end of the Concern was changed to Ingham, Stephens & Co. Whilst Ingham was in Leeds, he cast around for yet another nephew to work in Marsala, Joseph Whitaker being well settled in Palermo where he was too valuable to be moved. He chose another Joseph, an Ingham this time, rather a lugubrious individual and a bit weak, born in 1802 – evidently too ugly to be of interest to Old John Woodhouse. In due course two other Ingham nephews were summoned: Joshua, born in 1811, and one that bore his uncle's name, Benjamin, born in 1810. Thus – including the dead William – five nephews were employed in the firm at one time or other.

There had also been the possibility round about then of getting out another relative. This was a young cousin, again called Joshua Ingham, born in 1802 – the Ingham and Whitaker families liked to give biblical names to their children, in good North Country tradition. He was descended from Benjamin Ingham's uncle and lived at Blake Hall near Huddersfield, a house that had been a centre for Methodist preachers in the days of the Ingham of the Inghamites. Being well enough off on his own account, with the prospect of estates to manage in Yorkshire, he was not tempted by the offer of a job in Sicily.

Cousin Joshua Ingham is of literary interest, since it was he who in April 1837 engaged Anne Brontë as governess to his two elder children.[13] It was her first post and her experiences at Blake Hall are described in *Agnes Grey*, presumably pretty exactly, as the book started with the idea of being an autobiography. Her two awful charges are immortalised as Master Tom Bloomfield and Miss Mary Ann Bloomfield.[14]

In 1822 there were various references in the letters to the Santa Rosalia family. The Prince of Maletto lived in Catania and seemed constantly to have profited out of his sister's liaison with Ingham by borrowing money. However, from the tone of the letters from Palermo, he was obviously not very prompt at paying it back.

The first specific mention of the Duchess is suitably domestic, though brief:

*To Joseph Payne, Mazara*                                                    *15 May 1823*
I read your letter to the Duchess, who laughed heartily at your sending the pot without butter in it to the administrator.

Baroness of Mazara was one of her titles, and the administrator was in charge of her estates there.

Nobody seemed to have cared very much about Ingham and the Duchess living in sin. He was much in love, and one gathers she was a highly sexed woman. Palermitan nobles found Ingham too useful a source for borrowing money to want to antagonise him. The Duchess also had a strong will, and a sharp tongue for anyone who crossed her path. Her love of rouge made her appear an extraordinary creature to some, though – oddly enough – a number of men at that time seem to have found her desirable. For Ingham there was no other woman, or ever would be hence-forward in his long life.

For a while the Duchess's second son, Domenico, toyed with the plan of going to Marsala with Joseph Ingham, so that they could learn the wine trade together, but on Joseph's arrival in Palermo he suddenly changed his mind; maybe the aristocratic Sicilian and the dour Yorkshireman just didn't take to one another.

The Duchess had four sons: Federico, Domenico, Carmelo and Carlo. They all of course bore their father's patronymic, Ascenso. Only the eldest had a child, Francesca, who was the eventual heiress. She married Salvatore Monroy, Duke of Realmena, youngest son of the Prince of Belmonte. Of the four brothers Carmelo seems to have been a particular friend of Joseph Whitaker.

The Ascensos were pretty good spongers, and became worse as they grew older. Not that Ingham seemed to care, even though he hated such a thing in other people. Was he lenient through snobbery, or for love of their mother? It could have been either. Federico, known as the *Duchino* (Little Duke), received a handsome but temporary loan in November 1823 when he married Maria Lucchesi-Palli – a very good match, as she was related to the Prince of Campofranco, who had been the Viceroy the previous year.[15] Only a few months later, however, he was mildly scolded for not returning the money; indeed he seems to have been more careless about money matters than the Prince of Maletto. We also hear in this letter how 'Mama is leaving for Bagni di Lucca' for a thermal cure; and there is an ominous warning: 'I know well enough that there is a person in the city who is determined to sow discord between you and your wife, and to force a separation. You will know how to deal with this.' And that was that; we know nothing more. The marriage survived.

What was satisfactory to Ingham was the definite eclipse of the still eccentric Lee-Brown (he continued to sport peacocks' feathers whenever he knew there was a chance of running into his old enemy, and he drove about Palermo in a Sicilian two-wheeled cart, garishly painted with biblical names). Oddly, though, the man was to reappear in 1831 as a partner with of all people the Duke of Floridia, stepson of the late King, at the Zucco, a 3000 acre property near Partinico and a place still renowned for its wine. The Abbot at Marsala was probably by now dead, as we hear no more of him either. His place as supplier of wine from Church lands had been taken by the Bishop, a pompous *Monsignore*, of whom Ingham had a low opinion, expressed frequently in suitably vivid terms.

Actually Ingham had become a shade mellowed recently. All the same, nobody could have been more energetic in business, more expert at what is today called aggressive marketing. The wine that was sent to America on consignment would be followed by letters like whip-lashes, goading agents into more and more efforts. Ingham was getting richer, yet the times were still very worrying. Even old friends could not expect mercy.

*To Joseph Payne, Mazara*                                    *16 December 1824*

I take the liberty of informing you of my return to Palermo in good health. In consequence of the many failures which have taken place, I am under the necessity of calling in the funds which I have lent out. As such, I must apply to you and trust that you will be able to pay me the greater part, if not the whole, of what you owe me in a month or two at latest. I should be sorry to put you to any serious inconvenience, but necessity has no laws, and I can assure you that I am in absolute want of every dollar which I can collect either by fair means or foul.

Poor old Payne. He was unable to pay up. Another, stronger letter followed. It arrived on Christmas Day. Within a month he was dead of a heart attack.

As more Sicilian merchants went bankrupt, so more British merchants got a hold on the raw materials and industries of the island. There were relatively few Americans by comparison, Gardner being easily the doyen. Palermo and Messina were still the two main trading ports. Morrison, Routh, Valentine, Jeans, Horner, Taunton, Rose: these were some of the bigger names among the new merchants. Joseph Whitaker, being mean and thus able to save quite a bit of money, seems to have started up in various side-lines of his own. His future father-in-law, Sanderson, was greatly extending his essential oils business in Messina, the town he so much loved; indeed his firm, though Italian owned, is still flourishing strongly today under the same name, W. Sanderson & Sons.[16] Gardner's main interest was in the sulphur industry, the production of which in Sicily had risen over the years to four times in quantity, thus becoming almost a world monopoly. Originally it had mostly been shipped to Marseilles, but with the founding of sulphuric acid factories in the British Isles the greater proportion was now sent to England.

The chief paper factory in Sicily was owned by the Turrisi brothers near Palermo. Since it depended on rags, which were also an important item of export to England, the Turrisis soon found themselves clashing with Ingham, Joseph Whitaker and the once more affluent Oates, who were powerful enough even to persuade the Viceroy to alter the protectionist laws in their favour. The battle, a losing one for the Turrisis, dragged on until 1842, when they went out of business. A modern commentator has written, bitterly: 'In the name of free trade, British "merchants" not only monopolised Sicilian raw materials for industries in their own country, but ruined or scotched at birth any attempt at industrialization by Sicilian capital.'[17] A harsh summary, and not altogether true, as will be seen. A very great Sicilian merchant-industrialist-banker, Vincenzo Florio, was soon to emerge and become well established long before 1842.

In 1825 the British Chancellor of the Exchequer dramatically reduced the duty on wines, with the effect that marsala (and madeira) had a considerable advantage over French wines and rum. Ingham was delighted and began some experimenting.

*To Joseph Bickford, Plymouth*                                  *28 June 1825*
I confirm that our Marsala establishment is preparing a red wine in imitation of port which we could sell you at £10 a pipe. We sent a sample of red muscatel wine reinforced with brandy to Glasgow, and this has led to several orders. . . . If you can charter a vessel cheap to go to Newfoundland for dried cod, it would be well worth your while. Fish is always saleable in Naples. We can then arrange for the vessel to

5. The Quattro Canti, Palermo, c. 1840, looking down the Toledo. Church of S. Giuseppe in centre; on left Palazzo Bordonaro, on right Palazzo Rudinì (*artist unknown, in possession of W. I. Whitaker of Pylewell*).

6. Travelling by *lettiga*, 1824 (from W. H. Smyth's *Sicily and its Islands*).

7. Benjamin Ingham, aged eighteen in Paris, 1802.

8. Georg Wilding, the Hanoverian mercenary who married the Princess of Butera and became Prince of Radalì (*in the possession of Baron Luigi Chiaramonte Bordonaro*).

be loaded here with Sicilian produce including our Bronte Port, which we are sure you will find superior to the madeira lately imported into England, being free from the acid quality which such wines now inevitably have.

So Ingham had stolen the Bronte prefix from Woodhouse. Having plunged into the investment, it was worrying for him to hear from London that sherry had suddenly become popular, again because of the reduced taxes on non-French wines.

*To Richard Stephens, Marsala*                               *18 August 1825*
Your will see that the wine which Mr Woodhouse shipped on board the *Cherry* in April last has not been approved of, and that the rage in England is for sherry or for wines having a sherry flavour and a light colour. Now I am of the opinion that we could give marsala such a flavour by putting in it an extract from sweet almonds. You already have these extracts for making *rosolio* [a sweet liqueur]. I would recommend your making a trial upon a few pipes of wine to see how it answers.

Stephens was anxious to taste this sherry. At last, three weeks later, Ingham was able to write: 'My coachman has gone to the Consul's for a bottle, which will be sent to you if it can be spared.'[18]

The red wine for the 'port' came from far away: Vittoria, on the south-east corner of Sicily. Thither Stephens had to travel by ship. At the same time Ingham made the effort of investigating the resources of Alcamo, famous then as now for its black-veiled women and picturesque balconies. He found the place and its women mean and dirty, and could not face visiting the Arab castle's site; and the bleating of goats kept him from his sleep. Nevertheless he hired a mule and manfully rode some nine kilometres over the parched, silent mountains to see the temple of Segesta. Quite a pilgrimage in that heat. The Doric columns of the roofless building were duly inspected, but not the theatre on the hill. Luckily, for the return journey from Alcamo, he was able to hire a carriage and thus enjoy the beautiful, blessedly more verdant landscape, with its profusion of oleanders. G. W. D. Evans, a traveller of the period, wrote how 'carriage-travelling is a luxury almost unknown in Sicily'. It was indeed reckoned then that there were only 250 miles of carriageable road throughout the whole island, the best road – thanks (*pace* Simond) to the British army during the occupation – being between Palermo and Messina. The *lettiga* was reserved for 'the wealthy and the delicate'. Evans strongly denied there was any danger of brigandage on the roads, however 'execrable' they were; as he said, 'with regard to the danger upon which travellers in Sicily have so often enlarged, they may now be ranked with the tales of the nursery.' One fancies, however, that this was wishful thinking. Ingham of course always travelled with a more than adequate bodyguard.

The following year John Woodhouse died, aged fifty-eight. He had been suffering intensely from his gout and had been starving himself, so he died of sheer weakness. Indeed his last portrait makes him look like a survivor from a World War II concentration camp. A family mausoleum was built, in appearance rather like a marabout's tomb. Strangely, it was never consecrated until 1900. The whole thing was blown to bits by British bombs in 1943.

The disappearance of Old John, *Il Vecchio* as he was known to the Marsalese, made a great difference to Ingham's trade. Neither of John's quarrelsome brothers, Sam and Will, his heirs, had much flair for business. They died in 1834 and 1835 respectively, and the firm was divided between their sons, both minors. Thus control gravitated to an uncle, Humphrey Hervey, one of the trustees – not a happy situation. Hervey, known as Don Onofrio at Marsala, was a thoroughly bad if not corrupt businessman, and remained virtually in charge for some thirty years. It has been suggested that he deliberately tried to let the firm run down, so that he could buy it at a bargain price from the young Woodhouses, who were even more disinterested in it than their fathers, preferring their hunting and shooting. To make matters worse, Hervey appointed a series of disastrous managers, one being John Barlow, of whom it has been said: 'He seemed to have been more interested in social life and the ladies than anything else, as witness the many red heads scattered over that part of Sicily.'[19]

King Ferdinand, *Re Nasone* (King Big Nose) to his subjects, had died on 2 January 1825, after a reign of sixty-five years. His son Francis I meant well but was hopelessly inept. During his short reign the *Carbonari* and other secret societies flourished. Smuggling, arson, kidnapping, in spite of G. W. D. Evans, became ever more common in Sicily. The *lupara* or sawn-off shot gun, for shooting wolves, was frequently put to terrible use in village feuds. The word *Mafia* was not yet current, but all the ingredients were there.

The Austrians withdrew in 1827, and Swiss mercenaries were employed by the Bourbon Government as a supplementary police army – the southern Italians not being especially martial types. The presence of the Swiss did not much help the economy. But Ingham, with his insistence on a twelve per cent interest and three per cent commission, continued to prosper.

Tourists flocked to Naples; yet Sicily was still regarded as remote and somewhat outlandish, except for Palermo which could easily be reached from Naples by steamer. Travel books about Sicily continued therefore to have great popularity, especially Simond's and even the by now slightly discredited Brydone's. One learns from Simond that the population of Sicily then was around 1,800,000. 'Not a day has passed since our landing,' he said (in 1828), 'without our hearing someone lament the fall of Buonaparte and the retreat of the English.' He hastened to add that these complaints were 'not for the sake of either of them, but because the existence of one and the presence of the others maintained the Constitution; and above all effectually separated Naples and Sicily.' He summed up the island's plight as follows: 'Sicily now seems as completely a *tabula rasa* of depotism as Naples itself, and puts up with a good many more abuses. . . . It would still feed five times its own population, if that population were but left alone, and their industry not shackled by absurd regulations, the natural capabilities rising superior to bad husbandry.'

The seeds of revolution were still there, and were again ready to sprout.

# V

## Travellers and Romance

JOSHUA INGHAM is mentioned as being in Sicily in 1829, when he was eighteen, so one can assume that his next elder brother, always known in the Concern as Benjamin Ingham junior, and in the family as Ben, must have arrived a year or two earlier. Joshua took over the position that had been occupied in Marsala by his other brother, the gloomy Joseph Ingham, and remained exiled there more or less for the rest of his life. Joseph Ingham was sent to live in Boston,[1] as trade with America was developing to such a vast extent – his uncle had also been making some use of a Massachussetts connection started by the Ingham of the Inghamites (in spite of the great man having been opposed to the drinking of wine).[2]

If Joseph Ingham was thankful to escape from his overbearing uncle, he could not escape his letters. Wine, sumac, pumice stone, silk, bales of rags were coming over to Boston in quite large quantities. It is clear that the Concern had some brigs of its own at this stage. The unfortunate young man could rarely do anything right:

> *To Joseph Ingham, Boston*                    *4 June 1829*
> I beg you to be open and candid, and not expose yourself to any remark which will injure your character and standing, for in a country like America such things have great and serious consequences. The *Nestor* arrived here on the 31st. It is a great pity that you asked for the staves and cloths to be sent to Marsala and not to Messina. As regards the staves, I have examined them and have found them fair, but nothing equal to the lot that you sent us on board the *Pembroke* . . . many are knotty and not fit for casks. When we consider the high freight and duties (equal almost to the first cost in Boston) you will be aware that it is folly to ship to this country any other staves except those that are the very best dressed. The fact that you chose to send them in an American brig means that the seven bales of cloth will not enjoy the ten per cent reduction on duties allowed for British and other flags. . . .
> You acted very wrong in letting the wine on board the *Pembroke* go in Boston at the miserable price of 80 cents a gallon and also in selling it

exclusively to the house of Munsen and Barnard. Now all the other buyers will be displeased.

Over the next years Benjamin Ingham saw to it that Joseph was kept to the grindstone. With the market growing so quickly, he just could not afford to let him relax. Then on 8 October 1833 Joseph committed suicide at the City Hotel, New York. Few details are given, though we know that he shot himself and that the coroner's verdict was that the suicide was due to melancholy. Early in August he had suffered some 'deplorable accident' in Boston and had nearly died. There is a mystery about his will, which he made just before leaving Boston for New York. Eventually the will was admitted to be *bona fide*, and letters of administration were granted to a Mr Hodgkinson. However, the British Consul in Boston, George Manner, tried to gain administration of the estates and appealed against the will, 'with no other view than to secure his fees'.

We know that Ben was sent out to investigate this sad situation, but there are no details. He remained in America for two years, travelling extensively up and down the east coast. He was so successful that he soon became a kind of roving ambassador for the firm, visiting America nearly every year and often travelling to France, the Italian mainland and the West Indies. The three surviving nephews in the firm were therefore deployed as follows: Joseph Whitaker in Palermo, Joshua Ingham in Marsala and Benjamin Ingham junior free lance. Whereas Ben and Joseph were obviously of the right stock, Joshua's less dynamic character comes through rather imprecisely.

A letter written in April 1830 from Ingham senior to Joseph Whitaker has survived separately from the letter-books. It reads like a series of military orders and is more or less a summary of all Ingham's activities at that time. Evidently it was written just before he was due to set off on another trip to England.

The letter has thirty-four headings (sumac, barilla, liquorice paste etc). 'DO NOT FORGET THIS', which deals with the all-important mortgage business throughout the island. From this one learns that Anne Page, of the Prince of Wales Hotel, and her husband owe money, as do the Princes of Campobello (the ex-Viceroy) and Valguarnera, and that the Lenzitti bankruptcy affair is – not surprisingly – still dragging on. Two of the brigs used by the Concern are given as the *Ulisse* and the *Alessandro*. An estate of 580 acres has just been bought in the province of Caltanissetta. But the totally new development is a partnership with the Prince of Pantelleria, the patriot leader of 1848, in some sulphur mines at Girgenti, the modern Agrigento, in the arid, hilly country on the south coast of Sicily.

It ends characteristically:

And you will write to me every fourteen days, oftener if required. It remains for me only to repeat my most urgent recommendation that you devote the whole of your attention and care to the Concern and to subscribe myself

Yours most truly B. Ingham

One realises from this letter how Benjamin Ingham was keeping a grip on every smallest detail affecting the Concern. His memory must have been phenomenal. Not that he needed to worry about Joseph Whitaker's capabilities, or his interest in the work. Unlike his late elder brother William, Joseph was a fanatic for letter-writing. There was nothing he liked better than having an office run like clockwork, getting everything properly filed and pigeonholed, and pouncing on the inefficiencies of untidy minds. Gradually, in the succeeding years, he took command of those small details, and his uncle was shut out from them. This gave him the supremacy he wanted.

Ingham's particular emphasis on the sulphur trade, as shown in the April 1830 letter was, as always, shrewd and well-timed. By 1834 exports had almost tripled those of wine, and in that year there were at least twenty British-owned firms dealing in it. As it happened, for political reasons, at the end of the 1830s exports had begun to drop – but by then Ingham had no doubt made a great amount of profit. Among the main firms which survived the eventual slump were those of Gardner and Rose at Lercara, in the centre of Sicily, and Frank at Licata, near Girgenti.

James Rose was English, a muscular, smiling John Bull, grandson of a Woolwich lighterman. He had been sent to work for an uncle in Messina at the age of twelve.[3] Originally he had traded in citrus fruit, but in the boom years of sulphur had gone into partnership with Benjamin Gardner, American Consul in Palermo since 1825. Gardner, in spite of a rather forbidding demeanour, was well-known for his magnificent receptions. A compatriot of his, N. P. Willis, arrived in Palermo in June 1833 on board the frigate *United States* and described such a party in honour of the ship's officers. It was given in a palace at Bagheria: 'The crowd of carriages in the court, the gold-laced midshipmen scattered about the massive stairs and in the formal walks of the gardens, the gay dresses of the ship's band playing on the terrace, and the troops of ladies and gentlemen in every direction, gave an air of bustle to the stately structure that might have reminded the marble nymphs of the days when they were first lifted to their pedestals.' The table was 'loaded with every luxury of the season' and seated sixty or seventy people. Willis added: 'No cost had been spared and the hospitable consul (a Bostonian) did the honours of his table in a manner that stirred powerfully my pride of country and birthplace. All the English resident in Palermo were present; and it was the more agreeable to me that their countrymen are usually the only givers of generous entertainment in Europe . . . against the charge of hardness and selfishness urged upon our nation.'

There were 'one or two lovely girls' among the English and they, with the officers' wives, appeared to have thoroughly enjoyed dancing 'in the soft light of the moon'. Never had there been a gayer party, and the Americans left unwillingly, so as to be back in Palermo by midnight.

It was the age of travel on the grand scale by English aristocrats. The most stylish 'milord' in recent years had been the Duke of Buckingham, looking for antiques and other *objets d'art*. He came to Palermo in his sumptuous yacht, the *Anna Eliza*, and for a while stayed with the British Consul, Mr Lindeman. He was much fêted by the 'Viceroy', the Marquis delle Favare, and the excited nobility, whose general state of poverty somewhat dismayed him. The Viceroy was obviously anxious that the Duke should leave with a favourable impression of governmental progress, and to some extent he succeeded, though the latter in his often humorous diary, posthumously published, kept qualifying praise with such remarks as 'I am not defending arbitrary power – God forbid that any Englishman should do so!'[4]

Ingham naturally did the Duke proud, but the money spent on entertaining him proved also to be a good investment. 'The noble lord insisted on paying me five times the value for my collection of Greek vases sent me last year from Tindaris. He also bought the Duchess of Santa Rosalia's fine tortoiseshell toilet set mounted in silver that belonged to the late Queen Maria Carolina.' The Duke then continued on his long ambitious tour, with a secretary, a chaplain and a doctor on board. He had wisely brought plenty of gunpowder and muskets, in case of trouble from pirates. He climbed up Etna, saw Syracuse and Messina, then visited Naples and Malta. Next he sailed along the southern coast of Sicily. When he reached Marsala he found the inhabitants recovering from a severe earthquake, which had taken place three weeks before, having killed four persons. Stephens was abed with shingles, so it was that red-headed Don Juan, the Woodhouse manager Mr Barlow, who came to welcome him on board, with a present of wine – 'good in itself', mused the Duke, 'but to my mind very much injured by the quantity of brandy which they put in it, both for the American and British markets.' It was reckoned, he added, that Woodhouse exported 3000 pipes annually.

Not much was thought of the countryside around Marsala either scenically or archaeologically – 'no antiquities to be collected . . . in the evening the smell of the marshes was very distinctly appreciable on board, and perfectly explains the malaria' – the *Anna Eliza* set sail for Trapani. Mount Eryx and Segesta were duly visited, also the dread, penitential island of Pantelleria, before the return journey to Naples.

Another notable arrival in Sicily was that of Lord Ossory, later Ormonde, travelling with his friend Mr Odell. He also wrote up his experiences and published them many years later.[5] The two had a far less comfortable trip, indeed an exhausting one, travelling on mules – 'most provoking animals'[6] – and usually sleeping out in tents. Ossory was impressed by the beauty of Messina, but not at all by Mazara: 'Every house, says the proverb, contains a priest and a pig. We encountered thirty-four priests on our ride through it, but I took no heed of the pigs.'

They stayed at the Locanda Nuova at Marsala, 'a very fair sort of inn', and drank the 'first really good wine that we had tasted in the country', and as a result arranged for a cask to be sent home to Ireland.

In Palermo they went to Marletta's hotel, originally Madame de Montagne's, and like previous guests complained of the proximity of the Vicaria prison – the prisoners' begging, the nightly hailing of sentinels every half hour. Ossory was not nearly so 'hoity-toity' towards the Anglo-Saxon 'mercantile and professional gentlemen' as the Duke had been, overwhelmingly hospitable though they were. Indeed Ingham felt he spent 'too much time at the house of my friend Mr Gardner, after all an American.' 'Both young gentlemen,' he also noted, 'seem to enjoy driving up and down the Marina after nightfall, for reasons which one can but guess.'

The heavy baggage was forwarded to Naples on a brig specially hired by Ingham. It was now important for Ossory and Odell to travel light, as like many other British travellers they were curious to see Bronte and Etna. But, again like the rest, 'they were a bit disappointed in Bronte, its pile of rude houses surrounded by lava beds'. Etna was also in the actual process of eruption, and the 'constant fall of light ashes' and the sinister sound of thundering from the mountain did not encourage them to linger. So before long they were off to Messina, through thickets of arbutus 'throwing those of Killarney into the shade', on the homeward journey.

They passed red-roofed Maletto, 3100 feet high, where the lovely, wooded countryside was 'richly clothed with fine oaks, pines and poplars', with views of Etna. It was a pleasant contrast to the unlucky Bronte where indeed the inhabitants were then in an exceedingly depressed state – but not entirely the fault of Nelson and his heirs (as some later chroniclers would have us assume). In many ways, as Ossory had been assured by Ingham and his friends, the Duchy had been a back-handed gift to Nelson, for the hospital in Palermo, its previous owner, had allowed the land to go to waste. After Nelson's death the estate had been bedevilled by litigation with the Comune of Bronte. In view of all this, and of the fact that its Castle of Maniace was simply a romantic ruin, Nelson's brother – his heir – could not afford to do much by way of improvement, although agents were left in charge.

In 1835 Nelson's niece Charlotte, Lady Bridport, inherited the title of Duchess of Bronte, so she and her husband decided to visit the place personally. She was amused by the dress of the locals – the men's leggings and the slit up the back of their coats, and the women with white flannel shawls round their heads. Yet she was so overcome by the rigours of the journey by *lettiga*, the black volcanic landscape and the tales of atrocities in 1820, including beheadings and disembowelments, that she swore that she would 'never come back to the island unless there was a revolution in England, and even then would probably go elsewhere.' She loved the view from Taormina, poor and dirty though the town was; if she had been forced, whilst in Palermo, to stay at Marletta's no doubt her decision never to return would have been confirmed. In any case a revolution of sorts was to break out in Sicily itself in 1837.[7]

A distinguished visitor to Sicily at that time was John Henry Newman. He was well entertained in Palermo and on 17 February 1833 wrote to his sister Harriet how 'we dined last Tuesday at Palermo with Mr Ingham, one of the principal merchants', adding:

I ought to give you an account of an Italian dinner as we first became acquainted with it on board the steamer, after waiting until we were very hungry. First a course of cheese, pickles, anchovies, raw sausages of mule's flesh – then soup, then some boiled meat, then fish, then cauliflower, then a fowl, lastly pastry with a dessert. You are never helped twice. I see now the meaning of the English phrase, 'cut and come again'. Yet sometimes, as at Mr Ingham's, this dinner becomes quite superb. All over the South, according to our experience, after two or three glasses of wine, the cloth not being removed, coffee (one small cup) is brought in, which is followed by some liqueur, and so the entertainment ends.[8]

Newman then journeyed to Rome. He returned to Sicily, but his trip ended unhappily, for he became seriously ill in Syracuse and thought he was going to die. In May, as soon as he was fit enough, he hastened to Palermo, where he stayed at Page's Hotel, originally the Prince of Wales, favoured by members of the Woodhouse family when in Palermo. It is very likely that Benjamin Ingham, who in any case lived not far from the hotel, would have been one of the people to help him to get a passage back to France. Later Newman wrote:

I was aching to get home; yet for want of a vessel I was kept at Palermo for three weeks. At last I got off in an orange boat, bound for Marseilles. Then it was [on 16 June] that I wrote the lines 'Lead Kindly Light', which have since become well known. We were becalmed for a whole week in the Straits of Bonifacio [between Sardinia and Corsica, at which time the hymn was written].

When the British church was eventually built in Palermo, its first chaplain made 'Lead Kindly Light' a kind of sombre theme-hymn for his congregation.

On 8 November 1830 King Francis had died, to be succeeded by his son Ferdinand II, the man who was later known as King Bomba. Ferdinand was a much more vigorous character than his father, though his 'common manner and off-hand ways'[9] did not endear him to his 'better-class subjects'. He seems at first seriously to have wanted to carry through some reforms and to pay a little more attention to the woes of his Sicilian subjects. He visited Sicily in the summer of 1831, but almost immediately after his departure – and despite all the festivities and welcomes – there was another revolt, though only a small one, resulting in thirty-three arrests. His next visit, in 1834, looked at first as though it was going swimmingly. Paths were strewn with flowers; loyal subjects flocked with lanterns from Palermo to greet the Queen's carriage returning from the shrine of Santa Rosalia on Monte Pellegrino. Unfortunately, as so often happened in Sicily, an unforeseen disaster exacerbated public feelings: there was an explosion at the factory where fireworks were made for the *festa* of Santa Rosalia, and some people were killed and wounded. There were rumours (unjustified as it happened) of Neapolitan sabotage. When the King left

Sicily, it was felt that, when all was said and done, he had achieved virtually nothing to improve the island's lot.

Then in September 1835 the great composer Vincenzo Bellini died, aged thirty-three, not long after the first performance of *I Puritani*. He came originally from Catania, and his early death caused a sort of frenzy throughout Sicily, so that he suddenly became a nationalist symbol – indeed, in spite of the fact that he had died in Paris, the Neapolitans might almost have murdered him.

When revolt did break out once more, in July 1837, it was due not only to despair on the part of the poor, but to panic and ignorance – an ignorance shared even by universitity professors. For it was genuinely believed that an epidemic of cholera had been maliciously spread through poison by the Neapolitans.

Cholera was relatively new to Europe. There had been an outbreak in Ancona in August 1836 and it had soon begun to spread southwards in a most alarming way. By October it had reached Naples, where it raged for most of the winter. And it did not subside until March, by which time there had been 6200 deaths in the city alone. A short while later it broke out again and spread to Sicily.[10]

The hysteria on the mainland in 1836 as the cholera advanced had been almost as bad as it was to be in Sicily the following year, the chief reason being that the doctors were not sure how to cope with the disease. In Naples emergency hospitals and first-aid posts were hurriedly prepared. The King was completely overwrought. Indeed the bad state of his nerves was well illustrated by a much publicised incident involving Carmelo Ascenso, third son of the Duchess of Santa Rosalia.

Ascenso was an army captain at the time. During some manoeuvres under the personal command of the King he misinterpreted an order. The King was furious and at once spurred his horse, galloping up to Ascenso with a drawn sword. He struck out violently at the young officer, whose life was only saved by his shako, sliced almost right through. Ascenso 'bore the insult in silence, but at once left the camp and sent in his resignation'.[11] Nevertheless the affair caused such a scandal both socially and diplomatically that Ferdinand was compelled to recall Ascenso and make him a public apology. While this apology was taking place it was said that the King's rage was so great that he tore his gloves to ribbons. 'He never forgave Ascenso the humiliation of this apology, and deliberately thwarted his career on every possible occasion.' Ascenso never forgave him either.

The ravages of the cholera in Sicily were to be far worse than in the

Neapolitan provinces. In all 136,033 people died,[12] nearly a fifteenth of the population. And the xenophobia this time was not always directed towards Neapolitans but sometimes against foreigners in general.

Meanwhile Ben had been energetically coursing up and down America on his uncle's behalf. He was a genial-looking person and sturdily built, described as having a 'mild and conciliatory disposition'. Later he became slightly bald and sported a flap of hair over the top of the head. Nobody thought that he would ever get married.

There were fewer complaints now about the quality of the wine emanating from Ingham, Stephens and Co.; Woodhouse wine seemed quite definitely to have taken second place. Now it was generally conceded that Ingham had 'created' the main demand in the United States. Alfred Greenough of Boston justly told him: 'You have made the reputation of "Sicily", but the benefit of your success is reaped by others.' During this period outlets were also being explored in Australia and Brazil. Large consignments of wine were being sent to New Orleans, as well as to the previous main markets of Boston, Philadelphia, Baltimore and New York. In February 1837 the firm started its association with Messrs Barclay and Livingston of New York. This connection proved to be of vital importance, for one of the partners was Schuyler Livingston, whose brilliance as an investor was largely responsible for lifting Ingham senior to the status of a multi-millionaire.

Ben had boldly become involved in large-scale fruit dealing with a Daniel Draper of Boston. One senses that at first he was slightly nervous of his uncle's reactions, for citrus fruit had up to then been only of very minor interest to the Concern. All the same, he suggested that no less than 100,000 boxes of oranges and lemons might be sent to Draper. His hunch was well justified, and from then onwards the firm was deeply involved with the fruit trade in the United States.

Romance seems to have been in the air in 1836. The young English ladies of Naples and Sicily were put into a flutter by the news of the pretty twenty-year-old Penelope Smyth eloping with Prince Charles of Capua, brother of the King. Penelope was Anglo-Irish, coming from Ballynatra, County Wexford. She had been seen out riding various times with the Prince, who was well known for his weakness for Englishwomen. One evening at the Opera she complained of a sore throat and went home early. When the rest of the party returned, she had disappeared.

All this was thanks to forged passports arranged by a certain 'Mr

Patrick O'Conor of the Navy'. Penelope and her Prince were eventually married on 5 April, in traditional style – over the anvil at Gretna Green. It was very exciting, for King Ferdinand was at present widowed, with only one son, and Charles stood next in line to the throne. Unfortunately the Prince was immediately informed that his marriage was illegal and indeed that Penelope and any children would never be regarded as part of the royal family. Moreover, all his lands were confiscated, with the exception of the wretchedly poor estate of Mascali in Sicily. A life of wandering, harassment and bitterness now started for the couple. They had two children. Prince Charles died in 1862, Penelope in 1882.

Ferdinand himself had in fact decided to find a new wife. In the early summer of 1836 he paid a quiet visit to Vienna, where he chose for his bride the Archduchess Maria Theresa. They were married, again quietly, on 9 January, and a fortnight later he brought her to cholera-stricken Naples.

During that same summer Sophia Sanderson had become engaged to Joseph Whitaker. It had been an ardent but brief courtship. The soft-natured Sophia, who was twenty, was a bit frightened of Joseph and, it is said, had not the 'strength' to refuse his proposal. Obviously the match was a good one, with a rich uncle in the background, or rather foreground. Reading between the lines, however, one wonders whether she was really trying to escape from home, as her widowed father was himself about to make a marriage, unpopular in the family, to a Prussian lady named Bertha Aders.

Sophia was in Naples, staying with her uncle William Routh, another big merchant there,[13] in order to buy her trousseau, when the cholera swept down from the north. It was too late to get away; ships' captains were refusing to call at Naples. So she was marooned and the wedding had to be postponed. Joseph, unable to reach her, was frantic.

Meanwhile Uncle Benjamin had a plan of his own, which was to make an honest woman, or an apparently honest woman, of his Duchess. This was a secret, but it had not escaped Joseph, who had now reached his position of bureaucratic ascendancy and was strongly opposed to the 'marriage'. Part of a letter survives from Joseph to his elder brother, yet another Joshua, at Ossett. It shows that Joseph had more humour than one might have credited him with from his looks:

My dear Brother,
 . . . I now proceed to give you some domestic intelligence. In the first place I regret to inform you that I am still kept at this place what with

business and what with our interrupted intercourse with the continent owing to the cholera at Naples, while my intended better half is waiting for me in the city. And when I shall be able to join her there I know not. My uncle I believe is determined not to let me go till April which is the more provoking as in the course of a short time we shall absolutely have nothing in the world in the way of business to prevent my going – but as the Sicilians say – *pazienza* – which you will not be at any great loss to guess means in English, patience. The Other Marriage in the Family will take place *very* soon if we may believe what we hear on the subject. Should my uncle ever take it into his head to take the Lady over with him to England you would of course have an opportunity of making acquaintance with your new Aunt, and Ossett would no doubt be graced with her Grace's presence. You could not do otherwise than have the Old House put to rights somewhat to receive such a distinguished visitor, and I will take care to inform you beforehand in order that you may have plenty of time to order furniture etc., of which you will need the value of full £500 to make things at all befitting for the occasion. . . .

And now my dear Jos I must come to a conclusion for Ben is waiting for me to have our punch which we take regularly almost every night – and I am besides tired of writing, not being accustomed much to it by candlelight. Pray give my best love to my Mother and believe me always very truly

Your Aff. Brother,
Joseph Whitaker

The old boy released Joseph in March, the cholera epidemic apparently having come to an end. The story runs that he had planned his own marriage ceremony the moment his nephew was safely at sea. The ship departed; unfortunately there was a gale and it had to return to port – so Joseph caught his uncle in the act.

# VI

## *Awful and Unexplained*

WHATEVER form the ceremony took, there are plenty of reasons for supposing that the marriage between the Duchess and her *cicisbeo* was never made legal. Ingham did not claim any of her titles, which would have been worth his while, though he did take the trouble to obtain royal confirmation to the title of Baron of Manchi e Scala – his 580-acre *feudo* carrying with it the right to this distinction. There is no mention of the event in any of the letters, nor yet in *Whitaker of Hesley and Palermo*, whose author would have been quick to seize on such an illustrious connection.

True, in Ingham's will he refers to 'my beloved wife'. Otherwise the first documentary authority appears ninety-nine years later in Tina Whitaker's *Benjamin Ingham of Palermo*. In this pamphlet it is also claimed that Cardinal Pignatelli di Monteroduni gave 'hurried written permission', but such a statement does not help either, since Pignatelli did not become Cardinal of Palermo until 1839. No doubt they merely went through some sort of civil formula to satisfy tongue-waggers in the Consul's office. At any rate from then onwards the pair lived as man and wife. Ingham left his house in Via Bara, and he and the Duchess settled in the villa in the Piano di Sant'Oliva (where a glass office block now stands). The villa was simply proportioned and not especially large, in traditional Palermitan style, though probably built by Ingham himself since he refers to his 'new house' in a letter to Stephens in 1825. The house in Via Bara was made ready for Joseph Whitaker and his bride.

There is a statement in the pamphlet that 'before his marriage Mr Ingham, with his usual forethought, made the Duchess sign a declaration renouncing all right to any claim on Mr Ingham's fortune'. Perhaps this was the nub. When Joseph became engaged to Sophia Sanderson, the Duchess saw the chances of inheritance slipping away for her sons and their descendants. Ingham was fifty-three, a dangerous age for an active businessman – right in the coronary belt. She must have insisted on the marriage ceremony; he in turn would have gone through the performance of drawing up the declaration to satisfy Joseph. After the signing the document must have disappeared or have been destroyed, otherwise Joseph and

Sophia would not have worried so much about the inheritance when they began producing children.

One of the Duchess's wifely duties was to accompany Ingham to Marsala, where she took an immediate dislike to both Stephens and the *Baglio*, what with the 'trying fumes of the fermented grapes, the noise of the workers hammering at the cooperage and rolling out the heavy barrels of wine for embarkation in front of the house, the inconvenience...'[1] Thus Ingham had to look out for a country property that would please her. In 1840 he found Racalia, some five miles from Marsala, on a hillside overlooking the vineyards towards Motya and the Aegadean Islands, with a view of the fabled Mount Eryx away to the right. The long, rambling villa, which he enlarged, still stands today and is typical of an English expatriate's retreat, serene and unpretentious among tall trees, luxuriant shrubs, peacocks and fountains.[2]

The Duchess's unpunctuality was notorious – perhaps it was a way of asserting herself over the perpetually busy Ingham. On one occasion at least it brought them both luck. Some brigands were lying in wait for Ingham on the road along which he was expected to pass between Marsala and Racalia. The Duchess was to have accompanied him and was so late that the brigands got bored and 'decided that for that day he was not coming and went off'. Thus the story ends, and indeed there are no other references in the papers to Ingham being troubled personally by brigandage.

Sophia's mother, who had died in 1833, had been a Jeans, a name well known among the British merchants of Sicily, Naples and Malta. A brother had married into the Rose family, and she was also connected to Edward Gibbon Wakefield the colonial statesman, Priscilla Wakefield the philanthropist, Elizabeth Fry, the Bonham Carters and thus later, though indirectly, to Florence Nightingale. If the letters say nothing about the 'Other Marriage', they also barely refer to the occurrence of Joseph's and Sophia's wedding, which took place on 18 March 1837 at the British Legation in Naples. The Rev. Charles Lushington officiated – a good Anglo-Neapolitan name, for he was one of the six sons of Sir Henry Lushington, who until 1832 had been Consul-General for the Two Sicilies.

At least Joseph was spared his uncle's letters for three weeks. Ingham indeed seems to have been in a thoroughly bad mood, not the best way to start his married life – though there were good reasons. A brother had died in England, so Joshua Ingham was also – at this very inconvenient time, with Joseph absent – having to leave Sicily temporarily in order to settle matters in Yorkshire. The cholera scare was very aggravating, and commerce was being seriously affected. Benjamin Ingham grumbled constantly at the strictness of 'that greatest of Mediterranean miseries, quarantine', far worse than usual, on ships arriving from Naples, and indeed had sent an official letter to the Minister, the amiable William Temple, via Joseph Whitaker when the latter sailed on 3 March. Temple was Palmerston's brother, and such was his nature that it is unlikely that he personally would have taken much notice.[3] At any rate he was under a cloud with the King, who believed that he had connived at the elopement of his brother with Penelope Smyth.

Nevertheless Ingham's complaint was made in some desperation.

*To Dobree, Maingay & Co., Naples*                    *11 February 1837*
As to our Board of Health relaxing in their measures, it is useless to expect it for some time yet to come. They are as obstinate as it is possible for man to be, and continue to give fourteen to twenty-one days only to arrivals from Malta, whereas vessels from your port are made to perform their quarantine with the utmost rigour that their laws enjoin. It is clear that their hostility is founded more than anything on a pique which they have against Naples. We mention this in confidence as we would not wish our names to be made use of in any way. . . .

We are sorry to say that we perceive in the population generally, and in the higher classes in particular, a most unreasonable alarm of the malady.

The 'supremo magistrato' in Palermo who was in charge of the Board of Health was Ruggiero Settimo, that hallowed name in Sicilian history.

Just as worrying as the cholera, if not more so at that time, was the financial situation in the United States. There were already signs of a crisis ahead in that country – a crisis which in May was to turn into panic. The Presidential campaign was under way, and Jackson – who had been President for two terms – was being strongly challenged by the Democrats' candidate Van Buren.

During the previous six years there had been some 275,000 immigrants into the United States, and sales of public lands in 1836 alone had totalled nearly twenty-nine million dollars. Much of the best land had been paid for in paper money of questionable value, for quantities of new small banks had sprung up, with little real backing. In July 1836 the Treasury had issued its 'Specie Circular', which laid down that future government land could only be bought with gold or silver. This had only had the effect of encouraging a great deal of reckless dealing, not only in land but in various large-scale national improvements, such as railways and steam navigation.

All these troubles had been relayed in full to Ingham from Boston, and the letters were then passed on to Marsala.

*To Richard Stephens, Marsala*                                       *20 February 1837*

I fully agree with what Alfred Greenough writes of the great danger arising to commercial credit from these banks. . . . It is to be hoped however that a stop will be put to the rage for speculation in public lands and that Congress will adopt the suggestion made by the President to allow no sales in future except to actual and real settlers thereon, and to insist on payment in specie. The banks seem to be so deeply interested in such speculation as to be induced to prefer their own interest to that of the country at large . . . I have to add that, when Greenough writes of the immense distress if the United States Bank succeeds in its schemes, he is actuated considerably by party spirit and is evidently a thorough Jacksonian.[4]

On 4 March Van Buren was sworn in as President. Meanwhile the American trade balance had been becoming more unfavourable, and British investors had consequently begun to be frightened.

*To Heath, Furse & Co., London*                                      *6 March 1837*

As your Mr Heath is a bank director, permit us to observe that, however much it may be against our interest, as far as we are connected with the American Trade we are very glad to hear that the Bank of England has determined to curtail as much as possible the system of credit in all parts of the globe. Certain houses in London connected with America have been until lately granting so much to American houses as to absorb to a great measure most of British spare capital This has done an incredible injury to British commerce and shipping, to say nothing of the over-trading which it caused in the United States. We were not aware, until the return of our Mr Benjamin Ingham junior from the States, of the immense facility with which even young Houses there could obtain letters of credit from various agents acting for London houses.

*To Richard Stephens, Marsala*                                       *10 April 1837*

I send you some new papers and you will notice an important paragraph relative to the relief afforded by the Bank of England to the eight American houses in London and Liverpool. I am further informed that Baring's [Ingham, Stephens & Co.'s bankers], George Wildes and Thomas Wilson, all of London, and Messrs Brown of Liverpool had to show their books and that the extent of their obligations amounted *together* to nearly twelve millions sterling. But what alarms me is the letter from John Bibby in Liverpool. I am very apprehensive that there will be a great crash in the U.S.A.

There was, not surprisingly, an air of preoccupation in a letter written on the same day to Joseph Whitaker – the first since his marriage to Sophia Sanderson.

*To Joseph Whitaker, Naples*                    *13 April 1837*
I have requested Ben to reply to your former letters concerning quarantine and to keep you fully informed of the movements of the Board of Health. I presume you will be making arrangements to return to Sicily direct. Thus it will be of no great consequence whether you embark for Messina or Palermo. I should therefore recommend your availing of the first eligible opportunity in the near future for either place.

Shortly afterwards Ingham, on the advice of Heath, Furse, decided that 'prudence requires that we should have someone in America upon whom we can depend'. So it was decided that Ben should set out immediately on the brig *Attila* which was about to arrive from Genoa for loading to Boston. Ingham would rather have sent someone older and more experienced (Ben was twenty-seven). As he told Stephens, he would have preferred Joseph (aged thirty-five) and had in mind that he might go direct to America from Naples, but then he wisely decided that the 'father of the young lady might have objected to her accompanying him', so the idea was dropped, 'particularly as I did not like to lose time in waiting for an answer'.

One glance at the squalid *Attila* had been enough to make Ben decide that he could not possibly endure the long journey to Boston in her. It was settled that he should if possible make his way to Naples, whence he would go by steamer to Marseilles and then by land to Le Havre, 'as the packets sail from there every eight days to New York'.

Joseph and Sophia managed to get a berth on a steamer leaving Naples on 18 April. The hope had been that Ben would have been able to return in the same boat to Naples. But there was a disappointment:

*To Richard Stephens, Marsala*                    *22 April 1837*
The steamer has just arrived, but I see no chance of our getting our letters to let you know their contents. What is worse, the rigour of the Board of Health is such that we cannot either be permitted to go to speak to the passengers at the mole or at the Lazzaretto [quarantine building, built in 1628, but restored and enlarged in 1833]. I am however

sorry to hear that the steamer does not return to Naples but proceeds to Messina and Malta, so Ben will have to look out for some other opportunity for Naples.

*2 o'clock p.m.* I have been at the mole and have not only succeeded in speaking with Mr Whitaker and his young lady (both well), but in getting the letters. As for Baring's, I understand that after all they were not among those who received assistance from the Bank, as their credit derived from Lord Ashburton [of the Baring family]. It is evident that the crisis in America will be dreadful.

Dreadful indeed. When Ingham read all his letters he saw that 'in New York eight-five houses have failed, mostly among the dry goods merchants, bill and exchange dealers and shippers, and everything is at a stand.' His clients Wildes and Wilson were both in a state of liquidation.

During May many American banks found themselves totally unable to redeem the paper money that they had been issuing so liberally, and specie payments were therefore suspended. Several collapsed altogether. To make matters worse, later that summer, the harvest was bad.

All the same, Ingham could still see a brighter side to the situation. 'I am pretty sure,' he wrote, 'that with this crisis many who have been drinking champagne, high priced sherries and madeiras will be glad to drink wine that is not so dear.'

Ben had somehow managed to get a passage to Messina, and meanwhile the Whitakers had been told that they would have to spend twenty-five days' quarantine in the Lazzaretto. The newly-weds had only been there fourteen days when bad news reached Palermo.

*To Richard Stephens, Marsala*                              *6 May 1837*

It is with the greatest regret that I have to inform you that, in consequence of the cholera having again broken out in Naples, though only in a trifling degree, say eight or nine cases, the Board of Health yesterday resolved not only to send away all provenance from the Kingdom of Naples, but also the goods and passengers from the Lazzaretto. You will be well aware in what consternation I have been put on account of Mr Whitaker and his lady. I hear that the Board's resolution has been transmitted to Naples this morning by telegraph with a demand whether the King will sanction it or not. I trust he will not approve such extreme rigour. The *Cordone Sanitario* is also to be *riattivato* [put into being again].

It was a week before a reply came from Naples. The steamer's passengers would not have to return; instead their quarantine period would be extended to forty days, while goods would have to remain in the Lazzaretto for fifty. All Ingham's influence was used to get the Whitakers out earlier, but it was hopeless. Ruggiero Settimo would not release them 'one minute before the full forty days are completed'. Ingham was livid, fulminating against the bureaucracy and iniquitous regulations 'which no other country adopts – these people insist on treating cholera like the Plague'. He decided to submit a list of 'vexations, grievances and extortions' to the Neapolitan Government; 'if there is any justice in the Kingdom, this list will make everyone tremble in their graves'.

At last on 1 June the Whitakers were 'liberated', and only just in time. A week later Settimo, because of alarming reports from the mainland, decided that no vessels whatsoever from Naples would be admitted into the port of Palermo.

Then the trouble began:

*To J. Smithson, Messina*                                    *8 June 1837*
There is great alarm here since yesterday morning, in consequence of two watermen having fallen ill and died in a very short time from an excessive eating of tunny fish and other extravagances, which our wise Board of Health at once takes to be the cholera. The corpses have been sent to the Lazzaretto, where a post mortem examination is to take place. The police and some troops have been put as a *Cordone* around the quarter of the town where the men died, and orders have been issued to prepare hospitals etc. In our opinion there is no foundation for this alarm. . . . All vessels have been ordered to depart immediately.

The two watermen had arrived on the brig *Archimede* from Naples on 28 May but had illegally broken the *Cordone* 'in order to sell their merchandise and gain money'. Three days passed and there were more cases of suspected cholera. A strong scirocco was blowing and the weather had become extremely warm; this surely would 'make the germ appear' if indeed it was in Palermo. The Duchess became uneasy and persuaded Ingham to take her on one of the ships leaving for Marsala. Joseph was now left in charge of the office, so all the firm's letters quoted here during that nightmare of a summer were written by him.

Rumour leaked out that the autopsies on the watermen had indeed shown that they had died of cholera. Then on 14 June the doctor who had conducted the post mortems himself died of the same disease. Alarm swept the city.

15 June is considered to have been the day of the main outbreak in

Palermo. There is a letter of that date written by Joseph to his father-in-law, William Sanderson, in Messina. 'All sorts of arbitrary measures', he said, 'both on commerce and personal liberty are daily taking place.' Everyone in the Lazzaretto was to leave for the mainland immediately.

People in Britain, largely thanks to the *Cordone*, were ignorant of the situation in Palermo until they read a startling but brief article in *The Times* of 28 July, quoting another article dated 9 July from a somewhat sensation-mongering journal called the *Augsburg Gazette*. It ran as follows:

> Between eight hundred and nine hundred persons were carried off daily [in Palermo] by the cholera, and no one was found to remove the dead from the houses or the city. The people had plundered several stores and notified to the rich and to the nobles, who had fled from Palermo on the breaking out of the epidemy, that if they did not immediately return to the city to assist the poor, they would set their places on fire. Soldiers had been sent into the country to bring in provisions. The Cardinal, who was at the head of the Sicilian church, and the wife of the Viceroy had fallen victims to the epidemy. Several physicians who refused to visit cholera patients had been murdered by the populace.

So it seemed, at least, that Settimo's earlier caution had been justified.

For some days afterwards readers of *The Times* were treated with ever more horrific details. Typhus had now broken out. The 'lower orders' had refused to bury the dead as they considered such work degrading. 'Several hundred galley slaves' had been dispatched from Naples to do the job. Some five or six hundred soldiers had also been sent to Sicily. The King had wanted to join them but had been restrained by his Government. It was steadfastly believed in Palermo that the Neapolitans had been responsible for spreading the 'poison'. Bands of robbers were 'now masters of the city'. Cables of Neapolitan troopships had been cut, and people were roaming round the streets shouting, 'Death to the foreigners! Long live Sicily!'

How much of all this, which included dark references to 'unheard of excesses', was literally correct is difficult now to gauge. Some of the Paris newspapers claimed that the *Augsburg Gazette* had absurdly exaggerated the situation. This was no doubt true as far as Palermo itself was concerned, but anarchy certainly did 'rage' in its immediate environs and much of it has gone uncatalogued. Some innocent persons, such as chemists and bakers, lost their lives because of the poison theory, and it was a great moment for settling vendettas. According to the British Consul's report, written some months later, only 'three unfortunate citizens' were actually murdered in Palermo; they had been 'dragged through the streets and torn to bits by the mob'. By the end of the epidemic it was officially reckoned that over twenty-five times that amount of people had died through mob violence in the whole of the *Valle* of Palermo.

Many of the rich, like the Duchess of Santa Rosalia, did indeed flee. And the Cardinal Archbishop Trigona, did die – if any Cardinal had given 'hurried written permission' for the Ingham marriage, he would have been the one. He refused all medical aid, being firmly convinced that 'there is no remedy against this poison'.[5] Likewise the Viceroy's wife died. And she was the Princess of Campofranco, the relative of the wife of the *Duchino* of Santa Rosalia – the Prince having been Viceroy, for his second term, since 1835.

Joseph kept doggedly to his desk. He drank ice-water from Etna, supposed to be an antidote to cholera. His letters are a macabre commentary on the speed with which the cholera spread.

*To J. Smithson, Messina*                                           *19 June 1837*
We are sorry to say that deaths increase daily and we fear that the number will soon be such as to admit no longer to any doubt but that it is the real cholera and no other. The lowest class of people is obstinate in not giving the smallest credit to it being the cholera and are disposed to act roughly towards the doctors, who they say are merely killing their patients by wrong methods of cure.

A list of cholera deaths was kept at the Rotoli cemetery. Up to 22 June they numbered forty-four, and between 23 and 28 June they were 290. Joseph wrote to his uncle in Marsala to tell him that the 'morbus' had broken out in Malta on the seventh, the day of its first appearance in Palermo. He wrote also to his wife's relatives in Catania, the Roses, saying that he hoped that the report of a cholera outbreak there was not true. Palermo was now on the brink of terror. One can imagine the scenes in those narrow, dirty back-streets, sometimes only four yards across.

*To Benjamin Ingham, Marsala*                                       *28 June 1837*
The malady is increasing with us frightfully and has made rapid strides in the last four days. The number of deaths since last evening we are told are upward of 140, during the night only. It has shown itself in all parts of the city and is very bad in our immediate neighbourhood.

In fact, according to a later letter, the total deaths on the twenty-ninth were 158, with 212 new cases. The total number recorded at Rotoli between that day and 4 July was 2430.

The cholera had now reached Messina.

*To J. Smithson, Messina*                                                  *3 July 1837*
We regret to hear of the demise of your poor Mr Dunner. It is however our lot to acquaint you in return with two deplorable misfortunes, being the attack by cholera and the dissolution of our worthy friends, Mr B. Gardner and Mr W. Horner – the first was carried off on Saturday at about 4 p.m. The malady, we regret, has assumed a most terrific appearance, attacking all classes and all nations.

So Benjamin Gardner, the American Consul from Boston, was gone. Other foreigners, German and Swiss, 'met the like untimely fate'. One of the Ingham clerks died, and another was an invalid 'more through apprehension than anything else'. The Duchess of San Martino died, so did the Prince of Fitalia, brother of Ruggiero Settimo, and the Duchess of Cumia, the wife of the Director General of Police. Other casualties included: Nicolò Palmeri, the historian; Gaspare Vaccaro, who had been leader of the *Camere Comuni* in 1812; Domenico Scinà, Chancellor of Palermo University; the Marquis of Gallidoro, a mathematician; Pietro Pisani, a philanthropist.

The cholera reached its zenith in Palermo on 7 July, when 1801 deaths were recorded. John Goodwin the Consul-General, in his report to London, described the extraordinary aspect of the streets by day, virtually empty and with all shops shut except for those owned by apothecaries and confectioners – since ice-cream was also made from snow specially brought from Etna – who were making vast profits. At night there was the 'horrid spectacle' of death carts rumbling along the Toledo. Not only were doctors refusing to visit patients, but half of them had fled. Nevertheless, he said, the conduct of the clergy and of the higher authority – which included the Praetor, the Prince of Scordia (the title used by the then Prince of Butera), and the Director General of the Police, the widowed Duke of Cumia – deserved the highest praise.

Goodwin also admitted that many 'outrages' had occurred outside Palermo, but inside the city, apart from some ugly demonstrations, the situation was comparatively tranquil – thus giving the lie to the dramatic report by *The Times* correspondent (not, strangely, quoting the *Augsburg Gazette*, but purporting to have been written from Palermo itself) that the Viceroy, the Prince of Campofranco, had been 'massacred in the most barbarous manner' and that his body had been dragged through the streets and later quartered. The Prince, although 'null and inefficient', in William Temple's words, and hated by Palermitans for being the complete tool of

Naples, in fact remained safe and sound until he was belatedly removed by the King in October.[6] Indeed, the report only serves to show us now that *The Times'* foreign correspondents of those days could not only be fallible but capable of spreading dangerous malice.

The handwriting of Goodwin's brief letter of 8 July, still to be seen at the Public Record Office in London, is wild and scrawled, obviously the result of strain. He reported that the 'ravages continue with unabated fury' and that Mr W. Valentine, William Routh's partner, and a Mr March had 'fallen victims to the cholera'. He made the remark that it was noticeable that the mortality was greater among fatter people and among women, especially those who were pregnant.

Meanwhile *The Times* reported, this time correctly, that ten murderers had been executed at Misilmeri outside Palermo, including a boy who had been too small to hold a musket but whose job had been to finish off with a dagger those who had been felled by his elders. There were, according to *The Times*, only 2000 troops, 'most of them invalids', in Palermo, and it was thus impossible to keep control of the population, of whom '20,000 are rendered desperate by want'.

Now it was the turn of the *Augsburg Gazette* to claim 'ultra-cannibalism and other atrocities' in the *Valle*. *The Times*, needless to say, was sceptical and prudently decided to 'refrain from enumerating' these atrocities, 'because our Paris correspondent, better informed we hope, declares that there is scarcely a tittle of truth in those statements.' Poor Sicilians; whenever there were any upheavals of a particularly alarming nature, someone would always trot out this rumour of cannibalism. It had happened before and would happen again.[7] Who, it may even be asked, would relish the cadaver of a cholera victim?

The morbus had not increased very much around Messina – the city was relatively speaking, spared. This did not prevent unrest developing among the inhabitants, mindful perhaps of the devastation of the Plague of 1743 when nearly 70,000 inhabitants of Messina had died. Riots broke out on 12 July as a result of a Neapolitan packet forcing the quarantine with soldiers aboard, some suffering from cholera.

Joseph Whitaker wrote:

*To J. Smithson, Messina*                                     *20 July 1837*
We note there has been a fracas in which your mob has demolished the Health Office and the Customs House, but we are glad to hear that no other outrages have been committed. We trust that the English in particular may be respected . . . There have been several outrageous attempts at

disturbance in the villages of this neighbourhood and we regret to say that a great many lives have been sacrificed to the fury of the populace, who still will have it that the cholera is a poison administered by Government individuals. In some places troops have been sent in, and some Swiss have been got over from Naples, but the cholera has made sad havoc of their numbers. . . . We are glad to say that we keep quiet in the capital and the number of deaths is subsiding. The writer and his lady continue to enjoy good health, thanks to a merciful providence.

The atmosphere in Messina remained very tense. The *Augsburg Gazette* gave the rumour that 'the British flag had been hoisted' over the citadel. Anonymous pamphlets, referring to the 1812 Constitution, were being circulated in the city; the Government attributed them to the machinations of the Prince of Capua, since he was then in Malta.

*To J. Smithson, Messina*                                              *27 July 1837*
We hear that the King is dreadfully annoyed by your occurrences. Some people are saying that the large number of troops, with which the King in person is once again expected, is coming over not only to quell the disturbances but also for the purpose of setting you Messinese 'to rights'. . . . On this side we cannot but look upon the arrival of troops as a favourable circumstance, as it will put a stop to the anarchy which will take years to remedy. The population of Palermo is now reduced to between 30 and 35,000, what with deaths and absentees.

In a letter to Mr Routh, Joseph estimated that the deaths had now been some 23,000 in Palermo. This was in fact a little conservative. At any rate conditions seemed to be improving. Only sixty people had died on 25 July.

Meanwhile a 'sanguinary tumult', as the Consul termed it, had broken out in Syracuse. It was said there that Ferdinand, in order to retain the island of Sicily for Naples, had decided that it would be simplest just to annihilate the Sicilians altogether. The captain of the Lazzaretto and a priest were shot publicly in the main square, while the Intendant or departmental governor, Baron Vaccaro, was dragged from his hiding-place in the quarries and slaughtered, as were the police inspector Li Greci and his son, a tax inspector. A Frenchman from Toulon, Joseph Schwentzer, who ran a 'cosmorama' show in Syracuse, was seized and hauled off to jail with his eighteen-year-old Tyrolese wife, whose amazonian looks had already caused disapproval. On the way to the jail the Police Commissioner, attempting to protect the Schwentzers, was bludgeoned, stabbed many times, tied to a pillar and shot, along with a few of his friends. Later the jail was attacked and Schwentzer was himself horribly stabbed. His wife was then seized and executed with fourteen others, her baby being saved from a similar fate in the nick of time. Martial law was declared, but owing to the lack of troops was totally ineffective.

In Catania the yellow flag of Sicilian independence was flying. Royal statues were destroyed. However, further developments were not nearly so savage as in Syracuse, and some of the nobles joined the revolutionaries – quickly to change sides, when they heard of the approach of Neapolitan troops. As for the cholera itself, John Goodwin wrote to London saying that the 'ravages were awful and unexplained'. 400 people were dying every day, and the Vice-Consul William Rose, his brother John Rose and an assistant Mr Smith had all been 'carried off'. Indeed, apart from the Roses' sister, Mrs Leaf, who escaped the cholera, these three represented the entire British colony in Catania.

The unrest spread to the ever explosive Bronte and to Maletto, but there were none of the atrocities of 1820, nor any attempts at organised resistance. By this time it was obvious to most that any rioting in Sicily would be sporadic or impulsive, the result of sudden panics. Only the British merchants of Messina thought otherwise, and at the end of July they were demanding a man o' war from Malta for their protection.

*To J. Smithson, Messina*                              *3 August 1837*
Regarding the alarm which you have of some popular commotion in your city, we have made a point of communicating with Mr Goodwin and mentioning to him what you have suggested, but he does not feel disposed to interfere further than he has already done some days ago, which is to have acquaint the Governor of Malta[8] of the general state of Sicily, and to leave entirely to his discretion the steps to be taken of his government. He has however authorised Mr W. W. Barker [the Consul in Messina] to write if necessary direct to Malta. We all of us cannot but think that you are too much alarmed, particularly as you have a good garrison.

The luckless Consul Barker, a septuagenarian and only just recovered from a stroke, had had a hard time pacifying his merchants and ship-owners, and complaints had been pouring into the Consul General's office in Palermo. It was not his fault if Goodwin, whose caution was proverbial, was so unhelpful.

Earlier in the year Barker had been in trouble with some ships' captains, on account of the long and expensive quarantine that they had to endure. The captains had been so disgusted with him that they had complained direct to Lord Palmerston in London, saying that not only had Barker refused to see them but that he was not competent to act as Consul in such an important mercantile port. This was not the first complaint that Palmerston had received, and at the height of the epidemic a letter was already on its way to Goodwin, asking him whether Barker's state of health 'precluded him from discharging efficiently and in person the duties of H.M. Consul'. As it now turned out of course, Barker – admittedly a ditherer – had been perfectly right in refusing to ask the Board of Health in Messina to relax its quarantine regulations. The trouble was that being a poet, and a particularly romantic one at that, his temperament was not the sort that gave confidence to hoary old sea-captains.[9]

As for Joseph Whitaker, he was beginning to sympathise with the general sense of exasperation among his brother merchants.

*To J. Smithson, Messina*                                    *12 August 1837*
The resolution of the Governor of Malta to send the steamer *Confidence* to enquire after you all shows that they are a little more alive there to British interests than is our own pigmy authority here. This last is so very insignificant in his official capacity that we must not be surprised when he does leave us in the background.

So the merchants had only been granted a civilian vessel, not a man o' war. Joseph's letter included a *double entendre*, for he was referring to John Goodwin, who was small and slightly built, known as *Lo Zoppo* (the lame one) to Palermitans. Goodwin, a bachelor, had been appointed Consul-General for Sicily in 1834 and was to remain in Palermo for another thirty-two years. Later he became a good friend of both Joseph Whitaker and Benjamin Ingham, but he was a difficult man to get to know and his reserve often made people think that he was trying to shirk responsibility. He was also extraordinarily conscientious and soon developed a great sympathy for the Sicilian patriots against Naples.[10]

The next letter makes no mention at all of the situation in Sicily.

*To Heath, Furse & Co., London*                            *14 August 1837*
We have received letters from our Benjamin Ingham Junior who arrived in America on the 19th June. As might be expected, he gives a most gloomy account of the state of that country. We are however happy to say that we continue to be without apprehension for the safety of our numerous connections there, and it is also of great consolation to us to learn that our friends have made but few bad debts for us. We note that the President has been compelled to call a special meeting of Congress on the 1st September.

And that is also the last reference to the American crisis.

In Palermo, *The Times* correspondent deigned to admit, 'happily peace and security are restored'. Deaths had been reduced to ten or twelve daily; as a result 'no one yet seems disposed to resume business, and every man keeps himself confined within his own family circle.' 'A new loan', the correspondent added, 'is in agitation, and it is said that the house of Torlonia has already made considerable advances.'[11]

Shortly afterwards there was an amused reference in *The Times* to the *Augsburg Gazette* which was blaming the English for being the 'fomentors of the excesses in Palermo'; the Austrians were about to re-enter Naples 'for fear of British designs'. *The Times* then said that troops had reached Messina on 15 August and that the 'sanitary state' of the city was good. Indeed the cholera was fast subsiding both in Sicily and Malta (though it had broken out with considerable virulence in Rome and in northern Italy). A letter from Palermo on 20 August said that there had been no cases of cholera there for a week. Troops had taken possession of both Catania and Syracuse. 'Not a day passes in which five, eight, ten or twelve persons are not tried by a court-martial and shot. It is to be hoped that those measures will secure tranquillity for a long while.'

It was not until 21 October that John Goodwin could write to London announcing that Sicily and Naples were now in 'free pratique', even though there were still a few cases in the centre of the island. In the *Valle* of Palermo itself there had been 40,642 deaths from cholera; 80 people had been murdered, 650 accused of rebellion; there had been 140 death sentences and 90 capital punishments.[12] Since the Black Death no such scene of terror had been witnessed.[13]

Benjamin Ingham returned to Palermo early in September. Mercifully Marsala had been virtually spared the cholera, though it had been bad in Trapani. He had been occupying his time with writing a lengthy leaflet in Italian and addressed, as he put it, to the 'simple vine-grower'.

Tourists, not surprisingly, seem to have avoided Sicily for a while, but the cholera did not deter foreign visitors to Naples, which received over seven thousand even in 1837. Pompeii was now very much the additional lure, for *The Last Days of Pompeii* had burst upon the world in 1834. Few tourists were unenthusiastic about Naples; Dr Arnold of Rugby was however one of them and found the city merely enacting the 'fearful drama of Pleasure, Sin and Death'.[14]

It took a long while, needless to say, for the Sicilian economy to recover from the disaster. Local administration in many instances had virtually collapsed. King Ferdinand made genuine attempts to help with political palliatives. The Ministry of Sicilian Affairs in Naples would be abolished; in future Sicilians would be able to hold executive posts in Naples just as Neapolitans could hold them in Sicily. He re-established Messina University, with the intention of training more local executives. Delegates were sent to investigate corruption in the magistrature. In the following year, in September 1838, he himself set out with the Queen to Sicily and did a grand tour of the island. As a result of his visit, when incidentally Benjamin Ingham first met him, new roads were ordered, public banks were established in Palermo and Messina, taxes were overhauled, almshouses built and plans laid for land reform.

Another result of the King's visit was not so popular with some: the granting of a virtual monopoly in the sulphur trade to a Marseilles firm named Taix, Aycard. Exports of sulphur being four times what they were in 1832, Ferdinand had not surprisingly decided that the time had come to get some revenue for the State. His action was also directed against the British, whom he accused of exploitation.

Before the Taix, Aycard contract, forty-nine per cent of the entire production of Sicilian sulphur was sent to Britain. Forty-three per cent went to France, and the remaining eight per cent went mostly to Holland, the United States and Russia. The British merchants and shipowners (about 30,000 tons of British shipping were used in the trade annually) were immediately up in arms. There were rumours that Taix was not only a Carlist but an accomplice of the Duchess of Berry, the King's sister – the assumption being that he was therefore a natural trouble-maker on an international scale.[15] Palmerston retaliated by sending a furious note to Ferdinand, who himself flew into a rage on its receipt and as a result was barely on speaking terms with any British subject for a long while, the more so since Palmerston was also demanding that Ferdinand should pay for the Prince of Capua's debts in London. Macaulay, on his way from India, visited Naples and wrote on 12 January 1839: '. . . the King's birthday. The Court was attended by many foreigners. The King paid no attention to the English – not even to so great a man as the Duke of Buccleuch – but reserved his civilities for the Russians.' He added sarcastically: 'Fool to think that either the lion or the bear cares which side the hare takes in these disputes.'[16] One wonders how friendly the King's meeting could have been with Ingham.

Some of the rest of Macaulay's letter is also worth quoting, if only for an obvious reason: 'In the evening as I was sipping Marsala, and reading a novel called *Crichton* [by William Harrison Ainsworth] . . . in came

Verney to beg me to take a seat in his opera-box at the Teatro di San Carlo, which was to be illuminated in honour of the day . . . The Royal Family were below us, so that we did not see them, and I am sure that I would not give a *carlino* to see every Bourbon, living or dead, of the Spanish breed.'

British sulphur merchants put in enormous claims for compensation. Sicily herself began to suffer. Sulphur prices went up two hundred per cent and exports dropped by three-quarters, while alternative sources were being explored in Belgium, Iceland and America. As the Duchess of Berry had married Count Ettore Lucchesi-Palli, Ingham might not have been totally displeased by the Taix monopoly. One notes that the Duchess came to visit her in-laws in Palermo in the first half of 1839.

Adelaide, the Queen Dowager of England, also visited Palermo that year. She arrived in April on board H.M.S. *Hastings*, after some months' stay in Malta. She was 'labouring under a severe cold' and 'suffering much from the effects of the recent storm which lasted from the 9th to 12th.'[17] Eventually she managed to come ashore on the fourteenth, when she was able to visit some of the sights of the city. Later, after visiting Monreale, she received the families of British merchants. Consul Goodwin was presented with a gold snuff-box 'in token of her approbation'. Then she sailed on to Naples, where – in spite of the sulphur dispute and 'to the surprise of all' – she was enthusiastically received by the royal family.

1839 was a landmark in Ingham's business activities. On 1 May it was announced that from 30 June the firm of Ingham, Stephens was to have its own London office, to be run by Richard Stephens himself. Thus Joshua Ingham was now left totally in charge of the *Baglio* at Marsala. Stephens had somehow managed to leave Sicily and return to England at the height of the cholera epidemic in July 1837.

Then towards the end of the year there had been the sensational arrival of Ingham's brig *Elisa*, loaded with pepper from Sumatra. This was the first such cargo ever to come direct from the East Indies to the Kingdom of the Two Sicilies. Hitherto all spices had arrived by way of New England, as often as not via London. Such was the excitement that the cargo was allowed to be landed free of duty. Any prejudice against the English on account of the sulphur dispute was temporarily put to one side, and the King (who may indeed have been in Palermo at the time) invested Ingham with the order of St Ferdinand. The captain of the *Elisa*, Vincenzo Di Bartolo, was given the gold medal of civil merit, and the second officer, Federico Montechiaro, was granted the right to wear the uniform of the Royal Navy of the Bourbons.

The whole venture had been a typical Ingham enterprise. He was never a great innovator but always an adept at imitating and improving on other people's successes. Suddenly he had had the idea of bypassing the New England merchants. There had been a reference to the *Elisa* in June 1837 during the cholera epidemic, when she had been diverted to Leghorn. She had been built in Sicily, which was another cause for national pride. On 28 October 1838, loaded with wine and other merchandise, left for Boston with a crew of twelve sailors. Thanks to gales the journey took nearly four months. It took another five months to get from Boston to Sumatra, and five nearly to the day from Sumatra to Palermo, which the *Elisa* reached on 14 December 1839. The Sicilians had not felt very secure on the 'inhospitable shores' of Sumatra, where the head of the tribe wore a wickerwork hat and was suspected of having eaten a Frenchman, and had only stayed there sixteen days.[18]

The journey of the *Elisa* was hailed as a real voyage of discovery. Such foreign seas had been well explored by the British, Americans and others, but to the Sicilians they were totally unknown, which was all the more credit to the navigation of the intrepid Di Bartolo. Ingham must have profited vastly. A new and larger ship, renamed the *Sumatra*, of 500 tons, was bought and, first under Di Bartolo and then under Montechiaro, she brought back several cargoes of pepper and spices from the East Indies over a space of years. But 'finally, as usual, competition made the business no longer worth continuing.'[19] One wonders, indeed, whether the voyages of the *Elisa* and the *Sumatra* had something to do with the tradition still current among some that marsala is best after it has taken a trip round the world.

The other excitement of 1839 was the issuing of a prospectus by Ingham and others to form a company in order to buy the first steamship for Palermo. After the nightmare of the cholera, it seemed to give hope for the next decade. One of the co-directors was the banker Vincenzo Florio, now much on the ascendant and already approaching Ingham's position of power and riches; others were Duke Ettore Pignatelli of Monteleone, nephew of the late Princess of Campofranco (and descended from Cortes), and Gaetano Fiamingo, a merchant who acted as Russian Consul. The treasurer bore a well-known Palermitan name, Baron Gabriele Chiaramonte Bordonaro.

Letters of congratulation came rolling in, even from the Torlonias. The new steamship, which was built in Glasgow, was at first to be called the *Indipendenza*, but the Government felt that such a name would be too provocative, so it had to be changed to the *Palermo*. She was put into regular service in 1841.[20]

9. The Duchess of Santa Rosalia in old age.

10. Benjamin Ingham in middle age.

11. The *Baglio* Ingham in 1871, by Francesco Lojacono.

# VII

## *In Pursuit of Wealth*

TAKING into account the fact that King Ferdinand, because of the sulphur dispute, was on exceedingly bad terms with the British from 1839–40, it is perhaps all the more remarkable that Benjamin Ingham was allowed to dominate the steamship company. The *parvenu* Florio would have been another possibility for its head – Florio, who had built a *baglio* at Marsala slap between the establishments of Woodhouse and Ingham, and who was involved in many leading industries in the island, including sulphur and not least the fantastically successful exploitation of the *montoleva*, or means of preserving tunny fish in olive oil. Florio, indeed, later had his own shipbuilding yards and acquired a fleet of merchant vessels. He was to become one of the greatest figures of the nineteenth-century industrial revolution in Italy and Sicily, a legend in his time.[1]

The 'Sulphur War' actually broke out in April 1840, when Palmerston reached such a pitch of exasperation that he ordered the British navy to blockade Neapolitan ports and seize any Neapolitan or Sicilian ship wherever met on the high seas. 'No blood was shed in this somewhat ludicrous affair', wrote Rear-Admiral H. F. Winnington-Ingram, then a midshipman on H.M.S. *Talbot* stationed in Corfu, and the whole exercise does seem to have been treated by the navy in a somewhat hilarious spirit. Winnington-Ingram described how one would sail up to the Neapolitan ship, as though in complete innocence and flying false colours, which might be Austrian or even Neapolitan; then one would pounce, only hoisting the British flag whilst capture was being made. Not quite fair play, surely. . . . However, in this way many *traboccoli* or coastal fishing vessels were captured, and taken with the brigs and schooners to Corfu, 'there to have their rudders unshipped and sails sent ashore, pending the settlement of the dispute'.

The whys and wherefores of this Sulphur War are fairly complex. It was true that the King in August 1838 had 'abrogated suddenly an old-standing treaty on the exportation of sulphur', but it was also true that the British (and indeed the French) had cornered a very unfair share of the market. Nevertheless the suddenness with which the contract with Taix,

Aycard was made was quixotic, not to say despotic; the attitude of the aggrieved British to the nationalisation of the Suez Canal in 1956 might even be taken as a parallel – only by then the lion's teeth had been drawn. Not only were British merchants immediately out of business, shipowners and importers ruined, but 'the whole population [and this included children] of the sulphur districts have been thrown out of employment ... multitudes of these have become desperate robbers . . . persons cannot travel without an escort, and the number of arrests and executions has continued very great.'[2] All this in an area of Sicily that was otherwise practically barren, and in the words of Consul Goodwin 'destitute of timber, and diversified only by fruit-trees scattered around the villages', with 'few charms for the passing stranger, beyond the fantastic shapes of its cliffs and mountains.'[3]

When the British navy proceeded to blockade Naples, the King got into an even greater state of excitement. Twelve thousand troops were sent to Sicily, and he himself rushed off to inspect Sicilian military establishments. There was, however, little that he could do, especially as his friends the Austrians were not prepared to back him. Thus, on 21 July 1840, thanks to French mediation, the Taix, Aycard contract was cancelled, and an indemnity to foreign merchants was fixed by royal decree.

But the situation was still not entirely happy, since there remained an appreciable duty on the export of sulphur. On 25 October 1841 Goodwin wrote to Temple: 'A Petition to the King, praying for the total removal of the Sulphur Duty, has received the signatures of many many Mine owners and merchants. . . . The only English name which appears on the list is that of Mr Ingham. The other British merchants have declined signing, as the petition professes to come from Sicilian subjects.' An interesting commentary on the way Ingham identified himself with the natives. One notes, however, that in that year Ingham and Florio obtained majority shareholdings in the 'Chimica Arenella', a firm originally started by a Marseilles chemist, Augustin Pourri, for the making of sulphuric acid.

Among the first travellers to Sicily after the cholera epidemic was Frederic von Raumer, whose book was published in 1840. He found Messina flourishing and busy but 'Palermo, on the contrary, wears the appearance of an ancient, sinking capital, where the nobility itself is on the decline, and almost all are tumbling, with or without reason.' *Eheu* the days of Brydone! Ferdinand and his Government may at that period have been slightly maligned (some historians have presented them as an enlightened despotism), and certainly real efforts – even if they were rather crass – were made to try to make the Sicilians happier. Indeed, to Neapolitans the case was considered almost hopeless and hardly worth the effort. 'Whoever,' von Raumer wrote, 'wishes to learn what distress, what ruin ensue when . . . a perverse, selfish bureaucracy seats itself upon the throne – let him go to Sicily. One must be more than a Hercules to cleanse this Augean stable.' Hatred for Naples and everything it stood for had never been more violent.

Von Raumer noticed how in Palermo some of the princes were so poor that they 'scarcely know how to find themselves a dinner', and 'the jewels which they wear in company must first be redeemed with great difficulty by the pawnbroker.' He also added that 'many who are wealthy and not in debt have scarcely ever seen their estates, and never attend to the management of them.' And it was this listlessness on the part of the landowners that was another cause of the island's unrest.

Syracuse, after 1837, was in disgrace. As a punishment the 'seat of the district' had been moved to Noto. Von Raumer found the city of Dionysius, once the rival to Athens and antagonist to Carthage and Rome, 'anything but a handsome or thriving town'. When writing of July 1837, he said: 'The wealthy and the persons in office had fled precipitately, instead of fearlessly performing their duty. In that time of terror and excitement, there were of course no authorities whatsoever; the military shut themselves up in castles, and made no effort for the preservation of order. Is it then surprising that the populace, left to themselves, should have committed excesses?'

Another traveller, Arthur John Strutt, went to Syracuse slightly later, in 1841. He too found gloom. At a *trattoria* he spoke to the owner and found that 'the disasters of Syracuse had not left him unvisited, for all his customers had fled from the place, and he found the utmost difficulty in keeping up his tottering establishment.' When visiting Palermo, he remarked that 'there is still some degree of danger in the environs'. The sense of nervousness among the law-abiding and monied citizens did nothing to help the economy. Von Raumer pointed out that out of a population of some two million there were now 127 princes, 78 dukes, 130 marquises, innumerable counts (not to mention barons), 28,000 monks and 18,000 nuns. To make the situation even stranger, Strutt noted that some of the richer princes actually supported and fed the brigands who lurked in the neighbourhood.[4]

Strutt attended a New Year's Day ball at Consul Goodwin's. Some seventy to eighty British, French and other foreign merchants were present. He too could not but help noticing that in Palermo generally the English and Sicilian societies 'rather form bodies apart'.

Sophia Whitaker gave birth to the first of her twelve children, a boy, on 16 August 1838. He was tactfully christened Benjamin Ingham Whitaker. As other babies followed, at more or less yearly intervals, Joseph took pity on her in stuffy Palermo and bought a property, renamed Villa Sofia in her honour, on the border of the royal part of the Favorita, a short distance from Maria Carolina's Chinese Pavilion and almost in the shadow of Monte Pellegrino. It was a charming situation, with good quail shooting in season. Joseph became obsessed with gardening and laid out the estate with palms and rose trees. During the eighteenth century various noble families of Palermo, such as the Bordonaros, the Lampedusas, the Pantellerias and the Niscemis, had built villas in the area, known as the Colli. They came here for the *villeggiatura* or holiday season, in the spring and autumn. One of the most recently built and grandest of the villas, in Neoclassic style, was the Belmontes', on a high position above Arenella with a view of the whole sweep of Palermo bay towards the isthmus of Bagheria, and even of snow-capped Etna, a hundred miles away across the mountains.

There were villas clustered all round Palermo throughout the Conca d'Oro, the oldest group being to the south near Bagheria. It was in Olivuzza, in the autumn of 1845, that the seventeenth-century Villa Butera was rented by Tsar Nicholas I for his Tsarina Alexandra, who because of feeble health had been advised to winter in the south by her personal physician, Dr Mandt. The house was owned by the Russian widow of the Prince of Radalì and thus contained many northern comforts.[5] To many Sicilians even the word stove was unknown, so 'no little astonishment was caused by the whole of the Butera villa being provided with a heating apparatus before the arrival of the Empress, and indeed the Russian colony during the winter months used more wood in Olivuzza than the whole of Palermo.'[6]

The Tsar travelled out with her. Political and commercial rivalries with Britain in any case made it convenient for him to visit the Mediterranean just then. He only stayed in Sicily a short while, and returned via Naples, having meanwhile made a genuine effort at a 'reconciliation between the King and his Sicilian nobles and people'.[7] The Tsarina and her daughter, the lovely Olga, later Queen of Würtemburg, stayed on in seclusion at the Villa Butera, while the Tsarina's sister, the Grand Duchess of Mecklenburg-Schwerin, was at the Villa Serradifalco nearby. Although the Tsarina scarcely appeared in public, her entourage did something to revive the drooping spirits of Palermo's aristocratic society, especially after the arrival of Russian ships and the Grand Duke Constantine, fresh from a tour of the Greek islands and Mount Athos. The visit was the forerunner of many such royal sojourns in Palermo, that continued at least until World War I.[8]

Dr Mandt's presence proved to be a boon in one way, for Joshua Ingham was ill, one suspects with tuberculosis. The first intimation of the illness appears in a letter that concerned the reappearance of the unpopular Humphrey Hervey, who had been running the Woodhouse firm during the minority of the two young owners. Don Onofrio was bringing with him his sister and nephew.

> *To Benjamin Ingham jun., Marsala*                      *3 January 1846*
> Mrs Woodhouse with her son, young Will [aged twenty-four], and Mr Hervey arrived yesterday per *Palermo*. They had a fortunate escape, and not without much alarm, as the *Palermo* came in collision with the steamer *Stromboli*, doing each other no small damage.
>
> Unless Mrs Woodhouse herself comes to Marsala, you do not call on them: that is my counsel. You will be glad to know that Joshua has arrived safe in Messina by the *Mongibello* from Malta but has accepted Smithson's kindness of a bed in his house until the arrival of the *Palermo* on the 20th. I cannot make out anything positive as regards the state of his health. Stephens writes from London that Joshua will tell us of the new machines for curing [drying out] and cleaning casks; they should be an immense thing for us at the *Baglio*.

Ben was in charge of the *Baglio* during Joshua's absence. When Joshua reached his uncle on the twenty-second, he appeared to be better, but later there was reason for alarm.

> *To J. Smithson, Messina*                      *31 January 1846*
> We can only report on the health of our nephew Mr Joshua as being middling. The fact is that his complaint is one that will take months to get rid of entirely. We have been thinking of calling a very first rate physician, a Dr Mandt, who is here with the Tsarina. But Mr Joshua is not at all willing, though we hope he will be persuaded. . . . We are happy to be able to inform you of the arrival of the *Sumatra* in our port yesterday, all well but after a tremendously long journey of 170 days. Captain Di Bartolo on arrival learnt the sad news of the loss of his wife. . . . The cargo consists entirely of pepper, in 5471 parcels; being for the most part old pepper it will yield better than 140 cantars per parcel.[9] 1000 cantars will be for your market and this, and the balance will be for Naples. We cannot say what quarantine the wiseacres here will decide to give her. Nor can we say what price we may obtain here,

having only just commenced treating with our usual dealer, Signor Florio.

Everyone was still cursing the quarantine laws. At any rate it was now clear that an interview Ingham had had with the King the previous August had borne fruit. He had been to see him about a thirty per cent concession in duty being granted to vessels when they were *en voyage*. 'Our *supplica* was received with the greatest kindness', he wrote, 'and we were clearly given to understand that our case would be immediately taken into consideration.' He had clearly caught the King in an expansive mood, for it was the day after the publication of the decree abolishing the sulphur tax and of another reducing the *fondiaria* [land tax] in Sicily. The concession had been granted, and Ingham made good use of it when the *Sumatra* arrived with her cargo. No wonder he wrote: 'Our finances seem to be now more in prosperity.'

It was something of a struggle to get Joshua to see Dr Mandt, but at last he gave in. There were many worries on Ingham's mind: thieves at the *Baglio*, the sacking of the caretaker at the villa at Racalia, Mrs Woodhouse throwing her weight about ('I shall not be surprised at anything young Will Woodhouse did or may do under her influence'), the consequences of a fire in New York the previous year, where warehouses containing Ingham's goods had been burnt;[10] a tiff with the Duchess, who had refused to come with him to Marsala. There had also been trouble with the crew of the *Palermo*, a form of strike which had meant delays in sailings.

*To J. Smithson, Messina*                           *17 March 1846*

We fully concur with you that Signor Trifiletti, the Captain of the *Palermo*, must receive his demission.[11] We hope that Fiamingo will be the man to do the needful. You will no doubt have heard of the many placards posted at the office of the Administration and in the streets, chiefly aiming at Fiamingo[12] himself but at the same time very severe on the other members, not excluding our own countrymen. . . . What a misfortune that the boat should have been idle at this time. The *postale* brings regularly 80 to 100 passengers from Naples. Patience.

Our Mr Joshua appears to be getting on much better and has had the Tsarina's physician to see him several times. He will most probably proceed for Marsala, where the old scenes and a little more active life will contribute greatly to his recovery.

The Tsarina and suite left us yesterday for Naples, to the regret of the good Palermitans who had evinced towards her from the first the greatest respect and reverence. Her departure will be severely felt by many who have partaken of her generosity. Snuff-boxes and other presents, both in kind and in money, have been freely distributed, as was expected.

Joshua left for Marsala on 31 March on the schooner *Comet*. Ingham arranged for him to be accompanied by a doctor. Soon there was disturbing news.

*To Benjamin Ingham jun., Marsala*                    *16 April 1846*
I am sorry to hear Joshua had an attack of pleurisy, but I hope you will have called in the apothecary Giaconia for this complaint. I trust that your next intelligence will be favourable.

Within five days Joshua was dead. There is no doubt that Ingham – as in the case of William Whitaker many years ago – was greatly upset by his 'dear and ever to be lamented' nephew's death. It was discovered that Joshua had died intestate. This raised complications, since the *bagli* both at Campobello and at Mazara were in his name, and according to Sicilian law the estate had to be divided equally between brothers, sisters and parents. How Ingham managed to get round such an embarrassment is not recorded, but we do know that Joshua's personal effects in Sicily were valued at the considerable sum of £30,000.

Meanwhile the *Palermo* was laid up for three whole months. Trifiletti, after being sacked, prepared a *denuncia* 'in the most insulting language a lawyer could pen'. Then he found a job on board the *Mongibello*, the steamer which had brought Joshua Ingham from Malta to Messina. Ingham was delighted by a story that Smithson relayed to him about the 'gallant Captain being slapped on the face by an English lady on board, for being over amorous'. As for the *Palermo*, all ended to some extent happily, for Di Bartolo of the *Sumatra* agreed to become its new captain.

At Marsala Ingham realised that the Woodhouse firm, now more or less ironically referred to as the Great House, was 'determined to go the whole hog in the purchase of wine' under the supervision of 'that extraordinary female Mrs Woodhouse and her child, who is a nobody and not allowed to interfere in anything'. Don Onofrio all the while appeared to be enjoying himself at the Woodhouse *palazzo* in Malta, 'living like a king on his nephew's money'. It was given out that Vincenzo Florio was fully prepared to join with Ingham in doing battle against any resurgence on the part of the Woodhouses.

*To Benjamin Ingham jun., Marsala*                    *12 July 1846*
I have no doubt that our Mrs Woodhouse is determined to push the trade. If we may judge from the prices at which her agents are selling in

New York and in Boston, it appears that she is set to drive us all out of the markets. I would mention that I have heard that she has suffered herself to be completely humbugged by the intrigues and falsehoods of the Marsalese, who have induced her to buy their wines at extravagant prices [because the 1846 vintage was expected to be a bad one]. She has trusted too much in that infernal Bishop, who will pay dearly for his greed when he finds that he will get no custom from Florio or ourselves. I am reminded of that fine old English proverb: 'Put a beggar on horse-back and he will soon ride to the devil'. Likewise the Bishop.

The vintage was indeed bad. Mrs Woodhouse collapsed from the heat and retired from the scene altogether, but not without first sacking the firm's manager, Mr Barlow the ladykiller. She took her 'child' with her. African-type weather was not suitable for an energetic lady in Victorian petticoats. Tempers among the merchants became strained. 'Caution and delicacy seem now to be out of fashion among us', wrote Ingham sarcastically. The Marsalese also saw their opportunities. For the first time there are signs in the letters of displeasure with Vincenzo Florio, whose manoeuvres with the farmers were considered 'dangerous'.

*To Benjamin Ingham jun., Marsala*                   *27 October 1846*
You will do well to take *no* notice whatever of the lies which the *Capella*[13] in Marsala invent, as their only object is to get the *bagli* at loggerheads. They would not care a farthing if all the *bagli* were to get ruined in a few years, provided they can get their own price for their wine; in a word, they would not care if they killed their goose that lays golden eggs. Can you let Whyte [the new Woodhouse manager] know what I here write? I mentioned it yesterday to Florio at the *Borsa* [Exchange] and compared our situations just now to a man that is in a well with water increasing at the rate of a foot every year when it is already up to his knees; Florio agreed heartily with the justice of my remarks, being himself very low spirited.

The bad vintage was just one aspect of the whole agricultural situation. A succession of miserable harvests had brought about a grain shortage, only exacerbating the feeling of discontent against the Government. The year 1847 was one of anxious anticipation. Revolt was obviously inevitable. It only lacked the leaders.

By contrast, in the United States, Ingham's affairs were not only prospering but positively galloping, thanks to Schuyler Livingston. Ben had been right when he wrote to his uncle from New York in 1837 that 'from all accounts Barclay and Livingston sell more wine, sale on commission, than any other ten houses here.' Schuyler Livingston acted as Ingham's personal investment agent for over twenty years, and as such was the real architect of his fabulous wealth. He was another of those office-bound zealots – 'The man's whole life, from boyhood, was devoted to the mercantile profession. He had no ambition outside of it. In forty three years since he swept out the office as an under clerk, he has not probably been out of New York a week at a time.'[14]

Earlier in this book it has been shown how trade between Sicily and America at that time was mostly one way, so that barrel staves fell far short of balancing the payments. Ingham thus built up gigantic reserves of cash on the other side of the Atlantic, especially as transferring his funds to Sicily through London would only have meant a 'frightful loss' in commissions.[15] One assumes (most of the documents having been destroyed in 1943) that trade with the British Isles was at least as great as that with the United States, if not greater. At all events we know that Ingham instructed his London agents Heath, Furse to transfer as much of his British profits as possible to New York, provided 'they may be invested to pay not less than six per cent'.

As has also been already mentioned, the actual scope of Ingham's investments in America is obscure, again because of the bombings in the last war. We only have general indications, often just family tradition – such as his owning real estate on Fifth Avenue and tracts of farmland in Michigan. The bigger money seems to have rolled in during the 1850s. At first, in the early days, Livingston wisely concentrated on making use of the canal boom, again mostly in the states of Michigan and New York. Thus Ingham in due course found himself owning, for instance, stock worth $100,000 in the St Mary Falls Ship Canal Company. By 1844 most of the canals had been dug (1000 miles in New York State alone), and Livingston switched his attention to the railways. In this he had a great asset, for he was a close friend of Erastus Corning, a hugely wealthy merchant from Albany and for a while a senator (1842–6). Corning was, incidentally, president of the St Mary Falls Ship Canal Company. He was also president of the Utica and Schnectady railroad, 'by far the richest and most powerful of the railroads between Albany and Buffalo',[16] in which Ingham obtained a majority holding of 669 shares. In 1853 he consolidated nine railways, including the Utica and Schnectady, into one system, the New York Central Railroad. This new company was capitalised for $23,000,000 and thus became the largest public corporation in America. Ingham received compensatory stock; what with additions to his holding, by 1860 he owned $640,000 in the company, in other words nearly three per cent. Corning presumably was useful in other ways, and he must have been a particularly helpful ally when he became a Democratic representative in Congress.[17]

Livingston always seemed attracted to Michigan as a field of investment. In June 1850, for instance, we find him buying for Ingham $10,000 new stock issued by the Michigan Central Railroad Company, 'towards the completion of their line'. It was this company that in 1859 suggested that Ingham might lend a further $500,000, in other words just under half the sum required. Judging, however, from various lists made after Ingham's death, now in an extremely tattered and partially illegible state, other investments were spread widely over America – in Illinois, New Jersey, Missouri, Long Island. The book value of one such list, including forty-seven items, nearly all paying seven per cent, comes to $1,043,780, and this represented the share of one of three beneficiaries. Another list simply gives 'American assets' as totalling $6,506,261.

Let us not suppose, though, that Ingham confined his foreign investments to the United States. He owned stock worth at least £100,000 in the Lemberg and Czernowitz railway and almost as much in the Antwerp and Rotterdam railway. He had real estate in Paris and perhaps about £75,000 in French railways. As far as England was concerned, we know that at one time he had £40,000 in three per cent British Consols, plus the usual railway stock. 'Sundry assets' amounted to about £150,000. Yet when he died, and his will was proved, his English estate was given as 'under £14,000'. All very mysterious.

Then there was his property in Sicily and on the Italian mainland, not to mention the 'Concern' and the *Baglio*. The whole estate was almost incredibly valued at 18,500,000 *onze* on his death, nearly £9,000,000.

But this is drifting too far ahead. To return to Sicily in 1847, and the passions that were about to be ignited. This is not the place to discuss the European state of mind that led up to the revolutions of 1848. The Sicilian revolt was the first and, in a sense, the longest lived. At that stage in Sicily there was little popular interest (apart from among the intelligentsia) in the ideas of Mazzini and in the possibility of unification with the Italian north; freedom from the humiliation, the corruption, the stultification of Neapolitan rule was the simple aim. Perhaps the greatest outside event to spur on both Sicilian nationalists and Neapolitan malcontents was the accession of Pius IX. 'We were prepared for everything except a liberal Pope,' wrote

Metternich. On 17 July 1846, after a spate of reforms, there had been an amnesty in Rome freeing over a thousand political prisoners. 'Viva Pio Nono!' was a slogan now to be heard at any political disturbance, and Edward Lear heard it during a small insurrection in Reggio Calabria in September 1847.

Michele Amari's book on the Sicilian Vespers had had a tremendous impact on students. He had been forced to flee the country, to join other intellectuals in exile such as Francesco Crispi and Luigi Orlando. One of the most inflammatory documents of all was Luigi Settembrini's *Protest of the People of the Two Sicilies*, published anonymously. Only about 300 copies circulated – the rest of the edition having been burnt – but it 'flew from hand to hand'. Lord Napier, the young Chargé d'Affaires in Naples during the absence of Temple on a very protracted holiday, wrote on 25 July 1847 that 'The *Protest of the People* passed, it is said, to Sicily under the cloak of a friar and was presented to H.M. the King in the guise of a petition. It was tossed into Prince Scilla's carriage in the Toledo, and has reached the hands of all the Ministers and Magistrates.'

The revolt in Reggio had its brief, but more serious, counterpart across the Straits in Messina. Some fifty young men assembled outside the Senate, shouting 'Viva la Sicilia!' and the usual 'Viva Pio Nono!', and there was a clash with the garrison. Lear, having decided to escape from Reggio, had landed a mile away from Messina, 'out of reach of the guns': 'The revolt at Messina', he wrote, 'has occasioned the death of fourteen or fifteen men; but the Government has firm hold of the citadel. Distress and anxiety, stagnation and terror, have taken the place of activity, prosperity, security, and peace.'

Two days later he managed to get on a Maltese steamer heading for Naples. He exaggerated the number of deaths. Eight soldiers were killed and twenty, including the general, were wounded. Only two of the trouble-makers were wounded, whilst the rest fled. A couple of Neapolitan men-o'-war soon quelled Reggio, and when Messina was reached the place was quiet. Proclamations were posted offering money for the capture of the rebels, and there were some executions. General Vial was sent to Palermo, where he claimed to have uncovered a conspiracy; the ghastly tortures he thereupon inflicted were 'disgraceful to a civilised age'.

Palmerston had sent Lord Minto, Brydone's son-in-law, on a tour of some of the Italian mainland to encourage the Pope and other heads of states in their reforms. Whilst in Florence, Minto had been visited by Sicilian refugees who presented him with a 'memorial', reminding England of the 1812 Constitution and begging her to 'undertake the defence diplomatically of Sicilian rights which have been guaranteed by Great Britain'. As a result of this he was ordered by Palmerston to visit Naples, much to the displeasure not only of the Austrians and Russians but of King Ferdinand, thoroughly suspicious of Britain's designs on Sicily.

Lord Mount Edgcumbe, suffering from 'very delicate health', arrived in his yacht at Palermo on 10 November 1847. He was accompanied by members of his family, including his niece, Annie Macdonald. 'Fully prepared to expect public disturbances', he kept a journal, parts of which were eventually published in *The Times* and later reprinted in book form.[18] He witnessed two demonstrations, one at the Opera, but both were 'quickly terminated without the slightest violation of order', though for two days afterwards the streets were crowded and 'the population assumed a menacing aspect'. Rumour had gone around that the British Government was now, at last, on the point of intervening. Then, on 3 January, Mount Edgcumbe wrote: 'The *Gladiator* steamer, Captain Robb, arrived, and after remaining two days went to join Admiral Parker on the coast of Sardinia; the British merchants having made a request that the steamer should return on or about the 12th.'

The swift appearance of the *Gladiator* at such a crucial time, almost as if by chance, caused much excitement, as though it were a portent.[19] 12 January was the King's thirty-eighth birthday, and rumour was already current that this was to be the signal for a rising. The students were getting restless and the university was closed. On 9 January a stirring proclamation ('Siciliani all'armi!'), in fact a pure ruse and the work of a young man named Francesco Bagnasco, was posted on walls announcing that the revolution was planned for dawn on the twelfth. Meanwhile there had been more rioting in Messina.

At this point we are assisted by another diary, that of William Dickinson, Vice-Consul under Goodwin. Reputedly 'a great liberal' and viewed with some reservations by Ingham, who had written disparagingly about him to Dobree, Maingay two years previously – though perhaps not all that surprisingly since Dickinson's bank had failed in 1842.[20] On the night of the ninth he had recorded that General Vial had arrested several people, including the Duke of Villarosa and Professors Emerico Amari and Francesco Ferrara.

In an attempt to arrest Count Aceto, [he wrote, not very grammatically][21] living in the same palace with the entrance to the British Consulate, forcing the coach gate the police, being refused admittance either purposely removed the British arms over it, or the supports gave way –

the gate resisted the efforts made to force an entrance and the matter was abandoned. The officer in charge then gave the arms to the charge of a tavern-keeper on the opposite side of the street.

According to Mount Edgcumbe, this business of the British coat of arms was in fact accidental – 'two of the police officers producing as proof that it was so, their own heads broken by the fall'. The arms were replaced but there was a good deal of indignation in the town, 'the odium of which is all thrown on General Vial' (Dickinson).

One brief letter from Ingham exists for the following day. It shows pretty clearly that at that moment he was mostly on the side of the Bourbons, representing law and order.

*To W. Sanderson, Messina*                                    *11 January 1848*
We continue all quiet here, although we are living in curious times. Some alarm was felt, and is perhaps still felt, of disturbances being attempted tomorrow, but we hope and trust that the late numerous arrests, including several of the nobles, will have the effect of quelling these mad proceedings and assuring public tranquillity.

It has been said that the revolution broke out on the twelfth with the punctuality of a bill of exchange, though this was not quite true. When dawn broke, it was followed by a morning of uneasy quiet. The streets were again thronged; nothing exceptional occurred. One or two speeches were made. Then suddenly there were shots. Some nervous cavalry charged a crowd, but the troops were put to flight and in the process their commander, 'who happened to be son of the obnoxious Vial' (Mount Edgcumbe), was wounded. Furniture and hot water were thrown from windows. Shops were barricaded, but the people waited in vain for any sign of help from the gentry. It seemed that all might be over and, according to Mount Edgcumbe, the riot-leader Miloro 'sought refuge on board the *Bulldog* steamer, which had just arrived in place of the expected *Gladiator*.'

Consul Goodwin, however, caught sight of some sinister characters leaving Palermo that evening. He knew at once that they were off to stir up trouble among the outlying villages.

# PART TWO

# The Struggle for Freedom

# VIII

## *Revolution!*

LITTLE indeed happened during the early part of the thirteenth. But soon the crowds gained confidence and the troops in alarm withdrew into various strong points, such as the Royal Palace and the barracks. The crackle of musketry was heard everywhere, and at twelve o'clock the fort at Castellamare began its bombardment of the town. Nobles and gentry were now joining the rioters, and villagers from outside Palermo were pouring into the city. Dickinson wrote that by the evening of the fourteenth the ultimate victory of the people was beyond a doubt.

Captain Ashley Cooper Key of the *Bulldog* visited General Vial and the Viceroy, the Duke of Serracapriola, to protest against the bombardment on behalf of the British residents. He was received so enthusiastically by the Neapolitans that Mount Edgcumbe decided that, as a peer of England and a friend of several members of the Committee (as the provisional Government was known), he must put himself forward as mediator. This Committee included Ruggiero Settimo and the ancient Prince of Pantelleria. A correspondence between Mount Edgcumbe and Vial then followed, with Captain Key as emissary. Mount Edgcumbe's offer was not questioned, even if he had no political experience, for his rank made him indisputably the most important Englishman to hand in the emergency – just as in Naples nobody worried about the propriety of Lord Napier being the British Chargé d'Affaires during Sir William Temple's absence on holiday, though aged only twenty-eight and looking very much younger.[1]

The atmosphere in the streets of Palermo was becoming decidedly menacing, and Key was warned by the popular leader Francesco Santoro that he might be in danger if the *Bulldog* did not do something positive to stop the Neapolitan bombardment. Sinister armed men passed the Palazzo Butera, where the Mount Edgcumbes were staying, uttering threats against the English, and a young man on the roof of the palace was killed by a cannon ball. Then a shell actually passed through a room in which two ladies of the Mount Edgcumbe party were sitting. A meeting was hurriedly held between Goodwin and Santoro, with Dickinson present, and it was decided that all British residents and visitors must go on board the *Bulldog* that very afternoon at 5.30 p.m.

There are, perhaps naturally, no further letters from Ingham during this particular period. In a letter written during February we learn that he, with the Duchess and the Whitakers, did not go on board the *Bulldog*. Instead they took refuge on two schooners, owned by Ingham and happily in Palermo harbour, the *Lady Sale* and the *Juno*. The accommodation must have been a good deal more comfortable than on the crowded *Bulldog*, even if the *Lady Sale*, recently arrived from Newcastle, still had her shipment of coal on board. One of the group of fugitives, possibly the Whitakers, was shot at whilst embarking. The Mount Edgcumbe party climbed into the *Bulldog*'s paddlebox boat and were towed away by a cutter. Meanwhile a fleet of nine Neapolitan steamers had arrived, and the harbour was full of little boats landing troops. The Mount Edgcumbes were challenged, frequently and angrily in the twilight. They expected to be fired on, so at length Lord Mount Edgcumbe made known who he was. To his surprise an American voice cried out in reply: 'Pray excuse me, sir.' They were thereupon conducted to the *European*, a large American ship, where they found the American Consul, John M. Marston,[2] and his family with various co-national refugees resulting in such a dreadful crush that everyone had to spend the night on chairs and sofas.

The next day they were removed to the *Bulldog*, where despite Captain Key's kindness, conditions were not much better. 'Some of the ladies had to sleep in cots and on sofas, in a portion of the cabin curtained off in the evening, and they were in consequence unable to go to bed till late, and forced to rise very early, and deprived of many comforts deemed necessary on shore.' And there they had to remain for nearly three weeks.

The frigate *Gladiator* had now returned. Since her commander, Captain John Robb, was senior to Captain Key, various discussions were held on board with the commander of the Neapolitan reinforcements, in the presence of Mount Edgcumbe, still acting as Britain's unofficial mediator. Gradually the populace was gaining control of Palermo. It was expected that the Palace would be attacked at any moment; and while the consequences were being discussed 'a dance was held on deck for refugees and their servants, the band of the *Gladiator* accompanying', with sundry monks and nuns, also refugees, as spectators.

The bombardment was increased on the seventeenth, and on the nineteenth a formal protest was drawn up by the Consuls, including Goodwin and Marston, Ernest Busson for France and Gaetano Fiamingo for Russia. When the Palace was evacuated, the whole building – with the exception of the Palatine chapel – was ruthlessly sacked. The only remaining troops had been under the command of Domenico Ascenso, a major in the

*Cacciatori.*[3] All were thrown into prison – one assumes that swift action was taken by Ingham to obtain Domenico's release. Then the Finance building fell: this was the old Vicaria, another prison – octagonal in shape – having been constructed outside the town.[4] General Vial and the Viceroy escaped, hidden in baggage-waggons, and before the Neapolitan forces withdrew 4000 galley slaves were released from the new Vicaria – a deliberate attempt to create anarchy. The Mount Edgcumbes could see a long extended line of troops on the distant, blueish hills; the men were retreating with great regularity before a large band of peasants, who occasionally attacked them. Whilst this was happening tales of terrible barbarity and murders so inflamed the Palermitans that they rounded on the Sicilian police, or *sbirri* as they were pejoratively known, slaughtering any that got into their hands, with terrible ferocity – indeed the *sbirri* fared far worse than the Neapolitans. Santoro was said to be the real instigator of these ghastly doings; 'the British were horrified to watch bodies being dragged about and mutilated', children even being encouraged to take part 'as in a sport'.

H.M.S. *Vengeance* had arrived, under the command of Captain Lushington,[5] elder brother of the Reverend Charles who had taken the wedding service for Joseph and Sophia Whitaker. And the high-minded and very popular Ruggiero Settimo, now aged seventy, was made President of the Committee. The rest of Sicily had swiftly followed the example of Palermo and by the end of January virtually the whole island was clear of royal troops. The forts at Messina and Milazzo and that of Castellamare outside Palermo, under the Swiss mercenary Colonel Gross, were virtually the only strongholds left to the Bourbons – as usual the Neapolitans, the least soldierlike people in the world, had had to rely on foreigners to do most of their fighting for them.[6] Girgenti rose on the twenty-second and Catania on the twenty-fourth. At Girgenti there was a nasty report of the Neapolitan colonel having ordered some 160 prisoners to be thrown into a large hole and then lumps of burning sulphur hurled on top of them – these basic facts were confirmed by Vice-Consul Oates, except that in his report grenades were substituted for sulphur.

The situation at Messina was watched over by both Captain Codrington[7] of H.M.S. *Thetis* and the captain of the U.S. ship *Princeton*. On the twenty-ninth fifty soldiers and two rebels were killed, with the result that, according to Consul Barker, the town was bombarded anew 'in every direction', so that the property of the British sustained considerable damage, most of their main houses and warehouses being in the best part of the town, along the splendid Palazzata on the Marina, a row of half completed palaces begun after the earthquake of 1783.

It was on the twenty-ninth that Ferdinand suddenly announced that there would be a new constitution, that longed-for word. The decision had been forced on him by a revolt that had broken out near Salerno. A ship was hurriedly sent to Palermo to proclaim an amnesty.

Meanwhile the Palermitans had been constructing batteries opposite the Castellamare fort, a mere 400 yards away across the Cala, as the main harbour was called. On the arrival of this Neapolitan ship, Mount Edgcumbe made the mistake of deciding to return to land with his family. Annie Macdonald, a Miss Feilding and the two Mount Edgcumbe boys, aged fourteen and ten, went ahead; Lord and Lady Mount Edgcumbe with their little girl followed. Hardly had the second party settled in the barge of the *Vengeance* when fire opened up from all the Palermitan batteries. Annie Macdonald and the others had to scamper to the Palazzo Butera for safety, but the others only had time to take refuge on the *Bulldog*. Shells could now be seen bursting on the Palazzo. The *Vengeance* prepared for action, her ports up, the men at quarters, and her band playing patriotic tunes – including rather surprisingly the *Marseillaise*. Lushington, who claimed to have received terms from the Neapolitan commander, ordered the *Bulldog* to clear for action and place herself between the Fort and the Mole.

It was not a pleasant situation for the civilians on board, yet to Mount Edgcumbe the scene was exciting and gratifying, with the Union Jack proudly waving over the two ships. Indeed Captain Lushington behaved with very great bravery, sailing in a small gig to Colonel Gross's lines and successfully and amazingly obtaining his agreement to surrender, then steering the boat himself through shot and fire to the rebel batteries. He landed, and suddenly all shelling ceased. Then, accompanied by an enthusiastic mob, continually kissing him, he made his way to the Committee, and having ascertained that they were willing to accept the terms, returned to Colonel Gross.

Thus in effect ended the first stage of the revolution, and arrangements were made for the Neapolitans to embark for home under British escort. As it happened, when the time came, there was no trouble at all from rioters, and 'the people showed the best and kindest feeling towards their vanquished opponents, the gigantic Colonel Gross having to bring down his weather-beaten face to the level of ordinary men, that he might be kissed by dirty, whiskered mouths much oftener than could, even here (where the practice of men slobbering each other's faces is common), be thought agreeable'. Only the wretched *sbirri* continued to be persecuted. The odious Santoro, an obvious precursor of the *Mafia*, was put in charge at Castellamare, his presence there being regarded with considerable fear and disgust by both British and the Committee.

Mount Edgcumbe now decided to land once more. He found the Palazzo Butera in a much worse state than he had expected, several shells having entered the upper storey. Luckily, because the palace was so strongly built, Annie and her companions had been able to shelter downstairs out of danger. Indeed the ladies had shown courage and coolness 'rarely attributed to their sex', and when the firing had stopped they had bravely conducted the boys to the house of an American in the centre of the town.

The next morning there was a *Te Deum* in the cathedral. The Senate marched through the streets in full state, and Cardinal Pignatelli blessed the revolutionary flag. Dickinson noted that all the Consuls, except the Austrian, were present at the service; Consul Goodwin and Captain Lushington were received with immense applause, and the strains of 'Guerra, Guerra' from Bellini's *Norma* accompanied the ceremony. Many of the leading persons in society did Mount Edgcumbe the honour of coming up to his chair, and on his return to the Palazzo Butera his carriage was cheered. Later a special service was held at the British Consulate in the Palazzo Lampedusa.[8] All this excitement, however, was too much for the Prince of Pantelleria, who died in the midst of the festivities, 'the fatigue having hastened his end'.

Very likely the Ingham-Whitaker party also attended the *Te Deum*, for Captain Lushington at the height of the crisis on the fourth had ordered the *Lady Sale* and the *Juno* to put to sea for a few days, for reasons of safety. Thus Ingham and the others would have had the inconvenience of taking temporary refuge that night on the *Vengeance* or the *Bulldog*. Bullets were still flying around even after the departure of Colonel Gross and his men, and Ingham did not consider that danger had fully passed until 7 February. He settled down on that day to write his first letters.

*To W. Sanderson, Messina*                    *7 February 1848*
The patriots have completed their victories by the surrender of the Castellamare fortress, which took place after about three hours of brisk cannonading on Friday afternoon last, the King's troops being allowed to evacuate the place with all the honours of war and to embark on board the steamer for Naples. You must not be surprised at receiving letters from us by the *Palermo*, which left for your town last night. . . . The present will go by H.M.S. *Bulldog*.

*To Richard Stephens, London*                    *7 February 1848*
We regret greatly to say that we are still in a very unsatisfactory state,

particularly as all prisoners have been loosed from the jail. One might say that we are in exactly the same state as in the year 1820, and as you were then at Marsala we need not enter into further details. The only difference is that in 1820 Trapani, Messina and a great part of the island were against Palermo, whereas now the whole and entire population appears to be perfectly united and insists on having a separate parliament in Palermo. What the final result may be God Almighty alone knows, but this is certain, that unless some powerful foreign nation interferes we greatly fear it will take a long time to restore peace and tranquillity.

Ingham wrote to Routh in Naples to say that 'we are happy to be able to say that so far private property has been unmolested by the people, at least with trifling exceptions.' There was a great shortage of money, the banks being shut, though luckily the one where Ingham kept most of his 'effective' had not been pillaged. Lord Minto had now arrived in Naples, and it was clear that he was expected to come straight to Palermo.

Yet after nearly a month Minto was still in Naples. Mount Edgcumbe was asked to continue to assist him in his correspondence with the Committee, but after a while the former – in due course to be riled by sneers in the British Press about amateur diplomatists in Sicily – appears to have collapsed with a serious illness.

The fort at Milazzo surrendered on 12 February. Ingham now considered the revolution to be an accomplished fact. Naples could do nothing single-handed, he told Smithson, and help from Austria or any other power was hardly to be expected. Vice-Admiral Sir William Parker, the Commander-in-chief, had arrived in Palermo harbour with four lines of battleships and two steamers, reassuring though ominous. Meanwhile 'barbarous proceedings' continued daily, both in Palermo and Marsala. Stephens in London was told that there was an alarming number of assassins and robbers in every main port of the island.

*To Dobree, Maingay & Co., Naples*           *19 February 1848*

On Wednesday last no less than thirty-four poor unfortunate devils of the late police were taken from the prison where they were detained and sent into the other world, without any ceremony, and what is worse no resistance was made or could prudently be made. A thing that has given satisfaction to all well-disposed persons is the death of one of the most active and mischievous of the populace leaders, a certain Santoro, of whom we must say that we were greatly afraid, lest he would have called on us as well as on many others for a forced loan and in a way not to be resisted. He was shot by one of the other populace parties, we are of the opinion by some previous concerted plan in order to get rid of him as a dangerous character opposed to any settlement of our question.

*To Dobree, Maingay & Co., Naples*                              *24 February 1848*
We do not at all like the present state of affairs. We fear that the King and his ministers may yet cause us more troubles than we have given. As for his entertaining feelings of disgust towards this island for its unreasonable demands, you may rely that there are other more pungent reasons that influence his conduct and the minds of all Neapolitans when Sicily is the theme. The Neapolitans have been too long accustomed to oppress and squeeze out of her every dollar they can, to relinquish the power that they hold over her. Hence the poverty and wretchedness to which the country has been reduced. . . . Unless there is a guarantee against the wrongs ever again being committed, the Sicilians will never be satisfied, nor ought they to be.

Meanwhile in Naples the Government had rounded on the British: the fleet, it was claimed, had given assistance to the rebels; H.M.S. *Vengeance* had connived with the Sicilians: arms had been provided, possibly by private merchants.[9] Needless to say, as Napier told Palmerston, there were violent feelings among English residents on the subject.

In Messina, the position remained tense and serious. The Bourbon troops in the fort were still sporadically shelling the town. On the twenty-fourth Sanderson wrote to his friend Mr Turner, a merchant in Naples, that Messina looked like becoming a battlefield for all Sicily. 'Why destroy the city of Messina and a large amount of foreign property in it, principally British? It looks very like a hatred to our country.' And Smithson wrote the same day that there had been a thirty-two hours' bombardment, shells had been thrown into his warehouses in the Porto Franco, reducing every one of them to a cinder. The houses of the Germans were the most exposed, but their warehouses were stocked with British material and their 'portfolios full of goods sold during the last six months, and nobody pays'.

Captain Codrington naturally complained to the Neapolitan commander of the citadel, General Pronio, who chose as his emissary a member of the Acton family, Guglielmo, or William (nephew of the famous Sir John and thus a Neapolitan subject). But nothing transpired, and the shelling was even intensified on the twenty-fifth and twenty-sixth. Codrington reckoned that 30,000 *onze* damage had so far been done to British property. Later the British Government submitted a claim for just over this amount, including 14,000 *onze* owing to Smithson.

For all this there was still hope in Naples that some sort of settlement might be negotiated. Ingham, however, was deeply suspicious, especially when news came of yet another revolution, a clap of thunder he called it: the revolution in Paris on 24 February. Louis-Philippe, son-in-law of Queen Maria Carolina, abdicated and a republic was proclaimed. At once the political atmosphere in Sicily was recharged. The British residents became thoroughly uneasy.

Dickinson wrote in his diary:

*28 February 1848*

A confidential meeting was convoked at 3 p.m. of all the English merchants, at the request of Mr Ingham at the British Consul's, to take into serious consideration the position of things at Naples with regard to Sicily, as it was pretty certain (on the information he held) that Lord Minto by the procrastinating duplicity of the Government would retire altogether from the offer of mediator, and very likely the British fleet would also retire from their different stations in the Two Sicilies.

Under the circumstances Ingham proposed that an immediate application should be made to the Admiral for a man of war to be permanently stationed at Palermo, in order to protect British interests. He was strongly opposed by the rest of the British, led by a Mr Morrison who thought the proposal was premature. Far better to have someone visit Lord Napier immediately and simply to warn him of the possible dangers, which were indeed very grave.

This Mr Morrison was a popular figure, noted in 1848 for his remarkable wig. A Scotsman, dealing in liquorice paste, he was very much regarded as the wise man among the merchants, with the exception of Ingham of course who now resented being shown up as an alarmist, and who seems only to have given in because of a family connection – Mrs Morrison being Sophia Whitaker's first cousin.[10]

Ben was once more acting as consul in Marsala. Trouble seemed to be in the offing there too. His uncle told him: 'I see that the Sicilians are for an independent army, which can never be conceded to them. I dare *not* say this openly for fear of being taken for a Jacobin.' This was on 2 March. Ben was also advised to take in gunpowder and prepare the *Baglio* for defence.

As it happened, the Sicilians, more and more excited by the news from France, were now insisting on a completely separate kingdom, with not only their own army but their own flag and money. The most the Neapolitans were prepared to grant was a separate Parliament, with Ruggiero Settimo as Viceroy. Minto, having been present at the deliberations in Naples, was asked to take these proposals to Palermo and to use his influence in negotiating a peace. He arrived on 10 March, on board Admiral Parker's flagship the *Hibernia*.

A bright spot meantime for Ingham had been the fact that there was a good market among the British warships for coal from the *Lady Sale*. It sold at twenty-five shillings a ton. Then suddenly he won a victory over Morrison, for Dickinson wrote in his diary again:

*12 March 1848*

A meeting of the British merchants at Mr Valentine's and a requisition drawn up and signed, urging Admiral Parker to leave a ship of war here for their protection, should Lord Minto's mission prove unsuccessful and the fleet thereby be withdrawn. In the afternoon Admiral Parker called on Mr Goodwin and told him that, in the event of the fleet leaving sooner than was anticipated, he had taken care of British interests here. The requisition was received by the Admiral, and he promised to leave a ship of war, but not an eighty-gun ship.

Who was the wise man now?

Minto returned to Naples with an ultimatum that was so wounding to the King's pride that it was virtually certain to be refused. 'Plunder and robbery' were still only too common in Palermo and usually unpunished – the Committee seeming weak and curiously lacking in energy and courage.

The outlook was threatening indeed. 'As for trade,' Ingham told Robert Jeans of Catania, 'no one thinks of entering into engagements for the present. . . . We are in a pretty mess and no mistake, for the advices from Naples show clearly that the proposals from this side through Lord Minto will not be acceded to.'

*To Richard Stephens, London*                              *21 March 1848*

We have a most formidable fleet in the bay under Admiral Sir William Parker, consisting of 5 ships of the line and as many steamers, which is a great protection to us. We dare not venture to leave our houses after sunset and are spending near 2 *onze* per day on armed men to guard Mr Whitaker's and my house. If we sent to encash money we must have it guarded by two armed men to bring it to the office in a carriage and it was only yesterday morning at 11 o'clock that the American consul was sending to us about 116 *onze* for payment of some coals and the man by which he was sending it was robbed of it in the streets.

The 'advices' proved right. The small government steamer *Flavio Gioia* brought the depressing news that not only had the ultimatum been turned down but all negotiations through Lord Minto were to be suspended. A blockade of Sicily was now awaited, and as Ingham said 'the next move we expect will be to declare the throne vacant.'

Ingham's alarm about conditions in Marsala also proved to be justified. On the twenty-fourth there was a despatch to Captain Key from Admiral Parker telling him that the town had been in the hands of an armed mob since the twenty-first, and the British merchants had been demanding protection of their property. The plight of the British was corroborated by the American Vice-Consul who had just arrived from the town. The *Bulldog* was thus ordered to proceed to Marsala without any loss of time. Key's job was to find the British Vice-Consul (Ben) and to 'endeavour to obtain a correct list of the numbers of the British residents at Marsala, distinguishing the natives of England and those of Malta, with their occupations and the number of men, women and children comprised in the families'; and if necessary they were to be taken on board.

The arrival of the *Bulldog* must have instantly quenched the spirits of the mob, judging from a letter from Joseph Whitaker to Ben:

*To Benjamin Ingham jun., Marsala*                    *27 March 1848*
We have duly received yours of 26th by express through Mr Goodwin, and we write these few lines by return of the same. We are glad to hear you are again quiet . . . the *Bulldog* has returned but has brought no letter yet from you. My uncle has just gone on board to see Captain Key and hear his news. It is reported from Naples that the King has determined on collecting an army at Reggio, where several steamers have arrived with troops, and it is further said that His Majesty himself is probably gone there for the purpose of taking the command of reconquering the island. This as may be; Lord Minto and the Admiral have proceeded to Messina by the *Gladiator* with what object is not known, but they are supposed to put a stop to the fighting which we regret to hear has again commenced there. There is great news from the Continent which you will read in the *Cittadino* of yesterday.

The great news included the rising in Vienna, which resulted in the flight of Metternich, and the famous Five Days in Milan. Venice rose; her Austrian Governor was murdered. Revolt spread quickly right through northern Italy. The rebel Parliament had been opened in Palermo on the twenty-fifth, with Ruggiero Settimo as President of the Committee, and the King's offer, as originally brought by Minto a fortnight previously, was formally rejected. Messina was still the great source of worry, for the Bourbon troops there were as active as ever, and the bombardment of the town was continued at intervals. Mr Dickinson reported that a Mr Scalia had arrived from the town for money, bombs and ammunition; the Committee immediately placed ten thousand *onze* at his disposal.

*To J. Smithson, Messina*                     *27 March 1848*
We regret to hear that you had again recommenced fighting, as it is clear from the past that no effectual good can result therefrom. We shall be disappointed if things do not yet turn out aright for Sicily, as the news which has just been received of outbreaks at Milan and even at Vienna, the abdication of the Emperor, the flight of the Duke of Modena etc., will surely still cause the King to reflect and ponder well what he should do before having recourse to further coercion. The opening of Parliament on Saturday was rather an imposing spectacle, the members thereof proceeded at once to business and have been constant to their duty since.

In the north Marshal Radetzky was retreating into the 'Quadrilateral' formed by the cities of Peschiera, Verona, Legnano and Mantua. The King of Piedmont, Charles Albert, had mustered a large army, and volunteers were swarming there from all parts of Italy, including Naples and Sicily.

*To Dobree, Maingay & Co., Naples*              *31 March 1848*
Surely no ministry which your King may form can advise him to attempt now to reconquer this island, which is united to a man in resisting and fighting for their just rights. He must be prepared to entertain the main point in any settlement, viz. the independence of Sicily in fact and not merely in name. As for the news from the North, it is of so astounding a nature that one is lost in conjecture as to what the finale is to be or what to expect next. We have heard of immense failures in France and have just received the news that the Bank of France has actually suspended its payments, which we consider to be tantamount to a national bankruptcy. The house of the brothers Rothschild must suffer enormously.[11]

On 1 April the Mount Edgcumbes decided that the time had come for them to leave Palermo. They had not reckoned with a last-minute snag, for on that very morning Annie Macdonald eloped with one of the revolutionary leaders, Baron Alfredo Porcelli, a Colonel who had greatly distinguished himself at Milazzo. Apparently Porcelli 'fell madly in love' with her and his 'passionate pleadings eventually succeeded in persuading her to elope with him.'[12] One notes that he had providentially been an officer in charge of the Palermitan batteries that had opened fire on the Castellamare fort – fire that had occurred at precisely the moment when Annie was safely on shore, thus preventing the Mount Edgcumbes from being with her for a night.

Very early in the morning of the first Annie scrambled down the terrace of the Palazzo Butera to the public promenade, and she and Porcelli were married immediately afterwards in a nearby church. The two of them then rejoined her uncle and the rest of the party, but naturally the departure had to be put off. The next day there was a Protestant marriage service on board H.M.S. *Gladiator*, in the presence of Captain Robb, Consul Goodwin and Mr Yelverton, the chaplain.[13]

Lord Mount Edgcumbe at last sailed off, minus Annie, and arrived with his family in Rome a few days later. He was there until 18 May 1849; as far as danger from revolutions went, it was all very much a question of frying pan into fire.

For the next fortnight there was relative calm, politically speaking, in Palermo, though throughout the island and, even in Naples itself, there was a general drift towards chaos. On 6 April Consul Goodwin sent a despatch to Napier telling him of the great alarm prevailing in Palermo on account of all the robberies committed daily in the neighbourhood. Persons going out at night or even in the dusk were being stopped by armed men and 'plundered' on the spot, whilst others were being carried into the country and compelled to pay ransom. Now that the *Bulldog* had left Marsala anarchy and confusion had reappeared there. Later he wrote to say that the town was in the hands of an armed mob, so that British residents were once more applying for a man-o'-war 'to protect their lives and property'.

King Ferdinand had been forced to form a new Government under Carlo Troya and had even taken the step – some said it was crafty, others cowardly – of declaring war on Austria in support of Charles Albert. General Guglielmo Pepe, one of the leaders of the 1820 revolution and once a *Carbonaro*, returned to Naples and was sent up to the Po with a contingent of 17,000 troops. On 13 April the Sicilian parliament voted Ferdinand off the throne – in the words of Ingham they 'declared the King and his family decadent'. There was little that Ferdinand could do by way of retaliation. But Ingham was worried:

*To J. Smithson, Messina*                                    *15 April 1848*
Should the Neapolitan government declare its intention to blockade our ports, we have indeed boisterous times before us. What a pretty state of things to look forward to. The last news from England in respect of that ill-fated country Ireland is rather of an alarming nature. You may rely

that we shall have a kick-up in that country. After the declaration in our Parliament here we had a repetition of your proceedings in the matter of destruction of royal statues. One solitary marble remains on our Marina, happening to be of a different family.

Goodwin's despatch on the seventeenth included the following, by comparison:

The dethronement of the King by the vote of Parliament on the 13th instant was no sooner known than public joy found vent in deafening shouts, musical performances, and a general illumination. Early next morning all the statues of the Bourbons were thrown down and demolished, whilst the effigy of Charles II of Spain [the last Habsburg king of Spain] remained untouched and respected. The Duke of Genoa [second son of Charles Albert] is understood to be the personage to whom the crown of Sicily is destined to be offered.

On the eighteenth Joseph Whitaker told Smithson that the *Palermo* had sailed for Civitavecchia with '100 warriors on board to form part of the Italian grand army.' Also on board were Prince Granatelli and Luigi Scalia, the Sicilian emissaries to London, and Giuseppe La Farina and Emerico Amari, delegates to Turin (the other main delegates, Baron Friddani and Padre Ventura being already *in situ* at their respective posts, Paris and Rome). From the start of the revolution the *Palermo* had been in constant demand, carrying ammunition to Milazzo, making trips to Catania and so on; Dickinson had referred to her doing a tour of inspection all round the island and bringing the equivalent of £50,000 'in specie gold and silver from Trapani'. There was a feeling of euphoria. On the twenty-second Joseph remarked: 'The King has become as tame as a mouse. He no longer takes things with that high hand as he was wont and is regularly cast down in spirits. By the twenty-seventh the *Palermo* had returned, after a highly successful trip to Civitavecchia, Leghorn and Genoa. 'The envoys had been received everywhere with great honours, joy and acclamation – the fighting gentlemen equally so, being feasted in the cafés and hotels and not allowed to pay for anything.' On that day too poor old Ingham slipped on a cabbage leaf on his way to the counting house and sprained his ankle; leeches were applied and he was confined to the house, thus missing the ball on H.M.S. *Gladiator* the next evening – no doubt to him a mixed blessing. On the twenty-ninth Joseph wrote to Smithson telling him how sorry he was that there had been more firing, from the 'enemy' at Messina, causing the alarm to continue in the town.

The great and shattering event on the mainland was the famous Allocution of Pope Pius, also on 29 April, whereby once and for all the Papacy refused to take sides against Austria. This seemed a terrible setback to the cause of Italian unity. In Naples there had been some tepid elections and the new Parliament was due to open on 15 May. As that day came nearer, so unrest began to grow and the passions of royalists and democrats flared higher against one another. A civil war looked as though it was brewing in Calabria and Salerno.

Notwithstanding the dangers, the *Sumatra* sailed to Naples with a cargo of pepper for Dobree, Maingay. The sales were favourable. Then news came that Palmerston had 'indicated' that the Duke of Genoa would be acceptable as King of Sicily to the British Government, since he now considered Sicilian independence a *fait accompli*.

The warlike men of Bronte had also, and inevitably, been aroused. On 6 May Dickinson wrote: 'At Bronte Mr Thovez and family in charge of Lord Nelson's [i.e. Lady Bridport's] estate were obliged to fly for safety of their lives; convicts and some of the natives united there for plunder and rapine.' William Thovez had for a while been employed by Ingham in Marsala, at the time of the death of Joshua; he was married to a Sicilian, and in the usual, almost incestuous way became related to other British merchant families in Sicily by his daughter marrying John Jeans of Catania.[14] At any rate on 8 May the troubles at Bronte were over, for Captain Robb told Admiral Parker that the Duchy's steward had been reinstated and the guilty parties sent for trial to Catania. He added, however, that robberies were still taking place all over the island.

Then all was grim uncertainty once more. Revolution had broken out in Naples. A French squadron had arrived in the Bay, its presence at once starting the rumour that the now republican France had decided to help the Neapolitan liberals. Barricades were immediately thrown up along the Toledo. Strangers' carriages were turned upside down; paving stones, chairs, confessionals from churches piled on top of them. What happened next is sometimes attributed to premeditated treachery on the part of the King – hardly likely, since in the mounting hysteria he was obviously extremely frightened, even thinking of escape. While the first shots were fired, 12,000 troops massed in front of the Royal Palace. Then the carnage began. As Harold Acton has said, the details of the horrors committed, especially by the Swiss mercenaries, have been recounted so often as to be 'too wearisome to bear repetition'. People were thrown from windows, into wells, stabbed in bed. The Swiss had been goaded into fury by the deceptions and insults of their opponents, including members of the

National Guards[15] from the south; as they set fire to the houses, so the *lazzaroni* (that peculiarly Neapolitan form of layabout) would dash in and pillage the furniture, even pianos. The houses of the leading liberals were specially marked out. By the end of 15 May, when the situation was under control, it was reckoned that 19,000 people had died. And Ferdinand had at least learnt two lessons: firstly that the troops were subservient to him; secondly, that the people were not nearly so strong or so organised as he had feared. He immediately ordered the army under General Pepe to return south.

But the tocsin had been rung for the forces of reaction throughout Italy. When the details of the massacre reached Palermo, there were three days of mourning – combined with furious cries for retribution. Calabria was still in tumult, and there was wild and heady talk of sending Sicilian troops to help the rebels there. Ingham thought that such an act would be sheer inanity.

> *To Dobree, Maingay & Co., Naples*          *4 June 1848*
> We understand that Mr George Fagan is coming to Palermo by the *Porcupine* to represent to the men in power here the folly of their attempting to assist in the movement in Calabria, or to interfere at all with internal affairs of Naples; we therefore hope that the Sicilian forces will be called from Milazzo and all cause of a collision between the two countries done away with. The real fact is that we have sadly in Parliament too many hot-headed fools, who have nothing to lose and therefore care nothing about the consequences of their measures.

This George Fagan was the son of Robert Fagan, younger brother, or more exactly half-brother, of Ingham's ex-flame Estina. Like his father, he was liberal-minded, even fanatically so, and at the same time on the make – judging from the rather unsavoury manner in which he had once harassed old Consul Barker of Messina. He was now an attaché at the British Embassy in Naples, having been there since 1837.[16] On arrival in Palermo he went at once to see Marino Stabile, the Sicilian Foreign Minister, and we learn that among other things he conveyed Lord Napier's gratitude for what had been done to protect Lady Bridport's property, and also for the fact that British residents in Palermo were to be exempt from taking service in the National Guard.

Fagan could do nothing to dissuade the Sicilians from what was now a determination to send men to Calabria, about a thousand in all. It was a doomed expedition from the start. The King at once sent troops to meet them, and soon the local peasantry were beginning to regret the appearance of their Sicilian saviours. The inhabitants of Messina, across the Straits, were needless to say particularly worried. Smithson kept pressing for news. At first Ingham was not so sure that Ferdinand would have his way:

> *To J. Smithson, Messina*                               *10 June 1848*
> The only political item of interest comes from Mr Goodwin, that Great Britain would be ready to acknowledge Sicily as an independent nation immediately they will have chosen for themselves a prince to rule over them.

> *To W. Sanderson, Messina*                              *24 June 1848*
> King Ferdinand is in hot water. Whether he can hold his ground or not, you can rely that he will never give in. As for the standard of the English, we have no reason to complain of it in this city; but we ourselves take no notice of what they say or think of us here, as we know them too well and have the greatest contempt for the whole nation [i.e. Naples]. They not only expect everything from us but to have it done, how and when they like.

Goodwin was now not so sure whether the Duke of Genoa would be acceptable as King after all, though Fagan held the opposite view. There was a new movement afoot to have instead the seven-year-old son of the Duke of Tuscany. A great blow to merchants in Naples was the announcement that there was to be a forced loan – and foreigners were to be included. Karl Rothschild had to produce 30,000 ducats. Ingham, although resident in Sicily, was indirectly affected as Dobree, Maingay's share was 4000 ducats. Routh and Jeans had to find 800, and W. J. Turner (Sanderson's friend) 4000.

Ingham's temper, perhaps aggravated by the dislocated ankle, which had kept him at home for a month, was now getting very short indeed, as these extracts from Dickinson's diary show:

> *19 June 1848*
> Mr Ingham called a meeting at his office Wednesday morning of the British merchants to take into consideration the conduct of the Consul.

> *21 June 1848*
> At the meeting held in Mr Ingham's office, after some conversation, he decided that a letter (which he engaged to write) should be addressed to Lord Palmerston, setting forward the incapacity of our Consul to his post. On discussing the position of the present treaty and service of the National Guards, it was decided to address Lord Napier, Chargé d'Affaires at Naples, on the subject, in order to secure, on the recognition of Sicily, the full continuation of the Treaty.

12. Joseph Whitaker in 1841, by F. Patania (*in the possession of Major Sir James Whitaker, Bt*).

13. Emily Hinton, married firstly Benjamin Ingham, jun., then Marquis Medici del Vascello.

14. The *Sumatra II* in the Bay of Naples.

15. *Below:* Vincenzo Di Bartolo, captain of the *Sumatra*.

16. *Right:* Richard Brown Cossins with his second wife, Eliza Legge.

The Treaty was the original 'most favoured nation' treaty of 1816 – a treaty which had in any case been once thrown overboard, at the time of the sulphur dispute.

Ingham had precious little patience, either, for many of those in the Sicilian government. As far as he was concerned, a monarchy was the only means of bringing back order and prosperity.

*To J. Smithson, Messina*         *5 July 1848*
The very severe setback which the anarchists have had in France will serve as a good lesson to other nations, and we must say that we think it is doing so in this city where a republican spirit was beginning to manifest itself, particularly after the arrival of the French line of battleships from Naples. What has, however, tended more to check the spirit is the demonstration by our National Guard to have the constitution and election of the new King finished without further delay. . . . There are in Parliament sadly too many characters who would have never been elected in quiet times, and who have no object in view than the loaves and fishes.

*To J. Smithson, Messina*         *6 July 1848*
The want of money in the National Treasury is a most serious affair, and we do not see how it can be remedied as long as there are so many hungry thieves in employ whose only care is to rob as much as they possibly can. We dare not say more for fear of being taken for royalist [i.e. in this case, pro-Bourbon].

Strangely, the only good words were to be found for General Pronio, the Neapolitan commanding the citadel of Messina: 'that truly excellent person'. 'You perhaps have no contact with him', Ingham wrote to Smithson, 'but should the opportunity occur, without fear of passing for traitor, pray give him the writer's best compliments.'

The lesson in France was a reference to the four torrid June days when an insurrection had been put down by General Cavaignac with enormous casualties. Yet another victory for the reactionaries.

In Calabria there was disaster. Cosenza, the rebels' main centre, had fallen to the Bourbons. The local inhabitants had become totally exasperated with the civil war, and the Sicilians had no option but to escape – not to Messina or Milazzo, as Ingham thought might be the case, but to Corfu, which was British-owned territory. 600 of them had embarked on 6 July.

And now there was a new international incident. On the way to Corfu, the Sicilians in the brig *Gesù e Maria* were stopped, by the Neapolitan steam vessel of war, *Stromboli*, and the whole lot was captured. The 'lower orders' were taken to Reggio, the gentlemen and officers to Naples, where they were imprisoned in the Castello Sant'Elmo. It seemed that the *Stromboli* had followed the same technique as H.M.S. *Talbot* during the Sulphur War: a false flag – the British – had been used, hauling it down as soon as the brig was captured. Napier was most indignant. The Sicilians, who had had no food or water, had welcomed the British flag with immense relief and joy, and at once displayed their own ensign.

Nothing much did happen, though several angry notes were passed to the Neapolitan Government. Palmerston was realistic enough to appreciate that British ships had been apt to use this very technique in the past. At least the *Stromboli* was not flying the British flag *at the moment* of making the capture.

Meanwhile the Sicilian Parliament had been busying itself about this tricky matter of choosing a King.

*To W. Sanderson, Messina*                                      *11 July 1848*
Our Parliament has at last got through with its debates on the Constitution, and yesterday it proceeded to the appointment of a King, the same having fallen finally on the second son of Charles Albert, the Duke of Genoa, who is to be called by the name of Albert Amedeo the First, that of Ferdinand [the Duke's real name] not suiting at all and having been left out. There has been grand rejoicing and firing of cannon from the forts, which has been responded to both by the *Bulldog* and the inflexible French line of battleships, with 21 guns each. We are glad that this affair has been settled, as we think it paves the way for a final adjustment of all out troubles, since England and France will at once recognise our independence.

*To J. Smithson, Messina*                                      *20 July 1848*
The *Palermo* we understand leaves today for Genoa with a deputation to inform the new King of his appointment. You say that the news of his election caused little sensation in Naples, but we have reason to think otherwise. It is certain that the government there is annoyed beyond measure with the British and French fleets having saluted the new flag and King. . . . The two Admirals will not be satisfied to be mere lookers on should any invasion really take place of this island.

The two admirals were Parker for Britain and Baudin for France. Parker had written on the eleventh to Napier, from the *Hibernia*, saying that he intended to stay some days in Palermo in order to cement the better feelings now prevailing towards Britain. He might, judging from Dickinson's diary have had another reason for staying on.

*18 July 1848*

The ball, given by the English residents to Admiral Parker and officers of his fleet, turned out very brilliant at the palace of the Duke of Serradifalco in Olivuzza. Supper for 400 laid out in the villa, and well served. The ball broke up after daylight.

It was decided in the end not to send the *Palermo* with the delegation, in case of capture. Instead the French steamer *Descartes* was chosen, as less likely to arouse suspicion.[17] Ingham wrote:

*To J. Smithson, Messina*                                       *29 July 1848*

The *Descartes* returned from Genoa the day before yesterday, having landed the deputation there all safe, not however without having fallen in with three Neapolitan steamers which were lying wait in the vicinity and on the lookout for the *Palermo*. The steamers, some say there were five of them, are reported to have visited every description of vessel they met with, and in some instances fired at them, in particular a French merchant steamer. What a sad disappointment it must have been to King Ferdinand when he learnt the circumstance of the French steamer having taken the deputation over instead of the *Palermo*.

The *Descartes* had arrived at an unfortunate moment, just as Charles Albert had been forced to abandon Milan to the Austrians.

On 2 August Dickinson was told by Goodwin that he had 'received a hint that the mercantile body was dissatisfied' with him. This was obviously a result of Ingham's complaint to Palmerston on 21 June. On the next day there was a special meeting of merchants, at which it was explained that 'until the post service became regular with Naples, he [Goodwin] was to make up a bag by every steamer or conveyance for the better security of the letters from British merchants and residents' – for the matter of communications appeared to have been the original chief complaint.

There was another bombardment of Messina by Ingham's friend Pronio – 'unprovoked and barbarous', and on an 'unoffending portion of the town'. Several people lost their lives. This all contributed to the general feeling of menace hanging over Sicily. Would Ferdinand dare to invade? Ingham thought not.

*To J. Smithson, Messina*                                       *17 August 1848*

King Ferdinand has been deterred from his purpose of invading. There is a report here that the troops could not be relied upon or would not fight. We place no great faith in the saying that His Majesty will not spill another drop of blood. It is too well known that he lacks any feeling of compassion towards his ex-subjects. Can it be that Austrian aid is still looked for now that Charles Albert has been defeated? We hardly can believe that either England or France will ever submit to it. Lombardy will have again to undergo the rule of the barbarians, and right dear will she have to pay for her late revolution. But Sicily stands in our opinion on very different grounds. The British, as well as the French, have said 'Choose your king and we are ready to acknowledge you as an independent country.' Now the king has been chosen, and we cannot believe but he will accept, if he has not already done so. As for Charles Albert and the Italian campaign, the game is up and what a complete failure has resulted into the bargain. The capitulation signed in Milan is of a most disgraceful character. The fine Piedmontese army, which was to effect the regeneration of Italy and drive the Austrians back to their homes, has had to submit to terms as hard almost as their worst enemies could have thought of inflicting.

On 31 August Napier wrote to Palmerston that nine warships had left Naples the day before, 'with a force of 2,500 Swiss and a powerful train of artillery', under General Filangieri. It was clear that the invasion was about to begin. About 20,000 men were expected to be embarked at Reggio, and it was believed that they were to be landed at Milazzo and Scaletta, to the west and south of Messina.

It was just before this moment that the somewhat reactionary Charles MacFarlane, author of *A Glance at Revolutionized Italy*, reached Messina *en route* to Naples from Malta. He wrote:

> It was a brilliant morning in August that we entered the Straits of Messina, which I never before saw look so beautiful. The passage of the Dardanelles is monotonous and tame compared to this. The mountains of Calabria and Sicily were smiling upon each other, but fierce hostile bands were arrayed at their feet. The King of Naples was collecting an armament at Reggio for the invasion of the island, and armed Sicilians covered the heights behind Messina . . . the hatred between the belligerents [at the time of Murat] was love and fraternity compared to the passions which now reigned on either side of the straits. As we approached the citadel we saw troops of the King of Naples on some of the bastions. A Neapolitan war-steamer was cruising up and down. . . . A French frigate and an English war-steamer lay right in the port.

MacFarlane reckoned that Pronio could destroy half Messina 'in three hours of active bombardment', so short was the distance between the citadel and the town. He discovered that the city – contrary to newspaper reports and despite the British claims for damages – in effect hardly showed any marks of war, being 'far fairer and far larger than when I last looked upon it in the summer of 1827'. The magnificent houses on the Marina were 'all erect, all intact, shining brightly out in the morning sun'. When he landed, he found the place seething with a great crowd of fantastically dressed people, imagining themselves to be in uniform and all excited, boasting, arguing – 'I never head such vapouring as among these unwashed Messinese patriots. . . . In the main street the noise was astounding. It was a scene of Dante's Hell.' As for the English, they and the other merchants 'had nearly all withdrawn into the country, or had quitted the island'. The 'better class of the Sicilian gentry and nobility' had disappeared likewise. Vendettas, old grudges and private feuds were being gratified under the mask of nationality and patriotism. MacFarlane thoroughly disliked the way British naval officers were sitting in coffee-houses with the leaders of this revolutionary rabble – rabble indeed; why, one might as well give a constitution to a herd of tigers. Listening to public speakers ranting against the Neapolitans, he realised that there was an ancient and irremovable antipathy between the two races; it was like 'hearing an Irish orator in full peroration about the English'.

MacFarlane thankfully left Messina for Naples, having had his pocket picked. He arrived in time to watch the Bourbon fleet sail. There seemed no chance of British or French intervention; whatever his prejudices, he realised that, 'if that unhappy city [Messina] did not surrender or capitulate, it would be bombarded in earnest.'

He was proved to be right.

# IX

## *The Good Folk Appear Stark Mad*

T HE notorious bombardment of Messina, which earned Ferdinand his
nickname of King Bomba, began on 3 September. It lasted five days.
General Filangieri (sometimes referred to in history as the Prince of Satri-
ano) had sent advance warning from Reggio to the consuls, to give them
time to arrange for their nationals to escape. The British were taken on
board the *Gladiator*; we learn subsequently from one of Ingham's letters
that Smithson at first refused to leave his home, but later, and wisely,
changed his mind.

Consul Barker was also on the *Gladiator*. On the third he managed to
send a brief and excited despatch to Lord Napier, informing him that the
King's troops were actually in the process of landing at the citadel. The
town was being bombarded 'in every direction', and the fire was 'most
awful and chiefly directed against the dwelling-houses'. The Sicilians, he
added, were nevertheless carrying on a brisk cannonade in return. Indeed
they kept it up consistently for two days. Then on the fifth there were signs
that their ammunition was running short. The batteries did open up again,
but prospects for the defenders were obviously becoming far less hopeful.
From out to sea it was impossible to see how things were really going,
because of the smoke. The bombardment spread to the outskirts of Messina,
and Captain Robb reported that the whole of the beautiful country to the
south of the city appeared to be in flames.

A group of 300 Palermitan volunteers marched out against the citadel,
but it was a forlorn hope and they were easily driven back. By the evening
of the sixth the city looked all ablaze. The people were fleeing; some got
into small boats and rowed desperately to the foreign warships. The French
ships were 'crowded almost to suffocation' and the *Gladiator* was literally
packed so full that 'it was with difficulty that a passage could be formed on
deck'. Robb said that the bravery of the Sicilian troops had been fantastic,
in face of such an overwhelming force and with no real leaders of their
own. By the morning of the seventh Messina appeared to be deserted.
Even so, the bombardment went on for eight hours – and this despite the
fact that there was no answering fire from the Sicillian batteries. When

night came, the Neapolitans felt safe enough to enter, the flames having swept through the city unchecked for all this while. Barker told Napier that the shops in the main streets, as well as some private houses, were looted by the invaders, and that 'the most unheard of ravages were committed'; 'many British subjects are left homeless'; the Greek Consul had been stabbed, his house plundered and burnt down.

Reports vary about the number of Neapolitans killed – some say as low as 300, some as many as 1600. As for the damage to Messina itself and the number of Sicilian casualties involved, it was impossible for a long while to assess such things, especially since so many citizens had fled to other parts of the island. *The Times* later maintained that 'over a distance of about three miles not twelve houses had escaped destruction'. Captain Robb described the scene a month later to Admiral Parker, more explicitly and even more gloomily:

> It is really sad to go out into the country when at this season of the year it is usually so gratifying, in the direction of Catania, where the scourge of war has devastated for the space of four miles from the gates of Messina. Not a house is standing. I do not speak figuratively, but literally, every house, church etc. on the road and off the road have been destroyed, to say nothing of the destruction of two thirds of the town of Messina.

Consul Barker, in his official report three months later to William Temple (at last returned to Naples) said that the damage to Sicilian property alone was probably about five million dollars, or a million pounds. As for British subjects, the total losses claimed by them were about 44,500 *onze*. There were also many reports of atrocities committed by the Neapolitan troops – breasts sliced off, cripples slaughtered, women raped in churches. The ghastly rumour of Sicilian cannibalism had again shown up, but Barker said of this:

> I have no reason to believe that Swiss soldiers were put to death in cold blood and their flesh devoured and sold in the public markets, but I can assert that on the 3rd September the bodies of two soldiers killed in the combat were mutilated by the rabble and their limbs carried about the town. With the exception of this inhuman parade by the irritated populace, I have not heard that the Sicilians committed other acts of barbarism.

Milazzo surrendered some days later, after some desperate fighting by a few stalwarts; an American surgeon, by name Valentine Mott, courageously refused to leave, so that he could care for the wounded. Six weeks later, thanks to an armistice negotiated by the French and British, a line of demarcation was drawn from Barcellona near Milazzo, across the island to Scaletta, due south of Messina; this was the boundary for the Neapolitans. After that came neutral territory, and the Sicilians' boundary ran from Cape Tindari on the north to Taormina on the south-east. The armistice was to last until the end of March 1849.

Dickinson noted in his diary that in Palermo, as a result of the destruction of Messina, the public estimation of Britain had sunk by seventy-five per cent. And Charles MacFarlane, who by this time had reached Turin, told how Sicilians there were screaming with fury against the British. 'The treachery of 1815 is nothing to this!' they railed at him. 'Infamous England! . . . England has led us on in this revolution, and has now basely betrayed us! This is the second time! The third time will not come! . . . We will give ourselves to the devil rather than see the English there again.' In the view of the Sicilians Admiral Parker, having gone so far as to salute their flag, should have done something to prevent the Bourbons attacking. Ingham wrote:

*To Heath, Furse & Co., London*                    *12 September 1848*
You will have heard that Messina is again in possession of the Neapolitans, after having suffered immense damage from bombs and congreves [rockets]. We must therefore expect an attack on this city, unless there be the interference of foreign powers, which we sincerely hope for. This expedition from Naples would never have taken place had it not been for Lord Stanley[1] and others meddling with foreign affairs in the way which they did in Parliament about a month ago. We need not add that we are in the greatest alarm, and are endeavouring to put our property in safety, as far as practical, and are preparing to embark ourselves and families if necessary for our safety.

Ingham also managed to get a letter off to Smithson by means of H.M.S. *Sidon*.

*To J. Smithson, Messina*                    *13 September 1848*
. . . enormous expenditure has been going on here for the last few months, and little or no income to meet it. All sorts of measures have been tried, including the appropriation of church plate. . . . I am at a loss to express the unheard of barbarities which have been used towards your city by the King's generals in the late attack. Such cruel and revolting a

mode of warfare has been seldom if ever adopted before by any country. It has also been cowardly and wantonly destructive, inhuman, in short everything that is blameable and deserving condemnation by the civilised world.

He told Stephens that he was delighted that the French and British had decided to intervene. But:

*To Richard Stephens, London*        *23 September 1848*
. . . the King of Naples is as obstinate as a mule on the one side, and our leading characters on the other are bent on conditions that can never be amicably agreed to; the entire and absolute exclusion of the Bourbon race from the throne of this island. Moreover, there will be the greatest difficulty in calming down the passions of the so-called patriots, *letterati* and ultra-liberals, who will be reluctant to relinquish their power and hopes of wealth and to return to quiet and industrious habits. The worst of all are the *letterati*, who are in reality the principal authors of revolutions. . . . We fear that nearly all the money on the island will be disappearing. The paper money that is to be issued has no other security than the Parliament decree.

Somehow he managed to keep in communication with Naples, and even to ship off a few bags of dollars there by the *Porcupine*. Much later he sent 10,000 *onze* to H.M.S. *Vanguard* for safe keeping and told Stephens that he was contemplating sending 8–10,000 more. All the same, when he heard that a loan for Sicily was being floated in Paris, with a very favourable interest rate, he at once went into the question of selling £6,000 British Consols and risking the proceeds by reinvesting them in this very loan.

Ingham was now told by Dobree, Maingay that the English had become extremely unpopular in Naples too.

*To Dobree, Maingay & Co., Naples*       *6 October 1848*
We are most sincerely sick of revolutions and our only consolation is that we have never meddled therein either by word or deed of any shape. The French Rear Admiral has been here for the last three days in order to settle the line of demarcation. He has succeeded in this, although not without some angry discussion. It is therefore expected that the French too will have lost popular favour here.

Goodwin had warned Napier on 24 October that the revolution in

Vienna had produced 'strong excitement in the legislative body'. Actually that revolution was soon suppressed, as was a rising in Hungary. But in Rome there was more hopeful news for ultra-liberals. Following the stabbing to death of the Pope's minister Rossi, Pio Nono took refuge in Gaeta, in territory belonging to King Bomba and where the garrison was in the charge of bluff Colonel (now Brigadier) Gross, the Swiss defender of the Castellamare fort at the beginning of the year. On 2 February the Roman Republic was proclaimed.

But in Paris the matter of the loan was not turning out well. Russian interference had been mentioned. The Sicilian 'government was fast working itself to pieces and that for one good reason, the utter impossibility to find money wherewith to carry on the war much longer'.

Banditry too. At the end of November Ingham had written to Robert Jeans of Catania: 'It appears that you are much better off, in particular for what regards robberies and arrests of individuals for the object of extorting money to ransom them.' This was a reference, presumably, to the kidnapping at Marsala of the ex-Woodhouse manager Mr Barlow, described by Consul Goodwin as a retired merchant, and a Mr Alison, an accountant. Goodwin told Temple that they had been carried off to a lone house and kept prisoner for five days, at the end of which they were ransomed by their friends for 500 *onze*. 'The miscreants' were soon caught and tried; one was condemned to hard labour for life, another to 'twenty-five years close imprisonment in irons', two others to nineteen years' imprisonment and a fine of 300 ducats each.

*To W. Sanderson, Messina*                    *16 December 1848*
The last news from Naples is that the King has declined to enter into any negotiations until the result of the election of the President of France is known [this was to be Louis Napoleon, later Napoleon III]. We have no novelty here except the raising of a loan of 100,000 *onze* amongst the merchants and others of this city to enable the Government to carry on a little longer. Foreigners have not been called on. . . . The money serves principally for payment for the steamers bought in England and which we believe are now ready to be sent out.

These two steamers had been built for the P. and O. Steam Navigation Company and were the *Bombay* and the *Vectis*, of 1205 and 900 tons respectively. The purchase was being negotiated by the Sicilian delegates in London, Granatelli and Scalia, with an ambiguous character named Colonel Aubrey, ex Peninsular War, as intermediary – the aim also being that he should enlist and fit up 1200 English volunteers. Ingham found himself heavily involved, and by no means reluctantly. The deposit required was £25,000. Again in view of the very high interest offered, he soon agreed to lend £10,000 of this.[2] Stephens was to sell the necessary stock, and Dobree, Maingay were also told that 'we have been further requested by the Minister of Finance, Don Filippo Cordova, that you will render what assistance you can to Prince Granatelli and Signor Scalia relative to the steamers in question'. Ingham added, by way of reassurance, that the Minister ought before long to have plenty of money at his command, as he was in the process of demanding a large (though needless to say unpopular) forced loan from the Sicilians themselves. 'It is to be feared this will cause great discontent and make many a good *soi-disant* patriot turn his thoughts and wishes in a different direction, as indeed is already happening.'

The 'different direction' was of course King Ferdinand of Naples. A startling remark.

During December there had been discussions about raising a mercenary army, and Garibaldi was even invited to come to Sicily as Commander-in-chief. He was tempted at first, but Rome turned out to be much the greater attraction. General Giacomo Antonini (who had lost an arm fighting against the Austrians at Vicenza in May) accepted to take his place. He was received with immense excitement and Dickinson recorded that a great dinner was given in welcome at the Trinacria Hotel. Unluckily Antonini soon fell out with the Sicilians, and a month later he was substituted by a sort of Che Guevara figure, General Ludwik Mieroslawsky, a Pole who had fought in revolutions in Berlin and Poznan – not entirely a satisfactory choice, since he could not speak Italian.[3]

Another somewhat enigmatic person, also engaged in advising the Palermo Government on defence matters, was a rich, cantankerous forty-year-old Englishman, Colonel Hugh Forbes. He was attempting to raise a British legion. An ex-Coldstream officer, he was married to an Italian. Later he joined the defenders of Mazzini's Roman Republic. His autocratic manner did not endear him to his troops, though he was a friend of Garibaldi. A linen suit and white stovepipe hat seem to have been his favourite form of dress, even on the march.[4]

There were quarrels within the Government. Then, after all those weeks of wavering, the Duke of Genoa finally declined to accept the crown of Sicily. In Naples and Gaeta negotiations dragged on with the French and British; it was now suggested that Spain should join them as mediator. Ingham told Smithson: 'We are still in utter darkness and what the upshot of things will be we are altogether unable to make even a guess.' But to many outsiders the Sicilian cause was doomed.

*To Thomas Pate & Sons, Leghorn*                    *12 February 1849*

We regret to hear that you expected serious consequences from the flight of the Grand Duke [the Grand Duke of Tuscany had left Florence and was preparing to join the Pope at Gaeta]. The fact is that anarchy appears to be the order of the day in this island, as well as in nearly all Italy.

*To J. Smithson, Messina*                    *20 February 1849*

There is a rumour here since Sunday, when we had the arrival of the *Penguin*, a French steamer from Naples, that the King had finally accepted the basis of the proposals offered by Mr Temple [returned to Naples in November] on the part of England and France, and we cannot say that we think there is some probability of its truth, notwithstanding that nothing official has been received. An Adjutant of Admiral Baudin came over by the boat, and it is possible that the object of his visit is to prepare this Government.

*To Heath, Furse & Co., London*                    *23 February 1849*

We advise you of our drafts on you for £1000 in favour of Cavaliere Don Francesco Lanza [later known as the Prince of Scalea, a son of the Prince of Scordia; in this case a personal loan]. We also inform you of having taken the liberty to draw on you £8528.14. in favour of the Prince of Butera [i.e. Scordia; another loan to the Government], Minister of Foreign Affairs and of Commerce, which we request you will please place to our debit. We are quite aware that we are overdrawing thus on our account, but we have been desirous to profit of the favourable exchange which the Government pays us.

*To Potter Bros, Liverpool*                    *7 March 1849*

We are on the eve of important events, the mediating powers having finally come to an agreement with His Majesty, and the two Admirals [Parker and Baudin], with several ships of war, having arrived here yesterday with terms for approval or rejection by this Government.

The terms brought by the Admirals roughly speaking consisted of a statute based on the 1812 Constitution, a separate Parliament and a general amnesty except for forty-four persons, who included Ruggiero Settimo and most of the Sicilian Government. All acts put through by the Sicilian Parliament since the outbreak of the revolution in January 1848 were to be abolished, and the hated *sbirri* and intendancies were to be restored. On 7 March Ingham also reported the arrivals to Dobree, Maingay in Naples. 'They saluted the tricolour [Italian] flag, which we presume therefore, if all goes well, will remain that of Sicily.' The Sicilians, he said, seemed by no means disposed to give in. He then added a sentence, on the face of it disloyal – considering that he was writing to Naples – and typical of his ambivalent attitude during the latter months of the revolution: 'Nothing short of a good licking will bring them to their senses.' As usual, he felt he could write far more openly to Stephens.

*To Richard Stephens, London*                      *7 March 1849*
We are sorry to say the King of Naples is about to attempt the reconquest of this island and making preparations on an enormous scale. It will take place, no doubt, next month. In the meanwhile we continue in the same state as hitherto and perhaps worse. We have had the arrival of two Admirals from Naples with seven ships of war bringing the terms which the King has agreed to. If accepted, all will be settled amicably, otherwise there will be war to the knife. The writer has just been to Admiral Parker and had a long conversation with him on the subject.

Parker, it seemed, had told him that the terms were the only ones possible: a compromise in fact. The next day revealed that they had been scornfully, indeed furiously, refused by the Sicilian Government. Dickinson declared them infamous, and Parker wrote to Napier that so violent were the reactions that even the most moderate found 'insurmountable objections'. And Ingham wrote: 'As for ourselves, that is to say the English as a body here, we are by no means in an enviable position, either since it is to be feared that no little odium will attach to us in the part which we, or rather our Government, have had in concocting so unsatisfactory an arrangement.'
On the thirteenth Admiral Parker sent a message to Consul Barker to warn him that he believed that a 'renewal of hostilities will very shortly follow, with the disastrous consequences that may be anticipated from the overwhelming forces of the Neapolitans and the deficient means of resistance on the part of the Sicilians'. Vice-Consul Oates in Girgenti wrote to Goodwin: 'The people here of every class, old and young, will not hear of any "Transazioni". War! war! is the cry, and they are only waiting for instructions from Palermo to put themselves into activity.' And this was the attitude throughout the island. Temple and de Reyneval, the French ambassador, were so alarmed that they decided they must visit Palermo themselves.

*To R. Jeans, Catania*                          *17 March 1849*
The good folks here appear to be stark mad. We shall be anxious to hear

what the people in the interior, and particularly in your city and vicinity, say to the present state of affairs.

There was scarcely any need to ask such a question. Catania was in truth the most warlike of all the cities. But the end of the armistice was approaching.

*To Thomas Pate, Leghorn*                                                    *26 March 1849*

Here things are fast approaching to a crisis, and we may expect hostilities to commence shortly. Our Consul has just communicated to us that this port and adjacent places will be blockaded by the Neapolitans from the first day of April. We are not sure if Marsala be included.

*To Routh & Jeans, Naples*                                                *26 March 1849*

The arrival of Mr Temple and the French Minister has produced no good result that we are aware of. Indeed, we should say that it has rather added fuel to the fire, to say nothing of the disgrace that will fall upon the two nations from the failure, first of the two Admirals with a powerful fleet at their command, and now of the two Ministers representing the two greatest nations of Europe. . . . We shall be anxiously waiting for the advices on the threatened invasion by the Neapolitan forces. Perhaps the recommencement of hostilities in Lombardy will put off the sad day for a while longer.

Evidently Sicily had not yet received the news of the crucial defeat of the Piedmontese by Marshal Radetzky at Novara on the twenty-third. And worse: Charles Albert, disillusioned and broken, had abdicated in favour of his son, Victor Emmanuel II.

In anticipation of the Neapolitan blockade Admiral Parker sent warships to protect the principal ports of Sicily. Meanwhile preparations were being made to send British families by the steamer *Oberon* to Malta. Sophia Whitaker was to be one of the passengers, with six children, all under eleven. Ingham – partly because Ben was sailing for England – went to Marsala, leaving Joseph in charge of the office. The Duchess of Santa Rosalia also stayed behind. Perhaps she had been infected by the extraordinary sense of euphoria in Palermo, following the official rejection of the King's terms – as illustrated by a letter from a relative of Lord Ormonde included in his book, *An Autumn in Sicily*:

I never saw such excitement. The streets were crowded in all parts. As we went through the streets, thousands in every direction waved hats and handkerchiefs, crying out 'Guerra, guerra, ed ora.' It was as exciting as a bull-fight. . . . Many labourers have been working in the trenches, and ladies had set the example, the Duchess of Monteleone having used her spade and baskets.

Dickinson also watched the singing people – including both men and women, old and young, monks, priests and nobles – marching along the Cassero and the Marina, shouting 'Death to the Bourbons' and 'Viva la Sicilia'. The British were very much in favour for the nonce; 'When an English officer was to be seen, there was a clapping of hands and a general cry of "War, War!" ' Even the crypto-*Mafia* assisted: 'Crime disappeared, stolen goods were restored, brigands sent home rich citizens whom they had captured.'[5]

When Ingham reached Marsala, he wrote to Joseph saying that 'The people are now more warlike than ever, and in Mazara all are for war.' He was not so sanguine as Dickinson about the Sicilians' attitude to the British.

*To Richard Stephens, London*        *27 March 1849*

The *Elisa* does not make her appearance, which is most unfortunate, as there is every fear of her being captured by the Neapolitans. The Captain is unlucky, to say the least. The Consul having acquainted us that the Neapolitan Government intends to establish a blockade of this port and gulf and adjacent places from the first days of April, he therefore requested us to put ourselves and property in safety or to take the consequences. This is a most unpleasant state of things, particularly when we consider that, besides the horrors of war we have the feelings of the Sicilians very much against us since they pretend, and not without some reason, that the English are abandoning them to their fate. Some of the families have left and others, including Mr Whitaker's family, are preparing to leave as soon as the Admiral furnishes them with a steamer which he all but promised today. The armistice will expire on the 29th March, when we may look out for squalls. May all these troubles finish quickly, as we are regularly tired of revolutions and no mistake.

The *Oberon*, with Sophia Whitaker and her children, finally sailed on 6 April.

The Palermitans were worried about the arrival of one of their ships (the *Bombay*) from England. She just managed to beat the blockade, and Dickinson wrote succinctly:

       *28 March 1849*

The telegraph, this morning, announced the arrival at Trapani of one of the new Sicilian war steamers and its departure for Palermo. The *Palermo* went out to meet her and both came into port amidst the shouts and applause of the people congregated in every place, looking on the sea.

As for the *Eliza*, she also managed to reach port safely. The *Sumatra*, on the other hand, was safely out of the way, far away in fact: at St Helena in the South Atlantic. Indeed the much-bruited blockade looked as though it was turning out to be a flop – 'so far it is a dead letter, as no blockading squadron has made its appearance', wrote Joseph on 2 April.

The Sicilians soon realised, however, that Ferdinand was going to use his fleet for another purpose than a blockade: there was to be an invasion. A column of troops under the impulsive General Mieroslawsky was sent in the direction of Messina, whence the first attack was expected. The National Guard was mobilised and the students at Palermo University formed themselves into a special armed corps. It was reckoned that the Sicilian army now totalled 7,700 men.

The *Oberon* left just in time, for at that very moment Ferdinand was attacking, not in the direction of Palermo but towards Catania, both by land and sea. The first Sicilian outpost, the castle of Taormina, was overwhelmed almost at once, much to the annoyance of Mieroslawsky. This outpost had been under the command of Carmelo Ascenso, now a Colonel – he had left the Neapolitan army as soon as the revolution had broken out in 1848. Apparently (and probably rightly) he considered that it would have been impossible to defend it against the Neapolitan warships. Catania suffered 'an overwhelming bombardment', and after some very fierce fighting it surrendered. Joseph wrote:

> To R. Jeans, Catania                                  *9 April 1849*
> The news of your city having fallen into the hands of the Neapolitans we need not say has caused great gloom here. It is a sad misfortune and may be considered, we fear, the death blow to the independence of the country. What the people in power may now be for doing is more than we can say. The writer's lady and family are we believe still on the high seas for Malta.

Syracuse and Augusta, rather than experience Catania's fate, surrendered 'without a shot', and the Bourbons were able to march across the island towards Palermo, for the most part again without opposition. Then General Mieroslawsky was severely wounded at Castrogiovanni. On the fourteenth Admiral Baudin came forward with an offer to mediate, and on the fifteenth there was the dreadful news that not only had Genoa capitulated, but that the Austrians were advancing towards Florence and Rome. Not surprisingly, a dramatic change of attitude grew up among many people in Palermo. Baron Riso now headed a peace party, supported by Florio and other merchants.

The following letter is again, of course, from Joseph:

*To J. Smithson, Messina*                     *17 April 1849*

What will surprise you is that we have decided for peace here also. . . . Admiral Baudin offered to intercede for the Sicilians with the King, and this was at once accepted by Parliament and by the whole population with but very few exceptions. The Ministers and the Colonels had to submit to the will of the people, but wisely determined to save themselves by escaping to Malta, with their property, while there was yet time. The National Guard behaved nobly during the last five or six days, and we have no hesitation in saying have preserved this city from anarchy. For two or three days it appeared as if the people were either panic-stricken or determined to fight to the last and bury themselves in the ruins.

One of the colonels to escape to Malta was Carmelo Ascenso; Joseph obligingly arranged for a credit of 200 *onze* to be opened on his behalf with the Ingham agent, Pisani, there. There seemed little to hope for, by way of mercy, but the Sicilian Government held out for a general amnesty. Some of the leaders, indeed, among them La Farina, Crispi and Michele Amari, were in favour of carrying on to the bitter end – preferable far that Palermo should lie in smoking rubble rather than sue for mercy. When it became clear that the forty-four names were still to be exempted from any Neapolitan amnesty, Ruggiero Settimo resigned, and on the twenty-seventh he sailed for Malta in H.M.S. *Powerful.* Even before his decision there were signs that mob rule was again taking over in Palermo; 'mountaineers' from outside the city were swaggering about the streets, and there was some looting. These 'mountaineers', unfortunately, were the main supporters of La Farina and his friends. Joseph found life exceedingly uncomfortable. He almost longed for the Bourbon troops to arrive.

On the twenty-third, we learn from Dickinson, a deputation on board the *Palermo* was sent to Catania; included were a Count Lucchesi and the Marquis of Rudinì, father of the future Prime Minister of Italy. On the twenty-seventh Consul Goodwin was taken ill with paralysis. And on the same day Sophia Whitaker boldly decided to leave Malta and join her father, William Sanderson, once more widowed, in Messina; his house was still seven-eighths ruined and he had nobody to look after him and the ten-year-old Bertha, his daughter by his second wife.

Partly to thwart the Austrian advance southwards on the Italian mainland, the French had landed 9000 troops at Civitavecchia. Ferdinand, encouraged by this example, at once sent an army to Albano. Neither expedition was in fact to meet with initial success: the French certainly were not prepared for such fanatical resistance by the Romans. Yet the very report that the Neapolitans and the French were marching on Rome did much to dampen morale in Sicily. Baron Riso went on board the *Descartes* for a parley with Baudin; on his return, Dickinson tells us that the emotion among the populace was such that 'his horses were taken from the carriage, which was dragged up the Cassero to his residence'. Riso had become Praetor of Palermo, following the resignation of the Government on the thirtieth; two members of the new Government were Florio and Bordonaro.

Now the royal troops were closing in on Palermo. On 5 May Dickinson reported that Baron Gandolfo was 'massacred as a traitor at the fort of San Sacramento'. On the eighth he wrote: 'In the afternoon the head of a policeman stuck on a lance was paraded through the city. Later the right arm of a cavalry soldier on a pole with military accoutrements was conducted through the streets.' Once again such foreign civilians as remained in Palermo were taken on board their respective warships for safety. Joseph wrote:

*To J. W. Furse & Co., Naples*                                      *9 May 1849*
In Palermo Bay. We are unable to attend to business, as at present it is out of the question. Palermo is in a complete state of anarchy, and we, as all the other residents, English and other foreigners, are now writing on board ship, having left our homes on 30th April.

*To Dobree, Maingay & Co., Naples*                            *9 May 1849*
On the morning of the 7th the people were given to expect an answer had been received from the King granting a general pardon, and we believe had this been really the case all would still have terminated well. Unfortunately Filangieri marched his troops to Palermo at that very same time. . . . The disappointment was fatal; the lower classes rushed out to meet the troops, and a conflict began at once, and still continues. The result cannot be doubted, notwithstanding the Palermitans have turned out in far greater numbers than the royal forces, and will resist to the last. What we regret is the system adopted by Filangieri of burning all before him; already two villages have been set fire to in the immediate vicinity, and it is greatly to be feared Palermo will share the same fate. You can imagine what would be the horror and destruction in the city. Being under the protection of H.M.S. *Odin*, the French steamer *Descartes* and the American corvette *Jamestown*, we consider ourselves altogether out of danger.

Ingham, a little behind in news, since he was in Marsala, wrote:

*To Richard Stephens, London*                    *10 May 1848*

Where my family is I cannot say, as I have had no letter either from the Duchess or from Mr Whitaker for the last two posts. In Marsala all is tranquil and we have no other fear than from the robbers and assassins in the countryside, who are in a great number. What a pretty state we shall be in if the amnesty be granted to all the villains. We shall be as badly off as if in the desert of Barbary.

Later: We have just had a courier from Palermo with letters dated 8th inst. The people had begun the war against the troops which were in the vicinity of Abbate, a village about five miles from Palermo on the road to Catania and Messina. Mr Whitaker said that the village on the morning of the 8th appeared to be burning. You will thus see what a dreadful prospect we have before us if Palermo is destined to have the same fate which befell Messina and Catania, if not still worse. The people there are in great force, say upwards of 20,000, and the Neapolitan general will no doubt have to wait for reinforcements before he can attack them with vigour. The Duchess had taken flight to one of the monasteries. Mr Whitaker was on board an English schooner at anchor at Arenella, about three miles from Palermo, under the protection of three steamers. The *Powerful*, 84 guns, was anchored in the bay near Bagheria, thus leaving the field open for hostilities between the two contending parties. All continued quiet in Palermo, notwithstanding that the town was completely in the hands of the populace.

'Thousands of natives' had also now taken refuge on ships in the harbours. On the fifteenth the royal troops under Filangieri marched into the heart of Palermo; and contrary to all the wild alarums there was no fighting whatsoever. Joseph wrote at once, with considerable relief, to reassure his father-in-law. It was clear that he had long ago lost any sympathy with the rebels. He could scarcely wait to get back to the 'old footing'. 'We returned to our homes', he wrote in his usual rather pompous way, 'some on Monday, others yesterday, and are relieved to say that as regards ourselves we have met with no losses in any shape as to property or anything else.'

And here the letter quoted at the beginning of this book is reached: 'We are happy to inform you that His Majesty's troops took quiet possession of the forts of this city yesterday . . .'

The mad, uncertain weeks of so-called peace followed. Just how prepared were the Sicilians to submit again to the old régime? Were they mocking at the victors, or were they, like Joseph Whitaker, just glad to see a return to order and law of a sort? There was still danger from mob violence. The upper classes seemed ready to submit to the arms search, but the 'lower classes will deliver nothing, not even a knife, and we are now in their hands.'

At least credit had to be given to Filangieri for his 'forbearance and his judicious conduct in not chastising the many for the few who, bent on the plunder and sacking the town, were disposed to resist his entry.' The *Palermo*, after being at Catania, had gone to Naples bearing an armistice committee; now that she had returned, it was feared she might be confiscated by the Neapolitans, though such a course would have its complications, as so many foreigners held shares in her. Reports of brigandage were rife, especially in the area of Marsala and Mazara.

The feeling in Palermo of being in suspense went on far too long. Now there was even some crazy rumour that Prince Charles of Capua (grown into a portly figure with a huge beard) was going to be invited to wear the crown of Sicily. On the twenty-eighth Filangieri left with a number of his troops, it was supposed 'to assist in the campaign against the Romans' – Oudinot, after being repulsed with a loss of three hundred men, had arranged for an armistice during which Ferdinand had been chased south by Garibaldi. On the thirtieth Dickinson recorded in his diary that in Palermo there was still 'much talk and discontent among the people that no decrees or concessions have been published, all being thus but empty promises'.

It is necessary to skip very briefly over the events on the mainland, crucial though they were in the history of modern Italy. Oudinot, on 3 June started hostilities against Rome where 'the flower of Italian heroism had gathered'.[6] A month later, after battles immortal in the Italian Risorgimento, he had entered the Eternal City – 'one of the meanest deeds that ever disgraced a great nation'. Garibaldi, aided by Colonel Hugh Forbes, withdrew north with 3000 men. The Pope was thus restored to his temporal power, and the Grand Duke of Tuscany was able to return to his throne.

The *Palermo* was, at last, definitely confiscated. Other Sicilian celebrities decided that exile at the present moment was the wisest course; among them was the Duchess's youngest son Carlo, who had assumed the title of Marquis of San Martino – he went to Malta by the *Independent*, and as Ingham put it 'not voluntarily'.

On 28 June Ingham, still in Marsala, wrote to Ben in England.

*To Benjamin Ingham jun, Leeds*                                    *28 June 1849*
All is quiet here, and the judge has begun to arrest the notorious characters who have infested the countryside and amongst the rest the celebrated bandit Calotorto. The order for disarmament has been published
since 20th, and troops from Trapani are expected daily to see it enforced.
Everything goes on as usual in the *Baglio*.

The British were now being blamed all over again for the sense of
frustration still prevailing in Palermo. Not that they cared very much.

*To W. Sanderson, Messina*                                    *23 July 1849*
The *Odin* leaves us at last, we expect for good. Captain Pelham tells us
that all steamers going northwards will in future look in here to see how
we are getting on, which we hope will be sufficient for all purposes now
that order is restored.

*To J. Smithson, Messina*                                    *28 July 1849*
General Filangieri has returned with the powers of *Luogotenente* [Vice-
roy]. If we mistake not, the Sicilians will be highly pleased to see him
back, having an idea that he is disposed to govern with moderation and
mildness; but we will wait to see something of his proceedings before
we clap and rejoice. At the same time, however, we confess that we think
he is the right man to be at the helm in Sicily at the present moment.

Filangieri, 'the surest prop of the Bourbon dynasty if only it had been
content to lean on him,'[7] was indeed probably the only man capable of
dealing in a statesmanlike manner with the Sicilian predicament – not least
being the financial side. But he was to be frustrated by pettiness and intrigue
in Naples; and five years later he resigned in disgust.

# X

## *Entire Families Have Been Carried Off*

WHEN Benjamin Ingham 'retired' in 1851, most of the Concern's letter-writing in Palermo was naturally left to Joseph. One consequently misses that downright, arrogant style of his. Like any ageing tycoon of modern times, he contented himself with an eagle-eyed watching of profits, juggling investments, avoiding tax, switching huge sums of money here and there within the business, and teasing possible heirs. He however kept full control over his banking, and as the richest man in Sicily was often consulted by Filangieri.

Filangieri was indeed a statesman, and one of the few Neapolitan administrators still remembered with affection. He was married to a Moncada di Paternò and thus related to half the Palermitan aristocracy, including the Duchess of Santa Rosalia. Enormous banquets and balls, despite Sicily's near bankruptcy, were held at the Royal Palace, with full dress uniform *de rigueur*; Filangieri's gorgeous daughters acted as hostesses. Although many leading nobles were in exile, voluntary or otherwise, there was a spate of sparkling parties in Palermo's palaces, and the Duchess – who wanted her sons pardoned – saw to it that those in the Villa Ingham were among the most lavish. Her brother, the Prince of Maletto, had died, so his furniture and pictures had become her property; one of the prizes was a painting of the incarnation of the Virgin by Pietro Novelli that Murray's *Handbook* later urged British visitors to try to see. When Schuyler Livingston suggested that Ingham might care to visit New York to spend some of his millions, she refused either to accompany her consort or to allow him to be out of her sight for any length of time. So Ingham, after that one visit in 1809, never in his life went again to America, and it was left to the lucky Ben to play the prince on his uncle's dollars.

Meanwhile Joseph Whitaker kept up a *Barretts of Wimpole Street* atmosphere in Via Bara. At least his brood had a garden to play in at the Villa Sofia. Although Sophia had such a large family to console her, she never quite got over the loss of her third son, who at the age of five months had died after being dropped by his *balia*, or wet-nurse; the anniversary of his death in 1843 had always to be kept as a day of mourning. Like a good

Victorian *paterfamilias* Joseph was exceedingly devout. Church services were conveniently in the Palazzo Lampedusa in the Marina where Consul Goodwin had quarters. Such a locale, however, was hardly decorous; the services would be held in the saloon, decorated with frescoes of mythological figures, 'not always suitable in arrangement or decoration to the subject in view!'[1] To compensate for such garishness perhaps, all the little Whitakers had to dress in black for divine worship, however hot the weather.

Joseph had been making some shrewd investments himself. He also appears to have been quite heavily involved on his own account in the mortgage business. Even the Duchess's sons owed him money, though this did nothing to ease the strained relationship between his wife and aunt.

Ingham was now usually called *Barone* in Sicilian circles. For all his grandeur he was kind to humble folk including, as we have seen, visiting English people such as the Tidmans. He even invited the latter to stay at the *Baglio* when they went on a tour of the island, travelling having become much easier recently thanks to the roads built by Filangieri; and due tribute was paid in Tidman's diary to the 'truly English hospitality of my esteemed friend Mr Ingham'.

The *Baglio* at this stage employed 160 men and thirty boys under sixteen. Arthur Tidman described how 'the enormous enclosure of the *Baglio* with its high, blank windowless wall, and its loopholed towers at three of the four corners, gave more the impression of a fortified post than a wine establishment'. There was now a road between Trapani and Palermo, and a 'great artery' was under construction to Marsala – though in 1852 only the 'engineering part' had been finished and Tidman found that the stones still lying around on the road were 'of such Cyclopean dimensions as to be trying alike to the carriage and rider'.[2]

A surviving letter from the excellent and efficient R. B. Cossins,[3] the new manager of the Ingham *Baglio* who had been in Marsala since 1846 and was to remain in the firm's service for forty years, gives some information about the output of wine in the island as a whole:

'Mr Goodwin reckons the entire production of wine in Sicily at 180,000 pipes and in abundant years 400,000. The Marsala district produces 30–40,000 annually, half exported to Great Britain, Malta and other colonies, one third to other parts of the Mediterranean and to the U.S.A.'

Perhaps something over half of Marsala's output was handled by Ingham, Stephens. There had been a drop in output because of the fungus *oïdium* which had been devastating the vines; wine from Bronte was having to be used to supplement that from Marsala, as being the nearest in quality – thus further complicating the term 'Bronte Madeira'. Cossins' figure is rather more than that quoted for 1852 in Murray's *Handbook*, in which it is interesting to note that the value of Sicily's exports ran in this order: sumach £392,000, sulphur £361,909, oranges and lemons £191,151, oil £163,105, wine and spirits £105,827. These were followed by 'other fruits', silk, liquorice paste, essences, linseed, rags and manna. 'About three-eighths of these exports are taken by Great Britain', and about five-twelfths of the imports came likewise from Great Britain and her colonies. The value of trade with Britain was given in 1850 as £1,051,000; by 1856 it had more than doubled, to £2,448,000. Trade with the next most important country, France, increased from £355,000 to £1,070,000. The United States came third, increasing from £328,000 to £764, 000.

In 1854 ten banking firms in Palermo were listed as first class, one being Ingham and another Vincenzo and Ignazio Florio; a third was the English company of Prior, Turner and Thomas.[4] All these were entitled to take merchandise out of bond up to the value of 20,000 *onze*, leaving I.O.U.s instead of cash. There were seven classes altogether, in the second being the firms of Morrison, Seager and Gardner & Rose. In a category apart was Christian Fischer, the agent for the Rothschilds, whose vast loans in recent years had virtually saved Sicily from collapse.

Gardner & Rose were coming very much into commercial prominence in Palermo, and Morrison, Seager were the official agents for the government steamers that went to and from Naples. Both firms together represented the Anglo-Italian Company, which owned seventeen steamships of up to 1000 tons, all commanded by Englishmen and based on Liverpool. Vincenzo Florio features in most references to the main enterprises of the island. He was also managing director of the Royal Bank of Sicily, and (with Edward Gardner) on the *Borsa dei Cambi*, the body in charge of exchange control and price-fixing. Then, as something of a side-line perhaps, he was Consul-General for Bolivia. We also discover that he had become the main shareholder in the *Diligente*, the new name for the *Palermo* since its return from confiscation – though now it was relegated to trips around the island only, but still under the command of Captain Di Bartolo.

During the 1850s there was a considerable growth of German and Swiss interests in Palermo. The most famous Swiss firm, however, Fratelli Jung, originally dealing in sulphur but later involved in an enormous variety of merchandise, from canary-seed and pistachios to olive oil, did not get established until 1857.[5]

Two distinguished visitors to Palermo in the winter of 1850 were Lords Holland and Shrewsbury, the latter suffering much in the Villa Serradifalco, a 'long, single house and very cold'. The earnest, note-taking economist, Nassau William Senior, arrived on 6 January 1851. He had previously been in Naples, where he had witnessed part of the notorious trial of Poerio and Settembrini and had seen for himself the terrible conditions of the Neapolitan prisons, which became a *cause célèbre* thanks to the *Letters to the Earl of Aberdeen* by W. E. Gladstone,[6] whom Senior also met in Naples. He stayed at the comfortable and relatively new Trinacria Hotel, originally the private theatre of the Prince of Scordia, on the Marina[7] and recorded the many conversations he had with Consul Goodwin '. . . an old bachelor who has been here for sixteen years. He is very intelligent, and he has an excellent library which he communicates freely.' He also met many resident merchants including Messrs Rose, Gardner, Valentine and Morrison (but not apparently Ingham or Whitaker) and had a conversation with General Filangieri, who greatly impressed him: 'He is sixty-five, large, with a charming manner and address. If I were to be a slave I should not wish for a pleasanter master.' The state apartments at the Palace, he remarked, were very bare, with only modern furnishings and lacking all their ancient dignity, on account of the sacking by the revolutionary mob in 1848.

Prince Ernst of Radalì spoke despairingly of trying to improve conditions on the south side of the island. Sicily's problems in modern times, including the rise of the *Mafia*, have often been blamed on the absentee landlords of the nineteenth century, but the Prince's remarks do show that even those landlords who were rich enough to attempt to be progressive were inclined to be thwarted by apathy and superstition on the part of the *contadini*:

I built some farm-houses, but they lie empty. During many months they are infested by malaria. The farms are large; few less than 1000 acres, some much larger. I tried, at first, to take some into my own hands, and to adopt improved modes of cultivation, but it failed. I imported English subsoil ploughs; I gave double wages to the ploughmen employed on them, but they broke them to escape from the additional exertion which they required. I imported a movable thrashing machine. In order to take it from one farm to another my steward pulled it to pieces, and no one can put it together again. For some years I bred horses. I had an excellent English stallion, bought for me by Lord Lonsdale, and English three-quarter bred mares; but I lost more than half my colts from the negligence of my servants.

Senior heard much of the corruption and spying in Palermo, of dissolute priests and monks, the 4000 exiles, imprisonment without trial, the fear and the hatred. Travelling to and from Naples was deliberately now made as difficult as possible. The police were still so detested that 'if you were to be knocked down and robbed, and the robber were pursued by the police, everyone would help him to escape.' As he was told, 'we endure the evils both of despotism and of anarchy.' But he could not complain of lack of hospitality. Mrs Rose gave a 'piano dance' in his honour; he dined with the Shrewsburys and 'lounged' in the Prince of Radalì's garden, eating oranges. He was one of 200 people who called on the Duchess of Monteleone on her reception day; as the grand apartments in her palace were not open, 'a carpet dance was got up'.

After many a long, unblinking conversation, especially on the gory results of the 1837 poison scare, Senior regretfully decided that the people were 'scarcely civilised enough for the liberty of the press'. To this conclusion Consul Goodwin, loyal as always to his Sicilians, made the rejoinder: 'It must be admitted that when the liberty of press was obtained it was shamefully abused; but is this not always the case? Almost every liberty is at first abused. And you must recollect that the most active reformers were literary men. To them liberty of the press was everything.' An echo of that comment by Ingham in September 1848: 'The *letterati* are in reality the principal authors of revolutions.'

One imagines Senior on his departure mournfully shaking his head, not really much the wiser about the future of this turbulent island.

In spite of the financial crisis Sicily went through a period of fair advancement during the early 1850s. Not only were the new roads built and exports increased, but the harbours of Palermo and Messina were enlarged, schools and hospitals created, suspension bridges planned, nearly all due to the encouragement and foresight of Filangieri. Indeed he would have been able to have done more for Sicily had he not been constantly under criticism from the Government in Naples. Senior had recorded this comment about him from a noble Palermitan: 'If he were left alone he would make an excellent Governor. But he is constantly thwarted by the Minister for Sicilian Affairs at Naples, Cassisi. . . . Filangieri is neither a thief, a tyrant, nor a fool, and this is saying much for a Viceroy of Sicily.'

In October 1854 Filangieri resigned and his place was taken by a puppet-figure, the Prince of Castelcicala, who had been ambassador in London. After the balls and banquets, a grey dullness overtook Palermo, only enlivened by the plottings and secret meetings of would-be revolutionaries:

Such was the tyranny exercised by the authorities that even the cut of a beard, or the shape of a hat, was often regarded by the police as being the sign of membership of some secret society, and often led to the imprisonment of their wearers. The censor interfered everywhere and in everything, Liberal meanings being read into the most simple actions of the daily lives of the citizens. Many of the great houses in Palermo were closed.[8]

The British consulate was a favourite meeting place for the liberals. Goodwin once gave a dinner-party on Ruggiero Settimo's birthday, 'in silent honour of the great exile'. It had been tacitly agreed that there should be no mention of politics. When, however, a guest suddenly rose up and made an impassioned speech against King Bomba, Goodwin – always highly strung and nervous – was completely 'prostrated with horror'. Dickinson and another had to stay all night calming him. They had even been afraid that he might have committed suicide.

In Naples conditions were far worse. Ferdinand had not been unmoved by Gladstone thundering against his Government as the 'negation of God', but all the same nothing would prevent him from his policy of a return to absolutism. Sir Henry Elliot wrote that imprisonment could be made 'at the mere caprice of the police, from which there was no appeal . . . another frightful abuse was the arrest and imprisonment of men on secret private denunciation, more especially on that of the priests, who, when they wanted to get a man out of the way, sometimes with the most infamous object, accused him of *bestemmia* or blasphemy.' Naturally in such an atmosphere blackmail was common.

Senior had described some of the Neapolitan prisons. He had found men chained two by two in tiny cells, 'reeking with damp and swarming with vermin and loathsome reptiles'. All this had been enlarged upon in the *Letters to the Earl of Aberdeen*. It was estimated that some 40,000 people were brought in front of the Neapolitan courts after the end of the revolution in 1849.

Like any dictator Ferdinand could be fooled by sycophants. In October 1852 there had been, for instance, the spectacle of King Bomba receiving a thunderous and enthusiastic reception in Messina and Catania. After leaving the former city he had gone as far as to say that 'Messina will always be dear to my heart'. The British merchants, plaguing him for indemnities (sometimes over-exaggerating their claims)[9] as a result of the bombardment of September 1848, had formed a different opinion.

In the early summer of 1854 cholera appeared once more in Naples. It was to cause 7000 deaths there. A general quarantine, or '40*ne*', was at once enforced in Malta, but in Palermo it applied at first only to vessels arriving from Naples. The weather turned warmer, and soon the complaint, as Joseph Whitaker called it, became general all over the Mediterranean.

> *To W. E. Routh, Naples*                                     *7 August 1854*
> It is with extreme sorrow we learn of the sad ravages making in your city by the cholera, the last account received by the *Telegraph* being very alarming. Sincerely do I hope that you and yours will escape its deadly influence. Strict sanitary conditions are now being taken here for vessels coming from nearly every port in the Mediterranean.

Like Benjamin Ingham in the old days, he often now interspersed his letters with more general comments or politics.

> *To J. Smithson, Messina*                                   *10 August 1854*
> My Lord Lucan's silence [from the Crimea] on the subject of payment of wine[10] sold to him in April last, while he writes for a fresh supply, is exactly what we have experienced ourselves from other big folk, including the Lord High Commissioner at Corfu, Mr Ward.[11]
> We had not heard or seen anything of the immense failures you mention to have taken place in Yorkshire, or that so many as six houses went in a week in Bradford. . . . We hope that the capture of the three English merchantmen by the Russian steamer *Vladimir* will not prove true, nor yet the report from Malta of the Lampson Steamer Frigate having been captured.
> It is said that cholera in Naples, which had existed since the end of June, is better within the last two or three days. The last news of the 4th instant had been that the cholera was very bad.

The weather in Palermo continued very hot. 'Let us hope it pleases the Almighty that the cholera will not be of so dreadfully a malignant nature as it was the last time. We are all well in our circle, thank God.'

It was far too late to send Sophia and the children away – but where in any case would they go?

> *To J. Smithson, Messina*                                   *22 August 1854*
> The cholera seems to be a little on the decline in this city, although it is said to be the reverse in the neighbouring *campagna*. The deaths on the 17th were 365, the highest recorded. We hope you are still free from the scourge at Messina, although we are sorry to hear it had really broken out in Catania and Trapani. We are all, I am happy to say, pretty well

today, although Mrs Whitaker had rather a severe attack in the bowels yesterday, without however it developing into diarrhoea; under medical treatment it soon went off. I myself was also rather unwell most of last week, but thank God am now quite well again, as are all our children.

Joseph noted down that there had been 297 deaths on the eighteenth, 263 on the nineteenth and 269 on the twentieth.

*To J. Smithson, Messina*                           *29 August 1854*
We are sorry to hear that the cholera with you had assumed a most serious character, the deaths up to the 25th having reached the large number of 300. Here it is on the decrease, yesterday's report for Sunday being only 178 deaths. Business is quite at a standstill, most of the merchants and a great many of the shopkeepers having left the city, some for the country while others are on board vessels in the offing.

Joseph had not yet heard the bad news: Sophia's father had succumbed on the twenty-sixth. So had her half-sister, Bertha, aged fifteen.

The cholera epidemic in Messina was very serious, but not as bad as that experienced in Palermo in 1837. There is indeed no record of a sum total of the people who died from it there, although the maximum number of deaths in a day has been officially given as 474. The city, still in a ruinous state after the attentions of King Bomba, had lapsed into disgusting filth; the water-supply was tainted and flies swarmed everywhere, an ideal situation for a major outbreak, especially in high summer.

Mrs James Rose, the same who had entertained Senior, had left Palermo for Messina with her children two or three weeks before. She was one of Consul Barker's daughters, christened Sara Jane Eloisa but known to all as Lilly. She must have been an attractive person, judging by the affectionate memory that still lingers in the Rose family. Her husband had gone to England on business and had asked his partner, Edward Gardner, to send Lilly and the children to her father should cholera get bad in Palermo, for Messina had the reputation of being immune – thanks to the 'Madonna della Lettera', who was supposed to have promised that the inhabitants of the city would be under her special protection (in spite of the fact that more than half the population was swept away by the plague of 1743).

A month later James Rose, still in England, opened *The Times* and read that Robert Barker, son of the British Consul at Messina and most of the Consul's family, had died from cholera, all on the same day, 27 August. Lilly was dead; her unmarried sister Sophie had died, so had her other brother Frank. The Rose children were safe; perhaps they had been taken to Catania by Robert's Sicilian wife who had fled there with her own child. Lilly's mother's family, the Di Giorgis, were entirely wiped out; one of them used to act as Pro-Consul in Palermo in the 1830s when Goodwin was absent.

Tradition has it that Sophie Barker died in her father's country house. Her body was dressed as a bride's and taken in an open boat (by a fiancé?) across the Straits to be buried in the Lazzaretto in Calabria.

The decimation of the Barker family was a dreadful shock to the whole British colony in Sicily. Other compatriots' deaths followed soon afterwards. Following Bomba's ministrations in 1848, it was virtually the end of Messina's 400 years' reputation among the British as the most idyllic place of residence in Sicily.

Whether we should shed tears over Robert Barker, who was acting as Consul for Brazil, is a moot point. He certainly had far less charm than his sister Lilly. Indeed he appears to have been downright unpopular. His father had written to the Foreign Office in 1839 saying that he felt 'hoary old age growing upon me', and had suggested that he should be helped by Robert, then aged thirty-three. It was the second time of asking. In 1838 Palmerston had scribbled tersely on Barker's application:

> This is in other words asking me to appoint his son to succeed him which I cannot do. P.
> If he is unable by age or infirmity to perform his duties he should apply for retirement.

Possibly Robert Barker was simply considered to have dangerously revolutionary ideas: an ultra-liberal. There are references in consular papers to the Health Office in Messina accusing him and his father of 'having connection with Lord Cochrane' – 'mad, romantic, money-grubbing and untruthful'[12] Cochrane, Commander-in-chief of the Greek navy during the war of independence and therefore regarded as a natural trouble-maker by King Bomba.

So, after Palmerston's dusty answer, father Barker had to struggle on his own, against angry sea-captains, debtors and creditors, and some particularly annoying British flotsam called Causton, blatant scroungers who kept writing complaining letters about him direct to the Foreign Secretary. Then in 1851 there had been the humiliation of his enemy George Fagan being sent to Messina to deal with the British residents' claims. By 1853, although incapable of work, he was still Consul in name. It was then, at long last, that Robert was appointed Vice-Consul; even so the Bourbon

Government refused to recognise him, because – they said – of some report he had written in 1848. After Robert's death a clerk, Joseph Rickards, took over the work in the Consulate and eventually himself became Vice-Consul after poor, shattered old W. W. died in 1857.

By September the cholera was definitely abating in Palermo. Joseph told Robert Jeans that a government steamer had left for Messina 'with a number of physicians and other people on board to assist the dying and to bury the dead, also some police inspectors and men to assist in preserving order'. There were many anxious enquiries from clients:

*To Potter Brothers, Liverpool*                              *4 September 1854*
Business here is quite neglected, though the cholera in Palermo is fast decreasing after having carried off since the beginning over 4500 of the inhabitants. At Messina it has been raging with the greatest violence, almost as bad as what we experienced here in the year 1837. Our latest reports mention deaths on the 29th and 30th to have reached 499 and 574 respectively. Mr Sanderson, we regret to say, is among the number of victims. It is an awful thing, but God's will be done.

*To Capt. D. J. Phillips, Bark 'Resolution', Gibraltar*      *9 September 1854*
We are all still well, although the terrible visitation of that frightful malady is now fast decreasing. Mr Ingham and the Duchess are at Marsala, and are also well. Mr Benjamin Ingham junior is in England, just returned from the U.S.A.

So Ingham had once more deftly managed to retreat to Marsala at the moment of crisis. The figures for the deaths in Palermo may have been kept deliberately low. Between 10 August and 10 November the official total was 5334, of which 181 were foreigners. In Catania the total, for the period 31 August–31 October, was 1701.

*To Grants Balfour & Co., Genoa*                          *13 September 1854*
It affords us great pleasure to learn that the cholera in your city continues to decrease, and let us hope that as the warm season is past you will be free of it. Here we are able to report that the number of deaths for the last six days have been only 200, of which 46 were from natural causes. At Messina the ravages from it have been quite awful, but we rejoice to hear that it was fast decreasing, the deaths on the 10th having been only 44.

*To Potter Brothers, Liverpool*                          *13 September 1854*
We have to deplore the loss by the disease of our good friend Mr Valen-

tine and some few others of the colony, among whom the youngest daughter of Mr Seager. But how terrible have been the ravages caused by it at Messina, where entire families have been carried off, and we are very sorry to say that the lady of the writer's brother-in-law, Mr Thomas Sanderson, has also died.

Both Valentine – the son of W. Valentine who had died of cholera in 1837 – and Seager were Morrison's partners, and Miss Seager was Ben's godchild. Senior had drunk tea with Valentine in his 'charming house' on the Marina; they had discussed the iniquity of enforcing quarantine on vessels coming from the United States – Valentine believing that it was mere spitefulness, in revenge for the asylum given to Garibaldi.

Robert Sanderson, Sophia's other brother, had lost his father-in-law, Thomas Child. Joseph wrote to Routh (who had also been in partnership with Valentine) to say that Robert and Thomas were 'beginning to feel more courage' and 'were gradually reconciling themselves to the Almighty's will'. He added:

> *To W. E. Routh, Naples*                                          *18 September 1854*
> Many thanks for your kindness in providing us with bags of medicines, although I hope they will not now be wanted either by ourselves or by our friends. One half I am however sending down to Marsala where they have hitherto escaped. The malady has been quite near to them at Trapani, yet there has been no symptom of it either in the town itself or the immediate neighbourhood. . . . The authorities here have behaved beyond all praise and deserve the everlasting gratitude of the population, who on their part must also be said to have conducted themselves with great courage and admirable calm – a contrast indeed to the events of 1837.

The deaths in Palermo had now dwindled away to some twenty a day. By the twenty-seventh Joseph wrote to Potter Brothers to tell them that it had all but disappeared, though it 'continues its ravages in other places, particularly at Catania where the deaths on the 23rd were 77 and on the 24th 63.'

*The Times* of 25 September quoted an English naval officer who had called at Messina for a couple of hours whilst on his way to Constantinople in a French steamer:

> Not one shop or house in five is open, and the streets are almost deserted, for the cholera has been very severe indeed. Out of a population of 90,000 [i.e. Messina and its outlying villages] of whom full one half have

17. Giulio Tomasi Prince of Lampedusa, prototype of 'The Leopard'.

18. Corrado Valguarnera, Duke of Arenella and later Prince of Niscemi.

19. Baron Favara, father-in-law of Corrado Valguarnera, with two heroes: (*left*) Pietro Messineo, 'President of the Committee of the Barricades', and (*right*) Raffaele Di Benedetto.

20. Photograph of Garibaldi inscribed to Maria Favara, later wife of Corrado Valguarnera.

21. Sub-Lieutenant Joseph Nelson of Colonel Dunne's English Regiment, 1860.

fled [Filangieri reckoned two-thirds, including many doctors, police, priests, even grave-diggers], the most moderate computation puts the deaths at 9000; of the English residents, who amount to 70, 22 have died. The deaths when we were there were only 100 a day, though when the cholera was at its worst they amounted to 1200 [an exaggeration?]. Our doctors visited the hospitals, and their account of the state of them is terrific. Indeed the town is like one which has been stricken with the plague. One of the doctors said to me, 'Sir, if ever I meet your country-man, Gladstone, I will say to him "Here is a man who doubted the reality of the horrors you have told of in the prisons of Naples; but after what I have seen of the miseries of the hospitals, I can freely credit any-thing that is told of the barbarity of such a Government".'

It was not until 24 November that Consul Goodwin was able to tell his ambassador that there had been no cases of cholera for the past ten days on the island. The total number of deaths for 1854 was estimated at 27,101.

But the 'morbus' had by no means disappeared. It came back to Sicily in 1855, when 17,136 deaths were recorded.

One of the last letters to survive from 1854 refers to the cholera in the Crimea, where many thousands had also died. News of the death of the French field-marshal St Armand on 29 September, again from cholera, had just been received. The war now over-shadowed more provincial news.

*To J. Smithson, Messina*         *17 October 1854*
We await anxiously details of the battle for Sebastopol. Meantime we may be satisfied that our troops, both officers and men, behaved them-selves like British soldiers have always done and ever will before the enemy. Let the pro-Russians [presumably the Bourbons] say what they will.

The bombardment, unsuccessful, of Sebastopol actually began on that very day. 25 October was the day of the charge of the Light Brigade.

The ebullient and anonymous author of *Unprotected Females in Sicily, Calabria and on the Top of Mount Etna* visited Messina three years later. She found that the city's authorities had learnt their lesson: 'Within, Messina, for a Sicilian town, is clean and handsome; cholera having given the inhabi-tants severe lessons upon the danger of their former filthy state.' A new marble statue of King Bomba had also been erected.[13]

The Females had begun their trip in Palermo. They were in search of adventure, so did not bother much about the English colony, members of whom they found 'very backward', besides being too rich and apt to sing too loudly in church. Sicily to them was a romantic land where Spanish blood and chivalry still coursed strongly. And they were not disappointed, for some ardent gentleman who had spied them sightseeing in the cathedral actually sent a declaration of love to their hotel. Palermo was dirtier than Messina and all colour and tumult, the air in the narrow streets full of the noise of cracking whips from 'crazy carriages', whose drivers implored them to enter. There were dashing young men on glossy donkeys, picturesque beggars selling lottery tickets,[14] yellow-clad convicts clanking in chains. Paper fans waved in the confectioners' shops to keep off the flies; fruit stalls were festooned with pomegranates and Barbary figs; noblemen lounged in cafés, being 'too fine to walk, too poor to drive'.

Benjamin Ingham's life at this period was, needless to say, in some contrast to this vivid hurly-burly of the streets. He and the Duchess had decided that the house in the Piazza di Sant'Oliva was too small for them. Consequently in September 1856 he bought from the Prince of Radalì a large tract of ground slightly nearer to the centre of the city, between what are now the Vias Belmonte and Bentivegna. The money was paid to Radalì in England. On this site he built a great, modern *palazzo*.[15] The architecture of the new house was very plain compared to the elegance of Sant'Oliva. A photograph from the south side shows that it had two storeys, each with seven windows with their own balconies; to the east there was a conservatory looking across to the present port, with Monte Pellegrino like a Gibraltar on the left. In the foreground of the picture there is 'Square Ingham', also known in Palermo as 'English square', full of palms, yuccas, monkey puzzles and tropical plants. The street on the right, then known as Via Ingham, is the northern extension of the present Via Roma. And Palazzo Ingham is the present Hotel des Palmes, where Wagner stayed, though an extra floor, a sumptuous new entrance hall and a range of eleven windows instead of seven have been added.[16]

Ben, now aged forty-four, took over the Sant'Oliva villa. Perhaps this gives us a clue to the date of his marriage to Emily Hinton, who was nineteen in 1856. Her stepfather was Mr Wood, the owner of the third largest British *baglio* in Marsala and living in the Palazzo Derix in Palermo. Later *Baglio* Wood was 'absorbed' by the Ingham-Whitaker firm, no doubt because of this marriage.

Relations between Ferdinand and the British and French had become considerably more strained during the Crimean War, especially after Piedmont (or Sardinia as it was sometimes called, the crowns being united) had joined the Allies. Minor incidents were blown up on an international scale, such as when Mazza, the chief of the Neapolitan police, ordered George Fagan to leave a box in a theatre for quizzing him with his eyeglass. After the Treaty of Paris Ferdinand was virtually ordered by Lord Clarendon and Count Walewski, the French Foreign Minister, to declare an amnesty and open his prisons. When he took no notice, Britain and France broke off diplomatic relations. Then, on 8 December 1857, there was an attempt on the King's life by Agesilao Milano, a Calabrian, who succeeded in wounding him in the thigh with a bayonet.

Earlier that year George Dennis, later to succeed Goodwin as Consul in Palermo, had visited Sicily to gather material for his Murray's *Handbook*. Thanks to Goodwin, he managed to look inside the Vicaria prison. What he saw there simply underlined the barbarities exposed in a Neapolitan prison six years before in Gladstone's *Letters*.[17] A rule of terror, under Maniscalco, the Chief of Police, was in full swing in the city.

Secret societies – egged on by the exiles – were flourishing both in Palermo and Naples, and in Sicily there was a gradual growth towards the idea of union with the Kingdom of Italy, another name for Piedmont, in order finally to shake off Bourbon tyranny. Goodwin however was always in favour of Sicily retaining her autonomy. Among the most active agents of Mazzini among the Sicilian exiles were Crispi, La Farina and Rosolino Pilo, who with Pisacane and Nicotera was involved in a small abortive revolt in 1857. In July 1858 there was the famous secret meeting between Napoleon III and Cavour at Plombières, and war against Austria was planned for the spring of 1859. The next stage of the Risorgimento was about to begin.

Ferdinand, pallid, overweight and old for his age (forty-nine), was in very bad health. The strain of battling against foreign opinion had taken its toll. He also was suffering from the aftermath of Milano's bayonet wound. Some four weeks after the French and Piedmontese had declared war on the Austrians, he died, on 22 May 1859. He was succeeded by his son, Francis II, a very different type of person, 'vacillating, weak and priest-ridden'.[18]

Palermo in 1859 was more than ever a 'hotbed of conspiracy'. The Princess of Niscemi (sister of the Prince of Lampedusa, the prototype of the Leopard) was chief among the many nobles who kept patriots hiding in their houses. Baron Riso 'gave constant balls on the first floor of his beautiful palace in the Toledo, dancing serving as a cloak to meetings on the floor above, men in evening dress slipping upstairs between a gay valse or contre-danse to help in the making of bombs for the coming revolution'.[19]

# XI

## Garibaldi Cometh

THAT 'indefinite hope' soon seemed much closer to a certainty, especially when the Swiss mercenaries mutinied in Naples and their regiment was disbanded. Many of the fierier young nobles of Palermo, of the type of Tancredi in *The Leopard*, went into hiding. The atmosphere – the furtiveness and excitement mixed with impatience and sense of danger – was not unlike that in Rome during the German occupation of 1944. A gesture towards peace was made by the Neapolitans, by way of an amnesty for 137 exiled Sicilians, not one of whom however dared return; 'proof', as Henry Elliot wrote to Lord John Russell, 'of the entire absence of the sense of individual security which prevails here'.

At the end of grand dinner parties in Palermo the usual toast, with the champagne, would be 'Viva Verdi!', the letters of the composer's name standing for *Vittorio Emanuele Re d'Italia*.[1] In London Mazzini had long ago decided that Sicily, with her history of constantly rumbling discontent, every now and then erupting into violence, was the ideal starting off point for the great revolution that would bring about the unification of Italy. Garibaldi had also shown his interest in the suggestion that he should come to the island as liberator; on 29 September he wrote to the Revolutionary Committee to say that he would do so 'with pleasure, with joy', though adding the careful qualification that he felt the moment had not yet arrived – 'more intimate connections' were still needed between the Sicilians and himself. As for Cavour, he too insisted that, before he could sanction any sort of involvement, the people of Sicily must give definite proof that they were willing to stand up to their Bourbon oppressors on their own; as an encouragement (and what more tantalising one could he give?) he had indicated that Sicily would be given some sort of autonomy within a unified Italy.

Various conspirators landed on the island, usually from Malta, the most prominent being Francesco Crispi. Pretending to be an Argentinian with the name of Manuel Pareda, he carried his disguise almost to absurdity by wearing whiskers and blue glasses. His destination was Catania, where he was to lay plans for a revolution planned for 4 October. It happened that a

British naval squadron, under the command of Admiral Mundy, now virtually policing the coast of eastern Sicily, was in Catania harbour at the time, so the forty-year-old Crispi, in order to complete his pose as the eager South American tourist, even went so far as to join a party of the younger officers who were determined to 'scale the snowy peaks of Mount Etna'.[2]

Alas, the projected revolution failed completely, the police having been forewarned. When Crispi returned to Sicily on 11 October, in yet another disguise, he found that all his spadework had apparently come to naught.

Six weeks later Maniscalco was stabbed, though not fatally, at the entrance to Palermo cathedral. An inkling that this was likely to happen had already reached the British, thanks to some clandestine correspondence, sent from Leghorn to a merchant in Messina, that had been opened by the Vice-Consul Joseph Rickards. The gist of the letters had at once been forwarded to Elliot, their interception having been due to a suspicious visit to Rickards earlier on from one of Garibaldi's lady admirers, Maria Espérance Schwartz, known to the General as Speranza.

Rickards had shown himself a sterner and more down to earth individual than the Barkers (whose clerk he had been for sixteen years before 1854). But he was certainly less liberal-minded if we are to believe Madam Schwartz in her rather foolish memoirs, published under a pseudonym.[3] As she held a British passport, she had written – ever the conspirator – to Garibaldi asking whether she might be of any help. A telegram arrived: could she go to Sicily on a delicate mission? Then there was a letter, all very cloak and dagger, to be sewn into her skirt. But great disillusion. Disaster in fact! For Rickards, she found, was 'devoted to the Bourbon dynasty'. Before she was arrested that night, poor Speranza had to eat the proclamation, which was inconveniently written on very thick paper, and later she had to bribe her way out of prison. In spite of this episode, the clandestine letters were sent from Leghorn. 'The contents,' Rickards wrote to Elliot, 'surpassed my preconceived opinions. It appears the writer of these letters is an agent of a noted Italian general. . . . The landing of armed men in the island is proposed and the Committee are desired to send a formal requisition to that effect. The writer urges the strong necessity of first assassinating the Director of Police at Palermo.'

So 1860 arrived, the glorious year. The foreign community in Palermo, however, felt somewhat less elated. For the British, or at any rate for the young ladies and their mothers, the New Year brought a special excitement: the arrival of the sixteen-year-old Prince Alfred, later Duke of Edinburgh. A ball was given for him, and in the words of Consul Goodwin 'went off with the highest *éclat*'. Among those favoured to dance with His Royal Highness was Carrie Whitaker, aged fifteen.

There is a long description of that dance,[4] or rather of its aftermath, providing an attractive vignette of some of the people who attended it.

Midnight had struck – the music ended – the assembled people dispersed and a sudden silence followed the gaiety of a few minutes before. The gaslights were extinguished, and the moon remained motionless and alone to brighten the melancholy sea. The Marina was deserted, and at the windows of those Palaces stretching along the seafront, pale faces contemplated the scene of nocturnal silence, perfumed by the scent of orange blossom.

On one of the sofas sat Mr James Rose.[5] He was a heavily built man, grey-haired, of cheerful aspect, with traces of a smile on his face. As he sat talking, that face of rare contrasts became serious. He was speaking of the cholera of 1854, which took from him his young wife, mother of his children, numbering six sons and one daughter, Sophie, who now cared for her brothers as a mother.

He was conversing with a lady of a certain age, the Duchess Carcaci, who in her youth could not have claimed to have been beautiful. What was particularly noticeable about her was her slightly cross brow, a noble look and a slightly sarcastic smile. . . .

On the pouffe were seated two young ladies; one was Sophie Rose herself, aged twenty and possessed of all the graces that nature ever endowed a woman with. Her voluminous tresses were between blonde and light brown in colour, and contrasted well with the ribbon of black velvet which fell from her head to her waist. Her large blue-green eyes were surprisingly fine. . . .

Lyla [Harriet] Morrison[6] at her side was her senior by several years and taller, and seemed Sophie's antithesis. She kept her eyes constantly lowered – she was rather plain, in fact, not very careful in her dress, cold, with her lips opened in a perpetual smile. She never looked her friend straight in the face and gave the impression of being jesuitical. Curiously enough, Sophie Rose chatted to her as if blind to such defects, being very fond of her.

James Rose junior, two years older than his sister, his arms on the iron railings of the balcony, bent his tall figure so that he might the more easily converse with the young girl in a blue dress beside him. The light breeze would at times ruffle his brown hair, and the moonlight rendered more pallid the usual pallor of that most handsome face. His intense looks and sweet words of love enchanted the girl he called Maria, yet they were joy and poison to her soul. This girl was Maria Carcaci, a delicately made, small person, and while he spoke without a rest, she was silent, hardly breathing owing to her consuming love.

Not far from there were conversing Mr Morrison, Lyla's octogenarian father, and Mrs Joseph Whitaker, of most charming manner and always so kind, making strenuous efforts to raise her feeble voice so as to reach the deaf ears of the old man. Notwithstanding her efforts, she was forced to repeat the same sentence at least ten times in order to make it intelligible to him.

To console herself for her trouble, she looked with a greatly satisfied air towards the adjoining room, where seated at the piano two of her daughters, Ackie [Alexandrina, in deference to the Duchess of Santa Rosalia's name, Alessandra] and Carrie, were playing together, with variations, that well-known English song of the poet Moore, entitled 'The Last Rose of Summer'.

And so on. We are given to understand that William Rose, aged eighteen, 'of serious aspect with black eyes and hair' and standing erect by the piano, must have been jealous of Prince Alfred dancing with Carrie, 'with good reason called good-looking'. 'He keeps his eyes riveted on Carrie while thinking of the future.' And James Rose senior has designs on the jesuitical Lyla, who on the contrary told Sophie flatly that 'I would not spend an hour of my life with him'.

At the end of January one Enrico Bensa arrived from Piedmont with a letter of introduction to Antonio Pignatelli, related to the Duke of Monteleone, Benjamin Ingham's partner in the *Palermo* steamship venture. Bensa claimed to be a relation of Cavour and on intimate terms with Victor Emmanuel. He also bore secret messages from La Farina, secretary of the Italian National Society. His words had an electrifying reaction on Pignatelli and his young friends, who were urged to rise and prove themselves worthy of support from the north. The fervid excitement and the idealism grew. Discretion began to disappear. A future friend of the Whitaker family, Francesco (Ciccio) Brancaccio, wrote: 'Minutes seemed like hours, weeks months, and months years, in our impatience for action. Courage and gaiety were the special characteristics of the youth of 1860; not for them meetings in caves or remote houses; not for them oaths sworn in blood before a crucifix with a skull on one side and a dagger on the other. They preferred to meet in the open streets. . . .'

Such new recklessness was bound to have its consequences. There were arrests, including Brancaccio himself, who was committed to the Vicaria. On 2 March Mazzini wrote a famous letter, which was read to the Revolutionary Committee of Palermo: 'Brothers, I confess I no longer recognize in the Sicilians of today the men who flung down the challenge in 1848. . . . Dare, and you will be followed. . . . Garibaldi is bound to come to your help.' Such words were the required last fillip. Two main revolutionary groups were now formed, one proletarian and the other aristocratic, each collecting firearms and bombs, and each strangely enough headed by men with the name of Riso: Francesco Riso, a master plumber, and Baron Riso of Colobria, the owner of the palace on the Toledo. Francesco Riso's arms were stored in a building rented from the Gancia monastery, in the heart of the old city. The date for the beginning of the revolution was fixed for 4 April.

The British Government was now alerted to this 'first muttering of the storm'. On 18 March Commander Winnington-Ingram was sent with the *Argus* from Messina to Palermo 'to look after British interests'.[7] This was the same Winnington-Ingram who had been a midshipman on the *Talbot* in April 1840 during the Sulphur War. On board was another young Whitaker, Pip, aged ten, who had been spending his first year's schooling at St Julian's Protestant College in Malta. Because of the inevitable disturbances ahead, it had been decided to call him home, and as the steamer services had been suspended, he had been put on a brig heading for Messina, where his Sanderson relations were to transfer him to the *Argus*. The journey had been a thrilling one, lasting five days, and he had been accompanied by two young Anglo-Sicilian friends, Robert Frank and Robert Rose.

As a matter of courtesy, one of Winnington-Ingram's first duties was to call on the Neapolitan Viceroy, the Prince of Castelcicala, whom he considered far too old and 'unfitted to cope with the troublesome elements gathering around him' – the Prince, he added, had in his youth served with the British cavalry and had actually fought with the Inniskilling Dragoons at the Battle of Waterloo. On the same day he paid another essential visit, to 'the great Marsala wine merchant, Mr Ingham'; here he was introduced to a lady, anonymously referred to as Marchesa P—— and something of a firebrand as one would expect from her parentage, for she was the daughter of John Frost, the Chartist leader.

As a result of seeing Ingham, the Commander was invited to a conference of merchants at the British Consulate, 'to take into account the threatening state of affairs at Palermo, and to hear one of their number, a Mr Thomas [of Prior, Thomas and Turner], give evidence about the expected revolt.' Also present was a voluble Englishwoman, Madame Celesti, who claimed to be 'behind the scenes', and with a great deal of reason, since she was married to Michele Celesti, the Director General of Internal Affairs (her daughter eventually married Maniscalco's son).[8] 'Now I thought it necessary', he wrote, 'to make arrangements with our energetic Consul, Mr Goodwin, for the security of English life and property in the coming struggle.'

Winnington-Ingram kept a diary for the next seven months. The first entries ran:

*31 March 1860*

Heard that the police had been searching English houses for arms during the night, and that many foreign families, and also native ones, were about to quit the city.

*1 April 1860*

A report of 150 persons having been arrested during the night, and that great uneasiness prevails among the citizens.

*3 April 1860*

Outbreak of revolt expected tomorrow. Received on board Treasure on deposit.

*4 April 1860*

Firing heard in the town at daylight about 5 a.m. Sent an officer (Mr Coen) to learn the cause, and at 6 a.m. repaired on shore myself to find the revolution had commenced. Not many armed people were in the streets, but hot work was going on at La Gancia Convent.[9] which the rebels were defending. Troops, in companies, at the corner of the streets kept shouting 'Viva il Re', and the artillery were firing grape shot down the Via Toledo. I saw one man killed, and found the Consulate full of refugees. At 8 a.m. the firing had ceased. I then visited the British merchants who declined going afloat, so I returned to the *Argus* at 10 a.m. At noon, rumours were prevalent of further disturbances to take place at nightfall. Sent an officer with letter to the Consul, advising British subjects who wished to embark to do so before dark. Mr Thomas and family went on board a Danish schooner. The Whitakers, Marsala merchants, with their children [now numbering ten, and Sophia was eight months with child, her last], came to *Argus*. The firing recommenced towards evening, but was confined to the suburbs of the town. It is announced that the Friars of La Gancia Convent held out bravely, and had three of their number killed, but were finally overcome and made prisoners. The troops sacked the convent and hawked its books about the streets.

The plumber Riso with seventeen men had been waiting all night with their pile of arms in the Gancia building. When they heard the sinister noise of patrols the next morning, they took alarm and decided to attack. The monks tolled the monastery bells, and there was some hard fighting, Riso (mortally wounded) and his surviving followers were all captured. The monks were rounded up and sent to the Vicaria. Many of the home-made bombs, unfortunately for the rebels, had failed to explode.

But the revolution had begun. Riso had in effect ignited the furnace which by the end of the year would bring about the liberation of most of Italy. Scuffles continued in and around Palermo in a savage though haphazard way. Winnington-Ingram went ashore and there met Messrs Rose and Gardner, 'who did not conceal their sympathy with the rebel cause'.

*Squadre*, armed groups of peasants, some of them admittedly little more than bandits, harassed the Neapolitan troops in the surrounding countryside. There was a mounting desperation in the air, as though the peasants saw in their hated opponents the symbols of all the poverty, all the injustices under which they had suffered for generation after generation, and they were having their revenge. This was more than a political revolt, it was the beginning of a social revolution.

The skirmishings spread westwards, into one of the areas of Sicily nowadays most associated with the *Mafia*, to the orange groves and lush plains around Partinico and Camporeale where the towering sun-parched crags provided, as they still do, ideal refuges for guerillas. Some of the *squadre* dared even to creep into Palermo by night. Winnington-Ingram continued:

*10 April 1860*

See buildings burning in the neighbourhood of Bagheria. I walked up the Via Toledo and found a few shops open, and a good many of the lower class of the population lounging about the street. . . . We hear that the fires near Bagheria were caused by the soldiers burning insurgent houses. General Salzano[10] has issued another proclamation, in which he states that the troops defeated the patriots at San Lorenzo, near Mr Whitaker's country house. Many of the former – wounded – have been brought into the city.

Admirers of *The Leopard* will be reminded at once of that book's opening chapter, when the Prince of Salina is walking in the scented garden of
his villa outside Palermo and recalls the finding of a young dead soldier
from the Neapolitan fifth *Cacciatore* battalion. The boy had been wounded
at the battle at San Lorenzo and had crawled up to the Prince's garden
nearby, to die among the ants under a lemon tree; 'those swine stink even
when they're dead', the Prince's agent had said. Just as Lampedusa had his
own great-grandfather in mind as Salina, so the garden must also have been
based on that of the family villa, a pleasing, one-storey eighteenth-century
building, also in the 'Colli', white and saffron in colour and covered with
faded, though once probably garish, frescoes. The place is very derelict
now: the outhouses are crumbling, the shutters broken and a giant television aerial proclaims the twentieth century.

Later in the same chapter the Prince of Salina passes Tancredi's Villa
Falconeri, based on the present Villa Niscemi, a larger building and more
austere in appearance than the Villa Lampedusa, and still with the huge
bougainvillea described as cascading over the wall 'like swags of episcopal
silk'.

On 7 April five young noblemen had been arrested at the Palazzo
Monteleone, including Antonio Pignatelli and Baron Riso. They were
handcuffed and marched as felons along the Via Toledo to the Castellamare
fort. Maniscalco was all for them being executed immediately, but as
Castelcicala insisted that they must be tried by court martial, they were
transferred to the Vicaria, thus joining Ciccio Brancaccio, though put in
*camere serrate*, cells without windows. One of the young men was Corrado
Valguarnera, Duke of Arenella. The police had only had warrants for the
arrest of the other four, his friends, but when he had heard of what had
happened, he gave himself up voluntarily. And being the son of the Princess
of Niscemi, he was the original (or at any rate in part) of Tancredi, none
other.[11]

Lampedusa wrote of Tancredi as 'thin and elegant with a shy, quizzical
look', and Corrado's photograph fits that description. Corrado was remarkably handsome, with soft velvety eyes and dark hair combed straight
back from his forehead; he wore the fashionable side-whiskers, but had no
moustache or beard. Unlike the fictional Tancredi, he was in prison when
Garibaldi landed in Sicily a month later;[12] that other Tancredi, it will be
remembered, rushed off into the hills for his mysterious 'duel' with the
King, much to his uncle's disapproval – 'You're mad, my boy, to go with
those people! They're all *Mafia* men, all crooks.[13] A Falconeri should be
with us, for the King!'

Another to be arrested was Gabriele Cesarò, aged sixteen, The circumstances of the arrest of Padre Ottavio Lanza four days later were not very honourable. The old fellow was in a delicate state of health; Brancaccio said, 'Although he has a character like tempered steel, he is thin and sickly, and his body is frail.' With his family he had taken refuge on the American clipper *Tacconay*. A rowing boat came up alongside, with some police officers who demanded to be taken on board. Eventually only two were allowed up. Ottavio was reading in the *salotto*, and as soon as the men saw him they announced that they had come for his arrest in the name of Maniscalco – at the same time producing a letter of authorisation from the American Consul, Henry H. Barstow, There could be no argument and Ottavio departed for gaol 'amid the wails of his relations and the curses of the Americans on the Bourbon government'. The American and British residents in Palermo were so enraged by this unaccountable act of perfidy that a complaint was later sent to the United States Government, as a result of which the Consul was removed.[14]

On the fourteenth, thirteen of the Gancia rebels, including the father of plumber Riso were executed. Winnington-Ingram actually saw this happen, right opposite his ship's anchorage.[15] The incident outraged the population of Palermo even further, and the place where they were shot is to this day known as Piazza delle Tredici Vittime. Riso himself was slowly dying from the wound he had received ten days before. He did not know that his father had been executed, and thinking, presumably in his delirium, that he could thereby save the old man's life made long statements implicating Baron Riso and the other nobles – it seemed hardly possible that they would be able to avoid execution.

Not long afterwards there was a pitched battle between the *squadre* and the Bourbon troops at Carini, a few miles from Montelepre, a village crowned romantically by an Arab castle and made notorious in the 1950s as the bandit Giuliano's stronghold. The *squadre* were well and truly routed, and the whole revolt might have collapsed altogether had not Rosolino Pilo – like a messenger from Jove – suddenly arrived with the news that Garibaldi's arrival was at last really imminent. Pilo had landed secretly in Messina, where there had also been revolutionary demonstrations, but on hearing of the activities of the *squadre* had at once hurried westwards. His mission was not a moment too soon.

A third of the population of Messina was meanwhile reported to be encamped in the nearby hills. This was because of the rumour, following the demonstration, that the city would once more be bombarded. In spite of the panic, Vice-Consul Rickards remained stoically at his desk, though the families of the remaining British residents – those who were left, in other words, after the experiences of 1848 and 1854 – had mostly moved to Malta.

In the Colli the air was full of the 'nuptial scent of orange blossom'.[16] Flocks of quails were landing on Monte Pellegrino and in the sumac fields. The Conca d'Oro was at its most beautiful; but Palermo, with its shops shuttered and the streets deserted after curfew, was 'a city of the dead'.[17] All the same the very faintest rumour of an uprising would be enough for crowds, almost miraculously, to appear, and government soldiers would be daringly taunted with anti-Bourbon slogans. But the Neapolitans, Winington-Ingram saw, were making suitable preparations:

> *24 April 1860*
>
> Neapolitan steamers actively conveying troops here and there along the coast. Called on Captain Palmer, of the American steam corvette, *Iroquois*, and land with him. Found guards posted in the streets and sentries doubled. Little demonstrations were going on in the side thoroughfares, and cries raised for Victor Emmanuel.

At night the looming hills around were dotted with the crimson quivering fires lit by *squadre*, as though to menace 'this city of palaces and convents'.

Ben and Emily Ingham took the opportunity of slipping off to England on their way for America; they were accompanied by Willie, Joseph Whitaker's second son, aged eighteen. Ben was still Vice-Consul for Marsala, so the post was delegated temporarily to the manager, Cossins. At long last Garibaldi, or 'Piddu' as he was affectionately known to the Sicilians, could no longer be in any doubt that the time was ready for his landing. The story of his decision to set out, against the wishes of Cavour, has been often told. There had at first been a question of his going to his birthplace Nice, which to his fury had been ceded by Piedmont to Napoleon III. However, at last, on 5 May he and the immortal 'Thousand' – a strange assortment, mostly northerners, some being working men but many from official classes and including 150 lawyers – embarked at Genoa on two hijacked merchant ships of the Rubattino line, the *Piemonte* and the *Lombardo*.

News of Garibaldi's departure reached Sicily, and indeed Naples, soon enough. As the days dragged on the waiting began to seem intolerable to such an excitable race. Foreigners began also to feel the euphoria, and the British navy gave a small celebration:

*9 May 1860*

We invite the English residents in Palermo to a 'play' on board the *Argus*. Many ladies, and also officers from the foreign ships of war, attend the party. Our principal actor, an ordinary seaman, excelled himself in the *Thumping Legacy*. A grand supper finished the evening 'entertainment'.

Ingham and Joseph were among those who declined the invitation, but Mrs Gardner was persuaded to chaperone the Whitaker girls.

The next day the *Argus* and the *Intrepid*, just arrived from Messina, were ordered to Marsala: not collusion with Garibaldi and the Piedmontese, as the Bourbons later indignantly claimed, but to protect the British wine merchants, who had recently been forcibly disarmed by the military and were fearful of the 'numerous bands of robbers in the district'.[18] There had been the usual demonstrations in the town following Riso's revolt, and the Bourbon arms had been torn down; all the same it had taken a month before the Palermo Government could spare the men to go there. General Letizia had in fact arrived on 6 May, when he imprisoned most of the trouble-makers and conducted a general disarming, in which the British had also been included in a most peremptory manner – he had threatened to shoot Cossins unless he obeyed. The disarming done, he was suddenly summoned back. The merchants' appeal to the navy for help (which had reached Malta on a Woodhouse vessel), was therefore perfectly genuine – even though there was no doubt where their emotional bias lay.

General Letizia's recall seems now an act of lunatic bungling, for it was common knowledge that Garibaldi was likely to land between Marsala and Mazara. The way was thus left totally clear for him. Again one cannot help being reminded of 1944, when the Allies made their beachhead landing at Anzio and found the place totally bare of enemy troops.

Winnington-Ingram's dramatic, if laconic, entry in his diary for the eleventh has often been quoted. It begins:

*11 May 1860*

Anchored off Marsala in nine fathoms, and about two miles distant from the town. *Intrepid* anchors inshore of us. About 11 a.m. I landed with Commander Marryat[10] [of the *Intrepid*], and we both called on our Consul, Mr Cossins, and Mr Hervey (manager of Mr Woodhouse's wine establishment). . . . Whilst conversing with Mr Edwards (Mr Hervey's assistant), two Sardinian merchant steamers were reported to be coming in from seaward full of armed men. They steamed round the *Intrepid*, and then pushed on for the Mole. One of them got safely into the harbour, but the other grounded at its entrance. Shore boats came off the latter vessel, and she commenced disembarking a number of red-shirted men, and landing them near the lighthouse at the end of the Mole. A Neapolitan war steamer and a sailing frigate were in sight to the eastward. The former, with signals flying, was rapidly closing with the Sardinian. It was a critical moment.

A letter to *The Times*[20] further illuminates this account, so shorn of any frills:

It was a most beautiful day, bright sun and perfectly calm sea. Her Britannic Majesty's ships *Argus* and *Intrepid* were lying at anchor off the Town, having arrived about 10 o'clock that morning from Palermo, in consequence of some complaints that had been made by the English residents here against the Neapolitan authorities. Two paddlewheel steamers, which had been observed cruising in the offing most of the morning, at 1 o'clock steamed rapidly towards the breakwater, As they approached the shore they hoisted Sardinian colours, and were seen to be crowded with armed men, while field pieces were distinctly discernible on the deck of the larger one.

The men were not clothed in uniform but a large number wore bright red woollen shirts, without any jackets, and felt hats. On the bridge of the first steamer stood an individual, also in red, whose identity was then little suspected, but who turned out to be the illustrious General Garibaldi himself. . . . Every man was armed with a revolver, Minlé rifle and sabre, and many carried two rifles.

The Mr Hervey referred to by Winnington-Ingram was of course Don Onofrio, not manager but more like managing director. He and his wife were on a visit from Malta, where they really lived. So swift and smooth was the disembarkation on Old John Woodhouse's Mole that some junior British officers, eating ices in a café in the town, were surprised by armed men appearing in the doorway. At first they treated the matter as a sort of *opéra-bouffe*, having been told that to get permission to see Cossins they must first apply to 'an elderly man with a red garment on, and a wide-awake hat containing a feather and a tricolour cockade',[21] but they soon realised that the situation was deadly serious. Garibaldi had landed, and there was no time for jesting. What was more, Cossins was busy arranging for the Union Jack to be hoisted over the *bagli*.

The Neapolitan steamer was the sloop *Stromboli*, the very ship about which there had been the international incident in July 1848, when she

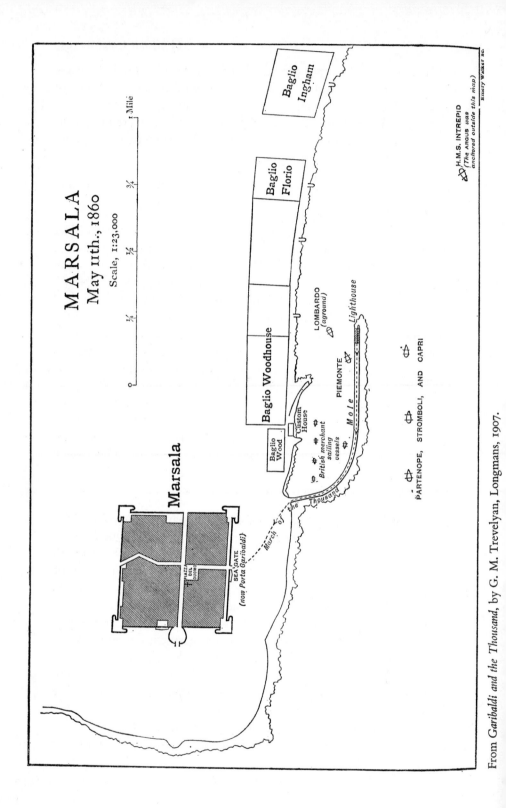

From *Garibaldi and the Thousand*, by G. M. Trevelyan, Longmans, 1907.

had intercepted and arrested the Sicilian rebels from Calabria. She had been towing the *Partenope*, which was left to follow on while the *Stromboli* sped towards Marsala. There seemed to be some doubt on board at first whether the red-shirts were British or not.

Winnington-Ingram continued in his diary:

> A boat was seen to quit the Neapolitan war steamer and pull towards the grounded Sardinian [the *Lombardo*, which had stuck at the entrance to the harbour]. She had not, however, reached more than half-way to the vessel, when a panic appeared to seize those in her, and a retreat was hastily made to their ship, which now opened fire upon the Mole with her heavy guns. Commander Marryat, Mr Cossins, and myself embarked at once in a gig of the *Argus*, and proceeded on board the Neapolitan to beg her Captain to direct his shot and shell clear of the British wine establishments. To our surprise, we found that officer to bear the name of a fine old English Roman Catholic family, and to be complete master of our language.

The officer's name was Acton: Gugliemo Acton, the same who had been General Pronio's emissary at Messina in February 1848 – later he was to become an Admiral, a Senator and Minister of Marine of the united Italy.[22] Although Neapolitan by nationality, he was obviously somewhat torn by divided loyalties; for all he knew the British warships might actually be assisting the landing of the Thousand. He seemed to Marryat 'excessively nervous and agitated', though impressed by his responsibility in the situation. His visitors received a promise that British property would not be injured, Acton 'pointing out to us', as Winnington-Ingram said, 'that his guns were laid for the Mole only, along which the red-shirts were seen making their way for the town as fast as their encumbrances would permit them'. In fact, all during the conference on board he continued his firing, and 'even offered a kind of apology for his shot going so low'. The British party left, but they were not out of danger.

> The Neapolitan sailing frigate [the *Partenope*] came bearing down upon our boat, and her officers hailed and waved to us to pull faster. Hardly had they done so when a veritable storm of shot and missiles of all kinds, delivered from her broadside guns, passed over our heads, but fell short of the Mole. One of her shot, however, entered Mr Woodhouse's wine establishment and nearly killed Mrs Hervey.[23]

Another letter to *The Times*, which must have been written from the *Baglio* Ingham, describes the feelings of the British:

*Monday, 12 May*

We were all in a state of alarm during the firing, as the shot and shell from the frigate went flying about in a most awkward manner – some into the town, some into Woodhouse's store, some into Wood's *baglio*, and one actually fell over our heads here on the terrace, into the sea beyond Salinella.

The *Capri*, 'a hired armed steamer in the service of the Kingdom of Naples', now appeared and also began firing wildly – 'we could not trace the course of her shot,' said Winnington-Ingram. An officer from the *Capri* then came on board with the impertinent demand that one of her boats should sail up to the Sardinian steamers and demand their surrender. 'He received a very decided negative reply', and the *Argus* merely 'shifted her anchorage nearer to the wine stores for their better protection'. In any case the disembarkation of Garibaldi's men, and of the crews, was completed soon afterwards, and the steamers were therefore left abandoned. The Neapolitans now decided it would be safe enough for them to dare to send their own armed boats to take possession – and this they did with 'cries of exultation and victory', much to the amusement of both Garibaldinian and British onlookers.

Heavy fire was still pouring on the invaders ('very fine men, many wearing the Crimean medal'),[24] dragging guns and ammunition into the town. Garibaldi, with hair flowing and his famous poncho round his shoulders, was a conspicuous figure, as he urged along his men, caring nothing for danger.[25] By the end there were only three casualties: two men and a dog, hit in the leg. 'Hostilities ceased at sunset', and Garibaldi spent the evening trying to rally the apprehensive inhabitants of Marsala. Since his supporters had the reputation of being *mangiapreti* (priest-eaters), it was natural that the bishops, monks and friars should be among the first to pledge their support. As a token of goodwill, the Jesuits were compelled to throw out their blankets one by one from their windows.

Commander Winnington-Ingram's diary for the next day began:

*12 May 1860*

At 5 a.m. the officer of the watch reported that the red-shirted troops were marching out of Marsala by the south road, and they numbered about eight hundred. Soon afterwards Consul Cossins came on board with the information that Garibaldi himself was with the landed force, and had sent a message requesting that I would receive on board the *Argus* the crews of the Sardinian steamers he had run away with him

from Genoa. This I declined doing, as it would have been a breach of
neutrality.

It was a fortunate decision, and an important one when the time came
for accusations of collusion. On that very day, indeed, the Neapolitan
Prime Minister Carafa was writing to Elliot that 'an act of the most barbarous piracy has been perpetrated by a horde of brigands' and that fire had
been 'obliged to be suspended because of two English steamers impeding'.
The Sardinian crews were in a state of some panic and had evidently been
given shelter in the *Baglio* Ingham.

Next there was a visit from Acton. He came to say that he had been
ordered by his senior officer on the *Partenope* to destroy the grounded
*Lombardo* by firing shot at her 'as she lay in line with the British wine
establishments'. Would Winnington-Ingram 'warn the people there to
keep clear'?

I requested him to destroy the vessel by some other means, as he would
now have no enemy to contend with, as Garibaldi and his men were in
full march on Palermo. He seemed surprised and disconcerted to learn
that the great revolutionary leader was present with the troops, and
went away muttering that he must obey his commander-in-chief's
orders. I sent an officer on shore to warn the residents at the wine
stores.

Needless to say, there was fresh dismay at the *bagli*, and 3000 dollars in
cash were sent from Woodhouse's for safekeeping on the *Argus*. 'The wives
and daughters of the employers were also about to embark, when I was
able to reassure them, and pointed out that their lives were no longer in
danger' – for the Neapolitans had now sent boats to set fire to the *Lombardo*.
Once more the miserable Sardinian crews beseeched him to let them come
on board; to this Winnington-Ingram made the unpopular suggestion that
they might in the long run be safer if they went after Garibaldi on his
march westwards. Just to make things more involved, he also found a
'Neapolitan agent' sheltering in the *Baglio* Ingham, 'he being afraid of returning to the town on the chance of falling in with the Garibaldinians'.
He met other refugees too:

When visiting Mr and Mrs Hervey at Mr Woodhouse's wine establishment, I was introduced to the American consul and his wife, who had
taken refuge there, so as to be under British protection. They had, nevertheless, a narrow escape from the fire of the Neapolitan ships, a shot

having passed close to the English flag flying over the stores, and another had gone through the wall of the latter and destroyed two large casks of wine.

A substantial party of patriot volunteers from Monte Giuliano (Erice) passed Marsala on its way to join Garibaldi. Trapani, being heavily garrisoned, could not send any men. The total number of volunteers from Monte Giuliano eventually came to about 700 – which must have left the little town just about emptied of able-bodied persons. Only 300 went from Marsala, and there were 600 from Castelvetrano. The Thousand, therefore, was soon in effect swollen to about 2500; even this was quite inadequate (especially taking into account their antique armament) in face of the Neapolitan forces under General Landi, now advancing from Palermo towards the small town of Calatafimi, near the haunted, lonely ruins of the temple of Segesta.[26]

Garibaldi was wise to have marched off without wasting time. If he had allowed his enemy to block the entrances to the hilly (and soon mountainous) interior, there would have been scarcely any hope for him. Before leaving, he had presented Cossins with the flag of the *Lombardo*.[27] The character of the acting Vice-Consul – alert and forceful – was just the kind that appealed to Garibaldi. And Cossins for his part had been swept with admiration for the general, so much so – the *Stromboli* having now steamed off, and Marsala being quiet again – he deemed it safe to ride into the hills after the Thousand. In due course he returned, his saddle-bag packed with letters from the great man, Türr, Sirtori and others for their wives and children.

The following day the *Partenope* also disappeared. Now it was the turn of Winnington-Ingram to feel that he could justifiably leave the town. He was worried about the fate of his unprotected countrymen in Palermo. Yet when he got there, he found the situation not quite as critical as he had feared, though people were clamouring for protection on board.

Earthworks had been thrown up on the Monreale road, and two thousand foreign troops in Neapolitan pay had arrived the previous day. Nearly everybody in Palermo seemed to be convinced that the *Argus* had gone to Marsala simply in order to help Garibaldi. Whenever Winnington-Ingram and his officers appeared in the streets, they were greeted with cries of 'Viva Argoose!' He of course visited his old friends the merchants, who to a man were insistent that he should stay on and guard them. Unfortunately the *Argus* was that evening ordered back to Marsala. As he sailed off, Winnington-Ingram noticed that the hills above Palermo were still 'ablaze with beacon-fires kindled by the patriots to denote the positions of the various *squadre* who had responded to Garibaldi's call to arms'.

He reached Marsala the next day, the sixteenth. The *Intrepid* had also left, and the population had meanwhile become much emboldened. Demonstrations were in full force, and tricolour flags were everywhere. For news had just been received of Garibaldi's dramatic victory at Calatafimi. Winnington-Ingram went by carriage to see Corlett's partner Mr Gill, who had a country house outside the city and was caring for the two Garibaldinians wounded on the eleventh. Whilst there he was brought a despatch from General Landi to the Viceroy that had somehow been intercepted. 'Help! Send us help immediately or we are lost', it began. But that help had never come. . . .

All the way from Marsala Garibaldi had been welcomed with wild enthusiasm. Bells rang in the churches. Monks and priests marched alongside. 'The populace take fire whenever they see him', wrote one of his supporters.[28] Baron Favara, the future father-in-law of Corrado Valguarnera, was among the local landowners who gladly allowed the motley army through their properties.

The Thousand passed among orange and lemon plantations, then climbed the mule tracks lined with agaves and prickly pears, through olive groves to an even more desolate landscape; deep waterless ravines, tumbled rocks, resembling 'the day after Judgment Day'.[29] On the thirteenth Garibaldi had reached Salemi, where he proclaimed himself Dictator of Sicily in the name of Victor Emmanuel. He stayed there until the morning of the fifteenth, and later that day, in parching heat, the battle had taken place. The fighting was fierce and cruel. Many of the Neapolitan dead were found to have bayonet wounds in their heads. Thirty of the Garibaldinians had been killed, and Garibaldi's own son, Menotti, had been wounded. And some of the bravest fighters had been the Franciscan friars.

Calatafimi created the necessary legend of invincibility. That night the victors slept on the battlefield, while General Landi's men hastened back to Palermo. Stragglers were hacked down by the peasants, telegraph wires were cut, supplies of food destroyed. The Neapolitans found themselves facing the full horror of guerilla warfare. Even Garibaldi's supporters were sometimes aghast.[30]

The Sicilians may have behaved savagely towards the Neapolitans, but the troops themselves had perpetrated some ghastly crimes. Garibaldi saw signs of these, the burnt-out houses, the charred bodies of women and children, as he marched from the valley of Alcamo – now more fertile – to

Partinico, only twenty miles from Palermo, defended by 23,000 troops.

The British families in the capital, needless to say, were becoming ever more apprehensive, especially as they still had no naval force to protect them. There are two letters from Joseph Whitaker for this period.

*To Maingay, Robin & Co., Naples*                                    *17 May 1860*
All communications with the rest of the island are interrupted. . . . As to the disembarkation being said to have failed, your *Giornale* as usual has given a false story. Far from failing, it was completely successful. Garibaldi in person with a respectable staff and a force of 800 to 1000 men, plenty of ammunition and stores and four field pieces, landed safely at Marsala the 11th inst. with hardly a casualty. It is also said another force has landed on the same coast somewhere about Sciacca, but it wants confirming. We are fast approaching a crisis, and that there will be a dreadful struggle everything around us does not allow the least doubt. The *Amphion* frigate is the only man-o'-war and cannot give protection to all the English on shore, and unfortunately no merchant vessels are to be found. The *Argus* is at Marsala to protect British subjects and property there. It is confidently reported that Garibaldi and his forces, including a large number of insurgents, will be arriving at Monreale shortly. The new *Luogotenente* General Lanza arrived day before yesterday, and Prince Castelcicala left us yesterday at noon. A report says that Lanza[31] has got the King's *alter ego*. We shall see soon what he may do, although we greatly fear that any concessions he may have brought or will offer will have arrived too late.

*To J. Smithson, Messina*                                    *17 May 1860*
We are in a complete fix . . . without any government or in a position tantamount to it saving the mere semblance by name. . . . The people are become so elated that nothing it is thought will now satisfy them, not even the constitution. We continue thank God quiet in the city as well as in the vicinity. How long it will last it is impossible to say, we fear not long and are therefore preparing our minds gradually for whatever may happen. Our Senior, alone in Palermo, is totally disdainful of danger.

# XII

## *Doomed to be Bombarded, if not Sacked and Burned*

ON 15 May Admiral Mundy had returned from his cruise to Valetta, where he learnt of Garibaldi's 'desperate enterprise' at Marsala and the march on Palermo. At once he applied to Admiral Fanshawe for permission to sail back to Sicily; this was granted on the eighteenth, so that evening 'by means of torches at the fair way buoys' the *Hannibal*, a screw liner of ninety guns, steamed out of the harbour. By midnight she was passing Gozo lighthouse 'with a moderate breeze in our favour, and with a sea as smooth as could be desired'.[1]

At sunset the following evening she was close to Marsala, where signals were exchanged with Winnington-Ingram.

The sea was no longer smooth, and the Admiral reached Palermo in wind and storm. He found the *Intrepid* and the *Amphion* waiting for him, also the French paddle frigate *Vauban*, and two small Piedmontese steamers. Consul Goodwin, greatly relieved, at once came aboard bringing with him a disturbing missive, an official circular in fact, signed by General Salzano and containing the warning that if an insurrection broke out in the city he would not be responsible for the 'consequences that might happen to foreigners who may remain in this city'.

Mundy decided that the time had come to recommend that the families of all British merchants and residents should take refuge on board the warships in the harbour. He also instructed Goodwin to tell the United States Consul that any American citizen would be equally welcome to the protection of Her Majesty's ships, 'if such should be their desire'. Meanwhile a strong note was sent to Lanza, expressing surprise at a circular 'which seemed to imply an inability or a disinclination to control the action of the troops'. Mundy was keeping a diary too, and he wrote:

The city is now declared in a state of siege, is deserted by the upper classes, all business at an end, and the shops entirely closed. Of the movements of Garibaldi nothing certain is known. He is reported to be in the mountains with his volunteers and armed peasantry . . . but what his numbers are, and what his plans, no one as yet seemed to know.

The next morning, the twenty-first, it was decided to take things further. At 8 a.m. Mundy fired a royal salute, 'hoisting the Neapolitan flag at the main'. There was an immediate reply from the guns of the Castellamare citadel. At 11 a.m. he landed in full uniform and drove in an open barouche to the Palace.

It was as if passing through a city of the dead, or of one decimated by plague. Containing two hundred thousand persons, not an inhabitant was to be seen, nor was there a vehicle abroad, save that which I occupied. Troops were everywhere posted, and the only sound which I heard was the tramp of the soldiery, who, either on patrol, or on guard, or on bivouac in the squares, held possession of the avenues leading to the forts and the military stations.

At the Palace he was first greeted by the notorious Maniscalco and then conducted to General Lanza, whom Mundy found 'replete with dignity and courtesy' though – being an octogenarian – very feeble in the limbs and no substitute for Castelcicala. There was a guarded exchange of views, but Garibaldi's name was never mentioned. Maniscalco, 'whose deeds of oppression and cruelty have long made him the terror of every inhabitant of this Island,' stood by the Viceroy's chair the whole while, but not a word was addressed to him. When Mundy left and reached the bottom of the staircase, he found that his hired barouche had been sent back to its owner and that one of the Viceregal carriages was waiting in its place to take him back to the Marina.

On his return to the *Hannibal* he decided to be more explicit and wrote to Lanza, deploring Salzano's circular and requesting ample notice if there was to be a bombardment of Palermo, 'in order that if possible the property of British subjects may be saved from destruction'. He ended with a tart sentence: 'I trust, however, that a measure so extreme and deplorable as the bombardment of an open town may not be resorted to.'

Meanwhile Garibaldi's troops were reported to be only eleven miles from the capital. Counting the *squadre*, they now numbered some 5 or 6000 men. On the twenty-first Rosolino Pilo had been shot dead near Monreale, and his loss was regarded as a severe blow for the Thousand – 'that brave Sicilian and Italian patriot, who thus died on the eve of the consummation of his life's work'.[2] Corrado Valguarnera di Niscemi and his four friends were moved to Castellamare, and there were rumours that their execution was imminent.

During the afternoon, [wrote Mundy] I received a communication from three young ladies of the Sicilian aristocracy, whose husbands were confined in the citadel on charge of high treason, requesting me to intercede with General Lanza for the preservation of their lives. These noble ladies, the Princess Pignatelli, the Princess Niscemi [*sic*, mother], and Baroness Riso, of course assured me that their affectionate husbands were themselves the victims of a conspiracy, and innocent as lambs.

He had to tell them that he could not see that he would be able to be of much help, but promised nevertheless to speak to Lanza when he had the chance.

A meeting of the principal British merchants had been arranged at the Consulate later in the day. Mundy came ashore to make an address. He explained his own views and the measures he had taken for the protection of their property, and concluded by urging that they and their families should go on board the British warships as soon as possible. 'Mr Ingham, the oldest English resident, now in his eighty-second year, married to a Sicilian duchess, and in possession of immense wealth in the Island, was the only opponent of this measure. He felt convinced the Royal troops would be able to maintain order, and he should therefore refuse to leave his mansion and seek safety in flight.'

The Admiral had got mixed over ages. It was the Duchess who was aged eighty-two – 18 May had been her birthday. Ingham was now seventy-five. At any rate he had been through far too many revolutions and scares of revolutions to want to go to all that upheaval. He did not care a rap for Garibaldi.

The Whitaker family went aboard the *Intrepid*. The ship was terribly overcrowded, and there was a strong north-east wind with driving rain. Those heaving decks were not an auspicious start to the life of the latest and last Whitaker child, Albert, only a fortnight old. Certainly others on board did not find Albert's wailing any comfort in their seasickness. The Roses went to the *Amphion*, all except for James Rose, the father – he too had decided to stay on shore, but not for Ingham's reason; being a fervid supporter of 'Piddu', he wanted to be sure of being in Palermo on the day of his hero's entry.

Ingham's point of view seemed likely to have some justification when Mundy received a reassuring letter from Lanza. Apparently, so the letter ran, orders had already been given 'to guarantee as much as possible the property of all strangers'. Lanza said he 'shrank' from the thought of putting the city to the horrors of a bombardment, though he did feel constrained to remind the British Admiral that if there was an attack on Palermo by the rebels he could not 'wait an instant to react with the artillery for saving the army I have the honour to command'. He also agreed that his Commander in Trapani should be ordered to return the weapons taken from the British residents in Marsala.

Five Neapolitan men o'war were now anchored off Castellamare. The American corvette *Iroquois*, under the command of Captain Palmer, arrived suddenly in the harbour on the evening of the twenty-second, so it became unnecessary for United States citizens – comprising mostly the Gardners and the Consul's family – to go on board British warships. As Mundy wanted Captain Marryat to hurry to Trapani to take possession of the British weapons in the fortress there, and to return them to their owners before any change of mind on the part of Lanza, the Whitakers were also transferred to the *Iroquois*, while other refugees from the *Intrepid* went to the *Hannibal*.

The following day Mundy had his return visit from Lanza, who came to the *Hannibal* dressed 'in full fig', as a correspondent wrote to *The Times*. Consul Goodwin was also present. Lanza made emphasis of the fact that he himself was a Sicilian by birth, and seemed indeed to be in a state of great distress. The request he now made was surprising: he asked whether Mundy would agree to act as mediator between the contending parties, so that an armistice could be arranged. Mundy very naturally refused, saying that he could not contemplate such a thing without first receiving instructions from Henry Elliot in Naples. He wrote:

I next adverted to the case of the nobles imprisoned as conspirators. His Excellency at once offered to set them at liberty if I would guarantee their good conduct. This was of course inadmissible – for who should rightly interpret the meaning of such a phrase? – but in the most courteous manner he promised me that their lives should be spared, which joyful intelligence Mr Goodwin undertook to convey to their wives.

Then General Lanza took Goodwin to one side and reiterated that he could not see any solution other than Mundy's own personal intervention. He also told him that if the Constitution of 1812 were to be proclaimed forthwith, he believed that might well be sufficient to pacify the people of Sicily. Mundy was appalled that Lanza should even think it was in a British Admiral's power to grant a constitution. The fact 'furnished ample proof of his unfitness for his post at such a crisis. A handful of adventurers were at the gates of the Capital, and a well-appointed army of 25,000 men was ready to attack them.' One vigorous effort by the Neapolitans would have been enough to scatter them.

Lanza finally left the *Hannibal*, 'to the salute of nineteen guns'. That night it was reported that the heights overlooking Palermo to the east were covered with bands of armed peasantry carrying the tricolour flag. The fires from their various camps now seemed provocatively close. Garibaldi was said to be near Misilmeri, just nine miles away. His attack was expected within the next forty-eight hours, or even the next morning. Count Tasca sent a message to Mundy to ask him if he would care to send an officer to watch and report on events from his 'lofty mansion' outside the Porta Termini, but 'this kind proposition I begged leave to decline'.

Tension was increasing with every hour. There were now fifteen foreign warships in the harbour – British, American, Spanish, Austrian, French, and Piedmontese. Behind them were some hundred merchant ships, crowded with refugees. A few of the Neapolitan ships were drawn up alongside the Mole, their broadsides swung ominously towards the Marina. It was quite clear that there would be no mercy for the city when Garibaldi's attack came. There was another visit, this time very tense, to the Palace to see Lanza. Again Maniscalco was present. He actually asked Goodwin 'if he did not think a population deserved to be annihilated, should they rise up in insurrection against the constituted authorities'. There follows a passage, again often quoted, in Mundy's diary:

> To this unexpected and ill-timed demand Her Majesty's Consul indig-nantly replied that he could not have supposed such a question would have been put to him; but that as Signor Maniscalco had chosen to do so, he had no hesitation in saying that when a people were tyrannised over they had an inherent right to take up arms, and to fight against their oppressors. This manly reply seemed to astonish the questor, and drew forth a remark from General Lanza that he did not imagine the English Admiral would endorse the Consular opinion. I declined enter-ing on the subject.

Mundy on his return could thus bring little cheer to his fellow country-men. Indeed he could only urge those remaining on shore to hasten to the warships. Again Benjamin Ingham refused utterly to budge. James Rose had for the time being disappeared. Mundy and Goodwin paid a visit the next day to the outskirts of Palermo, and from a tower they saw the burning villas of nobles who were supposed to be hostile to the royal cause. 'In whichever direction I looked, over this vast and richly cultivated plain, the smoke of ruins and devastation presented itself to my view, whilst the constant report of musketry and the distant sound of cannon showed that armed men were in collision on the slopes of the hills.'

Joseph Whitaker had managed to write a letter:

> *To J. Smithson, Messina*                                    *25 May 1860*
>
> We avail of the departure of H.M.S. *Assurance* to write these few lines, the chief object therein being to mention that we continue safe and well. . . . It is to be feared we are approaching events of far greater importance and we can only hope we shall come out of them scatheless as hitherto. We fear however the city is doomed to be bombarded, if not sacked and burned. The General in Chief has promised us that our houses and stores will be respected as far as possible. It is very fortunate that our Admiral arrived here so opportunely, as the Authorities cannot afford to treat so lightly with him as they did with the Consul.

On the afternoon of the twenty-sixth, at the same time as Mundy and Goodwin were visiting the suburbs, three young British officers – Lieutenant Wilmot, Lieutenant Cooper and Mr Morgan, a paymaster – had daringly gone on a sightseeing jaunt to Misilmeri. And there, to their surprise (as they said later), they had found Garibaldi having dinner with his men in a vineyard. The 'men' were in fact mostly youths, between the ages of fifteen and eighteen, dressed in red shirts and grey trousers. Also present were Menotti Garibaldi, 'a stout and tall youth of nineteen' with his arm in a sling as a result of his wound at Calatafimi, Ferdinand Eber *The Times* correspondent, Hungarian by birth, and two American officers from the *Iroquois*. Eber was far from being an unbiased war correspondent – but then most of his *Times* readers would have been sorry if he were; he had actually brought with him the exact details of the location of the Neapolitan troops outside Palermo and of the best ways of forcing an entry into the city.

Garibaldi was in tremendous spirits and busy signing autographs. A calf and quantities of onions were cooking on the fire, beside which was a barrel of marsala. He invited the three Englishmen to share some strawberries 'fresh from the bed', and then 'spoke of his affection and respect for the English people as a nation, and of his hope that before long he should make the acquaintance of the English Admiral'. After this he 'moved to his tent, which was composed of a worn-out old blanket, supported on pikes, before which a child, under the name of a sentry, was pacing to keep off the crowd'. The British and the Americans left together, but first one of the Americans presented Garibaldi with his revolver, which was carried by the General at the time of his entry into Palermo.

An amusing adventure. But Garibaldi's supporters were not all children, though like children most of them enjoyed plenty of noise and colour, armed as they were with old flint muskets, spears, scythes, and rusty cutlasses, tricolour flags – green, white and red – were displayed around the camp, while a host of musicians incited them to martial deeds.

Late that night, whilst Mundy was sitting in his cabin, a note was brought to him 'from an English gentleman, who, fearless of consequences, remained at his house in the city':

Dear Sir,
I hear that a rising will take place at two o'clock tomorrow morning, at which hour or soon after, Garibaldi will be near Porta Sant' Antonio, through which you went out this afternoon, prepared to force his way into the city with the bayonet. Prince Lampedusa will let an officer go up to the tower at the end of the Palace to get a view of the combatants.

The fearless gentleman must have been Rose, whose house was next to the Palazzo Lampedusa overlooking the Marina.

27 May was Whitsunday. Fire was heard on shore at 4 a.m. And sure enough an excited rabble, waving tricolour flags, was soon to be seen racing along the Marina.

Garibaldi had entered by the Porta di Termini, near the Porta Sant' Antonino, at the south end of the Maqueda, as predicted. The gallant Nino Bixio had been among those wounded in the storming of the high barricade. The insurgents, who included elements of the *squadre*, made straight for the Fiera Vecchia, where the 1848 revolution had begun. Soon they had reached the very heart of the city, the Quattro Canti, four beautiful seventeenth-century fountains, built in the period of Philip III of Spain, where the Maqueda crossed the Toledo. The appearance of the people on the Marina was the signal for the bombardment, and all the Neapolitan warships now opened fire indiscriminately on the city. Before long several houses were in flames. Church bells were ringing frantically. The big guns of the Citadel thundered off at regular intervals.

At the first reports of musketry, [wrote Mundy] I had sent the boats of the squadron on shore, to bring off any stray British subjects who might have still clung to their abodes under the hope of a pacific solution, and I gave directions that the aged Mr Ingham, to whom I have already alluded as steadily refusing to avail himself of our protection, should be made acquainted with the fact of one of the cutters being especially told off to convey himself and family to the *Hannibal*. It was destined, however, that he should pay the penalty of his obstinacy. The mansion of the

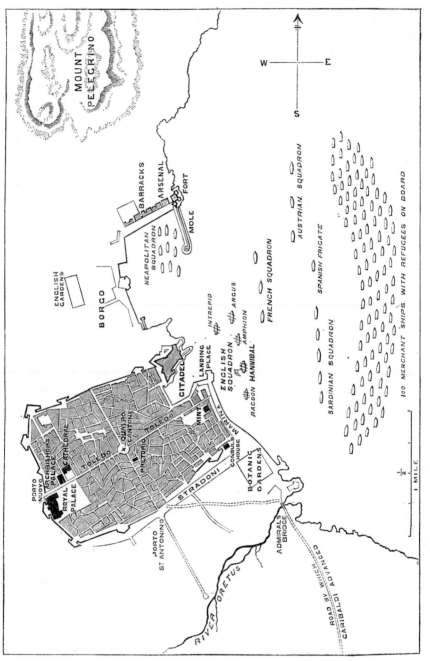

From *H.M.S. Hannibal at Palermo and Naples*, 1836 (facsimile).

great merchant was at some distance from the beach, and before he could make his arrangements for reaching the ark of safety, the tide of battle had flowed onward to the outer walls of his domain. He was now compelled to remain within their circuit, and to trust to the good feelings of the combatants not to molest a British resident.

As for Goodwin, he adamantly refused to leave the Consulate, 'confident that neither party would act in any way injurious to a man who for forty years [a bit of an exaggeration] had dwelt among them'. The red ensign floated over the building, while the courtyard and stables below were packed with women and children. There were now thirty-nine British refugees on board the *Hannibal*, the gunroom being set aside as a nursery for the children, 'an arrangement perhaps not quite convenient to the mids and naval cadets'. Captain Cockran of the *Amphion* had to curtain off half his cabin to 'the ladies of two of the principal firms of the city', including Sophie Rose and Ackie Whitaker, who had asked to be transferred from the *Iroquois* so as to be with her friend.

Soon the whole of the seawards section of Palermo, including the Palazzo Ingham, was in the hands of the insurgents, except for the Mint and Castellamare. Then the bombardment started up again. It was ironical that the Neapolitan warships and their guns, 95 cwt and 68-pounders, should have been British made. The helpless Whitakers watched smoke rise high above the mansion of their 'Senior'. Mundy wrote:

*27 May 1860*
At three o'clock in the afternoon the general bombardment of the ill-fated city, by sea and land, recommenced. My own cabin, at the moment, was crowded with the wives and daughters of the merchants, who had hoped to spend the rest of Sunday evening in quiet repose, instead of being spectators of one of the most awful scenes of destruction from civil discord that modern history has recorded.

Garibaldi was now known to have his headquarters in the Pretorio. 'Solid shot of large calibre were launched at the churches and public and private buildings in the immediate neighbourhood.' The lovely city of Palermo, praised by Brydone, Goethe and so many travellers, was now in danger of total destruction. Those far-famed baroque churches, dating from the Spanish occupation, not to mention the Palatine Chapel, Palermo's greatest masterpiece (should a shot go astray), might soon be lost to the world irrevocably. Captain Flores of the Neapolitan *Ercole*, we read, 'brought both broadsides alternatively to bear on the Toledo, and raked with his heavy metal the whole of that magnificent street from the Marina to the Palace Square.'

But when darkness came, the church bells were still ringing. The city was virtually all in the hands of the people, the main body of Lanza's troops being contained in the Royal Palace. 'All night long, the conflagration continued, but by midnight the bells had ceased to toll, and at that hour, as if by mutual consent, hostilities were suspended.'

During the morning of the twenty-eighth the galley slaves and political prisoners, including Ciccio Brancaccio, escaped from the Vicaria, which had been deserted by Neapolitan troops. Unfortunately Corrado Valguarnera and his friends were still under close guard in Castellamare; nobody knew whether they had yet been executed. Ciccio rushed at once to the barricades, while women and children began the plundering of the Vicaria – the sight of them being the excuse for a further vicious naval bombardment. Mundy agreed to a Neapolitan request to send Lieutenant Wilmot on a mission to find Garibaldi, to get the General to agree to a safe conduct for some of Lanza's men so that a conference could be held on board the *Hannibal*. Wilmot managed this without much difficulty, his British uniform acting as sufficient passport, and the General appeared glad to meet once more the young Englishman who had shared his strawberries at Misilmeri. Mundy had also asked Wilmot to visit the Palazzo Ingham. The old man and the Duchess were safe, and Wilmot gave this account of the scene:

With much difficulty I found my way to Mr Ingham's house, which is situated on the western outskirts of the town, near the English Gardens. The damage done throughout this district is very great, especially in the neighbourhood of Garibaldi's headquarters; but, strangely enough, the vast Palace of the Pretorio, which he occupied, had not a single shell in it, although a church, convent, and other public buildings, which formed the other three sides of the square were riddled, the convent being in flames and completely in ruins. The shells were still falling, and several times I had to shelter myself in a doorway till they exploded. It was also very unpleasant crossing the Toledo and streets facing the Palace and Mint, as the troops were constantly firing down them with musketry and field-pieces. Close to Mr Ingham's house there had evidently been a severe struggle. I saw several Royal artillerymen and horses dead, and still remaining where they had fallen.

The people seemed delighted to see a British officer in the streets, and

22. Catching a *sbirro* outside the Palazzo Tagliavia, Mure delle Cattive, the house of the American Consul, Henry H. Barstow.

23. The release of Corrado Valguarnera and his friends from the Castellamare fort.
Two drawings by Frank Vizetelly from the *Illustrated London News*, July 1860.

24. John Forester
Rose, c. 1876.

25. Corpses of
Zaraundi, Leone and
Lobue.

crowded the balconies, clapping their hands as I passed. They were loud in their entreaties to know if the English Admiral was going to stop the bombardment.

Everyone knew that far worse was likely to come. In fact the visit of Lanza's officers was cancelled, but at least Mundy managed to get the Neapolitans to halt their bombardment of Palermo from the sea.

Ingham's house was being used as a hospital. Some of the worst fighting had been in his garden. The legend runs that when the Duchess spotted a Bourbon soldier trying to cut down the young palm trees for barricades, she came out like a tornado and broke a bottle of marsala over the man's head, thereby knocking him out.

All during the next day severe street-fighting continued. Nevertheless there was no firing from the Neapolitan fleet, anchored now in line of battle right in front of the city. Reinforcements arrived from Naples in two large steamers, their decks and paddleboxes crowded with men. These turned out to be well equipped 'Bavarians', mercenaries of German extraction: a bad omen, and in light grey uniforms they quickly and efficiently set to work. On the thirtieth they forced their way past Palazzo Ingham and reached the rear of the Royal Palace.

Mundy had heard that Goodwin's life had been endangered the day before by a 13-inch shell exploding in his house. Much was his anxiety when the bombardment began again and he observed the guns of the Castella-mare trained in the direction of the Consulate.

Luckily the shelling did not last long. News then came that the prospect of a final 'desperate onslaught' on the Palace had inspired Lanza once more to seek Mundy's mediation, and this time he took the humiliating step of proposing a meeting on board the *Hannibal* with Garibaldi himself. Brave Lieutenant Wilmot was again the emissary, and in the process he found himself caught in the cross-fire between the Sicilians and the Bavarians – to make his presence known he had simply walked into the middle of the street waving a handkerchief. It was during a truce following this small battle that the Sicilian Colonel Giacinto Carini, who with Bixio was one of the commanders of the two battalions of the original Thousand, was badly wounded, 'whilst standing on the top of a barricade with a white flag in his hand, and restraining his own men from firing'.

The Bourbon delegates were Generals Letizia (who had led the punitive expedition to Marsala early in May) and Chretien, and the captains of the American, French and Piedmontese squadrons also came on board, Gari-baldi was dressed in the full uniform of a Piedmontese general. It was not an easy meeting. The three onlookers (the American being Captain Palmer of the *Iroquois*) were much annoyed when asked by Letizia to leave the cabin. Finally it was agreed that there should at least be an armistice until noon the following day. Little did the Neapolitans know how much Garibaldi was bluffing and that he was seriously short of ammunition. Winnington-Ingram, who had also been summoned aboard the *Hannibal*, saw that Garibaldi, on leaving Admiral Mundy's cabin, took Captain Palmer to one side 'and an earnest conversation ensued between them'. It transpired that Garibaldi was asking for ammunition to be landed from the *Iroquois* by night, but Palmer had 'pleaded his neutrality'. Be that as it may, some weeks later Henry Elliot noted that it was 'a curious coincidence that the American ship which was at Palermo during the siege was so short of powder when she arrived at Naples, that she could not even fire a salute'.

Garibaldi's son, Menotti, had also been on board the *Hannibal*. He was much admired by the refugee ladies, wrote Winnington-Ingram, and the fact that this 'fine-looking youth' had his arm in a sling seemed to make him all the more romantic. One of the refugees was Sophie Rose, who happened to have been on the *Hannibal* on a visit from the *Amphion*.

Joseph Whitaker sent a quick report back to Potter Brothers of Liverpool: the family was safe, and the armistice had been prolonged for three days. 'Our Senior bravely kept his house all through the frightful fighting. Although in black humour he is well, as is his Lady. The writer's children are restless on board ship, in view of this oppressive heat.'

During the armistice some British officers were allowed to explore the town and selected merchants were able to visit their homes. Again the officers were appalled by the devastation – a thousand yards of buildings in front of the Royal Palace were a crushed mass of ruins, still smouldering in its ashes. Luckily the little domed Norman church of the Eremiti had been spared, but many fine buildings, including the convents of La Badia Nuova and Dei Sette Angeli, while the palaces of the Princes of Cutò and Santa Ninfa had been sacked and burnt. There were tales of dreadful atrocities – bayonetings, crucifixions and immurings alive[3] – and the air was horribly infected with the stink of decaying corpses. Mundy sent his own surgeon Dr Walker, to deal with the wounded Garibaldinians, Carini and the Hungarian Colonel Tükory, dying from the effect of a badly amputated leg. They were at the Trinacria Hotel, in normal times still a favourite spot for British officers and run by the eccentric old Ragusa, 'an uncompromissing patriot'. Ragusa told Winnington-Ingram with indignation how Palermitan nobles had tried to flee, but had been stopped by Garibaldi's men.

On 2 June a dance was held on board the *Hannibal*. Two of the guests were the Colonel Stefan Türr, another Hungarian, a dashing cavalier to look at, with splendid twirled moustaches, and of course the handsome Menotti. 'The latter,' said Winnington-Ingram, 'was evidently making the most of his time with the fair sex and danced incessantly.' His chief partner was little Sophie Rose. Luckily we again have fragments of description of the young people on that enchanted night.[4] Sophie, 'beautifully proportioned and elegant in her movements,' had her 'voluminous tresses threaded with black ribbon, the ends of which fell to her waist; she wore an 'ample and long dress of finest lace, dotted with small flowers and green ribbons', while 'simple gold ornaments hung from her ears and neck, and bracelets clasped her wrists'. A delectable creature indeed for Menotti, who was exactly her age. Ackie, with 'light crispy hair and heavy eyebrows' and 'a determined look', her face 'pleasing' withal, was not so keen on flirting, as she was in love with Ben Gardner – unfortunately a love that was doomed. Carrie Whitaker, Ackie's youngest sister, had 'black hair, blue eyes, a coral mouth and rosy cheeks', with a 'modesty of deportment, an innocence of voice laugh and movement'; but she was a bit young for Menotti. Another Sophie, Sophie Whitaker, aged eighteen, was also one who danced with Menotti – a lively, humorous creature, though we have no precise description of her. Also present were the 'jesuitical' Lyla Morrison, Charlotte Gardner, Martha Gardner and Maria Carcaci, burning still with her 'consuming love' for James Rose junior. Of the young English civilians George Rose was much in evidence, also eighteen. He was as 'agile as a skylark' when he danced, 'always jovial and laughing'. We are told that his three younger brothers, the smallest being Forester Rose, aged seven – 'with dark hair, rosy cheeks, eyes as light as stars' – became obviously so tired by the end of the evening that they were all made to lie on a sofa 'showing much need but little willingness to go to bed'.

3 June was to have been the end of the armistice, so more refugees – bringing their beds with them – packed on board the foreign ships. A Baroness Giuliano, with numerous nephews and nieces, and an Irish priest, Father McGorman, had to make do with sleeping under canvas on the *Argus*. Still Goodwin – 'our brave old Consul, a complete cripple' – remained on shore; he sent news that General Letizia had gone to Naples for further instructions. Meanwhile the armistice was prolonged; and, needless to say, 'gaieties continued afloat and the young British ladies had a good time of it'. Perhaps the following letter from Joseph Whitaker went by Letizia's ship:

*To Maingay, Robin & Co., Naples*　　　　　　　　　　　　*3 June 1860*
We now write these lines to announce the termination of our difficulties
by the troops evacuating the Palace and Castle, taking with them their
arms and baggage etc. The armistice was to expire at noon today, and
great preparations had been made by the insurgents to renew the attack
immediately with vigour. Fortunately it was not destined to take place,
and we shall now be able to land and to return to our homes in peace.

May we beg of you to write to Messrs R. Stephens & Son to advise
them of the above news, and also request them to communicate the
same to Mr Benjamin Ingham Jr in New York, and to Mrs Tidswell
[Ben's youngest sister, Elizabeth], adding that the writer saw Mr Ingham
and the Duchess this morning and both are well, as is also the writer's
family.

There was some wishful thinking here. 'Difficulties' had by no means
terminated, but the very mention that some of the troops had already
withdrawn is interesting. The whole of the interior of the island was now
known to be in a state of revolt. In Catania particularly there had been some
terrible fighting, and the city had been 'given over to the troops to pillage
for thirty-six hours'.

But the extension of the armistice had been in reality an admission of
defeat by Lanza. The next day there appeared this announcement in *The
Times*: 'We publish today news which will gladden the heart of every
friend of liberty in Europe. The insurrection in Sicily is fully, and we trust
finally, victorious.' Again wishful thinking, but the article was illustrative
of the immense excitement that was sweeping Britain. 'Is Garibaldi the
greatest man since Adam, or is he not?' wrote Algernon Swinburne.
Admirers in Glasgow sent £3000 and £11,179; an individual in Manchester sent £450, and a club in Manchester sent 400 rifles of 'first-class
quality'.[5]

Letizia returned from Naples on the sixth, a sultry day, and it was then
that a capitulation was finally signed. Perhaps Vincenzo Florio had had
something to do with this decision; as the most powerful and richest of
Sicilian businessmen he had been summoned for advice to Naples by King
Francis. It was agreed by the Viceroy that the Palace and the whole of the
rest of the city of Palermo, except Castellamare, were really to be evacuated, and there was to be an exchange of prisoners. What was more, wrote
Mundy, it was stipulated that 'the noblemen who had been so long confined in the citadel, and whose lives had been spared at the instigation of
Mr Goodwin and myself, should be released.' A celebration was needed, so

that night 'we had theatrical entertainments on board, performed by the ship's company, and dancing till midnight'.

Corrado was therefore to be freed. Actually, judging from Ciccio Brancaccio's account, he and the others did not leave Castellamare for another ten days, when they were carried in triumph along the streets to the Royal Palace to be presented to Garibaldi. They had not in fact been all that badly treated in the fort, as Ciccio – who had courageously paid them a secret visit – had found out. Almost their worst experiences had been the receiving of secret messages from the outer world. These messages had been concealed in a chamber pot and afterwards had to be destroyed by each prisoner eating a portion – requiring a fair amount of determination.

The withdrawal of the Neapolitan troops was one of the most humiliating sights possible, and Mundy turned away from it in disgust. Some fifteen thousand men, cavalry and infantry, marched along the Marina to the Mole, waiting for embarkation. As they passed, ragged Garibaldinians contemptuously presented arms. That afternoon Mundy himself landed and went straight to see Benjamin Ingham. 'I found him in good health, and was glad to hear that his house had been respected by both parties. The officer of the Royal troops had requested him to keep his windows closed, and not to let anyone show himself; in that case he would answer that he would not be molested by his soldiers. There had been severe fighting in every direction around, but his mansion was uninjured.'

Generally speaking, foreign property had been respected everywhere, though 'one country house, belonging to Signor Fiamingo, who had married an Englishwoman, the sister of Frost, the Chartist leader, was threatened with sack and fire, and was saved by my sending an officer to give the lady protection as a British subject'.⁶ It was reckoned that up to 3000 men had been killed or wounded during the four days' fighting, and as many were in hospital as a result of exposure and lack of food. Approximately 600 civilians had been killed.

The letters from Joseph Whitaker are scanty just at this time. One learns that 'Garibaldi has behaved admirably and we hope he will remain here some time longer as without him all would go wrong in no time' (to Potter Brothers) and that 'we consider one third part of Palermo to be in ruins' (to Maingay, Robin). In a letter to Smithson he wrote:

*To J. Smithson, Messina*                                     *8 June 1860*
The idea and execution of it [the capture of Palermo] was both admirable and again worthy of the man who with so small a force ventured

upon and was able to accomplish so difficult a task. But his men were hardly more than 700–800, say 1100; although a large number of *squadre* was present, he derived but little assistance from them. You will understand from this that what may be called real fighting has been all, or nearly all, effected by the Italians [i.e. as distinct from the Sicilians], who have behaved like heroes, which indeed they are. When required they, English fashion, have recourse to the bayonet, which by the bye was successfully used both at Calatafimi and Palermo. Well may you say there has been ignorance on the part of the Neapolitan generals, but more than this, they and their soldiers have shown a cowardice the like of which history gives no example, and it will be the same at Naples as soon as the mine is sprung there, which will be sooner or later. Pray keep this to yourself, as we don't wish it to be published at large.

A sober account, befitting its sober author. One hopes that it at least gave some comfort to Smithson, who knew well that the next great battle in Sicily would inevitably have to be fought around Messina – whither many of the royal troops from Palermo had now sailed.

# XIII

## *Mercenaries, Victory and Blood Lust*

O N 8 June the *Argus* was ordered once more to the western end of
Sicily. She called first at Trapani, to find the tricolour flag festooned
on all the main buildings, and then sailed on to Marsala, that 'oriental city
lost in the sands',[1] where a great reception had been prepared. The Piedmontese Consul, Sebastiano Lipari, one of the chief wine-merchants,[2] had
hired rooms to give Winnington-Ingram an appropriate reception; among
the refreshments served were tricolour ices. In due course a grand ball was
held at the Woodhouse *baglio*:

'All the élite of Marsala were there, and a native poet composed an
impromptu ode in honour of England. It was received amidst loud shouts
of "Viva La Regina Vittoria", to which a suitable response was made. We
afterwards astonished the Marsalese by dancing "Sir Roger de Coverley"
with the English contingent of the party.'

Traitors were rounded up:

'The Marsala people routed from concealment four of the *sbirri*, or
detectives, employed under the late Government, and led them around
the streets with ropes round their necks.'

In the meantime the British naval squadron at Palermo was increased
by the return of the *Racoon* under Captain Chamberlain and the *Agamemnon*
under Captain Hope. Joseph wrote to Potter Brothers that he had
heard that revolt in Calabria was imminent. He also expected, he said,
that as before the 'enemy' would at all costs hold on to the citadel at Messina. Garibaldi was still in Palermo, waiting for reinforcements from the
north.

The day before General Lanza, in full uniform and covered with decorations, and accompanied by his entire personal staff, had come on board the
*Hannibal* to pay his final respects to Admiral Mundy. That evening he
sailed for Naples with his whole flotilla. The fort had been evacuated and
the white flag of the Bourbons was never seen again in Palermo. The whole
of the island, with the exception of garrisons at Messina (18,000 strong),
Milazzo, Syracuse and Augusta, was now in the hands of Garibaldi. On the
eighteenth the 'second expedition', 2500 men, had arrived at the town of

Castellammare del Golfo,[3] halfway between Palermo and Trapani. It was headed by the valiant Giacomo Medici, who had defended the villa of the Vascello in Rome for four weeks against the French in 1849.[4] Garibaldi immediately made him a Colonel and put him in charge of the first brigade of the sixteenth division.

This expedition consisted of three ships, acquired in the name of an American, De Rohan, and appropriately rechristened the *Washington*, the *Oregon* and the *Franklin*. With Medici on board the *Washington* were some figures of particular note: John Peard, to become almost a legend, thanks chiefly to British newspaper correspondents, and that indefatigable husband-and wife team, Alberto and Jessie Mario.

Peard, 'a fine, soldier-like looking man with the beard of patriarch' (Mundy),[5] aloof, accepting no pay, was often mistaken for Garibaldi, especially when he took to wearing a Calabrian hat. His life seemed to be charmed and he was to play a part of great importance thereafter during Garibaldi's campaign. Winnington-Ingram, on returning to Palermo from Marsala, was lucky enough to meet him:

*30 June 1860*

Anchored in Palermo Bay at 6 a.m. and found it full of warships. . . . On going ashore I found the city very gay, and the people busy in destroying the Castellamare citadel, which had taken such an active part in the bombardment of the town. Military bands were playing on the Marina, and all the beauty and fashion of Palermo were there in carriages . . . I met Captain Peard, a Cornish gentleman of property, better known as Garibaldi's Englishman, who had, for the mere love of fighting, joined the *Cacciatori delle Alpi* in 1859, and, being an excellent shot, did much execution amongst the Austrians.

The Marios were great supporters of Mazzini and thus fervent republicans. Jessie, *neé* White, was English, a brave and at that time boyish looking woman 'of fixed and fiery faith',[6] a kind of Florence Nightingale figure but rather lacking in charm. She and her husband had been in prison together in Genoa in 1857, afterwards marrying in England. As soon as they reached Palermo, they set about forming a foundling hospital for 2000 boys, an extremely successful enterprise run on military lines as a kind of junior version of the 'English Regiment' organised by another Englishman, John Dunne, who had come to Palermo to assist his friend Peard on the eighteenth. The 'Garibaldi epidemic' had now well and truly captured the British imagination.

The Regiment was basically designed to train some 600 *picciotti*, or

Palermo street boys, and like the foundling hospital was a great success. It began at first with eleven Britishers in charge – five officers, four cadets, a sergeant and a sailor. Unfortunately for the Marios, several of their children kept trying to desert to Dunne: 'at night, scrambling up on each other's shoulders, they managed to reach the lofty windows, where, using their sheets for ropes, they dropped into the street, ran home to change their Garibaldi uniforms for native rags, and presented themselves on the morrow to the recruiting officer to receive the *tre tarì*.'[7] Mundy had similar difficulties. When on 3 July he found two of his seamen missing from the *Hannibal,* he naturally and rightly guessed that they had 'deserted to the patriot forces'. Lieutenant Wilmot was sent to Garibaldi to demand their return – at once effected. 'This promptitude of action was just what I expected from the character of the man,' wrote Mundy.

Dunne was known to the Palermitans as 'Milordo', and judging from his photograph he certainly cultivated a supercilious air. He seemed to like to wear a thigh length coat with astrakhan collar and cuffs, a bit trying one would have thought in a Palermo summer. A tall man, he had commanded Bashi Bazouks in the Crimea, where he had – in the words of an *Illustrated London News* correspondent – 'displayed his wonderful powers of disciplining rough lives'. Alberto Mario described how Dunne would sit in a chair in the middle of the Marina, dressed in a suit of Indian silk (without the coat no doubt) and energetically and patiently drill his troops.[8] The activities of the English Regiment were watched with absorption by the Whitaker boys and especially the thirteen-year-old Joss – rather surprisingly in view of his own decidedly non-martial appearance in adult years. Indeed forty years afterwards Joss struck up a friendship with one of Dunne's cadets, Joseph Nelson, in 1860 a good-looking and athletic young man of twenty, in later life to become, more prosaically, an ear, nose and throat specialist in Belfast.

The second in command of the Regiment was Major Percy Wyndham, the real mercenary type, who had spent five years in the French navy and eight in the Austrian army (one hopes not fighting against Garibaldi). Sergeant Daniel Dowling, Irish from Kilkenny, was the most remarkable of them all, perhaps. He turned out to be a natural leader besides an expert at building bridges, constructing earthworks and so on; at Sebastopol he had been with the Royal Artillery.[9] Since the names of the other members of the English Regiment (including that of Joseph Nelson) are inclined to be ignored by writers on Garibaldi it is worth recording them here: the officers – Lieutenants Edward and Alfred Styles, Lieutenant Robert Walker; the cadets – Henry Archer, Alexander Patterson, who was aged only seventeen,[10] and one Clifford; and the sailor – Peter Cunningham. Glamorous figures all to the young Whitakers, and rightly so, as they acquitted themselves outstandingly in battle. Peard was also living at the Trinacria, likewise Carini and several of the wounded – 'Ragusa being the solitary and honourable exception who deigned to receive wounded into his house after the capture of the town.'[11]

But the most favoured of all the foreigners around Garibaldi was French: Alexandre Dumas *père*. At the time of the advance from Marsala he was on his way to the east on his yacht *Emma*, with a bizarre group of passengers including a nineteen-year-old pregnant bucket-maker's daughter, dressed in a violet velvet sailor-suit with sky-blue trimmings, sometimes introduced as his nephew. Dumas, as translator of Garibaldi's memoirs, was an old friend and no stranger to Palermo. So, on receiving the message 'Rally to the sound of my guns', he changed his plans and headed at once for Palermo, where on 9 June he and his colleagues were happily lodged in the Royal Palace, it seems in General Lanza's rooms. Garibaldi himself was content to live in a less sumptuous corner of the Palace. He was always a one for modesty. When he came on board the *Hannibal*, to thank Mundy for his part in bringing about the armistice, and to express his 'unbounded love for England and the British nation', his appearance was quite a contrast to Lanza's: a red shirt, a flowing silk handkerchief, grey trousers, a large curved sabre with a steel scabbard, and a Tyrolean hat with black plumes.

Dumas, the Marios, Peard, Dunne: there was never a question of any of them setting foot in the Palazzo Ingham. 'I turn my back on the infantile exhibitionists who infest this town,' Benjamin Ingham told Schuyler Livingston.

A Government had been formed with the help of Crispi. There were quantities of plans, for the draining of marshes, the building of villages, the creation of new hospitals and schools (the Marios' venture being one example), but there was little time to put them into effect. One minor reform was to forbid the use of the title 'Excellency' when addressing a superior – in *The Leopard* Salina is amused when Tancredi brings him a Tuscan general who calls him Excellency 'in utter contradiction' to one of the Dictator's first decrees. Garibaldi was anxious to press on with his conquests and begin the liberation of the mainland. In spite of this he delayed the process of handing over Sicily to Piedmont, partly because of the intricate personal struggle with Cavour, partly because he felt it was essential for the time being to keep Sicily as a base in preparation for the attack on the mainland. The situation was not helped by Cavour sending out Giuseppe La Farina, a tactless man and loathed by both Garibaldi and Crispi, on a mission with the express object of forcing Garibaldi to agree to the annexation.[12] Finally Garibaldi reached such a pitch of fury over La Farina that on 7 July he had him arrested and placed upon the Piedmontese Admiral Persano's flagship.

By this time the garrison in Palermo numbered about 8000 men. The foreign merchant community, besides Ingham, kept in the background as much as possible. As expatriates they were ambiguously placed – their lives and fortunes were necessarily tied to the country of their adoption, or indeed in some cases birth, yet it was no business of theirs to interfere. Everything had to depend on the presence of warships in the harbour. Like Salina, they observed the 'great show of joy' in the early stages: processions, tricolour cockades, everyone talking, haranguing, declaiming. They had watched the wounded being carried through the streets and heard the 'shrieks of Bourbon police "rats" [*sorci*, literally mice] being tortured in the side alleys.'[13] But soon the wounded were healed and the *sorci* were enrolled in the new police force. We do not know whether Joseph Whitaker or other merchants subscribed financially to the Cause. Probably not, and certainly not Ingham. The lack of interest among the Sicilians at large in this respect was becoming worrying to Garibaldi and his Government. By the middle of July only about £5000 had been collected. Henry Elliot said that he had met a 'Yankee captain' (Palmer?) who had been in Palermo and was an out-and-out sympathiser with Garibaldi, and that this man had told him that the Sicilians 'had done almost nothing to help in the liberation of Palermo'. Travellers, just arrived from Sicily, Elliot said, were full of contempt and indignation. 'I have not seen one single person,' he wrote, 'who has been there and who does not speak in the same way . . . they give little or no money, very few soldiers, and at the same time are full of envy and jealousy of their liberators.'

Commander C. S. Forbes talked of the 'froth and selfishness' in Palermo, Mundy of the 'apathetic and volatile character' of Sicilians. 'Scarcely a man of wealth or weight' had joined the standard. Meanwhile the *squadre* were clamouring for pay, and funds altogether were beginning to fail. The quarrel between Garibaldi and the Government in Turin about the question of immediate annexation was not helpful to morale either.

Of course there were exceptions. Dunne's Regiment and the very mention of *squadre* were proof enough of that. Then there were the young men from grand families like Ciccio Brancaccio and Corrado Valguarnera, both of whom were on noticeably easy terms with the victors; they 'with their friends Emanuele Notarbartolo and Narciso Cozzo, joined up in Türr's brigade.[14] But even these came in for criticism. It was said that the upper classes would only deign to fight for Garibaldi if they were given commissions. Goodwin noted all the familiar characteristics of 1848-9: the passion and the excitement in the beginning, followed by listlessness, disorganisation and lack of a sense of public self-sacrifice. In one of the Consul's increasingly wordy despatches – often larded with apt quotations from Burke, Adam Smith, Senior and the like – he summarised the reasons behind the Sicilian attitude of mind, the cynicism, deceit and savage despair that had grown up under the now defunct Bourbon Government and was still unchanged. The first was obvious enough: maladministration of justice, by which he meant corruption of the legal system, bribery of judges etc. The second: 'tardy despatch of provincial business', because of interference by the Intendant. Then: 3. obstacles to local governments at every turn in the making of roads and in public works generally, due to the 'monstrous system of centralisation'; 4. slowness with which public works proceeded when the permits had at last been given; 5. 'corruption of the clergy and ignorance of the people, involving on the one hand neglect of duties and on the other a want of moral and religious principles'; 6. grinding taxes on the poor.

As far as the peasants were concerned, there had been no miracle with the coming of Garibaldi; indeed there was now a glorious sense of having no Government whatsoever. In Palermo order was kept, but in the interior roaming gangs of ex-*squadre* were beginning to be a nuisance, and some landlords were forced to create their own private armies. People like Don Calogero, father of Angelica in *The Leopard*, were busy making fortunes.

To the Prince of Salina it would have been absurd so coolly to try to analyse the Sicilian predicament in the way that Goodwin had done. To him 'the violence of the landscape, the cruelty of the climate, this continual tension in everything, even these monuments of the past, magnificent yet incomprehensible because not built by us', were as much responsible. 'For two thousand five hundred years we've been a colony. Sleep, my dear Chevalley, sleep, that is what Sicilians want, and they will always hate anyone who tries to wake them.'

It is a little surprising that it was not until 30 June that royalist refugees of 'rank and stature' should claim asylum on board the *Hannibal*. Yet the fact that they were so far unscathed was a tribute to Garibaldi's magnanimity. Among them was Michele Celesti. Mundy was not all that helpful, but perhaps because of Celesti's English wife he arranged for him and three others to be sent to Malta on the *Intrepid*.

Earlier there had been an incident which had involved the honour of the United States. As Mundy wrote:

> Garibaldi was also much chagrined at receipt of intelligence of the capture of the American clipper *Charles and Jane*, with nine hundred volunteers on board bound to Palermo. This vessel was taken off Cap Corse by the Neapolitan frigate *Fulminante*, and carried under the batteries of the fortress of Gaeta, when the passengers were made prisoners. The American Minister had made strong remonstrances on the subject, and hopes were entertained of their release . . . doubts existed of the legality of the act.

The *Charles and Jane* had been in the company of a smaller Piedmontese vessel, the *Utile*. It was hardly surprising that the Neapolitans felt themselves entitled to take such action, since the men on board were intended to be supplementary to Medici's expedition. All the same they were technically in the wrong, since the seizure had taken place outside their coastal waters. The *Iroquois* was despatched at once, and in due course the men were released, to be shipped to Sicily on the *Amazon*, this time British owned, so that they were providentially able to take part in the Battle of Milazzo and kill some Neapolitans. Within three months of the taking of Palermo it was reckoned that 20,000 reinforcements came south from Genoa and Leghorn. In mid-July a shipload of British volunteers arrived on a merchant steamer from Liverpool, and earlier there had been another, principally of Frenchmen, from Genoa. C. S. Forbes wrote from northern Italy that 'such is the mania for going to Sicily, that the Piedmontese have been obliged to take very stringent measures to prevent the army deserting wholesale.'

Mundy decided that, after seven weeks, the time had come for him to leave Palermo, and on 7 July the *Hannibal* lifted her anchors and steamed out of the Palermo roads for Naples, where obviously British subjects would soon need protecting. First he paid his call on Garibaldi in the Royal Palace. He was taken aback to find him 'so thin and careworn, evidentally harassed in mind and devoid of his usual composure'. But then La Farina was about to be arrested. The *Hannibal* was some distance out to sea when she was overtaken, and a personal letter was delivered to Mundy from Garibaldi, a letter that was charming and flowery in the way that only Italians can express gratitude.

Meanwhile troops were gradually fanning out in the direction of Messina. Medici marched out of Palermo along the coast with 1800 men. Corrado and his friends in Türr's brigade reached the small and rather squalid village of Villafrati. There they met Dumas and his young mistress, and the two shared the same lodgings with them in adjoining rooms. Dumas did all the cooking, and his high-spirited Emile was an adept at chopping off flies' heads without injuring their bodies; she would also sit on his lap while he dashed off his articles.[15] At night there were pillow-fights. A merry war indeed.

Türr was obliged to give up the command of his brigade, as he was still suffering from the wounds he had received in 1859. His place was taken by Ferdinand Eber, who continued at the same time to manage to be correspondent for *The Times*, though for a while, admittedly, his articles became less frequent and decidedly less vivid. Later the young nobles resigned and joined a new battalion under Major Niederhäusern.[16] On 20 July they landed near Milazzo. 'The thunder of cannon informed us that the battle had already begun.'

The Battle of Milazzo was to Messina what Calatafimi had been to Palermo. Ironically the castle had been fortified by the British during the Napoleonic Wars. It was in a dramatic situation on the isthmus of a four-mile peninsula. The scenery along that part of the coast was exceptionally pictureque; being volcanic, the farmland was heavily cultivated, and out to sea there were views of the Aeolian Islands and Stromboli.

Medici clashed first with the Neapolitan General Bosco on 15 July. As soon as Garibaldi knew that battle was imminent, he hurried by sea to Patti in the *City of Aberdeen*, in the company of the men from the *Charles and Jane*. His appearance at Milazzo had an extraordinary effect on morale; 'there is an intimate communion of mind between Garibaldi and the masses that is positively electrifying', wrote Forbes, and Brancaccio saw him 'swimming in noisy admiration like a fish in water'. For sheer valour the Dictator's behaviour was magnificent. He would go charging ahead regardless of bullets, and on one occasion he seized the bridle of a Neapolitan captain's horse and with his sabre slashed the man across the neck.

It was reckoned that Bosco had 6500 men and Medici at first 4400 – though later this number was increased somewhat by volunteers. Bosco's downfall was partly due to the fact that he believed he was facing a force of at least 7000. It was one of the hardest fought battles in Garibaldi's experience. The Neapolitans, for a change, stood their ground very well, better – it was said – than the Austrians had ever done. Cosenz was wounded, and so was Corte, leader of the *Charles and Jane* contingent. Young Patterson was hit three times, and Wyndham was also wounded. Medici's horse was killed under him. Peard did tremendous work with his sharpshooter on the bridge, and suffered losses. At one desperate moment, Peter Cunningham, the sailor, asked Wyndham to pitch him over a seven foot wall into a vineyard where a Neapolitan detachment was known to be lurking. His sudden appearance had its effect, and the enemy 'scampered off right and left'.

The British cadre of Dunne's regiment now numbered thirty-seven. Dunne, feeling that his own men were not being quite vigorous enough and inspired perhaps by Cunningham's example, dashed up at the gallop and started throwing *picciotti* over walls 'like puppets'.[17] The Neapolitans again were terrified, shouting 'They can fly! They can fly!' By the time Bosco surrendered, about 750 Garibaldinians had been killed or wounded. As for Corrado and the Niederhäusern battalion, despite bayonet charges, showers of grape-shot, bullets whistling in the most unexpected directions, and some exceedingly reckless behaviour, it seems that everyone was unscathed. They had now been joined by Carlo Ascenso, Benjamin Ingham's fourth stepson. When the battle was quite over, they were sketched in martial attitudes by the correspondent of the *Illustrated London News*. A wounded Neapolitan, his face covered with bandages, was so stoical about his approaching death that they were moved to tears; the English correspondent, however, continued to draw, 'with that lack of feeling which so characterises that nation' – a comment which, in this second half of the twentieth century, must find an echo in many people's minds when faced with press photographs of horrific deeds of war.

The Marios were there with first-aid. They worked mostly in a commandeered monastery. Almost immediately they spotted some of their boys who had escaped from the foundling hospital. Alberto described how he saw three of them lying on some straw; 'on one of the beds abandoned by the monks, lay a little fellow asleep, an ice-bladder on the stump of his lost left arm.' The boy was only twelve. Jessie had been present at the amputation, and Mario recorded that the boy had said: 'I'll be good if you hold me, *signora*; if it hurts I won't scream. I'll only cry a little.' By the end Jessie had cried far more than he. Alberto continued:

"Are you angry with us, *Signor Comandante?*" asked one of the elder lads, taking my hand and stroking. "Such lots of our brigade were killed; our colonel says that after the battle of Milazzo, no one can say again that Sicilians won't fight."'

Alberto felt suddenly suffocated. He rushed out into the open air.

There had been three American officers at Milazzo: Dr Warwick, a captain from Richmond, Virginia, Lieutenant Joseph P. Agresta and Captain Watson. Another arrival there – English – was the Hugh Forbes who had sported a white stovepipe hat on the retreat from Rome, and who had meanwhile been in America, 'where he had had some peculiar dealings with old John Brown previous to the Virginia raid'.[18] He was no relation to Commander Forbes and, much to his disgust, had been left in charge of the garrison at Milazzo with 1000 men, while Medici advanced towards Messina. It was his idea that Edward Styles should go to London to help in the raising of a British Legion. Garibaldi had been easily convinced, even though Dunne was not in favour. Actually it would have probably been as well if Dunne's advice had prevailed. Styles had fought well at Milazzo but once in London he came to be regarded as corrupt and 'sinister'. The Legion, when it reached Italy, proved hopelessly amateur and a great liability.[19] Other volunteers arrived in groups or independently soon after Milazzo. Among them were Edward Bowra[20] and the author's great-grandfather and namesake, Raleigh Trevelyan, aged nineteen and eighteen respectively.

Milazzo was won on 23 July. After five days of negotiation General Clary surrendered Messina, and Medici entered on the twenty-eighth. All Sicily had now been conquered.

C. S. Forbes when he entered the city found it almost deserted, 'more like some city of the dead than the bustling Messina of former days, when the drums of your ears were almost cracked by the cries of itinerant vendors.' He ran into Rickards, the Vice-Consul, and over sundry *granite*, in the company of sundry thirsty Garibaldinians, listened to 'his history of the pains and penalties to which they had been subjected since Easter week'. Apparently there had been a general exodus at that time. Then confidence had briefly returned. Finally there had been another exodus when Garibaldi landed at Marsala. The various Consuls had been forced to stay at their posts, but Smithson, the Sandersons etc. had wisely made their escape to Malta.

Another arrival was Count Arrivabene. He had reached Palermo a few days before with 'a host of Englishmen, and two or three vivacious Irishmen, one of whom, though an amusing fellow, seemed to have sworn never to pay his bill at the hotel'. He joined Garibaldi as a war correspondent at his headquarters, the Punta Faro.[21] On Messina he wrote:

What a variety of uniforms. . . . Here comes by a well known Countess in a half-hussar, half-amazonian dress;[22] there the sharpshooters of Colonel Peard are parading in their brown blouses. Down below, several of Dunne's regiment are being drilled by their English officers, the elegance of whose red jackets contrasts with the rougher costume of their comrades. On the left of a dirty *osteria*, towards the beach, a hut has been constructed; and a large inscription tells the passer-by that the 'Albion Club' has been established there. British activity is never at fault: where there are ten Englishmen there must always be a club.

As for the Whitakers, all we know of them at this moment (apart from the fact that Willie was in the U.S.A. 'buying rags') is that on 22 July, at the very height of the Battle of Milazzo, Albert was christened by the Rev. Charles Wright. Ingham was sulking at home, trying to get his windows mended. 'There is not a glazier, let alone a pane of glass, to be had under this accursed régime,' he wrote. At the other end of the island, Winnington-Ingram was having a most enjoyable time. He had met the new governor of Trapani, who had been appointed on 22 June and who turned out to be Colonel Carmelo Ascenso. He had visited Segesta and Carmelo had helped him to buy coral, for which Trapani was famous. On Garibaldi's birthday, the nineteenth, there had been a big *festa* at Marsala, with illuminations at night and a 'transparent picture of Garibaldi landing' and, amusingly, being welcomed by enthusiastic Marsalese, 'who it is well-known were conspicuous only by their absence'.

We come now to a controversial episode. It is important to cover the affair in some detail, as being a kind of epitaph to Benjamin Ingham, on his life in Sicily, and also because of the effect even now on Anglo-Sicilian relations.

Amari's opinion of the state of security in the island had changed greatly during the past month. On 3 August he wrote that there was 'every sort of disorder in the provinces', though he was still able to add that 'in Palermo there is tranquillity as in time of peace'. It is strange that Winnington-Ingram, during the period of his happy sightseeing among Greek temples, did not make more of the ferment and growing brigandage in the island – one reads in his diary of thirty or forty men trying to attack and rob two Maltese merchant vessels at Marsala, yet even this might simply have been a question of collusion in a smuggling transaction between the captain and mainlanders. But perhaps ferment is too mild a word for what was happening at Bronte, on that very day of 3 August 1860.

As we have already seen, the people of Bronte, when roused to rebellion, had natures as inflammable as dry brushwood. Between 3 and 6 August events occurred in their town that far exceeded the atrocities of previous years. Giovanni Verga, himself born in Catania and a young man at that time, used them as a basis for his gruesome tale *Libertà*, written in 1882. The memory has in more recent times been revived by two leading authors, Carlo Levi and Leonardo Sciascia, who edited the section dealing with the uprising in the standard history of Bronte by Benedetto Radice.[23]

The story is a tragic one, a classic situation of ignorance, poverty, repression, and of the way blood lust can seize hold of crowds and make individuals do things of which they would have never dreamt themselves capable: a microcosm of the Sicilian tragedy, a Vespers on a small scale. It was Radice's contention that the special plight of the people of Bronte was due to sheer despair, and that their despair arose from the attitude of the people running the Duchy. When the uprising was put down, he believed that the horrible measures of retribution were taken simply in order to pacify the British. On the other side, the defenders of the Duchy's reputation have some powerful excuses. As for absenteeism, they point out that it was never possible, because of the war, for Nelson himself to visit Bronte. His brother, heir to the Duchy, was a clergyman and necessarily too occupied with his own calling to be able to travel. He died in 1835; the subsequent holder of the title, Charlotte Lady Bridport (who died in 1873) – as has been seen – could not stand the journey, so she continued to leave an English bailiff in charge. In any case, until 1847, her right to the Duchy was legally in doubt, because of a claim to it in England by the guardians of the third Earl Nelson which had lingered on for nine years.

The property had produced enough income to provide Lady Hamilton with £500 a year, but it did not raise the expected annual income of £3000 – it was a 'sour wilderness' that had been totally neglected by the previous owners, the monks, in the eighteenth century, following the earthquake of 1693. The inhabitants of Bronte maintained that King Ferdinand never even had the right to give the Duchy to Nelson, and that the common land was illegally enclosed. The Duchy administrators replied that it was perfectly in order for them to enclose this land; it was merely through lack of interest that the monks had allowed peasants to till it or graze their animals there. The expensive litigation that dragged on before 1860 hardly encouraged the efficient running of the property. Indeed a settlement was only reached in 1861, when Lady Bridport agreed to give up about one half of the estate. Members of her family began living at Bronte in 1870.

After Garibaldi's landing the people of Bronte, like all other Sicilians, received his stirring proclamation: 'To arms, everybody! Sicily will once more learn how to free herself from oppressors etc. etc.' The oppressors were of course the Bourbons, and the Bourbons had been responsible for giving the Duchy to Nelson. Palermo fell, and a new revolutionary committee was formed to run the town of Bronte. At last, the Brontini felt, the *beni*, or common land, would be redistributed. Yet there were delays. The town became divided between communists and right-wingers, the latter being automatically considered Bourbonists or *sorci* by their opponents. Then Milazzo and Messina fell. Criminals, escaped from the Vicaria prison, had reached Bronte. There were demonstrations, shouts: 'Death to the *sorci*,' 'We want the division of land,' 'Our blood has been sucked'. A municipal guard was killed. Stones were thrown. Then the houses of suspected Bourbonists were set on fire and looted, to the accompaniment of drums and 'Viva l'Italia! Viva Garibaldi!' Public buildings were burnt down. All this occurred on the night of 2 August.

On the third much worse happened. A lawyer, Cannata, whom Sciascia calls 'one of the most odious of the notables of Bronte', was dragged through the streets and burnt on a pyre in front of his son's house. Whilst still alive he was repeatedly stabbed, and a man from Maletto, called Bonina, when doing so licked the blood from his knife. According to Radice, Bonina then cut out the liver, which he ate. The truth of this disgusting act was later repudiated, and Radice said that he preferred to disbelieve it.[24] The passage in the book has given rise to angry controversy which continues to the present day.

Many other murders followed, usually in almost as horrid circumstances. One of those killed was an employee of Lady Bridport's, Rosario Leotta. Her overbearing bailiff, William Thovez, and his family had, needless to say, already fled, as in May 1848. This time they went to John Jeans, the Vice-Consul in Catania, who was to marry Thovez's daughter, Elizabeth (in 1868). Understandably Jeans was prevailed upon to appeal for help to Goodwin in Palermo. Goodwin in turn made representations to Garibaldi, who at once sent Nino Bixio to suppress this 'small dash of communism'.

It is appropriate now simply to quote a letter from Goodwin to Lord John Russell, the British Foreign Secretary:

*11 August 1860*

My Lord,

It is my painful duty to bring before your Lordship a proclamation by Major General Bixio, one of Garibaldi's lieutenants, which for hardship and severity is unexampled in Sicilian history. A rising of peasants for some unknown cause took place at Bronte on the 2nd instant and led to the loss of life and destruction of property. The head of the police in Catania [Colonel Poulet] hastened to the spot with eighty men, but finding he could not do good withdrew to the town of Adernò, whence, reinforced by two hundred men he returned to Bronte the next day and made a triumphant entry, most of the insurgents having taken to flight. Garibaldi, on receiving tidings of the outbreak, despatched a flying column under Bixio from Messina to Bronte. On his arrival at Bronte on the 6th instant Bixio issued a proclamation to the following effect.

'The Governor of the province of Catania, desiring that all persons may know how this Government means to reestablish order in *comunes* where attempts shall be made to disturb it, puts forth the following decree for public information. General Bixio by virtue of the powers received from the Dictator decrees that the town of Bronte, guilty of a breach of humanity, is placed in a state of siege. Within three hours from this forenoon, the inhabitants shall give up their swords and muskets under the pain of being shot for disobedience.

The municipality and national guard are dissolved and destined to be reorganised according to law respectively. The authors of the crimes committed shall be handed over to the military power to be tried by a special commission. A war tax is laid upon the town of five pounds per hour from 5.30 p.m. this day, at which the troops shall occupy Postavina, until the town shall be regularly organised. The present decree shall be posted up and proclaimed by the town cryer.[1]

*Bronte, 6th August, 1860.*

This manifesto has not remained a dead letter. Vice-Consul Jeans says it is reported that Bixio has tried and shot about thirty of the ringleaders. If this report be true, a feeling of horror and indignation will be expected throughout the island, which will be highly prejudicial to the revolutionary government.

It is right to mention that on learning that one of Lady Bridport's bookkeepers had been murdered by the peasants, I applied to this Government to seek out the murderer, and bring him to justice as quickly as possible.

I have the honour to be, etc.

John Goodwin

Later Goodwin modified the numbers shot by Bixio to six instead of thirty. He said that Jeans had reported that sixteen individuals had been murdered and forty-three houses partly burnt and sacked; 'the property of Lady Bridport in the Duchy of Bronte has not been interfered with.'

Bixio's behaviour was indeed a great slur on the glory of Garibaldi's Sicilian campaign. Although no doubt he had orders to be strict, and Garibaldi was obviously anxious to please the British, it is a bit hard that the British Government, or the Duchy, should be held responsible for the savagery of his conduct. By temperament he was a man who was notoriously impatient and pugnacious. He had for instance only recently challenged a colleague, Carmelo Agnetta, to a duel for insulting him on the parade ground. His fits of rage were terrifying. At the same time he was exceedingly brave; at Porta Termini he had been seen to cut a bullet from his chest. On arrival at Bronte, it seems that the rebels actually thought that he had come to help them rather than mete out 'justice'. His first main biographer[25] seeks to excuse his behaviour by producing another tale of cannibalism, this time very specious; he said that as Bixio was entering the square, a man was seen tearing with his teeth at the severed breast of a girl. Justice was very summary indeed. Arrivabene was told that when one of the ringleaders was brought to the General, Bixio in a fit of passion took his revolver and shot the culprit at once. C. S. Forbes gave a slightly different account. He said that the man was brought to see him whilst the troops were having breakfast after their long march. 'Having satisfied himself of the man's guilt, Bixio said, "Well, I can't disturb my men now," and drawing his revolver, shot him through the head.'

The tragedy was that many of the people who were executed by Bixio were not those who had perpetrated the atrocities. They were shot because they had been in positions of authority in the town before anarchy had broken out. One was the unfortunate mayor, Lombardo, who not only was innocent but had tried to halt the bloodshed. The village idiot was also despatched. The deaths of both gave copy to Verga. What was worse, Bixio had the men shot within twenty-four hours of the sentence, before there was any chance of appeal.

Eventually a new trial was held at the Court of Assizes in Catania, as a result of which, in 1863, thirty-seven people were sentenced, several to life imprisonment.

On 6 September Consul Goodwin wrote another despatch to Lord John Russell, this time enclosing a long letter from Benjamin Ingham, 'an eminent wine grower and merchant'.[26] The aim of doing this was to underline the state of weakness of the new Government in Sicily and to present a picture of the growing unrest and brigandage. To us this letter is especially interesting as giving a résumé of Ingham's possessions and social situation in the island. It also happens to be the last bit of Ingham's writing that we have left before his death – and there is not a trace of any lessening in the fire and energy that had characterised his correspondence ever since the days of the quarrels with John Lee-Brown.

*27 August 1860*

Sir,

On the outbreak of the late revolution in Sicily I was fully prepared and expected to find that the large amount of property of one kind or the other that I possess in different parts of the Island, part belonging solely to myself and partly to my large Wine Establishment in Marsala, and in other parts of the Province of Trapani and in the Bosco di Partinico, would be for the time exposed to great risk without sufficient guarantee and protection; but certainly I did hope that, as soon as the revolutionary state of the country had ceased, a dictatorial Government been formed, measures would have been gradually adopted for the public safety and the guarantee of all property. Such has not however been the case.

I nevertheless trusted that the local authorities would have the judgement and the power to put down and punish the excesses committed within their own districts, and accordingly I directed my Agents in different parts to apply to such authorities for protection.

But all applications have proved fruitless and to no effect, and it is therefore that I feel bound, in the quality of British subject, to have recourse to you to obtain that redress and protection, that every government extends to its subjects in foreign parts.

Having thus explained my motives for addressing you, I will proceed to give you a short account of the state of affairs here as far as my interests are concerned.

It is impossible to exact the payments of any Rents, and my Agents in the Province of Trapani write me that no one will pay Debts or Taxes of any kind, and that the government officials have neither the courage nor the power to enforce the payment of such arrears.

In the above mentioned province, and more particularly in the districts of Alcamo, Castellamare, Bosco di Partinico, Vita, Salemi, Castelvetrano, Campobello, and other parts where I hold property and lands, wine establishments, stores, rents, etc. etc., excesses of damage of every kind threaten not only the property itself but also the persons of those entrusted with the charge of it.

In Alcamo the so-called *componenda* [i.e. the organising body, a Spanish word: the *Mafia*] are in full force and my Agent there, by name Gaspare Ospedale, has several times received threatening anonymous letters, demanding under penalty of death, the payment first of

£300 and then of £400. To save his life he is compelled to remain within the walls of the town, and my interests are thus left without any-one to look after them.

Not content to stop there, but seeing that their insulting demands were not complied with, the malefactors proceeded to burn several houses in the Bosco di Alcamo.

In the country about Vita they openly robbed the wheat in the fields, as also the sumac leaf immediately on its being reaped. In short there is no limit to their robbery and rapine, nor has property any safeguard whatsoever.

The local authorities at whose hands redress is demanded clearly show their incapacity to afford it, by telling my Agents repeatedly that they require assistance from the Government at Palermo. Is such a state of affairs to continue?

Certainly it is out of the question to hope for the exacting of Rents this year, because they are either robbed by others, even by the Debtors themselves, if even Bailiffs could be found with courage enough to do their duty.

The vintage is near at hand, in the result of which I am largely inter-ested, being the proprietor of vineyards and carrying on an extensive business in wines and the juices of the grape in many parts of the Island – and who will now willingly consign or deliver up the produce for which I have advanced such heavy sums of money? and who is there to compel them to do so? and what guarantee have I in fine, for the produce of my Estates?

No one would be able to form a correct valuation of the many losses, direct and indirect, that I am suffering from the actual state of the country, and I must add that the well-being of an Establishment with such large means as mine has, and that supports so many dependants, must necessarily redound to the interests of the Island itself.

I see that at Bronte, where the interests of the heirs of Lord Nelson are likely to suffer, the energetic measures taken by Colonel Bixio were attended with great success and a complete restoration of good order, all of which I can attest myself, having experienced some damage to the property of my wife, the Duchess of Santa Rosalia, in the adjoining *comune* of Maletto. But if such efficient measures can be adopted and carried out in one Province there is no reason why they should not be practised in like manner in other and more necessitous cases, such as in the Provinces of Palermo and Trapani, where assassination, robbery, burning of property, seizure of persons, and the so-called *componenda* are the order of the day and of the most frequent occurrences.

I would therefore pray you, Mr Consul, to submit my above representation to the Provisional Government here, to whom I must look for redress and protection of my property and the people dependent on me; and I further hope that you will, as you have always hitherto done in similar cases under the late Government, have the goodness to acquaint with the state of things in this Island to the Minister of Foreign Affairs in London, our Minister Mr Elliot in Naples, and also Admiral Mundy at present in Naples, who is charged with the protection of British subjects in the Kingdom of Naples, and in Sicily, during the existing political troubles.

I have the honour to be Sir
Your most obedient servant
Benjamin Ingham

N.B. I would finally beg of you, Mr Consul, to impress upon the Government here, that the force which they have lately sent into the Province of Trapani has not had the desired effect of restoring good order there, nor has it made an example of severity in the nature required and absolutely necessary to put a stop to such iniquities.

Goodwin had assured Lord John Russell in his covering letter that Agostino Depretis, Garibaldi's pro-Dictator, had given 'energetic orders for Mr Ingham's estates and factories to be effectively protected'. One notes that about this time Depretis was writing to Garibaldi urging him to agree to the immediate annexation of Sicily by Piedmont.

Ingham's attitude to Bixio's methods at Bronte may cause raised eyebrows at this distance. Yet he was by no means alone. For better or for worse, other landlords, as a result of Bronte, had come to realise that co-operation with Garibaldi was the only way to cope with lawlessness.[27]

6 September was the day on which King Francis and his wife (the 'Queen of Naples' immortalised by Proust) fled from Naples. Garibaldi's troops had only crossed the Straits of Messina some four weeks before, on 18 August. On 7 September Garibaldi made his triumphal entrance into Naples. The Battle of the Volturno was fought on 1 October. On 21 October a plebiscite was held in Sicily and the vote was overwhelmingly in favour of unification – in *The Leopard* even Salina voted Yes. On 7 November Victor Emmanuel entered Naples as the first King of Italy. On the ninth Garibaldi went on board the *Hannibal* to say goodbye to Admiral Mundy. At dawn the next day he left for his cottage at Caprera in the *Washington*.

# PART THREE

## *The Inheritors*

# XIV

## *Viva La Vescovina*

IT was a new era in Sicily, and for the foreign colony too a time of enormous change. During the next decade or so many of the old stalwarts were to die. A fresh generation married, produced children, inherited businesses, formed others, left the island for good.

But first and foremost, the great divide, there was the death of Benjamin Ingham, at 6 a.m. on 4 March 1861, at the age of seventy-six. No cause is given on the certificate at Palermo (his death is unrecorded at Somerset House), though we know it was sudden. What was more, he was on the point of changing his will – indeed many people believed that he had already done so.

There is a mystery about this will. For at least a decade the old man had been keeping the family on tenterhooks about his heirs. Would his money go to the Inghams, the Whitakers, or even the Ascensos? The Ben Ingham juniors being childless, Joseph Whitaker's eldest son seemed the most natural candidate. Ben, who was one of the executors, had to sign an affidavit in London, twenty months later, before the will could be proved. Part of this affidavit is worth quoting, to give an idea of the furore that arose:

*15 November 1862*

The said Testator [Benjamin Ingham] declared that possibly he should decide on making another Will . . . and expressed his intention of placing it in the hands of the English Consul residing at Palermo. I further make oath that I have personally made enquiry of John Goodwin Esquire . . . and have also made diligent and careful search in all the places where the said deceased usually kept his papers of moment and concern, in order to ascertain whether he had or had not left any other Will, but that I have been unable to discover any such Will.

The man whom Ingham had been threatening to nominate as his heir was his second cousin, aged fifty-two and, although making quite a mark in his native Yorkshire, quite unsuited to inherit such vast and complex business interests: Judge Theophilus Hastings Ingham, a grandson of the

Ingham of the Inghamites. As it happened, the eventual legal heir was Joseph's second son Willie, aged nineteen. He was a lucky boy. Exactly how much his great-uncle left is difficult to gauge. Tradition in the family is that he left the equivalent of four and a half million pounds sterling, but this is obviously far below the actual figure. As has been observed, the Italian estate alone was valued at well over eight million, and as for the American . . . Not, of course, that Willie came into everything: he had to wait for others to die first, and then there were many individual legacies to be taken into account.

This is not the place to go digging into the adjustments over the inheritance that obviously took place within the family. The value, moreover, of the railway shares in America and elsewhere had dropped vastly by the time that Willie, over twenty years later, came fully into the possession of his property. By inheriting Manchi e Scala he had, incidentally, the right to the barony, though this was not confirmed by King Victor Emmanuel until February 1876. No provision was made for the likelihood of Ben and Emily Ingham producing offspring. It is said that Joseph's eldest son, Benny, was overruled because of a talk he and Willie had been having with their great-uncle a few years previously. They had been discussing a journey which the boys had made. Benny had reached the destination first because he had paid to go over a toll bridge. Willie had said that he had walked the extra three miles rather than have to pay at the gate. Such shrewdness on the part of Willie made an immediate appeal to Ingham, who promptly altered the will in his favour (it was Benny in later life who had the reputation of being mean). Actually, like all the young Whitakers, Willie turned out to have little head for business. Perhaps Ingham, before his death, had come to sense this and had decided to leave his money to someone of his own name who had already proved himself a success in life.

The Duchess of course was well provided for, and her four sons received decent legacies. She was left the house in the Piano Sant'Oliva, with any contents belonging to Ingham, for her lifetime; not only was the Estate to pay for repairs but it was also to find the money for all household provisions, including food. Evidently it had been Ingham's intention that she would have as few worries as possible, for it was stipulated that she was to receive a payment of about £20 every ten days in addition to further monthly and annual allowances. The house on Vias Bara and Lampedusa (now always referred to as the Casa Lampedusa), which included the Banco Ingham and the *Scagno* (office), was left to Joseph. Since there is no mention in the will of the Palazzo Ingham, one assumes it was bought originally in

Ben Ingham junior's name, as he and Emily went to live there – having had to move out of the house at Sant'Oliva to make way for the Duchess; Square Ingham was renamed Square Emilia in Emily's honour.

The residuary estate, including the business, went to Ben and Joseph in equal shares for their lifetimes, afterwards passing to Willie, who also received a big sum on reaching the age of twenty-five or on his marriage, whichever was the earlier. Willie does seem to have made an attempt to learn the business but after a while he lost interest, so presumably it was handed over to his father and Ben in return for some lump sum, or even as a gift. As for the Duchess's sons, their chief advantages were in having all their debts wiped out. Carlo and Domenico were the most favoured, though Federico, who was now the Duke of Santa Rosalia, would appear to have owed the most money to Ingham. The will stressed that the money left to the brothers Ascenso and to Federico's daughter, the Duchess of Realmena, was only out of 'good friendship and personal regard'; if there were any 'discussion or obstacle', then they at once forfeited their rights to the legacies – special mention was made to Federico, who was no doubt a bit of a trouble-maker. As for Carmelo, if Ingham thought that, by dint of being a regular soldier, he was any the less in need of money, he was mistaken. The next generation was to be pestered by his begging letters (though not so much as from Domenico). Indeed, he was driven when quite elderly to find a rich wife to set his finances aright, though in this he bungled, for the lady of his choice, Lady Louisa FitzGibbon, was similarly desperate to find a spouse to save her from ruin, brought on by her extravagance, and each only discovered the other's penury after the marriage.[1]

Benjamin Ingham was buried in the Lazzaretto Acquasanta cemetery. In 1949 that cemetery was closed and his body was moved to the new Protestant burial ground at the Vergine Maria, given by Garibaldi as an act of gratitude to James Rose for the benefit of the British and Protestant community.

Schuyler Livingston also died in 1861. The job of investment agent for the estate was taken over in New York by the Anglo-American house of W. C. Pickersgill and Co. Erastus Corning, however, continued to manage the land holdings in Michigan which had been obtained as a result of the St Mary Falls Canal venture; when he died in 1872 they stayed in the hands of his son. From the few documents available it is obvious that huge sums continued to be paid in, thanks to Livingston's careful investments. On 5 July 1862, for instance, collections of $10,000 (all from interest, dividends etc.) were credited by Pickersgill to the 'estate of B. Ingham'; three days later further collections of $4876 were reported. Between 28 October and 4 November they came to $13,605.[2] Judging by the fall in value of the investments twenty years later, one is forced to deduce that the Pickersgills were not nearly as nimble-minded as Schuyler Livingston.

In the summer of 1863 Joseph Whitaker, now sporting a great bushy beard, but without a moustache, went to England with some of his children, including Benny, Sophie, Carrie and Pip, who – again as noted – is to loom fairly large ahead. One object was to buy a property in Yorkshire, and another was to put Pip, or Peppino as he was more usually known,[3] in a school near Epping. The search for property was abortive, but eventually he acquired Hesley near Rotherham, where a typical mid-Victorian mansion was later created, complete with Italianate tower and surrounded by a variety of fir trees. A bunch of his letters written to his cousin Ben during this trip, in tiny, scratchy handwriting, are still in existence, and show that he had a character rather more human than one would suppose from his photographs. For instance, there is his anxiety for Benny, evidently deeply upset at not having been the heir. Then there is an amused discussion about how to deal with the Rev. Charles Wright, the chaplain in Palermo; everyone wants to get rid of him, but the Roses and Gardners have scruples about the man's feelings. The Roses and Thurburns are in the same hotel, much to the delight of the Whitaker girls – Mrs Thurburn had been the eldest daughter of Consul Barker and was thus the late Mrs James (Lilly) Rose's sister. The references to the Duchess in the letters show that she was keeping the estate on the hop. For instance:

*7 September 1863*

The repairs to the dining room at St Oliva ought to be done immediately, and it cannot be helped if a heavy bill of costs will be the result. It is regretted that the old lady had no pudding sent her by anybody and she will of course put it down as a 'mancanza di rispetto' [lack of respect] especially on the part of Joseph [i.e. himself].

Then an important step was taken:

*28 September 1863*

I see you were in receipt of my letter from Scarborough advising about Benny remaining permanently in England. You would naturally be surprised at the news and the suddenness of the step taken, but I cannot doubt that it will be for his good.

The letter ended:

Please say to my wife that we had a nice letter from Peppino, that he had been put into the same sleeping room with the Roses and Willy [William Beaumont, later known as 'Beau'] Gardner, and was as happy as could be expected. The Roses as usual have got themselves into a scrape. Peppino has already acquired a mouse and a pet stag-beetle. . . . When you see the Duchess please give her my salutes.

Pip/Peppino was a funny, introverted little boy. Already he was show-ing a passion for natural history, later to bring him real distinction. On the eventual acquisition of Hesley in 1864, Benny was put in charge of its management and of supervising the building of the house, which was made over to him. Pip spent many happy hours there. Thanks to his craze for birdsnesting, he became an expert at bird identification.

It was Pip incidentally who recorded later that the Duchess, his god-mother, was in the habit of loading him and others with lavish presents, and charging the bills to the firm. He also once surprised her at her toilet and discovered that she was totally bald – hence the thick, jet black wig.

The Pickersgills, because of the Civil War in America, had decided to come to London. The moment they met, Sophie Whitaker and young William Cunliffe Pickersgill, aged eighteen and nineteen respectively, fell in love. There was no hiding it. Sophie was warned 'plainly' by her parent that 'perhaps there would be a disappointment in store for her'. Neverthe-less a luncheon was arranged. Although the subject was not mentioned throughout the meal, all was settled afterwards in private between the fathers in 'as smooth and as agreeable a manner as possible'. No disappoint-ment at all therefore. Joseph wrote later to Ben:

*20 October 1863*

The question of money matters has not yet been touched on, neither has there been anything said of a positive nature in regard to when the marriage can take place. This latter point will, however, no doubt be talked over, and some understanding come to thereon, before we leave England . . . I may mention that the old people, I mean Grandfather and Father Pickersgill, will wish that William should have his future position chalked out, and provided for in some way or other, which at present cannot be determined beyond that it is to be one in business. Were the American troubles over, New York would solve the question at once, as William would be made a partner in the House immediately, but I fear we cannot expect this to happen awhile.

Sophie and William were a well-matched couple: lively, handsome, mischievous, with very twentieth-century faces. They married in 1865. Poor William seems never to have settled to a job, as a result of which he has forever been branded as 'rakish'. He died, suddenly in 1869, of tuberculosis. They had one son, whom they lost when only a few months old. Sophie was badly affected. She lost all her *joie de vivre* and people even wondered if she would ever recover.

From the point of view of romance, that autumn of 1863 was a hectic one for the Whitakers. Joseph had been interested in acquiring some Egyptian stock (because of the imminent opening of the Suez Canal, in 1869). He wrote to say that he had been seeing 'a Mr Christian, well acquainted with Egypt and its resources', who had given good advice, as a result of which £13,500 worth of stock had been bought. This was Ewan Christian of Alexandria. He fell for the black-haired, vivacious and rather birdlike Carrie Whitaker, who had by now shed her admirer William Rose (later to marry Martha Gardner); and they married in 1864. Then, just at the time of the Pickersgill engagement, Willie Whitaker arrived from Palermo. Shortly afterwards he met Louisa Ewing, a nice conventional girl, the daughter of the Bishop of Argyll and irreverently nicknamed by other Whitakers *La Vescovina* (the female bishop); he married in 1865, on the same day as Sophie married Pickersgill, thus conveniently coming into his money before he reached the age of twenty-five.

But there were other, serious matters to be discussed in the letters – politics in Sicily:

> *28 September 1863*
>
> It is very gratifying to think that public safety and tranquillity will be improved greatly by the vigorous measures being taken by General Govone to put down brigandism. The neighbourhood of Palermo has been too long infested by all sorts of malefactors, worse perhaps than any other part of the Island. It looks as if Government's rule will have to be one of constant rigour, pretty much the same as in former times. The fact is the people are not fit for a constitutional government, and never will be, in my firm belief. I wish I could hold a better opinion of them.

Harsh words from one who had lived for some forty years as the guest of Sicily. Yet every friend of the country was at this period both baffled and saddened by the way its inhabitants were reacting to their newly acquired freedom. There were so many tales of murder, banditry and kidnapping that tourists were becoming thoroughly alarmed. George Dennis was forced to admit that 'whatever the faults of the Bourbon government, it at least had this merit, that it kept the roads throughout its dominions as secure for the travellers as those of Northern Europe'. Like Goodwin in earlier days he analysed under headings some of the reasons for the state of disillusion. For instance the 'policy machinery' was not yet in working order, a nice understatement. Then, and very true, the Sicilians had suddenly had a strong arm lifted from them and found instead that they were in a state of complete subversion – they had gone from 'abject political slavery, when the police had the monopoly of committing outrages against persons and property', to constitutional liberty. Another problem was the fact that the Government was 'bad at securing malefactors'; at Christmas 1862, for instance, 127 prisoners had escaped from Girgenti gaol. Lastly and most important, there was the hated conscription, which had had the effect of driving youths into hiding in the mountains.

What Dennis did not add was that Sicilians were being faced with taxes that to them seemed just as bad as before – they were tired of being told that they must make 'sacrifices', which they considered to be beyond their means. Worse still, Cavour had decided against self-government for them. The northern administrators had proved mostly out of sympathy with the people, ignorant of their customs and even of their language. Gang warfare now became common. Smuggling was everywhere, often with the connivance of customs officials. Prisons were a scandal. The very way the tax system was administered bred graft, corruption and terrorisation. Life was becoming cheaper than ever. In two years there were 1500 murders in Palermo. The age of the *Mafia* had truly begun.

It had not really been Garibaldi's fault that things had gone wrong. He was not an administrator, and his main concern in 1860 had been a military one: to conquer the rest of southern Italy. There was a curious incident in June 1862 when he returned to Sicily, ostensibly to revisit the old battlefields. He had been greeted in Palermo with enormous enthusiasm, even relief. In Marsala he had made it clear that the total unification of Italy, the capture of Rome, was still the first thing in his mind. 'Roma o morte!' was the cry, even in the cathedral. 'Napoleon must leave Rome. If necessary, we must make a new Vespers.' It looked like 1860 all over again, and at the end of August he led some 3000 supporters into Calabria. At Aspromonte he was twice wounded and then captured. Lampedusa refers to this incident, when the governmental commander, Colonel Pallavicino, comes to the ball in the Palazzo Ponteleone; the Colonel had even gone so far as to kneel before the defeated Garibaldi and kiss his hand – a controversial episode, but typical of what practically any Italian would have felt in such a predicament.

The Ponteleone ball, one of the most famous scenes in *The Leopard*, was held in November 1862. It had seemed then that the clock had been safely put back. Palermo was 'passing through one of its intermittent periods of social gaiety', and people were never tired of 'congratulating one another on still existing'. 'Heavenly! A dream! Like the old days!' said those girls like crinolined monkeys. They were mistaken of course. Not just because of the 'bomb manufactured in Pittsburgh, Penn' which in 1943 was to blow to pieces the reclining gods on the painted ceiling of the ballroom,[4] but for a more immediate reason. Pallavicino told Salina that on the Italian mainland 'never have we been so disunited since we've been reunited'.

It was D'Azeglio who said that unification was a process of making Italians dislike one another. He is also credited with saying that union with Naples was like going to bed with someone with smallpox.[5] Until 1860 regionalism and nationalism could coexist happily, but now hard politics had taken over from idealism. The Civil War in America was providing some unpleasant lessons about coexistence at that very moment.

Banditry was a symptom of the unease not only in Sicily but in Italy proper, especially in the south. Richard Cossins' letters from Marsala at this period are full of references to it, though the town appeared to be quiet. He recommended increasing the height of the *Baglio* wall for 'best security'. On one occasion trouble seemed about to break out, but it was scotched thanks to thirty carabinieri descending from Trapani during the night and making several arrests.

After Aspromonte there had been martial law in Sicily for a while. And in 1863 General Govone had been given powers which would have enabled him, if he had so desired, to behave in as summary a way as Bixio at Bronte. There was indeed a kind of reign of terror. It was of his arrival that Joseph had written so approvingly in September.

Some travellers nevertheless dared to venture to the island. Mr and Mrs Moens arrived in Palermo on 12 January 1865, not realising what adventures lay in store for them. They came from Marseilles, with a boat-load of adventurous Americans, 'very amusing and sociable' (except for one old man 'shunned by his fellow-countrymen' and who had 'just amassed a large fortune at the oil springs') and made straight for the Trinacria, which they found all very comfortable. Ragusa was attentive as usual, and commendably particular 'about the people whom he admits to his table d'hôte; one Sicilian was turned away because, to my great disgust, he expectorated incessantly while sitting opposite to me at table.'[6] At the Sunday service held at Consul Goodwin's the congregation numbered about a hundred persons. Once more, as in decades past, there were tales such as how most of the splendidly dressed aristocratic Palermitans, in their gay carriages on the Marina, were in reality so poor that they had 'not a decent room to receive a friend in'.

In no time the Moens were becoming thoroughly alarmed about brigands. 'Neither the rich Sicilians nor the English dare drive half a mile out of the town.' 'We hear a great deal of brigands, and are told that all the peasants carry guns, and the country round Palermo is in a most unsettled state.' The day after they had climbed up Monte Pellegrino, a Marchese Guccia was captured, to be released after a ransom had been paid. 'These atrocious affairs seem to be matters of everyday occurrence here. . . . Scarcely a week passed without a fresh instance, but not one fourth of the cases are ever heard of. It is only when a man of note is taken that any fuss is made.' A story, only too typical of the Sicilian character, was told by 'our Italian master'. He had been in a church where a murdered man was lying on a bier, near which the widow and her child were kneeling: 'After a burst of frantic weeping she joined the child's hands together and made him repeat after her a solemn oath to the effect that when he grew up he would take deadly vengeance on the murderer's nearest relative. She ended by a solemn and fearful curse on the child should he fail to keep the vow he had taken over the dead body of his father.'

Then there was the hair-raising account of the 'capture of Mr ——, an English merchant, two or three years ago'. Since Mr —— was large and stout and spoke Sicilian well, he could have been James Rose, though his present-day descendants vehemently deny it. He was accompanied in his carriage by his daughter, who could also therefore have been Sophie. About a mile outside Palermo the carriage was suddenly surrounded by six men, who 'threatened to shoot him, if he did not get out of the carriage quietly and go with them' – particularly impudent, in view of Garibaldi's respect for Rose and the fact that he was then acting as British pro-consul. He was dragged over 'walls, fields and ditches, until at last he fell through fatigue and said he would go no farther'. Then the bargaining began. At first his captors demanded £1000, but eventually he managed to beat them down to £50. Meanwhile Miss —— had been left crying bitterly in the carriage, with the muzzles of brigands' guns pointing at her over a wall. A priest passed and took no notice. Eventually she had the courage to drive home. 'Many men were taken up on suspicion, and thrown into prison.' Mr —— was asked to go and try to identify them. 'This was endangering his own life however; for had he been the instrument of their conviction, their relations would have shot him – so he declared he knew none of them, and they were consequently released. In a few days several men called on Mr —— to thank him, and his watch was returned.'

Later, after some more scares, the Moens met the Rev. J. C. Aynsley and his wife in Syracuse. The four decided to continue travelling on the mainland together. At Battipaglia, after visiting the temples at Paestum, they were surrounded by armed men, 'some like serpents creeping through the standing corn'. Messrs Moens and Aynsley were carried off, and the ladies sent back to Salerno. A ransom of £17,000 was demanded. A long saga followed, but not so relevant here. Enough to say Aynsley was released early, but Moens was kept prisoner two months and let go after £5100 had been paid.

Conditions in Sicily were becoming ever more nerve-racking for expatriates. Part of another letter from Cossins to Ben gives a fair indication of the atmosphere:

*16 August 1865*

I am just sending a couple of lines to give you a copy of a 'gram received on Monday afternoon from Florence –

'*Vice Console Inglese*, Marsala
British flag must not be hoisted over wine stores
Herries'

I am very alarmed about this. I imagine there could be no objection to our hoisting the flag over a British dwelling house attached to a wine stores. We could even convert the rooms over our *Baglio* gateway into a dwelling house for this purpose. I suppose Mr Herries will be writing to give you an explanation of the above 'gram and I shall be anxious to hear what he has to say. We ought certainly to know if we have the right or not to hoist the British flag over a British residence in case of danger, or any act of violence being threatened, and if he does not explain this our Consul in Palermo should get us this information.

The weather continues excessively hot, which is bad for people's tempers. One notices it in the streets. I was very sorry to hear that your good dog Neptune had died. Dogs that have been brought up in cold countries cannot stand the intense heat of summer in Sicily. The clerk is duly commissioned to get a good whelp for you, the off-spring of a fine shepherd dog, reared among the temples of Selinus [Selinunte].

Emma[7] joins me in best regards to Mrs Ingham and your goodself.

Yours very obediently

Richard B. Cossins

By 1866 it was clear that real trouble would be erupting very shortly. There had been a panic when paper money had been introduced. The new tobacco monopoly had been violently unpopular. Then the famous Santa Rosalia festivities, the very essence of the life of Palermo, were abolished. And to make things generally more insecure for citizens, troops had been withdrawn for the war against Austria.

The Duchess died on 8 January 1866, *da un tratto* (from a stroke). She was eighty-seven. It must have been a blow to her bachelor sons. No wonder, later that year, Joseph had to give £100 to Domenico as *elemosina* (charity). Willie and the Vescovina took possession of the house, put in gas lighting and spent £230 on its redecoration. They moved in for the birth of their first child on 3 April and then launched on a series of brilliant parties. Their house expenses for the year trebled those of the Joseph Whitakers and quintupled the Ben Inghams'. It was Willie who later erected the charming little bandstand, in the Pompeian style, that still stands today among the palm trees in the Piazza Castelnuovo. He did this to prevent the space in front of his house being built over.

September arrived. It had been known for some while that armed bands were massing in Monreale and that they were in communication with malcontents in the city, but according to *The Times* correspondent the blindness of the Prefect Torelli had been almost criminal. The offer of assistance from the National Guard had been rejected, and on the night of the fourteenth there were very definite signs that some 'iniquitous and ill-advised enterprise' might occur. All the Prefect did was to 'sequestrate a journal' and arrest its editor for warning the people of approaching danger. Two nights later some 2000 men, under a Colonel Bentivegna, secretly entered the city.

For four days there was anarchy. Once again houses were looted, and there were acts of horrible brutality, especially against the police. The Prefect and the Commander-in-chief, with such armed forces as had been left in the city, shut themselves inside the Royal Palace. Cholera reappeared.[8] Demands for a republic were openly heard. It was a strange, murky episode to the historian. Bolton King said: 'though there is much that is dark in the history of the revolt, there can be little doubt that in the main it was the work of the same clerical-anarchist alliance which had scourged the Neapolitan provinces five years before.' And to quote *The Times*: 'Six years of constitutional government, badly administered, had not taught them patriotism.'

The Willie Whitakers found themselves in the thick of the fighting. As for the next fortnight communications with the outside world were closed, the Vescovina's proud father submitted some of her letters anonymously to *The Times*. They were very feminine with some all too hasty judgements on the poor Sicilians. The first letter was headed 'On board the S.S. *Rhone*'. The riots had started on the Sunday, she said. All during Monday and Tuesday bullets had been 'whizzing about', and a man of war had begun to 'throw shells', some nastily close. In fact those three days were the most unpleasant she had ever spent in her life. She and Willie, with the nurse Harriet and the baby (who was in a state of delight, thinking that 'every shot and shell was for his amusement'), had tried to shelter in the cellars, but they had been driven out by scorpions:

*20 September 1866*

On Wednesday morning, however, it was so dreadful that we thought it better [at 6 a.m.] to risk it and try to get on board a ship, so we bundled out as fast as we could, and went in the carriage half way down the Inghams' street. There we saw a ship lying just facing the street, and some men told us to get out of the carriage, which we did and ran as hard as ever we could into a boat and came off here, but we had a narrow escape and cannot be thankful enough. We are now on board a Liverpool steamer, but she goes tomorrow and we shall have to get on some other. . . . The rebels are in possession of the whole town except the prisons, the palace and the castle; they have made barricades in the streets, but it is so dreadfully difficult to get at these wretches for they are not in the streets, they are shut up in the houses and fire down on the soldiers. The National Guard is on the rebels' side! And it is so difficult to get anything to eat. They say they cannot hold out at the palace, for want of food.

She added that Mr and Mrs Whitaker, her parents-in-law, were still at home in Via Bara and unable to get away. As yet there was no sign whatsoever of a British man o' war, absolutely shameful, and all the telegraph wires were cut. 'One man-servant came here today and he says our house is perfectly riddled with balls.'

Her next letter was written a week later. By then the government forces had arrived 'with a vengeance', more and more every day. She could see shells bursting near their house. Most of the 'country invaders' had sneaked away during the night:

*27 September 1866*

The townspeople got rid of their arms somehow, and pretended they had never done anything at all. Oh, it does make one so angry! Those horrid cowards who a few days ago were fighting against the soldiers are now calling out 'Viva l'Italia! Viva Vittorio Emanuele!' and putting out the Italian flag just because they are too frightened to do anything else. If I had anything to do with the Government I would give up Sicily altogether, and not own such a set of rascals, as they all are, every one. I hate the very sight of our own servants; they are just as bad as the rest. When they were robbing the Garibaldi School, we saw our groom go in and get a musket. Willie went and took it from him, and has just gone now with him and made him take it back. I wonder how he likes that? Yesterday we went to see the poor Garibaldi School, and it is too shocking; they have not left one thing except the walls, even torn out the very gaspipes to make bullets, and anything they had not time to take away they have broken to bits, and such a nice place it must have been. At the hospital it is just the same. They even took the mattresses and beds from under the sick soldiers. These Sicilians are not like human beings, they are more like beasts; but I don't think they will try this again. There are 20,000 soldiers here now, and there are to be 60,000 quartered in Sicily. None of the higher classes of the Sicilians had anything to do with it; but fancy what those wretches did – they took a number of gentlemen here prisoners, and made them go about with them, and mix them up in it, when they had nothing to do with it. The few poor soldiers who were here at the beginning held out very well, but they were so few. Their principal care was to guard the prisons, because the wretches tried hard to let the prisoners loose. There are 2400 people in prison, and fancy if they had escaped! But the soldiers managed to keep the prisons, though they were nearly starved, and the Palace, where the Prefect, the General and all the authorities were glad to eat horses! The poor *Sindaco* [the young Marquis of Rudinì], they took everything out of his house and burnt it in a heap, made barricades of his carriages, and killed his horses – barricades are everywhere, the pavements torn up, and numbers of houses half ruined by cannon balls and shells. Everybody says that the priests are at the bottom of it, and it was from the convents and churches that these wretches fire principally.

The day before her letter, the Vescovina went on to say, a state of siege had been proclaimed in Palermo. Nobody was allowed out after dark, and anyone found with arms on him was shot within twelve hours. There were more cases of cholera among the troops; she prayed it would not spread, 'but the town is in a filthy state'. She continued:

> We have not had much damage done to our house happily. We have got a good many bullets in the drawing-room and sitting-room, but nothing broken which cannot be mended, such as windows, shutters etc. There are some pretty big holes in the walls, which is tiresome, as it has just been all newly papered. . . . The Inghams' house is dreadfully damaged, but luckily it is to the bedrooms not the drawing-rooms. A great deal of the furniture is quite spoilt by cannon-balls. Five of those horrid things of triangular shape, they call them 'granate' here, I don't know what they are in English, went into the house; one room they say will have to be newly roofed.

There were still no British ships at Palermo, though there were supposed to be plenty at Syracuse. The Whitaker in-laws had stayed on shore all the time, but had only had one bullet in the house. Of course they had been 'dreadfully frightened': 'every shot fired from the castle seemed to whizz close past them – which, indeed, it did, but their house was not touched.'

The gentlemen who had had to 'go about' with the rebels had included Baron Riso and the debonair and newly married Corrado Valguarnera. They had been coerced, as they later claimed, into forming a provisional Government. Knowing Corrado, however, one suspects that they had leapt at the fun of a new revolution. In yet another letter, written on 28 September, the Vescovina summed up: 'A revolution one can hardly call it, for it was not for any political cause, only these Sicilians are, one and all, a most discontented set of people, and the lower classes are all thieves and robbers.'

*The Times* correspondent gave the date for the appearance of the first troops as the twenty-first. The slaughter on each side, he admitted, had been considerable, the most desperate fighting having been around the Porta Maqueda. Areas round public buildings had been raked with gunshot by the fleet. Many people had taken refuge in the monasteries. Then

General Cadorna[9] arrived at the head of more reinforcements. During the past week deaths from cholera had amounted to an average of a hundred a day.

The revolt came to be known as the *Sette e Mezzo*, due to the fact that it only lasted seven and a half days. Later, a most extraordinary letter, dated 6 October from Cadorna to 'His Excellency the President of the Council of Ministers', namely Ricasoli, was also published in *The Times*. He confirmed what the Vescovina had said about the sacking of the hospital. 'The Dominicans,' he added, 'issued forth from the hospital, red flag in hand, and after an interview with the rebels pointed out those among the sick who were Sicilians, that they might be spared from the massacre that awaited the Northern Italians.' He also confirmed about the destruction of the Garibaldi Institute and said that two houses belonging to Rudinì had been sacked. Then:

> Very many of the soldiers were massacred in the most barbarous manner. An artilleryman was found nailed up at the Vittoria Barracks most horribly mutilated, his eyes having been plucked out etc. Near Sant'Antonio a *carabiniere* who had refused to cry 'Viva la Repubblica!' was nearly killed by blows on the head and poniard thrusts, after which the monks lighted a large fire into which they threw the dying man. Near the Convent and at Monreale the flesh of the soldiers was sold at so much per pound . . . nearly all the convents and monasteries gave shelter to the insurgents, and the monks themselves were seen to fire upon the troops, and with guns and knives to attempt to force an entry into houses supposed to be favourable to the Government. At Misilmeri a certain Sartorio was sentenced to be bitten to death, and the women set upon him and literally tore him to pieces with their teeth, leaving him a ghastly and bleeding corpse.

One of the insurgents tried to wrest a musket from a man he was killing; he recognised the man as his son and at first he was horrified – then he carried on. The tortures were disgusting. Even the nuns led bands of ruffians. 'Nearly all the convents were hotbeds of rebellion and to them Palermo owes the frightful scenes enacted within its walls.'

So the horrid rumour of cannibalism had been raised again. Nothing more has been heard of this selling of flesh. It must have been pure sensationalism, though it was odd for a man such as Cadorna to have been so gullible. As for the incident at Misilmeri, it had been a castration. Enrico Fincati referred to the incident eleven years later when writing of other events in the town:

Looking at those ugly alleys, rough and dark, I could not restrain a shudder when I thought of the scene of cannibalism [sic] during the seven days of revolution in 1866. Puah! . . . every hag I saw seemed to have a piece of *carabiniere* flesh between her blackened fangs. . . . Oh unfortunate martyrs to duty! Are any of you remembered today? Does anyone recall the unbridled savagery of those ignorant people, who lost all sense of morality and had fallen below the level of brutes?

A subscription was launched on 17 October by an anonymous Englishman (Rose?) to help wounded soldiers and the families of those who had fallen. 'Especial thanks are due to the excellent English gentlemen Ingham and Whitaker.' The Italian Government had now duly received the alarm signal. Rudinì, who had behaved so courageously – refusing to treat with the rebels whilst his own house was burning – was made Prefect. All his translations of Macaulay's works had gone in the flames; it was said that his wife never really recovered from the shock of the experience. In 1868 he went to Naples, again as Prefect, and his place was taken by Giacomo Medici, whose reputation had been more than ever enhanced by his brilliant advance against the Austrians in 1866, compelling them to give up the South Tyrol. Medici combined the duty of Prefect with that of Commander-in-chief, remaining in Palermo for over five years. Thus Palermo was virtually under military rule. But as *The Times* said: 'The evil is social, and the sword cannot reach it.'

Corrado Valguarnera had married Maria Favara on 16 April 1866. She was aged fifteen and was given a tutor after her marriage. Latin was one of her subjects, and she went on studying even after her children were born. An intelligent, rather serious-looking and very warm-hearted girl, her looks were far from those of the lush, gypsyish Angelica as portrayed in the film of *The Leopard*. Her father Baron Vincenzo Favara was a large man, 'very strict and sour-looking', and it was said that he would not allow his men to touch a hair on the tail on any of his cattle when they moved from summer to winter quarters.

Early in that same year Lyla Morrison married James Rose. Prudently, perhaps, the wedding had taken place at the British church in Paris, for the event was a tremendous blow to Sophie Rose, who at that New Year's dance in 1860 had been so blandly assured by Lyla that her father was 'of no interest'. As a result of their conversation Sophie had decided to refuse the hand of a suitor; for she had felt that, as a matter of duty, she could not leave her widowed father and young brothers.

A party was given for British and Americans in April 1867. Maria

Carcaci wrote another word-picture of the event, which must have been somewhat gloomy.

In that same room, on that same central piece of furniture, is seated Sophie's friend; no longer does she bear the name of Morrison, but that of Lyla Rose. Mr Rose is seated beside her, and they both amuse their few months old baby girl, Edith, who now cries and now smiles, while being held in her mother's lap. In the adjoining room at the piano, where once we saw Ackie and Carrie Whitaker, are now seated Bella and Mary Morrison, younger sisters of Lyla; but being unable to play, not a sound comes from the instrument. William Rose, now a man, is near them and shows openly a partiality for Bella, who reminds him of Carrie Whitaker, the love of his youth and now wife of another, enjoying the stately parks of England, while enchanting everybody with her lovely looks.

And Ackie whose face once showed so much strength of will? Ackie Whitaker passes her days weeping in solitude. Why? Because for her the world has no longer any joy since Ben Gardner has been lost at sea, vanished with the vessel in the waves. . . . But the oldest of the Roses, who charmed all those who came in contact with him, where is he? He is no more – drowned while enjoying a bathe. James Rose junior is no more!

The elderly Duchess Carcaci has been dead two years now. Mr Morrison still lives, more decrepit and deafer than ever. And Mrs Joseph Whitaker, with the same brave efforts, but with rarer success, endeavours to make him hear her voice.

In a corner of the room, are two young women, sisters by affection, but not by blood. One of them is Sophie Rose – the other, Maria Carcaci. Do not imagine, O reader, that they give themselves up to lamenting their lost happiness, which is irreparable. No! Sophie, with the dignity of a dethroned queen, keeps silent before strangers, while recalling to her mind her lost kingdom and her father's affection robbed from her by the deceitful Lyla. Maria, after exhausting the spring from which came her tears, has taken up her burden and goes forward in her sad life, without fear or hope. But who would search in her heart would find there, written in letters of blood, the name of James Rose junior.

The deceitful Lyla bore James Rose senior another child in 1868, and in that year he died. Old Mr Morrison, Lyla's father, was far from crack-ing up. He never, for instance, wore an overcoat, even in the coldest weather. In 1867 he lost his partner, Seager from cholera; still undaunted he set out in his eighty-first year on an extended trip to England and Scotland. He was accompanied by an employee, Camillo Lojacono, grandson of the great Sicilian financier Michele Pojero who had been associated with Florio in all the early commercial ventures. Lojacono wrote of him on this trip as 'quest'uomo impareggiabile e mummificato che muovevasi come un giovanotto nonostante i suoi 80 anni suonati.'[10] Later he said: 'Mr Morrison was a gay companion, particularly after sunset. He seemed much younger than me, and his rosy-blonde wig and dyed beard completed the illusion.' By 1870 Ackie Whitaker had recovered from her grief; she married Morrison's son William, her second cousin, rather a dim person who carried on the shipping business after his father's death in 1873.

Cholera continued to be a terrible scourge in Palermo; 7873 died from it altogether on this occasion. During 1866 and 1867 both Joseph and Ben gave generous donations to subscriptions 'pei poverosi cholerosi'. Both were in the habit of giving big sums to charities. In December 1866 each donated about £20 to church expenses (Willie gave £8). Ben seems to have been mainly responsible for the building of the entire church at Ossett and in 1869 he gave £500 to the Ripon Cathedral restoration fund. Then it was decided that the time had come to erect an English church in Palermo, so Joseph and Ben volunteered to build one at their joint expense.

The spot chosen was opposite Square Emilia. Foundations were laid in 1872 and, thanks to the enthusiasm and energies of a Colonel Henry Yule, another Palermo resident, the church was opened for divine worship just before Christmas 1875; it was a typically English late-Victorian affair in yellow sandstone, a notable contrast to Palermo's other architecture. The architect was Henry Christian, cousin of Carrie's husband and responsible for the alterations at Hesley. Willie dutifully donated windows in memory of his great-uncle. The font was the gift of Mrs Beech of Poughkeepsie, New York, the children's heads on the corbels being those of Gordon Morrison, Ackie's third son who died in infancy, and Prince Max of Baden.

Two other important deaths must be recorded for this period: Vincenzo Florio in 1868 and John Goodwin in 1869. Goodwin died *en poste* and was succeeded by George Dennis the following year. Vincenzo Florio died worth something over a third more than Benjamin Ingham, as far as their respective estates in Sicily and Italy were concerned. There was no doubt about his heir, for his able and brilliant son Ignazio was already his partner.

In 1860 Vincenzo had been made a *consigliere comunale* (councillor of the Comune of Palermo), and in 1865 he had been president of the Camera di Commercio and the Tribunale del Commercio. In 1864 he had become a Senator, and he was also a governor of the Bank of Sicily. He was one of the most powerful and able men that Sicily had ever produced.

The story of the rise (and fall) of the house of Florio awaits its biographer. Vincenzo and Ignazio were in the main literally responsible for the industrialisation of Sicily. Up to 1860 many of their enterprises had some backing from the British. But when in that year, after Garibaldi had left, the 'Banco di Circolazione' was formed, modelled on the National Bank, under the aegis of the Florios, Bordonaro, Pojero and others, there was no attempt to draw in Ingham or any in the British community. A sign of the times no doubt. In any case the Banco di Circolazione never in the end came into force – quite why, one does not know.

The *Baglio* at Marsala, the *tonnara* and fish canneries at Favignana, the Oretea iron foundry, ceramics, armaments, shipbuilding: these, beside their banking and the merchant fleet, were the main sources of the Florios' wealth. In 1860 they owned five steam vessels:[11] by 1877 Ignazio had twenty-seven and soon he had ninety-nine – he was limited to this number by law, but had a model made in solid gold to 'make up' the 100. In 1881 Ignazio merged his fleet with Rubattino of Genoa.

Ignazio Florio had been born in 1838, Dignified, affable, quiet, he had the ideal flair to carry on his father's work – he was a very different man from, say, Joseph Whitaker, but then Joseph had not inherited so much capital. Vincenzo had the genius, but Ignazio was the entrepreneur. Moreover Ignazio married into the aristocracy, and his wife, *née* Baroness Giovanna d'Ondes, was the sort of person who knew how to use wealth to a dazzling effect. The scale of their entertainments encouraged the great families of Palermo – the Trabias, the Scaleas, the Mazzarinos, the Cutòs, and indeed the next generation of Whitakers – to attempt to compete. In 1873 the vast Politeama Garibaldi was begun on the Piazza Ruggiero Settimo, facing the Willie Whitakers; it was not finished until 1892. Not content with this building, the Palermitans – ignoring the terrible poverty of the back streets – planned an even vaster theatre, the Teatro Massimo, designed by Filippo and Ernesto Basile, with a huge dome and massive Corinthian portico, and mostly underwritten by the Florios. It was finished in 1895, having taken twenty years to build, and had a stage which in size was only exceeded in Europe by the Scala and the Paris Opéra. By then, thanks to a large extent to Giovanna Florio, Palermo was at her fashionable zenith and had become a byword for elegance.

# XV

## *The Mafia Supreme*

AFTER leaving prep. school Pip had been at Harrow, and in 1867 he returned to Palermo to work in the family firm. He was seventeen, shy, fair-haired, not bad-looking, a scholarly young man in a dilettantish way and still very keen on natural history, though at the same time – in a typically British fashion – an ardent sportsman. For a while, after his sister Ackie's marriage, he was the only member of that large family to be living at home, all the others being either married, working elsewhere or at school in England.

He has left a nostalgic little account of happy *villeggiature* at the Villa Sofia between the years 1868 and 1881. He also explains why in Palermo they preferred to take a *villeggiatura* in the spring – and perhaps also in the autumn – instead of in the summer:

> I shall never forget the delight of going to the country after a winter's experience of town-life in Palermo. Long before my father's fiat had gone forth, fixing the day for our departure, I began to anticipate with keen excitement the coming change. . . .
>
> By the beginning of April the Sicilian spring had already set in. The country on all sides was bursting into fresh leaf, the first swallows of the season had put in an appearance, and the little green tree-frogs had started their nightly chorus, varied by the whistling notes of their larger speckled-grey congeners. In town signs of spring were also visible, and a few straw hats and white 'duck' costumes might already be seen in the streets. The *villeggiatura* season had at last arrived and the Palermo *villeggianti* of all classes, from the titled owner of some magnificent old *casina* to the humble *impiegato* [clerk] renting a modest four-roomed dwelling, hastened to pack their family goods and chattels and wended their way countrywards. . . . The hottest months of the year were, not without reason, spent by most people in town, for Palermo, situated as it is, on a wide spreading bay, facing north-east, is in summer an exceptionally cool town, enjoying a refreshing sea-breeze by day and an equally cool land-breeze by night. Its streets, too, are well shaded, thanks to the lofty *palazzi* and other spacious buildings

flanking them, which themselves maintain an equable and comparatively pleasant temperature, even in the hottest weather. Fortunately the dreaded *scirocco* does not often blow during a normal Sicilian summer. . . .

When my father purchased the Villa Sofia in 1850 – the year of my birth – the flower garden, or *fioreria*, was limited to the small square plot immediately in front of the house, with its *vasca*, or fish-pond, surrounded by four lofty cypress-trees. The remainder of the property was, at that time, mainly given over to the cultivation of olives and prickly-pears, with some orange and lemon trees. Gardening was my father's hobby, and the laying out of the new grounds afforded him intense enjoyment and interest. Every tree and shrub was planted under his personal supervision. A narrow lane on the other side of the garden wall united the Via della Favorita with the village of Resuttana. It was very little used and consequently most solitary, to such a degree, indeed, as to be positively dangerous in those days when brigandage and *Mafia* reigned supreme. I well remember one Autumn, when my father and mother were absent from Palermo, I used daily to go out to the Villa Sofia alone and received a series of threatening letters, one of which, signed with a skull and crossbones, indicated that very lane as the spot where I was enjoined, under pain of death, to deposit a large sum of money hiding it under a particular stone indicated in the letter. I knew well enough who was the head of the local *Mafia*, so I sent him a message saying that the letters had been deposited at the *questura* [police station] giving the name of the man, in case I was killed. I had no more trouble after this.

The fine pepper-tree walk, with its large carob tree at one end, which formerly existed on the east side of the house has disappeared, as has also the adjoining long path, with its vine pergola, a favourite haunt of ours when the grapes were ripe. I also have pleasant, not to say greedy recollections of a certain fine peach tree. . . . In the late summer and early autumn, I used often to ride out to the Villa Sofia of a Sunday morning, for a breakfast off prickly-pears, under the old carob trees, a meal preceded by a bathe in the *gebbia* or reservoir.

When in the country early hours were naturally the order of the day. My father, at all times an early riser, used to be up by 6 o'clock, and after a cold bath took his 'constitutional' in the garden, preparatory to driving into town, to his office. Except on Sundays he used always to breakfast in town, and his carriage was ready for him every morning at 7.30 in spring and at 8 o'clock in autumn. His punctuality was proverbial – so much so, that some of our friends living on the Colli road used to tell me that they were in the habit of setting their clocks and watches by him. . . .

My younger brother Bob and I, both rather great smokers, used – after he had come home from school in England – to make good use of our little smoking-room, giving on to the long terrace, although I remember, when dining late, being in the habit of going downstairs and finishing my pipe or cigar in the stables or in Don Emilio's[1] rooms, opening on to the garden.

Like most of the Palermitan ladies, my dear Mother, when in the country, used generally to spend the day quietly at home, seldom going into town and but rarely paying any visits. It was customary among the ladies to get over all their formal duties before leaving town, for once the *villeggiatura* had commenced the season was at an end and one was supposed to be 'out of town', even though one's country house might be within a few minutes drive of Palermo. Among the *villeggianti*, however, should they happen to be living near each other, friendly calls were made and of course one's intimates never completely abandoned one, though all society functions and duties were over for the time being.

One of the most pleasing recollections connected with our *villeggiature* is that of the quail shooting in the spring. Through the kindness of General Medici, then Prefect, my name was included in the list of a few privileged sportsmen who had permission to shoot in the royal property. For some years I continued to avail of this permit, and although it was not often I made more than a very moderate 'bag', I nevertheless spent many an enjoyable day in the Favorita, with my dogs and gun. About that time I had several good pointers, and used to amuse myself by training them. On one red-letter day I got 82 of the little birds to my own gun. . . .

The Favorita undoubtedly was a Godsend for us living at the Villa Sofia, and to me in particular, for seldom a day passed without my going there at least once during the twenty four hours, either on foot or on horseback. In the autumn, as well as in the spring, I used to go after woodcock, but I never had much luck with the long-bills, and the guns were generally more numerous than the birds. Still, it was always good healthy exercise, and the fresh autumnal mornings were most enjoyable, either for a tramp through the woods, or for a gallop on the race-course, which had then not been long instituted. *Eheu fugaces, labuntur anni!*

General Medici had become a considerable friend of the Whitakers and Inghams, and was a frequent guest especially at Emily's numerous parties at the Palazzo Ingham, where he would enjoy a good American cigar over a rubber of whist. It had been hoped by the Government in the north that a strong man of his calibre would prove the answer to the *Mafia*. But it was not to be the case. During the 1870s the *Mafia* developed into a virtual reign of terror. Medici had always to be accompanied by a large armed escort whenever he went any distance outside Palermo. It was his belief (like Filangieri's) that large-scale expenditure on public works could solve the Sicilian predicament. But the basic problem was still the same: that desire for 'sleep', a weariness – and more specifically despair, a desperation arising from a deep-engrained poverty centuries old, mixed with ignorance, superstition and the people's own natural hotblooded-ness. The grievances of the peasants were still being exploited by an often illiterate and corrupt middle-class, bent on gilding its own coffers, and the result was as Gavin Maxwell described it eighty years later, when the *Mafia* had a sudden resurgence, a protection racket on the grand scale. Vendettas and revengeful murders flourished; whole families were wiped out (such as the Frattuzzi and Stoppaglieri in the area between Bagheria and Monreale, a feud which started in 1872 when a Frattuzzi made the calamitous mistake of denouncing a member of the other clan to the police), and people would be terrified of admitting to a drop of some tainted blood. Not that the aristocracy was exempt by any means from contamination. There was the famous case at the communal elections of Villalba in 1881. The Marquis of Villalba, who was in league with the *Mafia*, took his precautions ten days beforehand. Some 218 citizens were qualified to vote, so he locked them all into a granary, releasing them eight at a time so that they could be conducted to the polls under armed escort. He was elected.[2] As for the police, the corruption among them was so great that when Diego Tajani in 1871 accused Giuseppe Albanese, the chief of the police, of conniving at various crimes, including murder, there was an attempt to silence him by the government.

All this was muddled with the Sicilian cult of *omertà*. The *Mafia* demanded blind obedience. Family ties, graft, knowing the right people in the right places, these were taken for granted, as the very fundamentals of life. But everyone, of course, was united against common or garden petty crime.

Sidney Sonnino, in his excellent, sensational (at the time) and still very readable book on the Sicilian peasant, considered the *Conca d'Oro* in 1876 to be totally in the hands of the *Mafia*. Lush and fertile though the district was, Palermo's very history, and the fact that it was the capital and domicile of the nobility and aristocracy, had brought the *forunculo* (boil) of the *Mafia* to a head more than anywhere else, giving it a particular form of suppuration.

Rome fell on 20 September 1870. Medici, as the hero of the Vascello, could not be there with General Cadorna to be among the first to enter the Eternal City. In August of that year Mazzini had arrived in Palermo, to preach republicanism. His views could have been dynamite in all that discontent, so Medici had to order his arrest. Actually the Palermitans had taken remarkably little notice. Three years later, full of honour and acknowledged as one of the great figures of his time, Medici left Palermo for a life of semi-retirement in Florence.

In October 1872 Ben Ingham was in Paris, staying as usual at the Hotel Meurice. During lunch on the fourth he suddenly choked, and by 2 p.m. he was dead.

His English estate, as in the case of his uncle, was less than might have been expected, this time 'under £40,000'. The eventual beneficiaries were the children of his sister, Ann Brooke, but naturally Emily came in for the greater share, including the Palazzo Ingham and its contents. Judging from the firm's account books he had been very generous to her since the old man's death. In 1867 he had, for instance, given her a pair of diamond earrings that had belonged to the Marchesa delle Favare; they had cost him £1600, and a few months afterwards she had been given more jewels worth £140. Emily, since the death of her stepfather, was also in her own right the owner of the *Baglio* Wood in Marsala and the Palazzo Derix in Palermo.

Within a very short while Emily was married again, to General Medici. It must have been a civil wedding, as no official records have come to light. One hopes, at least, that it was not just a case of *concubinaggio*. One tradition persists that they were married in the Prefecture at Palermo, which would have been within ten months of Ben's death. Pip wrote later that the wedding had taken place at General Radaelli's villa in Florence in 1874, and that he went up there to give the bride away.

The Medicis never lived in the Palazzo Ingham, for in April 1874 it was sold for 20,000 *lire* to Cavaliere Enrico Ragusa, son of the famous Salvatore of the Trinacria Hotel. Ragusa slightly added to it and turned it into the Hotel des Palmes, which name it still holds, the palms being in the exotic garden in Square Emilia, by now affectionately known in Palermo as 'Lo Square'. In 1882 he still further enlarged it. Emily sold the

*Baglio* Wood to Ingham Whitaker (as the firm had been known since 1868, following Stephens' demise) and it became henceforward the residence of the firm's managers.

In 1876 Medici was created Marquis of the Vascello. He was already a Senator and had been *aiutante di campo* to Victor Emmanuel. Two years later he became *aiutante* to Umberto I, and Emily was made a lady-in-waiting to Queen Margherita. Thus, if there was any irregularity in their union, it was concealed from the royal family. Shortly afterwards the King agreed that Medici's daughter by an earlier liaison should be the heir to the title, since Emily was well into her forties and presumably past child-bearing. But here there is another mystery, for not only is there no record of this earlier marriage, but there is no trace either of the daughter's death, or even of her name – she must have died before her father, for the title went to his first cousin, Luigi.[3] At any rate the Medicis lived in Florence, in a house still known as the Villa Emilia, belonging originally to the Dukes of Mecklenburg and afterwards to the Trollope family, who gave it the *aspetto nostalgico di un castelletto inglese*.

It is necessary at this stage to chronicle yet more marriages and deaths. Benny, at Hesley, married his cousin Caroline Hudson in 1871. He was, it seems, becoming steadily richer, and steadily meaner. In the same year Sophie Pickersgill – great relief to all – remarried. Her second husband was very different from the gadabout William, in fact another distinguished Garibaldinian hero, Corrado Tommasi-Crudeli,[4] a widower with a walrus moustache and a bald head; he was by then a professor at Rome University where he worked at the Institute of Anatomy and Physiology that he himself had founded. 'Cruel Thomas' had been wounded at Milazzo, where he had been commanding a battalion in Cosenz's division, and again at Messina. In 1866 he had been in command of the National Guard in Palermo.

Then in 1872 Charlotte Gardner, eldest daughter of Edward Gardner (who had died in 1862), made a spectacular match. She married Baron Gabriele ('Nenè') Chiaramonte Bordonaro, nephew and heir to the financier Bordonaro[5] who had been partner to Ingham and Florio in so many projects, and who had bought up great quantities of Radalì land.

In 1870 Ewan Christian died, and three years later Carrie married his cousin, Henry Christian, the architect. The Vescovina died, aged only thirty-one. Willie left Palermo the following year, and the Sant'Oliva house was let. Just before he went he arranged for a pipe of marsala to be sent to the King in Rome – in grateful thanks, no doubt, for the barony just conferred.

In 1878 Willie married again, his second wife being perhaps the best-looking of the Whitaker ladies, Rita Sartorius, daughter of Admiral of the Fleet Sir George Sartorius, who had fought at Trafalgar and commanded the Liberal fleet in Portugal in 1832. Two years before the Vescovina's death he had bought Pylewell Park, an early eighteenth-century house near Lymington which he had boldly proceeded to enlarge and Victorianise, unfortunately with the help of Henry Christian. The Vescovina and he had not been getting on too well, and in consolation she had acquired a Sicilian admirer. Willie's jealousy had made him decide to give up Palermo altogether. He himself died in 1893 and it was his son, also called William, who was mainly responsible for so magnificently laying out the huge garden, to this day full of his rare shrubs, flourishing in the almost frost-free climate of the Solent.

Whilst dealing with family chronicles, let us briefly also glance at the fortunes of the Woodhouses. Humphrey Hervey's wife had died during a heat-wave in August 1861, and Hervey, so Cossins had written, had been so affected 'that he could not be made to believe the reality'. As a result he lost interest in the firm, and a very good thing too, for it had reached a parlous state. The situation was saved by Sam Woodhouse's second son, Fred, who went out to Marsala for five years in 1867 immediately after leaving Eton. It was he who persuaded his father that there was still a decent future in the wine trade in Sicily, and who convinced him to buy the half share in the business owned by Will Woodhouse and Humphrey Hervey.

Sam's nominal capital had been £100,000 and he had been content to receive a regular income of only £800 gross out of this. Fred was now granted a quarter share of the profits. The firm under his direction flourished in such a spectacular manner that by 1874, on his marriage, he was earning £4000 a year. In due course he was joined by two of his brothers. Their prosperity continued steadily until the turn of the century.

According to Sonnino Ingham, Whitaker was still the largest wine firm in Marsala, employing 300 men. The district around was split into numerous tiny farms surrounded by vineyards. The *inglesi* lent the farmers money, fixed the price of wine each season and controlled every detail of its sale. Some years were of course bad, as a result of which most farmers had never been able to catch up with repaying their loans and were thus chronically in debt.

By and large the British and other expatriate residents had been left in peace by the *Mafia*. If there were any threats, they were taken light-heartedly, witness Pip's accounts of his *villeggiature*. We also have the Woodhouses' boast that their family was never once endangered. However in 1876 the whole foreign colony had an exceedingly unpleasant jolt. What seemed to be a fairly local matter was to result in angry snarls between the Italian and British Governments.

In northern Italy there had been a growing sense of guilt about the situation in Sicily. Crispi had maintained that in the past fifteen years she had suffered a worse oppression than she had ever known under the Bourbons. 1876 was the year of the alarming report by Sonnino and Franchetti revealing that not only was brigandage now an accepted state of affairs throughout the island but that the ruling classes were heavily implicated. A correspondent to *The Times* wrote:[6] 'Almost everyone, from the proprietor to the day labourer, is in league against the authorities and in the interest of the brigand. The brigand may be outlawed by the Government but he is not outlawed by society.' Needless to say, the correspondent added bitterly: 'If an Englishman ventures to speak, Ireland is thrown in his teeth.'

Several distinct bands were operating, one west of Alcamo, many to the east of Palermo along the north coast, and a quantity around Sciacca and Girgenti. The most famous of all brigands in the mid 1870s was Antonino Leone, who had the chilling reputation of being an invincible marksman, and who operated due south of Palermo in the desolate, craggy area between Lercara Friddi and Villalba – these places being the birthplaces of two notorious post-World War II *Mafia* chiefs, Lucky Luciano and Don Calò Vizzini.[7] Leone, a little, burly, brown man, born in 1842, with black eyes, a small head and curly black beard, had had a price of £1000 on him since 1873, when he had 'sequestrated' Baron Porcari for thirteen days, receiving a ransom of £2600 for his pains.[8]

On 4 November 1876 John Forester Rose, the youngest son of James and Lilly Rose and born before the year of the cholera epidemic, set off by train to Lercara, forty miles from Palermo and the site of the sulphur mines owned by the firm of Gardner Rose and Co. A strong, straight-backed, moustachioed young man, he was accompanied by his brother George and some others. Instructions had been given for a groom to meet him with his mare at the station, since Forester preferred to ride instead of driving in a postal carriage.

Lercara, 2000 feet above sea-level, north-facing (hence Friddi, meaning cold), numbered in those days some 12,000 inhabitants. It was considered by Sicilian workers to be a prosperous and impressive place (despite the smell of sulphur), what with its factories, warehouses and relatively grand villas inhabited by foreigners, its wide streets and public gardens – though to Murray's *Handbook* it was a 'miserable town of mean hovels'. The railway was situated in the valley below. Forester took a short cut, while the carriages made their way up the precipitous road. Suddenly he was confronted by four armed Sicilians, 'dressed like country gentlemen'. One of them seized his bridle; then at gun point he was made to dismount and get on another horse, while another man took over his mare. The mare, however, was difficult to control, and during the confusion, as Forester was to write later in his official statement for George Dennis:

> I caught sight of the three carriages slowly creeping up the hillside beneath us, and thinking I should be safe if I could only reach them, I resolved to make a dash for it; so throwing myself from the saddle, I rushed as hard as I could down the hill towards the carriages. The brigand who was leading the horse I had left, fired at me as I ran, and the bullet whizzed past me, but I reached the carriages without injury. I shouted for the *carabinieri* but none were in sight. They had left the carriage road for a short-cut up the hill, and were nowhere visible. I felt sure, nevertheless, of my safety for I thought the usual patrol of the soldiers must be somewhere near at hand. Meanwhile two of the brigands, one who I afterwards learned was the notorious *capo-banda* Leone, and the other leading the horse from which I had escaped, approached the carriages. The passengers, some twenty in number, had now got out and stood in a crowd in the road. Seeing the brigands approach I appealed to these people for protection, but in vain.

George Rose kept quiet and nobody gave away his identity. A correspondent to *The Times* continued the story:

> With the utmost audacity and self-possession, this man [Leone] rode alone into the midst of the passengers, singled out young Rose, with cool impertinence upbraided him with treating him very badly by this attempt to escape, and compelled him at the muzzle of his double-barrelled breechloader to remount the horse from which he had just escaped, apologizing at the same time with mock courtesy for the inconvenience to which he was obliged to put him.

The perfect highwayman. Forester was then forced to ride off with the brigands. They rode for several hours, and on one occasion they were approached by a body of *militi*.

Leone instantly pulled up, and made us lie flat on our horses, and the *militi* passed us in the gloom without perceiving us. . . . We continued our ride till 2 a.m. on the 5th when we came to a halt. My own mare not being accustomed to a protracted journey of sixteen hours, fell beneath me twice, and was left behind, Leone promising that she should be well cared for and restored safely to Lercara. I have reason to believe that she had been purposely kept without food by my groom, Lo Sairo, whom I believe to have been in league with the brigands, in order to render me a more easy prey, if I should take alarm on first encountering them and attempt to escape. We now all dismounted and I was led to a cave where a fire was made and we had supper. I have no idea of the situation of this cave but it must have been at a considerable elevation for the cold was intense. It was now that I asked the chief his name, and he told me he was Leone ['Sono il brigante Leone.'] I also asked him what amount of ransom he intended to demand for my release. He replied by requesting me to write a letter to my brothers, telling them to send half a million of *lire*, or 40,000 *onze* (nearly £20,000). I represented to him that such a sum was utterly out of the question. I threw the pen away, and refused to write. He insisted, but I was resolute in my refusal, telling him he had better kill me at once, than utterly ruin my whole family. He gradually came down in his demand to 10,000 *onze* (£5000) declaring he would not take less, and for this sum I was obliged to write. . . . My brothers sent a reply that it was quite out of their power to pay so large a sum.

In this grotto we remained nine days, waiting for the arrival of the ransom money. But the presence of troops in the neighbourhood prevented its delivery. We fared tolerably well here, receiving a supply of provisions daily, which we cooked ourselves with charcoal. We received the papers from Palermo, and heard the rumours current in that city relative to my capture. Who brought the food and information I cannot tell, for I never was allowed to issue from the grotto. One day a dog came to a hole in the roof of the cave, and barked at us. The brigands not choosing to fire, killed him with stones. On another occasion while in this cave we heard the tramp of soldiers over our heads.

Forester noticed that, although the brigands boasted constantly of the number of people they had killed, they all wore crosses round their necks. Negotiations with the Rose family continued. For eleven more days he was kept on the move, 'taking the greatest care during the day never to stand up or to expose ourselves for a moment.' The horses had disappeared. They walked at night, sometimes in cold heavy rain, and by day they hid among thickets or rocks, always in a new place. Then, thanks to the 'good offices of an influential member of the *Mafia*', Forester's brothers managed to get half the ransom, £2500, to Leone, the understanding being that the rest would be paid at a later date.

Forester was conducted to a spot three miles from Sciara, where Leone 'took an affectionate leave of me, embracing me warmly, and giving me directions as to the road I was to pursue to reach the station.' At the same time he was presented with a third class single ticket, and his cap, mantle, cuff-links and watch were returned to him.

The attitude of Sicilians had been anything but contrite while this had been going on. Forester's capture had been the subject of a dialect ballad sold in the streets of Palermo. It treated Leone like a modern Robin Hood: 'This brave man stole from the rich. . . . If he sees poor people he has compassion on them,' etc. etc.

Indignant letters to *The Times* now appeared. As one correspondent, who signed himself 'Exile', pointed out: 'The last and least thing which a *capo-brigante*, like Leone, has to dread is, perhaps, the being denounced to the authorities, even for the sake of £1000. Those who know Sicily well are convinced that not one of the multitude of people who are acquainted with Leone's person could be tempted even by such an enormous reward, as this would be to a Sicilian, to betray him to the Government.' In December a joint 'memorial' was sent by the British resident merchants in Sicily to Lord Derby, the Foreign Secretary. It was demanded that he should urgently approach the Italian Government about 'taking prompt steps for repressing the lawless system which exists.' They pointed out that a considerable proportion of the island's population, including 'some of the higher classes', had a 'wide-spread sympathy with the brigands', while for many there was 'a mysterious dread of their vengeance, which prevents and paralyses any ordinary efforts to put down the system.' Since Forester's release a Signor Tasca had been captured, at the very gates of Palermo. The memorialists then went on to make precise suggestions as to how the Italian Government should deal with the menace. First, they said, the province in which an act of brigandage had taken place should be held responsible for paying not only the ransom, but a fine of an equal amount to the Government. Second, the troops employed should be northerners not Sicilians.

Sensible suggestions no doubt, but the Italians were outraged – and, one must admit, with some reason. Was the British Lion now assuming responsibility for telling them how to run their internal affairs? Among those Deputies who expressed the greatest indignation in Parliament was Rudinì, in spite of the fact that he had been one of the most vocal in urging that something should be done about suppressing the brigandage in Sicily. After all, he pointed out, the British merchants did not have to live there if they did not like it. *The Times*[9] was scornful about 'wounded dignity' and the so-called 'hospitality extended to British residents' – 'There are Italian soldiers and statesmen who would soon restore order if they were fully supported by the Government. Two or three such men as Medici, invested with full powers, would extirpate brigandage without material difficulty.' It was said that the irritation in the Italian Parliament was mainly because Forester Rose had only been released 'upon payment of a large ransom' and 'now being free does not inform of the whereabouts of his captors, notwithstanding the fact . . . that all who have trod the road which surrounds the gardens of the Conca d'Oro . . . know how, from step to step, crosses are to be seen sculptured on the walls, and signifying that here such and such a one was assassinated for having denounced such another to the authorities.'

Forester, resting in Cannes, was now stung into writing a letter to *The Times*. He most certainly had given a full statement to the authorities on his release, and his brothers had gone straight to the Prefect when he had been captured, this Prefect advising them to take whatever steps they thought necessary. It must be confessed that his letter is not entirely in line with family tradition, when one takes into account that influential member of the *Mafia* who had acted as intermediary. At any rate feathers were before long smoothed down. And in due course Leone paid a nocturnal visit to the Rose household, leaving a present of game for Forester with a polite note reminding him that not only had he been promised a new-style American repeating carbine but the second £2500 had not yet been paid. But Forester was in England, This note (without game) was twice repeated.

The Roses were, needless to say, anxious in case some other member of the family might meanwhile be sequestrated. Luckily for them, however, in September 1877 Leone was killed, betrayed by an accomplice whilst he was waiting for yet more ransom money. When he had realised he was trapped, Leone had seemed stupefied and quite unable to use a dreaded carbine that he already possessed. A *carabiniere* blew out his brains from a distance of four inches. Two of his accomplices, Zaurande and Lo Bue, originally herdsmen, were also killed, but a third, Randazzo, was brought to trial. Forester had returned to Palermo, and in some trepidation he not only gave evidence but identified him. Then Randazzo escaped from a prison van, in a most sensational manner, and there was real panic. No reprisal followed fortunately, though he was never re-captured, 'it being current at that time that he had made his way to the U.S.A'.[10]

Forester Rose married Lizzie Gardner in 1882, yet another link between the two families. Alas, by then the firm of Gardner Rose and Co. had collapsed. Its demise came in 1879; for the past four years sulphur prices had been dropping very rapidly, partly because of drastic competition from America – also the long overdue security laws for the mines had caused financial difficulties. The previous year had seen another crash, in a different field: the firm of Morrison. William Morrison was in bad health, and his father-in-law, Joseph Whitaker, was generous with loans, paying out some £100,000, which at least saved him from bankruptcy.

Joseph's third son Joss was in Marsala, helping a 'Cousin Joe', great-nephew of Benjamin Ingham. From the firm's account books we see that he bought a cutter and spent a lot on cigars, so he must have enjoyed himself (Pip's money went on dogs, and Sophie Tommasi-Crudeli spent a lot on sweets – at Christmas the family bought about £150 worth of them). Here he met an extraordinary brown-skinned girl, Euphrosyne Manuel, known as Effie, aged nineteen, from Malta and of Greek ancestry, niece of Cousin Joe's wife.[11] She was as mischievous and energetic as the good-hearted Joss was stolid and pedantic. It was an attraction of opposites and on 4 June 1881 they were married.

Effie was keen on riding and tennis. She also had a magpie interest for collecting *objets d'art* (Joss collected majolica, so at least they had this in common). Her taste in furniture was decidedly oriental. And she had very little reverence for the aristocracy. Not long after her marriage she was calling on her mother-in-law at the Villa Sofia, who was entertaining some aged princess; Effie crept up behind the princess's chair and crowed like a cock. This is just one of many such stories. No wonder she refused to live in dull old Marsala. Joss therefore had to persuade the bachelor Pip to take his place.

As Pip was becoming interested in archaeology, he did not mind having to spend some while in Marsala, where he started a collection of Phoenician and Roman fragments. He made frequent trips to the small, flat island of Motya or San Pantaleo, five miles from Marsala, and the site of one of the great Phoenician strongholds of the western Mediterranean. There was another reason for getting away from Palermo: he had hankered after one Alice Bennett, whose family came from Leghorn, and had lost her to Beau Gardner. All the same he still had to go to the capital occasionally, and on one of these visits he met and fell in love with Caterina, or Tina, Scalia, also a very individual girl though with tastes quite different from Effie's. One gathers that old Joseph was not very pleased about his son's interest in her.

Tina had been born in 1858. Her father, General Alfonso Scalia, was a Garibaldinian hero, and her mother, a stout, socially ambitious woman, had been born – like Tina – in London, the daughter of a Tuscan exile. Tina had been trained as an opera singer, and there were already hopes of appearances at the Scala. Tall, rather dreamy, long-faced, admittedly no great beauty, she had a charm and intelligence which appealed to 'interesting' people. Pip and she were married on 30 June 1883. There was no question, unfortunately, of finding a younger brother to come to Marsala, as the next in line, Robert, was hopeless at business. So Tina had to spend the first year of her married life at the *Baglio*, which she detested quite as much as had Effie and the Duchess of Santa Rosalia. Indeed she was only able to return to civilisation thanks to the death of her father-in-law, which occurred on 17 October 1884.

Joseph Whitaker died aged eighty-two. Among his many charities (he seemed to spend up to £200 a month on them) he and Sophia, his wife, were particularly remembered for the *Educatorio* Whitaker, near the Zisa and intended as a home for girls from poor families.[12] His British estate amounted to £640,390 18s 4d, and on his death, of course, the remainder of Benjamin Ingham's trust reverted to Willie. Broadly speaking, after leaving £1500 a year to each of his daughters, he divided his effects among his sons, with the exception of Willie, being already a multi-millionaire, who was simply left a gold watch and chain as a 'token of affection'. The wine business at Marsala and other businesses and property in Sicily were left jointly to Joss, Pip and Bob. The church was left to Joss, with an endowment of £6000. Their mother was to have the right to live in the Villa Sofia, but just a year later she died at Pylewell.

Bob was now courting Maude Bennett, sister of Pip's ex-flame Alice. Maude was very pretty and flirtatious, gay and fond of parties. She had been born in 1860 and when Garibaldi had been imprisoned at Varignano after Aspromonte, she and her sister used to be allowed to bring him puddings and cakes. The story goes that Bob offered her a bunch of lilies-of-the-valley after church, it being understood that if they were accepted she would marry him. But Maude felt so little for Bob at that time that, much as she loved lilies-of-the-valley, she refused him. It was the chaplain's wife, Mrs Burbidge, something of a professional matchmaker, who claimed to have persuaded her that she would be a fool to turn down such a rich suitor. After all, the Bennett girls had been practically penniless, their father dead and their mother, as Tina scathingly said later, 'of lowly birth and remarried eventually, for convenience's sake, to a Mr Saunders, an American widower, being the head of some workmen for the improvement of the port of Spezia'. So Maude and Bob were married on 1 March 1886.[13]

On the death of Sophia Whitaker, it was decided that Bob should take over the Villa Sofia, which like other Whitaker houses was promptly enlarged and embellished. Joss kept the Casa Lampedusa, and at Effie's instigation he erected an enormous *palazzo* in the Venetian manner on the adjoining garden along the Via Cavour. Pip and Tina, on the other hand, bought some acres of land on the northern outskirts of Palermo and proceeded to build an even bigger and statelier house, the Villa Malfitano, with a huge ballroom and reception rooms in the style of Louis Quinze and Louis Seize – all surrounded by an ambitious garden, whose exotic trees and shrubs far surpassed in quantity and variety those in the old Square Ingham.

The stage was now set. There were three rich Mrs Whitakers ready to rule Anglo-Palermitan life. Three Mrs Whitakers with very little in common.

# PART FOUR

*Princes of the Revolution*

# XVI

## *Exiles*

TINA WHITAKER attempted to start a diary soon after her marriage, but like many another would-be diarist she in no time lost the stamina. Then in June 1894 she made another effort. She foundered, started again, and finally six months later at last managed to turn it into an almost daily habit. In later life, conscious that she had been unusually fortunate in meeting important and gifted people, she also began writing retrospective 'pen-portraits', mainly with a view to incorporating them in an autobiographical book to be called *Memorie di una sopravissuta*.[1] This book did not come to pass, really because she was never much of a person for marshalling together facts and figures. She did, however, publish a volume based on her parents' reminiscences up to 1870; this was *Sicily and England*, which came out in 1907.

She was devoted to her mother and made no secret of the fact that she loved her far more than she did her father. Obviously she felt she owed more to her maternal, i.e. grander, ancestry, the Anichinis, rather than to her father's family, the Scalias, however spectacular the latter had been during the great days of the Risorgimento. Her mother's father, Pompeo Anichini, had been born in Pisa in 1782. He was a liberal and one of those who had welcomed Napoleon's troops when they had entered Florence in 1807; according to Tina, he actually then took service under Napoleon. He also had literary tastes, Filippo Pananti the poet being one of his friends.

Tina would profess a disdain for 'Trade', but the plain fact is that her much revered grandfather, Pompeo Anichini, was one of Benjamin Ingham's clients in the early 1820s. He not only bought wine from Ingham but – even more degrading – rags. He also was a victim of Lenzitti's bankruptcy in 1825. In his early days in Tuscany he was republican and anticlerical, though his life was 'governed by strictly Christian principles'. He took to producing inflammatory books and articles against the Catholic hierarchy, and about the time that Napoleon was an exile on Elba he was excommunicated and his writings were publicly burnt in the Campo dei Fiori in Rome by order of the Pope. It was swiftly hinted to him in Florence that he should leave Tuscany as soon as possible. He travelled to Sicily, Spain and Portugal, and finally reached London, even before Ugo Foscolo, regarded as the forerunner and doyen of the nineteenth-century Italian exiles.

Tina draws a veil over his marriage and nowhere mentions her grandmother's name. One deduces that he must have married around 1820. There were three children: two sons, Alfonso and Federico, who died young, and Giulia Cordelia, Tina's mother, born in 1824 and known as Giulietta until she became too plump. Anichini's wife died soon after, possibly as a result of Giulia's birth.

When Tina herself died, the obituaries described her mother as a Contessa. This however is not borne out in *Sicily and England*. Pompeo Anichini belonged to a distinguished family, though not a noble one; when Grand Duke Leopold came to the throne of Tuscany in 1765, he not only conferred several new titles but 'recognised' the old patrician families, among whom Pompeo's father, Cesare Anichini, was included. The Anichinis were the direct descendants of a Giunta Anichini who in 1423 was 'elected as candidate for the position of three chief governors of Florence'. Later, long after the publication of *Sicily and England*, Tina lighted on a passage in Gibbon's *Decline and Fall* which led her to assume that she was descended from the Anichinus who migrated to Tuscany from Rome in 47 B.C. after the assassination of Julius Caesar – and possibly there was some truth in this, a clue being that Cesare and Pompeo were for generations used as Christian names in the family.

Anichini had rather a fine face: high forehead, aquiline nose, clean-shaven, slightly humorous. In London he formed 'many lasting friendships': such great personalities as Mazzini (to whom he dedicated a pamphlet), Pepe, Arrivabene, Gallenga being frequent visitors to his house. He also knew Gabriele Rossetti and Antonio, later Sir Anthony, Panizzi. Indeed he sympathised with all patriots and exiles of whatever nationality and whether or not their ideas coincided with his own. Thus he became friendly with Lord Dudley Stuart, the head of 'a powerful group of Englishmen who espoused the cause of the Poles'; Lord Dudley's niece, Lady Townshend, and her eldest daughter, Lady Anne Sherson, were the 'greatest friends' of Giulia's girlhood. Naturally Anichini, like all leading Italian émigrés, was welcome at Holland House. Life was hard for the exiles, but liberal-minded English society enthusiastically took up their cause. Dinners, balls and receptions were given in their honour and it was considered fashionable to have a patriot at one's party. Thus the motherless Giulia became accustomed to move in the grandest circles in London.

Anichini eventually became naturalised British. He certainly had a fluent knowledge of English. One of his pamphlets was on the evils of divorce; it was published in 1836 and dedicated to Lord Brougham.[2] Much as he admired London, he said, as the home of liberty, he was horrified by its immorality; the middle classes were 'cheerfully exempted from the lash of my censures', but he was appalled by the 'disgusting licentiousness of high life' and even more by the 'iniquitous and heart-sickening depravities which rule the conduct of the low class'. On the one side there was Lady Winnington offering to society 'the soul-grieving unchristian exhibition of appearing in the Ecclesiastical Court, a suitor for the dissolution of her marriage on the ground – I tremble to think of it – I scarcely am able to write the black words . . . on the plea of impotency. Gracious God! And yet it is true.' On the other hand there was Mary Brown who in 1835 appeared in Lambeth for having pawned her wooden leg for three shillings in order to get 'beastly drunk' on gin.

Tina always represented her grandfather as having lived in a state of genteel impoverishment in London. Yet he continued in the wine and rags business, for Ingham wrote in 1829 promising to call on him. The Anichinis lived at that time in Spanish Place. Pompeo aged early; Mr Mills of the music shop in Bond Street used to watch Giulia – a lush, black-haired girl – taking her father on her arm on his daily walk, and he would wish that 'when he was old he too might have such a daughter'. Giulia was stout nearly all her life, but said Tina, 'the head and shoulders were perfect, and the lovely complexion and soft skin she kept to the last'; 'her total absence of gesture', moreover, 'showed how deep was her English education'. The Italian exiles 'absolutely idolised her', as well they might, for her pictures make her look a real *bel pezzo di donna*. That picturesque individual Gallenga sent her a special poem when she was only fifteen. A young attaché at the Turkish Legation, Cabouli Pasha, in time to become an ambassador at St Petersburg, offered to become a Christian if only she would marry him. Then there was the case of Mr De Burgh 'who was much in love with her, but whom my grandfather had forbidden the house, as he had the reputation of being a *mauvais sujet*. My mother was one day interviewing prospective housemaids, when, to her horror, a gaunt-looking female, who had just entered the room, threw up her veil and rushed forward to clasp her hand. It was De Burgh, who had resorted to this subterfuge in order to speak to her'.

Giulia also had a great attraction for her own sex, much as she objected to 'exaggerated feminine friendships'. There was the 'extraordinary infatuation' displayed by Mrs Woodhouse Currie, related to Sydney Smith and daughter of Lord Lyveden; she used to send notes, flowers and presents at all hours of the day. Marie Fox, the adopted daughter of Lady Holland to whom she behaved so 'disgracefully' after her marriage to Prince Lichtenstein, also admired Giulia very much. Madame Bini Puzzi declared she was like a Santa Caterina; Lady Galton said she 'looked almost divine' when playing her harp; Mrs Cowper Smith was 'at once fascinated by her charm'. Her accent in French was so pure as to be praised by Monsieur Brachet, instructor in French to the Empress Eugénie, and she was a 'first-rate musician'.

Among Giulia Anichini's particular friends were the chatterbox Lady Morgan, author of *Italy* and several novels and travel books, as well as a hostess (unkindly dismissed by some contemporaries as a 'snob and a tuft-hunter');[3] Mrs Inwood Jones, Lady Morgan's niece, nicknamed Mrs Inward Groans because of being 'rather inclined to fault-finding and be-moaning her fate';[4] Mrs Mostyn, daughter of Mrs Thrale; and the third Lady Combermere, wife of one of Wellington's generals whose upright figure was to be seen riding in the Park almost daily – 'his perfectly made wig, and the rouge upon his cheeks, giving him from a distance, an extraordinary appearance of youth'. 'All strangers of note' flocked to Lady Combermere's house at 48 Belgrave Square, for not only was she a clever musician, but an 'excellent amateur painter and a first-rate linguist'. Alas, she had a 'propensity for sarcasm' which overcame her better judgement; 'her epigrammatic remarks in some cases made her lifelong enemies'.

Lady Ely, whose friendship with Arrivabene in 1860 was inadvertently to lead to his release in Naples,[5] gave Giulia her first ball-gown, 'trimming it herself with carnations'. 'When my grandfather's affairs were found to be in hopeless confusion, and his health entirely broken down, my mother bravely resolved to give singing lessons.' It was Lady Ely who helped her to find pupils. Giulia never sang at public concerts. Instead she preferred to invite her friends to a *fête champêtre* in some garden lent her by a friend, such as at Lady Webster's Granard Lodge, Roehampton, or Mr Woolley's Prior's Bank, Fulham. Once Lord Londonderry even sent 'a band of the Guards' to accompany her.

Pompeo Anichini died on 28 November 1850. He had already met Alfonso Scalia, a young Sicilian exile who had distinguished himself in the 1848–9 revolution, at the house of Mrs Milner Gibson, friend of the Brownings, Dickens, Garibaldi and Mazzini. 'An attachment soon sprang up' between Alfonso and Giulia and they were married on 30 November 1852, 'my mother having insisted on this long period of mourning'.

The Scalias had lived for several generations in Palermo, all worthy citizens and respected, and although leaving reputations *senza infamia e senza lode* not one of them had displayed any intellectual powers. An uncle of Alfonso, Raimondo, had been administrator for the Trabias, another for the Cattolicas. His mother, however, came from livelier stock. She was born Caterina Serretta and had been initiated into the Carbonari as a *giardiniera*, as women associates were called, in a 'gruesome cavern near Naples': an ordeal 'before which the strongest men might shrink'. Tina writes of her as 'highly sensitive, courageous and of a patriotic temperament', in strong contrast to the 'placid indifference' of her husband. Francesco Vassallo, the patriot, used to relate how in 1847 the Scalias' house was entered by Neapolitan soldiers, in search of compromising papers affecting Luigi Scalia, the eldest son, known to be one of the heads of the Liberal party – and whom we have already met as one of the delegates to London in 1848–9. At last the soldiers reached the room in which Luigi and Alfonso were destroying the papers, Caterina bravely stood in front of the door. 'When ordered to stand aside, and let the soldiers pass, she cried: "You must first shoot me, and pass over my body!" The soldiers had no orders to fire upon a woman, and by keeping them at bay she saved her sons who escaped by the window.'

Luigi Scalia was born on 15 November 1806 and Alfonso on 23 April 1823. There were two sisters: one called Giulia, a good-natured person who in later years bore the brunt of running the household, and Adelaide, who married the patriot Vito Beltrani[6] and died of scarlet fever at the age of seventeen, only a few months after giving birth to a son, Martino. This Martino also achieved fame as a patriot and for two weeks in 1860 was in the Vicaria in the same cell as Ciccio Brancaccio. When the Scalia father died in the great cholera epidemic of 1837, Luigi became head of the family and took a job as agent for the Princess of San Cataldo, selling her sulphur for delivery to Licata. Alfonso as a child had the reputation of being a 'pickle'. He would climb over rooftops and switch round pots and pans in people's kitchens, when the owners were absent, or run about naked except for a skirt and headdress of white peacock's feathers, plucked from some old relative's cherished pets. He found it impossible to apply himself to serious study, so the family decided to send him to sea for some years.

The Scalia household in the Piazza Marina was always a favourite haunt for the revolutionaries, and it was here that Baron Casimiro Pisani (a relative), Giacinto Carini[7] (married to a first cousin of Luigi and Alfonso) and Antonino Minneci met at daybreak on 12 January 1848, the date of the eventual outbreak. Alfonso was then twenty-three and a captain in the Sicilian merchant marine.

On hearing the first shots they shouldered their guns and went off with my uncle Luigi Scalia. My father was about to follow them when his old uncle, Raimondo Scalia, barred the door and tried to keep him in. Whereupon my father drew out a pistol and declared he would blow his brains out on the spot if they would not let him go. 'Let him pass and do his duty,' cried his heroic mother. The door was opened and he followed his brother.

Martino Beltrani, being only eighteen, was however successfully held back. Alfonso was away for three days and nights. On his return he was able to report that he had taken three prisoners, one of whom was a major in the Neapolitan army.

On 13 January the provisional Government was proclaimed, with Luigi Scalia as a member. The following day he was at the meeting in the town hall, with Ruggiero Settimo, the aged Prince of Pantelleria and all the chief Liberal nobles and citizens. Alfonso managed to get a post in the artillery under Colonel Giacomo Longo, just escaped from prison; one of his colleagues was Alfredo Porcelli, who later eloped so romantically with Lord Mount Edgcumbe's ward. It was their battery which bombarded the Castellamare citadel. They were at Milazzo and after its fall removed the captured war material for use against Messina. Alfonso was now a major. He had an 'extraordinary power of sleeping' and 'during the siege of Messina a friend found him placidly asleep, although a bomb had fallen into the room where he was lying'. Afterwards Longo, Alfonso, his cousin Ercole Scalia and others went on the ill-fated expedition to Calabria. When things started to go badly Alfonso was sent back to Palermo to beg for help, being apparently the only person capable of making the journey, owing to his knowledge of seamanship. The trip saved him in fact. Longo and Ercole Scalia were among those captured in the brig *Gesù e Maria* by the Neapolitans and condemned to the galleys.[8]

Luigi Scalia and Prince Granatelli meanwhile had been sent to England, as Sicily's representatives. They had, as we have seen, sailed on the *Palermo*; Baron Pisani was one of the delegates to Turin. According to Tina, Granatelli caused some consternation among polite society in London because of his table manners; he would scratch his head with his fork and stir his coffee with his little finger, even at official banquets. Not so the clothes-conscious Luigi, whose 'courtly manners were in pleasant contrast with the uncouth ways of the Prince'. During the twelve years that he lived in England he made many important friends, including Lords Palmerston and John Russell. Indeed he enjoyed a great deal of hospitality

– too much, his enemies were to complain. After the brutal recapture of Messina by the Neapolitans an urgent SOS was sent to Scalia and Granatelli 'to urge them to greater efforts'. Palmerston invited them to stay at Broadlands, but nothing could be done. As Luigi wrote to Torrearsa: 'Ogni nostro argomento detto col sangue agli occhi e l'anima sulle labbra non poté ottenerci migliori promesse da parte dal Governo inglese.'[9]

Alfonso had been despatched again to Messina, to prepare for the Bourbon attack. 'He was, however, once more sent in hot haste to Palermo to procure money and ammunition [the Mr Scalia mentioned in Dickinson's diary]. Parliament immediately voted him 10,000 *onze* and this sum was placed in his charge. He returned with the supplies to Messina on the 3rd September, and took part in the last efforts made by that heroic city to maintain its independence.' When the patriot troops fell back to Milazzo, he and one other were the only two officers who refused to withdraw – 'my father declaring that he would fight until he had no ammunition left'. But the next day, 'unable to withstand the overwhelming numbers that were coming to their attack, they realized that further resistance was both useless and foolhardy', and they abandoned the town.

Back in London, Michele Amari, who had been Minister of Finance in Palermo, arrived on a special mission, the object of which was to push the Sicilian representatives to greater efforts. 'Great historian and orientalist as he was, apparently he had been inspired by political ambition . . . he undoubtedly became jealous of the position occupied by my uncle . . . this petty envy and jealousy is made abundantly clear in one of his private letters to the Marquis Torrearsa, in which he openly accuses my uncle of being lukewarm in the cause, adducing frivolous reasons by way of proof, one of them being his late rising in the morning.' (So sleeping heavily was a family failing.) Although Tina says that 'my high-minded uncle seems to have been quite unaware of this treachery of his friend', she does however admit that he 'went to the theatre constantly, especially to the opera', even though these visits were supposed to have been for a purpose ('Went to the Haymarket Theatre', runs an entry in his diary, 'to try and distract my thoughts, but it was impossible!'). Luigi was also blamed by the Sicilians for the P. & O. ship *Vectis* not being ready in time for delivery with the *Palermo* in the crucial month of March 1849.

After Mieroslawsky had retreated from Taormina, Alfonso was in command of the artillery forts at Catania, whilst they were being bombarded by four Neapolitan warships. Two of the warships were so seriously injured that they were forced to leave. 'I was told by one who was present at this spirited defence that when the guns under my father's command suddenly ceased firing, Mieroslawsky turned to the head of his staff, saying "Le canon cesse de tonner! Ce pauvre Scalia doit être mort." The pause, however, was only momentary.' This victory earned Alfonso many congratulations in high places.

As the situation in Sicily became ever more hopeless, Amari returned to Palermo. Luigi and Granatelli implored the British Government to intervene. All they received were sympathetic cluckings from Palmerston. Even after Palermo had fallen, and the patriots had fled, the delegates hung around Carlton Gardens. Palmerston kept them waiting for more than an hour; he seemed very embarrassed and told them simply: 'You must wish for better days; there is no more hope now.' He admitted that France had betrayed Sicily and that England had abandoned her. 'Now all is over!'

Alfonso came to join his brother in London. Imprisonment and worse lay in store for any patriot who remained, as in the case of young Bagnasco who had written the proclamation of 12 January 1848 and died subsequently under torture, some say by poison. The Neapolitan ambassador to London, the Prince of Castelcicala, at once opened 'a campaign of prosecution' against Luigi and Granatelli. First they were accused of embezzlement, in connection with the two ships bought for the rebels, then he brought them to trial in an English court for 'manning a ship in British territory and engaging men to fight against the King of Naples'. False witnesses were brought over, but Luigi and Granatelli – having admitted perjury – were acquitted on 6 July 1849. For the Bourbons to have won such a case would have been unthinkable.

Alfonso Scalia and Giulia Anichini had two marriages, one Roman Catholic and one Protestant, since Giulia had been brought up in the Church of England. In those days, said Tina, the Vatican did not 'raise the difficulties now existing', and her parents agreed that any sons would be brought up Catholic and any daughters would be Protestant.

Tina glossed over the troubles in their early years of marriage ('A petty thought never came to them' etc.). The fact was that Alfonso was less interested in society life; gossip bored him – especially in a language which he could at first barely understand. Neither was he used to such impecunious living. Giulia, now aged twenty-eight, found herself having to see less of her own friends, who in any case found Alfonso strangely rough and unconventional. Instead the house (in Wyndham Place) was filled always with arguing, excitable, hungry émigrés, for whom she had endlessly to serve the essential *pasta*. Alfonso was a year her senior, in appearance amiable, rather baggy-eyed with much hair over his ears, not nearly so handsome as his brother, and with a 'sense of humour rare for a Sicilian'; a good raconteur, in his daughter's words he was 'in principle an aristocrat but in practice a democrat, and adored by the lower classes, to whom he was ever ready to give the benefit of his advice'. The trouble was that his 'outlook in life was tinged with an eighteenth century insouciance', a contrast to Giulia's 'high tone of mind induced by the early Victorian code of manners'. But they were a generous couple. Luigi lived with them, and large dinners were given every Sunday, so noisy that neighbours sometimes sent servants round to complain. When Caterina Scalia died of the cholera in 1854, it was a terrible sadness to her sons that they could not go to Palermo. Entertaining stopped for a while. It was lucky that Alfonso had a job – in the P. & O., thanks to strings pulled by Luigi and to his experience in the merchant navy – to take his mind off his grief.

The Crispis were frequent visitors at the Scalia household. Signora Crispi's heroic devotion to her needy husband greatly impressed the Scalias. Of peasant background, she was to be the only woman among the famous Thousand on the voyage to Marsala. It was therefore a shock when Crispi, after he had become a 'brilliant and successful lawyer' in Florence, caused the marriage to be declared invalid – though 'undoubtedly she had been a great trial'. Then there was George Fagan, who returned for a while to London from Messina in 1852 and was eagerly welcomed by the exiles. The year previously he had helped Panizzi to visit the Neapolitan prisons, following the publication of Gladstone's *Letters to Lord Aberdeen*; he also played a large part in the plot to rescue Settembrini and Poerio.[10] Alfonso saw much both of Panizzi and his friend Sir James Lacaita, 'the Italian Englishman', who was on very close terms with Gladstone and at the time engaged in cataloguing the library at Chatsworth. Guglielmo Libri, the mathematician, and his wife – 'he so big and ponderous, phenomenally greedy, she so small and refined' – were visitors too; the Scalias would never believe in the truth of the scandal about Libri, that he had stolen valuable books in French provincial libraries – even though his crimes were proved after his death. The Marquis d'Azeglio, Piedmontese ambassador at the Court of St James, was friendly, but naturally had to keep his distance for political reasons – 'his calm, deliberate manner, combined with a certain natural reticence, gave one a higher idea of his intellect than perhaps he deserved'. More forthcoming were two young attachés, Corti ('so plain') and Maffei ('so good-looking'), themselves future ambassadors. Count Carlo Arrivabene, Baron Marochetti the sculptor (who modelled the bust of Panizzi at the British Museum), the Prince of Scordia and Damiano Assanti were other *habitués* in their time. Assanti, 'one of the most popular of the patriots', was to cause a sensation when, as a senator in the days of the Unity, he was challenged to a duel by Nicotera; Alfonso Scalia was his second.

The exiles were in the habit of meeting at the shop of the Italian book-seller, Rolandi, to hear and discuss the latest news. 'Mr Quaritch once told me that it was while he was a poor assistant there that he gave a sovereign to the Italian cause, so much was he impressed and wrought upon by the conversation and enthusiasm of the patriots. "And you have no idea, Madam, what a sovereign meant to me then."' Alfonso, in this world of bibliophiles, soon became infected himself. Not only did he become a collector, but he turned into an expert bookbinder and gilder.

Luigi's hobbies were botany and the flute, 'upon which instrument,' says Tina, 'he played fairly well'. Tall and fair, he was singularly like the composer Bellini, so much so that on one occasion, when he had gone to hear *Norma* in Milan, he was mistaken for the great man, 'and to his great discomfiture made the object of popular ovation'. The Scalia family belonged to the Moderate party, known as 'Malva' to the more advanced Liberals and Republicans. Thus Luigi never joined the Mazzinians, and 'although a personal friend of the Caldesi, Crispi and Aurelio Saffi, politic-ally he was entirely at variance with them.' Naturally he kept in touch with Palmerston, whom he nicknamed 'Cucca' (owl), and Lords John Russell and Minto.

Chief among the Scalias' English friends of the period was Mrs Lynn Linton, the authoress, then Elisa Lynn. Tina believed that at one time this rather earnest-looking but volatile and gifted lady nearly married Luigi and that only their dramatically opposed political views kept them apart. Since Mrs Lynn Linton was held in such very high esteem by Giulia Scalia, and eventually by Tina, who felt that she had exerted a strong influence over her, it is necessary to give a few facts about her early life.

Born in 1822, she was the daughter of a Northumberland vicar. She came to London in 1845 to be a 'woman of letters'. Her first books were un-successful, no doubt because of her lack of knowledge of the world, but her vehement eloquence and sharp, impulsive pen soon made her into a person of note. She went to Paris as a newspaper correspondent, returning in 1854, when she met the Scalias, entering wholeheartedly into the *polemica* at Wyndham Place. 'This brilliant authoress', Tina wrote, 'whose chival-rous nature always rose and rebelled against injustice, whose flashing eyes and heightened colour, when roused to enthusiasm or revolt, was a real stormy petrel in their midst.' 'Tumultuous articles' were being written in the *Saturday Review* and 'powerful essays' in the *Queen*. An agnostic, a medium, an admirer of Buddhism, a passionate defender of Zola, bitterly jealous of the success of George Eliot though in other respects generous-minded, she was reckoned by Rider Haggard to be 'one of the very ablest and keenest intellects of her time'. 'She was a great lover of the beautiful, especially in the human form, irrespective of sex. She was, however, totally lacking in sense of humour, and although appreciative of music did not understand it.' In 1858 she married the widowed James Linton, an engraver, it was said to test her educational theories on his children – not surprisingly the marriage was brief. It was then that she launched into her best period of fiction writing.[11]

Lady Morgan and Mrs Milner Gibson were still faithful friends. Poor Giulia was not always able now to accept their invitations. One evening, however, she was persuaded to go alone to a *soirée*, in order to sing to the Duke of Wellington. 'After the *Adieu* of Schubert, the Iron Duke was moved to tears, and thanked her warmly for the great pleasure she had given him. A few minutes later he was dozing on the sofa.' But not everyone grew old so gracefully. When Giulia called on the American-born Princess Elizabeth Bonaparte-Patterson, first wife of Napoleon's brother Jérôme, she found her weeping before a mirror. The Princess raised her face and said in French: 'Ah, my dear girl, you do not know the sadness of growing old when you have been so beautiful as I!' But Giulia had the right reply: '*Altesse*, if one is to suffer as I see you suffer now, I am happy to be less beautiful than you.'[12]

There was something about Giulia that appealed to 'confirmed bache-lors', or would-be bachelors who in the days of foolish youth had allowed themselves to get married. Abraham Hayward,[13] 'much sought after for dinners because of his brilliant conversation and ready wit', struck Tina disagreeably in later life because of his self-importance, sarcastic manner and 'keen eyes in a shrivelled body'. Percy ffrench was a more desirable person and a much closer friend:[14] of medium height, slight, fair, 'with an attractive Hibernian vivacity, a living proof that cold dignified reserve is not an indispensable evidence of high breeding.' 'Overpowering in his tirades, a bad listener and a witty writer of letters', he remained intimate with the family until his death. It was thought that his diplomatic career had been marred by his being too taken up by the 'intoxicating froth of society'. As one friend told Tina: 'I believe if I was going to Timbuctu, Percy would be able to give me a letter of introduction to a great friend there.' Then there was Sir John Harington.[15] a dandy, and musically minded; he was bald soon after he was twenty and known as the man with the least hair and most hair-brushes in London.

People, people. Giulia knew Lady Acton, widow of Prime Minister Sir John, and her two nephews, Harold and Roger, brothers of the Guglielmo who commanded the *Stromboli* when Garibaldi landed at Marsala. Admiral Sir George Sartorius, whose daughter Rita later became Willie Whitaker's second wife, was one of Luigi's special cronies. Among musical friends there was first and foremost, Madame Puzzi, who had made her operatic début in London in 1827, singing in Rossini's *Mosè in Egitto*; one of the useful aspects of her passion for Giulia was the fact that she organised the concerts at Apsley House. As for Edoardo Vera, the composer, famed for his wit and repartee, he would say that he only held three persons sacred: the rightful Queen of Italy, his sister and Giulia Scalia. Lesser fry paid appropriate court: Ciro Pinsuti, also a composer, 'a diminutive little person, refined and gentle in spite of his avariciousness'; and the mezzo-soprano Pauline Viardot, 'whose intense ugliness was such a drawback that she wisely refused to appear in opera parts requiring grace and beauty' – though this did not prevent her from being Turgenev's mistress.

There were many more. Several of the patriots – Mariano Stabile, Michele Amari, Baron Friddani, Carmelo Agnetta (so poor that he was reduced to selling *salami*) – had settled in Paris, and the Scalias were in the habit of paying them visits once or twice a year. Usually they stayed with Giacinto Carini, since he had married Alfonso's relative: 'handsome, fascinating, distinctly profligate Giacinto', the founder of the *Journal Franco-Italien*, and such a contrast to his son, the future Monsignor, 'so modest and shy'. It was at the Carinis' that Alfonso and Giulia met Dumas *père*.

For the Scalias these exciting days lasted until 1856, when Giulia became pregnant. Her first child was a boy, but he died almost immediately, a dreadful blow. On 12 November 1858 Tina was born – Caterina Paolina Anna Luisa. She on the contrary was a strong child, blue-eyed and light-haired, and baptised an Anglican. A baby in the house made life more restricted, and entertaining more difficult; trips to Paris were no longer possible. Alfonso was in any case getting worried about money. He would have been gloomier had he not been convinced, like all his friends, that the hour of liberation for Sicily had very nearly arrived.

# XVII

## Successor to Adelina Patti?

THE exiles in London were able to keep a continuous though guarded correspondence with their families in Sicily. For the bourgeoisie the Palazzo Scalia was still one of the most patriotic centres in Palermo. Alfonso's sister Giulia bravely kept the household going; she also opened a school for girls, 'where many distinguished men, who would not take office under the Bourbons, gave lessons, and thus gained means of sustenance' – one of these being Baron Pisani, who in fairness can hardly have been much of a teacher with his reputation for being a man of few words.

Most of the conspirators were people who had been too young to take part in the 1848 revolution. Night after night they met in the big *salone* of the Palazzo Scalia. Martino Beltrani would be there, and Baron Pisani's son. One of the most dramatic, not to say reckless, was another Scalia relative, the soft-voiced Giuseppe Caputo,[1] who perforce spent most of his time in hiding. He was a Mazzinian and, when not yet seventeen, had helped to smuggle arms to Sicily from Liverpool. He was also an accomplice of Agesilao Milano, executed for attempting to assassinate King Bomba. After being exiled to the convict island of Ponza, he took part in the plot to rescue Settembrini and the rest. In the ensuing, extremely bloody fight he was wounded and captured, only to be released after the coming of Garibaldi in 1860.

In February 1860 it was finally decided that the two revolutionary committees in Palermo, the nobles' and the bourgeois', must in some way unite. Ciccio Brancaccio and Corrado Valguarnera were chosen as emissaries for the former group, but only a few days before the proposed meeting Brancaccio was arrested and shut in the Vicaria. After a while he was joined in his cell by Martino Beltrani Morello (cousin of Martino Beltrani Scalia), a burly black-haired young man who read Byron because he was in love. Then Riso, Corrado and their friends were arrested, and old Baron Pisani became the obvious president of the unified committee. Garibaldi landed and three days later, on 14 May Martino Beltrani Scalia was apprehended.

Martino Beltrani Scalia was the 'dear friend' of Brancaccio's childhood,[2] and it was soon arranged with the head gaoler that he also should be transferred to the cell. He had been on the point of setting out to join Garibaldi at Gibilrossa. Brancaccio nicknamed him Martino Il Bianco to distinguish him from his cousin, whom he called Martino Il Nero. There was now no space left at all in the cell; the young men had either to sit on the beds or squat on the window-sill. Martino Il Bianco was likewise in love – with Marianna, Baron Pisani's daughter – so he too took to reading Byron. In due course the others rather regretted having him there. 'The day after his arrival he broke a wash basin full of water, flooding everything. Later, he broke a glass and another article which modesty prevents me naming.' Worse, unlike the other two, he liked going to bed early and getting up early, when he would be very noisy. To compensate, however, he had arranged with his family for letters written in lemon juice – decipherable when held over a candle flame – to be smuggled into the prison. Thus they learnt of the death of Rosolino Pilo and of the approach of Garibaldi. But it was the ringing of church bells that finally made them realise that deliverance could not be far off. This deliverance came on 28 May, as has already been described, after the Neapolitan soldiers had escaped from the Vicaria, in terror of their lives.

'Swift as a flash of the most brilliant summer lightning', wrote Tina, 'the news of the fall of Palermo came to the waiting exiles, and all those who were able hastened to take part in the final fighting.' Alfonso Scalia had been one of the organisers at a grand meeting of 300 exiles at St Martin's Hall, London, held on 4 May, to raise money for the expedition which everyone knew would surely come soon. But Garibaldi's landing must have taken him by surprise, for he did not arrive at Palermo until 1 June, in the company of the young Rudinì, who observed him stoop and kiss the soil of his native country. 'It was a time of intense emotion . . . and to my father, after eleven long years of exile, his mother dead, so many dear ones gone, and above all, his greatest friend, Rosolino Pilo, just killed at the gates of Palermo, the moment was indescribable.'[3] He hurried to join the Garibaldinian forces and on 25 June the Dictator made him a lieutenant-colonel in the artillery. Luigi Scalia had stayed behind in London to negotiate the purchase of some British frigates.

Information about Alfonso's career during the next months is unfortunately vague, not to say mysterious. After Milazzo he was in the great encampment on the Punta Faro near Messina, whilst waiting for the crossing of the Straits. He took part in the bombardment of enemy ships between 21 and 23 August. He was promoted again, to full colonel, on

15 September. A short official biography[4] claims that he then rejoined the combat forces preparatory to the Battle of the Volturno, in which he took part. On 1 November he was at the siege of Capua under General Orsini, and it was here that he gained an important medal, the Ordine Militare di Savoia, awarded for acts of continual personal bravery.

The whole campaign must have been an anticlimax for the Scalias, which is why no doubt Tina gives so few details. In *Sicily and England* there is this terse remark: 'Neither he nor his brother were rewarded by their country as they deserved to be; the revolution of 1848, and its bitter consequences to them both, were forgotten by the Italian Government, and Garibaldi had his own friends and followers to put forward.' She also says that Alfonso caught pneumonia, the result of exposure on the battle-field, and that this decided her mother – taking Tina with her, and accompanied by her Canadian friend Lady Filmer[5] – to hurry out to Naples, where they arrived just in time for Garibaldi's glorious entry on 7 September.

If Alfonso had been ill in Royalist Naples before 7 September, then he must have been taken prisoner. Since he was definitely also ill after Capua, Tina may of course have been confused in her dates. In any case Giulia and the faithful Lady Filmer must have settled to go to Naples before they knew about Alfonso's pneumonia. They took the train to Marseilles and then went by boat. During the journey there had been a dreadful storm and the boat had been obliged to shelter in the harbour of the little island of Monte Cristo. Lady Filmer had been convinced that they were about to be drowned and had begged Giulia to come and pray with her. She had been sincerely shocked when Giulia refused, saying that she was far too seasick and Lady Filmer must do it for her. Lady F. was indeed a shockable person. Later, though she found it impossible not to be moved by the cheering and 'tumult of joy' of the roaring Neapolitan crowd, she could not but be appalled by the sight of 'women pressing forward to kiss Garibaldi's white cloak and holding up their children for a blessing.'

Yet Naples was a dangerous place to live in for a while. The whole city was 'running mad with flags, daggers and red shirts.' Commander Forbes wrote that the people had 'roused themselves into a state of frenzy. . . . When I was in the Café d'Europe a priest rushed in with frantic gestures, his eyes starting from his head, with a banner in one hand and a knife in the other, uttering horrible and inarticulate howlings.' A man, who did not cry 'Viva Garibaldi!' when told to do so, was 'ripped open by another enthusiast' and died on the spot.

Lady F. was one of those who, under a soaking umbrella, watched the royal entry into Naples on 7 November. It was a glum affair, very different from that of two months before. On the previous occasion Garibaldi had come without troops, 'surrounded only by his staff and accompanied by his faithful English friend, Colonel Peard.' Now everything was stiffly formal and the streets were lined with regular troops. Lady F. remained with the Scalias at the Hotel Vittoria until Alfonso was well enough to be moved to Sicily. 'As soon as they asked for their bill, the landlord absolutely declined to present it, saying that he had been amply repaid by the honour of receiving one of Garibaldi's heroes.'

As for Luigi Scalia, when he finally managed to return to Sicily, he was almost immediately sent back to London on a special mission with the Prince of Pandolfina.[6] Later he was elected a member of the Parliament of the United Italy, sitting at Turin, but 'after a very short time he found it impossible to carry out his parliamentary duties satisfactorily because of the great distance between Piedmont and Sicily, the crippled condition of his finances, owing to his long exile, rendering it necessary that he should give his private affairs constant personal attention.' He therefore retired to Palermo, where he led a quiet, uneventful life until his death in 1888, 'occupying from time to time important positions of trust in the financial and municipal government of the city.' He took an active part in repressing 'that foolish rising, the *Sette e Mezzo*, in 1866, and for this he was awarded the silver medal for civil valour.'

Little Tina was not in good health during the winter of 1860–1, so her mother decided to remove her to London. Alfonso, however, went to Piedmont and thence to Canobbio near Lugano in Switzerland, to act as second for Carmelo Agnetta in his famous duel with Nino Bixio on 17 November 1861.

Agnetta had reached Genoa after Garibaldi had sailed for Marsala. He was given guns and ammunition by the National Committee and (against the advice of Medici[7]) despatched to Sicily in the *Utile*. On arrival at Palermo he was told that Garibaldi wanted to inspect him and his followers in the Piazza Pretorio. Whilst they were waiting there for the Dictator to arrive, Bixio came tearing into the square and peremptorily informed Agnetta that he must provide an escort at the funeral of Colonel Tuköry. Agnetta did not recognise Bixio, who was in any case in civilian clothes, and therefore refused. Bixio slapped his face. At once Agnetta drew his sword and, if he had not been restrained, would have slashed the other down. Garibaldi was furious and ordered Bixio to be placed under house arrest. It was agreed that personal animosities must be put to one side whilst the campaign was in progress, but a year later Agnetta resigned his commission in order to challenge Bixio to the duel. As both were renowned as crack shots, there was naturally much consternation among fellow Garibaldini.

Bixio advanced with his arm inclined upwards, holding his pistol high; Agnetta, on the other hand, held his arm pointing downwards with his pistol low. At the barrier, Bixio slowly lowered his pistol while Agnetta raised his. When the mouths of the pistols were on the same level, Agnetta shot at once. Bixio was unable to fire at all because his adversary's bullet had smashed his hand.

The hand that had been wounded was the very one that had slapped Agnetta's face. This was recognised as divine justice, and the two, one is assured, became friends and remained thus for the rest of their lives.

Tina's earliest recollections of London were of moving from Wyndham Place to 3 Hanover Terrace, near Ladbroke Square, where the air was considered healthier and open fields were within ten minutes' walk. Pheasants were often to be seen in the square (Tina also remembered picking watercress in Sloane Street). Alfonso returned to London, but the winter of 1861-2 was so miserably cold that it was decided that he should go back to Italy, where he entered the regular army, still as an artillery colonel. Giulia and Tina stayed behind, so for the next five years husband and wife were separated.

In 1864 Garibaldi made his triumphant visit to London, where he stayed at Stafford House, the house of the Duke of Sutherland. Tina in later years vaguely remembered the bellowing of the vast crowd and the fact that she was made to wear a red shirt. The only recollections she had of being brought to see the General were that his breath smelt of garlic and that when he took her on his knee and asked her if she spoke Italian, she cried: 'Si! Viva Garibaldi!' Now Giulia Scalia's most intimate friend was Madame Graham, once a milliner and whose parents had been in Louis-Philippe's *entourage* at Palermo. They 'adored' one another so much that Abraham Hayward said: 'It is fortunate that Giulia *is* charming. Pauline Graham sings her praises so perpetually that otherwise one might get suspicious.' Tina remembered Madame Graham's round figure, 'French to the last and surrounded by French servants', with a black wig and little sharp, beady eyes. The Graham household was a centre for Orleanists, and Giulia thus had the satisfaction of being introduced to various royal personages. She also met there that ubiquitous and popular society figure, Hamilton Aïdé,[9] a bachelor who dabbled in painting, poetry, the composing of songs and the writing of plays and novels, and who in due course became a friend of Henry James. Little did Giulia think that one day he would be her daughter's great confidant. She also, as in old days, went frequently to Holland House, where princes and grand dukes seemed to lurk in every garden walk.

Alfonso, acting now as a general, was in command of the 40th Infantry Brigade at the mouth of the Po in the campaign against the Austrians in 1866. The following year, his rank confirmed, he was assigned to Florence, where he was joined by Giulia and Tina, who did not recognise him and were amused by his broken accent in English. It was here that, for the second time, he acted as a second in a duel: in that between Assanti and Nicotera. The latter was wounded in the head, and one of Tina's habitual pleasures was to climb on a chair to look at the scar, 'much to my parents' consternation'.

In Florence the Scalias were often at the fabled Villa Salviati, which belonged to the two great singers, Mario and Grisi, then in their fifties. 'Their hospitality was unique. It was never known how many guests would avail themselves of the general invitation to lunch or dinner, given on Sundays.' Tina's memories of Grisi, quick tempered and now rather stout, included driving with her in a carriage and seeing the road from the Villa almost lined with beggars, 'gathered there to await her passing and the invariable handfuls of coppers.' 'I remember so well one day in the winter of 1867 how, after persuading me to sing, she kissed me enthusiastically and clasped a gold bracelet on my arm. Then as a reward she sang "The Last Rose of Summer". I was only eight years old, but how well that scene remains in my mind – the world-renowned singer singing for the pleasure of a little child! The exquisite pathos of the words seemed to sound a lament for her own past glories.' In Tina's view Grisi was a great tragic actress and it was fitting that she should be buried in Paris near Molière and Racine – 'If Giulia Grisi had not been a singer, she would certainly have been one of the greatest interpreters of these two authors.'

Mario (whose real name was Count Giovanni de Candia) and Grisi were living in sin. Everyone knew this, but their fame, wealth and generosity were quite enough to counteract the scandal, as far as accepting invitations was concerned – asking them back was a different matter. The Scalias left Florence for Leghorn in 1868, and a warm correspondence was kept up with Grisi and her three daughters, known as the Grisettes in Florence.

Grisi's last letter was from Wiesbaden in August 1869. She was there for the mineral waters, as she was feeling very depressed. Maurice Strakosch the impresario came to hear the Grisettes sing but even he could not cheer the mother. The whole family, she told Giulia Scalia, was going to St Petersburg for the winter, as Mario had an engagement there; it was his farewell performance: 'I would far rather be in our villa at Florence, and that you were with us, *carissima mia*, so that we could all play charades!'

At the end of October they set off for Berlin, *en route* for St Petersburg. On the way there was a railway accident, which greatly shook Grisi, who had been advised by her doctor not to travel. She died at the Hotel du Nord in Berlin on 25 November.[10]

Another letter, of a very different sort, has been preserved for that year. From a certain Ernesto Pinedo, obviously something of a busybody, it is addressed to Alfonso, and shows that whereas Bixio may have forgiven Agnetta he had certainly not forgiven Agnetta's second. It also shows that Alfonso had been involved in a slight military scandal:

*Pisa, 28 February 1869*

*Carissimo Generale,*

For the last two years, as you know, I have been with H.E. General Cialdini attached to the Staff and personal secretary to the General. I therefore am acquainted with all the unfortunate incidents which occurred during the recent manoeuvres, and I know too how much you regret them and are worried about the consequences, especially now that General Bixio has taken over the command in Leghorn. I now have the very pleasant opportunity of informing you . . . of a very confidential letter written by H.E. to the Minister about you, advising him that an old feud exists between you and Bixio, which in the present climate does not make it advisable for you both to remain together. To send you to another post would not be convenient, since . . . it might seem as though you were being punished. The General says he now absolves you on every count . . . despite the gossip in newspapers . . . that you were only slightly hasty in the initial attack at the Borgo San Lorenzo manoeuvres, and that he put you under arrest without knowing who was really in command, and that he released you that evening. He concludes his letter in a very flattering manner and suggests that, rather than removing you, which might be interpreted as a smear on your reputation, an effort should be made to make peace between you and Bixio . . . I beg you to treat this letter with strictest privacy and to tear it up as soon as you have read it.

I shake you by the hand etc. . . .

Whatever the outcome of Cialdini's letter, Alfonso was taken away from Leghorn that year. He went to Terni – not much fun for Giulia, who complained violently of the danger there to her child from malaria. So Tina was conducted to London by her mother, and there was another separation, this time of two years. Alfonso next went to Messina, and in 1872 he was quartered in Palermo, a five years' assignment. Giulia and Tina were summoned again. They all lived in the Palazzo Scalia, which Giulia found below her standards, in spite of its semi-aristocratic past.[11] There was every sign now of her becoming a difficult person. She missed her smart London friends – 'Italy to her had always been a sentiment rather than a reality . . . she was a stranger in her own country'; Tina often found her in tears over a letter from England. Giulia said she could never get used to the way 'persons of minor rank' might call on you at home, before they had even been introduced.

On landing at Palermo, Tina's first impression had been of a string of black bands, draped over the shuttered shops in Corso Scinà. These were in honour of Ben Ingham junior, who had just died in Paris. She and her mother occasionally visited the Villa Sofia. Joseph Whitaker rather terrified her; he was so methodical and would be annoyed if she picked flowers in the garden. As for Pip, he seemed to dismiss her as a mere hobbledehoy – he was, moreover, interested then in Alice Bennett, whom Tina found 'so very refined', quite a contrast to her own future sister-in-law, Maude. Old Mrs Gardner, widow of Edward and mother of such a tribe, was good-natured but rather common. 'But how we enjoyed her iced water-melons, as we sat chatting or playing cards on her fine terrace at the Palazzo Angiò, overlooking the Marina!' Dr Burbidge, the chaplain, was a 'scholar and a dreamer', once a master at Rugby, too prone to taking laxative salts which occasionally prevented him from appearing at church. 'His sermons sounded clever, but were really almost without meaning. In fact they tended more to raise doubts than strengthen belief.' The bossy Mrs Burbidge was a lively and sympathetic woman of the world, though 'she had a rather morbid mania for female relationships, and I should say was totally unfitted to be the wife of an English clergyman.' The wife of George Dennis, the Consul, was Irish, a hearty soul who 'indulged too freely in the joys of the grape fermented'. 'She was a connoisseur of lace and I suppose had sung nicely in her youth, though after dinner she would insist on singing "The Low-Backed Car" in a quavering, squeaky voice. Her husband we all regarded rather as a middle-aged Apollo, with beautiful silky white hair. We girls were very sad when he was transferred to Smyrna in 1879.'

Giulia, needless to say, found most of these English people very inferior. She was lucky therefore to be introduced to the chief hostess in Palermo at that time, the Princess of Scalea, 'a most charming creature, very thin, very cultivated, speaking all languages and married to a broad-minded husband who did not mind her liaisons with the Duke of Cesaró and Count Capace'. 'In Casa Scalea all foreigners of distinction were presented, but in a day when the fact of an aristocratic name alone was the necessary card, the Scaleas welcomed those who excelled in science and the arts.' After a while Giulia would be invited there perhaps twice a week.

The years 1875–8 were especially important for Tina, for it was then that her father was stationed in Naples. He must have been a success in Palermo, for in 1876, at the time of the capture of Forester Rose, a correspondent to *The Times* wrote saying that Sicily needed a strong man like Scalia to stamp out the *Mafia*.[12] In Naples Tina was able to study music and take singing lessons in earnest. At first she studied under Lauro Rossi, the director of the Conservatorio, though with disastrous results: for he insisted on teaching her both the contralto and soprano parts in his own operas *Cleopatra* and *La Contessa di Mons*, as a result of which she strained her voice. She then transferred her favours to one Guercia. Adelina Patti came to sing at the San Carlo, and Tina heard her in *Traviata* and the *Barbiere*. 'Oh the beauty and agility of that voice, the perfect diction! As an actress in *Barbiere* she was quite unique, though in *Traviata* I felt something was wanting in the grand moments; the voice had pathos, but it could not give one the *soul* in "Alfredo Alfredo".' Maurice Strakosch was in Naples, though about to cease his association with Patti on her marriage. He wrote to Giacinto Carini prophesying a great career for Tina; he said that she had all the necessary qualities for taking Patti's place and he would be ready to star her, if only she would go on the stage – 'Patti was then devoted to the tenor Nicolini [she later married him] and was singing with him. His abandoned wife came to Naples with the children, to implore her to give him up. It was rumoured that Patti simply answered: "Je l'aime et je le garde", and one evening in consequence the Neapolitan public hissed her.'[13]

The Scalias had a large flat in the tumbledown, Government-owned Palazzo Salerno. The gossip among the military families there was formidable, but Madame Scalia remained resolutely aloof from it. It was annoying for her when Lilian Praed, the daughter of the poet Winthrop Praed, came to stay with them. 'She fell in love with a Colonel Cabini, an undesirable person, who would take no notice of her. She eventually made his acquaintance in a museum and *would* marry him, although they had never been introduced. My parents were not present at the marriage.' The Commander-in-chief was General Pettinengo, 'a good general, but timid in the ordinary ways of life, in awe of his subordinate, General Emilio Pallavicini (supposed by all to be the son of Carlo Alberto).' Pallavicini was having an affair with Baroness Mazza, the wife of the chief of staff, so ugly that she *tuait les mouches au vol*, though she had a good figure. Two colleagues who became life-long friends were future generals: Edoardo Arimondi, in course of time the hero of Adigrat in Eritrea, and Alberto Pollio, then the youngest lieutenant in the Italian army and an eventual *Capo di Stato Maggiore*. Pollio had a beautiful baritone voice; he was rather beautiful himself too, with a 'poetic romantic nature', and they sang duets together. One of the sights of Naples for a while was the Countess Mirafiori, the King's morganatic wife. 'Fat and common she used to drive about *à la daumont* [with four horses], her postilions garbed in blue velvet and silver.' And so on, and so on.

The next move was to Parma, *quella città graziosa*. Tina, now aged twenty, tall (nearly six foot) and English looking, and her mother were a great social success. Indeed Tina went to fifteen balls in a month there.She also made her first début as an artiste. Enthusiastic notices followed a concert in which she had appeared – *voce vibrata, espansiva, simpatica, chiara* etc. After that people would gather under her window to listen to her practising.

There was another interlude in London in the summer of 1879, so that Tina could be launched in the Season. She sang at the Queen's Hall, and the *Illustrated London News* pronounced her 'a new and most promising prima donna'. At Lady Molesworth's – 'quaintly named Andalusia; her husband had picked her up on an excursion boat to Ireland, and had sent her to a first-class school before marrying her in 1855, the year he died' – she went to a musical evening. 'The rooms were packed and the company was in complete silence, while a fair young man almost whispered out his songs, by then the rage. He was Paolo Tosti, already the king of drawing-room melody. Even Giovanni Battista Gordigiani [also a composer and singer, died 1871] could never have rivalled his attractive personality, his verve and amusing conversation which drew around him not only the people of the great world but painters and poets too.' In 1880 Tosti became music teacher to the British royal family, and for the rest of his life he was Tina's staunch ally.

Meanwhile Alfonso had been moved, alas, from Parma to Cuneo, almost as dull as Terni. Thus Madame Scalia and her daughter, on their return from London, lingered in Turin so that Tina could have lessons from

Virginia Boccabadati – 'the great personifier of Linda de Chamonix and afterwards singing mistress at the Pesaro Conservatorio, founded by Rossini's will, until she quarrelled with Mascagni'. They travelled to Bologna for more lessons under Ferlotti, the famous baritone, with Luigi Mancinelli, the conductor, accompanying. Triumph – in other words the Teatro Scala – seemed to be round the corner. At a charity concert in Cuneo Tina had 'an absolute ovation, young men trying to take the horses out of my carriage to drag me home, and then coming outside my windows to serenade me.'

So it seemed like a setback to her career when her father, who had now the rank of Lieutenant-General, decided to leave the army and retire to his native Palermo. Maybe he had been influenced by the fact that his sister was dying of cancer. At any rate she died soon after their arrival, and there followed a long period of mourning. Only close friends and relations, like Padre Isidoro Carini, Ciccio Vassallo and Ciccio Brancaccio, visited the house. At Carnival in 1881 Tina was allowed out in society again. Yet in a sense she had a lonely time. 'My mother was always very strict about my girl friends. Both she and my father said that women did each other a great deal of harm. Indeed my mother was really my only intimate friend throughout my girlhood. Carolina Notarbartolo [daughter of Emanuele, Corrado Valguarnera's companion in 1860] and Lily Belmonte, the daughter of the Prince of Pandolfina, were quite close to me at that time. After our first meeting Lily sent me a little note, "La sympathie est une fleur dont le fruit s'appelle l'amour".' Palermo was now becoming a fashionable place to winter in. The Palazzo d'Orléans had been lent by the Duke d'Aumale to the Grand Duchess Vladimir of Russia. Her brother, the Grand Duke of Mecklenburg-Schwerin and his lovely Duchess, just married, were at the Villa Belmonte below Monte Pellegrino. It was a thrilling time, and Lily would take Tina to meet the Russian royalties. Both girls were bewitched by the Grand Duchess Vladimir and her black pearls. Once they were at her feet, gazing up at her, when the Grand Duke had to reprimand them: 'Je comprends que vous soyez sous la charme de ma sœur, mais ma femme aussi est charmante quand on la connaît.'

Tina afterwards would repeat two stories, both typical of the sort of thing that amused her:

The Grand Duchess Vladimir's son Cyril was a sweet little boy. After Ekaterinburg he proclaimed himself the head of the Romanov family. But even as a child of about two and a half or three he had a naturally autocratic manner. When the Princess of Butera stooped to kiss him, he drew back with regal dignity and said: 'On ne m'embrasse pas, madame.' At that same tea-party Anastasia, the Grand Duchess of Mecklenburg, who was doing the honours, offered my mother a second cup, which she declined with a smile. At this a General sitting next to my mother whispered that it was not etiquette and that he had just got through a third cup, which he had no wish for.

The King and Queen of Italy came to Palermo,[14] and with them Alberto Pollio. When Pollio found Tina no longer interested in him, he turned his attention to Lily and actually fainted when he was repulsed. Five years later Lily married one of the richest men in Italy: Duke Leopoldo Torlonia.

The Scalias' old friend Mrs Lynn Linton also descended on Sicily and stayed at the Hotel de France. She was hardly one to be interested in the Mecklenburg-Schwerins, and in any case, with her peculiar round spectacles and forthright way of speaking, was not all that presentable in such circles. A solution was found when the Whitakers lent her their villa at Racalia near Marsala. Then the impresario Ricordi offered to get Tina an audition at the Scala. It happened just at the time that she became engaged to Pip.

When she was an old woman, Tina would be asked if Pip had fallen in love with her because of her voice. 'Not a bit of it. We met at a bathing establishment. Pip's pointers kept leaving him and following me, so he thought I must have something.' His proposal had meant that she had to choose between a possible career in opera or a life of luxury as the wife of a potentially very rich young man. She had chosen the latter.

In 1881 the Hotel des Palmes was visited by a group of distinguished guests: Richard Wagner and Cosima, with their three children, and Daniela and Blandine von Bülow, Cosima's daughters by her previous marriage. They arrived on 5 November (except for Daniela, who came later, after an unhappy time in Rome). Wagner had been suffering from eczema. From the point of view of his health, the visit was a great success and he felt rejuvenated. 'Am I really sixty-eight? It cannot be,' he kept repeating. It was at the Hotel des Palmes that he completed *Parsifal*, on 13 January 1882.[15]

Tina did not like Wagner.

His personality was not at all pleasing to those such as I who did not know him well. He was arrogant and domineering, and his total want of consideration for the feelings of others jarred on me considerably. The exaggerated hero-worship which Donna Cosima always encouraged made intercourse even less agreeable. I remember one day when we called on them at the Palmes, suddenly the Master stopped speaking almost as if he was in ecstasy. Donna Cosima immediately whispered: 'Je crois que le Maître va avoir une inspiration. Il faudrait que vous nous quittez.' Very quietly, without saying goodbye, we crept away. Rachele Varvaro, who lived opposite, told us what happened on the occasions of the inspiration: depending on what *kind* of inspiration it was, a coloured veil was thrown over him, that his visions might be roseate, or not, as the case might be.[16]

Others in the suite were the artist Joukowski, working all the time on stage designs and costumes, and young Joseph Rubinstein, 'a disciple of the Master and ever ready to minister to his smallest whim'. Tina was invited to sing before Wagner at a big reception given by Count Tasca. 'I sang songs from Wagner's early days in Paris, "Dors, mon enfant" and "Mignonne", and then the dream of Elsa from *Lohengrin*. I can still see the Master by the piano, looking so pleased with the interpretations, jumping and shouting for encores without waiting for the rest of the audience – which embarrassed me exceedingly.'

Wagner said that Palmes was too expensive. When he and his family moved to the Prince of Gangi's villa in the Porrazzi, the proprietor of the hotel demanded compensation for the months that had been booked ahead. Wagner had stoves put into the villa after the boy Siegfried caught a fever. It was there that he directed an orchestral audition of some extracts from *Parsifal* at a party to which we were bidden. Prince Constantine of Russia was also present. One bit especially pleased Wagner and after a *bis*, he demanded a third repetition. This was too much for the Prince who rose, saluted and departed. . . . I became intimate with Blandine, the first to break away from the family fold. Donna Cosima often spoke to my mother about a husband for her. At last, with the help of Count Tasca, Count Biagio Gravina was found, a member of a great family that had fallen into financial extremes. Was Blandine happy? Was it right that this very young, sweet, blonde creature of the north, ignorant of the practical world, should be tied to a man she knew so little, without even a tiny home? At any rate Biagio was very popular with his friends, and she became a perfect wife, supporting her position with dignity.[17]

The Wagner family went to stay at Acireale for the engagement celebrations. Here Wagner was able to watch Garibaldi on a gala visit, of almost operatic splendour, just two months before the hero's death. They then made their way to Messina, where they left Sicily on 13 April. But Wagner had less than a year to live. He died in Venice on 13 February 1883.

While Pip was courting Tina, all his letters had to be addressed to Madame Scalia. The marriage was delayed because of the death of Joseph Whitaker, the 'missing corpse', at Marsala.[18] The reception was at the Hotel Trinacria, and there were ninety-one people at the wedding breakfast. She and Pip spent most of their honeymoon in England; since Tina and her mother had never for a single day been separated, Mama came too.

And it was about a month later, at the end of July 1883, that Lampedusa made his Leopard, Don Fabrizio Prince of Salina, begin to die on the balcony of that same hotel with its view over the harbour and the metallic sea towards Monte Pellegrino.[19]

# PART FIVE

## Living as Princes

# XVIII

## *Flowers from the Grand Duke*

MADAME SCALIA detached herself from Tina and Pip when they reached England. There followed a furiously social time for the honeymooners, and Tina recorded in her diary that during a single week they slept in five different houses. Naturally they went to Hesley and Pylewell. They also went to see Grayshott Farm near Hindhead, a new house that one of Pip's (at present) bachelor brothers, Ingham Whitaker, had recently bought and was converting into Grayshott Hall – Tennyson had lived there from 1866–7.[1] Then Tina wanted her husband to meet some of the grand friends of her youth, and on a few of these occasions they would happen to run into Madame Scalia. It was at Lady Howe's that the three of them discovered the jovial and enormously fat Duchess of Teck (mother of Queen Mary). The Duchess was said to weigh 240 lbs. Her greeting was not quite the sort they expected: 'Ah, Madame Scalia, I see neither of us has grown any thinner since we last met.'

Mama also turned out to be staying at the house of Sir William Siemens the electricity king near Tunbridge Wells, when Tina and Pip called there. Sir William had a 'most noble and charming character, with a singularly benevolent glance through gold-rimmed glasses.' His dining-room was sensational. 'It was lit by electric light, quite a novelty, in the form of bunches of grapes, decidedly Bacchanalian though not especially tasteful.' The Siemens strawberries were also forced and ripened by means of electricity. 'I tasted some but was not in this instance impressed by the wonders of science.'

Elsewhere they encountered, and used, a telephone for the first time. Mama rejoined them for the return journey, via Venice and Florence, where they saw much of the now widowed Emily Medici.[2] It was quite touching to see Emily surrounded by the General's gun-dogs, but not so pleasant having to sit through meals with the slavering animals' heads resting on the table. They arrived in Palermo for news of an engagement, and a truly spectacular one it was: between the thirteen-year-old Giulia Florio, daughter of Ignazio, and the twenty-one-year-old Prince of Trabia – a familiar situation, great wealth allied to a title. The marriage, however, did not occur for another two years. Giulia was a sweet, attractive and serious-minded girl. Like Maria Favara, Corrado Valguarnera's wife, and now known as the Princess of Niscemi, she had had very little conventional education and at once set about teaching herself Latin and Greek.

Pip now took his bride to the *Baglio* in Marsala, an experience which she so much detested. There was no social life there whatsoever, and Mama stayed behind in Palermo. The smell and the noise were frightful. What was more, Tina was pregnant. For four weeks she was even alone, whilst Pip went on a trip to Tunisia at the behest of his father, who had suddenly become seized with the idea of acquiring a tunny fishery at Monastir. The sending of troops into Tunisia by France in 1881 had caused an uproar in Italy, and the fury – headed by Crispi, now Minister of Interior – had been even greater two years later when the country became a French protectorate. It is thus rather a pity that we know no details about the Whitakers' motives for trying to start up a business over there; maybe it was simply because they wanted to set up a rival to the Florio *tonnara* at Favignana, whose enormous success Joseph must have been watching with envy.

Pip also spent much time on Motya. The extraordinary thing about the island was that hardly anybody had bothered to excavate it, and virtually no historical records existed. The Phoenician town there had been destroyed by Dionysius of Syracuse in 397 B.C. after a grisly siege, the surviving inhabitants being transferred as slaves the following year to Lilybaeum (Marsala). It was a curious, flat, haunted place. Pip could make out a circuit wall, gates, even – he thought – remnants of temples and houses. But most intriguing of all was the underwater causeway for wheeled traffic that linked Motya (only three quarters of a kilometre wide in any direction) over the shallow, weedy lagoon to a necropolis on the mainland. It was then that he conceived the ambitious plan to acquire the island for himself; and it would not be an easy task, in view of the many peasant small-holdings, jealously guarded.[3]

For Tina life was suddenly brightened by a visit from the Mecklenburg-Schwerins. They were charming, and she made Pip write to Joss about persuading his parents to lend the Villa Sofia to the royal couple. Nothing, however, came of this . . .

She was back in Palermo by June, so that she could have the baby in the Casa Scalia. It was a girl, born on the twentieth and christened Sophia (after Pip's mother) Juliet (after Madame Scalia, i.e. Giulietta) Emily (after Emily Medici) Eleonora. Everyone called her Norina. Her hair was dark, so it was assumed that she took more after her Italian ancestors. Then in September, when the worst of the hot weather was over, Tina journeyed back to Marsala with her baby. Almost exactly nine months after her arrival there another girl was born, also in the Casa Scalia, on 6 June 1885: Cordelia (Madame Scalia's second name) Stella Georgette Edith (the last two being the names of Carrie Christian's two daughters). She was fair-haired, obviously more of an Anglo-Saxon than a Latin, and known always as Delia.

Madame Scalia was worried lest more births would follow in the same rapid succession and decided on a frank talk with Pip. The story of this encounter may or may not be apocryphal. She insisted that from then on-wards Tina would sleep in the same room as herself, and that if Pip wished to gratify his beastly lust he had better do so on his mother-in-law's body.[4] At any rate there were no further children.

Meanwhile old Joseph Whitaker had died. Delia had been born at the beginning of a cholera epidemic, so the family took refuge in Sorrento. The epidemic was really the continuation of the one that had raged in Naples in the autumn of 1884, the seventh major outbreak in Europe, when there had been 1000 cases a day; Axel Munthe later wrote a book about it, *Letters from a Mourning City*,[5] as an attempt to arouse the European conscience, because of the squalor in which most of the city's population lived. Whilst Pip and Tina were at Sorrento, they heard of his mother's death in England; Pip at once hurried back.

Joseph Whitaker's British estate must have been undervalued for pro-bate, for each of his seven sons (i.e. Willie excluded) found themselves in-heriting about £200,000, on top of the substantial sums that had already been made over to them. As Joss, Pip and Bob in addition shared all the business interests and property in Sicily, they had become very wealthy in-deed. The one who came off worst was Ackie Morrison, with six children and a husband who had nearly gone bankrupt. At least Sophie Tommasi-Crudeli and Carrie Christian had husbands who were earning good salaries. Tina, dreading Marsala, now suggested that the three heirs to the Sicilian estate should take turns at the *Baglio*. Such an arrangement, how-ever, did not at all suit her sisters-in-law, and in any case both Pip and Bob now decided that they were not particularly interested in running businesses. As Joss had a genuine affection for the 'Concern', it was decided that the other two should simply be sleeping partners: ultimately a disastrous solution, since Joss – dear old bumbler that he was – was just about the last person in the world to fit into the shoes of Benjamin Ingham.

The three Mrs Whitakers now set about establishing themselves in society. Maude was the pretty one and had the least brains. Needless to say, her parties were considered the most fun. The Villa Sofia was enlarged and altered by her brother-in-law Beau Gardner. Effie, with her Eastern looks, made herself more exotic with sequins, ostrich feathers, earrings and tiaras. She was also able to indulge even more in her eccentricities: she collected vast quantities of Trapani coral, Greek vases, tortoiseshell work and every sort of bric-à-brac which could not possibly all be displayed, specialised in furniture inlaid with mother-o'-pearl, and went about with a parrot on her shoulder and a silver scoop for its droppings on her wrist. Her Venetian-style palazzo was designed by Henry Christian; tremendous sums were paid for obtaining different marbles from all over Italy, and in front were great lawns lined with palms and banana-trees. As she loved tennis, she made Joss buy more land at an old orange and lemon grove that he owned at Sperlinga on the outskirts of Palermo, where she built three courts and created a large garden, again filled with palms.[6] Although she mixed a lot in princely circles, her friends were varied. In other words she was not a snob, or not much of a one.

Tina's house, Villa Malfitano, was easily the most ambitious and the most impressive. The architect was Ignazio Greco, and the noble style of the house might best be described as Belgrave Square architecture, being based on the Villino Favard[7] on the Lungarno Amerigo Vespucci in Florence. Actually it was Pip, with his meticulous eye, who was more concerned with the details of the erection of Malfitano and even of its furnishing. Tina (anything but meticulous) had decreed that her basic requirements were a large ballroom, a conservatory, the Louis Quinze drawing-room, the Louis Seize drawing-room, a billiard-room, and nine bedrooms (in addition, of course, to a dining-room etc.) and she was happy – more or less – to leave it at that. Very little of the furniture was old, and the house inside was thus perfectly of its period: late Victorian, with a hint of art-nouveau. Madame Scalia was to have her own suite of rooms. The General, on the other hand, was to live separately in a house (known as the Villino) specially built for him in the garden; he enjoyed his freedom and, as he had a taste for the ladies, made sure that it had easy access to the street, which was not the case with Malfitano itself.

The *Piano* of Malfitano consisted of seventeen acres and lay at the end of the Via Dante. Its name was said to derive from the fact that it belonged once to Amalfitani, or people from Amalfi. Negotiations to buy it took place during the winter of 1885–6. The owner, Cavaliere Beneventano of Catania, said that it was beneath his dignity to sell but he would exchange it for a property of equal value in Catania; this therefore had to be done. The house's first stone was laid by Norina, aged nearly two, who tossed back a glass of marsala before she could be stopped. The family spent the first night there on 18 February 1889. According to the account books, it seems that the basic work – building and decorating – must have cost at least £20,000.

Pip was now in the happy position of being able to indulge freely in his true interests. His expedition to Tunisia, and all the shooting of game there, had made him very interested in ornithology. His time at Marsala had resulted in a passion for archaeology. Now that he was faced with making a garden and park, he also became – thanks to the Villa Sofia head gardener, Emilio Kunzmann – interested in botany. Eight palms were actually transported from the Villa Sofia, but hosts of other rare plants were acquired from Tunisia, Sumatra and other places abroad. These were white judases, howeas, yuccas, washingtonias, dracaenas, nolinas, bamboos, papyruses. Today a *ficus magnoloides* that he planted has a span of 135 feet and is supposed to be able to shelter 3000 people. The huge mansion must indeed have looked odd in 1889, full square in the *Piano* with tiny, newly planted trees all around.

It had been conceived as a house for entertaining in, and on the grand scale. Tina was also looking ahead, to the days when she would be launching her daughters. Entertain she did, and it must be confessed that, as far as attracting *haute société* was concerned, she easily outshone her sisters-in-law.

In 1887 the Pips, as they were known in the family, went to London for the summer. This was to be an established routine, with Pip himself going to Scotland in August for the grouse. But 1887 was also the year of Queen Victoria's Jubilee, and Tina was presented at Court by Lady Downshire, who was married to a grandson of old Lord Combermere. She had collected her dress and train in Paris from Mr Worth on the way from Italy. 'The great man deigned to come and see my dress on me and was not pleased with the way some roses did not match others on the brocade. He spoke indignantly and volubly in French, but with a miserable accent. He had of course begun life as a salesman in a small haberdashery shop at Bawtry in Yorkshire, and had then been an apprentice at Swan and Edgar.'[8] Tina was quite caustic about the pushing and shoving among the smart ladies. The Queen became easily tired and now and then would retire, so that the Princess of Wales could take over. Naturally everyone was keen to be presented to the Queen herself, and her appearances would result in a sort of panic.

It was a brilliant season. At nearly every party there would be a clutch of gorgeously bejewelled Indian princes. Thanks to Lady Ely, now Mistress of the Robes, Tina and Pip were able to attend the great court ball, given in honour of the foreign crowned heads who had come to London for the Jubilee. As they watched the opening quadrille, they little thought that four of the royal personages would 'soon be lying in lonely graves'; these were King Louis of Portugal (1889), the Crown Prince of Germany who became Emperor Frederick III for three months, 'so splendid in his white uniform' (1888), the Archduke Rudolf 'who died so romantically and tragically at Mayerling' (1889), and Duke Amedeo of Savoy, at one time King of Spain (1890).

Madame Scalia and Tina lingered in London until the late autumn, then went to Cannes for a month. Pip had gone back to Palermo, to prepare for his second trip to Tunisia. He was evidently becoming tired, if not bored, with social life. His notorious vagueness and lack of punctuality might even have been deliberate. For all that most people agreed that he was 'a sweet little fellow', upright and kind-hearted. He now sported a beard and looked quite professorial, especially as his hair was growing grey.

And who should be at Cannes but the Mecklenburg-Schwerins. . . . It was at this point that Tina made her first attempt to begin her diary.

> *Cannes, 12 December 1887*
> The Mecklenburgs have been very *empressés* and kind to us – he, as ever, simple and genial; she, cold, in general, but to us very charming. We met there at lunch a Captain Perceval,[9] a so-called lady-killer. I did not care for him.

Later Tina wrote that the Captain was supposed to be 'the Grand Duchess's too intimate friend.'

> *Monte Carlo, 13 December 1887*
> Arrived here yesterday evening – Grand Hotel. At the station at Cannes we found two lovely bouquets awaiting us from the Grand Duke: one for Mama – carnations, yellow roses and mimosa; mine – pale roses and lilies of the valley.

> *Rome, 14 January 1888*
> Poor dear Uncle Luigi is no more! At his great age [81] it was to be expected, despite his wonderful constitution. In the Scalia family there is great longevity, and I have heard of uncles in past generations lasting over a century.

She herself was nearly to complete her century when she died.

> *Rome, 21 January 1888*
> Yesterday Mama and I, by special permission through our cousin,

26. General Alfonso Scalia.

27. Madame Scalia in widow's weeds.

28. Luigi Scalia.

29. Edward Gardner.

30. Pip Whitaker.

Monsignor Carini, went to see the exhibition of the Pope's presents [consolations for being the 'Prisoner of the Vatican']. It is not yet officially open, and the confusion is amusing, as is the extraordinary variety of gifts. Next to beautiful stoles, mitres and exquisite embroideries, one finds heaps of preserved fruits. Again, I saw a large box of pale kid gloves for a lady's evening dress; further on, admirably worked cushions, jewelled rings obviously of great value, massive gold tiaras, and then again a box of baby's socks! One is struck by the incongruity of the Sultan of Turkey sending a present – such a glorious diamond ring. And the Queen of England sent a present, and the Czar of Russia. One cannot help realizing that these presents are given to the Pope as consolation prizes by those various countries which did *nothing* to help the Papacy retain its temporal power. His Holiness's position is like that of some *petite maîtresse délaissée*, whose lover – to console her for her loss – gives her an *écran* with a very valuable *parure* as a parting gift.

Since they were in mourning, they could not be presented to Queen Margherita as planned. It was sad, for the Queen said she had been looking forward to Tina singing to her, having remembered hearing her in the old days at Parma. However they did manage to meet, in her red hung drawing-room, the intellectual hostess of the day, Laura Minghetti – she had been born an Acton, a sister of Guglielmo, Harold and Roger, and was the widow of Marco Minghetti, a distinguished writer on art and literature and Prime Minister from 1873–6.[10] Most people were terrified of Donna Laura, but not so Madame Scalia and Tina. Walburga Lady Paget, ex-British ambassadress, known as Wally in British royal circles, wrote of her: 'I instinctively felt that she took my measure as we met, and that she did not find the result quite satisfactory.' When, however, one reads how Lady Paget (quite a warhorse, in looks and attitude) was garbed, one is not altogether suprised. 'Oddly enough, I remember exactly what I was wearing that evening – a perfectly simple dress, of very thick white silk, and a wide sash of rose pink ribbon round my waist. This was not the fashion of the day. . . . In my hair I had a wreath of purple grapes with many coloured leaves, and a bunch of the same pinned, with a knot of rose ribbon to my waist.'[11] Donna Laura, for all her dark blue eyes and Byzantine features, and her many adorers, was to Lady Paget a cynical, calculating, ambitious woman; people left her 'with the impression that they were forever enthroned in her heart when she had never even taken the trouble to find out their names.' A lesson sadly learnt by Tina and her mother.

Tina was beginning to miss Pip, who was now in Tunisia with a brother,

Arthur, also on a jaunt without his wife. It was odd to her that he disliked Rome, especially since his favourite sister Sophie Tommasi-Crudeli lived there. She next went to Naples to hear some opera, and was back in Palermo by the end of February. She had been away for ten months: a measure of her lack of interest in the progress of Malfitano. The extraordinary thing was the way the house turned out so successfully and so comfortably – all credit, therefore, to Ignazio Greco. As usual, there were a number of charity concerts in which to perform, and as usual they earned her extravagant praise: 'Quanta passione! quanta intelligenza! quanta arte fina!' 'Quale inestimabile tesoro di voce!' 'Voce divina!'

Soon she, her mother and Pip were on their travels again. At least half 1888 was spent away from Palermo. The children, Norina and Delia, were proudly shown off; 'the chicks have been much admired and petted', she wrote in Florence. Inconceivably, Tina did not return until six weeks before she was due to move into Malfitano. They had spent Christmas and the New Year in Rome. 'Mama and I were presented to the Queen, who was as gracious as always. Peppino was booked by the Marchesa Villamarina [lady-in-waiting] as having been presented without the trouble of going, which much delighted him.'

Whilst in Venice, during a glorious October, they had been pleased to come across the small, bearded figure of Hamilton Aïdé staying in the same hotel. 'As we drifted, often aimlessly, in a gondola, a great friendship was forged. . . . I had once thought him prim and conventional, but at Venice I suddenly saw him as singular and unconventional.' Tina would have found him even more singular, no doubt, if she had overheard his private conversation with his friends John Addington Symonds and Horatio Brown, 'lovers of fine wine and handsome young men'.[12] Tina does not say, in her very haphazard diary, whether she met Symonds on that occasion, but she wrote later that she had been uneasy with Horatio Brown. As for Aïdé, he seems to have been rather of the type of Sir Edward Marsh in post-World War I London: an amusing and informed talker, spruce, debonair, cosmopolitan, kind to young people with talent and full of a genuine joy of living. He lived in a flat in Hanover Square, knew all the duchesses, all the actresses, all the successful novelists and musicians. When he entertained, there would frequently be a strip of red carpet outside the door, to proclaim the expected arrival of royalty.

*Venice, 20 October 1888*

Mr Aïdé was telling us today that his mother knew the Piozzis well and easily understood how Mrs Thrale forfeited the affection of many of her friends, including Dr Johnson, by her second marriage to a singer from

Brescia. The Piozzi *ménage* was by no means an unruffled one. Passages of arms – or rather tongues – of a violent kind frequently ensued between husband and wife, especially at cards. But Mrs Piozzi generally had the last word.

Aïdé was invited to Malfitano, as one of the first guests. 'And thus began a series of almost yearly visits to us, never less than one month, sometimes even two.'

General Scalia was highly pleased with his Villino. He professed to have taken up spiritualism and held séances there, the ladies in the big house only rarely being invited. The renowned medium Eusapia Paladino, a Pugliese, came on various occasions. Tina found her fat, plain, common (needless to say) and not even interesting looking.[13] 'These séances usually took place in a darkened room, and I was never allowed to be present. There is no doubt that she had some mysterious power, often enhanced by trickery. I noticed during daylight performances that she always asked the men to hold her hands. In later years she was caught cheating, by which time she had become celebrated in both London and Paris.'

Pip sometimes attended the séances. He was trying to persuade his father-in-law to come with him to Tunisia. The General was very much a man's man. He preferred roughing it on travels and never dreamt of going on those lengthy sophisticated jaunts round Europe with his wife and daughter. For a while he was president of the Bellini Club. His hearty manner and amusing talk made him much in demand in the *salotti*. Often he would be asked to mediate in duels, and being a quick-tempered fellow himself he was apt to be challenged now and then. Indeed he had become a highly respected public figure in Palermo; one of the positions he held was president of the Manicomio (lunatic asylum). Madame Scalia complained that he did not push himself enough – he never asked for favours, otherwise Crispi or Rudinì, successively Prime Ministers, would willingly have made him a senator. The fact that his standing was held in considerable esteem by Crispi is indeed made clear by a highly charged letter from the Prime Minister on the subject of the slave trade in the Red Sea – Crispi was annoyed by a public pronouncement by the Antislavery Committee in Palermo.

This Committee had been formed in 1888, as a result of the crusade launched in Italy by the French Cardinal Lavigerie, Primate of Africa, and strongly supported by Leo XIII. Lavigerie had visited Palermo and had delegated the initiative for the crusade to Cardinal Celesia, who became its

President. He was a politically minded man and a strong supporter of a reconciliation between the Papacy and Italy; thus his manoeuvres were watched with suspicion by the Italian Government, whose relations with France had been strained ever since the occupation of Tunisia. As the capture of Massawa in Eritrea had patently forestalled France's designs, any outcry by the French about the slave trade in the Red Sea could only be regarded with suspicion.

The Vice-Presidents of the Palermo Committee were the Duke of Verdura, mayor of Palermo and a Senator, and the Prince of Scalea. Pip recorded that he subscribed 500 *lire*. The women's section of the Committee was organised by the Princess of Torremuzza, with the help of Madame Scalia, who organised a concert, starring Tina as principal soloist with a chorus of society ladies – a *successo clamoroso*.

Crispi's letter to the General went as follows:

> *Rome, 23 July 1889*
>
> *Mio caro* Alfonso,
>
> An Antislavery Committee has been formed in your town. A number of our friends have joined, and I have nothing against it, as everyone is free, under a Liberal government, to think or act as he thinks best. This Committee has published a supplement to no 6 of its bulletin with an article entitled *The Ingenuous Italians*.
>
> Please read it.
>
> The booklet is anonymous, but what is important is that all the members of the Committee are responsible.
>
> I cannot believe that my friends should treat me so badly, and I can only think that none of them have read my speech to the Senate on the 27th June, a speech that was interrupted by warm applause on several occasions.
>
> Italy, with the agreement of Britain, has ships in the Red Sea and in the Indian Ocean for taking action against the treatment of slaves, and has proved by her deeds that she knows how to apply herself to the requirements of humanity and civilization, when others simply proclaim them with words.
>
> My speech was published in the newspapers and I am sorry that I have no copies to send you. I shall only say that what I said was correct in form and substance . . .
>
> *L'aff.mo tuo* F. Crispi
>
> P.S. Verdura, a member of the Committee, although I have spoken to him about the article, affects to ignore it.

The article had been intended as a sarcastic reference to Crispi's speech, in which he had attacked Lavigerie for his political motives behind the crusade. The Cardinal, he said, was simply an agent for his own country, and unfortunately many Italians, out of the highest motives, had been *ingenuous* enough to give money to him, little realising that their cash would be spent in a way that would not be to their country's interests.

General Scalia was still doing his bookbinding, and his work was greatly admired. At the National Exhibition in Palermo in 1891–2 he was awarded a silver medal with diploma. Unfortunately he was also a bit of a spendthrift. Not only was he heavily in debt to Pip, but he managed secretly to get large sums out of Joss.

1888 was a worrying year at Marsala: a bad vintage, taxes increasing and phylloxera spreading. Although phylloxera had appeared in Messina in 1880, it had not yet reached western Sicily, despite alarms. It had first been noticed in Italy in 1875, but the original, main outbreak in France had been in 1865. So with possible disaster ahead, the Monastir project seemed even more financially desirable. Pip in fact went out alone to Tunisia, without much success from a business point of view although he had obviously enjoyed himself greatly. He had begun taking notes on bird behaviour, later to form the basis of a two-volume work, *The Birds of Tunisia*, published in 1905,[14] and brought back several skins which he had stuffed in Palermo. Joss became impatient and persuaded General Scalia with his friend Andrea Guarneri to go to Monastir in October 1890. Guarneri was a prominent figure in Sicily and eventually became Vice-President of the Senate. He was indeed one of the last protagonists in favour of federation for Sicily with Italy, as against unification. There was much excitement and legal documents were signed, but the whole thing eventually collapsed over some question of legal entitlement. At any rate, phylloxera still had not reached Marsala, and seemed to be drifting northwards. When it struck Austria-Hungary in 1892, a new and valuable market was suddenly opened for Italian wine.[15]

If Joss was nominally in charge of the wine business and thereby bungling the overseas sales, the efficiency of the *Baglio* was entirely due to Richard Cossins, still energetically in the saddle as manager. He also ran the five auxiliary *bagli* at Campobello, Musciuleo, Castelvetrano, Balestrate and Vittoria. This last was used for the distillation of wine into the strong spirit for the reinforcement of young marsala. The other four were depots for the temporary storage of new wines brought in from the surrounding countryside, to be transported the following spring to the main *Baglio*. There were now twenty-seven stores for wine and one for cognac, and two distilleries. Some innovations were the use of steam power for pumping the wine, and of mechanical fans for drying the casks.

A eulogistic lady wrote to Tina that she almost 'cried with the excitement' of seeing the garden at the *Baglio*: the 'lilac-flowered Paulownia, the great vine almost smothering the summer-house . . . so wonderfully eastern-looking, that long adobe wall with red tiles studded with watch towers.' Tina, one imagines, did not share her enthusiasm.

The following year there was the usual summer visit to London. Tina briefly picked up her diary again.

> *Grayshott, 25 September 1889*
>
> Here we are, enjoying a visit to Ingham, a kind and thoughtful host. Will he ever marry? I begin to doubt it. On our journey to London we encountered poor Emily Medici at Lucerne: *Madrina* [godmother] Emilia, as the children call her. To think now she lives insensible to all joys and sorrows, a living death, and that a few days will probably end all [she died of a stroke on 4 October] . . . I do hope that Norina will not grow up as nervous and sensitive as she promises! Real nerves are a great drawback to happiness and, coupled with her noble heart, they may make her into a miserable woman. Delia is sure to get on. She takes to any stranger and is so *leggiera di carattere* that I feel that the inevitable troubles of life will sit lightly on her.

Poor Norina, how prophetic were these words. And how wrong she was about Delia.

Details of the Pips' lives are scanty just at this moment. They went to Paris, where the exhibition was 'in full finale swing'. In November they were staying near Turin at the Mandria, owned by Giacomo Medici's nephew and heir Luigi, who had also inherited the Marquisate. The Mandria was an eighteenth-century villa with some 7500 acres, and had been acquired by Giacomo Medici from King Umberto. Pip had gone there for the stag shooting, and it was a very great success. The Marquis gave him a few red deer to keep in an enclosure at Malfitano; some of these animals had Wapiti blood, as a result of Victor Emmanuel II having introduced the breed to the Mandria.

Then came 1890: national bankruptcy seemed to be looming; there was another visit to Tunisia, this time accompanied by General Scalia; plans were laid for a daring (and worrying to the womenfolk) lion-hunting trip to Eritrea, officially an Italian colony in that year. In Palermo there were *tableaux vivants*, garden parties, a costume ball, a flu epidemic, etc. etc.

Many English travellers arrived with letters of introduction. Tina had 'another charming visit from Hamilton Aïdé', who one day brought to lunch the surgeon Sir Morell Mackenzie 'with an uninteresting daughter, caring for nothing but boating . . . the father looks a very clever man, but hardly the polished courtier one would fancy to have played the all-important part he did in the tragic reign of the Emperor Frederick [Sir Morrell had attended the Emperor whilst he was dying of cancer of the throat].'[16]

Then on 27 May Ronny Gower arrived in Palermo for the first time – Lord Ronald Sutherland Gower – with an introduction to the Josses. As he had been in Paris with Percy ffrench (who had 'paid a score of visits each day – how he does it I cannot understand')[17] and later in Algiers, within a day or so he received a letter from Tina asking him to visit Malfitano 'a splendid but unfinished house with tapestries on the staircase from the Palazzo Colonna in Rome'. He found Madame Scalia 'a dear old dame', and there was much talk of Percy ffrench, Hamilton Aïdé and Lady Holland. As a result, he too was asked to stay.

One of Tina's nieces by marriage used to say: 'Tina always attracted people with bad reputations, like Ronny Gower.' Certainly Gower thereafter was a regular visitor to Malfitano and Tina became fond of him. Obvious points in his favour were that one sister was the Duchess of Leinster, another had been the late Duchess of Westminster, and a third was the Duchess of Argyll, mother-in-law of Princess Louise, daughter of Queen Victoria; the Duchess of Northumberland was his niece. His mother was Harriet Duchess of Sutherland, who had lost her head over Garibaldi whilst he was her guest in London in 1864. Like Aïdé he was a dilettante and artist. Queen Victoria admired his sculpture, and in 1888 his Shakespeare Memorial at Stratford had been unveiled by Oscar Wilde, a fact which was conveniently ignored when his *Old Diaries* were published, although Wilde had been a friend since 1872; indeed Gower was the original of Lord Henry in *The Picture of Dorian Gray*.[18]

As *The Times* said after his death, none of his many biographies, which included Joan of Arc, Marie Antoinette and Gainsborough, 'could have been called adequate' – he 'travelled over ground which others had worked to better purpose'. Actually, according to the anonymous author of the scandalmongering *Things I Shouldn't Tell*, he never wrote a line of any book attributed to him (except presumably those based on his quite interesting diaries). As for his statues, 'without a single exception they were the work of Madrassi of the Boulevard Montparnasse. . . . Ronny, unaided, could not have modelled a nose, not even a Jew's nose appraising a precious stone.' A glorious and uninhibited hoaxer in fact, though to be fair his royal niece was not above 'assistance' – the statue of Queen Victoria by the Round Pond being attributed to her though in reality done by Sir Edgar Boehm, who ghosted it.[19] But Gower was a scintillating guest to have in the house and Madame Scalia was amused by his arrant snobbery and the way he would preface remarks with suspect phrases like 'As the Queen of Würtemburg wrote to me yesterday', 'As the King of Saxony told me at breakfast one morning,' 'As I hope to hear from the Prime Minister by next week's post.' Yet all this business of appearing to be in the know was given an aura of credibility when he received a letter from Hamilton Aïdé announcing that he would like him to be the first to hear that the great explorer H. M. Stanley had become engaged to Dolly Tennant, Aïdé's relative.

Tina thought that the tips Gower gave the footmen on leaving Malfitano were unnecessarily generous. On reading this comment one's suspicions are aroused, especially after Mrs Grosskurth's recent revelations about Symonds, who disapproved so strongly of the attitude of both Wilde and Gower towards the working classes – 'fair ground for sexual exploitation'. In passing, it is perhaps worth noting that the model for Prince Hal on the Shakespeare Memorial was a young American soldier named Perrin, who became Gower's lover in 1879.[20]

Last dinners and receptions in Palermo. Then the Pips set out for London by way of Rome, Carlsbad, Frankfurt, Cologne, and Brussels. The journey was marred by Mama getting ill. Rooms in London had been booked at the Berkeley, where an invitation for the Stanley wedding was waiting.

The wedding, in Westminster Abbey, was the social event of the year. Stanley, aged forty-nine, looked terrible, as he was suffering from both gastritis and malaria. Of course old Hamilton Aïdé was fluttering about – Dolly's mother was his first cousin. Mama's ill-health continued all through the summer. For Tina there was, however, one special excitement: the publishing of her novel *Love in the Sunny South*, little more than a long story really, the author's name simply being given as 'Tina'. It had been Mrs Lynn Linton who had urged her to try her hand at fiction – and it was Mrs Lynn Linton who was landed with the work of editing and tidying up. The result was not something that made Tina especially proud, with good reason, and in later years she very seldom chose to refer to it. The story, needless to say, centred on a charity concert in a town in Southern Italy. The beautiful Elvira is loved by her brother-in-law, who is shot in a duel by her husband . . .

*London, 2 October 1890*

To celebrate the book we went to see Lady Dunlo [society lady, whose wedding had had much publicity the previous year] act *Venus*. Mrs Linton came with us. We were surprised to find Lady Dunlo not so very lovely, although she has a certain grace.

Hamilton Aïdé spent the night with us on his way to Ascot. His journey with Mrs Tennant and the Stanleys seemed to preoccupy him. Stanley, however, is becoming rapidly civilized under the influence of his wife.

The journey was to America, where Stanley had 120 lecture tours arranged. They reached New York on 29 October, rather overwhelmed by the din and unsightliness. Although a special pullman car had been provided, complete with kitchen, drawing-room, three state bedrooms and a piano, Aïdé soon became exhausted. He wrote to Tina that he now regretted very much having forgone his visit to peaceful Malfitano. Dolly began to show her fire by quarrelling with the impresario. The newspapers were insulting to Aïdé. 'Mr and Mrs Stanley', wrote one reporter, 'are accompanied by a gentleman with whose name the flies appear to have taken liberties.'

By the time Tina had written again in her diary, the Pips had already gone from London.

*Paris, 16 October 1890*

We left London the day before yesterday. We spent a pleasant day with Lady Downshire at Easthampstead, Aïdé being of the party, his last before leaving. Lady Arthur Hill sang us her new composition and we had music all the afternoon. . . .

Last night, here in Paris, we went to the Opera, and heard Melba in *Hamlet*. She is a pupil of Madame Marchesi, and very young still. She has the same clear, bell-like voice of Patti, and the pathos in her voice does not make one notice that she is still a little cold. Still, it is a mistake for an artist to feel too much. I remember Strakosch telling me that Patti when she made her début was quite a *stick*.[21] Yes, the secret of life is to play ably on the keyboard of others' feelings, leaving our own in repose. To *act*, but only to act, not to show our feelings. Indeed, when we feel the most is when we generally should show the least.

This was Tina's last entry for nearly four years.

# XIX

## Simpatica *and Rather Sad*

A PATTERN for some while ahead was more or less established: the end of December (probably after Christmas) until mid-May at Malfitano; June in London for the Season, with perhaps a visit to Switzerland on the way; July to September elsewhere in England and in Scotland; October travelling on the Continent; November in Florence; most of December in Rome.

Sophie Tommasi-Crudeli now had a *salotto* which in a modest way rivalled Laura Minghetti's. Her friends were inclined to be more academic than literary or social, and many were Germans. They included such eminent persons as Bruno Chimirri (law) and Senator Francesco Brioschi (mathematics and engineering), both at times in the government; Senator Pietro Blaserna (physics); Wolfgang Helbig (Secretary of the German Institute in Rome) with his huge, mannish Russian wife, who looked like Martin Luther; and Ferdinand Gregorovius, the German author of many books on Italy and an honorary citizen of Rome. Tina, having found Donna Laura not quite as agreeable as she had seemed on their first meeting, naturally favoured her sister-in-law. She also herself kept up a kind of patriots' *salotto* at Malfitano, in deference to her father, but it was more formal and centred round Sunday luncheon, as in the old days at Wyndham Place. Her most frequent guests were Ciccio Brancaccio, Ciccio Vassallo and Baron Fucile.

In the autumn of 1891 Tina coincided briefly in Venice with Ronny Gower, who was staying with Horatio Brown and his mother. She had to hurry back especially early to Palermo, to be in readiness for the opening of the National Exhibition where she was to sing before the King and Queen – their first visit since 1881. Gower went to Rome, and here he discovered Symonds, unflagging in energy despite his precarious health, with his faithful gondolier Angelo, 'a fine, rough, rather bulky-looking Venetian, who follows him like a shadow'. Tina had suggested that Gower should bring Symonds, with of course Angelo, to Palermo, but alas the invitation was not taken up.

Gower reached Malfitano by the end of November. 'Nothing', he wrote in his diary, 'could be more beautiful than this place, a huge white stone building surrounded by gardens commanding beautiful views of the distant hills, the town and the harbour. My windows look out over the famous plain of the Conca d'Oro, and Monreale at the top of a violet mountain.' (Now, eighty years later, these views are all but shut out by cliffs of apartment blocks.) Cranes and Purple Gallinules (water-hens), *Porphyrio coerulens*, had joined the Mandria deer.[1] Pip employed twelve gardeners.

As for Effie's garden at Sperlinga, this had become one of the sights of the city; here there were no less than twenty-five gardeners. 'Till three years ago Sperlinga was a waste bit of land; now it blossoms like the rose, and the views from every side are beautiful.' All sorts of little tiled nooks had been built at strategic positions. The Via Cavour palace, pink and white, was virtually complete; and with even more bedrooms than at Malfitano.

Meanwhile there were *flambeaux* processions by night and parades of Garibaldini up and down Palermo, in honour of the Royal couple. The tenor Francesco Tamagno had been engaged to sing in the same concert as Tina in the Politeama – he was now at the height of his fame.[2] For some reason the reigning soprano refused to sing the duet from *Guarany* with him. It was Tina who was eventually persuaded to take her place, having at first refused because she had been afraid of the power of his voice. Tamagno had said: 'But I shall be *tenore di grazia*; you'll see.' The King sent her a special good luck message: 'Prosit', and indeed he and the Queen were the first to applaud. All went splendidly and Tamagno kept to his word. Blandine Gravina was one of the most enthusiastic with her congratulations. Gower wrote: 'Mrs Whitaker took the lion's share at the concert, sang admirably, and much applauded by a full house.'

Now that Palermo was becoming such a fashionable place for rich foreigners during the winter, one had the feeling the National Exhibition ought to be the beginning of a new age of brilliance and prosperity. Ignazio Florio had died on 17 May, and his eldest son, Ignazino, or Don Ignazio, as he was soon to be known, aged twenty-three, was his heir. Very handsome, immaculate, unmarried, full of the Florio business drive, fond of sport and good living, the brother-in-law of the Prince of Trabia to boot, he was the *autentico principe azzurro*, the real blue prince. He and his sister were outstandingly the leaders of social life. In Palermo alone he employed 6000 people, so that, out of a total population of 250,000 it was estimated that 16,000 dependants 'ate his bread'.

Ignazio married in 1892. His wife was not from one of the great aristocratic families, nor by any means from one of the richest, though a woman of considerable beauty: the 'divinely lovely' Franca Jacona di San Giuliano.[3] She was a natural hostess in the grand manner and had, moreover, a warm and unaffected character. Then there was a brother, Vincenzo Florio, born in 1883. Whereas Franca was virtuous, he most certainly was not; but like her he knew how to spend money, and this fact also helped to make Palermo, in the early part of the twentieth century, one of the most sparkling capitals of Europe.

Yet in the early 1890s a general gloom lay over Italian national life. Bankruptcy seemed inevitable. Crispi had fallen in January 1891 and the Right had come into power under that other Sicilian, Rudinì, wearing the mantle of Minghetti. In Sicily the *Mafia* was as strong as ever. Throughout the western end most people had to go armed; brigandage and murder were still common. Local toughs, in classic *Mafia* fashion, held unassailable positions and expected tribute. Workers, to protect themselves against unemployment and the rising cost of living, in the larger towns formed themselves into *fasci*, the equivalent of local trade unions. The ruling classes were thus becoming fearful of the 'Socialist scare'.

Ronny Gower visited Monreale, where he went to see the boys' reformatory school and listened to its brass band led by the son of the brigand Leone. Then Pip, who had become quite friendly with him, took him to Marsala. They stayed in the *Baglio*, 'more like a fortress or prison than a wine factory', and were rowed across to Motya, of which Pip now owned about a third. Most of the island, Gower noted, consisted of vineyards, dotted with olives, carobs and almond trees; Pip had been introducing the agave ('like huge goats' horns') for commercial purposes. The peasant inhabitants, about sixty in all, stood in a row to meet them. Pip said that the eminent excavator of ancient Troy and discoverer of the 'treasure of Priam', Professor Hermann Schliemann, who died in 1890, had been there for a fortnight in 1875, though without achieving very much of importance. He indicated to Gower the weed-covered causeway, only two feet under water, and various other, partially excavated ruins. It was at Motya, he said, that the *ballista* – the instrument for throwing stones against beleaguered cities – had first been used, an invention as revolutionary as that of artillery. His stories of the sacking of Motya and of the subsequent crucifixions were blood-curdling. 80,000 men and 3000 boats had been used for the attack, and wheeled wooden towers, six stories high, had been used by Dionysius to cope with the high houses, for which the town was famous.

At Marsala they ran into the widowed Jessie White Mario. As a patriot she had been admitted to a Malfitano Sunday lunch. She had not been impressed. After glowering round the dining-room she had looked at the marguerites on the table and had said tersely: 'I see we are among monarchists in the house' (referring to Queen Margherita). Gower found her altogether too aggressive and positive, too full of her own works, albeit kind-hearted. She had just been visiting some sulphur mines and was justifiably full of terrible tales of overworked children; it was still legal for boys of ten to work in them. Some miners' families lived in caves; sulphur prices were falling and with them the standard of living; terrorisation by the *Mafia* was there at its worst. Reforms were being impeded by the vested interests of *latifondisti* (big absentee landlords).

Gower was thankful that she was not invited with him to Benjamin Ingham's country house at Racalia. He loved its setting and peacefulness. 'The villa is a long rambling villa standing high, with pretty shaded pergola walks, terraces and clear fountains; the sunsets from the garden are glorious. This is the place Mrs Lynn Linton, the novelist, fell in love with, and where she said she would wish to end her days.' Harry Clark, employed by the Whitakers as a trainee and later to become their manager, escorted him up Mount Eryx where Gower wanted to 'worship at the shrine of the Earth Mother', and then came back to Palermo with him.

*Malfitano, 2 January 1892*

I rode up Monte Pellegrino, in this wise, young Clark and Mrs Whitaker's nephew, Alexander Morrison, walked up, accompanied by Mrs 'Effie' Whitaker, who although not a sylph, walked up and bounded down the hill with wonderful agility. My donkey was a first-rate 'moke', and carried me up in good style.

In town Effie was only to be seen driving in a brougham. Occasionally a hand would appear, scattering the husks of parrot seed. She was now the mother of four, and a pretty tyrannical one. Joss, known to those at the *Baglio* as O.P. or 'Old Particular', after the brand of marsala, applied himself at snail's pace to the family business, and insisted on using a quill pen and sand instead of blotting paper; he could sometimes be very irascible. Gower paid him a duty farewell visit, then was off to the fleshpots of Algiers.

When summer came, the Pips met Gower once more, this time in London, where he took them to the unveiling of the Jubilee statue done by his niece Princess Louise. And this is virtually all we know about 1892 in Tina's life. No doubt she also saw Hamilton Aïdé and J. A. Symonds, who accompanied Gower to Stratford to see his Shakespeare memorial. Angelo went with them. Then the quartet moved to Castle Howard, to stay with Gower's relative, Lord Carlisle. 'J. A. Symonds' gondolier, Angelo, is a thorough impediment to his master on his travels, but is occasionally a source of amusement, as, for instance, when he told Johnnie [Symonds] of his horror at finding himself alone in the house with five-and-twenty maids.'

In April 1893 there was another *serata di beneficienza* with Tina singing pieces from Rossini, Offenbach, De Leva and Wekerlin, and sundry princesses and duchesses appearing in *tableaux vivants*. That summer she managed to persuade old General Scalia to come to London. It was his first visit since the grim winter of 1861. They took him to see Mrs Pat Campbell, 'bursting forth in all her glory as Paula in *The Second Mrs Tanqueray*. 'I was very taken,' Tina wrote, 'with her impassioned utterance, toned down by her British education. A wonderful actress indeed! I hear she refers to Hamilton Aïdé as "the world's governess". His men friends call him "Titums".'

The effect of London on the General was not good for his health. His wife decided he must go to Langen Schwalbach for the mud baths. And as Princess Louise and the Marquess of Lorne had gone there, it would naturally be all the more agreeable. By a strange chance the Whitaker-Scalia party stayed in the same hotel as Her Royal Highness.

Meanwhile things were still not all happy politically in Italy and Sicily, to say the least. The Marquis Emanuele Notarbartalo, father of Tina's girlhood friend, had been murdered on a train, presumably because he was about to uncover some scandals in the Bank of Sicily of which he was a director.[5] There also had been unrest among Sicilian peasants: police had been attacked, tax offices burnt down etc. Rudinì had resigned in May 1892 and had been succeeded by Giolitti, Crispi's Minister of Finance. Then the scandal broke. It was revealed that Tanlongo, head of the Banca Romana, had issued duplicate bank notes worth 62,500,000 *lire* for the profit of himself and his friends. Giolitti totally exonerated him and made him a Senator. When Parliament pressed for a full investigation, it became clear that several of its own members had received money from Tanlongo and that Giolitti himself had been compromised. Giolitti resigned, in spite of being acquitted of 'personal dishonesty', and prudently went to Switzerland for a rest.

Sicily was on the verge of revolution. On 12 December Pip and Tina at Schwalbach read in *The Times* that eight rioters had been killed by troops in Palermo and fourteen others had been wounded. The infuriated mob had thereupon captured the town clerk and his wife and cut off their heads, which they proceeded to parade on pike round the town. Houses had been burnt down. A dreadfully familiar story. Was 1893 any more civilised than 1866, or for that matter 1820? When peasants began taking over land owned by *latifondisti*, the employer classes became really alarmed. Crispi, once more Prime Minister, declared martial law in Sicily and initiated measures of ruthless severity, including mass deportations.

Because of the national crisis, Crispi declared a 'truce of God' in the feud between the Vatican and the Italian Government. The revival of the Triple Alliance with Germany and Austria-Hungary by Rudinì had been a blow to the Pope, who had regarded Austria as a special ally (Franz Josef had actually offered him asylum in 1882). Crispi initiated some informal talks, in which Monsignor Isidoro Carini was able to play a certain part. By agreement with Crispi, Carini invited Alfonso Scalia to Rome to help in the discussions.

It was a very great honour. A snag was that Tina had been engaged to sing before Princess Louise and some German princesses. Nevertheless she nobly abandoned this engagement, and the whole family came hurrying down from Schwalbach to Rome. In fact the talks ended in failure. They were still in mid-stream when Alfonso Scalia caught pneumonia, from which he died on 4 March 1894. He had suffered from a 'weak chest' ever since he was wounded at Capua. Umberto I sent Madame Scalia a special message of condolence. The body was removed for burial in a special little Gothic chapel in Santa Maria di Gesu outside Palermo, and a great number of senior army officers, senators and deputies were at the funeral. Crispi sent a wreath inscribed 'All'amico carissimo'.

Probably Tina was right when she complained that her father had never received enough recognition from his country for his services during the Risorgimento. If he had been less of a sybarite, he might have been more successful. To put it politely, he emphatically did not appeal to women of his own class, and vice versa.

All this while Pip had been in Tunisia, on his most ambitious journey yet. He had taken his tents and camping equipment by train to Tebessa, where he had hired camels for the trip to the Roman city of Gafsa. In 1893 he had also ventured to Gafsa, though he had not been so well prepared, and had gone as far as the Algerian frontier. Ostensibly it had been a 'shooting tour', looking for mouflon and other game, but many a rare bird had also fallen to his gun – a Green Sandpiper, Egyptian Vultures, some Hoopoes and Sand-Grouse, an Algerian Bush-Babbler and assorted chats, wagtails, finches and larks, the skins of all of which had been preserved. In 1894 he had headed for the oasis of Nefta, on the edge of the shifting sands, and then had skirted round the southern edge of the Chott el Djerid and made for Gabes, his point of embarkation. He had been delighted with the success of the journey, and his collection of skins of the Tunisian avifauna was now becoming quite comprehensive.

Both trips resulted in articles for the British ornithological magazine *The Ibis*.[6] Pip gave general descriptions of the countryside and his experiences, with detailed notes on the bird species he had encountered. He had been urged to do this by two of the leading ornithologists of the day, Philip Sclater and E. Cavendish-Taylor, who had both become impressed by his field-work. His style was easy, yet vivid, communicating enthusiasm and a sense of wonder. He could have been an excellent writer of travel books.

In June Tina settled down once more to keep her diary in earnest. Her chief motive was to leave some record for her children. Although only thirty-five, she had a presentiment that she would not live long. She also wanted to make her diary a kind of confidant; it was, she confessed, almost an impossibility, certainly an agony, to expose her intimate thoughts to other people.

Needless to say, having started with such firm intentions, she let several weeks pass before she picked up the diary again. Thereafter she kept writing in a desultory way until 1928, when she was aged seventy; sometimes a year might pass with barely an entry. In 1940 she began again. Many of the entries are of course of family interest only, and this fact alone has made it all the more necessary to be stringent in selecting from them.

After the usual summer in England and a further, rather morbid return to the mud baths of Schwalbach (for Tina's benefit this time), they travelled to Lucerne and then to Lake Como, where they were confronted by endless rainstorms.

*Bellagio, 1 October 1894*

We had hoped to go to Cadenabbia to be with the Stanleys and Mrs Tennant, but the hotel there was full. However we have managed to see mother and daughter often. The mother adores Dolly and was determined she should marry a celebrity. But is Dolly really happy? One has to admire the husband's strength of character and incredible tenacity, but his poor, beautiful wife has to bear with his ill-temper as well as his ill-health. During the ceremony at Westminster Abbey he had to

31. Tina Whitaker in her court dress designed by Worth.

32. Malfitano in about 1889.

33. Malfitano from the air, 1946.
(*Photo: Col. Giulio Lipari.*)

34. Palazzo Whitaker, Via Cavour, exterior.

35. Palazzo Whitaker, drawing-room.

36. Effie Whitaker and her parrot.

37. Maude Whitaker in court dress.

38. Villa Sofia.

remain seated, and one could quite clearly see the suffering on his face. There is no chance of children, which is a grief to Dolly.

Indeed ugly rumours of marital rows between the Stanleys had reached the world outside. A reporter from the *Herald* tracked Stanley down and had the impertinence to ask whether it was true that he beat his wife. 'Dolly Tennant said she would marry a lion,' a kind friend remarked, 'and she certainly has married the king of beasts.' In 1896 they adopted a boy, Denzil, aged one, and this helped to settle the marriage a little.

The rain drove the Pips south. They found another old friend and patriot, the octogenarian Sir James Lacaita, one of the great figures in Anglo-Italian liberalism, ever since the days of the *Letters to Lord Aberdeen*. Dear Sir James Lacaita, with his 'soft, incisive voice and careful diction.' Although an Italian citizen (and now a senator), he had for a while been naturalised British and had been knighted by Gladstone for his help in the Ionian Isles question in 1858.[7]

*Florence, 27 October 1894*

Such a charming visit to Sir James today. We were alone, except for Janet Ross [the intellectual queen among Florentine expatriates].[8] How bitterly (and rightly too) he spoke of the unveiling of the monument to Agostino Depretis. 'It is to him that we owe the defeat at Lissa [the naval reverse against the Austrians, 20 July 1866]. It is because he was Prime Minister [1876–87] that we are in these financial straits now.' And then again about King Umberto's sad tendency to the *Sinistra* [Left]. . . . He said that Massawa [i.e. Eritrea, where a war against Abyssinia was imminent, thanks in part to arms and money lent to the Abyssinians by the French] has already cost us one hundred million. In 1867 he had proposed that the Italian Government should make an offer of four millions for Sarawak in Borneo, having written a confidential letter to Rattazzi, as Prime Minister, on the subject. I gathered that the then Miss [later Baroness] Burdett-Coutts had urged him to do this. She was a friend of Sir James Brooke, the Rajah of Sarawak, who had left Borneo that year; it was her idea that an Anglo-Italian company should take over the administration of Sarawak, which might eventually mean an Italian protectorate of the whole island. Rattazzi had sent for Sir James Lacaita and had said that he dared not put a refusal in writing, since he would not like it to be known that he had lost a good opportunity for Italian colonization. 'I think all the money Italy can dispose of should be spent on improving the empty tracts of land in Sardinia, Calabria and Sicily, before she encourages emigration and colonisation abroad.' And right he has proved to be. . . . I once met Rattazzi at Leghorn. I had heard so much against him, but my prejudices faded before his clear, quiet, straightforward look, so full of intelligence. He possessed both will-power and self-command, a rare combination in an Italian.

*Rome, 3 November 1894*

Arrived the night before last and found General Pelaez [once General Scalia's A.D.C.] waiting at the station. Sad meeting, he was devoted to my poor father. The conversation nearly all on the same subject: useless regrets, vain longings to have done differently to what one did. . . . Here at the Grand Hotel we watched Zola and his wife dining at a table near ours. There is something *acaraître* in his expression which disappointed me, something small and mean I would rather not have found. Perhaps it is the key to his wild, almost abject, craving to be an *académician de France*. And the wife? I wonder who she is.[9] Not that she interests me, excepting as being Zola's wife. She looks *bourgeoise* with a great desire to be thought a lady. Otherwise a blank, a nonentity.

*Rome, 6 November 1894*

So many friends: Monsignor Carini, Martino Beltrani, Rudinì. Princess Belmonte came twice, bringing her grand-children, Teresa and Giulio. She knew the pleasure she would give me to see the children of my dear dead friend. Brilliant Lily Belmonte, still more brilliant as Duchess Torlonia [she died in 1891 and the Duke remarried a year later], now forgotten except for a few friends. And we saw our friend General Arimondi, proud and pleased at his battle gained so gloriously at Agordat [December 1893], always the same, hearty and simple. He said, with usual modesty: 'The greatest pleasure I have had is to be able to prove to my friends that I have not been unworthy of the affection bestowed on me.'

A few years later Tina wrote one of her pen-portraits of Arimondi:

He was a Piedmontese and of modest origin – his father was station master at Ivrea. He worked hard and was tenacious of purpose, in the way that Piedmontese habitually are. When I first knew him well he was already carried away by colonial dreams for Italy in Africa and was learning Arabic hard. . . . In November 1894 we invited him to dine at the Grand Hotel with Monsignor Carini, and I remember one comment by the latter in answer to a question: 'My dear general, we historians merely relate the material that you soldiers provide for us.' Arimondi at that time did not want to return to Africa, because he disliked the idea of serving under General Baratieri [Governor of Eritrea], whom he considered incapable. He had also told Crispi that he wanted to resign as he did not agree with the government's policy in Eritrea. However after some days he came to say goodbye. 'I was summoned to an audience with the King,' he said, 'and he has ordered me to take up my command in Africa.' He was sad but resolute, the perfect soldier. That was the last time we saw our friend. He wrote to us last on the 20th January 1896 [the very day of the fall of Makallé to the Abyssinians], during the tragic epilogue of our African campaign – it was a scribbled note; he was seated on his baggage and writing on a stone. On the 1st March he died horribly in battle at Adowa. The retreat had already started, and his batman had brought him a mule to mount. The officers asked him to hurry. 'You go,' he said. 'My place is here.' Almost immediately after this he was hit on the knee. He fell on a large slab of rock on which he had been standing with General Baratieri at various stages of the battle. There he was hacked to death by the advancing dervishes, drunk with victory.

The Italian casualties at Adowa had been nearly 11,000 out of a force of 17,000. It was an appalling defeat, but at least the courage of the troops had left Italy's honour unstained. As a result of the disaster, Crispi fell, once more to be replaced by Rudinì, and Baratieri was court-martialled.[10]

Whilst the Pips had been away from Palermo, an obliging Monsignore friend had been going through General Scalia's effects at the Villino. Tradition has it that he removed many 'pornographic love stories in beautiful bindings'. Pip had decided to take over the building as a museum for his objects excavated at Motya and the bird skins acquired in Tunisia. We do not know whether he had his 'amusements', like Joss, in the town. Tradition also has it that Joss kept a regular *cocotte*; clean sheets would be sent in advance to announce his visit.

Ronny Gower came to stay for a month, thrilled that his Westminster niece had married Prince Adolphus of Teck (Queen Mary's brother). He had just been paying a pilgrimage to Leucaspide, Sir James Lacaita's house near Taranto. Hamilton Aïdé, dressed in a shiny waterproof that looked like grey satin, had also been there. Gower had found Sir James in acute suffering, praying for the end, which in fact came on 6 January. It was he who had telegraphed the news to Janet Ross.

Tina wrote in her diary:

*Malfitano, 20 January 1895*

Horatio Brown arrived with Ronald Gower, and I am reading his life of Symonds [who had died on 19 April 1893, attended by Dr Axel Munthe], the second volume first – I did not know enough of him to care about his boyhood. A sad, sad life, with the restless longing of an invalid for health and strength, the sense that his works were not appreciated in the way he had hoped, and that he had failed to produce all that he should have done. How many of us have such feelings! When I was twenty I believed all that was prophesied for me that the musical world would echo out my name. Now the struggle has been not to become bitter at the disappointment I have undergone. I am resigned to be nothing, to have produced nothing, to have done nothing of which my youth and energy made me dream. I am content to live in my children as the future, in my mother as the present. My husband does not require me.

Gower, in his diary, wrote that Horatio Brown was accompanied by 'his faithful gondolier Antonio', who presumably also stayed at Malfitano. Tina's next entry ran:

*Malfitano, 27 January 1895*

A great shock to us. Monsignor Carini is gone. Can it be true what they say: that the black party at the Vatican have made him disappear by poison?[11] Hamilton Aïdé has now arrived at Malfitano. He bicycles each morning in the garden for exercise. He wants the girls to call him 'Uncle Hamilton', but this they refuse. They are too old-fashioned he says.

*Malfitano, 27 February 1895*

Last day of Carnival. At Mrs Gardner's I saw Maude who looked tired after so many gaieties. I do not wish you [i.e. Norina and Delia] to read this until you are married. I want you to remember that a mother's duty to her child begins before its birth, and Maude is expecting hers within three months. Hot rooms, vitiated air, late hours, an appearance of a good figure kept up too long: all these are dangers.

Tina had objected to Pip going to Tunisia for the third year running, so a Mr O. V. Aplen was sent on a collecting expedition in his place, this time along the coast to the Tripolitanian frontier. White-collared Flycatchers and Crested Larks now fell to his gun and their skins were duly transported to Malfitano.[12] As for Gower, he had gone to Florence, where he called on Hamilton Aïdé's friend, Bernard Berenson, just becoming famous and 'rather too positive in his judgements about early Italian art'.[13] In Venice he was joined by his new protégé, Frank Hird, a journalist, aged twenty-one. Horatio Brown took them to *Charley's Aunt* in Italian; they were accompanied by Antonio the gondolier and Luigi the butler.

Returning to Tina:

*Malfitano, 14 April 1895*

How many people have brought letters of introduction this winter. I realize now how careful one has to be in bringing together conationals who have not previously met. It is quite a mistake to think that English like one another abroad. . . . Maude has been very ill lately. I have been rereading what I wrote about her behaviour during Carnival. Let us hope all will go well.

*Malfitano, 19 May 1895*

Anxious days have I passed nursing dear Mama. I am thankful to say she is better now, though still weak. Robert and Maude have a little son. He seems none the worse for all that he went through before his birth. Yesterday in the billiard room I had cause to reproach Delia for selfishness. I trust she will grow out of this fault. Norina, as usual when her sister is scolded, melted into tears.

Fifty-five years later Tina wrote a footnote to this comment in the diary: 'Nobody could call Delia selfish now!'

Madame Scalia was frequently ill during the summer, so it was decided that she should be taken to Bad Homburg for a cure. At Malfitano she had busied herself with destroying old letters and papers, which seemed to Tina to be a worrying sign.

*Homburg, 11 September 1895*

At lunch the Duke of Cambridge sits at a table next to ours: a good hearty hale burly country squire. He has with him Mr Christopher Sykes, a mild fair edition of the well-known Mayendorf of the Russian Embassy in Rome. We have several times seen the Grand Duchess Mecklenburg-Schwerin; she brings messages from the Grand Duke, who is in bed, saying that he has listened to my singing with much pleasure. Not so a biscuit maker, whose name I do not know, who resides on the 3rd floor with his daughter suffering from delirium tremens (!). He sends pencil notes saying that music disturbs them.

*Florence, 13 November 1895*

Every year I have met Janet Ross and every year our friendship has been allowed to sleep on, nursed by our mutual esteem for Sir James Lacaita. Now that he is gone, it is all the stronger and will not break I think, so long as I do not mention the name of Ouida. She does not like the biography of Symonds and says it gives quite the wrong impression.[14]

This feud between Janet Ross and Ouida was of twenty years' standing and centred on the Marquis della Stufa, Janet Ross's *cavaliere servente* or lover. Ouida published a novel, *Friendship* (1878), in which the gentle Stufa, the domineering Mrs Ross and herself were but barely disguised. The legend that Janet Ross thereupon horse-whipped Ouida, publicly outside the Circolo in the Via Tornabuoni, has never entirely been substantiated; some say she did this because Ouida had spread the rumour that she had her lovers' names tattooed on her thighs.[15] Walburga Lady Paget described meeting Ouida in September 1893: 'She received me in a dreadful white nightgown, trimmed with lace, and a black cape. Eight dogs kept up an infernal noise, and went on mistaking the lace frill of her nightdress for a lamp-post.'[16]

*Florence, 15 November 1895*

*Sic transit.* Percy ffrench told me the other day a little anecdote worthy of record. A year or so ago the Empress Eugénie was passing through Paris. She was stopping at, I think, the Continental. Percy, who knows her well, called and sent up to know whether she would receive him. The answer came: 'Le numero 102 vous recèvera!' . . . Dr Baldwin, speaking of Axel Munthe, gave a definition of him which came home to *me* very strongly: 'We know he is a great man and capable of great heroism. The trouble is that, having done a sublime thing, he feels he must cry it out from the house tops.'

*Malfitano, 26 January 1896*

At Villa Sofia they have been very sad. The baby boy they were so proud of was taken from them on the 1st January, after a fortnight's illness. He had little vitality from the first. So all that I wrote about a mother's duties before the birth of her child has proved totally justified.

*Malfitano, 10 April 1896*

Percy ffrench has really left us, after a visit of *fifty* days and *fifty* nights, to use his expression. It has been a dull stay for him, for Mama has been ill and I have been in constant attendance on her. ffrench however has found his own amusements; he is a thorough southern Italian. . . . I must write about the honour we received last Saturday when the Empress of Germany visited us, accompanied by the two young Princes and a numerous suite. Franz [von Rekowski, German consul in Naples and married to Pip's first cousin, Louisa, daughter of Robert Sanderson] called on Peppino at 9 o'clock to say that if we would send our carriages he would bring the Empress that same morning. I was in bed and had just time to dress when at half past 10 she arrived. She remained nearly an hour; I sang to her Rossini's 'Assisa a pié d'un salice', Tosti's 'Si tu le voulais' and 'Spingole francesi', which amused the young princes. Mama accompanied the first piece by heart, and of course I sang it without music, which made a great impression on the Empress. We were all charmed by the graceful simplicity of her manner. The Crown Prince [Wilhelm] looked to me a very *intellectual* boy. The second [Eitel-Friedrich] is fat enough to be the son of Prince Gangi.

Twelve days later Percy ffrench died in Naples. Tina left the event un-recorded, but remarked some while later that his effects totalled just over £57,000.

Then, on 13 May 1896, came the dreadful thing: Madame Scalia died. It was shattering to Tina. She could not even bear to turn to her diary. Gower, when he heard the news wrote: 'I cannot imagine her poor daughter's life without her mother, so wrapped up was her spirit with hers.' When eventually Tina did begin to write again, the extraordinary outpourings were like those of some bereaved lover: 'The sun has gone from my life . . . Ah, my beloved, my heart, my home was only in you . . . What am I to do, where am I to lean?' It could have hardly been very cheerful at Malfitano for Pip and the girls.

*Malfitano, 23 January 1897*

How can I expect to be understood in my grief? How can I turn for consolation to those nearest me? Peppino does not want me very much. Maude is busy making preparations for a ball only four months after her step-father is dead. Effie. How can she understand? She has now asked her good mother for a month's stiff visit for the first time in *ten long years*. This mother whose only fault is not being very refined!

Effie at least did her best to make life better for Norina and Delia, how-ever strict she was with her own girls. When she came to Malfitano for dinner, she would put a nightdress over her evening frock and have pillow-fights with them. People were horrified by the way Norina and Delia were molly-coddled. Before they went out, they were always bundled into coats and made to put on galoshes. If it was raining, their temperatures would be taken first. Norina was supposed to 'have the looks' and to be the 'clever one'. Before dinner she and Delia would be brought down like pretty dolls and made to play on their mandolines.

No doubt it was Pip's idea that Tina should be made to turn to good works. She was already to a certain extent involved in her in-laws'

*Educatorio* Whitaker. Following a scheme to launch an animals' protection society, she and Pip now started an institution known as the *Infanzia Abbandonata*, or refuge for waifs and strays – about eighty children, two-thirds being girls, either orphans or children of people in prison or in hospital. Countess Maria Wilding di Radalì gave the land in Via della Croci and Ignazio Greco was commissioned to erect the prison-like building. The Municipality was also persuaded to give its support. As usual in Sicily, a man had to be the figurehead in a public concern such as this, so Pip was President, although Tina did much of the work behind the scenes. The animals' protection society was, laudably, concentrated at first on cab horses and stray dogs. The two societies together were run under the title of the Sicilian Society for Humane Education.

A curious episode also helped to divert Tina's mind from her grief for a short while:

*Malfitano, 26 January 1897*

I am sure Joss is not telling the truth. It was in the papers that Audrey [his third daughter, aged ten] was riding in the Favorita, accompanied by Ninuzzo the groom, when four men suddenly came out of the bushes and set upon Ninuzzo and tied him to the horse, making off with Audrey. Someone went to ask Joss for the ransom (80–100,000 *lire*); Joss paid up at once and Audrey was returned home, unscathed. Now Joss says it is all an invention.

The kidnapping of Audrey was and is still a mystery. There seems every good reason to believe that there was some element of truth in the story. Such was the power of the *Mafia* that Joss did not dare even to confide about his hush money to his closest relatives. Another very upsetting incident that was also hushed up was when a human hand, thrown over the wall at the Villa Sofia, landed at the feet of Maude as she walked in the garden. Nobody dared make a fuss in case it was a threat.

*Wimbledon, 26 July 1897*

I have laughed again! A whole week has passed since I heard that sound, the first time since the day of my great bereavement. . . . Emily Luck [Effie's actress schoolfriend] asked me if I was sorry to leave Wimbledon and glad to go to Bavaria. My answer 'It is quite indifferent to me personally where I go, what I do' brought forth the exclamation: 'I am sorry for you.' Why? Truly I care for nothing now.

Yet soon there was something of the old spark in the diary.

*Florence, 15 October 1897*

I am reading Ouida. I love her. I love her for her marvellous perception and sense of colour. Above all I love her for her love of Italy. So many here turn a cold shoulder and are unwilling to continue paying for her luxuries. To what a point her want of sense of value of money goes is illustrated by her calling on Madame de Tchikacheff [widow of the great traveller] one day in her smart Victoria and two bays, and asking her to lend – five *lire*!

*Rome, 14 November 1897*

I met Marianna Bülow [daughter of Laura Minghetti]. She is so simple, bright, intelligent and unaffected that one would hardly credit her with such a past: having her first husband [Graf Karl Dönhoff] living with Lenbach the painter, then although there were two children getting her marriage annulled in order to marry von Bülow [Graf, later Prince Bernhard von Bülow, eventually Chancellor of Germany], and coming as Ambassadress for Germany to Rome. It was her mother who remade her life and arranged all these wonders . . . Dr Munthe introduced me to Mr Rennell Rodd [later Lord Rennell of Rodd, ambassador in Italy 1908–19] recently returned from Abyssinia. I was glad to hear that he thinks the French overrate their power with Menelik [the Emperor, father of Haile Selassie], who is alive to the power of Italy and anxious for friendly terms. Rodd impressed me as having a clear and practical intelligence; his modesty and great charm may however mar his career, in this decade where *blague* and self-assertion are half the battle won!

*Rome, 15 November 1897*

I wonder how it is that Giulia Trabia can make friends of 'certain people', and that I cannot. I mean the Bob Whitakers. I have come to the conclusion that as these people are relations of ours they show themselves *as they are*, and with her, *en guants jaunes*. Thus she does not see them in reality, but only with the varnish they have learnt to put on in a society to which they do not belong.

*Malfitano, 28 December 1897*

The police have at last got hold of a number of criminals, some of whom are supposed to have kidnapped Audrey. Joss still maintains that the affair was all an invention, and I have never dared ask little Audrey about it, as reviving the memory may be harmful. There has been a barrier of silence all round Via Cavour, and even the servants refuse to utter.

Lady Paget came to Palermo in January. She mentioned the '*simpatica* and rather sad Mrs Whitaker' who took her about everywhere; 'she cannot recover from her mother's death.' Tina arranged for her to meet Giulia

Trabia, 'this extremely pretty and clever woman who captivates everybody by her goodness and gentleness.' The baroque and Louis XV furniture in the Palazzo Butera, Lady Paget felt, was among the best to be found anywhere. The walls were covered with gilt and golf-leaf, the tapestries were embroidered with pearls. Even the princess's bedroom, hung with red damask, was bigger than most people's drawing-rooms. The footmen wore silver mitres and had the family crest embroidered on their stockings.

For the next four years Tina wrote somewhat infrequently. Her dislike for Maude intensified. The family wandered round Europe, with a retinue of nurses, governesses, valets and lady's maids. In London they usually stayed at Claridge's. People such as Princess Aribert of Anhalt (later known as Princess Marie Louise), the Empress Eugénie, Mrs George Keppel, Lady Warwick and the Duke and Duchess of Schleswig Holstein visited Palermo. Mrs Keppel came with Mrs Ronnie Greville in the McKeown yacht and told Tina that she did not 'care' for foreign society 'which explained why she was not very amiable to the various Sicilian ladies presented to her by the Trabias'. Lady Warwick refused to know any Sicilians at all. 'These great lights of England feel they cannot shine so brightly out of their usual background.' Eugénie had bought the yacht *Thistle* from the Duke of Hamilton; there is a wonderful description of her, in flapping widow's weeds, in Lampedusa's *Two Stories and a Memory*, when she called at the Florio villa (a bizarre hotch-potch of Arab-Sicilian-Aragonese-floreale architecture) on Favignana at 7 a.m. to say goodbye to Don Ignazio and Franca. 1897 had been once more a year of dreadful harvests. The resultant increase in the price of bread in 1898 produced some alarming rumblings of discontent. There were clashes with the police and martial law was proclaimed in various cities. In Milan barricades were thrown up; eighty people were killed in riots and 450 wounded. On 18 June Rudinì resigned – his efforts to help Sicily had been half-hearted and disappointing.

*London, 28 June 1898*

Just before leaving Rome I saw Rudinì, as usual flatteringly pleased to see me and full of reproaches for not letting him know of our arrival. Now that his ministry has fallen and the Left has come in, I fear we shall not have the punishments required for the late riots. Why did he disgust the Right by taking in Zanardelli [as Minister of Justice in a reshuffle of the Government in September, mainly to intensify the anti-clerical campaign]? Better to have fallen last year with his colours flying than to bear such ignominy now.

Here in this hotel we have Mrs Minto Elliot [travel writer,[18] mother of the Marchesa Chigi], bracing herself for a visit to Princess Mathilde [Countess Demidoff, niece of Napoleon I]. She is far from well; undoubtedly her health is failing. This weakened condition gives her a quieter dignity, which if she had it in earlier years would have let her reach the considerable intellectual position she deserved. Still one is grieved to see that famous energy giving way, that lively, once irrepressible, vitality dying. My mother used to say: 'Mrs Elliot will die in a ball-room'; but no, she is finishing her life a lonely and somewhat isolated old woman, her spirit broken at last, with no home love around her.

*Mandria, 2 November 1898*

A joy to have this week of sunshine after three months of rain in England. The Comtesse de Paris here, *bonne bourgeoise*, smoking cigars and going out deer stalking with Pip. Her daughter Hélène [Duchess of Aosta] is with her and infinitely more regal. We also have General Cagni [father of Captain, later Admiral, Cagni, celebrated for his journey to the North Pole with the Duke of Abruzzi]. He is full of anecdotes and yesterday gave us a nice one. The Rudinìs have just sold their villa to the Russian ambassador and have moved to a new house. The Marchesa at the same time secured a little dog, which she has christened Tòtò, the same name as her husband's. Of this her friends are not yet aware, and one calling on her enquired after Tòtò (naturally meaning her husband). She, thinking of her new pet, promptly answered: 'Thanks, he is well, but he is not quite house-trained and is rather dirty, which is trying.' Tableau——.

Then to Florence. Lady Paget was busy at work on her highly outspoken memoirs. She would invite selected ladies to tea and read them extracts.

*Florence, 30 November 1898*

Another interesting reading at Lady Paget's. The same ladies there as last time, plus the Duchess of Sermoneta. Much about the Queen and John Brown, but one realizes that these memoirs cannot be published for a long time to come. Lady Paget read an episode about one of her drives with the Queen, who graciously turned to the ladies and said: 'Where shall we drive today?' – and John Brown was distinctly heard murmuring: 'Drive to Hell'.

Lady Paget says she was *née* Hohenthal. One deduces that she was born in Saxony in 1839. For a while she was maid of honour to the Princess Royal, as Princess Frederick William of Prussia. It was in Berlin that she met her fate and married Sir Augustus Paget [ambassador in Rome 1876–83]. . . . We drive constantly in her Victoria, dachshunds on knees and feet. Her clear cut features are seen to a great advantage against an always artistically arranged widow's veil.

Another bachelor had joined the group of regular house-guests at Malfitano. This was the rotund, talkative, clownish Alick (the Hon. Alexander) Yorke,[19] a member of the Royal Household. His great-nephew, Sir Victor Mallet, became British Ambassador in Rome many years later (1947–53); he describes Alick Yorke in his book based on the diaries of his own mother, Marie Mallet, who was lady-in-waiting to Queen Victoria from 1887 – matters are not minced; Yorke was an 'elderly pansy', scented and bejewelled, always extravagantly dressed, but kind and hospitable. Herewith Tina's pen-portrait:

Alick Yorke, second son of Lord Hardwicke, was a good friend and paid many visits to Malfitano. The first time I met him was in 1879 in London, at a party of Lady Combermere's. This dapper young man, on his arrival with a flower in his button-hole, was greeted by his hostess: 'Why Mr Yorke, you look like a rose!' This was a malicious remark by the old lady, as it was well known that art was called in to accentuate his pretty complexion. And yet, despite this foible, he was practical and full of altruism, besides being much beloved by his cousins, who ran into hundreds. He was inimitable as a comic actor. How can one forget his putting into practice 'You should see my coat-tails flying' as he skipped across our amateur stage in the ballroom at Malfitano? Or sitting on a chair where some wicked boy had put a pin pointing upwards? He had a great tendency, however, to serious recitation, which was not always, alas, so successful. One evening we arranged an audience of our Sicilian friends for him. The comic parts were a great success, and they all pretended to understand enough English to enjoy the jokes which he illustrated with inimitable mimicry. But when he recited Gray's *Elegy*, peals of laughter greeted him at the most tragic parts. He looked not unlike Queen Victoria, whom he imitated remarkably well. The Queen, who liked him, got to hear of this and one day surprised him by asking that he should do the imitation (opening a garden fête) in front of her. Her comment afterwards was: 'We wish that to be the last performance.' He had been the devoted gentleman in waiting to the Duke of Albany for many years. On the Duke's death the Queen attached Alick Yorke to herself.

According to Sir Victor Mallet, the imitation was almost certainly the episode which gave rise to the famous 'We are not amused.'

Another new friend was little Alec (again the Hon., and later Sir, Alexander) Nelson Hood,[20] who bore the title of 'extra gentleman usher to Her Majesty', a former equerry to the Duchess of Teck, and a bit of a writer. As the son of Lord Bridport, he was Nelson's great-great-nephew; after his father's death in 1904 he became Duke of Bronte. Since the early 1870s he had been living for part of the year at Maniace, which he had greatly altered and modernised. He too was unmarried and belonged to the Aïdé-Gower-Yorke set; another attraction for Tina was the fact that he knew and admired Mrs Lynn Linton. Then there was Frank Hird,[21] cherubic and pert, with a very different social background. Tina called him 'The Bébé'. Again we turn to a pen-portrait:

I met this distinguished journalist for the first time in the early autumn of 1897, at the old Lord Warden Hotel at Dover, on our return journey to Sicily. A violent storm kept us there for the night, and we found Lord Ronald Gower in the Hotel with Mr Hird, who was helping him with his book on Sir Thomas Lawrence. I was at once attracted by this brilliant, buoyant youth, on the staff of the *Morning Post*; already, by his personal initiative at the age of only twenty-three, he had fired his paper to start the famous home for down and outs. The next morning, in unexpected calm and sunshine, I sat with my new-found friend on the beach, by a glittering, smooth sea, while waiting for the boat. He admitted that politics interested him greatly, and I was struck by the maturity of his opinions and keen sense of humour. The *Morning Post* had no correspondent in Rome, strange to say, so I asked if a letter of introduction to the then Prime Minister, Rudinì, to grant him an interview would help to obtain this post. This fitted in with Frank Hird's plans, as he had just accepted to accompany Lord Ronald on a short tour of Dalmatia and Italy, including Rome. The interview was published and Lord Ronald's friend, Mr Dunn, the editor, at once gave Frank Hird the post of correspondent.[22] An invaluable friend from the first was Mr Wickham Steed, correspondent of *The Times* [and its editor from 1919–22]. They came together to Palermo for the 50th anniversary of the breaking out of revolution on the 12th January 1848. We invited Frank Hird to stay, and amid jokes and laughter the time passed quickly. A conundrum was produced by our guests. Which of the two correspondents is the most powerful? Answer: the *Morning Post's*. *The Times* has only one steed (Steed), whereas the *Morning Post* has a whole herd

(Hird). Just a very few weeks later Frank Hird threw up his engagement, on Lord Ronald Gower's offer that he should live with him as his adopted son!

Such camping around made life more cheerful at Malfitano. Gower had met Frank Hird in June 1893, when he was secretary to Lord Thring and afflicted with rheumatic fever; he had come to visit the boy in bed. The entry in his diary for 2 February 1898 ran: 'My heart is very happy tonight, for I have just received a letter from Frank accepting the offer I made him through Mr Dunn last week, of coming to me . . . as my adopted son. "I congratulate you both," Mr Dunn said, when he learned from me my intentions.' It seemed that Dunn had been on the verge of transferring Hird to Vienna.

Gower had in fact recently suffered a severe epileptic attack and had been told by his doctor to take things more restfully in future. Presumably this had something to do with his decision to settle down with Frank.

A long gap followed in the diary. Tina gave her views on some of the authors whose books she had been reading: Walpole, Stuart Mill, Ruskin. She wrote at length about the Dreyfus case, and of course repeatedly referred to her dead mother – 'such a very unhappy life was hers, full of trials and disillusions, a husband most erratic in his peccadillos'.

*Marienbad, 12 September 1899*
At last a chance to write of our stay in London. I took the girls to the Lowther Lodge children's fancy dress ball, but they did not enjoy it – they were shy among strangers. I made the mistake of dressing them as Boulogne fishwives. I say mistake because it gave them the appearance of being of a different class to the majority of the others, all dressed in silks and flowers. It was the first time since my great parting [i.e. Madame Scalia's death] that I had been at any major gathering. The impersonality of being a chaperone made me feel almost as if I were another person. . . .
  The Prince of Wales here. Frau von Püfendorf sat with us at the next table during lunch. She was so excited, poor dear, that when she found she was not facing him she put white violets on her back.

Delia in particular must have hated the party at Lowther Lodge. At the bottom of the page there is written, in different ink: 'With what pleasure can I now truly say that Delia's sulking is a thing of the past. She has outgrown this objectionable trait.'

In Palermo that winter there was some excitement over a visit of British doctors to the Villa Igiea, a beautiful property by the sea that had been acquired by Ignazio Florio from Admiral Sir Cecil Domville (who romantically is said to have bought it for a Sicilian mistress from Acquasanta). Florio had commissioned Basile, under the general supervision of the Savoyard Baron Alberto Fassini, then a needy hanger-on[23] distantly related through his wife to the Duchess of Santa Rosalia, to build a vast T.B. sanatorium here, with 180 rooms, distinctly *fin de siècle* in conception though also a bit like a medieval castle; it was to be run by Professor Vincenzo Cervello, who had revolutionary ideas for treating tubercular patients. Fassini proceeded to spend far too much, and the British doctors told Tina that it would never pay. 'Far better to turn the place into a casino, as at Monte Carlo.' Then Cervello's ideas were discredited. Florio, with dramatic suddenness, therefore changed his mind about having a clinic at all. Instead he had the whole place transformed into a luxury hotel, which at once became the very centre of social life for the international set. Indeed he was so pleased with what he had done, that in due course he decided to live in part of the hotel with his family.

Old friends paid their lengthy annual visits:

*Malfitano, 8 March 1900*

Ronald Gower and Frank Hird have been with us five weeks and left this morning [in good time before the embarrassing arrival of Oscar Wilde?].[24] Hamilton Aïdé is still remaining on a few days; they all get on so well and are happy with us. The other evening Ronny was teasing Hamilton about having his German servant Hey in the room while he dresses. He declared he felt sure he had him there even during his bath, and that he supposed Hamilton had a trick of playing with the soap, and that Hey was there to prevent this. The next day Ronny favoured me with this sketch [see page 304].

We had a little party a few evenings ago: Franca Florio etc, sixteen to dinner, and then some people afterwards to see a hypnotist. It was predicted that Hamilton will die quite a sudden death. Hird, having at present an extremely happy life, would only be miserable if he married; the poor boy did not seem very pleased at this – I rather fancy marriage enters into his view of the future. And Ronald Gower? Oh, well, as he leans so much on Hird, and is so fond of him, he would accept even the wife I suppose.

There had been much chatter that February about the execrable behaviour of the Duke of Orleans – Marie Mallet in a letter had said that the

Queen was very angry; the Duke was a 'mean little beast and ought to be kicked out of the British Isles'.

> *Malfitano, 20 May 1900*
> Hamilton Aïdé has sent me this extract of the order of the day which his club proposed to pass for expelling the Duke of Orleans in consequence of his congratulating Willette for his obscene caricatures of the Queen: 'That the conduct of H.R.H. the Duc d'Orléans has been such as to endanger the character, good order and welfare of the St James' Club.' Not a noble undertaking for the pretendant to a throne; any ordinary gentleman would shrink from such low conduct to a woman. But the Duke is indeed a 'pauvre sire'.

A few days later Tina wrote of the death of one of her husband's brothers-in-law.

> *Malfitano, 30 May 1900*
> And so Corrado Tommasi-Crudeli is gone to his long rest! He passes away with little regret left behind him [Sophie had died in 1899]. One of the most brilliant intellects of Italy, one of the men whose mental capacities and great culture fitted him for the highest posts in the nation, but who by his capriciousness and tendency to satire made himself too many enemies ever to succeed. A clever person has always a multitude of envious, jealous people around him, people who wish to profit out of him without admitting his worth.

39. Five Whitaker brothers
*Left to right*: Bob, Albert, Pip, Joss, Ingham and Arthur.

40. Tina: Edwardian heyday.

41. Delia and Norina as Breton
fishwives.

The visit to England was short that year, and the Pips spent the early autumn in Switzerland.

*St Moritz, 31 August 1900*

Tamagno is in the hotel. I reminded him of our duet, and tomorrow he is to sing in a requiem mass for that same King Umberto cruelly murdered by an anarchist [Bresci, from Paterson, New Jersey, on 29 July at Monza]. Tragic end to a good reign. Umberto's personal bravery was his chief characteristic. It was typical of him that, on receiving the first wound in the clavicular, he stood up and faced the enemy, who was thus able to shoot him through the heart. . . . Our stay has been a pleasant one, the hotel full of Jews, from Rothschilds and Sterns *down down* to Loebs and Manuels [Effie Whitaker's family]. Indeed all the guests are Jews except dear Hamilton Aïdé and the Hohenlohes. Hamilton said that Lord Rosebery, when his first-born came into the world, gazed carefully at its nose and said: 'Le jeu (Jew) est fait, rien ne va plus' [his wife was a Rothschild].

In 1900 phylloxera at last reached Marsala, the worst year for all Italy Having drifted northwards, in 1899 it turned south again and hit Puglie, soon afterwards spreading to western Sicily. To some extent the wine merchants were prepared. It was a disaster of course, and no wine was produced in the area – again reinforcements had to be brought from Bronte and the eastern part of the island. With the planting of new American vines one hoped that situation would soon right itself. The market did get going but the demand was patently slacking off.[25] Perhaps the new vines just did not provide the same taste or quality. Marsala's peak of wine production had been in 1870 with a total output of approximately 50,000 pipes, Ingham exporting about 6200, compared to Florio 3400 and Woodhouse 2100. Between 1901 and 1905 Ingham was only exporting about 2000 pipes a year, and the others in proportion. The popularity of marsala *all' uovo*, invented somewhat later in Milan, seemed a step towards vulgarisation and debasement.

Tina was beginning to lose interest in her diary again. Indeed there is hardly an entry for the entire 1901. Then, perforce, she had to make herself launch wholeheartedly into the world again. Norina, aged seventeen and a half, had 'come of age'.

*Malfitano, 15 January 1902*

Last evening Norina made her début in Society at her Uncle Joss's ball. The Sicilians, strange to say, were punctual, and when we arrived at 10.30 there were already many couples dancing. . . . Norina and Diana

[Theodoli] received many cotillons and I could hardly get them away at 4 a.m. When we returned to Malfitano, they woke up Delia who had sulked all day [again?]. And what a contrast seeing her in her white nightdress compared to Norina in all her beauty. Then Diana told of all the successes they had had, but Delia could raise no enthusiasm and just said that one should never trust a man!

Delia had been told that she must wait until the summer of 1903 for her coming out. Meanwhile suitors for Norina began appearing at Malfitano; in London she was presented at Court. Tina had to entertain on a suitably grand scale and be prepared to stay up all night as chaperone. She did her best. Norina was not going to suffer from the disadvantages that Tina and Madame Scalia had in their youth; she had parents rich enough to launch her in the highest rungs of society.

# XX

## *Your Majesty Commands*

DELIA's 'coming out' was a bit of an anti-climax. The Pips arrived in London too late for her to be presented at Court – perhaps in any case she was glad, as she was suffering from acne. Then both she and Norina were struck down by chicken-pox, so all celebrations were cancelled.

Ronny Gower and Frank Hird had settled, some three years ago, in a large, Virginia-creeper-covered house called Hammerfield[1] at Penshurst, Kent. Tina arranged to take a furnished house nearby. Knole, Penshurst Place and other stately homes – not to mention Hever Castle, in the process of being converted – were conveniently close. The Empress Eugénie had of course left Chislehurst years ago and was now at her strange mansion at Farnborough. All the same one felt somewhat in her orbit, especially as her lady-in-waiting, Mrs Hippisley (sister of Dame Ethel Smyth) was constantly at Hammerfield – a 'living Romney' she was, said Ronny, who was writing a life of that artist. One afternoon Mrs Hippisley, in the company of the Duchess of Alba and Count Clary, drove over in her motor-car, bravely persevering in spite of a puncture, to invite Tina to tea the following week 'in the name of the Empress'.

*Tonbridge, 21 September 1903*

Went over to Farnborough Hill[2] to tea with the Empress Eugénie. I took Norina, who was asked when Peppino refused. The Empress was in a way disappointing, not even a beautiful wreck! Nor very *grande dame* in manner. Most *agréable* and bright, no pathos or deep shadows of past sorrows, either in tone of voice or manner, in spite of the sad view of the chapel containing the tombs of her husband and the Prince Imperial. Only at one moment, during the hour of constant conversation with her, did I notice a touch of regret for the great past gone for ever. It was as we were taking leave. She led me to the window to look at the beautiful and extensive landscape. 'Très beau, n'est-ce pas? Et si vaste que je puis bien m'imaginer que tout ce que je vois est à moi!' We chattered of Palermo gossip, of Mazzarino whose infidelities as a husband seemed to amuse her, of the Florios, Trabias etc., nothing serious except for a while about the horrors going on in Macedonia.

'Ils sont des barbares, les Turcs, et les Chrétiens se valent.' We spoke also of Percy ffrench, but she evidently does not care to dwell on those who are gone.

Pip was far too preoccupied with his great opus, *The Birds of Tunisia*, even to be tempted by tea with an Empress. The book, elaborately produced with many colour paintings, was nearing publication.[3] Praised by ornithologists, for the layman it was a model of what a readable scientific work should be; thorough and cultivated, it remains the standard work on the subject to this day. Altogether some 365 species or subspecies were described, most being represented in his collection of stuffed specimens in the Villino which had been turned into a museum; this collection was later extended to cover all the birds of the Mediterranean littoral, and in that respect was described in *The Times*, over thirty years later, as 'the finest in the world'. Pip had recently sponsored (in 1901) an ambitious expedition by a couple named Dodson and Drake to Tripolitania, a country on which Italy had territorial designs, thus insuring a certain amount of press coverage. Nobody had bargained for such dramas. Apart from sandstorms and running out of water, they had narrowly escaped being massacred in an ambush.[4] One of their Turkish guards had died from exposure, guns had become phosphorescent during electric storms and they had been wrongly imprisoned by the Governor of Fezzan.

Pip (who had been given the title of Commendatore by the King of Italy) took very little part in social life if he could help it. Robert Hichens,[5] at that time recently revealed as the author of *The Green Carnation*, wrote how at smart lunch parties at Malfitano he would suddenly appear towards the end of a meal, slipping with hardly a murmur into his place between two princesses. On another occasion, at the Grand Hotel in Rome, Hichens noticed a plate of chicken bones outside Pip's room. The time was 6 p.m. 'Ah', said Delia, 'Papa must have just finished luncheon.' No wonder Pip was known as the 'late Mr Whitaker'.

That winter Walburga Paget came to stay in Palermo. Tina wrote:

*Malfitano, 21 January 1904*

Lady Paget has been and gone. Her visit has been a most pleasant one, her presence full of charm. She is an agreeable guest, throwing herself with zest into the interests of those around her, without (as many would think she would be) being in the least *obsédante*. But her visit has tired me, her powers of observation and keen insight to things and people *aiguisent* my mental capacities. . . . She urged much the girls marrying early. She said the more time passes the more difficult they will be to please. In many ways I regret that Norina refused young Gangi. Apart from the feeling that she was asked for herself and not for her money, it is a good respectable family, where her refinement and delicacy of feeling would be appreciated. Of course there would be the difference of religion, but we would not object to her becoming R.C. I personally could not subject myself to such a change: to have a different faith to my beloved mother's.

One turns to the counterpart of this entry: Lady Paget's version. The house she found suitably palatial, and the garden impressively exotic. Minor things irritated her though, like the tiny writing desk in her bedroom. The butler, she said, belonged to the *Mafia* – 'he protects the house and sees that nobody is stabbed'. She did not like the way Pip kept some hawks in cages; he was described as gentle, retiring, determined, 'in the pink of neatness and refinement', going around smiling and making little noises, but taking no notice of anybody if he did not want to do so. Tina was charming, spiritual, distinguished, at times extraordinarily energetic, looking and behaving like an Englishwoman, still in deep mourning for her mother, after nearly eight years. What was the secret of Tina's charm? Lady Paget decided that it was due to her ready sympathy and unworldliness. Others would say that it lay in her sheer oddity – Tina was not a person (as she herself had admitted) to lay bare her soul to anybody, so one never knew quite what she was thinking. Her face might seem severe at one moment, and suddenly, unexpectedly, a joke would pop out. If people bored her, she found it difficult to hide that fact.

As for Norina and Delia, Lady Paget described them simply as 'two languid girls', whose greatest wish was never to leave Palermo.[6] Frank Hird was staying at Malfitano too – she obviously found him bumptious. He had written a costume play, *Mrs Ashley's Opinion*, in which the girls were made to act. She had never been to anything so amusingly haphazard. Up to the last minute all arrangements – scenery, clothes, invitations, supper – were never seriously considered. It was a good thing that the audience was not critical. . . . Then to Marsala, which Lady Paget considered a thoroughly wretched place, and she felt heartily sorry for the English who were condemned to live there. On the other hand she raved about Racalia and its view. She went to Favignana to see Franca Florio who was recovering from the loss of two of her children from typhoid (or so Lady Paget said, the actual cause of the deaths having always been a mystery – some maintaining that they were from sleeping-draughts administered by a nurse).

This tragedy was and is still indeed held to have been the turning-point in the Florio saga, when Don Ignazio realised that there would be no direct male heir to carry on the business, his brother Vincenzo being too much of a playboy[7] – from then onwards Ignazio began noticeably to lose interest and money was recklessly squandered. To Lady Paget, Franca in spite of her grief seemed amazingly beautiful, like a lovely English girl not yet out of her 'teens. As for the *floreale* decorations of the Favignana villa, the energetic northerner certainly did not take to them; they were an 'unpleasant and over-expensive version of William Morris's least good phase'.

In 1903 there had been a possibility that Edward VII might call at Palermo in his yacht *Victoria and Albert*. Instead, in his quixotic, typically regal way, he had gone to Rome, to pay a 'private and informal visit' to the ninety-three-year-old Leo XIII (who died in July that year). It was a curious period. Spring after spring Edward and Kaiser Wilhelm sailed round the Mediterranean in their respective yachts, ostensibly on pleasure cruises, but in reality – as the whole world knew – playing just a new version of the power game. The Kaiser loved spectacle and protocol. He felt that his visits helped to secure Germany's political dominance in the world. Edward knew how to act like a king but was the opposite to his nephew; his manner was urbane and calm, and he actually showed a dislike for organisation and uniforms. His visit to Rome was regarded with great suspicion by the Kaiser, who at once followed there as soon as Edward had left. In the same way that autumn, a week after Edward had been the guest of Franz Joseph at Vienna, the Kaiser appeared in full panoply of state.

Again in 1904 there was no sign of the British King. Yet he was obviously keeping in touch with his nephew's movements:

> *Malfitano, 25 March 1904*
> The Chamberlains' visit. Mr Joe has altered since we knew him in Rome, before he became a celebrity. He has lost that brilliant expectancy which characterised him in those days. Now he is very much the man who has *achieved*. But he has retained much simplicity of manner. We invited the Trabias to meet him. The Prince asked if it were true that he was here because of the German Emperor, who is expected next week. Joe answered: 'I am not waiting for him, I am preceding him.' A *double entendre*! [Chamberlain and the Kaiser had not taken to one another when the latter visited Sandringham in 1903.]

The Kaiser's visit must have been disappointing, for it was barely recorded in Tina's diary. Perhaps he was not feeling well enough for the usual formalities.[8] A year later, however, his arrival was an important occurrence for her. . . .

Meanwhile the question of Norina's suitors remained inescapable.

> *Malfitano, 20 April 1904*
>
> More marriages talked of for Norina. Prince Carini comes forward as the rival to the Pietratagliata boy, who has nothing to offer. *Intanto* I must chronicle an incident. Peppino was told the other day that a gentleman from Catania wished to see him. As he sometimes gets rare birds from there, he immediately concluded that the visit was something to do with his favourite hobby and at once had the visitor taken over to the museum. The man, clearing his throat, in an embarrassed tone said: 'I have come from my cousin, Prince Grimaldi. He has one son and would give him four millions if he made a suitable marriage. Now we hear you have two charming daughters . . .' Tableau, and Pip saw no rare bird that day but instead had to explain that in England people do not barter their daughters.

Carini 'hung around' for some years, protesting his love for Norina, but stupidly queered his pitch by proposing to Delia half-way through his wooing.

> *Malfitano, 2 June 1904*
>
> Last week we had a visit from Maude Valérie White [composer and author of popular songs, including 'Home Thoughts from Abroad', 'Ye Cupids', 'Soft Lesbian Airs', etc.] and Robert Hichens. She is devoted to him, in love with him. But he?! He has much friendship for this gifted creature, but I don't see my way to imagining more. She throws such verve, such *élan* into her playing. I think in her orchestration she is more wonderful than Mascagni.

Well might Tina have put that exclamation mark. For Robert Hichens was a protégé of Alec Hood and associated with a curious, mostly German group of homosexual 'baroni' that had settled in Taormina.[9] At any rate Hichens, then aged forty, soon became one of Tina's closest friends.

> *Abetone, 18 July 1904*
>
> Today at lunch I met Duke Torlonia. He was motoring through here with his wife and I was introduced to *her*! It was a painful emotion, and I gaped at the sharp, angular profile of his second duchess [Lily Belmonte having been the first]. Yet she has a pleasing smile and nice eyes, and I know she is a good step-mother. . . . Robert Hichens has just arrived, to finish *The Garden of Allah*, and is obviously overwrought by the

climax. His is a curious nature, matter and spirit both powerfully developed, but he gives preference to the former. I am half amused by the trouble he takes to persuade me that I still have some life to live! [Tina still believed in her own early demise]. . . . I have drifted into the still waters of life which one generally does not reach until later [she was 45]. I have much to be thankful for. The tumultuous feelings of unsatisfied longings were not a happy situation.

The diary continued in its discursive way. Tina was getting very worried about the situation in Marsala, where the family was losing money. Neither Pip nor Bob were in the slightest bit interested and treated her efforts to 'talk shop' with maddening condescension. Joss was simply bad-tempered when she interfered.

*Grayshott, 14 September 1904*

Came here after three days at Claridge's which we really must give up, as it is too expensive. Five guineas for our rooms, and out of season. With our Marsala deficits we are obliged to be economical. I wrote a long business letter to Joss from Abetone. . . . Aileen [eldest daughter of Bob and Maude] is here. Pity her mother does not try to keep her in hand. Oh what manners with men, young and old! An erratic letter from Robert Hichens. How curious our friendship. *Scotta ovunque si tocca*, he burns wherever one touches him. His keen sense of humour, however, combined with that extreme melancholy, make a specially attractive mixture for me. . . . Our new ambassador in Rome is to be Sir Edwin Egerton. I liked the Curries [Lord, previously Sir Philip, Currie, ambassador 1898-1902], although he – and especially she [the novelist Violet Fane[10]] – were not born to be diplomats. After dinner they presented their dogs to the company. One, she said, was a 'maiden aunt' and had orange blossom about its head because it was 'about to be married'. At least Sir Edwin will be a relief after the Berties [Sir Francis, later Lord, Bertie, ambassador in Rome 1903, in Paris 1905-18]. How could Lady Bertie, as a daughter of an ambassador of the old school [Lord Cowley], be so ignorant of good manners?

With all the excitement over the approaching publication of *The Birds of Tunisia*, Tina's thoughts were also being turned to things literary. Ronny and Frank were urging her to publish a memoir of her parents – the book that was eventually published in 1907 as *Sicily and England*. Frank, by now well accustomed to ghosting Ronny's works, had promised to help her. She did not quite bargain for the social whirl ahead, when the family settled at the Grand Hotel in Rome for the Christmas Season.[11]

*Rome, 28 December 1904*

A rather hard day. Went to the Vatican with Lady Paget in an attempt to see the new Pope [Pius X] to implore his interest in the plight of birds which Italians blind to make them sing better.[12] In the afternoon tea at the tiny Princess D'Avella's, [the 'least interesting' sister of Prince Doria], and in the evening a dance at the Meyers' at the Palazzo Brancaccio, American Embassy. Certainly the lady of the house takes no trouble to do the honours. She is however good-looking, well dressed and not common. Donna Nicoletta Grazioli, with her big nose, seemed set to dazzle the world in an orange velvet dress, and Donna Maria Mazzoleni in violet spangles looked fagged out but graceful and her eyes large as ever. Why should these two women remain afloat, and so many others, who have committed far less faults, such as the Duchess San Teodoro, sink for ever? The girls were pleased to go to the party and the Marquis Calabrini was most kind in finding constant cavaliers. I bored myself.

In subsequent entries one soon learns the gossip: what Tina meant by 'faults'. Nicoletta Grazioli, always exquisitely dressed and belonging to the very smartest set, had been thrown out of the house, 'literally like a servant', by her husband because of her affair with the Duke of Camastra, the Prince of Trabia's younger brother, thereby dividing all Roman society. Maria Mazzoleni, tall with a 'wonderful' figure, and who entertained practically every evening, was openly the mistress of Ferdinando Belmonte, Lily's brother. As for Teresa San Teodoro, by birth half English and the mother of the beautiful Princess of Teano (later famous as Vittoria Sermoneta), she had once been married to a Colonna but in her own words 'felt that I could no longer live in that family':[13] she had thereupon moved out of the Palazzo and had reverted to her father's title, San Teodoro, taking a Professor Lanciani as her lover. Her drawbacks were that she was a bit dotty (people said she was sane only three months in the year), not *chic* and no hostess.

*Rome, 2 January 1905*

Cards, cards at all hours. Cards to return. And good wishes and postcards. Frightful! Had a pleasant conversation with Prince Ruffo. He seems an intelligent boy and well informed. I am sure Norina entertains no ideas of him. Alberto Theodoli is obviously interested. He is intelligent, bright, but – I should think he is chiefly looking to the *beaux yeux de la cassette*. It is horrid to think of one's children sought after for only that reason. . . . Belmonte came before dinner and talked to me of the girls. He too wanted to find out about dowries and our general intentions, the usual Italian idea of marriage. We were fortunately interrupted by Florio's servant rushing in to say would we go at once and see Franca Florio dressed for the court dinner (the girls had said they wished to see her). She looked very beautiful with her plastron of diamonds and her magnificent white and strass embroidered dress and train. Afterwards that plain Maria Bardesono [who acted as lady-in-waiting to Franca] wished to impress on me how well-read and intellectual Franca is. I did not know what to say!! The women of the house of Villarosa – Franca's mother was the daughter of a Villarosa – are proverbially wanting in brightness, just as the men look all the same, are overbearing and *mafiosi* [i.e. with a small m, handsome].

*Rome, 14 January 1905*

Had our audience tea with Queen Elena. She has improved since the early days of her marriage and is gracious and amiable, but dull. She talked chiefly of her babies and her education of them – intelligently I admit, but is it a subject for a sovereign to make her only one? Yesterday I gave a tea, about 100 people came. It was animated and considered a success. At the end the girls had a *tour de valse*. . . . Lunched with the Countess of Somaglia, more *bonhomie* – in spite of her high-pitched voice – than her sister Duchess Massimo [both sisters of Prince Doria], who however has the looks one associates with high breeding.[14] In the evening I was invited by Robert Hichens and Hamilton Aïdé to meet Mr and Mrs William Sharp. Mr Sharp is so good-looking and attractive! I wonder if he is the author of the Scotch poems [as 'Fiona Macleod']. Hichens says he denies it, but that is useless, there are too many points towards it.[15]

*Rome, 6 February 1905*

Pressure is put on us to return to Rome for the end of Carnival. If the girls wish it, Pip and I are willing to execute ourselves. In the evening the Rudinì ball. A great success; both Rudinìs are very popular and I hear the Laboucheres are delighted at the success of the marriage, [Dora Labouchere daughter of 'Labby', the British journalist and Radical M.P., had just married the son of the Marquis of Rudinì]. The girls much enjoy themselves. A very pretty cotillon.

The Pips returned to Malfitano, bringing Hamilton Aïdé with them. Ronny Gower reached Rome soon afterwards and noted in his diary that Hamilton had found 'the Whitaker girls in a state of complete idleness'. But within three weeks they were back at the Grand, and the whirling and the chit-chat began again, among all the great names – the Dorias, the Odescalchis, the Boncompagnis, the Theodolis, the Chigis, the Caetanis.

*Rome, 1 March 1905*

How many people ask whether Ignazio Florio is half ruined! What nonsense I say. Still P. says he has lost many millions since the death of his father, and certainly he has been foolish in his friends – a set of impossible people for entrusting one's most important business. I am glad to hear Vincenzo is *accorto* [careful], and means to look into things seriously, though he is very young, only 21. I hear the Russian woman [Hélène Bariatinski] has been a good mistress to him, and has taught him to be less extravagant, unlike the chief one [unidentified].

Vincenzo's mistresses, like Ignazio's, were legion. Ignazio's most blatant mistress was the beautiful and rapacious Lina Cavalieri,[16] a soprano. It was because of her, some said, that Franca was in compensation given a necklace of 300 pearls.

*Rome, 6 March 1905*

Last day of Carnival. We dine with Gwendoline Somaglia, and afterwards she gives a large *après dîner*. Prince Altieri [a Serene Highness] was there. He is introduced to the millionairess Miss Walsh, brought by Princess Poggio Suasa, an ambitious American *née* Josephine Curtis [her granddaughter Emanuela de Dampierre married Don Jaime, the eldest son of the King of Spain, in 1935],[17] and immediately devotes himself to her. We all go on, not Miss Walsh, to the Austrian Embassy ball – which is very fine, not too crowded. Countess Lützow asks if I notice the absence of Americans at her dance, and alludes bitterly to the Miss Wardours putting themselves in the front row at the Court ball. The cotillon was charming and ended up with really beautiful Empire umbrella handles being given as presents to the ladies.

This descent on Italy by American heiresses again makes one think of *The Leopard* – of the *nouveaux riches* Sedaras and Angelica.

The firm of Ingham, Whitaker and the various Florio enterprises may have been feeling the financial draught, but it was nothing to the panic and despondency that had overtaken the Sicilian peasant class. Emigration had been a feature of life in most regions of Italy for some decades, but 1904 was the year in which for the first time the highest number of emigrants were from Sicily. It was a 'spontaneous act of protest against intolerable conditions'.[18] The greater number of these unfortunate persons were from isolated regions, in the mountains of the *latifondi*. Sometimes villages were reduced to a fifth of their population in a year. As many as a million and a half Sicilians had left their country before the Great War broke out.[19] By 1904 three-quarters of them would be heading for the United States, Brazil or Argentina – into the maws of new Benjamin Inghams.

Florio tried to help unemployment in Sicily by reviving the sulphur industry, in collaboration with some British financiers. The company, 'Sulfur', was founded in 1896. It went through a period of boom but collapsed after ten years. American sulphur had cut the Sicilian product by half.

The labour shortage that resulted from this emigration at first meant even worse hardship. By 1907, however, money sent from *americani* was making a noticeable difference to the economy of some villages. After a while a few *americani* even returned, bringing on the credit side new ideas and standards of living, but also a more sophisticated form of crime.

The Pips returned to Palermo, and peace of a sort.

*Malfitano, 10 March 1905*

Alick Yorke asks me which I prefer of my Palermo sisters-in-law. I say undoubtedly Effie. She is frankly what she is, and Joss is as kind to a common sailor as to a peer of the realm. The others are snobs to the soles of their feet and – well – I doubt Maude being sincere and truthful quite. Robert is self-centred. Apart from his wife's successes and his dancing, he has no other interest except a collection of precious stones, though he can be witty in a way when he takes the trouble.

Yesterday Lord Albemarle brought in Mr and Mrs Miller Munday and their party, including the Duke of Leeds and Mrs Fritz Ponsonby, from the yacht *Narcissus*. Mrs M. is a niece of Lady Shannon, who is furious I hear at her son's marriage with the unknown Miss Gardner. Discussed the thing with Alick Yorke and he agreed with me that had Mrs Gardner and Maude been ladies they would have found out if the Shannon family wished the marriage, and not hurried it on in that extraordinary way!

This acid comment referred to the marriage of Lily Gardner, daughter of Beau Gardner and therefore niece of Maude Whitaker, to the Hon. Edward Boyle the previous year. Frank Hird wrote a letter that was much appreciated:

Dear Madame Tina,
The news of the Lily of Palermo is surprising.

> Beat the drum and sound the cannon
> Lily mates with noble Shannon.
> Skill and patience she has shown
> As the seasons fast have flown.
> For years she's simmered at her toil
> Now she's come upon the Boyle (boil),
> And Lily with the prefix 'Hon'
> Will grace the world of London *ton*.
> So beat the drums and sound the cannon
> To drown the howls of hookèd Shannon.

Don't let the young woman or her cousins or her aunts know of this effusion. They will have me up for libel. . . .

Yours ever affectionately,
The Bébé

Tina stuck the letter in her diary with a note appended: 'Certainly her vulgarity and bad manners can hardly have been an attraction, but she is a fine creature with heaps of the animal spirits so highly appreciated in a certain set in London society nowadays!'

Love was very much the topic everywhere. . . .

*Malfitano, 20 March 1905*

It is said Miss Walsh's marriage with Prince Altieri has fallen through, on account of the Walshes assigning the place of honour at their dinner to Countess Giannotti instead of to the Prince's mother! It is also said that Mrs Arthur Paget, recently arrived from London, now has a grand English marriage to offer the Walshes.

So Adelina Patti is to be given the *Légion d'Honneur*. I remember only too well her behaviour in Naples in 1876 with her lover Nicolini. Also how she refused to sing at the Schilizzis' house, so that the dying brother Luca could hear her once more – and yet a few evenings before she had accepted their flowers at the Opera, in the shape of a cushion fastened at each corner with bunches of rubies, diamonds, emeralds and sapphires.

What a day with Valentine [Rousseau, daughter of the French Consul]. Arranged a meeting for her with Peppino Scalea, she having obtained permission from her father to speak to him once again, to say goodbye for ever! 'We won't be long, Mrs Whitaker,' Valentine said. I sat one hour patiently in the Louis XVI drawing room, while they sat together in the Louis XV one. At last it was over. He, however, seems far more in love than she; he *wept* after. What folly on the part of Baron Rousseau not to sanction this marriage. She is pretty, she is good, she is intelligent, but she has no dowry.

Baron Rousseau was the retiring French Consul and had absolutely refused to countenance a marriage between his daughter and Peppino.[20] 'Je déteste l'aristocracie', the crusty old martinet told Tina, 'et surtout l'aristocracie sicilienne.' It also appeared that he disapproved of the past *amours* of Peppino's mother, the Princess of Scalea. In fact, Peppino was an outstanding character, of great probity; he might have belonged to one of the chief families of Sicily, but he was very liberal-minded (unlike Valentine). At any rate, the Baron's *diktat* by no means killed the romance, which kept up at gale force for many months ahead.

Meanwhile the Kaiser, *en route* from his mischiefmaking trip to Tangier, and his family had arrived on board the *Hohenzollern* from Messina and Taormina. It was, in a sense, a climax in Tina's life. Franz von Rekowski telephoned to say that the three German Princes would like to come in the evening. So a ball was hurriedly arranged.

*Malfitano, 4 April 1905*

In the quadrille *Il Contessone*[21] [Countess Mazzarino] dances with Prince Adalbert (the sailor, good looking, alert and amusing, the only one to have inherited his father's brilliance). Giulia Trabia dances with Eitel-Fritz (tall and rather heavy), and Norina is her *vis-à-vis* with Oskar (shy), both these latter princes being difficult to talk to. The party is a great success, although we were not prepared for Royalty. The house lends itself to these great occasions. How proud my mother would have been! The princes asked our girls for photographs, but I would not allow this. I cannot have Norina and Delia behaving like little actresses.

The next day there was a party on the terrace of the Palazzo Butera. The Pips were invited, but none of the other Palermo Whitakers.[22] It was an extremely formal affair, the Kaiser in a blue uniform covered with decorations and medals, the Empress in a light yellow silk dress and a large black hat with a long, white, trailing feather. The three Princes were also in uniform and had to stand to attention by their father's side, while the guests were presented. 'There is discontent,' wrote Tina, 'because the Wardours, as Americans, and Countess Rucellai [also American] were presented to their Majesties.' Tina did not mention the fact that there was also discontent because she was presented, many representatives of leading Palermitan families not even having been invited.

DELIA BY NORINA

*Malfitano, 6 April 1905*

In the afternoon the battle of flowers. We have barely time to dress for dinner, which is at 8 p.m. A pleasant and simple entertainment on board the *Hohenzollern*, so different from other Royal dinners I have been to. The Emperor and Empress on deck to receive us. Trabias, Tascas and Mazzarinos our fellow guests. After dinner P. has a long conversation with the Emperor, ranging from the growing of potatoes by electricity to reforms of the British army – his suggestions regarding the latter, he complained, had been ignored by King Edward. Curious being! His egomania destroys what could have made him the greatest man of his age. After dinner we are shown the cinematograph, with himself constantly to the fore.

On that very day King Edward, accompanied by the Queen, left London for Marseilles. There followed a short cruise, which significantly included Algiers. He avoided Sicily once more, as the Kaiser's family had been ensconced for so long at the Albergo Timeo at Taormina – part of the German fleet having been anchored at Giardini below.

Tina was not very well. She was also working on her book. The girls, however, were thoroughly absorbed by *belle époque* society in Palermo. And there was much gossip of Valentine and Peppino: 'He is oh! so in love with her, and she *thinks* herself in love with him, which is one better than being really in love.'

*Malfitano, 20 June 1905*

Norina's birthday, and I am seedy again. The girls and their father entertain in the garden: the usual *toute Palerme*. An expedition in Vincenzo Florio's motors is arranged, and after much pressing P. agrees to take the girls. They greatly enjoy it, and fly about, from Monreale to Mondello. I worry at home!

Then to Switzerland, in the company of the Trabias.

*St Moritz, 8 August 1905*

I cannot decide who are the most objectionable, the Americans or Jews who swamp this place. These latter make a sort of yearly international congress here. Certainly they try to be forgiven their riches by accepting our traditions and recognising old Europe and her ways. Whereas America tries to force her insolent love of luxury upon us, and dominates us with arrogance, and through the beauty of her women and their *esprit*; and ends, I fear, by winning the day.

We met Matilde Serao [the much-translated novelist and journalist] ugly *à faire peur*, but with the compensating attractions of ready Neapolitan repartee, tearing spirits, and the ability to speak on a variety of topics. She asked us to hear Giusti sing again. I was really impressed by the beauty of his voice. I said why not be on the stage, but his answer was pathetic: 'I am too grotesquely stout. I should be ridiculous.' I told him the story my mother used to tell me of the great Tachinardi. He was really revoltingly ugly. At his début in Florence, early in the 19th century, the public on seeing him began to hiss; upon which he advanced and said: 'Ladies and gentlemen, you have come here to hear me, not to see me. If after I have sung you are not content, I bow to your judgement.' His admirers became fanatics, and he was the great tenor of his day.

*Lausanne, 2 October 1905*

Invited Matilde Serao to tea yesterday to meet Princess Niscemi. She is the most extraordinary personality: vulgar, loud, fat and brilliant in conversation, which most celebrated writers, as we all know to our cost, are not. Who of us has not spent a trying half-hour of dullness near a celebrity of the literary world?

Then back to Italy:

*Mandria, 1 November 1905*

The death of Henry Irving comes as a sorrow to many. I remember sitting next to him at a supper given by Hamilton Aïdé and thinking he looked more like a statesman than an actor. Surely there is not a little lacking in sense of proportion in the great national grief evinced at his death! Truly this is an age of play actors.

42. Frank Hird,
Hamilton Aïdé and
Lord Ronald Gower
at Villa Malfitano.

43. Benjamin Ingham's
house (small building
in centre) in the Piazza
Castelnuovo, formerly
Piano Sant 'Oliva.
Among the palms the
'Pompeian' bandstand
given to Palermo by
Willie Whitaker. In
foreground the quad-
riga of the Politeama
Garibaldi.

44. Tina, Tuffy-Too and Alick Yorke at Malfitano.

45. Family group, Malfitano, March 1908
*Left to right, back row:* Pip, Cecil, Maude, Norina, Arthur. *Front row:* Dorothy, Joss, Aileen, Bob, Delia, Boots, Ben (Benny), Effie, Euphrosyne (Syne), Tina.

46. Franca Florio greets the
Kaiser.

47. Reception for the Kaiser at the
Palazzo Butera. The Princess of
Trabia centre, hatless, shaking
hands; Norina on right, in dark
stole.

48. Norina.

49. Delia.

50. Edward VII, Queen Alexandra and Princess Victoria at Villa Malfitano, 26 April 1907. Delia far left, Tina next to the King, Norina behind him; Pip next to the Princess. His Majesty's Consul, Sidney Churchill, remained seated.

... The Countess Robilant is here and very friendly. My prophetic eye sees in her attention to Norina the desire to secure for her brother-in-law Luigi a well-dowered wife, who is at the same time a *lady*. At least she is not looking for Americans, with only money to recommend them.

*Florence, 17 November 1905*

To tea with the Gigliuccis; nice people, and intelligent without the irksome pretension of it. I could not help thinking of the story of the old Countess – she was Clara Novello the great singer – and her anger when one of her sons wrote to say he was about to marry a young Jewess called Mozley in Liverpool. She at once sent her other son to rescue her lamb, when lo! he wrote to say he had fallen in love with the sister and was about to marry her. They both turned out well.

This story might well have been part apocryphal, though Clara Novello's sons did marry two sisters, both Jewish. Contemporaries of that period remember only too well the chorus of girls after a Tina story: 'But Mama, that is not quite true . . .'

*Florence, 30 November 1905*

Lady Paget came yesterday, full of the assault she had received by the *Accalappia Cani* on Monday. She told me of the brutal way these men tore her dogs away from her, and then how she rescued one of the animals, which bit her in fright. Evidently they are given 90 cents for every dog they catch.

*Florence, 11 December 1905*

Sir Thomas Dick Lauder [a well-known Anglo-Florentine] amused me by telling me of his first visit to Mrs Labouchere. In his bread and butter days he had much admired the lady when she was 'in tights' [i.e. on the stage, as Henrietta Hodson; she had also helped to launch Lillie Langtry in *The Fair Encounter*]. Should he or should he *not* say so to this individual with a somewhat pugnacious cast of features? With considerable pluck he decided in the affirmative. Mrs Labouchere at first looked inclined to be offended; but he went on so insinuatingly to remind her of her many charms, in her different costumes, and then even repeated some special ditty of hers. This was too much, and breaking out into smiles Mrs L. began also to sing the verses.

We then talked gossip, mainly about Sandra Rudinì and D'Annunzio, who has squandered all her money on horses, dogs, carpets and extravagances beyond imagination, without a thought for her two children. And now he has become the lover of the Marchesa Luisa Casati. In March he was seen at the theatre with both women.

To explain. Sandra, or Alessandra, was the daughter of the Marquis. Tall, masculine, habitually dressed in a riding-habit and top boots, a morphinomaniac, she had supplanted Eleonora Duse as Gabriele D'Annunzio's mistress in 1904. She was in fact just as extravagant as her swashbuckling lover. If he had a hundred suits and used a pint of eau de Côty a day, she bought her riding-habits from Paris at £80 apiece.[23] There was no doubt of D'Annunzio's genius, but his hyperbole and love of the limelight were just the things that Tina felt she must detest.

*Florence, 12 December 1905*

Went to see the poor Duchess of Sermoneta, *née* Howard de Walden, known as the Ugly Duchess in the family (she married the Duke when he was blind!) and now alas with good reason. She is a terrible spectacle after a fourteen months' illness. A singular and dreadful disease, sores eating her up and breaking out all over her except her face. She lay, covered in rough bath towels, in a sort of chaise-longue. Her attendant told me that her patience and resignation are really most admirable. I was with her half an hour and never a word of complaint fell from her mouth.[24]

There was a chatty letter from Frank Hird:

*Hammerfield, 12 December 1905*

My dear Madame Tina,

Your chapters have been typed and I am sending them by registered post today. Laurence Binyon, the reader at Constable's, wrote only last week, asking when I thought he might see the book. As for your suggestion about sharing profits, let us be quite clear. I won't share – so there! After Constable I suggest you try Macmillan and then Bell.

Yes, my play is done, but I am having difficulty with getting neighbours to act in it. A little girl, the daughter of the rector at Hever, wrote to say her parents would not let her act because some other people, the Cubitts, would not do so. . . .

Ronny had a wonderful time with the Hippy-Pinky [Mrs Hippisley] and the Empress yesterday. He was taken to the Harmsworths.

Your ever affect.
The Bébé

A fortnight later she received a letter from Ronny, full of the up-heavals that this wretched play had caused in the household. He added:

*Hammerfield, 30 December 1905*

On Thursday we had lunch with the Latham Browns at Hever Rectory. Apropros of this, Frank has announced his wish of marrying the daughter (who after much fuss was persuaded to take a part in his play), which has taken us all by surprise, the more so since he has seen so little of her this last year. I tell him that, although I do not encourage the idea, I want him to consult his own happiness and I hope he will do nothing rashly. He says the young lady is not aware of his attachment but that he has spoken to the parents on the matter. Let us hope for the best, especially as he says that he would wish them to continue living in this house after the marriage.

So the hypnotist's prediction looked like being fulfilled. Actually it was the 'little girl' who brought the romance to an end – she jibbed at a *ménage à trois*.

*Rome, 30 December 1905*

Had a few people to dine – Medici [Luigi, owner of the Mandria] and Ferdinando Belmonte, who has just been included in the Ministry after the last reshuffle. What next! The triumph of mediocrity. And dear frog-faced old Chimirri, hard at work on his new law for Calabria and at last about to pass into the Senate. Rudinì is furious with this Ministry [it fell on 30 January, the Prime Minister Fortis being accused of subservience to big business]. Incidentally, I was told a fine story for my book about the time when he and his parents had to take refuge in Naples early in 1860, because of his association with the liberal nobles in Palermo and the danger of imprisonment. One day the police entered the Hotel de Rome, where the family was staying. It was evident that they did not know the young Marquis by sight, for the officer in charge said to the father: 'We have a warrant for the arrest of your son.' The old man, with marvellous presence of mind, turned to Antonio, as if he were a secretary, and said in a peremptory tone: 'Be good enough to fetch my son, who is wanted by these gentlemen.' Antonio bowed and withdrew, and so made his escape. . . .

Visits and cards. Will they never end? P. and Delia went to 'bridge' at Countess Somaglia's. Lady Pirbright, who Robert Hichens says looks like something that has just popped out of the mayonnaise,[25] and Princess San Faustino, amusing and red-haired, were there. 'Jane', as this last is called, did not ask us to her New Year's Eve party. She is an odd woman, fat, dressing like Mary Queen of Scots, trading on a sort of *prime-sautier* wit, but I think *au fond* she is only the usual American snob. The Spanish ambassador lives, as she does, in one of the numerous Palazzo Barberini apartments. He has always rather ignored her, and the other day when he met her he said: 'This Palace is so agreeable, so quiet.' She answered: 'Yes, occasionally one hears a noise, and one learns that a Spanish ambassador has died.' (His two predecessors have died in the Palace.)

*Rome, 7 January 1906*

We went last evening to the Doria reception. It was faerie indeed. The rooms that have just been done up I thought delightful, though Duchess Massimo seemed affected and said they had been her mother's bedroom – but the Prince was young when his mother died and may be excused for not having waited another generation to sweep away any intimate memories, memories sacred to so few! [Tina still kept her mother's rooms shut up at Malfitano.] The Princess, so English [daughter of the Duke of Newcastle] and Orietta, the pretty vivacious 18-year-old daughter of the house, whose eyes remind me of those of her aunt Gwendoline Somaglia, stood of course at the entrance, with the Prince not far off. The mother dressed as usual very simply. The daughter was in pink velvet and chiffon and looked radiantly happy [it was to have been her coming out party but instead celebrated her engagement]. The rooms were beautifully lighted, never trying to the eyes, and the crowd never too great, but *animated* – one saw it was made up of people pleased to have come, to see a great Roman house open again. One noticed how more than ever the 'blacks' [Papal aristocracy] and 'whites' [Italian aristocracy] are mixing. To me the evening had a special interest. Teresa Torlonia [Lily Belmonte's daughter] made her début in the world. She is like her mother, and was of course shy and held herself badly, looking fragile and pale. Mrs Baldwin from Boston was there; a *hard, determined* face, handsome still; Doria, making no secret of his devotion, and introducing the Milanese [Count Carlo Borromeo, Orietta's fiancé] to her. Will she get through the social barrier here? Her daughter, the famous Gladys Deacon [eventually Duchess of Marlborough] is handsome, but her eyes are too wide apart, and although she has a beautiful figure there is want of grace in her movements. However, when I think of the Marchesa Casati (who at present is in this hotel) and her *fama rubata* of charm and beauty, I bow down to Miss Deacon. . . .

I was told the other day the *exact* story of the Crown Prince of Germany's ring. He was driving —— in a dogcart at Blenheim and complained that his ring cut into his fingers. She offered to pull off his glove and remove it while he held the reins in his other hand. On their return from the drive, she said she would keep the ring as a souvenir; at this he demurred, saying it had belonged to the Queen, his grandmother, and that he could not give it to her. But she was obdurate and kept it. The rest is known, how the German Ambassador, sent by the Emperor, requested her to return the ring – which she was obliged to do.²⁶

*Rome, 9 January 1906*

To Donna Maria Mazzoleni. So she floats on *malgré* her liaison. *Che mondo!* I am sorry for Princess Belmonte who would wish to see her only son married, but on the other hand, Donna Maria makes no *wife* miserable and she does not keep him from his mother. What I despise is the woman who comes into a happy household and steals the husband from his wife.

*Rome, 19 January 1906*

To the Queen's for tea. Pleasant, long. The Queen is improved, more at her ease. Fassini says a shy queen is charming. I differ. She addressed us in Italian for the first time and delighted the girls by saying they looked very Italian. It is amusing to see all the Queen's ladies offering cakes. Princess Viggiano [French] was the most queenlike of all, more even than her sovereign. Vittoria Teano, the lovely, gay, black-haired, black-eyed princess, of whom posterity will talk. She looks especially well in the evening but is a little affected in her movements, a silly closing of the eyes while speaking [she was short-sighted] a general straining for effect. . . . Queen Margherita, on the other hand, was in brilliant form the other day, telling us amusing stories about letters she receives from Americans. One woman wrote recently asking if she had any old jewels to sell. The Duke of Abruzzi has had many offers of marriage [from Americans] etc. etc. Talking of Princess Poggio Suasa, we agree that Americans have an amazing power of assimilation. One sees them one year looking quite common, and the next they have all the varnish of a fine lady, carriage, movement, even tone of voice (sometimes) altered. . . .

Bugnano [Duke Ferdinando of Bugnano] wishes to marry Norina. The vanity of the man! I don't think he has a chance.

*Rome, 22 January 1906*

The other day calling on Countess Somaglia, Caterina Moncada [Princess of Paternò, daughter of 'Tancredi'] talked of our footman whom she recognised downstairs and told people, to their astonishment, that he used to be her playmate as a child – he was the son of their coachman and a stable boy. Strange companion for the child of a princely household.

*Malfitano, 17 March 1906*

Effie has had a bad fall from her horse. Went to see her today – lying in bed with the parrot sitting on top of her. She really is extraordinarily fond of that bird. Bice Lampedusa [Duchess of Palma, mother of the author of *The Leopard*] has been here, complaining about Effie's servants [the Joss Whitakers and the Lampedusas being neighbours]; they look in through her windows and shout rude things. I noticed that Bice was wearing the bracelet that Ignazio Florio had given her. Poor Franca! . . . We are overdone with people bringing letters of introduction. Dear Hamilton is here, which is a blessing. Princess Aribert [Marie Louise],[27] with Miss Crofton and Alick Yorke have arrived from Ceylon. Sir Augustus FitzGeorge, who is of course the morganatic son of the Duke of Cambridge, amused me by saying that she and her sister [Helena Victoria] are not liked in the family – *mauvaise langue.*

Effie had broken her hip, and this was to lead to severe arthritis. She was indeed devoted to her parrot; she took it to London and had been seen by a journalist shopping in Bond Street with it on her shoulder. Antique dealers said that she had trained it to laugh at their prices. During tennis parties it used to be allowed to fly about the trees, until one day it was shot as a joke by Vincenzo Florio.

*Malfitano, 26 March 1906*

A big lunch for Prince Louis of Battenberg.[28] Tea at Franca Florio's. Then our party. The Trabias to dinner, Mazzarinos and Camporeales. A great success. As for Princess Aribert, she danced with all the *piccioni* [pigeons], the name given by general consent to the dandies of the town, and we stayed up quite late. She is very intelligent, with wide and ready sympathies for all those around her; and she is interested in nearly everything that comes into her reach!

The happy princess left to stay at the Aostas' in Naples. She wrote a flatteringly intimate bread-and-butter letter, signing herself 'Louie'.[30]

It was indeed a lovely moment for the girls: race meetings, picnics, *tableaux vivants*, boxes at that stupendous building, the Teatro Massimo.[31] The King and Queen paid a state visit. The Empress Eugénie appeared suddenly at Malfitano and dashed round the garden, livelier and younger-looking even than three years ago at Farnborough. Tina laboured at her book. And the agonising romance between Valentine Rousseau and Peppino Scalea continued.

*Marsala, 20 June 1906*

We arrived here on Tuesday with Princess Niscemi, Professor Salinas [Director of the National Museum] and Guido Jung [of the Swiss merchant firm][32] after a glorious visit to Selinunte. The Professor was a stimulating, enthusiastic guide. Clear blue sky and sea, the ruins standing out in the arid scenery of summer. Here and there a patch of ginestra, cleverly planted as if by chance by Salinas. Guido Jung wanted to bathe, but I would not let him leave us, as I was sure he had not got a bathing costume. We could not keep the Princess waiting.

We spent the day on Motya. Salinas enthusiastic over two flights of steps which P. has dug up lately. The next morning he told us that he had been thinking of Motya during the night and hoped that he might be able personally to supervise the excavations during the summer! Motya occupies all our thoughts. We settled about enlarging the house on the island. I am struggling to keep back from extravagant expenses. I say we cannot consider anything until the Marsala question is settled. The girls' future *must* be considered! . . . Three 'pigeons' came to pay us, or rather Norina, a visit on the island.

*Marsala, 22 June 1906*

At last everything has been arranged about Valentine and Peppino, and he is gone to Paris. But what a foolish man the Baron. She the mother – dear sweet creature – does not count. As I told her, the Princess's conduct was not worth taking into consideration, and Valentine must not hope to have the Villa Scalea left to Peppino, with all the art treasures it contains when the time comes! [In fact the beautiful eighteenth-century villa in the Colli did become Valentine's in the end.] . . . Young Salvo Ugo [Marquis Ugo, a 'pigeon', great-nephew of 'Tancredi'] sent to enquire if there is any chance of his being accepted by Norina. She declined. That makes four since January, not counting Guglielmi who evidently found out he had no chance and retired.

Not a mention of a proposal for Delia. The time for travels had arrived. The London Season was now definitely out of favour. After more worries about Marsala, whether or not to sell the wine business, they left for St Moritz. Tina grumbled again about Americans and what she called the *haute juiverie*. The presence of Guilia Trabia was at least a compensation.

*St Moritz, 11 August 1906*

Countess Santa Fiora [King Umberto's last mistress] as usual here, not even *des beaux restes* of the once beautiful woman who caused Queen Margherita so much jealousy. Yet there is a jolliness, a brightness about her which makes her very attractive, and her conversation is always cleverly adapted to the people she is with. I saw Trabia, not easily amused or kept in good temper, really enjoying himself for quite a long time with her the other evening.

The Pips rented a Whitaker nephew's house in Curzon Street for the autumn, thereby missing Aileen's wedding in Palermo – 'poor silly little Aileen, losing her head for a soldier'. They saw *A Winter's Tale*, with Ellen Terry in the lead, wonderfully graceful though past sixty summers. Tina, however, was not feeling at all well; her back was hurting her. One afternoon she settled to writing down some candid remarks on her in-laws, providing a useful résumé.

*26 Curzon Street, 13 September 1906*

To begin with. *Benny*, the eldest, born in 1837. Married Miss Hudson. She had money and was clever, with a great sense of humour, very pretty except for her mouth which spoiled her. Pity she had not had a cultured education. *Ackie*: married late a Mr Morrison, a merchant of Palermo;[33] not a good marriage. He eventually failed and settled in England here at Eastbourne. A good-natured fellow who became very popular and was several times mayor. *Willie* married when very young, the daughter of the Bishop of Argyll. Not a happy marriage. His mother told me that, the morning after a ball where he had proposed, he showed her a white lock, saying: 'See my hair has turned white in a night.' She was a charming creature, but they were not suited to each other. Then he married Rita Sartorius. Again they were totally unsuited to each other. He had, it must be said, a difficult temper, as so many Whitakers have. Rita charming, artistic, good – really good – but impractical. *Carrie Christian*, sweet and amiable. Her first husband I did not know, her second was a delightful philosopher but not suited to her. She associated herself with a Captain Bagot, ten years younger; he died this year, a few months before her husband. In her double trial she has been very brave. *Joss* comes next, generally known as Uncle Joss. Kingly, obstinate, takes infinite trouble to help his neighbour. His wife is half Greek, half English, father of Jewish origin [pure supposition of course on Tina's part]. We call her Mrs Tennis. She likes to pose as being totally heartless. Passionately fond of curios and with a love of acquisition, probably inherited from her paternal side! She did her duty to her unborn children so that they would come healthy into the world – *poi basta!* *Arthur* took a legal degree; very good manners, diplomatic. He is rather in awe of his Welsh wife, Emmie. She is extravagant, but never for herself, has rather a violent temper that makes her forget at times that she is a lady.[34] *Robert* comes next. Can be amusing. He lets life slip through his great indolence. He loves sprawling on the floor and reading a book. His great loves are his wife and youngest child [Beatrice, known as 'Boots'], so much so that he would be waiting to give the former a glass of port on her return from her early morning rides, with the *adorateur* of her early married life at a time when all the town talked of this (?) friendship.[35] She was the daughter of people of quite a low station in life. It is curious to note that both Joss and Bob should have married beneath them, with such a perfect lady as their mother, and with such charming sisters. Maude has got on wonderfully in the world; by her pretty manners, tact and good temper, she gets credit for being intrinsically worth far more than she is. She is really *au fond* selfish, and her good nature is chiefly exploited for the benefit of those from whom she can get some return. She is not sincere, so one never knows quite where one is.

Curious coincidence, while writing the above I receive enclosed from Frank: 'I must have a truly wicked disposition. I am always seized with a wild longing to stick pins into Aunt Maude to see how much of the *varnish* will crack. Don't tell anybody I said so, because there are things one ought to keep to oneself.'

Three couples had been missed out: the Tommasi-Crudelis, both of whom were dead; Ingham and his Swiss wife Berthe, who lived at Grayshott; and the youngest brother, Albert, and his wife, Eileen (Irish, daughter of Mrs B. M. Croker the novelist) who had recently bought a large mansion, Babworth Hall, in Nottinghamshire. Albert had so far had the most adventurous life of the brothers, having fought in the Afghan War.

Tina and Pip were invited to Hammerfield for lunch, in order to discuss her manuscript with Laurence Binyon. On the way down by train she began to feel 'all wrong', so much so that she had to be put straight to bed. Everyone was charming.

*Hammerfield, 14 October 1906*

The housekeeper had promptly decided I must not move. Frank brought roses. Ronny gave me his books to read. The next day Ronny and Frank went off to a lunch given by Mr Astor, a house warming of Hever Castle, to see what new gold can do when allied to old stone. Alick Yorke was there. They told me that after being shown over the gorgeous rooms, Alick – as usual thinking much of his food – sank into a chair and exclaimed: 'Will lunch *never* be served?' At last some little chimes were heard, and he at once asked a relation of the house what they were. 'The gong.' 'I am thankful indeed,' said Alick. 'I feared they were my insides.'

The illness kept her indoors on her return to London. She felt guilty, as Pip was chafing to get to Motya and the girls had decided that they hated England. At last it was decided: she must have an operation. Norina sat by the bed holding her hand until she was overcome by the chloroform.

All went well. Reading between the lines one understands that the operation must have been an hysterectomy. Naturally it was a question of weeks before she could be moved from the nursing home. Frank sent cheering news: Binyon had said that her book was 'one of the most interesting works of its kind that had passed through his hands since he had been reading for Constables', of course he would publish it. Frank shrewdly also sent a cutting about D'Annunzio's new play in Rome, *More Than Love* – just the sort of thing to amuse her. The play had been 'a most humiliating failure, a glorification of unscrupulousness and personifying the sort of worship which D'Annunzio's disciples accord to him'.

*London, 10 November 1906*

D'Annunzio is a true degenerate. How could Sandra be his mistress? He is not worth the sacrifice. Of course Eleonora Duse hates her and must certainly have organised the claque to boo and whistle the play. So much for our 'gifted author'. [Sandra parted from him in January. Six years later she took the veil as a Carmelite nun.][36]

. . . Still flat on my back, but improving. Lovely bunch of white lilac from Lady Headfort, apparently well satisfied with her daughter-in-law, Rosie Boote that was [a Gaiety girl], after her visit to Scotland. New wine in old bottles. Then a visit from Maude Valérie White, *bohème jusqu'au bout des ongles* as usual, pining to get away to her Robert [Hichens] in Taormina – he of course is with *his* Alec Hood at Maniace.

So Tina was keeping up her spirits. She was moved to the Hans Crescent Hotel, where on 10 December she had the great shock of seeing Hamilton Aïdé come staggering into her room, obviously very ill indeed. The nurse gave him brandy and hot soup, then Pip arranged for him to be taken in a cab to his new rooms in Half Moon Street. The next day they had the verdict: double pneumonia.

*London, 11 December 1906*

No better news of dear Hamilton up to late last night. He wanders a great deal, reciting Shakespeare, talks of this hotel and fancies ladies are coming to call, such as Mrs Godfrey Pearse [*née* de Candia, one of the Grisettes], to discuss the biography of her father, Mario, the singer. I have written to Hey to beg him to get a male nurse.

*London, 14 December 1906*

So all is over! Poor Hamilton passed onward yesterday morning. The only mercy is that he did not suffer in the least. He was totally un-conscious of his condition. When his cousin Mrs Tennant, who was much affected, leant over him and said 'Dear Hamilton, we shall meet again soon,' he replied: 'Yes, my dear Gertrude, the best hour is luncheon time.' He asked for his opera glasses, thinking he was at the play, criticized actors and admired some ladies in the boxes; then he thought he was teaching a young friend to act, or that he was receiving guests and making introductions, always fancying he was very busy and very occupied. Gradually his strength diminished and he sank into a state of coma. Luther Munday [theatre director, artist, related by marriage to Aïdé] said: 'Dear Hamilton, if you hear me and are free from pain, do say "No pain",' and he murmured the words quite distinctly: 'No pain.' He died quite quietly at 3 a.m. without a gasp. He was the kindest of beings. It was a life spent in good. When he could help a struggling artist or writer, it was his greatest joy – and if he was sometimes misguided in his judgements, his intentions were ever of the kindest. He was just 80.

Later Tina wrote a long pen-portrait of Hamilton, who left her some of his water-colours.

'Vice he shrank from, even in the abstract; that is, even in conversation, ugliness in any form was to him more than repulsive, it was intolerable. He was free from the curse of shyness, which he insisted was really a form of self-consciousness.' Sarah Bernhardt, the Trees, Irving, Mrs Kendal, Wyndham were all his friends; he apparently spent quiet weekends at Rye alone with Henry James, who had known him since the early 1870s;[37]

Janet Ross and Sir James Lacaita used to call him *Ricciolino d'amore* because of his curly hair. As for Hey, his faithful servant:

> He took his mission seriously. Who was better turned out than Hamilton Aïdé? Whose silk hat more shiny, whose spats more immaculate? My housekeeper-maid used to say: 'To see Mr Hey clean Mr Aïdé's boots, ma'am, is a poem.' How this faithful servant warded off the undesirable encroachers on his master's ever-ready purse! It was he who gave him bicycle lessons at Malfitano, typed his writings and no doubt criticized them. After one of Hamilton's tea-parties, he asked if in future he might be informed what class of person was expected. He came to see us before we left, on the 1st January, and I could scarcely believe it was he, he was so aged. His rather stern, cold and forbidding demeanour had given way to a quiet despair. He soon fell into a decline and died of a sort of consumption, only a few months later. Luther Munday said to me: 'If ever a man died of a broken heart, Hey did!'

The weeks passed –

*Malfitano, 21 March 1907*

The Rudinìs are gone. Well, little Lea is a wonderful woman, and a lucky one, when you think of her past: her great love affair with Rudinì, which perhaps even hastened the complete madness of his first wife (her great friend); then her marriage, and he Prime Minister twice; a Collaressa [a courtesy title, as her husband had the Collare dell'Annunziata, the equivalent of the Garter], their illegitimate boy recognised, and the world at her feet. She is a devoted stepmother [Carlo, husband of Dora Labouchere, and Alessandra were children of the first wife], and above all is *senza posa, animosità o fiele,* brimming with life and energy. She was amusing about the Marlborough scandal. When the Duchess was in Paris with Lord Castlereagh, the Duke wired he would not have her back. But the Duchess took no notice, and it was Lady Castlereagh, as her best friend, who saved the situation. The personal intervention of the King and Queen finally put an end to talk of divorce.[38]

Colonel and Mrs Cornwallis-West here, on their daughter's yacht [i.e. belonging to Daisy Princess of Pless], with the Duchess of Westminster [their other daughter]. This latter is certainly more than pretty; she reminds me of a picture of Lady Hamilton: bright, animated but *childlike* – even her little letters show this. Mrs Cornwallis-

West was, as usual, brilliant, filling the room with radiancy and buoyancy.

Then came one of the great moments, greater than the arrival of the German Royal Family in 1905: the visit of Edward VII and Queen Alexandra to Malfitano. It caused not a little flutter, mainly because of its unexpectedness, following so soon after a gala evening of *tableaux vivants,* organised by Tina and Giulia Trabia and involving all the smart 'beauties' of Palermo – Franca Florio, the Princess of Petrulla, the Duchess of Bissana, Norina, Delia, Maude Gardner etc. The King, it was thought had been intending to go to Rome, but in his usual autocratic way he had changed his mind. Then Pip was not at all well, Norina had a rash, and – even worse – the newly-married Peppino Scalea was on the danger list from blood poisoning in the foot.

*Malfitano, 25 April 1907*

Early in the morning we telephoned for news to Casa Scalea. Swelling increasing, high fever. Franca Florio sent me her motor, as I did not feel strong enough for a long carriage drive. I found poor Peppino S. pale green, with dry parched lips and burning hands, vomiting continually. Still he thinks of others, and when he heard I had come by motor, he begged me to tell the chauffeur to drive slowly and carefully.

. . . The King and Queen of England arrived yesterday afternoon. My Pip still with feverish attacks, so decide not to write our names in Royal book. Their Majesties visit the Cathedral, Cappella Palatina etc. In the afternoon they go to Sperlinga (Joss not there in time to receive them!), then to the Favorita and to Villa Sofia (Maude *quite* ready to give them tea). Then to the Football Club to witness a match between the men of the *Victoria and Albert* and the Palermo team. No preparations made, no good society to meet them; Pip, honorary president, in bed. In the evening P. insists on our names being signed in the book. Churchill [Sydney Churchill, British Consul] in consequence says that their Majesties, with Princess Victoria, who I hear is suffering from neuralgia, will wish to visit Malfitano. Can we give them lunch tomorrow? The King wishes to lunch *al fresco.* I say this is impossible. P. cannot lunch out in the open air. But P. says it is to be, and I have to give in!

The King had told the Prefect of Palermo that he and the Queen had come strictly as 'tourists'. His appearance in civilian clothes and a white bowler made a particular contrast to the German Emperor's uniform. They sped disconcertingly fast around the city, stopping at shops, visiting the sights (they went to the Catacombs twice). On one occasion they ran into a demonstration of shoemakers who were on strike; the men – according to *The Times* – 'respectfully saluted them and decided on the spot to postpone their agitation during the Royal visit, out of deference to their Majesties'. Then, having lunched at the Villa Igiea, they found the *Victoria and Albert* guarded by *carabinieri,* whom the King at once asked to be removed.

*Malfitano, 26 April 1907*

*Slightly* better news of Peppino Scalea, but we are still very worried. Spraggia [the doctor] comes; I implore him not to allow P. to lunch out of doors. But I am outwitted – it is not to be. Very anxious, very worried. It is a warm spring day, but the wind is fresh and strong. The table looks poor and tawdry;[39] *pazienza,* but oh! the anxiety about P. The Royal party are announced for 1.30; they arrive at 1.20. We are ready to receive them. The King is announced as he gets out of his motor. . . . Lunch *al fresco* was a success *malgré* the wind, and we were very cheery – nothing stiff. The King, walking with me towards the table, said: 'How shall we sit, Mrs Whitaker?' To which I at once answered: 'This is humble soil, but British soil. Your Majesty commands.' He seemed much pleased and at once settled our places at table, taking the head of the table and placing me at his right and Norina on his left. At Homburg, where one summer we had the table next to his every day at Bitters Park Hotel, I noticed how quickly he arranged his various guests every day. At dessert he teased De Martino [later ambassador in London] for eating three *fichi d'India,* asking where he would like to be buried. It struck me how much more friendliness and pleasant intercourse there was between the King and his followers than between the German Court and their Sovereign. After lunch we strolled down into the garden: I asked permission for a group photograph to be taken, and the King took great interest in it, and insisted it should be beneath a *palm.* The Queen I thought very amiable, far more so than I had expected; all the more credit with her affliction of great deafness, which as we know makes ordinary mortals suspicious and irritable. The King's good-humour and good temper were most evident; he kept calling out to the Queen about some little item of interest, which I am sure she more often than not did not hear. He seems to me to be a man of clear sound intelligence, though not as *clever* as I had imagined in view of the considerable position he has taken in international politics. His commonsense and tact triumph over the German Emperor's brilliant intellect, which might even be genius.

After all, it was the Emperor who initiated the idea of the spring cruises; and who is now profiting by his example, reaping the real benefit? . . .

They remained just two hours with us. I did not ask for their photos, as Maude did (although they were only a quarter of an hour at Villa Sofia). The King complied with her request, but the Queen forgot.

P. none the worse for his lunch in the open air. The King saw he did not look well and insisted on his putting on his overcoat. We spoke of dear Hamilton at the lunch, and the King said he understood he was the son of Lord Melbourne, from whom he had inherited his many gifts. I had never heard of this before. I always understood that he was the son of a Greek ambassador who had been killed in a duel.

The following evening the *Victoria and Albert* sailed for Naples.

# XXI

## Some Horrors; and for Norina – Auletta

PEPPINO SCALEA recovered, though it was a fortnight before he was out of danger. Tina and Pip for the next years were endlessly fussing about their own health. One reads time and again in the diary about 'tiresome' fevers, being 'confined upstairs' or spending days on chaises longues. At any rate in May the family set off for Marsala. There had been an exciting and highly important discovery at Motya. Pip's ailments disappeared immediately.

*Marsala, 11 May 1907*

A small necropolis on the north side of the island has now been proved to exist. It is outside the fortification walls. We had thought that the only Motyan burial-ground was at Birgi on the mainland. A large funeral vase, surrounded by small ones, has been brought to light. In fact there are *two* strata of tombs. The lower stratum consists of cinerary urns placed in holes cut out of the rock, with a stone sarcophagus above.

Pip deduced that the two strata belonged to different periods, while the sarcophagus probably belonged to yet a third period. In his view the little terracotta urns, with lids like saucers, could even have been for the ashes of sacrificed babies or small animals. Obviously the large vase in the upper stratum would have held the ashes of an adult, the smaller surrounding vases containing pieces of entrails. The necropolis was without doubt the original burial-ground of the early Phoenician settlers, in the days when Motya was a comparatively humble settlement. When the colony grew and the town became larger, it had to be abandoned and the new site was selected at Birgi.

There was no restraining Pip any longer over Motya. Tina's remonstrances about expense were totally ignored. Professor Salinas was even urging him to start a small museum on the island. As she was beginning to feel 'seedy' again, she returned alone to Palermo.

*Malfitano, 2 June 1907*

On Friday evening went to hear Vivien Chartres, a child of twelve,[1] play the violin at the Massimo. Giulia Trabia, indeed everyone said

51. *Tableau vivant,* 'The Triumph of Light' grand finale, on 8 April 1907.
*Left to right:* Duchess Maria of Bissana, Amalia Villafranca, Costanza Vannucci, Maude Gardner, Franca Florio, Princess Maria Petrulla, Annina di Montereale (later Florio), Stefania Pajno.

52. Harriet (Enrichetta) Caetani, Duchess of Sermoneta, third wife of Michelangelo Caetani and daughter of Lord Howard de Walden.

53. Giulia Trabia.

54. Ignazio Florio, the 'blue prince'.

55. Giulia Trigona, murdered
2 March 1911.

they could never get over the wonder of this most gifted little girl. She simply held the whole theatre enthralled. Such pathos, such originality in the interpretation of an ordinary melody, such brilliant technique in the most difficult pieces of bravura. It is true genius. The other day the child was rushing about in the garden here with Sofia and Giovanna Trabia, begging for five minutes more, and now the deep sentiment of womanhood, of a woman who has suffered, loved and lost, coming from those long hands, as she moves one to emotions such as Kubelik cannot even do.

The Pips arrived at Claridge's on 1 July – 'P. *at last* quite pleased to be in England' – just in time for the sensational news of the theft of the Irish Crown Jewels, only four days before the official visit to Dublin by Edward and Alexandra on board the *Victoria and Albert*. Since this affair was to have greater repercussions on Tina's world than she ever dreamed of at that time, one must dwell on it in certain detail.

The Ulster King of Arms, who was in charge of the jewels, and who kept the key of the strong-room in his pocket, was Sir Arthur Vicars, aged forty-three. He was unmarried, a kindly if foolish man, and friendly with Frank Shackleton, brother of Sir Ernest Shackleton the explorer. Shackleton was handsome and a con-man, though it took some while for his friends, who also included Ronny Gower and Frank Hird, to realise this. Someone later described him as 'utterly and totally depraved'. Vicars, however, was at that time so dazzled by the young man's charm and looks that he made him one of his Heralds.

On 6 July the jewels, valued variously at £15,000, £54,000 and £80,000, and including the insignia of the order of St Patrick, were found to be missing. Shackleton on that day was staying at Hammerfield, and the Duke of Argyll (the erstwhile Lord Lorne) was one of his fellow-guests. The news of the theft broke in the newspapers on the eighth, and the Duke read out the story in *The Times* to Shackleton as they travelled back to London by train. Needless to say, the royal visit to Dublin was not a happy one, and the King was even more angered when two months went by without very much apparent effort being taken to recover the jewels. Vicars was quite adamant in declaring that the keys had never once been out of his pocket. Indeed a commission to investigate the affair was not held until 6 January, with the result that Vicars and Shackleton were removed from their posts. The jewels were never recovered, and nobody was charged. As far as the public was concerned, the theft remained one of the great mysteries of the Edwardian era.

Even a quite recent book, published in 1965, did not give the solution, though the innuendoes were clear enough.[2] There must have been too many people alive who did not wish the embers to be fanned all over again. It was left, three years later, to a veteran Irish journalist, Bulmer Hobson, who covered the case at the time, to be the first to say what nobody else apparently had dared to put in print.[3] The jewels were stolen by Shackleton in complicity with one Captain Richard Gorges, both of whom were accustomed to attend drinking parties at Dublin Castle. One night, long before the fatal 6 July, they plied Vicars with so much whisky that he passed out. Whilst he was in this state, they took the keys from his pocket, opened the strong-room, removed all the jewels, then replaced the keys. The jewels were then taken by Shackleton to Amsterdam and pledged for £20,000, with the proviso that they would not be broken up for three years.

Shackleton and Gorges had met during the Boer War in South Africa, where Gorges had been 'caught red-handed with a drummer-boy'. King Edward is reported to have said: 'I will have no scandals!',[4] which is one reason no doubt why the thing was hushed up. For it had been hinted that the truth could shake the country in a very different way. To be blunt, it would involve a great number of 'influential homosexuals', and presumably the King's brother-in-law, the Duke of Argyll, would have been implicated, whether in fact he was a homosexual or not. The resulting witch-hunt would have had far more drastic consequences than those following the Oscar Wilde case. Shackleton did crash in the end, but for a different reason. Meanwhile, although Vicars soon became suspicious of him, Ronny and Frank were in cheerful ignorance of the real nature of their Machiavellian friend. They even took him travelling abroad. When Ronny's man of business died in November 1907, Ronny – still having epileptic fits – decided to give Shackleton power of attorney over his affairs, especially since Frank was ill with scarlet fever. This decision meant that Shackleton virtually had complete freedom over all the money and investments. He had told Ronny that he would have doubled his capital by the time Frank recovered.

*Claridge's, 10 September 1907*
Ronald Gower's garden party at Hammerfield. Lovely weather, great success. Special train; we fill two carriages. Robert Hichens, Alec Hood, Sir Donald Mackenzie Wallace[5] and self in one compartment. . . . We are very gay. On the spot we find the Duke of Argyll. Everything is beautifully managed by Frank. His little play very pretty. He

is excited about the Dublin jewels and worried for his friend's sake. I must say Sir Arthur Vicars seems to have treated Shackleton abominably.

And there we let the story rest for the time being.
The Pips had moved briefly to a furnished house in Surrey.

*Hindhead, 18 September 1907*

We go to tea with Effie and party at Greatholt: charming farm turned into a delightful house, and a picturesque young garden. I am taken over the house – and notice that Effie and Emily Luck sleep together. Curious arrangement! Can my early suspicions be true? Joss in another part of the house.

Tina, having failed to prove that Effie was Jewish, had now decided that she was a lesbian. The truth was that Joss snored, and Effie could not bear to sleep anywhere near him.

*Hindhead, 20 September 1907*

We all pack into the Fiat and go on to Grayshott, where we find Conan Doyle and his fiancée. I introduce Frank, as C.D. is leaving this neighbourhood and going to live near Hammerfield. He is like a big newfoundland, with an attractive simplicity and indeed all the delicacy of feeling appertaining to that canine breed. He looks so happy now. When I last saw him at Grayshott, he brought an almost half-witted invalid of a wife to dine. There was something pathetic about the situation, and in all the care he still lavished on the lady. He looked older then, though it must be several years ago.

Post brings me excellent reviews of my book. Only one protesting voice is heard. Long visit from Lady Wynford. We sympathise in many ways but differ strongly about Prince Scipione Borghese, who has just successfully travelled from Pekin to Paris in a motor [the journey took exactly two months, in an Itala Fiat]. I charge that there is no great merit in this fact. It does not advance science or help humanity, and if it really is dangerous it is only foolhardy and comes from a morbid desire for notoriety. How different to the Duke of Abruzzi. I am proud to be his compatriot.[6]

Some self-analysis:

*Claridge's, 20 October 1907*

The Empress Elisabeth of Austria said: 'There is in every human life a moment when one inwardly dies.' Yes, this is very true of many people, though indeed there are some who fight and live to the end.

I am not posing, as perhaps Robert Hichens thinks, when I say laughingly: 'I am dead.' It is true. I am dead to all the ambitions of my early youth, dead to all the hopes that were inherent in it. Dead, dead. I look back on the strength of my desires, in those golden days when I dreamed of the success with which I was to repay the hard sacrifices my mother had so willingly undertaken for me.

It was a very social period. Thanks partly to Princess Marie Louise, there were many introductions in Court circles. As a result, no doubt, the following spring there came this bombshell of a letter:

*Private and Confidential*          *10 Wilbraham Place, 12 March 1908*
Dearest Tina,

I was asked in confidence by a friend if I knew any one wanting to be nominated a peer in the next gazette. Merely a matter of figures (might be got for £60,000). I thought perhaps this might suit you; if so I would put you in direct communication with the party concerned, but let me know as soon as possible. If you don't care about it, perhaps your nephew of Pylewell would, and if so would you ask him? But please note it must be strictly *entre nous*, for it has been known that though things had been all arranged they have been 'stopped' owing to their 'leaking out' beforehand.

I hope this will find you all flourishing.

With love to all

Yours affy Emmie

There followed a telegram, dated 18 March: 'DID YOU GET LETTER OF THURSDAY – EMMIE.' It has not been possible to establish who this Emmie was. 10 Wilbraham Place was a new block of flats, and the rates books show that it was almost entirely inhabited by lone females, spinsters or widows. At any rate Emmie had hardly left much time for Tina to reply. It was a crucial moment in British politics. Campbell-Bannerman, the Prime Minister, was ill and it was likely that he would not be able to resume public life.

Another urgent letter followed:

*Private and Confidential*          *10 Wilbraham Place, 20 March 1908*
Dearest Tina,

I wrote you a letter over a week ago headed as above and *sealed*. Getting no answer I thought it might have strayed. So I telegraphed 2 days ago to know if you had received it but received no reply.

If the matter does not interest Mr Whitaker, would you kindly wire me 'No' on receipt of this – for I have to give in the name by Sunday, for the friend [Asquith?] who is 'in the know' is leaving for Biarritz [where the King was staying incognito] on Sunday. *Entre nous* the price is really £100,000 but I was told it might be got for £60,000 and a member of my family was thought of, but it can't be managed, so I thought of you.

I hope you are all well – I suppose you are kept pretty busy with H.R.H. Princess M.L. about. Love to all

Yours affy Emmie

Tina noted in her diary that she had answered that the Whitakers were all staunch Conservatives and would not 'care to come to terms with a Liberal Government'. Moreover, Pip had no sons. She had however passed the message on to 'the Pylewells'. 'One is never sure,' she unfairly wrote, 'when human vanity is involved.' But the chance had been missed. No Whitaker acquired a peerage.

That winter in Rome everyone had been talking of the Nasi case. Tina was visited by her cousin, the octogenarian Martino Beltrani, who told her that he was sure that Nasi must be condemned and that indeed he hoped that this would happen – 'it would be a lesson to others'. The case had dragged on for three years. Nunzio Nasi, a native of Trapani and deputy in Parliament for that town, and a former Minister to boot, had been impeached for embezzlement. His attitude had been typical of the southern way of life – jobs for friends, the occasional small sum from public funds judiciously spent in rewarding followers, suppression of adverse local press comments. Nothing unusual in *Mafia*-land. He was enormously popular in Sicily, needless to say, and when he was sentenced to eleven months' imprisonment and four years exclusion from public life, there were bitter demonstrations against northern 'foreigners', even some wild talk about another Vespers. His constituents promptly re-elected him. He was unseated and again elected, whereupon Parliament accepted him and he continued to sit until his death.[7]

Conditions in Sicily were in fact very gradually improving, thanks chiefly to the return of the *americani* with money in their pockets. A man who had been an under-gardener at Malfitano startled his former employers by calling on them in a motor-car; he had also invested in a dozen gold teeth. 'Later we heard he was hand in glove with the *Mafia*.'

In April 1908 G. M. Trevelyan was in Palermo collecting material for

his *Garibaldi and the Thousand*. When he wrote to his father, Sir George
Otto Trevelyan, of his intention to follow Garibaldi's route from Marsala
to Palermo, on foot, the old man and his wife became very alarmed, the
more so since G.M. had suddenly and unexpectedly inherited money
from an English aunt in Taormina. Surely the *Mafia* would be alerted?
Worse, G.M. was intending to take three companions, one of whom was
his elder brother Charles, the others being Bertrand Russell and Aubrey
Waterfield. So a careful and patient letter had to be written to the parents:

> Mama's fears that I could in any way be endangered are quite
> beyond the scope of all possibility. There are no bandits or organised
> robbers, and 'agrarian crime' like that of Ireland is all that is wrong;
> it is very spasmodic, there has been none of it this year, and it never
> touches foreign visitors. I have talked over the question of safety with
> Churchill and the Whitakers, who are doing everything for my
> convenience and happiness. They all say the same thing, that with
> *four* of us as there will be, the walk from Marsala will be four times as
> safe as safety itself. To take gendarmes would be to insult the country,
> to arouse curiosity, and to give one an uneasy feeling that whenever
> the gendarmes went away, one would remain a marked man in the
> eyes of the people, who would naturally wonder who it was that had
> needed gendarmes.
>
> In fact Churchill's expression that 'the whole island was talking of
> Mrs Cacciola's [his aunt] will', only meant what such expressions do
> mean, the chatter of the well-to-do classes, *mainly* of course in the east
> of the island whence he had that day (or the day before) returned. The
> peasants between Marsala and Calatafimi will never have heard the
> word Cacciola, still less that of Trevelyan. I would not have written at
> such length on so clear a matter, but that I know in England it may
> seem different to you, and I want finally to disabuse you of the idea
> that there is any danger whatever.
>
> You can see for yourselves that nothing short of organized bandits
> would attack four English youths – and there have been no such
> bandits for years.

Tina wrote in her diary about this time:

*Malfitano, 5 April 1908*

George Trevelyan is here, working up his Garibaldi in 1860. Had a
long talk with him the other day after lunch; made him a sort of
description of the unselfishness of the patriots; how I was brought up

to think that if one had no money to give to a poor person, one should give a trinket, but that it was *natural* to do this, and not a merit etc. etc. All at once I heard a great sob, Trevelyan had been so deeply moved that he was weeping. It was a curious moment – absolute, though emotional silence on my part. Then he recovered himself and went on asking questions. Such is the man of strong feeling who is writing of those great days, and of those great men of whom, as he truly said, Garibaldi is but the *culminating* expression.

G.M.'s description of that afternoon's talk, in a letter to his brother, went as follows:

Here is a scheme of education, recounted to me yesterday by Mrs Tina Whitaker, wife of a wealthy English Marsala-wine merchant and queen of this town, but *née* the daughter of a very poor Sicilian exile, in the fifties. She said to me in her simple, believable manner: 'My people never had a thought about themselves. They never kept a shilling or a piece of jewellery or shirt or a coat in the drawer if a brother or sister in the cause was needy and at hand – and that was always. *All* the exiles I knew were like that. None of them except Crispi had a touch of personal ambition, and when the cause was won they retired to obscurity leaving the jackals to fight for the spoils. I sometimes look round at this great house and wonder how I came here. That *I* should have married money! *When I was a girl I was never told to be unselfish or given to understand that what my parents did was virtuous. I never saw anyone acting or feeling otherwise and thought it was natural and that everyone was like that.*' She has found out her mistake in that now. She is the life and soul of what philanthropy there is in this town, and makes her daughters (good ordinary girls) carry it on. But they are not of her world or of her tradition. She gets into corners with one or two of her old veterans and they weep and laugh together over this new Italy which they bought with their common blood and tears, which reverences but *knows them not*. That was a system of education, but not reproduceable in our conditions of life. The conditions are too artificial to be reproduced.

The walk started in mid-April. Considering that G. M. Trevelyan was such a stickler for exactitude, it is slightly surprising that he did not choose 12 May, the date when Garibaldi had left Marsala. Maybe the Sicilian heat had to be taken into account. The Trevelyan brothers were tireless, oblivious of hardship; if Bertrand Russell or Aubrey Waterfield dared to stray a few yards from the correct route they were sternly called back to heel.

Lina and Aubrey Waterfield had been living at the Palazzo Derix, the one that had been inherited by Emily Ingham from her stepfather. They had originally chosen Palermo as their first home because they felt it was a good place in which to work. Lina gave as another reason the fact that 'an old friend of my aunt, whom I also loved, lived there'.[8] From what Tina said later it was clear that Aubrey had collapsed on the great walk.

*Malfitano, 30 May 1908*

The summer has come early. This morning Lina Waterfield and her husband are gone off to Marsala for a more leisurely look at Garibaldi's landing-place. Aubrey had been ill with fever and now has an abscess. I am glad, poor things, they are out of that hot stuffy room. Oh! the horror of it. I went to see them on Sunday. He was lying on a sort of deck chair, the room littered with paper. The table had a big bouquet of faded flowers in the middle. Tins and empty bottles all over the place. Fly papers, covered with dying flies. Such is the interior where Lina writes her book on Palermo for Methuen, a book which is to breathe poetry and the traditions of past beauties [but which never came to pass].

Quite a contrast to life at Malfitano.

Tina collapsed once more.

*Malfitano, 2 June 1908*

We have had a houseful with Alick Yorke, Hugh [a bachelor Whitaker nephew, attaché at the British Embassy], Sir Frederick Milner and his daughter Doreen [later Marchioness of Linlithgow, Vicereine of India], and little Princess Fafka [sister of Lady Egerton, the British Ambassadress, who was Russian]. They have been very gay; I in bed the whole week. What society is coming to though. Miss Milner changed round Alick's pyjamas with the Princess's nightgown, and both emerged from their rooms with these garments on (over their other clothes fortunately) and danced all down the corridor hand in hand and into my room. Pretty odd since they had only met the day before. I laughed until I could no more, to see Alick's pink face coming out of the frilled baby nightgown. . . Alick told us a story of Queen Victoria last night. Lady Erroll (very Low Church), who was trying to console the Queen in a bereavement, said: 'After all, Marm, we shall meet again, and even shall we see Abraham and Jacob.' 'I will *not* meet Abraham, Lady Erroll,' answered tersely the Queen.[9]

NORINA BY DELIA

*Malfitano, 4 June 1908*

Norina is as usual – or rather more than usual – surrounded by candidates for her hand. De Seta seems to have taken a proper place in her mind, but she realizes he has no position to offer, no career and is of lowly birth [he was the son of an ex-Prefect, created a Marquis in 1896]. The little *Duchino* Pietratagliata one does not take seriously. He is clever, an only son, and from a good old family,[10] but he is supposed to cheat at cards and is not very honest. Peppino Gangi is very keen on her, but though he is a prince now only two generations ago the Mantegnas [the Gangi family name] were mere moneylenders who bought their title just after the Union. All the buying and selling of titles within their family denotes a lack of breeding. A Count Montelupo from Naples has put himself to the fore, but with no success; he is nice-looking but over forty and has had too much success with women in Naples. Count Luigi Robilant has just turned up on his ship, the *Vespucci*, but Norina does not seem inclined to change her mind, at least for the present. Manfredi Gravina [son of Blandine] came over for a few hours from Naples the other day. He is a friend of both girls for the present, nothing more. P. and I agree we should like him as a son-in-law.

Thus spoke the descendant of republican revolutionaries, and one who was married to a man who had made his money out of trade.

People who remember those days describe the radiance with which Norina would enter a ball-room: arms outstretched, eyes afire, casting smiles in every direction. Delia would always be following, arms by her side, like a lady-in-waiting. It was understood that her hour of glory would come only when her sister was married.

Time had arrived to prepare for the visit to England. After much discussion the motorcar was sent ahead, in spite of 'two awful years at Marsala'. 'We *must* economise, or we shall be ruined!' True enough, exports had dropped by one-sixth. The Woodhouse firm was also in the doldrums – not that the owners had cared, until recently at any rate. Old Sam had died in 1891, whereupon Fred and his two brothers had each inherited a third share of the business. They used to take turns to pay annual visits to Marsala in the spring. Fred, however, was the only one who learnt Sicilian properly and who knew anything of the mechanics of the firm. Gradually even he began to lose interest; after all, by 1900 he had increased his personal capital to well over £100,000. The firm was left therefore mostly to the manager, while the three partners lived happy lives as English gentlemen, with large country houses and all the shooting, hunting and entertaining they could wish for. With the fall of their income at Marsala, however, they were now becoming worried, though the crisis did not break until 1912.

In 1906 or 7 one of Fred's sons, Robert,[11] had visited Malfitano. Tina had done her duty entertaining him and had been affable though distant. For one thing he was 'no match for our beloved Norina'; for another he 'lacked any artistic qualities'.

*Basle, 5 July 1908*

On our way to England. Left Palermo on the day of our silver wedding. Pleasant dinner on board with Prince Scalea, Vincenzo Florio, his inseparable friend 'Becco di Siringa' [Point of a Syringe, i.e. Ciccio Lampedusa, uncle of the author and so nicknamed because of his shape], not to mention 'Stinkydusa', as the girls call him, [Ferdinando Lampedusa, another uncle, who suffered from the same affliction as his father, Prince Giuseppe of Lampedusa, known as 'Piedifitusi' or Stinking Feet]. Crowds to see us off: Annina Montereale [of the Alliata family] thankful no doubt of the excuse to see Vincenzo Florio, – the *fiançailles,* though not announced, are practically settled. He will make a better husband than has been his brother, but he has no *senso morale. Pleasure* alone rules the day. If it is true that the Florios have lost so much of their money, how will they adapt their lives? . . .

Rome a night. Hugh left with us for Vallombrosa to join the Egertons who cannot bear to be without him. The Ambassador, whom Hugh calls the 'Old Noodle', is simply devoted to his young unpaid attaché, whom at first he did not want to have. Hugh ought to have more manly pursuits and not dedicate himself so much to jade, tapestries and *objets d'art.* Of course I do agree that he arranges his rooms beautifully.

Hugh Whitaker was the son of Willie's second wife, Rita Sartorius, and a young man of extraordinary taste and character, perhaps the most intelligent of the younger generation, with the exception of Audrey, Joss and Effie's daughter, who was a gifted 'cellist. Tina seems to have been a little alarmed by him. At any rate he lent the Pips his house in Curzon Street for the summer.

*26 Curzon Street, 25 July 1908*

On Hugh's recommendation went to see Maud Allan dance at the Palace Theatre. We were in a big box near the stage, so saw her well. The first dances were graceful, but I could not lose sight of her large *flat* foot, and the movements were monotonous. In *Salomé,* where she appears naked almost, one sees the great beauty of her back and torso; quite like the Venus Callipyge in Naples, but the scene though powerful is gruesome and revolting.[12]

Alec Hood, since the death of Queen Victoria, had been private secretary to the Princess of Wales (the future Queen Mary). He now wrote from Marlborough House to say that H.R.H. would like to call on Tina – 'quite a *private* visit'. There was the usual flurry. Hugh himself had been forewarned and, knowing of the Princess's reputation for 'taking a fancy' to the most valuable antique in the house and expecting to be given it as a present, had discreetly arranged to remain well out of the way in Germany.

*26 Curzon Street, 14 August 1908*

The Princess of Wales paid a pleasant visit. We found her neither dull nor silent, as some had said we should. We got hold of Cecil [Hugh's brother] to help to receive her. She thanked me for my gracious words about her mother, and said she had read my book with much interest. She is tactful, said the right thing to us all; spoke with Pip of his island

and his excavations, looked over the girls' album with Norina before signing her name. To Cecil of his racing and big game shooting, and at the end sent a message to Hugh about his jade collection. *She* has a head on her shoulders, and will make a good Queen. Everyone says it has been a most brilliant and wonderful Season. But what gossip, what immorality. The Duchesses of Rutland and Sutherland inviting Lina Cavalieri to their balls and parties as an honoured guest!! The King's displeasure with the latter Duchess is worth recording. She was to have sat next to him at a dinner but had to send word she was ill and could not go. The hostess, knowing nothing, turned to His Majesty saying how she regretted that this sudden illness prevented the Duchess coming. The King at once said: 'A very good thing. I hope a long time will elapse before I see her again.'

*26 Curzon Street, 8 September 1908*

Again hoping to get rid of Marsala, or better, turn it into a company. Frank, who has been staying with us, tells us that Mr Shackleton is to see Florio, to see if he can come to terms for taking over all his business. He has begged Shackleton to include us if possible. But this is not easy, as Florio is a complicated affair, and how much he may require ready money we don't know; a lot of capital has to be found. Dear Frank as usual has been most kind and devoted to our interests.

*Rome, 16 December 1908*

A long gap. We stayed at the Mandria, where Prince Alfonso of Bavaria took a great fancy to Norina.[13] Three weeks in Florence. We are staying at the Excelsior, fearing the quarantine at the Grand. Our friends have been overjoyed at the Duke of Abruzzi's engagement to Miss Elkins [American] being broken off. He seems to have been really in love with her. At the Mandria he was most charming; no gentleman in waiting, not even a valet.

Hugh has bought his beautiful tapestries for 52,000 francs, also the Aubusson curtains. His taste is wonderful and unerring. Alas! he keeps to his own set in Rome and makes no efforts in Society.

On 28 December there came the news of the appalling earthquake at Messina. It had happened at 5.20 that morning. In under forty seconds practically the whole town was in ruins, and a tidal wave twenty feet high had swept over Reggio Calabria, where the devastation had if anything been more total. Nobody knows even now quite how many people died in Messina; the most conservative estimate seems to be 77,000, but the figure could have been nearly 100,000, out of a population of some 150,000 for the whole *Comune*. 20,000 were killed in Reggio.

During the last half of the nineteenth century the buildings had grown in height and splendour, with surprisingly little heed for what had happened in the great earthquake of 1783. There had been tremors in 1894 and 1907, but if these were warnings they went unregarded. The Palizzata – the magnificent row of palaces along the Marina, that had so intrigued Lord Ormonde in 1832 – had been rebuilt to three storeys. On that December morning it was reduced to something like the ruins of Cassino in 1944. Terrible stories flooded from the Press: of the groans and cries of trapped people under 'dunes of rubble'; of fires burning for a fortnight, until extinguished by torrential rain; of the 'insupportable stench' of decay and roasted flesh; of the heavy pall of smoke and dust; of vicious looting; of dismembered limbs hanging from masonry; of young girls being kidnapped for Neapolitan brothels; of criminals escaping from prisons; of bloated bodies in the sea. When the Countess Nicoletta Canciafera's body was dug out, it was found that she had eaten her own fingers out of starvation – she was the sister of Bice Palma (Lampedusa). Her husband also died. One child was trapped for twelve days under her parents' bodies, which were being pecked by famished poultry. A woman, crazy with fear, was seen rushing around the ruins cradling her baby's severed head. Another woman who lost her child kept her husband alive by suckling him at her breast.[14]

Arthur Cheney, the U.S. Consul, and his wife were killed. Mrs Ogston, the wife of the British Vice-Consul, was killed. The British chaplain, the Rev. Charles Huleatt, his wife and entire family of four children were crushed to death,[15] as were Mr and Mrs Walker Oates, their children and governess. The U.S. Vice-Consul, Joseph Peirce, his wife and four children were buried beneath a three-storey house; 'a huge wave completed the destruction', and it was impossible to save them. The Sanderson family, fortunately, was away from Messina at the time. Out of sixty guests at the Hotel Trinacria only six survived; some of the women died by jumping out of the windows. The cathedral had been wrecked, and the twenty-six monolithic granite columns, brought from the Temple of Neptune at the Punta Faro, were smashed to pieces.

Giolitti, again Prime Minister, declared martial law. The Russian cruiser *Admiral Makaroff* and the American merchantman *Washington* were on the spot and their crew was able at once to help in the relief. British warships were hurriedly despatched from Malta. It was said that 15,000 people were dug out within the first two or three days. Relief poured in from all over the world, especially from the Americans, who built a temporary shanty town for survivors. A Lord Mayor's Fund raised £160,000. Alec Hood was at Taormina and took a lead in relief work; later he was decorated by the Italian Government. Meanwhile the shocks continued, and it was a very long while before any form of order could be reached.

A correspondent of *The Times* visited Messina on 7 January:

> And over all was the same awful silence. I did not see one hundred refugees. There are about two thousand left who mostly sleep in ships in the harbour, while perhaps six thousand are on the hills behind the town. The rest are dead or have fled. Or they are dying. The crowning horror is the belief, nay certainty, that under some of these hideous masses of fallen bricks and stone are human beings who are slowly perishing. Three more persons were dug out today.

As far as the British colony was concerned – the few descendants of those who had lingered on after the horrors of other great disasters – this had to be the last straw, and it virtually disappeared. Indeed the ruins of the earthquake were still to be seen thirty years later. In 1943 the Allied bombing brought new misery to Messina. 5000 people were then killed and the rebuilt cathedral was set on fire, the remnants of its mosaics and frescoes being finally destroyed.

The Pips went to Naples to help in settling refugee families. Then to Palermo, where the *Educatorio* Whitaker and *Infanzia Abbandonata* had necessarily become main centres for relief:

> *Malfitano, 10 January 1909*
>
> Work, work, work every day, all day, and yet one seems to do nothing. We find our society world really doing wonders; the *Comitato delle Dame,* formed for giving out clothes, works splendidly. On Tuesday 5th I receive a wire from Chimirri, telling me to help form a local committee of the *Patronato Orfani Regina Elena* [Queen Elena's Orphans' Fund], I receive also a telegram in same terms from Countess Spalletti, the *Patronato's* President in Rome, and I am to meet Prince Scipione Borghese who will be arriving with full instructions. . . . The Committee includes among others Princess Sant' Elia, the Marchesa De Seta, Franca Florio, Madame Notarbartolo and self. Princess Sant' Elia declines the presidency, so I am elected. I ask for time and say health will not allow my accepting. We however arrange a meeting at Malfitano that afternoon to talk things over, and again meet next

morning at the Prefettura. I accept presidency after pressure *temporanea-mente*. That afternoon I ask Prince Borghese if Giulia Trabia (now in Rome) could be added to the Committee, as in her I saw the permanent President.

*Malfitano, 20 January 1909*

The unidentified babies are the most difficult cases to deal with, and are most pitiful. As whole families have been swept away, it is in many cases hopeless to try and trace the parentage. Alfonso Scalia [cousin] told me that he had undertaken to meet the Red Cross trains at Catania arriving with wounded; on the third evening after the catastrophe a large basket was handed out, with fourteen babies wrapped in cotton wool, six were already dead. I have myself been dealing with the case of a child of six months, a boy, with '*tesoro mio*' embroidered on his shirt; he was brought to the children's hospital, wrapped in a sheet with the initials V.G. on it, having been given by a soldier to a woman, and found in Corso Garibaldi. That is all we know. Pip's appeal for money for the *Infanzia Abbandonata* has so far brought in £1200 from England.

The labour went on for many months. The Princess of Trabia agreed to become President. Some of the ladies had their eyes opened – 'the depravity of Messina was far beyond the usual behaviour of the lowest classes in a big seaport.' Franca Florio and the Princess of Sant' Elia soon proved to be broken reeds. The Princess of Torrebruna adopted an unknown orphan. At the *Infanzia Abbandonata* young girls became pregnant and had to be married off hurriedly. Tina put forward an idea for an orphanage at Messina with a *fattoria* (farm) attached. It was accepted enthusiastically by Chimirri, who was head of the *Patronato*, and the French ambassador promised a donation of 300,000 *lire* in the name of his country.

Then trouble hit Palermo.

*Malfitano, 14 July 1909*

We shall be thankful to leave this town. The last days have been excited by riots in the streets, fomented it is said by Florio and the *Sindaco* Trugini against the proposed *Convenzioni Marittime* [strikers had been replaced by the *Società di Navigazione*; Florio was perhaps fomenting trouble to give the port of Palermo an advantage over Naples]. P. on one occasion had his carriage surrounded by the mob, and they began unharnessing his horse. But he was recognised, and they called out 'E il Commendatore Whitaker. Lasciamolo passare.'

[It's Commendatore Whitaker. Let him pass.] So they reharnessed his horse and he was sent off in triumph with much applause. The Florio-Montereale wedding had to be put off a day or two in consequence of the riots. P. and the girls attended the ceremonies, also a *small* evening party at Casa Florio. Things had to be quiet – much as the Florios love display – on account of all Vincenzo's financial troubles. Ignazio has refused to come to an agreement with the banks and remains with a heavy mortgage on the *tonnare*. How will it all end?

Tina had for long hankered after a permanent *pied-à-terre* in Rome. Of Malfitano she wrote: 'I wish I cared more for our home, for it is undoubtedly beautiful.' That July therefore she and Pip acquired 44,000 square metres of Monti Parioli, with the intention perhaps of selling two-thirds of it five or six years later. Even she did not dream how successful such an investment would be. After World War I Monti Parioli became the most fashionable suburb of Rome, a position it still holds. Shades of Benjamin Ingham and Fifth Avenue.

*Claridge's, 2 September 1909*

. . . this dear old hotel, nice but expensive. Gwendoline Somaglia constantly with us. The Mazzarinos are here now, also Tosti. The latter is going to make Delia sing to him. Great agitation. Alas! I am glued to my bed. Hugh came to see me. No career – pity, but too much money and independence. Lady Cardigan's memoirs create a great sensation. So many people whose mothers and aunts are treated shamefully.[16] I am reminded of the story told me by Alick Yorke of the famous *cocotte* 'Skittles'[17] in Victorian times: 'Let us drink to the health of the head of my profession, the Countess of Cardigan.'

Tina was indeed really ill. She had cancer of the breast. Should she or should she not have an operation? She dreaded the thought, and especially the chloroform. The doctors pressed and tried to frighten her with the consequences of waiting. She decided against, and a nurse said: 'Mrs Whitaker, one sees you have the fighting instinct in you, and that you are the daughter of a soldier.'

They returned to Rome, where the doctors actually said an operation was inadvisable. Tina could not face moving from the Grand Hotel.

*Rome, 7 March 1910*

Still here after two months. On arrival found the Mazzarinos again, Madame Giovanna Florio and all the Trabias. Giulia more than kind in chaperoning the girls. There is an infinite charm in her, a charm that carries all before. People discuss who is the greatest lady in Rome – she or the Teano. Although Giulia is only a Florio by birth, and living in a hotel, she gains the day. Above all she is clever. She has all the subtle cuteness necessary to cope with the so varied a society as that in Rome, and she has an ambitious husband, *qui sait se faire valoir,* though personally shy. Giulia's only strong feeling is her maternal one, so she is not hampered otherwise by over-sensitiveness. I emphatically do not like the Mazzarinos. I hear they call me 'La Caprazza' [nannygoat].

Robert Hichens was pleased to be asked to one of Donna Maria Mazzoleni's parties. He admires her much. She is still a wonderful-looking creature, of a fine race with a force of a lioness in her eyes, that has enabled her to fight for her lover – and keep him. Norina is now flirting with Ferdinando Rospigliosi. They meet at the Sala Picchetti, skating. *Not* serious, I am glad to say. I can do nothing for the girls! 'Mais pour vous vos filles sont une idée fixe', Countess Santa Fiora said to me the other day when she came to see me. I met the Countess again two days ago on the bridge of the Pincio, and we sat together and had a long talk. There is a coarse side to her which jars on me, but I cannot help admiring her. *Elle a su vieillir,* and this is a great deal for a woman once the most beautiful of Rome.

The Tostis are gone. She is full of the house they have taken in Via Veneto for next winter. I shall miss them, or perhaps more her. She has such a charming desire to give me comfort through theosophy and Buddhism. On her last visit she told me an amusing story. She was going to marry Tosti – it had all been settled at last [they had been lovers for a long time]. He had a cold and she was reading the papers to him, when the Duke of Connaught was announced. She slipped away and hid in a sort of cupboard next to the hall; the Duke mistook the door, and discovered the lady! All she could find to say was: 'Well, sir, it really is all right, we are going to be married in a fort-night.' I, knowing the *dessous des cartes,* was amused at this story; poor Percy ffrench often told us the difficulty mutual friends had to make Tosti see that the patience, *et plus,* of Berthe deserved reward and recognition.

Tosti (who had been knighted in 1908) had been impressed by Delia's singing the previous autumn and had agreed to give her some lessons. Some say now that he had a crush on her. 'How he loved a joke,' Tina wrote many years later.

He always was making Delia sing his 'Baciami' [Kiss Me], asking if she had studied it with sufficient *concentration*. Norina said once: 'Indeed she has. She has screamed out the words so much I wonder the floor waiter hasn't come in and offered himself.' . . . His lessons were invaluable. Great artists such as Calvé and Melba did not disdain to go to him to pass over their part before starting on rehearsals of a new opera.

Tina was operated on two months later, at the Anglo-American nursing-home. 'The blank of illness and the relief of long tension. The chloroform given so well, so differently from in England, where I suffered the tortures of consciousness long after the rigidity of death had set in. This time barely a gasp – then sleep.' She went to Vallombrosa for her convalescence. Her diary lapsed, and she did not return to Malfitano until the end of February 1911: twenty months' absence.

Not surprisingly she left unrecorded the drama that had enveloped Ronny Gower and Frank Hird. The previous Christmas (1909) they had invited Shackleton to Hammerfield for Christmas.[18] Another guest was Josephine Browne, an ageing spinster from Tavistock whom Tina had met there at the time of her collapse. Miss Browne regarded herself as a mother-figure in Shackleton's life, and in return he was helping her with her investments. Already he had taken control of some £13,000 of her money. She now said that she had another £1000 to spare, which sum Shackleton easily persuaded her to hand over, subsequently saying that he had placed it in the Celtic Investment Trust financing a firm with the suspicious title of the North Mexico Land and Timber Company. When, in April, she suggested he might come to Tavistock to discuss her money, he simply shut her up: 'For goodness' sake, don't ask me now. I am so tired.'[19]

Shackleton had an overdraft of £40,000, for which Ronny Gower in part stood security. The rest was secured by 60,000 shares in the City of Monte Video Public Works Corporation. When Shackleton took over £5000 belonging to Ronny in exchange for some Monte Video stock, Frank Hird became worried, and with reason, for a few weeks later the directors of the Corporation were sued by a creditor. On 6 July 1910 it was found that the Corporation owed £943,000. On Shackleton's appearance a month later at the Bankruptcy Court it was reckoned that his own debts amounted to £85,000. After he was declared bankrupt he had the impudence to walk over to Frank Hird and Josephine Browne and grin in their faces. Frank pursued him and Sir Ernest Shackleton, shouting insults. He then wrote a series of libellous postcards to Sir Ernest – so libellous in fact that if he had not apologised in time he would have been prosecuted.

Ronny was ruined. Hammerfield, his furniture, his pictures, all his possessions had to be sold. On 8 March 1911 he too went bankrupt. Needless to say, the Sutherland family rallied, and Frank worked hard at his journalism to support him. As for Shackleton, his public examination had been postponed until 11 May. When that date came he failed to appear. He had fled the country.

Also, needless to say, Tina gave up trying to find buyers for Marsala. It had been a lucky escape, to say the least, and for once Joss's pig-headedness had been useful. He was one of those people who believed that if one did not reply to a letter it 'answered itself'. Tina had had to apologise to Frank Hird for his dilatoriness, just before leaving London:

> First I must explain that Joss will make *no* effort to get rid of the Concern, or even to turn it into a company, though he has consented to agree with his brothers if they accept any good offer or proposal made. By the will of the father, the business was left equally to the three brothers, but by *verbal* consent Joss as the elder one works it. We believe that at present Woodhouse, who have several sons, would not be willing to join, but Florio are certainly interested. The actual value of the *Baglio* Ingham and its surrounding must be about 6,000,000 *lire*. The Cinzano firm, who are making an enormous fortune in *Piedmontese* Marsala (besides the vermouth) in South America, might well be willing to take us in hand. After all, if the law, at present being pushed, passes for the protection for the name of Marsala, they will be obliged to have a *baglio* in Sicily.

One can imagine the letter being discussed at Hammerfield during that Christmas of 1909. Perhaps the passing of the law also had something to do with saving Ingham-Whitaker from the clutches of Mr Shackleton. Not that Cinzano were, for the time being, interested in acquiring it.

At Chamonix the Pips met the Sermonetas and got to know them well. At last Tina had found the ideal match for Norina. Roffredo Caetani, the second Sermoneta son and brother-in-law of Vittoria Teano, was the 'handsomest man you ever saw', with a shining, courtly character. Both his mother and grandmother were English. The Caetanis were among the greatest families in Italy. They were intelligent and talented. They had a superb palace.

Unfortunately, as Roffredo's sister has since said, 'Roffredo had only to smile at a girl – and he was always very nice to them – and she thought she had been chosen.' Or the girl's mother thought that her daughter had been chosen.

The months passed. Geneva, Lausanne, Stresa (to see the Duchess of San Teodoro), Mandria and Venice, packed with the bright lights of London society: the Duchess of Westminster, Lord Anglesey, Lady Radnor, Lady Juliet Duff, Lady Bective. This last (known as 'Queen') had become decidedly aged – in her zenith her sloping shoulders had caused her to be known as the 'beautiful champagne bottle'. When Delia was made to sing to her, she was so moved that she cried. 'It makes me think of the past. Oh, Tina, the harm one has done!'

*Rome, 3 February 1911*

. . . then to Florence. Busy time, seeing Janet Ross, Lady Paget, Lina Waterfield etc. Berenson reproached me for not letting him know I was there. He is certainly *simpatico,* but has many enemies. People say that Americans on his affidavit accept the authenticity of any picture, and that as he gets ten per cent on these commissions he does a good trade. *Chi lo sa?* If one believed everything in this world, few reputations would stand.

Pip left Rome after a week for some digging at the Cappiddazzu[20] on Motya, and we follow *subito dopo le feste.* Why have we stayed on? I suppose we are fulfilling our destiny, whatever that may be.

The gossip of the town is about the Trigonas, who reached a crisis a fortnight ago, when she came to Rome *with her lover* del Cugno, to resign as lady in waiting. But the Queen would not accept her demission. Not even Giulia Trabia can persuade husband and wife to make

THE CAPPIDDAZZU BY DELIA

peace – he is still having his affair with the actress from Scarpetta's company, and all the details were passed on to his wife by the usual kind friend in Palermo by means of an anonymous letter. Del Cugno is a cavalry officer and certainly very handsome. I would never have allowed Norina to go riding with him if I had then known the truth! In any case the Trigonas are now arrived at the Quirinale to do their usual February *servizio,* as if nothing was wrong between them. I really feel it is a mistake that the Queen has made. She should have let a little time elapse – such a public scandal, and such a precedent too, that the faults of a husband should make the faults of the wife condonable. How times have changed! Poor Teresa San Teodoro, now in this hotel, for years hiding her head under sackcloth and ashes, and this little woman *braying* out her shame before the world.

Scandal it was, but there was cataclysm round the corner. Countess Giulia Trigona was another of Bice Palma's sisters.[21] An attractive woman, black-haired and with a sweet disposition, she had married Count Romualdo Trigona of Sant' Elia in 1895 and was now aged thirty-four.

When she found out about her husband's romance there had been some terrible scenes. A legal separation had been discussed. Meanwhile she looked for consolation, soon to be found in Baron Vincenzo Paternò del Cugno, elegant and dashing, two years younger. They had met at a Florio reception. The flames leapt and he followed her to St Moritz, Frankfurt, Perugia. But he was a gambler and constantly needing money, which the Countess at first gladly provided. Then she felt remorse and tried to shake him off. In order to make her jealous, he pretended to be one of Norina's most ardent courtiers, with the immediate result that Tina asked him to dinner at Malfitano. His ruse succeeded and Giulia Trigona – 'lovely as a woman can only be when she is in love' – took him back. All her friends now got to know of her 'shame'. As she was a lady-in-waiting she decided she had no option but to resign. But the Queen refused and even arranged for Count Trigona to be at Court at the same time.

By the end of February 1911 arrangements for a separation had been revived. Del Cugno demanded that the Countess should give him part of her settlement money, to pay for some new debts. When she refused, he forced her to meet him anonymously at a small hotel near the railway station.

*Malfitano, 3 March 1911*

In the paper we read of the grisly assassination of poor Giulia Trigona. It happened yesterday in Rome at the Hotel Rebecchino, a fourth rate inn of ill repute. There del Cugno stabbed her viciously in the back and then pulled her to the bed and slit her throat. He was determined that all the world should know of their liaison, and at the same time to drag her down to the lowest depths by making her accept such a rendezvous. How could she have agreed to this last degrading meeting, when the deed of separation with her husband had been signed that morning, with the *distinct* understanding that, and promise on her part, that she would break with her lover? It now seems that Giulia never told the Queen all the truth when she came to Rome, and only spoke of the husband's faults and failings, dismissing her own as mere *flirtations*. It is believed that towards the end of her *servizio* she had confessed everything to the Queen, but it is not quite definite yet. Public opinion is much against Romualdo, as to avoid a scandal he took her back, and then later agreed to the deed of separation on condition that a part of her share should be given to pay *his* debts too. She was a poor, pretty, refined, witty creature, one of those eminently frivolous and inconsequential things who are bound to bring their men ruin and despair, unless ruled with a firm hand from the start.

Del Cugno had stabbed the Countess yet a third time after cutting her throat. He had then shot himself 'through the temple'. It was all very classical Sicilian, a question of honour: one of those terrible primeval reflexes.

But miraculously, incredibly, he had not died. On 27 June 1912, when he was recovered, he was sentenced to life imprisonment, with five years' solitary confinement. Ignazio Florio and Bice Palma were witnesses. Bice never recovered and for the next quarter of a century scarcely returned to Sicily. The event is thought to be one of the great formative factors on the character of her son, who often accompanied her on her wanderings abroad.

Thirty years later, in 1942, del Cugno was freed by Mussolini. He attempted to get in touch with some of his old friends, including Norina, but was firmly repulsed. He died in 1949, aged sixty-nine.

Another death, less violent but also a shock:

*Malfitano, 21 March 1911*
On Wednesday last at 7.30 p.m. dear Alick Yorke arrived from Syracuse and Egypt, where he had been with Hugh. He seemed fairly well, though very tired, and we noticed much thinner than he used to be. All Thursday he kept well, wrote letters in the morning, and in

the afternoon walked in the garden and saw friends who came to tea. He dined with us as usual, having put on a violet velvet suit of which he seemed very proud; he also wore a large buttonhole of a pale green orchid with violets round it.[22] He was however upset, having missed two rings which he said must have been stolen at the Savoy Hotel in Cairo, as he had noticed a woman prowling rather suspiciously about near his room the last night. He went to bed a little before us, saying he felt worn out. On Friday morning at six Pip was awoken by the servant for whom Alick had rung a little before – it seemed that Alick was suffering from something like a violent attack of indigestion and want of breath. P. sent for the doctor. Then at 8.30 a.m. Alick began to suffer again. At 9 the servant called us hurriedly, but before we could reach the room, all was over. The breaking of a small blood vessel at the back of the head had caused immediate heart failure. . . . Thus has disappeared a good man, a true Christian believer, the soul and life of the last ten years of the Victorian court.

And then yet another death:

*Rome, 25 June 1911*

Rumours of increasing cholera in Palermo. On the 18th, Sunday, we called on Madame Florio to say goodbye and found Annina sitting with her mother-in-law, looking ill and complaining of pains, terrified of cholera. We thought nothing of it, but the next day, on going to Maude's for a garden party, we were horrified to hear that poor Annina was dangerously ill with the disease. Nothing could save her, and on Tuesday the 20th she was dead. They say Vincenzo behaved splendidly, attending her, rubbing her, trying to snatch her from death until the last moment. Thus ends the short life of this good little creature, who was so devoted to her husband and whom he adored. Before dying she begged him to marry again, and he said he would never find anyone to love him the way she did.

1911 was the year of the last cholera epidemic in Palermo. It is not possible to assess the number of deaths as the Municipality abolished the cholera books after the Union – all the cholera deaths being henceforward registered with the others. Vincenzo did marry again, but there were no children. As his marriage with Annina had also been childless, the Florio dynasty in the male line was ended.

It was Teresa San Teodoro, now so odd-looking that boys ran after her in the street, who broke the sad news to Tina: Roffredo Caetani had married an American from Connecticut, Marguerite Chapin[23] – later

well-known, in post World War II years, as the brilliant foundress of the
multilingual literary review *Botteghe Oscure*.

*Pylewell, 20 October 1911*

So passes a dream for the girls. Charming Roffredo! The Duke and
Duchess wished him to marry one of them, but he never seriously
thought of it. How happy I should have been! The years pass, Norina
[now aged twenty-seven] is losing her good looks, which were of the
*beauté du diable* order, and she is not one who will marry for the sake of
marriage, though Delia perhaps will.

*Rome, 15 January 1912*

Whilst in London I went to see poor dear Lord Ronald in the charming
house at Hampstead where he has been installed. It is dreadful to see
him stricken in body, looking so so sad, and yet so handsome in his
bed, almost like a marble statue, so white and still. Frank is very
courageous.

Baron Wrangell [a middle-aged Russian widower with children]
turned up at Pylewell to see Delia and I tried not to encourage him too
much. Joseph, a young man in the Guards (nice), proposed to her and
she refused [a cousin had to do it for her]. She may take it up again!
He seemed upset and has consoled himself by going off with Hugh to
Ceylon.

*Rome, 10 February 1912*

P. hates the Grand Hotel, with all its scandals and *pettegolezzi* [gossip],
the rarefied air. He would be glad to have a house of our own. It is
however convenient for the girls to be here; they can always find
chaperones, and often there is an unexpected dance or game of bridge.
How I wish they would marry happily! Roffredo's wife, an insignificant American with bright eyes, makes me realise even more that he
might have been content with one of them. They are not easy to
please. I must say the Sermonetas would have been the only family
really suited to them.

We made the acquaintance of Durini [Marquis Ercole Durini]. He
is not right for Norina: too rough and noisy. Also a Marquis Francesco
Auletta has been making up to her, but he is far too Neapolitan. Being
descended from Giorgio Castriota Scandenberg, he is a pretender to
the Albanian throne. He is also, they say, descended from Saint
Gennaro.

As it happened, the affair with Auletta was to prove by far the most
serious of any so far.

On 29 September war had been declared by Italy on Turkey, with the object of acquiring Libya as a colony – the only North African country available. Speed was important, if Italy was not to be forestalled by the French or Germans. Tina's heart-throb of the 1870s, Alberto Pollio, was Chief of Staff and her friend the Marquis of San Giuliano, a Sicilian from Catania, was Foreign Minister. Maybe these facts influenced her when she wrote: 'I am one of those who think the time has come for Italy to assert herself.'

The conquest of Libya did not prove quite as easy as had been expected.

*Malfitano, 20 February 1912*

We find all our friends deeply engaged in attending to the wounded and sick soldiers. Giulia Trabia and Maria Niscemi are admirable, if possible too devoted, taking common soldiers about etc. The Princesses Fitalia [Polish] and Sant' Elia less *entirely* engrossed. They are *femmes du mondes* and keep better control over their feelings. Rose Camastra [French, descended from Marshal Ney and Princess de la Moskowa in her own right] most devoted of all and caught *rosalia* [German measles] from a soldier.

The Scipione Borgheses came to lunch, and afterwards we went to Sperlinga to watch the tennis. Suddenly Effie, who was playing, shouted to us to be quiet, as we were all talking. When the Prince kept on, she volleyed a ball straight at us. Fortunately no one was hit. Effie is not liked by the Sicilians who do not take to her eccentricities very kindly, but I have to explain that this is not the way that all English ladies behave.

*Fiuggi, 3 July 1912*

We find Chimirri delighted at the success of this place, which he created, as he did Vallombrosa. But we were very sad at leaving poor Maria Niscemi, hopelessly ill ['a wretched spectre' – *cf.* Angelica in the last chapter of *The Leopard*], with four or five months to live. Cancer. She will be a great loss to the city, as well as individually to her many friends, among the first being Pip and myself. She had a ready sympathy for anyone in distress, without any pettiness or jealousy. After the Earthquake disaster her work was untiring, and last summer, during the cholera epidemic, she was completely fearless of contagion, attending personally to the working of the several soup kitchens in the town, always to be seen ladling out soup and testing its quality. The whole of this winter she has worked energetically among the wounded from Tripolitania. She went on without rest and was still working when we left for Motya early in May, though she must have known she was ill. One day she said to me: 'Ora sono stanca, molto stanca!' [Now I am tired, very tired.] When we returned at the end of the month, she was lying in a darkened room, and the doctors had given their verdict, though she is *supposed* not to know it.

*Fiuggi, 12 July 1912*

On the 9th at table d'hôte lunch San Giuliano announced the taking of Misurata. He read the despatch with us all standing around him and amid enthusiastic applause, the waiters joining in. The band was called and the *marcia reale* [royal march] was played. San Giuliano seems well contented with the situation, and that the war should continue. All we have to do, he says, is to be careful not to tread on any big power's toes, and to play a steady *advancing* game.

Turkey ceded Libya at the Treaty of Ouchy three months later, though Italy's troubles there were by no means at an end.

Auletta had followed the Pips to Fiuggi. Tina watched him and Norina 'mooning about' with certain amusement. It was a shock when he turned up in Munich. Kind friends sent roses to the train when they left. 'For Norina – Auletta!'

So there really was something afoot. Tina could not help being worried. He was by no means the ideal match. In fact she found him rather stupid. Yet she did not want to upset Norina, if she was really, at long last, losing her heart. On the boat to Folkestone they met Gwendoline Somaglia and Duchess Massimo, who told Tina that their nephew Filippo Doria was in a nursing home. After Roffredo nobody could have been more desirable than Filippo as a son-in-law.

*Claridge's, 28 August 1912*

Sent Norina to see Filippo Doria on his back. For two years he has had tuberculosis of the spine. Cruel irony of fate. The only son of that great house!

Maria Niscemi died. Hugh was engaged to the shy but 'devoted' Lady Helen Bootle-Wilbraham: all very satisfactory, as not only was she Lady Radnor's granddaughter but a cousin of the Duchess of Sermoneta. But Filippo did not ask to see Norina again.

Tina was keeping up a lively correspondence with Robert Hichens and carefully treasured all his letters, which do not reflect a very endearing character. His protestations of friendship seem false and each letter is full of vague invitations which could not possibly be accepted – 'Tell me how you are. Why not come to Sicily *now?* Bring your motorcar and stay here at Taormina for *weeks.* I long to see you.' One has the impression, perhaps unfairly, that Robert Hichens, at that time, mattered most to Robert Hichens. He was loyal to poor ailing Maude Valérie White – 'she is in London to produce a ballet in which Pavlova will dance' – and of course to 'the Duke', Alec Hood. *The Garden of Allah* was 'doing wonders' in Chicago. It had earned him £1600 in the first three weeks. In a surprising burst of confidence he told Tina that his investments now brought him about £1300 a year and 'I am *earning* at present £10,000 a year.' *Bella Donna* was running in New York and was about to be performed in Australia.

Hichens did not care much about the fate of Ronny Gower and Frank Hird. Indeed he seemed anxious to dissociate himself from them entirely, although the Sutherland family features often in his autobiography.[24] They had 'simply made themselves ridiculous'. Shackleton had at last been arrested. He had been tracked down in Angola, where he had been working as a manager on a plantation. 'May it all now come out properly!' wrote Tina. But this was not to be altogether so. His case was heard on 21 January 1913. He was accused of defrauding Miss Browne of £1000 and of conspiring to defraud Ronny of £50,000 and Frank £6000. As a result he was sentenced to fifteen months' imprisonment. The furies had caught him up. He emerged from prison a broken creature, but the matter of the theft of the jewels remained officially unsolved.

As for Sir Arthur Vicars, he had retired to blessed obscurity at his sister's home, Kilmorna, in County Kerry. But in 1921 he was taken out of the house in his dressing gown and shot by a gang of thirty men of the I.R.A.; Kilmorna was burnt down. Captain Gorges, Shackleton's accomplice, was arrested in 1915, apparently for revolutionary activities. During a struggle he killed a policeman. He was found guilty of manslaughter and sentenced to twelve years' penal servitude.

Auletta came to Palermo, staying at the Palmes. He was shown off at both the Villa Sofia and Via Cavour and met with general approval. But . . . Just why was Tina uneasy?

That he is likeable there is no doubt. A gentleman in every sense of the word. Yet his character is weak. He has no *cultura*. He gambles, or used to be a gambler. What if he gets hold of Norina's money? And if he has a rich father-in-law to pay his debts? There are plenty of men here in Palermo who want to marry Norina. Will they not be jealous and try to ruin him at the gambling club?

CROSSING THE CAUSEWAY TO MOTYA BY DELIA

Against these objections of course there was the tempting possibility that if Norina married him she might even one day be a Queen. No wonder the poor girl suddenly became 'seized with terrible palpitations, her whole mucous membrane affected and swollen'.

Most of May was spent on Motya. Further excavations were proceeding at the Cappiddazzu. Pip was also turning his attention to what he termed the *cothon*, a small artificial basin which he thought might have served as an inland harbour to shelter Motyan ships during bad weather. If he was correct, he said, then it was something unique among Phoenician and Carthaginian ports.[25] A number of urns, beads, weapons and steles (engraved slabs used as gravestones) had also been unearthed. Not that Tina was so very interested. Meanwhile at Marsala there was a lot of talk about the plight of the Woodhouses. It seemed that Fred's two brothers had overspent themselves wildly, even using up some of the firm's liquid capital.[26]

What a relief to get back to civilisation.

*Fiuggi, 15 July 1913*

Beautiful new hotel. Many acquaintances coming and going. The Duke of Sermoneta and I witnessed from a little distance the meeting of the Marquis of San Giuliano with Signora Giolitti. He with a very low bow kissing her hand. The Duke said: 'A traverso la mano della moglie, bacia il piede del marito' [By means of the wife's hand he kisses the husband's foot]. The Countess Santa Fiora's conversation really amuses me. She has just returned from London, charmed by Harrods' Stores. And dear Chimirri is always so benevolent in his calm judgement of things and people. Auletta arrived just as we were leaving. I had a few words with him on the subject of Norina. Will he succeed with her? I cannot press her. Although he gambles (a vice I hate and dread more than Women), I think he might suit her, if only he would give this up. Ferdinando Belmonte, also at Fiuggi, spoke to me very highly of Auletta's way of playing – never getting in a rage etc. All Auletta's set like him and speak well of him. Others say he is full of debts, though not at all serious. Chimirri against him.

Festivities in honour of Maria Mazzoleni. Truly she is the apotheosis of those who stray from the paths of virtue. That she has great personal charm there is no doubt. Yet her beauty is gone, and I fear she is losing Ferdinando Belmonte for ever.

The tension over Auletta gave Norina a bad attack of asthma. After London, Tina took her to Switzerland for a cure, but as soon as they began to make preparations for a return to Italy the asthma started up again, worse than ever before.

*Rome, 14 January 1914*

The doctor wishes that Norina should take 20 inhalations of water from Salsomaggiore,[27] so we stay on here whilst P. goes to Motya. This suits Countess Negri who is most anxious we should meet a young diplomat, Count Miniscalchi. Nothing comes of it however. Baroness Pollio has a *progetto* [project] for Norina, a very attractive young officer, but my beloved Norina I fear will not marry a soldier [a mistaken prophecy] – she wishes to be *urged* and I cannot do this. Auletta plays about, but still less can I urge a gambler. And yet, and yet, in many ways I still feel he would suit her. He would be patient with all her fads and fancies. But *she* must be the one to wish it. She is so fine, so subtle, and she lost her chance (if she ever had it) with Roffredo.[28]

Auletta is never mentioned again in the diaries. When they returned to Palermo, Norina suddenly recovered. 'Very gay days – she stands the fatigue well.' There were receptions at Malfitano for the officers of Russian and British warships. Sir Rennell Rodd, now British ambassador in Rome, and 'Lady Rude' stayed three nights. He was 'proud of his fine nation' but seemed 'sad and grave' at the prospect of approaching war. Not so the Duke of Abruzzi, who came to Palermo as Admiral in command of an Italian naval contingent and was staying at the Villa Igiea. 'The first evening he danced entirely with our girls, and Norina settled he should dine with us to show them some tango steps, which he is not allowed to dance in public (though I think an indecent *one step* can be far worse!).' A quiet time on Motya, ruffled by a letter from Robert Hichens prophesying civil war in England that autumn: 'The millions of poor people cannot any longer stand the sight of the fantastic luxury of the few.'[29] Rome again, where Tina went to see the Duchess of Sermoneta. 'She wanted us to go to Fiuggi. There would have been a last chance with Livio [the youngest Sermoneta son], who has just been named Minister to Persia. But would we wish one of our girls to go there? They have neither alas! health. Doctor advises the Engadine for Norina.' Tina also saw Gwendoline Somaglia 'in her terrible predicament: entirely paralysed on the right side, having totally lost her speech and unable in any way to express herself, though her eyes are as intelligent as ever. Good kind friend, good woman in every way. Why should she suffer so cruelly?' To watch thus was almost like witnessing the passing of a whole epoch. And so it was; for the day was 28 June, when Archduke Franz Ferdinand was murdered at Sarajevo.

To the Engadine the Pips went, for a belated celebration of Norina's thirtieth birthday, and they were still there, perched high up in this playground of the wealthy, when the Great War broke, crashing and thundering in the countries around them.

*Campfer, 4 August 1914*

Since the 31st, when the sudden exodus of visitors and hotel servants (German) from St Moritz began, we have lived in constant emotion. The panic has been most strange, people leaving by rail in cattle waggons only to find themselves blocked at Basle and having to sleep in station waiting rooms. Those going back to Italy have gone to Chiavenna. . . . Pip is ever calm, and we for the present are not thinking of leaving. All our little affairs seem so petty compared to the horrors ahead. The only drawback is the difficulty in getting news – and money. Many rich Americans are marooned here because the banks won't cash cheques. There are only five men left in this village – all the others are gone for mobilisation. The housemaid on our floor has gone home today to help her father fetch in the hay. Giulia Trabia and her girls are gone down to Chiavenna.

*Campfer, 8 August 1914*

Four days since I wrote. We live on the *Corriere della Sera* for news. Today the taking of Liège by the Germans is announced. England has declared war. The Swiss seem to fear an invasion from Italy; their sympathies are clearly all with Germany. Italy maintains her neutrality for the moment, but a general mobilisation is expected next week notwithstanding. We personally are waiting on, as we rather dread the heat in Italy. Italians leave daily, the frontiers being still open. The British and Americans are begged to wait until provision is made by their governments for their safe return. In this hotel there are only nine guests left.

Stunned, hardly comprehending, they made their way slowly south by stages: Chiavenna, the Mandria, Florence, Rome. Meanwhile the French and British were in retreat. It was announced by San Giuliano that Italy would be neutral. The first young Whitaker was killed in action: Harold, second son of Arthur, 'shot down when patrolling' at Ypres – only a few weeks before Harold's mother had stoically written to Tina: 'We are glad our sons have such a fine foe to fight.' The Marquis Imperiali, the Italian ambassador in London, spread gloom at the Grand Hotel by saying that the war must inevitably last for years. Pip busied himself with writing a pamphlet on the causes of the war and the British point of view, with Tina translating it into Italian for him.[30]

*Rome, 5 December 1914*

Bülow is returning as German ambassador, to persuade us to stay neutral. This morning I met Camporeale [i.e. Bülow's brother-in-law]. Very sad, none of his usual joking. He told me Prince Doria has been suddenly seized with a fit and is supposed to be dying. They had been at school together in England. He saw him only the other day at the Senate, and Doria greeted him with his inevitable 'Hullo Piccadilly' – Camporeale's surname is Beccadelli and the boys called him that. It seems that Filippo intends to marry or has married the Scottish nurse who attended him through his long illness. At least it will be a better match than his uncle's, Lord Francis Pelham-Clinton, who married an impossible person and had to get a divorce. It is from the Newcastles, or rather from his grandmother, the Duchess, that the queer side comes. I remember my mother used to talk about the Duchess who was the only child of a Mr Hope of Deepdene – she was supposed to be very naive and just before our marriage said: 'The only wedding I have ever been to was Papa's and Mama's.'

A small section of the highest classes of Italians still preserve their allegiance to Germany and Austria, asserting that in those nations they see the guarantee of the continuance of aristocratic principle. Great Britain's tendencies point distinctly towards those liberties which will be detrimental to hereditary privileges. As a party, however, they do not count, in the great wave of popular enthusiasm for Italy's eventual participation in the great war of regeneration. Had an unpleasant evening last night. We and Giulia Trabia generally sit behind Luisa Mazzarino and her friends at the Grand. I went over to speak to her. Matilde Serao was there. Alas! They began pouring forth in favour of Germany.

*Rome, 25 December 1914*

Having done my best to avoid Luisa Mazzarino, I met her today on the wide stairs leading to the hall where we all sit. She stopped to embrace me, saying: 'Oggi, carissima, per il Santo Natale siamo tutti uguali' [Today, dearest, for the sake of Holy Christmas we are all the same].

Bülow's efforts were to be of no avail. As tension rose in the country, the secret Treaty of London was signed, with the promise of the eventual cession of the Austrian-owned Trent and Trieste to Italy. The British disaster at Gallipoli and the driving back of the Russians from Galicia increased the sense of urgency. The Italian Government resigned. There were ugly cries of 'war or revolution'. The memory of Garibaldi was invoked; D'Annunzio arrived in Rome and symbolically kissed Nino Bixio's sword in front of the Capitol. Then on 24 May 1915, amid general elation, Italy declared war on Austria.

56. Excavating at Motya, Delia sits on her Union Jack cushion. Pip at rear. Cav. Giuseppe Lipari-Cascio with white dundrearies.

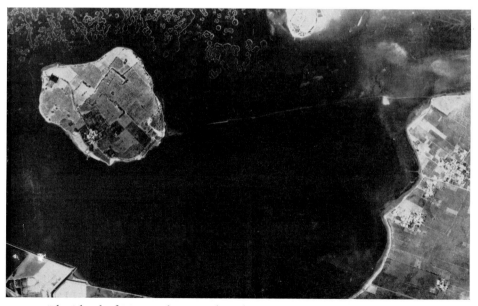

57. The island of Motya, showing the submarine causeway, running due north. *Cothon*, top left corner; Pip's villa, bottom left; Cappiddazzu and North Gate, bottom right corner. (*Photo: Col. Giulio Lipari.*)

58. Mussolini with General Antonino Di Giorgio as Minister of War, 1924.

59. Visit of George V, Queen Mary, Prince George (Duke of Kent) and Princess Victoria to Malfitano, 16 April 1925. Pip and Tina between the King and Queen; Sir Alexander Nelson Hood behind the Queen; Di Giorgio next to the Princess, Norina behind; Delia far right, without hat.

# PART SIX

## *Princes of Fascism*

# XXII

## No Ordinary Ambitious Climber

DURING the war a great deal of Tina's energies were taken up by an organisation in Palermo known as the *Alleanza Femminile,* of which she was Vice-President, and she obviously enjoyed the responsibility. Her particular interest was the care of 4500 children of soldiers at the front – housing, education, health, food. Later she became involved with finding work for soldiers' wives. She also founded a crèche for the babies of working mothers. The Villa Igiea was turned into a hospital for British officers; Lady Rodd was President and Tina Vice-President.

Two more nephews were killed in the first months of 1915: Trevor, another of Arthur's sons, and Hubert, only son of Joss and Effie. Trevor had died in a submarine somewhere near the Kiel Canal. Hubert had died at Gallipoli. Both were aged twenty-four. The tragedy about Hubert was that he was the only male among the children of the three families of Palermo Whitakers.

Livio Caetani was killed, so was Ottavio Tasca, one of the 'pigeons'. Sigismondo Giustiniani Bandini, a nephew of the Trabias, was killed on the very day of the Armistice. Raffaele Pedicini, who had married Audrey Whitaker, was wounded at Caporetto. The effect of the death of Gian Giacomo Somaglia on his poor mother was truly horrible – 'speechless, she can only show her sorrow, or rather give vent to it, by continual moaning, or even screaming'. Manfredi Trabia, after having been wounded early in the war, was killed by a bomb that exploded in the piazza of a small town near Treviso. His brother Ignazio was taken prisoner, and it was only discovered in 1919 that he had died. Jack Whitaker, Albert's son, was severely wounded and also taken prisoner, but survived.

The third Trabia brother, Giuseppe, died unmarried many years later. So the titles and property of the great house of Trabia and Butera passed to the female lines.

The excavations at Motya had more or less to be halted, particularly as Professor Gabrici, the new Director of the Palermo Museum, had actually gone so far as to forbid them. Pip, normally mild and slow to anger, was furious at such 'petty persecutions'. The visit to Motya by his friend, Dr Thomas Ashby of the British School in Rome, had been virtually wasted. Professor Gabrici now maintained that, since Motya was a site of national importance, any excavations must be done by Italian archaeologists. Useless for Pip to point out that the island was his own property; that he had had the initial enthusiasm, the perseverance and the capital; that he was British and wanted the British School to do the excavating. It was fortunate at least that the war prevented an open quarrel.

Among Pip's latest discoveries had been some pebble mosaics of a griffin and lions. The fact that they were so rare, denoting very early Greek work, did nothing whatsoever to help towards melting the steely heart of Gabrici. Pip therefore consoled himself during the war years by working at the manuscript of his book on Motya, a true labour of love and eventually published in 1922.

For Tina one bright spot at the time was the discovery that her sister-in-law Maude had 'toned down'. She also approved of Boots,[1] 'a dear little thing', born in 1898; 'How different from the days of Aileen: mother and daughter rivals in flirtations, and the daughter allowed to run wild!' As for Effie, she had taken Hubert's death very hardly. Not that it made any difference to her consistently hostile attitude towards her three daughters. If, for example, one of them came to wish her good morning, her expected retort would be: 'What's good about it?' Teresa San Teodoro continued in her letters to rub in the salt about Roffredo, e.g. 'Strange that the Duchess of Sermoneta should not be going to Florence for the event of the Caetani infant. I fear she is going to be disappointed in that American daughter-in-law and am sorry for her.'

Teresa's house on Lake Maggiore was filled with wounded. 'I live a most interesting life,' she wrote in 1916, 'seeing operations daily.' As for her daughter Vittoria Teano, 'she sits on her island and does nothing for anybody. I really shall be glad when she goes, sad to say, as her stolid presence oppresses me. And she is never loving to me, who have ever loved her so dearly. There you are far richer than I, for you possess two loving daughters who feed you daily with their faithful affection.'

Tina's diaries throughout the war were fairly scanty, concentrating mostly on the bare recital of news. Partly for this reason, partly because of the war's physical remoteness from Sicily, those years have to be treated somewhat summarily here.

Each summer (at first), whatever might be happening at the front, the Pips took to the mountains – either Fiuggi, Varese or Gressoney-St-Jean. All war work was dropped. Personal health became the priority.

*Varese, 9 September 1915*

We await news of the attack on Gorizia [not captured until August 1916]. A grim, alpine winter seems certain for our troops. . . . We hear of the death of Donna Laura Minghetti. At Fiuggi last month she was wonderfully clear of mind and reading Aristotle, with faithful old friends around her – Senators Chimirri, Blaserna and Casalini, her 'knights of the Round Table' as Chimirri said. I understand that, like King John of England, she fell a victim to some excess of food. Well do I remember those large imprudent plates of strawberries and cream, those *pizze napoletane*. Poor Chimirri so feared for the results and seemed weighed down by the responsibility of his friendship for her. On the 24th May, when Italy went to war, she is supposed to have said: 'All last winter I was the Bülows' mother. Now I regard myself simply as Minghetti's widow.'

1916 was 'long, tedious and cruel', 'ever the din of war in our daily life.' G. M. Trevelyan, with the Italian Red Cross at Gorizia, wrote to Tina of the tragedy of the ordinary soldiers, particularly her 'compatriots' the Sicilians, undergoing sordid and weary misery for a 'cause that had never been intelligibly explained to them'. In August 1917, whilst some of the fiercest fighting of the Italian war was happening on their eastern front, Frank Hird – who was in the Church Army – called on the Pips at Gressoney. Ronny had died in March 1916, his estate being valued at £2241. 8s. Latterly they had been living in a small house at Tunbridge Wells. Tina found Frank still full of jokes; it was a delight to meet him again. He proposed to Delia, but was rejected.

When winter came that year, the prospects for Italy seemed ugly. During the seventy-mile retreat from Caporetto she lost 340,000 men in killed, wounded and prisoners. An equal quantity arrived at the Piave without arms or in a state of total disorganisation. Lina Waterfield has written[2] that she heard from Tina that a Sicilian friend [*Il Contessone?*] had said that, when the Germans won the war, she proposed to give a ball in honour of the Kaiser. Tina was one of the bitterest critics of Cadorna,[3] who had been replaced as Commander-in-chief by Armando Diaz. She found him 'pig-headed to the last'.

As the daughter of an old soldier, I feel I am entitled to say this. May history give him the place of incompetence that he deserves. After playing up to the lowest elements in journalism, he now finds he had been abandoned by them. I cannot forget being told that his promotion years ago trembled in the balance, as he was considered incapable by the majority of his colleagues. At Pollio's urgent appeal in his favour, he *was* promoted. Alas for the consequences.

*Malfitano, 18 January 1918*

Italy's soldiers have retrieved their honour magnificently [by holding firm along the Piave], put in jeopardy by the narrow-minded Cadorna – but at what a cost. I always considered that Cadorna ought to have been kicked out when we had the crisis following the failure in the Trentino in the Spring of 1916. By chopping and changing his officers, he made them strangers to their men. The Italian soldier likes to make his officer into a *hero,* and will then be ready to die for him. The Third Army [which retreated in notably good order from Caporetto] was saved by the personal influence of the Duke of Aosta, who at the risk of an open quarrel with Cadorna refused to allow it to be interfered with. . . . Now Russia, democratised to the lowest ebb, is treating for a separate peace with Imperial Germany, the only state that still holds back the fatal wave of democracy, which is swaying the destinies of all the thrones of Europe. Yet surely a rotten republic such as the United States is already showing us democracy's perils. And France, splendid as she has been in her resistance and patriotism, does she not show that democracy and integrity in administration do not go together? Give me good hereditary traditions of rectitude, and let every opportunity be given for the really great mind to emerge from the lowest classes. In the Roman Church one sees many invaluable lessons to be accepted. . . . We fight on with the word Liberty on our lips, Liberty both collective and individual, but woe to the day when, by gradual concessions to the proletariat, we wake to find we have given ourselves over to the rabble. I turn to our greatest Italian statesman of modern days, Crispi. A hot-headed republican lawyer in the upheavals of 1848, he died the friend of Bismarck, and was with him the co-creator of the Triple Alliance: monarchist to the strongest degree! We cannot forget what great service he rendered his country in 1893-4, when once again at the helm, after the ignominious fall of Giolitti, he grappled with the rising so-called *fasci* of the working classes, realizing that under these apparently simple guilds, there was the birth of a dangerous coalition preparing for revolution.

To the end of her life Tina remained a staunch supporter of Monarchy. Her diary at this stage is filled with such True Blue *riflessioni filosofiche,* as she called them.

Early in 1918, whilst in Rome, she had been asked if she would take over the Presidency of the *Regione Infanzia* of the *Unione delle Donne Italiane*. It was an honour, but she turned it down. Firstly, she said, because of her health; secondly, because she bore a foreign name and felt that would be a disadvantage. Her hypochondria was getting ever worse, only exceeded by Norina's – even Tina was startled when Norina, watching some young people romping around, said: 'It makes one feel young again.' The scourge of Spanish 'flu did not help matters. As war made travelling to the north more difficult, the Pips had – prosaically for them – to spend August 1918 at Rocca di Papa, above Frascati: 'This dirty little place where rubbish from the house is just thrown out in heaps by the roadside; there are no W.C.s and the near woods are covered with mantraps. If we survive our visit here without fevers it will be a miracle.' Alas for the smart hotels of St Moritz and Marienbad.

All thoughts of marrying off Norina and Delia had long been given up. Tina spent gloomy hours musing over her mother's grave at the cemetery in Palermo. 'Oh my dearest, I could not have hoped to have kept you until now!' When at last the news, the glorious news, of the Armistice arrived, the family was ensconced in the Royal Hotel in Rome (because of the dangers of 'flu at the Grand).

*Rome, 13 November 1918*
In this bewildering tumult of joy, in a world bled white, among nations that have crumbled, I survey *myself*. What do I matter, have I mattered? As a wife I have perhaps helped to forward my husband's interests. As a *mother* I have failed. The girls are not married, they are not really happy. They jar on one another, though they love each other dearly.

Now aged sixty, she could only watch the antics of the bright young things with disdain:

*Rome, 18 November 1918*
From our window we saw the wonderful sight of Generals Diaz and Badoglio standing in a motor car with a seething crowd around them as they slowly progressed down the Via Nazionale. In the meantime Society, not realizing that we are on a bed of hot coals, prepares for mad amusement, throws off the heavy cares of those past years and rushes to buy evening dresses of 2000 *lire* and hats at 350. One looks around and sees the wounded, the orphans, the widows awaiting our help. . . . But the so-called upper classes are heedless to these calls of humanity. The Red Cross nurse of yesterday puts aside her uniform, prepares to dance and takes up her life of four years ago. God help us.

The highspots of the diary in 1919 were the visit to England, where they found 'dear old Claridge's as comfortable and quiet as ever' (dear in both senses, lunch being 7s, small dinner 10s 6d), and the possibility of Hugh – on the verge of a distressing divorce case – taking over the running of Marsala, where the bunglings of the manager Massey had caused even more chaos than usual. But after all Hugh did not seem to have 'quite the genius of a Benjamin Ingham'. In Palermo there was 'large unrest as everywhere else'. 'Young fellows returning from the army expect one knows not what and will not accept work unless largely paid. We cannot find a young footman for instance . . .'

The great ballroom at Malfitano had been silent now for many a year. Indeed Palermo was far less of a fashionable centre for the European rich. The Villa Igiea was once more the smartest spot. Stories of 'half naked dancers' there scandalised Tina. However, in the autumn of 1920, something happened which at once gave a fillip to social life in Palermo: the arrival of a young, high-spirited prince of the royal blood, in the shape of Prince Amedeo, Duke of Puglie, aged twenty-two.

The Prince had been sent to Palermo to finish his university studies – in 1931, on the death of his father, he became Duke of Aosta. He was quite exceptionally good-looking, very tall, and soon became accustomed to breaking hearts. His aide-de-camp in Palermo was Nino Medici di Marignano, who earlier in 1920 had married Nerina Gigliucci, granddaughter of Clara Novello. The whole party stayed in the splendid Villa Orléans. As Nerina was a friend of Boots Whitaker, and as Boots was pretty, lively, uncomplicated and aged twenty-two, it stood to reason that the Villa Sofia should feature more in the life of Prince Amedeo than Malfitano.

Maude may no longer have been 'flirtatious', but at least she knew how to give parties, the more impromptu the better. She thought nothing of telling the cook in an afternoon that fifty people were coming to lunch the next day. There was a lack of formality about the Villa Sofia which young people enjoyed.[4] Then the Villa Igiea was not so very far off; one could always go on there after a party and watch the apache dancers of which Aunt Tina so much disapproved.

Nerina Medici has left descriptions of her stay at the Villa Orléans.[5] It was all tremendously sumptuous, the floors of majolica, the fires of delicious-smelling orange wood, private drawing-rooms for everybody, barefoot black servants in orange shirts and blue fezzes, breakfast out of doors under cascading bougainvilleas. There were trips out of town to Agrigentum and Monreale. Nerina was introduced to the Princess of Trabia, the 'dearest person you can imagine', with enormous charm and warmth. 'Boots is having the time of her life,' noted Tina on 10 February 1921, 'and is off with the Prince, the Medicis, some young men and women for a three days expedition to Mount Etna. People tell me the Prince said 'Sono tutti così snob, che li porto dove voglio' [They're all such snobs, that I take them where I want]. The journey was indeed all very strenuous, with the worst part on foot, nights spent on mattresses in rest-houses, and only candles for light. And the Prince was always followed by his huge Alsatian, Mowgli.

When Prince Amedeo's younger brother, Aimone, Duke of Spoleto, arrived, there were other exciting trips. Boots went everywhere with them.

*Malfitano, 28 March 1921*

Coming out of Church saw Boots looking so ill, with no voice. On Good Friday her mother told us that she had not been able to shake off the chill caught during the wild expedition to Selinunte and Marsala with two Princes a fortnight before. A picnic at Mondello, dancing at the Villa Sofia, until it was time to accompany the Princes to the boat, wound up Easter Sunday. *Addio* to those mad two months of gaiety.

*Malfitano, 4 April 1921*

We have Cecil staying with us now. He was rather shocked I gather at the goings on of Boots and the Princes. Poor little thing has been in bed a week, trying to recover from all her fatigues. Her mother is to blame, as all that can have come out of this flirtation is that Boots may have lost her heart to this undoubtedly *simpatico* Duke of Puglie. The goings on at Marsala and on Motya, according to Pace [Professor Biagio Pace, an archaeologist and a leading light in the Colonial Office in Rome; he had helped to arrange for the house on Motya to be opened up for the royal party on a bathing visit] were almost unbelievable. I thought at first Delia was foolish not to have given in and gone with them, but I now realize that our girls would have been out of place. I hear that, on returning from Church, Boots actually fainted.

News now came that Frank Hird was engaged to a 'nice young lady, suitable in every way and with money', called Gladys Sinclair. Unfortunately this view of Gladys was not altogether shared by the Pips when they came to meet her. The 'young lady' was aged forty-two and to them she seemed strident, unattractive and jealous of Frank's old friends. Worse, she had less money than Frank had expected. He had married her, it seemed, on the strength of a recommendation by one of his cronies, her uncle, a Colonel Hugh Sinclair.

Another friend had been made. This was General Antonino Di Giorgio, a small, somewhat self-important Sicilian, unmarried and aged fifty-four, with a great war record behind him, not only in the colonies but during the war on the Ortigara and Monte Grappa. He had proved unusually attentive the previous winter.

*Vallombrosa, 8 August 1921*

General Di Giorgio came to Palermo both for Norina's and Delia's birthdays. In Rome we saw him practically every day and he took the girls out in the evenings. Does Norina care about him? He saw us off at 8 a.m. when we came here on the 11th July. She seemed very miserable, *crying* half the journey. I pretended not to notice. Again the other day she was upset when she had a letter from him saying he was going to Sicily. She answered it but said nothing to us.

*Vallombrosa, 19 August 1921*

On the 16th we were surprised by a visit from General Di Giorgio. Norina has had two or three letters from him, with red eyes afterwards. I was alarmed and mentioned this in a letter to Valentine and Peppino Scalea; I said I could not understand that she should have anything more than friendship with the General. They wrote me on the subject saying they thought he is *épris* with her, but that there was some *malinteso* [misunderstanding]. Did I do wrong and precipitate matters? Well at all events, he had it out with her on a moonlight walk. Norina said *no*, that she wanted only friendship. Late that evening she went into Margherita's [Margherita Bordonaro: daughter of Gabriele Bordonaro and Charlotte Gardner] room and cried. M. asked her if it was that she could not make up her mind, and she said yes, that was the difficulty. . . . I feel I am responsible in a way, because I feel sure the Scaleas urged him to come up here. He left yesterday, having spoken about the affair to Delia and saying he wished to speak to me. So I broached the subject, meeting him yesterday morning. He left at 12 by train with a send-off of friends and acquaintances. 'Funerale di prima classe', he whispered to Delia and me. But is it really at an end? Does he care for her? Does she perhaps doubt this, and so hesitate? I feel that she does not wish to confide in me.

*Baveno, 14 September 1921*

P. and I both considered that we would have liked Norina to have a quiet month to think things over without seeing him, but gave in, and he stayed until the day before we left. They seem as if they were coming to an understanding, but I feel I cannot urge her. He has many friends, is a charming fellow, is a great patriot, a brilliant soldier (though, they say, quarrelsome) and politician, but will he make a good and faithful husband? I doubt it; yet everybody thinks I must not discourage her. She will be a miserable old maid if she does not marry. Why oh! why did she not meet her fate when she was strong and young and full of life? Are her sufferings hysteria, or is it general weakness? Her doctor urged last winter that she should marry for her health. I am tormented and worried beyond description. Di Giorgio has asked permission to come here and may turn up any day from tomorrow. Ought I to speak to her before he comes? I feel I am letting her drift, and yet what am I to do? No good pointing out that he is only nine years younger than me. After all she is a woman of 37. Yet she does not seem to realize that at his age a man is likely to look upon matrimony from a practical point of view and that she must not expect too much romance from him.

*Baveno, 18 September 1921*

So it was the *Scaleas* who hinted, on introducing him to us, that he might have success with one of the girls. He thought it would be an easy conquest, having been successful in illegitimate love affairs throughout his life (mainly I believe with dark, rather common, flashy-looking women from Naples), and fixed his attentions on Norina. He did not make open love to her, as others would have done, but insinuated himself into her affections. He would pretend to ask her privately for advice on important matters, such as which army post to accept, and kept her constantly in a flutter. Her tears at our departure in Rome last July moved him, and he realized, I gather, that he had burnt his wings on the flirtation, which he had intended should end prosaically in a marriage of a calm kind without romance or great love.

*Rome, 12 November 1921*

I have not written of *the* event in our family! Di Giorgio, whom I now call Antonino, had a long conversation with Norina, and on the evening of the 22nd he brought her into Pip's room and introduced his *fiancée* to us. That morning he had had a lengthy talk with me by appointment, and the business part had been settled. The next morning I suggested announcing the engagement, but Norina would not hear of it, when I had even prepared the first batch of letters, 28 in all. Her shyness lasted some days. Nothing was said even when Prince Aimone and the Duke of Puglie met the girls for lunch with Antonino at Pallanza! . . . At Milan I had Norina examined by Professor Pescarolo who found nothing organically wrong and said that marriage and a new life would be the best thing for her. I cannot help feeling anxious, though I am thankful to see that so many of her little fads are disappearing. Happy couple they indeed appear to be, after so many misunderstandings covering a year.

*Rome, 18 November 1921*

Antonino is trying to settle up about the Villa we are building on Monti Parioli. He and Norina may want to live there [the property had increased by over five times since the Pips bought it]. And now we have a terrible *sciopero* [strike] which paralyses everything. There has been the fascist congress here these days, and in some row the black-shirts killed a railwayman. So now we have a dearth not only of the railways but of trams, cabs and newspapers. What a ruin for the country. Foreigners will avoid Italy this winter, but that is the least of it. Industrial enterprises are hung up and disorder reigns. There is no discipline and no order. The Government is helpless against the *fascisti*. Antonino says that never should they have been permitted to hold their congress in Rome.

It was at this congress that the fascist party was officially born. When its programme was published, the swing to the extreme right was shown to be decisive. Mussolini's ideas, conceived in reaction against communism, were revealed as a menace to the whole existence of the liberal state.

Antonino accompanied the family to Palermo. Effie, still with a parrot on her shoulder – in Palermo she was known as Mrs Whitaker *Pappagallo* (Parrot) having actually appeared as such in a society column before the war – and Joss were on the same passenger boat. It was a dreadfully rough crossing. 'Antonino was obviously charmed to have a family to look after. One sees it is a novelty for him. Whatever happens, I have a strong man at the helm.' But, Tina noted darkly, he suffered often from dyspepsia, which 'as we all know is bad for the temper'. As usual, on returning to Palermo, her first visit was to the cemetery. Would her mother have approved of the marriage? 'My father would have been delighted at all events.'

The wedding had to be postponed because of Norina's 'flu. Then there was a landslide at Antonino's native village, San Fratello Acquedolci, near Messina. It was decided that Peppino Scalea, now mayor of Palermo, must perform the civil marriage ceremony at the *Municipio* on 4 February, and for this he had to be summoned specially from Rome. All the presents were displayed at Malfitano, and Di Giorgio made a great point that they must not be cleared away until his brother had arrived. Very inconvenient, as the Protestant ceremony was to be held in the redecorated ballroom on the next morning, Sunday. Then in the evening Pip 'was seized with a sort of collapse, with violent shivering, and gave us a great fright.' But it was only 'nerves' and he recovered in time for the Catholic church service on Monday morning. 'An agitated wedding,' Tina with reason described it, as the couple set off for a three weeks' honeymoon on Motya.

Norina wrote every day to her mother. All this excitement was somewhat dashed by the death of Ben Whitaker (Benny), Pip's eldest brother. He had been on a visit to Palermo and had collapsed and died on his way home at Mentone. Then there had been the gloom surrounding Princess Beatrice, who was at the Villa Igiea. Just as she was about to motor up to Malfitano for lunch, news came of another disaster: her son Prince Leopold had died. 'Of course, like his uncle, the Duke of Albany, he had had scrofula and only one skin. He was lame and, as with the Queen of Spain's children, always very delicate. Coburg heredity!'

Antonino, who half sympathised with Mussolini, had returned to politics. Suddenly he went dashing to Rome. There was a new Government with Luigi Facta Prime Minister, and he wanted his military future clarified. When, however, he was offered the job of Commander-in-chief at Florence, he prudently refused it. Much of northern Italy, thanks to fascist terrorism, was in a ferment, and he realised it would be best to await the outcome.

But he had to be back in Palermo for a dramatic event:

*Malfitano, 22 April 1922*

Yesterday was a memorable day. Peppino Scalea had a duel with Empedocle Restivo, President of the Chamber of Commerce, who had written him an insulting letter because he had not been asked to accompany Peppino to Rome in order to invite the King to inaugurate the new port here in Palermo. Restivo is a bad lot and I suspect a real *Mafioso*; being a lawyer, he knows how to be dishonest 'legally'. He had never before taken the smallest interest in the affair, on Peppino's various visits to Rome, so Peppino had taken Rajan instead. We had two days of excitement as Antonino was one of the seconds for Peppino and got him to have Camastra [Peppino's first cousin] as the other. This was a happy move, as Restivo in his letter had said that Trabia [Camastra's brother] had an *eterno rimorso* at using his influence to make Peppino mayor. In the meantime, all Thursday having been passed in trying to avoid the thing, the duel took place yesterday morning in Vincenzo Florio's garden. Very early our girls phoned poor Valentine, who knew nothing and was sleeping out at Tommaso Natale (with the children, who have whooping cough), telling her that I wanted to speak to her, and that as I had to give an urgent answer to someone – would she come here at once and we would send the car for her? She accepted; all went well, and when she arrived we were able to give her all the news, that the duel had taken place, with only a scratch on each side. . . . We had a dinner in the evening for the Scaleas, General Basso (C-in-C, Sicily), General Lisi Natoli (from Messina) and Colonel Streva (Antonino's colleague from Somalia and Libya days). *Intanto* electricity remained in the air, and Norina and Antonino had their first serious quarrel over a futility. Norina almost had hysterics. He would not give in. Delia was mixed up in it, and they could not go to the Rosenthal concert as previously arranged, Norina being too upset.

Tina had become very intrigued by Antonino's character. 'He is no ordinary ambitious climber, but a self-made man concerned not with the piling up of a fortune but solely with the good of his country.' English relatives thought him strutting and bossy, typical of the sort of man who got on well during the Mussolini era. Tina saw him now as a kind of super-man.

He had been born on 22 September 1867 and had gained two bronze medals in the Eritrean campaign of 1896, the first at Adowa and the second at Aga. In 1908 he went to Somalia. A later biographer[6] makes much of his valour during this period, and how he was responsible for smashing the legend of the invincibility of the Mad Mullah. His subsequent exploits there, however, were drenched in mystery, and even Tina was unable for a long while to get at the truth. It seems that he quarrelled with the Governor of Somalia, possibly over the matter of purported cruelty to *askari* troops, and that this resulted in a court-martial, much publicised in the Press; after all he was only a major, and the Governor (Carletti) no doubt resented his characteristically dictatorial manner. But Antonino's reputation was redeemed in 1912, when he won a silver medal in Libya and received friendly letters of congratulation from Cadorna.

In 1913 he entered politics. When the war came he fought on the bloody summit of the Ortigara, on the Trentino frontier, in command of a contingent of *alpini*. The Ortigara was over six thousand feet high, and the action one of the grimmest. On 26 October 1917, when the retreat from Caporetto was in full flow, Cadorna wired him in Rome to take over two divisions. The success of this *Corpo d'Armata Speciale* was the glory of Antonino's career. When Tina wrote of Italy's soldiers retrieving the honour of their country, little did she realise that one of the chief heroes would become her son-in-law. According to Tina, he was amazed, on arriving at the Front, to find that certain letters he had written to Cadorna, warning him of political opposition in Rome, had been deliberately suppressed. Then came the Grappa, which D'Annunzio described as the 'sublime altar of expiation'. Antonino took part in the attack at Montello in June 1918 and his unit was one of the first to cross the 'sacred river' in the final great battle of Vittorio Veneto. For these various exploits he was honoured with the 'supreme decoration' first of *cavaliere,* then of *commendatore,* and finally of *grande ufficiale* of the Order of Savoy. In 1921 he became 'disgusted' with politics, from which he had just retired at the start of his courting of Norina.

*Malfitano, 7 June 1922*

As we were preparing to leave Motya, a message came from the Mayor of Marsala asking Pip whether he would permit a visit to Motya being included in the itinerary of the King to Marsala. Naturally we said yes, but I – fearing the excitement and fatigue for P. *if* it came off – thought we had better be away and get Antonino to do the honours. . . . Yesterday A. was at the King's inauguration of the port and in the evening there was a *serata di gala*. Antonino and Norina had a box with the Scaleas. She really looked extremely pretty, and the King and all his entourage kept gazing up at them. . . . Poor Delia meanwhile having a dull time. . . . Then today Antonino put on full uniform and went with Norina to the Favorita, to see the King give the gold medal to the Aosta *Brigata,* which won it under Antonino at the famous defence of the Grappa after Caporetto. Very unjustly no special invitation was sent to Antonino. His heroism was never properly acknowledged afterwards. And Badoglio, the cause in great part of the original débâcle, was given an army to command! When Lord Plumer was here this winter he said on leaving: 'Tell Di Giorgio on no account to give up his career. He is a *brilliant* officer.' Joffre said that the defence of the Grappa had no parallel in history except in Marshal Ney's famous retreat from Moscow. . . . Poor little Boots is better, but still far from well. She had thought of going to the Villa Scalea for the reception in honour of the King, but said she did not feel up to it, and that she had fever. Poor soul. She pays dearly for all her mad gaieties last winter.

Unfortunately we know next to nothing of the King's visit to Motya, apart from the fact that it was a 'great success' and that 'Pip and Norina stood the strain well'; Tina, who had never liked the King, stayed away, on the plea of being 'seedy'. There were no hitches and it all lasted two hours. And so, at last, the time came for that leisurely journey to London. It was quite like times of yore.

*Rome, 28 July 1922*

Here we find the Marchesa Imperiali, quite pleasant, bitterly regretting her husband being turned out of England [as Ambassador]. He has been replaced by Giacomo De Martino [the old pre-war friend],[7] whose wife is totally unfit for such a post. She was in Palermo last winter to meet a lover, and besides her loose conduct is also of low extraction. Orlando [Vittorio Emanuele Orlando, Sicilian, Prime Minister 1917–19] has been playing bridge with Delia. Somehow *il s'écoute*, as the French say, and there is a want of depth of character in his face, though clearly he is very intelligent and quick. I only had one little talk with him, on Poland. He said Poland's ambition to be united at once may be her undoing. Never will a powerful Germany submit to having her finest province cut off from her to give Poland a sea port. Princess Jane San Faustino is as usual full of go and complaints, and most amusing. At present she is against what she calls the 'free love couples', though some have got it more or less straight. The Palfis are at long last married. Dora ex-Rudinì [she had divorced Carlo Rudinì] is now married to Prince Odescalchi; he has got himself into an awful mess over the war – a traitor to his country [Hungary], and to Italy [getting off military service by saying he was Hungarian in Italy, and vice versa.][8] At any rate he has now succeeded in getting an Italian passport, though Belmonte says society will never receive him. Dora is very clever, not for nothing the daughter of Labouchere; she is rich, attractive and I should say unscrupulous. She is also much in love with her husband and means to see him through, and is starting a weekly political and social paper, like *Truth* [Labouchere's paper] I suppose. She is also buttering up the Vatican, and able as she is to grease every one's paw there is little doubt that the couple will be floated very shortly. A large house and some good dinners go a long way.

*London, 26 September 1922*

Antonino has been very impressed by the London buses. Yesterday he had an audience with the Prince of Piedmont, who is in London, but he would not accept an invitation for himself and Norina to the Embassy, as he considers the Ambassador has been rude to him, not asking him until now. The De Martinos have made all sorts of social *gaffes* and are quite beneath the situation. To Italians the talk and gossip about Princess Yolanda has been painful: going to a noisy, small hotel and running about with a group of cavalry officers, attending Ascot races very badly dressed etc. Last, but not least, Antonino has been humiliated by the sight of Carlo Schanzer, as Italian minister for foreign affairs, hanging around for a fortnight, waiting like a lackey to be received by Lloyd George.

On 23 October Tina was in Rome. 'Italy seems to be returning to the old days of the Guelphs and Ghibellines,' she wrote. 'The country is overrun by different factions, the fascists being by far the largest. . . . How long will the mask of monarchy remain? *Fascismo* may however split on this. The army is fascist now and may decide to remain monarchical. . . . The old fox Giolitti still commands the situation, the Prime Minister Facta and his weak government being entirely subservient to him.' Whilst in Florence she had seen black-shirts brawling in the streets outside the hotel and two people killed. But this was nothing to the terrorist tactics that were going on elsewhere. To the ordinary citizen all was confusion, communism being the greatest fear. On 24 October there was a huge fascist congress in Naples, and it was on that day that the famous 'March on Rome' was decided upon. On the twenty-eighth a state of siege was declared throughout Italy. On the thirtieth Mussolini became Prime Minister.

*Malfitano, 25 November 1922*

We arrived here on the 20th. Rome was quite calm, and Mussolini settled in his exalted position. How long will the wave of quasi universal praise last at his feet? Will not the breakers rush ahead and carry him off his pedestal? Or is he so great, that he can stem the tide of malcontents and those with disappointed ambitions, who must rise up inevitably against him? He trampled, in his speech to Parliament, on the dignity of that assembly in a way no other man had ever done before. He was received by the Senate with joyous acclamations, not a word of reproof rising in the defence of those institutions of the State that he had crushed. Italy has indeed fallen low, for such a consensus to be possible. Those two days when it was obvious that Facta's government would have to succumb were truly wonderful. On that memorable morning of the 28th, when we woke to find the state of siege proclaimed, it seems matters proceeded as follows. The Ministers sat in conference all night. In the morning Facta was sent to the King with the document to sign, but his Majesty refused at once to do so and said he must think it over. When Facta returned to the other Ministers he was told that the proclamation had already been sent out and wired all over Italy, and that he must return and insist on the King signing at once. This he did, but the King at once jumped down his throat and said: 'What, you have dared to do this without my signature? This is unconstitutional. I now absolutely refuse to sign the decree.' Facta returned, and it was then that overtures were begun to form a fascist ministry under Salandra [Prime Minister in 1916]. . . . But Mussolini showed his colours, and Facta was seen to be in tears. May this new era bring the regeneration we all hope for.

*Malfitano, 29 November 1922*

Lady Rodd has turned up with two little grown up daughters, to shew them Sicily she says, though I think chiefly to see Prince Amedeo. Oh these foolish mothers. A repetition of the Boots episode, though let us hope in a less pronounced form. Professor Biagio Pace is full of excitement about his *fascisti*. He told us he went to the Naples meeting and was given the order to form the group destined to occupy the Palazzo Chigi, the Ministry for the Colonies. . . . The Greek Ministers of King Constantine have been tried, condemned and shot. And while this awful condition was going on in their country, here in Palermo the King and Queen of Greece were accepting little tea parties and going to the motor races, in three cars one of which belonging to Commander-in-Chief Basso. They came here in September, when exiled from Athens, on a British man o' war. At first they took refuge in the Hotel des Palmes and then passed to the Villa Igiea where after two months they still are. Giulia Trabia is much interested in the sadness of the ex-Queen Sophia. She asked me to tea last week to meet them. She, the Queen, has large grey-blue, very sad and patient eyes. He seems stunned, or more likely indifferent. It is a *banal* face with little expression. Indeed the execution of his Ministers has not seemed to turn the even tide of his life. Frank Hird writes me that the entourage in Switzerland was most undesirable. Here the King's chief outside interest seems to be watching the vulgar dancing at the Villa Igiea. They have their three daughters with them: the Crown Princess of Roumania [Helen], who I thought quite charming, pretty, simple, very intelligent and observant; Princess Irene, aged 19, nice-looking but with the King's dull expression [Prince Aimone's future wife, married in 1939]; and a small child aged nine [Catherine], whom I have only seen at prayer, as they frequent our English church – Audrey played the violincello very well indeed for them yesterday. I am glad, as Effie cut them at Sperlinga, on account of Queen Sophia being the sister of the Kaiser. Prince Amedeo is now always with the Greek Royal party. Will they tame him? He certainly is most attractive, but now he should rein himself in, be more the Royal Prince. There is only one life between him and the throne, if throne there is to be!

*Malfitano, 12 January 1923*

Yesterday morning the ex-King of Greece died, suddenly at the Villa Igiea. They were actually on the eve of departure, on a short visit to the Duchess of Aosta in Naples, *en route* to settling in Florence. They tried to assure people who went to see them that they had always been faithful to the Entente, and that it was only the intrigues of Venizelos who made out the contrary. Time will show, but it seems unlikely. . . . The evening before there was a picnic dinner at the Villa Igiea, and the princesses joined the party after. The King sat up a little later than usual and seemed pleased to see them enjoying themselves. The next morning he was dead . . . Prince Amedeo is in Rome for three months' cavalry lessons. Better so for Boots. She quite realizes that the flirtation is at an end, and does not now wear the bracelet he gave her.

*Malfitano, 21 January 1923*

Norina up and about again after her little mishap [a miscarriage, the only mention, even of a pregnancy, in the diary – she had been frightened at a circus when a lion-tamer could not get his head out of a lion's jaws], which kept her on the sick list since Xmas. Antonino returned home from Rome on Thursday. He seems to think well of Mussolini, but the army is not pleased to see Diaz as Minister of War. Will Antonino ever get very involved with Mussolini, as he should be? It is doubtful. His health may even be an obstacle.

*Malfitano, 24 March 1923*

Two brothers gone in less than a fortnight. Arthur had been getting gradually worse since a relapse in January. . . . Bob was seized with a more or less sudden illness on the evening of the 12th. He had attended

Church the day before, in seemingly perfect health. On the Monday Maude refused to see Giulia Trabia because he was not feeling well; Giulia had called to condole about Arthur. On that night he became much worse and made Maude send for the doctor, who at once did a *piqûre* of camphorated oil for the heart. . . . A week later it was all over. It seems that Maude had been told that the heart was wrong two years ago, but he – knowing nothing – continued smoking his usual ten cigars a day. The meeting of Joss and Pip on the stairs of the Villa Sofia was painful, the two much older, losing that younger brother whom they loved.

*Motya, 7 May 1923*

We left Palermo on the 1st, but slept at the *Baglio,* as our train was $2\frac{1}{4}$ hours late. The railway people, in anger at Mussolini having moved the May Day holiday to the 21st April (*Natale di Roma* – Rome's birthday), gave us a sabotage experience at the numerous small stations between Castellammare and Castelvetrano, pretending the engine had broken down and keeping us waiting, while they mended – nothing. There is something hysterical in Mussolini's speeches that makes me tremble. Yet his lieutenants and entourage are immensely inferior to him in ability and character. All hangs on the life of this one man, as indeed it must always be where a government is a dictatorship. . . . Princess Yolanda married on the 9th April: a cavalry officer, Count Giorgio Calvi. They say that the King is to be congratulated on allowing his daughter to marry the *Milite Ignoto* [Unknown Soldier]. . . . Antonino and Norina are in Rome. He has been named head of the mission to escort King George V in Rome. Must keep notes on Antonino. Talking of Plumer versus Cavan he said, the other day before leaving, that there was such a difference between the two men. After Caporetto Antonino was under the former, who took a close personal interest in all he could tell him. When General Cavan came, he received Antonino in an untidy bedroom, then just waved him off, saying, 'The head of my staff will settle everything', and never bothered to enquire about anything. . . .

Somehow I doubt whether Antonino will enjoy his week with King George. He hates paying attention to *details*, saying that he is only interested in the big things of life. Alas, the every-day train is made up of small things . . .

In fact Di Giorgio enjoyed the experience very much, and King George created him a K.C.V.O. He was impressed by Queen Mary's knowledge of ancient Rome, which far exceeded his own. Unfortunately the King was struck down by violent stomach trouble, the English papers blaming the crowded programme, the heat and the change in cooking. When the party went to hear *The Barber of Seville* at the Costanzi Theatre, the lights were never lowered for the whole period, as a result of which the King insisted on leaving at the end of the second act. The next day he stayed behind at the Quirinal while Queen Mary did her duty sightseeing: San Clemente, San Paolo fuori le Mura, the Baths of Diocletian, the Borghese Museum etc. 'Miss Brown, the famous governess who has wielded such influence over the Queen of Italy was introduced to the British Sovereign.' A visit to the war cemeteries in the north followed – being Royal was much more of a duty than in the days of Edward VII, who kept everybody guessing about his next movements. And on the return of the King and Queen to London, they were greeted at Victoria by a special contingent of fifty English fascists.

Tina, having once been so bitter against Cadorna, now took the fashionable line of leniency. Thanks to the testimony of those who had served under him, it was realised that he had been maligned and that his downfall in 1917 had been partly engineered politically.

*Motya, 20 May 1923*

In this polemic with Foch claiming the honour of having advised the Italians to hold the line of the Piave in the retreat after Caporetto, I believe that there is *no doubt* that the great feat was due to Cadorna and Cadorna alone. How far Mussolini is right in refusing to 'reinstate' him is more difficult to decide. Diaz [the Minister of War, who succeeded Cadorna in 1917] cuts a very poor figure. Cadorna, unfortunately, loved those who fawned on him, and Diaz was one of those. Now Diaz is ennobled as 'Duca della Vittoria' [Duke of Victory], but he was always a figurehead and will remain as such in history.

A surprising volte-face, but one realises from the diaries that Tina's thinking was totally influenced by Antonino's ambitions. He had his eye on Diaz's job. By pressing the cause of the great rival Cadorna, he hoped to topple the Minister of War. It had been suggested that both Cadorna and Diaz should be created *Marescialli d'Italia* [Marshals of Italy], but Cadorna had let it be known that he would only accept this distinction if it was acknowledged that he was the senior – after all, he was eleven years older than Diaz.

*Motya, 28 May 1923*

Antonino hurried to Rome yesterday. He has been asked by the

Government to advise on the discontent in Sicily – it is an impossible
situation where no patriotic association can exist unless it be affiliated
to fascism [Antonino had also in fact gone to vote in favour of the
abolition of secret societies, i.e. in particular the Freemasons]. Throughout her history Sicily has been accustomed to dealing with dominations
for which she does not care, and it will not be easy to crush her independence of thought and action if she has a mind to resist. . . . Delia
very busy threading Phoenician beads.

During the summer, whilst the Pips were in Switzerland, Antonino
was frequently summoned to Rome by Mussolini.

*Igls, 4 September 1923*

The political horizon is again dark, the immediate cause being the
massacre of the Italian general and others whilst on the interallied
mission for the delineation of the Greco-Albanian frontier. Mussolini's
strong protest and request for a high indemnity met with a general
approval, but his occupation of Corfu is a breach of the treaty of 1864.
. . . The Paternòs [the Trabias' daughter and son-in-law], who have
been in Munich, bring the news that Yugoslavia is preparing for war,
siding of course with Greece against Italy. Ugly clouds are indeed all
over the world. Antonino has been told that the League of Nations,
which is at present sitting, will actually formulate a protest against
Italy [as indeed happened; Corfu was evacuated on 27 September].

The next pages of the diary are full of the sense of confusion that still
lay over Italy. 'Yet in a year of power and adulation Mussolini has not
lost his head. His grip on the better kind of Italian has most decidedly
strengthened. Rome was not built in a day, and the regeneration of
Italy cannot be expected even in one or two years.'

*Malfitano, 25 November 1923*

In bed a week in Florence. Saw no one at first but Blandine Gravina,
whom Berenson unkindly calls a 'foolometer', I know not why [because
she spoke in such a highbrow manner and made everybody feel
ignorant]. She says her German affairs are not so bad, as the law gives
a tenth of all that Cosima Wagner receives to each daughter, even the
Bülow ones. The operatic direction at Bayreuth has decided to give
Donna Cosima one per cent on all performances of Wagner's operas.[9]
Later I managed to see De Filippi [traveller and explorer married to an
American] who was disgusted by the local fascists. Luckily he was not
in a *vin mauvais* mood.[10] He said it is impossible for any self-respecting

person to take part in politics. He described his first meeting with Mussolini, said he went there to ask help for important scientific publications. Went without any presentation. M. said 'Who are you? I don't know you.' 'Mi gioco la pelle recevendo così chiunque senza saper chi sono' [I risk my skin receiving someone like this without knowing who he is]. All Antonino's interviews with Mussolini have led to no special *incarico* [appointment], in Sicily. In the summer he refused the post of High Commissioner, and I am thankful that he is not in that particular hornets' nest. Sicily is indeed in a deplorable condition, political rivalries causing worse chaos than if fascism had the upper hand [the fascist party not yet being the dominant one in the island]. Biagio Pace has set his heart on being Antonino's secretary and on becoming a deputy [member of Parliament]. But there are no signs of an election. If fascism is to crush all other parties and dominate the country, let us hope that the Augean stables of fascism will be cleaned out. Otherwise poor Italy!

In fact an election was called for 6 April, and Antonino was personally asked to stand for Messina. Mussolini, universally known as the Duce, had meanwhile passed through an appropriate 'reform' of the electoral system.

*Malfitano, 26 January 1924*

On the 12th Mussolini made a speech for the unveiling of a memorial stone to Crispi. He said: 'Prendo in consegna l'anima di Crispi' [I take in trust the soul of Crispi]. This is his *fourth* incarnation. First, in Parliament on his advent to power, he felt he personified Cromwell. Later on, I forget on what occasion, he said he felt he had the soul of Napoleon. Last summer, on closing the parliamentary season, he announced that he felt that Cavour dominated his being. Who next?

Meanwhile, light relief. Queen Marie of Rumania had arrived in Palermo. 'Being English, she had said she hoped to meet the Whitakers.'[11]

*Malfitano, 1 March 1924*

I asked if H.M. would care to see Malfitano, and on her saying yes, we arranged lunch for following day. I made Effie also offer Sperlinga, where she accepted to go to after lunch here. Queen Marie certainly is worthy of her fame as a *charmeuse,* and she *knows* it. She said sovereigns have the duty to gain sympathies and lay themselves out to captivate those they come in contact with. One can see that she is quite tactful, of ready and wide sympathies, intensely human. Her lady in waiting told me, that she has never, in all the years she has been with her, heard her say an unkind or hard word to any of her dependants. I asked the Queen her impression of Mussolini, who had lunched with her the other day in Rome. She said: 'Excellent. He is a strong man, and we got on splendidly, as we understood each other. We are both unconventional; we go straight to the point, and we are both hard workers.'

Tina's contribution to the Election was to write an 'anonymous pamphlet to the people of Sicily, approved of by Pace and Antonino'. She advised her readers to vote in favour of Mussolini, in the interest of stability. Meanwhile Antonino had been promised by Mussolini that he would be made Minister of War if he were successful in the Election. Of this success there was obviously little doubt, for on 30 March Antonino was ceremoniously presented with the freedom of Messina. Tina was a bit worried because his speech did not please the ultra-fascists – perhaps Mussolini would have second thoughts about the promise. At any rate the results of the Election were overwhelmingly in favour of the Government:

> Of course there was trickery, and the absent and the dead were made even to vote, but mostly it was the pure expression of the will of the country, to give this new régime its chance.

Pace, naturally, was one of those elected.[12]

*Malfitano, 5 April 1924*

The Prefect telephoned the news of Antonino's *nomina*, as Minister of War, to Norina yesterday at about 4 p.m. She was expecting it. So our hard work of the past four months has been crowned. We went to a Mahjongg party at the Salvos', Norina surrounded by congratulations. On our return home we found that Antonino had telephoned from the Ministry. So he must be already *insediato* [in office] . . . Effie, I understand is still negotiating to buy the Lampedusa picture frames [a reference to the death of Carolina Lampedusa, the prototype of one of the two penurious and eccentric sisters in the last chapter of *The Leopard*; Effie had been interested in a pair of enormous tortoiseshell and silver frames, the only remaining heirlooms that the sisters had to sell].[13]

*Malfitano, 6 May 1924*

Mussolini is among us! Antonino arrived on Sunday morning and yesterday went out to meet the great man at 9. Norina joined them for lunch at the Scaleas. All went off very well, no *gaffes* or hitches. Pip and I received him at the *Infanzia Abbandonata* at 4.15. In his silent way, Mussolini seemed pleased, and was certainly sympathetic towards the children. His face is less hard than I had expected; it is very strong but there is pathos, and kindliness, in those piercing eyes – Norina notices that there is a tired look now, which was not there when she met him last May at the Quirinal. He had, it seems, a wonderfully enthusiastic welcome on arrival, as indeed has been the case everywhere during the entire fulfilment of his heavy programme. Delia went to the reception, and was also presented to Mussolini. Thaon de Revel [Minister of the Marine] was in such a rage about having no place assigned to him to hear M.'s speech, that he would not go to the Prefect's dinner. Pip and I hope to escape for a little peace on Motya tomorrow.

*Motya, 12 May 1924*

So cool after the awful scirocco in Palermo. Mussolini, however, told Norina at the Trabias' lunch that he did not mind it. 'The hotter the better for me.' The fact that he chose Antonino as his Minister of War is a *sign* of his character. It guarantees a desire for law and order, under an unbiassed head of the army. Only a superior mind would call in Antonino for the great reconstruction. A triumphal arch is to be raised in Antonino's name at Mogadishu [in Somalia, thereby eliminating the shame of his court-martial in 1908].

Tina was well and truly swept away in her admiration for her son-in-law – for his intelligence, his patriotism, his culture, his lack of rancour. The Press hailed him as the 'saviour of the Grappa'. Banquets were held in his honour. Norina of course had to go and live in Rome. The Matteotti murder was alarming though. It 'nearly precipitated Mussolini into the dustbin', and that would have been the end of Di Giorgio as Minister.

Just before Norina left, she suffered a dreadful attack of asthma. Thus, when the time came for Tina, Pip and Delia to go to London, the thought of leaving her alone and suffering was 'almost more than I can bear', especially as Antonino would inevitably be seeing so little of her during the summer. Towards the end of the summer Norina became so worried about herself that she decided she would just have to meet her mother on her return journey through Switzerland.

*Berne, 12 September 1924*

Norina joined us last Saturday, but I fear she lets her nerves get the better of her. The famous Dr Kocher,[14] recommended by Duchess

Ada of Sermoneta, says it is the thyroid gland which is out of order, and she must have a long course of injections, or have the gland removed. The latter she will not hear of, and the first cannot be done at present as the blood tester has gone on his holiday. Kocher therefore suggested a mild course of injections for the present to see how she responds and yesterday he gave her one. She was however terribly upset, because he did not wash his hands after the patient before us had left him, and because he shook hands with us with our dirty gloves on. The result was that she ended, on return to the hotel, in a hysterical attack, and could not even be got down to dinner. Ica Pignatelli truly says this atmosphere of illness is sufficient to make the few people who are well feel ill.

They stayed at Berne for two more weeks. Norina became ever more neurotic. She would only be injected by a special needle that had not been used on anybody else, and everything had to be sterilised in her presence. Meanwhile news came that Antonino was on a secret trip to the French frontier, travelling under the name of Signor Rossi. It seemed that, despite his earlier promises, he had been unable to persuade Mussolini to grant Cadorna his seniority over Diaz. Or had he lost interest, now that he had achieved his ambition and Cadorna was of no further use to him? Then, general consternation, it was discovered that the official ministerial apartment in which the Di Giorgios were to live 'brought bad luck'. So a new one had to be found, but this turned out to be too gloomy with 'ugly early Victorian furniture'. Naturally Norina insisted that the apartment was thoroughly fumigated before she set foot inside it.

*Malfitano, 8 December 1924*

Antonino is far from well with dreadful rheumatic pains. His illness has come at an inconvenient moment, when he is busy completing his plans for the reform of the Army. The Opposition has widely spread it around that he has been pretending to be ill, in order – at first – to be absent from the Council of Ministers when they met after the riots of the 4th November. Mussolini is getting more and more trouble from the Opposition, and is unable to keep the extremists of his party under discipline. Gradually he has had to part with nearly all those who were close to him. Can he withstand the force of public opinion? For Antonino it makes his army reforms all the more difficult to get through. Besides the now strong political opposition to this government, he has to contend with the old Generals in the Senate who cannot grasp the altered methods required for modern armies, and with the personal envy and jealousy of those who have been in power and have failed – and who nevertheless hope some day to take his place.

The omens were indeed bad. Antonino was being attacked in the newspapers. Not only General Giardino, the Governor of Fiume, but Cadorna had turned against him.

*Malfitano, 3 April 1925*

Yesterday Norina telephoned that, instead of allowing a vote at the Senate, Mussolini made a speech withdrawing Antonino's plan for 'further investigation'. So he has not upheld him as he might. The Opposition, however, has been violent and formidable, and of course Cadorna being against made a great impression – Cadorna's behaviour has been disgusting, encouraging Antonino until he got all he wanted out of him, and then throwing him over like an old shoe. Worse than Giardino, who is frankly a very ambitious *arrivista* [careerist]. Well, we must wait and see, but Antonino has very many enemies. He will of course resign, and we shall hear this evening or tomorrow if Mussolini accepts his resignation outright or asks him to wait.

Di Giorgio's speech to the Senate had lasted two days, from 1 to 2 April. There was really no option but to resign, and very shortly afterwards Thaon de Revel also handed in his resignation. Mussolini, who was already Minister of the Interior and Foreign Minister, now also assumed the role of Minister for all the Armed Services.

# XXIII

## Liberty Curtailed

ANTONINO retired to Malfitano after the shock of resignation, but not to peacefulness. Boots was about to marry a Scottish baronet, Sir Torquil Munro – 'on the rebound', Tina naturally assumed. The Whitaker family was thus in some state of fuss. Then:

*Malfitano, 12 April 1925*

On Friday afternoon we were sitting quietly at tea when little Bronte [Alec Hood, 'quite a pet, like a little band-box duke on the stage']¹ and Sir Derek Keppel called. They had arrived the evening before with George V and Queen Mary on board the *Victoria and Albert,* and said that they thought the Sovereigns would wish to visit our garden. They suggested tea, probably Monday.

The King had had a bad bronchial attack in February, so bad that for thirteen days he could not write in his diary. The doctors insisted that he should go abroad, and eventually he surrendered to the idea, even though foreign travel was 'repugnant' to him.² All official functions were to be avoided. He and the Queen went to Syracuse, Messina and Taormina, where they had lunch at Alec Hood's house, La Falconara.

The Queen, as usual, went sightseeing. She even surprised Delia by descending on her little charity shop at the *Infanzia Abbandonata.* She visited the Botanical Gardens, the Museum, San Giovanni degli Eremiti and the Villa Orléans. Both lunched at the Villa Igiea as guests of Ignazio and Franca Florio. When they arrived at Malfitano, at 3.30 on Monday the thirteenth, accompanied by Princess Victoria and Prince George (later Duke of Kent) it was raining so hard that they could not even go out into the garden. The next day all the Pips, including Antonino and Pip's youngest brother, Albert, and his wife Eileen were invited to lunch on board the *Victoria and Albert.*

*Malfitano, 14 April 1925*

. . . a rush, as I had to go to the Villa Sofia to see the exhibition of Boots' trousseau. Some very pretty things: tea gowns, cloaks, lingerie. The della Grazias had been asked on board, as Alec Hood said that the Queen wished to see her, but *no one else was to be asked*. Antonino sat on the Queen's right and Pip on her left. Hermione della Grazia [English, daughter of Lord Powis]³ sat on the King's right and I on the left. The King did not seem to care to talk of local matters, or of Sicily, and of course I could not direct conversation, but had to accept His Majesty's own drift. We spoke lengthily of young Prince Umberto [the Prince of Piedmont], of whom he seems very fond. He however dislikes Admiral Bonaldi [the Prince's tutor] extremely and thinks he has been far too strict with him. He said he was thankful of the freedom that he himself had enjoyed as a boy, being treated at school as others were. (I did not like to remind him that he was not brought up as heir to the throne, though of course one realises that the etiquette of the court of Savoy is far more aloof and stiff than that of our British Royal House). He had actually seen Umberto being made to salute his father on informal occasions. He further said – which I thought very true – that it was a mistake to have kept the Prince for so many years under the same tutor, and that, however good, Admiral Bonaldi should have been changed when the boy was fifteen, so that his mentality should have an opportunity of expansion and not remain in the one groove. He called across the table to Antonino to ask whether he did not agree that Bonaldi was a tyrant, and recounted how, on the day that he and the Queen went to Tivoli, he asked the King of Italy to allow Prince Umberto to go with them. Then he said: 'When the Prince and I were getting in the car – would you believe it, Mrs Whitaker – the Admiral thought he was coming too. But I put my foot down and said no, and that I only wanted Di Giorgio in the carriage with us.'

Some of this rings rather oddly, one might dare say hypocritically, now that one knows how much the King himself was a stickler for discipline within the family. Another subject on which he of course expounded at much length was Antonino having just left the Government. He said 'In England no Minister would have thought of leaving the Cabinet under the circumstances, but I think Di Giorgio was *quite* right. As to both Cadorna and Diaz, they are no good, and I always heard this.'

On speaking of the freedom of British Royalties' education, he mentioned the Prince of Wales, and I said something of his ranch. He at once replied: 'I don't approve of it, because it creates jealousy in the other colonies. He has quite enough to do looking after his Duchy of Cornwall.' He spoke also of the marriage of Princess Mary versus that of Princess Yolanda, who had married beneath her, 'while our daughter's husband's family is as good as ours, and is a really great family.' He went on to say that the King and Queen of Italy, though so good and giving such a good example of morality, live too much out of the world and have no influence on society – which society (in Rome), he understands, is rotten to the core. 'Only a few families faithful to the Vatican are really respectable.' He spoke against the 'fast set' in England in connection with the daughter of Lord Huntingdon, Lady Marian Cameron, now at the Villa Igiea, and said 'she belongs to that Melton Mowbray set.' Of course that is the set the Prince of Wales is now in. The King said he will have nothing to do with divorced ladies at his court.

Speaking of their visit to Rome two years ago, King George complained that at the dinners he always had the Italian Ambassadress, the Marchesa della Torretta, at his side. 'I get enough of her in England,' he said, 'where I am obliged to put up with her.' He personally showed us all over the yacht, even the bedrooms and bathrooms. He said it was still as it was in the days of Queen Victoria. Showing us the cabin of his sister, Princess Victoria, he said: 'You see she has found it exactly as when she was with her father down to every smallest detail. Naturally we gave it to our daughter until she married, but now my dear sister returns to have it as before.' I found Princess Victoria charming and so intensely human. Speaking of her first visit to Malfitano, she seemed quite *emotionée* and said it all came back to her when she had visited it with King Edward. She said: 'If the great King had lived there would have been no war.' With Queen Mary I did not have much conversation, as of course Pip and Antonino sat by her, both at tea and lunch. She struck me as having a certain reticence in speech, though at Malfitano she was keenly interested in all around her.

The Marquis Pietro della Torretta, it is worth noting, was a Lampedusa, an uncle of Giuseppe Lampedusa. He had been Foreign Secretary of Italy under Bonomi from July 1921 to February 1922. His wife's first husband had been a Latvian, by name of Boris Wolff, and naturally her daughter, Lucy Wolff, lived with the Torrettas at the Embassy in London. Young Giuseppe Lampedusa was invited to stay, and one evening whilst the ambassador was at Buckingham Palace Lucy was told to entertain him. It was then that the young people discovered that, intellectually, they had many things in common, in particular a love of Shakespeare. Seven years later they were married.

As for Lady Marian Cameron, she came into the news the very next morning after the lunch party on the *Victoria and Albert*. A shot was heard at 2 a.m. following a dance at the Igiea, and she was found with a bullet in her left lung. 'It is said that, on hearing that there had been a theft at the hotel, she loaded her pistol before going to bed and it went off! But there are other theories, involving suicide and a faithless German prince. The King has been much interested, as his head doctor, Lord Dawson of Penn, had been called up to the hotel during the night.'

*Malfitano, 19 April 1925*

At lunch on the 16th we were told that the King and Queen would be coming at 4 p.m. to see our garden. We left Pip to do the honours and all went off to Boots' civil ceremony at the *Municipio* where Antonino was one of the *testimoni*. Then back here and found the Sovereigns in the garden. They took tea and heard Delia sing 'The Queen of the May' by Tosti. Then we hurried off to a family reception at the Villa Sofia. At 7 p.m. I went to Via Cavour to inquire after Joss, who that morning had had some sort of seizure, giving us a terrible fright. . . . Mercifully the next day Effie was able to give the King and Queen tea at Sperlinga. . . . Then yesterday, in glorious sunshine Boots' wedding came off! The usual difficulties about Roman Catholics attending a Protestant wedding. A very few ladies braved the Cardinal's veto, but there was a large number of men. Crowds went to the Villa Sofia for the reception, a good old free fight for food and drink. . . . On Monday morning, at cock's crow, the *Victoria and Albert* steamed away. The Queen, I was told, was on deck in her usual white dress and with a pale blue parasol. A regal figure at all times. Alec told me that at Taormina an old woman shouted at her: 'Viva la Sposina!' [Long live the Bride].

The only shadow over this event was a new quarrel with Maude, who was accused by Tina of 'trying to make mischief between us and the Josses over the visit' – something to do with not telling them about having to sign their names in a book if they wanted to meet the King and Queen. Tina, quite obviously, looked upon herself as a sort of privileged friend of the Sovereigns, and it was she who 'organised' the tea party at Sperlinga. When she asked Lily Boyle 'if she thought Maude would like me to write to Bronte about a visit to the Villa Sofia', she was met with a snub: 'Oh no, Aunt Maude has done it herself.' Tableau.

The next months were overshadowed by Norina's renewed asthma.

She had her nose 'scraped' by Dr Pescarolo in Turin, 'all to no purpose'. Joss had a stroke. Part of the land on Monti Parioli was sold satisfactorily and the villa there began to be used by the family. Antonino was made Commander-in-Chief of the armed forces in Florence.

*Rome, 9 November 1925*

He took up his post at once owing to the fearful riots there [the October 'blood-bath']. A fascist had been shot for violating the domicile of a socialist. In reprisal the fascists murdered two socialists, taking them out of their beds by night and deliberately shooting them dead before their wives and children – one an ex-member of parliament, a *decorato* and *mutilato di guerra,* besides being an old friend of Mussolini in his socialist days. In such times we live. . . . Great things as usual here. On the 3rd the grand fascist *festa* of their – revolution, shall we call it – and march on Rome. On the 5th we heard that on the day before Zaniboni, also a Socialist ex-member of parliament, had made an attempt on the life of the dictator [one of four within eleven months]. It seems that the government will take the line that he was a maniac and not that he was part of a plot. Several important arrests have been made. Lina Waterfield, who is correspondent for the *Observer,* is here and distinctly more than ever anti-fascist. She says sooner or later Mussolini must reveal himself. At present his programme is taken from old King Bomba's: *feste, forca e farina* [lit. feast-days, gallows and bread = bread and circuses].

Mussolini's laws of 1925–6 effectively crushed political life for nearly twenty years, making Italy into a police state.

There was news that Boots had congestion of the lungs after a ball at Inverness. 'It is doubtful whether she will be able to winter at her damp though beautiful Scottish home.' And Tina could not resist adding: 'After all those follies committed in the wake of the Duke of Puglie, she will have to be doubly careful.'

So much gloom. Norina was constantly ailing and had to stay at Malfitano, as a result of which she barely saw Antonino. For all that she had to be prepared to entertain her husband's friends when they came to Sicily. Padre Semeria, for instance: a smelly, bearded, 'very open-minded' priest, who asked for money, whether for himself or the orphanages he founded is not clear. 'I think he must be ill. He drags his feet, and yesterday at lunch fell asleep, actually snoring, in front of Princess Fitalia.' Then on 5 May 1926 'poor dear Joss ended his suffering'. His death showed that the affairs of Marsala were in a hopeless muddle. Pip, now aged seventy-

60. Malfitano. The Garden front, 1971.

61. The Louis XV drawing-room.
(*Photos: Dante Cappellani, Palermo.*)

62. Villa Belmonte.　　　　63. Villa Valguarnera, Bagheria.

64. Villa Palagonia, 'the villa of the monsters', Bagheria.

(*Photos: Gioacchino Lanza Tomasi.*)

six and quite frail, was faced with taking over the office management, and luckily in this he was aided by the younger generation, in particular by Audrey and Raffaele Pedicini, now a general. Yet after only a few months it was realised that the wine business was doomed. Not only was marsala going out of fashion but there was the 'mad competition' from nearly a hundred other firms. Exports were a third of what they had been in 1910.[4]

The Florios were in similar predicament at Marsala. Indeed the general collapse of nearly all their enterprises had been almost as spectacular as when old Vincenzo had launched them. America, once the greatest market for citrus fruit, was now exporting it to Europe. She was also one of the world's largest sulphur producers. Palermo was no longer of particular consequence as a port. The vast industrial combines in the north of Italy had taken advantage of modern machinery and electric power and were building national monopolies. Ignazio Florio himself was simply not interested in new ideas.

As for the Woodhouses, they at least were making some efforts to hoist themselves out of the slough, in spite of heavy debts to both the Banca Commerciale and the Banca di Marsala. Robert and Mostyn returned after the war, each spending about seven months in Sicily. They were much liked by the Marsalese – witness this story, told by Robert himself:

For many years it had been the custom that the three principal firms – Woodhouse, Florio, and Ingham Whitaker – should fix the price of the grapes which they bought during vintage, *after* the vintage was finished. New ideas crept in, following the 1914–18 war, and in due course it became the custom for the three firms to agree upon the price among themselves, and to announce it just before vintage began. In 1926 the price was duly published at the beginning of September. Several of the younger peasants decided that the price was too low, while many of the others were quite content. Literally civil war threatened, for the discontented faction declared that they would shoot anyone taking grapes in, while the others said that they would shoot anyone trying to stop them. The notorious Prefect of Sicily, Cesare Mori, called a conference in the town hall at Marsala, which was attended by hundreds of armed men. No progress was made and turmoil reigned, until Lionel Hamilton, the Woodhouse manager, asked whether they would accept as final a decision given by Don Roberto Woodhouse (the writer) if he were summoned from England.

They all agreed, in spite of the fact that I was one of the principal interested parties and was to be the arbitrator in our own case.

Thus I suddenly received a cable asking me to go to Marsala at once, giving no reasons. I duly started next day, and four days later stepped out of the train at Marsala at 1 p.m. On getting into our brougham, I asked Hamilton why there was such a crowd at the station and was told that they had come to see me arrive. I then learnt that I was expected to make immediate enquiries and to have my decision as to what I considered to be a fair price ready to be read out by the Prefect at noon the next day in the main square at Marsala.

I made hurried investigations, made my decision, and at noon next day the people accepted it without question.

In August 1926 Antonino was appointed Commander-in-chief in Sicily. The Pips only heard of it through reading the announcement in the paper. Apparently Marshal Badoglio was 'very put out' and told Antonino as much; he had already publicly announced that General Romei would get the job.

So Norina and Antonino would henceforward be living in the Royal Palace at Palermo.

Antonino's opposite number on the civil side was the Prefect Mori, appointed by Mussolini with the express purpose of crushing the *Mafia*. Mori had once been a policeman and it was indeed appropriate that he should have been called Cesare, for he was the very prototype of a sawdust Caesar. Soon the Sicilians realised what sort of person they had to deal with. Crush the *Mafia* he did, and very effectively, but his methods were on occasions not dissimilar from those used by the Inquisition. Torture by electric shock and salt on wounds after flogging were just two refinements. Several individuals would be arrested for a single crime. On mere hearsay, people were rounded up and shipped to the penal islands. At first he was attacked as a *sbirro,* but as the terror increased it was found best in villages to greet him with triumphal arches bearing the words AVE CAESAR. Such great *Mafia* chiefs as Don Ciccio Cuccia, mayor of Piana dei Greci,[5] and the 'Queen of Gangi' were arrested.

In 1927 Mussolini was able to announce to his parliament that the war on the *Mafia* had been completely successful. Actually, of course, the *Mafia* had been but temporarily subdued. The Society of Terror had been terrorised into silence. And various ringleaders had fled to America. Thus, when an English traveller, Ashley Brown came to Sicily, he was able to say that brigandage was a thing of the past. '*Fascismo* and *Mafia* cannot flourish together.'[6] Palermo's population now totalled 420,000, Marsala's 76,000, out of a total of 4,225,000 in all Sicily. It was Taormina which boasted the largest Anglo-Saxon colony on the island. There was not even a British club in Palermo. The setting of the Conca d'Oro was still perfect of course, but Palermo's chief failing to Ashley Brown was the poor use she put to her incomparable sea front. The Marina was 'as dreary and ugly as any town could boast'; Palermo seemed determined to turn her back on the sea. What a shock such remarks would have been to old Brydone. Though perhaps he would not have been surprised at Palermo becoming the 'noisiest city in the world'.

'Gradually,' wrote Tina, 'the country comes more and more into Mussolini's iron grip.' The mayors were no longer to be elected but were to be appointed by the Government. She was worried about the position of the monarchy. The king was being pushed into the background, without any apparent protest. Were Mussolini's ambitions turning out to be in the full sense Napoleonic? Yet, although she recognised that he was 'totally unscrupulous', he was still a genius, 'in everything, at the head of everything, pushing and encouraging every initiative for the good of the country'. One just had to look back at the anarchy towards which Italy was drifting in October 1922. 'Individuals may have suffered, but Italy has gained so enormously that we can but pray for the continuing life of this wonderful man, who by avoiding civil war has done so much to create an atmosphere of greatness for the country in the eyes of the world at large.'

It took a while before Mori's true nature was apparent to her.

*Malfitano, 23 January 1927*

The great excitement in Palermo at present is the dismissal of Cucco, the Secretary-General of the *fascio* for the Province. He drew his bow too far, and it has snapped. The Prefect Mori is doing *splendidly,* though I would have preferred that he had not accepted presents for New Year: a horse, a gun etc. etc. All sorts of horrors are put down to Cucco: that (being an oculist) he induced diseases in soldiers' eyes – for money – so that they should not go to the war. The unravelling of the mess of the *imboscati* [shirkers] in wartime will be no simple task, if undertaken thoroughly. As far as Cucco is concerned, it is difficult to say how much truth there may be in what is probably based more or less on circumstantial evidence. His enemies are legion, and of late his swollen head made him most unpopular. Great pressure will no doubt be put on our Dictator to save him, but it is hoped that Mussolini will uphold the Prefect. His circular to the Prefects of all the provinces of Italy clearly says that they are to do their duty and allow no interference from fascist secretaries. It would seem the day of the secretaries is over, and in many provinces a general *purification* is a necessity. The country awaits the realization of the ideals which fascism has proclaimed, and which Mussolini has sustained. If the system of Corporations succeed, and Syndicates are able to work,[7] a great era for the world might begin. People will realise that communism cannot survive, and that another form of guarantee for the community must take its place. . . . A visit from Manfredi Gravina [now Italian delegate at the League of Nations, and from 1929 until his death in 1932 High Commissioner for the League of Nations in Danzig]. His deafness increases, which consoles me a little that he is not my son-in-law.

*Malfitano, 31 January 1927*

Norina and Antonino went yesterday, at last, to their nice little apartment at the Royal Palace, he having arrived from Rome the day before by *air*; he loves the flying, and the only inconvenience he says is the noise – padded compartments will no doubt soon eliminate even this. Antonino had been called to Rome by Mussolini. We have not been told what exactly was wanted of him, but Mussolini was very friendly and kept him over an hour. Norina is better but not well; no asthma, but always some ailment. Pip closes the office for good and all today. It is sad for him, and had not Raffaele been so impossibly excitable, he might even have kept it on. . . . What a terrible fate Delia has been spared. I had asked Antonino why we did not see so much of Colonel Streva. It seems that A. had urged he should marry her, but Streva refused as he already had a black wife in Somalia with three children!

Robert Woodhouse was taking the lead in Marsala, following a strange little incident. Suddenly the Banca di Marsala told Lionel Hamilton that the firm's 1,000,000 *lire* overdraft must be paid back at once. Robert was in London at the time, and he thereupon arranged for the money (over £100,000) to be paid to the Bank. He wrote later:

We did not tell Hamilton what we had done till later. The next thing that happened was the arrival of a cabload of directors from the Banca di Marsala asking to see Hamilton, who was much alarmed. However, greatly to his relief, the directors explained that they were most distressed by the wiping out of the overdraft. They begged that their letter should not be taken too seriously. Hamilton said that their letter must have offended Casa Woodhouse, and that was why they had paid off this paltry million. The directors then assured him that they were more than ready to loan him any sums required, and as a result our credit was never again questioned as long as we remained in the country.

The smaller wine firms, besides being engaged in 'various illegal activities', were divided into two warring groups. Most of them kept two sets of books, one for the eyes of the tax inspector, the other for their own private use. Robert succeeded in reconciling these two groups into forming a consortium, a difficult job as he refused to be a party to this system of cheating the tax-man. He went to Rome to see the Minister of Agriculture, who produced such impossible terms for the consortium that it had to be abandoned. Robert then realised that, if he was to avoid bankruptcy, he must sell out entirely. Thanks to his friend Commendatore Fra, managing director of Fernet Branca in Milan, he was able to open up negotiations with Cinzano, who professed themselves ready to buy up not only Woodhouse, but Ingham Whitaker, Florio and all the other firms in Marsala. The Whitakers were prepared to accept, though the terms for each firm were complicated and different, involving an assortment of middle-men.

*Berne, 10 September 1927*

We are here to consult Dr Kocher for Norina. The responsibility of urging her to do this cure is great. So many consider him a charlatan. We came from Florence, packed with noisy *legionari americani,* both sexes, who drink and dance. They arrive in batches of 80 and stay about three days. I suppose they get through their sightseeing all right by day but their evenings are given up to rowdiness. By contrast we went to see Mrs George Keppel at her house. All good looks gone, but still attractive in manner. No pose. . . . Robert Hichens motored over from his villa. Always a pleasure to see an old friend. Strange, in a way, his life centred round this Swiss family. I am told they are *terre-à-terre,* though the man, who is the chief attraction, writes also.

Tina was referring to the Knittels. John Knittel was the son of a poor Swiss pastor but by his good looks and energy had at an early age done well for himself in London. Hichens met him at a private showing of the film of *The Garden of Allah* and immediately fell for this live wire – 'tall, clean shaven, with thick hair and a robust frame'. Knittel confided in Hichens that he wanted to write. Within the year he and his wife set up house with Hichens, and the ménage continued for some twenty-five years. In due course John Knittel became famous internationally as the author of such novels as *The Torch, Into the Abyss, Thérèse Etienne* and *Via Mala*. 'It all reminds me very much,' wrote Tina, 'of dear Ronald Gower and Frank Hird, even if a bit more complicated!' Alec Hood was cynical about the relationship: 'Of friend Hichens I hear little these days,' he had said earlier. 'He is always with his *fidus Achates* (let us hope he is *fidus*).'

*Berne, 27 September 1927*

This cure is fantastic. Kocher is overworked with no time for *individual* cases. One feels it is done on a formula, and has simply to hope that it does no harm. His mind is on operations, and the organisation of the Clinic is entirely in the hands of a Mademoiselle Brousse, his assistant, who does about 150 *piqûres* a day; it is obligatory that these should be done at the Clinic. She keeps accounts, looks after the books, and her temper is at times most difficult. It is she who decides when the doctor sees his patients, not according – alas! – to any new symptoms they may have developed, but to her humour. In consequence flowers and presents are showered upon her, not to mention tips. And somehow she keeps her Princesses, Ambassadresses, wealthy Americans from North and South. Is it a sort of hypnotism, or are these serums really worth it? One wonders when or if Kocher sees any poor or middle class people.

Janet Ross died, aged eighty-five, 'a legend of physical and intellectual vitality and character'. Tina missed her very much.

*Malfitano, 20 January 1928*

We return to find our head servant Giovanni in prison for *associazione a delinquere* [belonging to a gang of criminals]. The Prefect Mori continues his work, but it is a formidable task. Antonino has had divergences of opinion and certainly Mori has not behaved well, trying to shift the odium of unpopular appointments on to him.

Pip had given up any serious excavating on Motya. At his age he could not cope any more with the obstructionism from Gabrici that had developed into a bitter feud. Yet a niece-in-law was delighted one evening to see him and Tina dance a polka back and forth the upstairs corridor at Malfitano, the entire length of the house, with Delia clapping her hands in accompaniment. Tina was now in her seventieth year. She was still liable to break into full operatic song – 'too loud for a drawing-room', they said at Pylewell – after dinner. Her appetite was enormous.

'At one moment you would see a huge pile of spaghetti in front of her. When you looked again, she had gobbled it all up.' She liked sitting on the floor in front of the fire and amazed people by being able to stand up without using her hands. More disconcerting was the way she would smooth her dress over her missing breast, saying: 'You see, I am just like a man.'

The sale of the firm took place on 1 March, following a great deal of tension with Effie over the division of proceeds. It seems to have been based on a trust of sorts, with a Commendatore Gervasio as the financial intermediary. A sum of at least 9,000,000 *lire* was involved, about two-thirds in cash and the rest in the form of shares in Cinzano and the new firm, spread over three years at an agreed price per share – not a very satisfactory arrangement, as it turned out, when the great slump hit the western world in the summer of 1929. Robert Woodhouse, however, had a more adventurous time. His arrangement was to sell out the firm 'lock, stock and barrel' to the 'audacious' financier Gualino, for £100,000. The first £50,000 was paid in advance, but Robert's suspicions of Gualino had been aroused so much that he decided to spend £500 at Lloyd's in insurance premiums on the second half.

When the *Fisco* [Treasury] in Rome demanded £8000 from Robert, he decided he must act quickly – grab his money and get out of the country. The demand was completely spurious and it would have been hopeless ever trying to cross swords with fascism. On arriving in Milan, needless to say, he received a message that Gualino had changed his mind. Commendatore Fra was called in, and together he and Robert went to Turin, where an open cheque for about £46,500 was extracted from Gualino. There followed some complicated adventures, including an evasion of thugs who were obviously following them. When the Banca Commerciale refused to cash the cheque, it was sewn into Robert's sister-in-law's stays. Thus they escaped to safety with the money, leaving behind at the *baglio* all the old Woodhouse furniture, family pictures and the silver spoons and forks made from cracked Maria Theresa dollars that Old John had decided were unfit for paying his peasant clients.

Some while later Gualino was arrested by the fascists, as a 'danger to the state'. After a spell in prison, he was exiled to the Lipari islands for an indefinite period. When Robert visited Italy in 1938, he was informed that Gualino was still 'in exile'.[8]

*Malfitano, 15 April 1928*

Antonino has told me in confidence that for some months past he has had doubts about the Prefect's methods in crushing the *Mafia*. Many leading figures in Sicily have come to him, with all manner of revelations about injustices. Suddenly, just a month ago. Mussolini summoned him to Rome and asked his opinion: if he still approved of Mori as much as he did a year ago. Antonino felt it his duty to say that unfortunately this was no longer the case. Mussolini asked him to specify, but he replied that he would prefer not going into details, and that Mussolini had better make enquiries himself. This is all we know, except that after a few days Mori was sent for by Mussolini. Of course the total collapse of the accusations against Cucco and twenty-seven others on the score of dishonesty have made a great impression on many people, and no doubt on Mussolini himself. Antonino did not advise that the Prefect should be sent away, but merely suggested that his methods should be altered.

Tina did not realise how serious things had become for Antonino.

*Malfitano, 2 May 1928*

Antonino has resigned from the Army. Asked by the head of all things [Mussolini] if he was satisfied as to how things were going in Sicily, he spoke out his doubts, and strengthened his words by a 'memorandum' saying that the police were encouraged to exceed their powers. All this was private, or so he thought. Mussolini however sent for the Prefect, and told him to modify his zeal. Immediately on Mori's return to Palermo the town was filled with gossip of the basest kind. The Marchesa De Seta [friendly with Italo Balbo and Mussolini], who now rules the Government of Sicily, went to Rome and had an interview with Mussolini. She then sent word to the Prefect that all was well and he could feel perfectly secure. On the strength of this, he publicly cut Antonino at the unveiling of Pitrè's statue.[9] Antonino, knowing nothing of these backstairs intrigues, complained to the Duce, who said he would receive him. He found Mussolini actually believed the calumnies against him, and there was a row. Antonino would not lower himself, to try and justify such ridiculous things. For instance, it was said that he had removed the Military Hospital, simply to please his wife's family, and knowing that he was thereby incurring wastage of money for the War Office! So he is going into private life, having resigned on the same day he returned to Palermo, the 24th April. A broken career on the eve of promotion to an army. He also leaves Parliament. . . . And Mori on his birthday is being treated like royalty by the shopkeepers of Palermo, who send him presents of food, which he has graciously distributed to the poor.

From a later entry it does seem as though Tina had been complaining to Antonino that conditions at the old Military Hospital, which was next to Effie's house in Via Cavour, were a disgrace, and no doubt she had been right. The decision to resign was quite a shock to Norina. 'He does treat her very much *à la Sicilienne* – wives not supposed to know anything about their husbands' careers, or be capable of helping them.' In his last months in office he had been particularly interested in the question of the reafforestation of Sicily – a very worthwhile project, abandoned on his resignation.

So he retired to Acquedolci, to write his memoirs of the Great War and grow sisal – the latter being an interest he had acquired from his father-in-law Pip, who had introduced the plant on Motya. Unfortunately his chief work, *La Battaglia dell' Ortigara*, was not published until after his death.[10] He now shunned Palermo, which was awkward, because Norina felt too ill to spend much time in Acquedolci, preferring the creature comforts of Malfitano. Indeed, even during their sojourn at the Royal Palace she had not been able to play the hostess to any extent.

*Berne, 7 July 1928*

Antonino feels the blank of his broken career. He can never be re-installed, unless some unexpected crisis occurs. Did it suit the Duce to believe the lies told against him? After all, the 'régime' has to stand, and for the present *individuals* must be sacrificed if they do not bow down unconditionally to it, even to its often unjust exigencies. In the long run, however, the laws of the State must guarantee the freedom of individuals. . . . In Rome I was pleased to see Lina Waterfield. She had come, I gathered, chiefly to report on the *tribunale speciale* trial of communists and others convicted of being against fascism. She said rather sadly that what pains her most, loving Italy as she does, is the mildly satirical acquiescence of the Italian people.

*London, 24 September 1928*

What stories about Lady Sybil Graham [the British ambassadress in Rome] and her rivalries in love with Vittoria Sermoneta [ex Teano]. Waiting in a mackintosh outside the Palazzo Orsini [where Vittoria lived] for her *innamorato* to reappear. She was at Dr Castellani's clinic – now *Sir* Aldo Castellani – when Antonino went there on account of his inflamed liver. She said: 'There are four great men at present in the world, all Italian: Mussolini, Marconi, D'Annunzio and Castellani.'[11] Her face is so *cold*; as Norina remarked, if she chose, she could freeze someone to death.

*Florence, 28 October 1928*

I have been a great admirer of Mussolini, even when he behaved so badly to Antonino. I felt that Antonino had misjudged the situation. He should not have been so brusque, with local fascism against him. But now! Really, the ceremony of yesterday, the Duce burning 140,000,000 *lire* [a 'receipt' from the *debito pubblico* (public debt) to strengthen the *lira*] on an altar [the Altare della Pace in Piazza Venezia] is entirely ridiculous. Like a *pochade* [pornographic farce]. And yet serious fascists stand by and applaud, and the people show no signs of objecting. Surely an extraordinary situation for a civilized country.

Tina had further misgivings when she heard that Mussolini had issued a circular to Prefects ordering them to 'economize in every way on all philanthropic institutions', which was 'in open contrast to the lavish sums granted to *all* Fascist institutions.' She saw this leading to 'favouritism and bribery'.

The villa on Monti Parioli was now virtually finished and had been handed over to the two daughters. By now three lots had been sold for building, fetching about £50,000, and £10,000 had been spent on improvements to the house. Cadorna died, and Norina wrote to say that Antonino felt it very much. 'After his ungrateful conduct, I find this most extraordinary.' Then another death, closer to hand.

*Malfitano, 16 April 1929*

Poor Maude died almost suddenly on the 3rd February. . . . She was a loving mother, though not always a judicious one. She was devoted to the daughters of her sister [Alice Gardner], to whom – and to her brother-in-law – she had owed her education. She was an agreeable and very popular member of Palermo society, by which she was much beloved; she was hard and not *sincere* with those she did not care for. In appearance she was always amiable, and certainly very tactful.

The Duce, Tina wrote, was still absolutely against Antonino; all who hoped to rise in favour 'fight shy of A.'. Then out came the crux of it all: 'The Duce chooses to believe that Antonino's brother [Domenico, mayor of Castel di Lucio and a small farmer at Acquedolci] was implicated with the *Mafia*, and that A. had a quarrel with the Prefect Mori who would not agree to save him.[12] It is even said that Antonino slapped Mori's face. The lies are innumerable.' No further details are given. One has an uneasy feeling of no smoke without fire.

February 1929 was an important month for Italy, for the Lateran

Agreements were signed. These consisted of the Treaty (*Conciliazione*) and the Concordat. By the former the Papal state was reestablished round St Peter's, and various financial reparations were made. By the latter Roman Catholicism was confirmed as the religion of the state. Both were ratified in June. Not that the political path ahead was exactly decked with lilies.

Pip, Tina and Delia went to La Bourboule for the summer. It was new country for them, and they did not like it.

> Three people went up to Bourboule
> In order to keep themselves cool.
> Though they often were ill
> And had more than their fill,
> They stayed weeks on top of Bourboule.

Tina had a letter from Walburga Paget, now aged ninety. The brave old thing was living in Gloucestershire, her elder son having recently died. She wrote:

As for poor Giulia Trabia [whose last son, Giuseppe, had also died – from eating oysters in North Africa], I often think of her – my heart bleeds for her. If she could only realize that this life is but a school for us to form our character, and that everything in this world is *finite* and we only think we carry over our own spirits because *they only* are eternal. If she could only grasp that, she would understand that God sends us only the things we can bear, and that they are for our good, and that she is sure of meeting again her beloved ones. These convictions have helped me to bear the great griefs of my life.

Just two weeks after receiving this letter Tina and Pip had the shock of reading in *The Times* that Lady Paget herself had died – she had been reading a newspaper and somehow it had caught alight from the fire. The flames had spread to her clothes. 'With great fortitude she struggled to a bell which she managed to ring.' A butler came quickly, but too late. She was badly burnt and suffering from shock. The next day she died in a nursing home in Gloucester.

The obituary in *The Times,* among other things, told how Lady Paget had been responsible for recommending to the Prince Consort that Princess Alix of Denmark might be a suitable bride for the Prince of Wales. 'After a good many political and other impediments had been overcome, the two Royal families met at Brussels. Queen Victoria was immensely taken with Princess Alexandra, and the Prince's proposal followed after luncheon next day.' Lady Paget, the obituarist continued, 'belonged to a world, already obsolescent, that was absolutely swept away by the Great War. It was a world in which "Society" in most European countries meant a small set of aristocrats and diplomats who spent their lives in expensive amusements, sport, intermarriage and the painstaking observance of an elaborate etiquette.' A world that had also meant much to Tina's mother, Madame Scalia, but had proved just that little out of range.

Tina was assiduous at recording deaths, and more were to follow:

*Rome, 30 November 1929*

Whilst in Florence we heard of the tragic passings of three friends in four days, all related to one another. On the 18th little Peppino Gangi, regretted by many but not by his wife and daughter. Then Prince Trabia, whom we had seen so much of lately, as he was so intimate and *premuroso* [solicitous] always towards Antonino. And at Trabia's very funeral Peppino Scalea, whose death we have felt *much*. Valentine is the girls' dearest friend (apart from Margherita Bordonaro). Peppino devoted his life to the city of his birth, until fascism interfered; he was modest, simple, unpretentious, without a vestige of snobism, a real hard worker, scrupulous in all the duties he undertook, a true liberal.

Tina was fast beginning to lose interest in her diary. She felt she no longer had the energy or the will to keep it up. After all, there was no younger generation to care about what old grandmother had said. Perhaps the girls would pass on the diary to Frank Hird, who might use it as a sequel to *Sicily and England*. . . . So on 8 June 1930 she stopped writing. 'I find suddenly I have nothing more to say.'

She had plenty to say of course, and settled down at once to her *riflessioni filosofiche*. But the diary, apart from one passing piece of scandal about Lady Sybil Graham, was left alone for ten years:

*Rome, 20 November 1930*

Heard more about the arrest of Lady Sybil and her *paramour* at the Hotel Marini about ten days ago. The couples were lined up in the hall. When – being without a passport – she announced herself as the British ambassadress, the lady next to her said: 'Allora, io sono la Regina d'Italia!' [Then I'm the Queen of Italy!] Sir Ronald Graham [her husband, the Ambassador] went next day to Palazzo Chigi to complain of the raid and to say that his wife had a right to meet her stockbroker where she chose. The *Questore* Angelucci was sent away at once. All this from Andrea Serrao [family lawyer] who relished a good story.[13] Shades of Emma Hamilton!

In 1930 she imagined that her life must be nearly over. She had in fact lived through rather more than three-quarters of it.

There was a useful little summary of the state of the *Mafia* in the *riflessioni*:

I must allude to the great work being done against the *Mafia,* which hitherto held western Sicily in its mesh. The *Mafia* came originally into being – though not at first by that name – long before the unity of Italy, as an assertion of self-defence against government tyranny and oppression; but gradually it degenerated into an association of evil-doers spread over the greater part of the island. Murder, rapine and total lawlessness prevailed unchecked, while landed proprietors, in order to be able to visit their estates were obliged to pay a heavy toll for safety – not only for their own persons, but for the fruits of their lands and the cattle grazing on their fields. In pre-fascist days the worst class, the scum, was protected by the government to secure its votes for the elections. These elections were the bane of the country and have now been done away with, swept aside by Mussolini as a mere heap of rubbish. First the local administrative elections were abolished, and now the parliamentary ones are controlled through the Grand Council. Time will show whether the country will gain from this curtailing of liberty. . . . The fascist methods have been extolled by some of the most prominent of British journalists, but it should be realized that an evil of such long standing as the *Mafia* cannot be scrapped in a few short months, or even years. Grave injustices have been inevitable in the wholesale imprisonments that have taken place under this repression, and the trials have been totally inadequate. The innocent have been left lying one or even two years in lurid prisons, owing to the insufficient number of judges. Although legislation in Sicily has not been divorced from that in the rest of Italy, the methods employed – alas! – have been drastic and merciless. The sparing of the upper classes has led to grave discontent, and important *Mafiosi* have been left at large, some actually in power – while underlings and their dependants, far less to blame, receive heavy penalties and long years of imprisonment. So the *Mafia* is not yet destroyed. Under the ashes there burns and smoulders the fire of resentment. . . . At Enna for instance 100 people were arrested and thrown into prison, and then only 14 finally convicted. The innocent men returned home to find themselves ruined, and faced with starvation. . . . Out of the 156 socialists elected to Parliament in 1919 not one of the 52 constituencies in Sicily sent a member of that party. There had hardly been any need felt for the fascist *squadristi* in the island, and up to the very eve of the march on Rome only a handful of young enthusiasts had adopted fascism. . . . Mussolini's work in Sicily is but begun and he has not been so well served at the outset in the carrying out of this vast undertaking as he himself thinks. . . . The want of roads all over the island makes the problem of increasing cultivation an extremely difficult one to solve, even if safety from the *Mafia* is insured. Miles on mule track to go to the fields, and total want of hamlets for inhabitants, are indeed a barrier which cannot be got over by an 'edict'. They require massive expenditure over many years.

The *riflessioni* covered scores of pages. A large section dealt with Mussolini's dramatic new law restricting emigration. Another with Italy's worsening relations with Britain, that reached a climax with Sanctions in 1936, and another with colonialism.

On 17 April 1932 Antonino Di Giorgio died, as a result of a gall bladder operation. People said he had been killed by love, for the operation had been kept a secret from Norina. The death was shattering to all three women. They dressed in black and avoided social life as much as possible – unkind persons gave them a nickname: *Le tre vedove Di Giorgio* (the three widows of Di Giorgio). Norina took to spiritualism. Again there were gossipy stories. It was said that in 1935 she had received a message (at a séance in Serrao's office) to the effect that the 'little mishap' was now twelve years old and doing very well at his lessons.

Di Giorgio like Benjamin Ingham had been a pusher; his personal ambition had come first. Both had used the social ladder to get ahead. Di Giorgio had set his sights on politics, Ingham on commerce. Di Giorgio had tried too hard and too fast. In any case it is easier to be unscrupulous in business, and to get away with it, even if happiness does not result.

Pip perhaps felt less deeply about Antonino. He was also getting old mentally (he was nearly eighty-two). There was a moment of awkwardness at Antonino's funeral when he applauded the mares. This was his summary of Antonino's character: 'Want of tact and excessive self-assurance combined with an uncompromising nature have marred his career. In the matter of the *ordinamento* [the proposals for the reorganisation of the Army], with slight modifications the bill would have passed, but he would not apparently modify it, and this excessive rigidity irritated people and set them against him.'

So he could still write clearly at times. His health genuinely had to be watched. In August 1928 he was to have given an address on Motya to the Royal Association in Cardiff, but at the last moment Dr Ashby[14] had to read his paper for him. Such excavations at Motya as had taken place since the war had at first been mostly under the auspices of Cavaliere Giuseppe Lipari-Cascio, also a pretty ancient character, with splendid white dundrearies – a son of the Piedmontese Consul who had entertained Winnington-Ingram with tricolour ices in June 1860; later Biagio Pace had been chiefly responsible.

A mournful letter survives from Pip to his sister-in-law Emmie, Arthur's wife. She had been asking about the family's history in Sicily.

> *Malfitano, 10 March 1933*
>
> It is sad to think how the British colony here, and generally throughout Sicily, has dwindled gradually away and is now almost non-existent. Throughout Italy, however, I understand it is the same, but after all I suppose one cannot complain if the Italians now find they can do without us.

Tina slipped a letter of her own into the same envelope. She wrote:

> The *Educatorio* Whitaker building has been given these days by the Government for a home for ex-prisoners, with workshops for them to earn a living. We heard of it quite by chance, and Pip is now requesting that he should be permitted to withdraw the busts of his father and mother. Last spring, when Antonino was still living, the Government being anxious to repair the injustices done him, and wishing to approach him, I suppose through us, proposed that the *Educatorio* should be turned into a model school and our name remain. Of course it is all altered, and I should not be surprised if Motya is taken from us. We take it all very calmly. It seems to matter so little.

Most of the other charities in which the Whitakers had been actively interested had now been absorbed by the State: for instance the Animals Protection Society and the *Casa del Marinaio* ('Sailor's Rest'). Pip, however, continued to act as President of the *Infanzia Abbandonata*. In his will he left a million *lire* for Tina to distribute to Palermo charities. Presumably most of it went to the *Infanzia Abbandonata,* which was spared Mussolini's displeasure.[15]

Tina, with the aid of Pip, was working on the monograph of Benjamin Ingham. It was published in 1936, but Pip never saw it in print, for he died on 3 November that year. His residuary estate, including Malfitano and Motya was divided between Tina and the daughters. The Monti Parioli house had already been made over to Norina and Delia, and was known as Villa Di Giorgio. Among his other bequests was the sum of 100,000 *lire* to his godson Manfred Pedicini, Audrey's only child and the current blue-eyed boy in the family – usually referred to as the 'dear little one' in Tina's diaries of the 1920s. The church building was left to Audrey and Delia, with a special donation of 300,000 *lire*. His English estate amounted to £110,338 16s 8d. There was a moving passage in the will: 'My darling wife during all these years of our life has been a pearl without price, always so loving, so good, so unselfish. We shall meet again D.V. in a land where there is no parting.'

The obituary in *The Times* was long. It mentioned Motya and his museum of bird skins, by then quite famous and all carefully labelled in his neat hand.

Until the war [it continued] there was probably no house in Europe where one met so distinguished and cosmopolitan a society as at Malfitano. Mr Whitaker and his brilliant wife had a gift of hospitality peculiarly their own. It is difficult to describe the atmosphere they created at Malfitano except by saying that here you had a husband and wife, very much of the world, whose outlook on life was kind, sympathetic and totally unworldly.

There was also a long obituary in *The Ibis,* written by David Bannerman and praising Pip's 'delightfully written books with their wealth of field notes, so obviously the work of a true lover of wild life'. 'Kindness and uprightness shone through him. . . . He had a passionate love of children, animals and flowers, and had only to hear of neglect . . . to leave no stone unturned. Nothing was too much for him to do for poor or rich alike.' Pip's contributions to *The Ibis* before the war had been very numerous, one of the last, typically thorough, 'On the Great Invasion of Crossbills in 1909',[16] showing how very extensive were his ornithological correspondents throughout Europe.

He died in Rome, on his way from Switzerland, and his body was not moved to Palermo until 1938, by which time the family tomb, containing spaces for four coffins, had been built in the Protestant cemetery at Palermo. It was underground, with a modest structure above, and every now and then one of the three bereaved ladies would descend there to sit and pray.

Effie continued to reign cantankerously at Via Cavour. Because of her arthritis, she spent a great deal of time on chaises longues. Her younger relatives, great nephews and nieces, considered her an 'old terror', though friends remember visiting her in bed at a sort of levee, her huge tummy heaving with laughter. Aileen had overspent herself, and as Boots had remarried and gone to live in America, the question of getting rid of the Villa Sofia now arose. The house, however, was not sold until 1953, when it was converted into a hospital.

Two further deaths increased the sense of isolation at Malfitano. Frank Hird died in November 1937, two years after the publication of his *chef d'œuvre,* a life of H. M. Stanley; the book had been based on papers made over to him on Dolly Stanley's death. He asked that his ashes should be placed with Ronny's at Rusthall Cemetery, near Tunbridge Wells. Gladys Hird had also said in her will that she wished to be in the same grave, and in due course her request was respected. At Somerset House Frank's estate is shown as £258 18s od only. It was typical of Gladys that she should have pestered Tina for Frank's letters, and that when Tina rather wearily complied she should have written again asking whether it was not possible that there could have been some more.

The other death was that of Alec Hood, also in 1937. He had been one of Tina's most regular correspondents during the last eighteen or nineteen years. His last letter had been, appropriately, in connection with Queen Mary:

> *Maniace, 10 December 1936*
> It is like H.M. to have sent you that thoughtful letter of sympathy [about Pip]. I think her visit to Malfitano was one of her pleasantest memories of the cruise. How much one's thoughts go out to her in this most lamentable 'crisis' [the Abdication].

As an 'old courtier', he of course was totally against 'her' – Mrs Simpson. Within a few months he was fatally struck down by bronchitis.

A mellowed Robert Hichens kept up his correspondence from Switzerland, where he was still living happily with the Knittels.

> *Zurich, 23 March 1939*
> The coronation of the Pope must have been very wonderful, but I could not help thinking how preposterous is the life of the Vicar of Christ in comparison with the life of Christ and His teachings. . . . Swiss guards, trumpeters, ostrich feathers, crowns studded with jewels, robes stiff with gold, a throne to sit upon. . . . I could not help thinking of *Aïda.* . . . The fact is that most of us are up to the neck in sheer

worldliness, which only falls away when we come face to face with Death. I cannot remember one day in my life, since I was quite a child, when I have not thought about death. . . . Alas, dear friend, I cannot come to Italy with the present régime. I am too English for that. The enemy of my country is *my* enemy. Some day surely the tyrannies will pass and Europe will be able once more to draw a deep breath.

Mussolini declared war on Britain and France on 10 June 1940. In October he invaded Greece. Tina and the 'girls' were in Rome. About that time she began her diary again, and kept it up intermittently until the end of her life. She had just passed her eighty-second birthday. Norina was fifty-six and Delia fifty-five.

# PART SEVEN

## *In Retirement*

# XXIV

## Besieged in Rome; Mists and Suns

O N 9 June 1940 John Leslie, an attaché at the British Embassy, had called on Tina to say goodbye, for it seemed that Italy's declaration of war on Britain must be imminent. 'He still does not believe in his leaving, though he told us that he had had his berth ticket assigned to him for departure. He added: "But the date is not filled in." The next day war was declared, and all the British were packed off on board ship.'

Tina and the girls had not seen Malfitano for nearly two years. As all British property was to be confiscated, the house was hurriedly transferred into the name of Norina, who had Italian nationality. The villa at Monti Parioli was already legally half hers. Motya produced problems; the Government would not recognise the island as belonging to her unless she agreed to leave it to Trapani or Marsala in her will. As for the Villa Sofia and Effie's *palazzo* in Via Cavour, there were no possible loopholes. There were confiscated without argument. The Bank of Sicily took over the Duchy of Bronte, later handing it over to an earnest but inefficient body known as the *Ente per il Latifondo Siciliano,* which immediately set about creating a gimcrack hamlet, within sight of Maniace and christened the Borgo Caracciolo – a deliberate insult to Nelson's memory. At one stage Count Ciano attempted to buy the Duchy, for one-sixth of its actual value.

Norina was now virtually bedridden. Tina, mentally very alert, was weak physically. So it fell to Delia, the 'poor child' as Tina persisted in calling her, to organise the household, which included – surprisingly, for an English family in wartime – two Germans: a maid-housekeeper called Teresa and a nurse for Norina, *Schwester* Weisskopf. Faithful friends called, but it was an ingrowing, almost secret household. Down in Rome itself, in her flat in the Via Savoia, was old Effie, also nearly bedridden, with her widowed daughter Audrey looking after her.

Tina seemed to have found it difficult to get into the swing of diary-writing again. At first she contented herself mostly with transcribing extracts from newspapers. She also went on listening to the British radio – in spite of Germans in the house.

*Rome, 30 November 1940*

So now Chamberlain is gone, without seeing the end of this dreadful struggle. . . . How well I remember my mother speaking of the peace terms of 1870: 'All well and good for Alsace, but France will never be resigned to losing her Lorraine.' Bismarck even realized his mistake, and tried to remedy it. Germany is astute enough to remember, and therefore forces the Lorraine people to leave their homes and starve in Poland, or in miserable so-called Free France, so that their country can once and for all be entirely Germanized. . . .

Today is my dearest mother's wedding day, 88 years ago. Yesterday Norina was brought a small bottle of Broncovedrina, smuggled through the Swiss diplomatic bag, for her inhalations against asthma. Made by a Jewish firm, expelled from Germany and recently from France. . . . We lead a very quiet life. Of course people don't care to come up here for tea in the dark. Besides, Norina is not well, and seeing people tires her. She has so many business letters to write! I had a visit from Madame Elvira Cimino yesterday, an out and out bundle [Fascist] and head now of the *Donne Laureate ed Artiste,* but discouraged and *sfiduciata* [disheartened].[1] How different from a year or two ago when I last saw her. Can this ghastly brutal destruction of the world's civilization continue much longer? Delia and I generally hear the radio at 6 p.m. It ends with God Save the King, for which we religiously stand. . . . Audrey just returned from Palermo. She is fundamentally good, unselfish, true and just, but she has no backbone. A pity. Emily Luck said of her once: 'She is intellectual, but not intelligent.' She has a good and devoted son, anti-bundle but unfortunately with the same drawbacks. They are too wrapped up in themselves, and in their music and painting.

Half the Italian fleet was destroyed at Taranto. In France Laval fell. Badoglio resigned as Chief of Staff, after the invasion of Greece. Haile Selassie re-entered Abyssinia. All these events were faithfully noted in the diary. 'The fall of the régime even seemed to be on the cards, but now the storm of discontent and disgust at the failure in Libya is already fading. Better this government than the Germans, people say.' Yet by 1 February 1941 Tina was writing: 'German penetration of the country is passively accepted. Troops in Sicily. Hitler follows in the steps of the Prussian Emperor, whose dream it always was to gain a foothold on the Mediterranean seaboard.'

*Rome, 6 April 1941*

I am proud of being a British subject, and love and admire beyond words the country of my birth in exile. I resent those English-born persons, married to Italians and living in Rome, who would dare to hide the nationality of their birth. I consider my object in living is to prove that Britain is Italy's natural ally. . . .

Germany attacks fiercely through Bulgaria. Germany three times heavily bombards Belgrade (after being declared an open city). Britain takes possession of Addis Abeba, with a promise to protect the Italian population of 40,000. The Governor, the Duke of Aosta [Prince Amedeo],[2] sends messages of thanks to General Wavell, and the military leave the town in the hands of the Italian police. The British hoist the Union Jack on entering. The British navy not able to prevent Germany from landing powerful troops at Tripoli, in order to retake Cyrenaica for Italy. What reward will Germany expect?

I decide my poor old brain must give up following events; I shall not read the Italian papers, except the Vatican one, the *Osservatore Romano*; and I shall avoid as much as possible listening to the radio.

After much difficulty Delia managed to get a permit for the family to spend the summer at Castel Gandolfo, near the Pope's palace. Then, with some foresight, she bought two *poderi* (small farms) near Albano and Velletri, in case the food situation became worse. Tina continued to write things in her diary which could have caused serious trouble were it discovered.

*Castel Gandolfo, 2 August 1941*

Some animals from the country wanted to know what was going on in Rome. So a cow went there, but soon returned. 'They milked me dry and have sent me away.' Then some sheep went, but they soon returned. 'They sheared off all our wool, and fearing worse we got away.' Then a donkey decided to have a look in. He returned hurriedly after a short time, saying: 'Don't keep me. I have to return to Rome as I've been made Duce.'

I spend many hours thinking, obliged to lie on my back for my head. How long can it last, or rather *I* last? What use am I? But I must not complain when I think of Madame Cimino, so suddenly struck down, deaf, nearly quite blind, and almost speechless. D'Annunzio gave her his gold medal for patriotism before the advent of Fascism. She was so ardent, saw everything everywhere, and is now going to the dogs. She is 78, and I 83. I have left my memoirs too late to put them together properly. I could have found plenty to publish that is not in *Sicily and England*. Quite young, I remember being taught to say and act in this sense: 'Forgive and forget'. But I always answered: 'There is no merit in that. My motto is *Remembering is to forgive*'. . . . What a hospital we are here. An irony of fate in this beautiful place. A fine large house. An unique spot. And on top the difficulty of feeding selves and fairly large household, twelve people in all. Delia overworked and now on the sick-list.

They returned to Rome. Then on 19 November, 'that terrible night', something happened which put both Whitaker families in grave peril: Audrey's son Manfred, aged twenty-seven and serving in the Italian army, was arrested for 'spying'. The news was brought to Tina by her lawyer Serrao. Norina, as the wife of Antonino Di Giorgio, was naturally expected to pull strings – which she did. Her collapse, bringing her near to death, was at once attributed by Tina to the strain.

The Rector of the American Episcopal Church in Rome, Padre Hiram Gruber Woolf, was arrested at the same time as Manfred.[3] Both were sent to the gloomy Regina Coeli prison. It was said that a letter from Manfred containing secret information, destined for a third person [the American Consul?] had been discovered in the Padre's flat. Until the trial by the Fascist Special Tribunal both men were held *incommunicado*. The Padre managed to write a letter to his servant and it caused some alarm at the U.S. Embassy about the treatment he must be receiving in that antique place. 'I understand now,' he wrote, 'why so many people go mad in prison.' The months passed without any sign of the trial. America declared war on Italy. Tina, distracted in any case by Norina's illness, remained curiously aloof from the drama, simply noting: 'We hear through my maid, who heard it from Effie's Swiss one, that for some time Manfred has been unofficially engaged to a very rich girl, clever though plain, daughter of Finocchiaro Aprile [Emanuele, brother of Andrea, the Sicilian separatist leader].[4] The girl and her father go every day to see Audrey.' In March Norina had another very bad attack. 'The asthma never leaves her, except under *piqûres* and drugs. She gets hardly any sleep. Delia five nights without even going to bed.'

The trial was at last fixed for 11 May.

*Rome, 12 May 1942*

Manfred's trial has done Norina's nerves tremendous harm, as did his arrest last November when she was at last getting better. His poor foolish mother is naturally in mad anxiety, though through a devotee of Antonino's we hear he will get off lightly. To save him, they will make out he is half-witted, which he certainly is not! I take the view that, the régime having been so generous to his mother and grand-mother, both British, a *gentleman* should not betray its laws of hospitality.

At least Manfred's life was spared, if that meant 'lightly'. He received a sentence of thirty-four years' imprisonment, 'without the benefit of clemency'. Padre Woolf received the same, but the process of condemning him was just a formality and the next day he was granted the King's pardon; for it had already been arranged that he should be exchanged for five officers and 120 sailors of the Italian merchant navy. Everything was precisely timed so that he could leave Italy at once on the same ship as the few other Americans still remaining in the country.

*Rome, 31 May 1942*

Still anxious about Norina, who had a sharp attack of asthma last night in the drawing room, and had to be given a *piqûre* there and then. Afterwards she slept three hours on end. The maid, tired out, has after six or seven years become rude and offhand, so Norina has ordered her to leave. As usual I am not allowed to help or interfere! Then we are not sure if Delia and I can have permission to go to Castel Gandolfo for the summer months. In the meantime doctors say it is essential for Norina to get away from the heavy air of Rome. . . .

Teresa is at Malfitano, with Lilian [Monypenny, English but Sicilian born, and a needy dependant of the Whitakers] to help. An Anglo-German alliance in full wartime. Everyone is on edge and anxious. Teresa has lost a nephew in Russia and his brother – if alive – is still there. The last heir to the great house of Caetani [Camillo] died last autumn in Albania, in that awful and useless push. He was the only son of Roffredo, now known as the Prince of Bassiano. Nassau William Senior in his diary of 1851 met Michelangelo Caetani, the great Dante scholar and Roffredo's grandfather, who praised the qualities of the British race and compared them to the best Romans of old days – of whom traces survive in Roffredo. . . . Delia went to see Effie and Audrey on Friday. She found the latter more depressed than last time. Effie not pleased with my letter, and said she was elated by Manfred's great qualities!! It seems strange that the Finocchiaro Aprile family should still wish for the marriage of their only daughter to him. We hear that Audrey and the girl's father are leaving no stone unturned.

With difficulty another permit was obtained so that the family could go up to the Alban Hills once more for the summer. It was obvious that despite the sentence Manfred's life was still in danger. Audrey was still hoping for a pardon, or at least for some mitigation of the sentence. In desperation she sent this cry of anguish to Castel Gandolfo:

*Rome, 4 September 1942*

My dear Delia,

I have just telephoned to the Villa for news and was glad to hear that Norina was better after her bad attack last week.

I know you have many worries and anxieties, and that Norina is not well, but I am alone in my terrible misfortune. You are my only blood relations and it is only natural that I should write to you, to implore you for the help which only you can give – and which I really do not see why you should deny me. After all, I can assure you that, although such a short time has passed – though to me it seems an eternity – those same people of the Regiment, the judges and authorities who have or are going to examine my 'domanda di grazia', are changing their first hostile and severe views on the whole question and have expressed sympathy and generous consideration even to the point of revising the whole thing. In fact Nene [Manfred's fiancée], who had at first been refused permission to see him has now been informed that she may do so, and an influential person who sent the communication said that the permit had been granted 'dopo riesaminata la pratica' [after the case had been reexamined].

Now I have heard that during the first part of the trial nothing was done to help Manfred because it was understood that 'la famiglia stessa se ne disinteressava' [his family was not going to help him].

The atmosphere has changed and my domanda is under consideration, and the whole affair is being reexamined. I am sure that if only that friend of yours [Colonel Fagà, head of the fascist secret service][5] could put in a good word, a generous one in his favour, the result might definitely be positive.[6]

Manfred has been a fool but not a guilty one, and no harm did his foolishness do to his country, and this was clearly stated by the Court itself. He has been punished and will continue to be punished for the rest of his life, but far beyond his deserts. What he is suffering now will leave traces for all time.

It is an act of charity that I beg from you, a thing that strangers offer me constantly. Must I be abandoned by you all in this desperate moment of my life? It is only during these long months that I have learned something about the terrible life he is now leading, and which you cannot possibly imagine. I implore you therefore to see or write to your friend, and I shall be for ever grateful.

Mother is not feeling well, her pains are worse than ever, and her eyes are giving her trouble – she is so tired, poor dear, and is in very low spirits.

Audrey had to wait ten days for Delia's reply, which also came by hand:

*Castel Gandolfo, 14 September 1942*

My dear Audrey,

Your letter distressed me a great deal. I would have answered it sooner but the very afternoon it arrived Norina began getting much worse, and she has been very ill these last days. As you can imagine, I have not had a minute free from anxiety, and I have been in constant attendance. I do not think you realize what she suffers and what it means to see her suffer *all* day and *every* day. A life condemnation battling for breath.

Do not think, dear Audrey, though, that I do not feel deeply for you. All you are going through must be terrible to bear. At least you have the constant *hope* for the near future, and that keeps you going. He is young and has his good health to assist him. *We* have no hope of health for Norina given us by the doctors. As for being *alone,* we have less real help I consider in all our worries than you have. . . . You have the blessing of the Finocchiaro Aprile family, constantly helping you and with such influential friends. . . . I am afraid I cannot ask Norina to do anything at present. Besides, what she *could* do, she did most willingly and *immediately,* when you yourselves feared the worst might happen, to the detriment of her own health. I do not remember if I told you that when your terrible misfortune occurred, and I having gone to you (against the lawyer's advice), your mother sent me home in a hurry saying: 'They will *shoot* him if Norina does not save him immediately.' We were all naturally dreadfully upset, and Norina got our acquaintance to come that same evening. . . . The next day he particularly asked me *not to leave the house.* Then on the following day the police came anonymously to enquire about us, and asked our servants what relationship there was with you. . . . Also, when Mama and I had to apply for a permit to come here for the summer, they at once pricked up their ears and asked if it was your family. I do not think you realize that our position is now a very delicate one, just because we *are* your relations. I think it is unfair of you to say that we have 'abandoned' you or 'denied' you help. . . . I am sorry, my dear, we can do nothing more. It is much more likely that you will succeed through your own friends' intervention. The name of Whitaker is no longer what it used to be. . . . I am sorry your mother is suffering. Mama too is very shaky.

Tina decided that she should also write:

*Castel Gandolfo, 16 September 1942*

My dear Audrey,

. . . You will have received Delia's answer to your letter, which upset her very much, and which I must say not only pained and grieved us, but also *surprised* us; we had been told vaguely that you considered no one helped you, but did not think it was meant for us, until your letter for Delia came, and so she felt obliged to refute the accusations you make. At the time of the tragedy I myself thought that both dear Uncle Pip and your father would have disapproved that the hospitality accepted by their two families [i.e. from Italy] should have been ill requited; they were true gentlemen of the old school. For this reason I could not write to you at once, and eventually did so to your poor mother for you all, and I tell you this now, sad as it is for me to do so. We are thankful, however, that influential authorities give you hope of revision, and *at all events,* dear, you must in your great sorrow take courage in the certitude that when Peace comes (whoever wins) things will be altered and judgements very quickly modified.

In the meantime you have to take care of your health, thinking M. is young and will be able to give you in your unselfishness the joy of a happy old age. I enquired of your doctor about you, and he said that mercifully your organs are quite sound. . . . We were told that many people in Palermo were nervous after the *sentenza,* especially when they heard that you were about to go there and might want to see them. . . . I consider that, in all this pitiful story, those immediately around you, in their anxiety to give you comfort, hid the case as it really stood from you.

Poor Delia is worn out mentally as well as physically, and I don't know how she managed to write you the long letter she sent. Constant nursing all day, a meal at any hour, accounts, household worries etc, and she will not let me help. Teresa here with bad sciatica, Giovanna [the maid] ill in Rome and now off to Turin, for the great sorrow of the death of a young favourite niece, only complicate matters. We don't know when we can return to Rome with our Norina getting weaker and more desperate with the incessant asthma which gives her no rest unless she is under drugs. No doctor can understand the case, nor the reason for this mysterious malady of which asthma is only one of the symptoms. At least, dear, you have the blessed 'faith beyond all understanding', for which *we* pray in vain! . . . Love to you both and tell your dear mother I never forget all her loyalty to Uncle Pip when there were difficulties over the closing down of the business [a dig at the behaviour of Audrey's late husband, Raffaele, who had considered that Effie was being unfairly treated in the settlement].

Audrey wrote back briefly:

*Rome, 18 September 1942*

My dear Delia,

I have received your letter and the only comment I wish to make is that I had no feeling of resentment. I simply appealed to you for much-needed help, never thinking that you should have resented what I wrote in my great distress. I hope and trust God will help me.

This exchange did not, as might have been expected, bring on another relapse for Norina.

*Castle Gandolfo, 16 October 1942*

Prolonged summer weather. The real deep blue Mediterranean sky of the famous *Ottobrate* [family holidays in October]. Norina actually sitting out in the garden for half an hour after lunch. Manfred has been moved to Civitavecchia. His unfortunate mother went to Regina Coeli and found that he had gone. She is more than ever distressed at hearing that conditions are so severe for *political* cases; she says they even use the rack as a form of punishment. . . . Mine is an unhappy old age. As a daughter, by general consent, I was all I could possibly be. As a wife, my husband's words on his will prove, I feel, that I was faithful and helpful. As a mother, although devoted to my children, I have been a failure, and am made to feel it. I did all I thought was right for their good, their education, their enjoyment, but somehow, in spite of so many offers of marriage, especially to Norina, I did not manage things properly for them. I have been left without the joy of grandchildren, and my daughters have no one to care for them if they are spared to live to my great age. Because of this, they are resentful towards me. I have to swallow bitter pills as a dependant in the house. I am a discontented grumbler, not appreciating what they do to look after my health. I am also getting deaf, and often do not hear what Delia says, which irritates her extremely. Norina has clearer diction.

*Rome, 5 November 1942*

Audrey came for lunch. A painful meeting. She is so pleased with her son's disgraceful behaviour. One feels deeply for her mother, and in a way for her, although the chief fault is hers, poor thing. Yet she seems still so self-satisfied. He is not even a bundle, yet she has written three times, it seems, to the Duce!

The entries for the next months are missing, and resume with the landing of the Allies in Sicily. On 11 June 1943 the island of Pantelleria had been taken, the only Allied casualty having been 'one soldier bitten by a mule'. Its capture was shortly followed by that of another island: Lampedusa, which surrendered to a British airman who had landed there by mistake when his plane ran out of petrol. D-Day for the invasion of Sicily, Operation 'Husky', was 10 July, preceded by a violent bombing of all the main cities on the island. The landings were at Licata and Gela. Four of the five German train ferries across the Straits of Messina were sunk. Only the shell of Messina's cathedral remained. Her University library was also badly damaged, though luckily the valuable collection of Greek manuscripts had been moved for safe keeping to Bronte. Catania was also heavily battered. The museum at Marsala, which included many objects from Motya, and the Woodhouse *baglio* were completely destroyed. All the Woodhouse, Ingham, Whitaker and Florio papers in Marsala were lost. The town of Trapani was devastated. The Roman gymnasium at Syracuse was badly damaged, both by bombs and civilian vandalism. Palermo, however, suffered the worst fate of all. Great areas of the town were laid flat, and more than sixty churches, most of them baroque, were destroyed or grievously damaged. As General Patton himself said, for two blocks in depth from the harbour practically every house was a pile of rocks.[7] Fishing boats had been blown clean out of the water. The Butera Palace was gutted and part of the Whitaker *palazzo* in Via Cavour destroyed, as was the whole of the Lampedusa house next door. The Lampedusa Palace on the Marina, with its gilt balconies, its painted ballroom, its Murano chandeliers, was flattened. Patton moved into the Royal Palace. Malfitano and the Villa Sofia were unscathed.

Towns such as Messina and Catania suffered even further damage during the Allies' whirlwind campaign. The little medieval town of Randazzo, used as a last strong point by the Germans, had a catastrophic hammering. Its neighbour Bronte scarcely suffered, though the castle of Maniace had been pillaged by the Germans and a number of treasures from the Nelson-Bridport collection, including portraits, were stolen or defaced; Field-Marshal Kesselring had written his name in the visitors' book.

On 19 July there was an American air attack on the outskirts of Rome. It lasted four hours, people said that many civilian buildings were hit instead of the intended military targets. The sixth century basilica of San Lorenzo fuori le Mura, one of the seven pilgrimage churches of Rome, was nearly obliterated.[8] Mercifully Norina remained calm, but Delia annoyed Tina by going up to the top of the tower to watch the bombs falling. Gradually the news of casualties filtered in. One young friend had been killed. Others had been severely wounded, including Tina's accountant.

*Rome, 29 July 1943*

The great event has come! On Sunday evening [25 July] we heard at 11 o'clock that Mussolini had resigned, and that the fate of the country was in the hands of the little King. The *Gran Consiglio Fascista* [Fascist Grand Council] had lasted from 5 p.m. on Saturday until 3 a.m. on Sunday [resulting in a vote of lack of confidence in Mussolini]. From Dr Randegger[9] we heard details. He is attending the Prince of Piedmont's children and was in fact with them on the afternoon of the terrible American raid. He stayed with the children and the Princess, in Red Cross uniform, in the royal *rifugio* [air raid shelter]. On Sunday he was at the Villa Savoia [the King's residence] and saw Mussolini's car in the courtyard. Dr Randegger later was told that when Mussolini came out he asked why the car was not waiting for him in its usual place. The ex-Duce was then told that the King was sending him in a Red Cross car to a villa outside Rome for safety.

Mussolini had not just resigned; he had been arrested. The Red Cross car was a closed ambulance. The villa outside Rome was a *carabinieri* barracks. And Marshal Badoglio was to take over the Government.

*Rome, 14 August 1943*

A week of anxiety in these tremendous hours. The excitement on the 29th gave my beloved Norina a complete *nuit blanche*. Sometimes she appears to be in a state of coma, at others she is so brave and smiling, saying that when the war ends her ambition is to be able to go to a cinema for the first time. Biagio Pace, needless to say, is full of the pillaging and horrors perpetuated by the Allies in Sicily. We shudder when we think of our people at Malfitano. The weather stifling. This is the first time that we have been unable to escape to the mountains during the summer months. Delia, on hearing of the fall of the Duce, switched on the B.B.C. and spent the evening listening to *Swiss Family Robinson*. . . . The King and Badoglio are losing time. Soon it may be too late to save the monarchy.

The Allies entered Messina on 16 August. Sicily had been won in thirty-eight days. On 3 September General Montgomery crossed the Straits, and on the eighth the Italian army surrendered.

At once the German troops encircled Rome. Badoglio and the Royal Family took refuge in the Ministry of War. In the early hours of the ninth they escaped to Pescara, where they were taken on two corvettes to Brindisi. On the same day the Allies landed at Salerno.

On 8 September Delia also decided to keep a diary. It was Norina who suggested she should do this, in detail, as their mother now wrote so spasmodically. Tina had become obsessed with the importance of gathering her memories together, especially of famous men she had known such as Crispi, Rudinì, Lacaita and Tommasi-Crudeli, and spent weeks transcribing her old diaries for Antonino D'Alia, a retired diplomat, to type out. She also preferred to pour out her *riflessioni filosofiche* than occupy herself with recording such baffling and quickly changing war news. Delia hated writing, even letters; but she studiously did her home-work every day until 6 June 1944, just after the Liberation. She described their feelings of 'mixed joy and misgivings' on that night of 8 September; Teresa had left for Germany in the morning 'in floods of tears' as another nephew, her favourite, had been killed in Russia and she wanted to be with her sister in Munich; 'cannons' boomed in the distance all night; there were perpetual rumours of Allied landings nearer Rome; the whole city was in a ferment of anticipation.

DELIA

*Rome, 10 September 1943*

The worst day of all. The thunder of the guns has been so loud that the house often shock. Early in the morning I saw great preparations to decamp at the Croatian Legation[10] – their villa is just opposite ours; a huge bonfire was going on, in which all the archives were being destroyed. Our servants said the Minister himself had presided. Later, I noticed all the windows had been shuttered, so it would seem that they have flown – but how will they get away, with the fighting all

65. *Left:* Street scene, the Papireto (where the papyrus once grew), Palermo.

66. *Above:* A game of football in the courtyard of the derelict Villa Lampedusa.

67. Villa Niscemi, showing the bougain-villea 'like swags of episcopal silk'.

68. Tina, aged ninety-five, with Delia, at Monti Parioli.
(*Photo: Villoresi, Rome.*)

69. Delia in 1966, under the *Ficus magnoloides*, in the garden at Malfitano.
(*Photo: Michelangelo Durazzo.*)

round Rome? . . . I spent my day running up and down the tower. I saw a column of smoke towards San Giovanni, or San Paolo, and then balls of fire (like white stars) going gracefully up in the sky and falling slowly down in the distance behind our horizon (the trees of Villa Borghese), perhaps on the Via Appia. Complete chaos everywhere. Marshal Caviglia [veteran of Vittorio Veneto, War Minister 1919–21] tries to come to terms with the Germans, but at 1 p.m. we hear on the radio that he has failed. Then at 2 p.m. the radio suddenly ceases altogether in the middle of a bulletin. Evidently the station has been seized by the Germans. We are informed that all army officers have left their posts and have told their soldiers to save themselves as best they can, dressed in plain clothes. . . . Panic reigns still. Friends telephone that fighting is going on under their windows. Late in the evening Randegger comes to reassure us. Says an armistice is being negotiated with the Germans by General Calvi di Bergolo, son-in-law of the King, so that the town should not be invaded but be considered a *città aperta* [open city]. No civilians dare leave their homes. But Randegger also told us he had seen Tiger tanks streaming past under his windows in Viale Parioli for two hours incessantly that afternoon. He has been to say goodbye to Von Bergen at the Vatican, as a new *chargé d'affaires* has arrived, Dr Rahn, a friend of Himmler, who Schwesterina [*Schwester* Weisskopf] says is hated in Germany.

Two young soldiers took refuge temporarily at the house, 'frightened to present themselves at their barracks'. People were being shot in the streets without provocation. By the thirteenth German troops were all over Rome. Gradually shops reopened, but there was a severe shortage of food. Then it was announced that Mussolini had been dramatically rescued by parachutists from the Gran Sasso and had been flown to meet Hitler in Germany.

TINA

*Rome, 19 September 1943*

Mussolini is supposed to have spoken yesterday from Berlin, in the name of a republic for Italy. I shall refuse to listen to that speech. Monarchy alone can save this country. The King must abdicate, and the Prince of Piedmont take his place. Delia, being English, dare not venture out of our gates. At least our cook has been able to purchase a fowl and some green apples. We are now 17 persons in this house. Schwesterina has presented me with a small lemon, given her by a German soldier.

Princess Mafalda was rumoured to have been carried off to Germany as a hostage: a rumour that turned out to be true, and she died at the Buchenwald concentration camp in August 1944. Count Volpi, the hugely rich Venetian industrialist, ex-Minister of Finance and once Governor of Tripolitania, was also arrested – 'his porter was threatened with a revolver at his head and thus forced to admit that Volpi was hiding in his own house'. The deportation of young men for forced labour had begun. Carmine Senise, the head of the police, was arrested for failing to give a list of Jews in Rome. All the Ministries were reported to have been mined. 'Diabolical' things were happening in Naples, where 100 civilians were said to have been shot for jeering at German soldiers.

### DELIA

*Rome, 29 September 1943*

This morning we were told that on the 24th they tried to capture Filippo Doria at his palace, but he managed not to be found and is in hiding somewhere.[11] Mary Vivaro [Mary Borghese Princess del Vivaro, sister of Tina's girlhood friend, Lily Belmonte] has been told that much of her furniture at her Castello [at Pratica di Mare] has been broken up and thrown out of the windows. Her administrator saw various young women – dancing for the Germans' entertainment on her beautiful dinner table!! We also hear from there that the Germans are taking all the cattle they can – some they kill, some they even send to Germany in aeroplanes. More important is that they are taking all the *carabinieri*. Our friend Fagà has let us know that he is now in hiding. They have done a round-up at Ponte Cavour. A terrible story there. While searching for *carabinieri* in a big house in that area, they found a young man concealed in his apartment. The mother tried to save him and put herself forward to protect him, so they simply pulled out their revolvers and shot her dead.

### DELIA

*Rome, 16 October 1943*

Deportation of Jews! Tragic episodes! Randegger's uncle-in-law and his family taken off at 6 a.m., small children and all. His daughter, aged 17, who had fainted seeing her father slapped by a German, on coming to, and seeing an Italian officer near her with a German one, looked at him and exclaimed '*venduto*' [sold, i.e. a traitor]. An old man of 80, who slipped on getting out of the motor van in which they had been transported, fell on the first step, upon which the German officer in charge kicked him to get him out of the way; when they

picked him up, they found he was dead. And so on, and so on. . . .
Things are getting worse every day, and people are desperate. The
Allies advance so slowly [Naples had been taken on 1 October] and
have barely crossed the Volturno yet. The poor wretches in hiding in
the woods are suffering from the continual rain and cold. Some young
men in Rome have even had themselves walled up we hear. . . .
Randegger said he considered it very dangerous for us keeping Ignazio
Di Giorgio [nephew] here in hiding. He said we risked everything,
especially as Mama and I are British. Said they might come and search
the house. A client of his, a Pole, had been to get a certificate of bad
health (I gather he is consumptive), as he had been warned by someone
at the Swiss Legation that the Germans might be carrying off all
foreigners. So Mama and I might be included. Everyone is busy
hiding their jewels, silver, clothes, anything else they care about. One
feels like so many *condannati* [condemned] awaiting their fate.

TINA

*Rome, 17 October 1943*

Oh, the British slowness! When can we hope to be delivered? Delia
is a true Britisher, though with some of the better qualities of the race.
She is *fiacca* [sluggish] beyond conception. Never down until nearly
mid-morning. . . . Wives and mothers of *carabinieri* in tears in the
streets, as they watch their men being taken to Germany.

DELIA

*Rome, 22 October 1943*

Today I screwed up my courage and went out, for the first time since
the 19th July air raid. I went to see Aunt Effie, whom I heard was
alone, Audrey having left some time ago 'for an unknown destination'
(luckily though it seems A. has a friend at the Zoo who manages to
send her mother meat which should have been for the poor bears
[lions?]). I found Aunt Effie in bed 'waiting for the Germans', whom
she was expecting any moment to carry her off. She was a pitiful
sight: a cripple, with a maid she does not care for and no one else to
talk to. She said: 'Why aren't you in hiding? Audrey is.' Worried
about Mama. She has no energy, and Randegger says her heart is not
what it should be.

It was reported that there would be the death penalty for anyone who
was caught concealing soldiers. Police dogs were being used in searches.
So Ignazio had to leave, much to his wife's distress; 'like a hunted animal'

he set off for the Allied lines. Badoglio's villa was given over to refugees and his belongings were to be auctioned. News arrived that many of the Jews who had been deported had already been killed. German, especially Austrian, troops were deserting and alarmed civilians by knocking on their doors to beg for clothes. The Grand Hotel was said to have been dynamited in case of a German withdrawal. By December butter cost 250 *lire* a kilo, sugar 90 *lire,* and olive oil 450 *lire* the bottle. By Christmas hunger was 'staring Rome in the face'. There was a curfew at 5 p.m. It was forbidden to use bicycles. Guns were mounted in the Via Veneto opposite Norina's Hungarian dentist. At least a joke could be made. His clients told him that they could no longer come, as they were terrified of having their teeth machine-gunned.

TINA

*Rome, 12 January 1944*

We heard last evening the terrible condemnation and death of 5 of the 19 members of the *Gran Consiglio,* who had been taken prisoner after the return to Fascism [Mussolini's son-in-law Ciano was one of those executed, with Mussolini's assent]. Norina is fearfully upset at this act of barbarism and actually cried.

Then, on 23 January, there was the thrilling report that the Allies had landed at Anzio, only thirty miles south of Rome. The Alban Hills were being pounded by Allied bombers. German tanks and lorries packed with troops rolled incessantly down the Corso in Rome. Sirens every other minute. Velletri was said to have been mostly destroyed by bombs. What of the *poderi* near Albano? Were they safe? 'People now discuss their political views freely in the streets – after 22 years of complete silence.' Schwesterina had to be on duty at the railway station, to receive those of her compatriots who were too gravely wounded to be sent to Germany.

DELIA

*Rome, 29 January 1944*

No advance at Anzio I am afraid, and we are feeling very depressed. In fact Schwesterina tells us she had met a German officer who said in 8 days the Allies would be pushed back into the sea. Alas, we have heard that Signora Bartoli, who looks after our main *podere* for us, was killed in that terrible raid on Velletri. It appears she was standing in a queue of 150 people at a butcher's, when the raid started, and all were killed. The little town is in ruins. Our *contadino* must have been killed too, as he always drove her to Velletri in his trap. The horror leaves one stunned. He is a father of five young children, with a foolish ignorant wife. I (who never dream now) had two vivid dreams two nights running. The first: that we were told to clear out of our houses in 24 hours, as they were all going to be burnt down, and I could not find a place where we could go to. The second: that the Germans broke into our house and, after ransacking the whole place, said I was to leave with them. On my protesting and begging, and saying my mother and sister were ill, and would die if I were not there to look after them, one of the German officers raised his revolver and shot them both, saying sarcastically, 'There I have settled that difficulty for you at once.'

TINA

*Rome, 2 February 1944*

Hardly know what to write. The battle is raging – how can it end? So near, and yet so far are our liberators. The Germans are still holding the heights above Cassino and above the coast on the Adriatic. 2000 prisoners, we hear, walked through Rome from the fighting line, chiefly British and making the V sign. Giovanna [the maid] saw one who said in broken Italian: 'In due o tre settemane tutti inglesi a Roma' [In two or three weeks all British in Rome]. Everything of military value is being destroyed, so that the Allies will find nothing when they come. And in the meantime the Allies hit the surroundings of Rome mercilessly, as indeed they must. The Vatican has lent lorries to the *Governatorato* to bring flour for bread into the starving town.

DELIA

*Rome, 3 February 1944*

Guns, guns all night, but now silence of the dead. People are in a frenzy about the 'man hunt'. Yesterday part of the Via Nazionale was roped off, and the troops seized all men as they came off the buses, young or old. We are told that it is intended to make Rome a second Stalingrad. The villa at Castel Gandolfo where we stayed has been partly destroyed by bombs; all its contents have been broken up or removed. It was such a beautiful villa. Albano too is in ruins and the inhabitants have been evacuated.

The Princess del Vivaro asked if Delia could house a cow – 'an enormous silvery white one with long horns' – and its calf from Pratica in the garage. The offer was gladly accepted, for it would mean milk for Norina. Then more 'refugees' arrived: sixteen chickens and two turkeys. 'It is no joke to feed all these animals.' The black market was in full swing, and butter now cost 450 *lire* the kilo. With the lack of medicine, Norina's asthma increased and her head began to swell.

### DELIA

*Rome, 13 February 1944*

After a period of quiet yesterday there were aeroplanes continually overhead, and bombs bursting in the direction of the Castelli [the Alban Hills]. About 8.30 a regular battle near Rome, the sky lit up by flares and myriads of small sparks of light, and bombs bursting made our windows shake. At night, too, fighting must have gone on, and this morning ditto, as one still hears the explosions caused by big guns. The news from the B.B.C. was a little more hopeful – but people are disgusted and tired of hoping, and say they don't care any longer who wins, as long as they can have peace. I am afraid the Allies are doing themselves a lot of harm by so much bombing, which is very often in useless places.

### TINA

*Rome, 2 March 1944*

The days crawl on, more or less sadly, from the point of view of military news. Our *contadino* at the other *podere* has survived, but most of his family have been killed. Madame Hodert's lovely villa on Lake Nemi which we occupied in 1940 has been smashed up. And Schwesterina has been ordered by her Embassy to return to Germany. What shall we do? It is so difficult to get a good nurse these days. Fear of water being cut off. A new man hunt. Our 'second doctor', Dr Rocco, witnessed a terrible scene. A young woman, pregnant, rushed to a lorry to embrace her husband who was being deported. A German Guard pushed her back violently. She tried once more to reach her husband, upon which the guard drew a revolver and shot her in the face. I counted the sirens ten times this morning. Bombs falling, aeroplanes constantly overhead. Everybody in the house, except we three, in a panic. We had to send some of them down to the *rifugio,* some early Christian catacombs beneath the house that we opened up recently.

### TINA

*Rome, 25 March 1944*

We see no one of course these days. In Rome water is being sold in the streets. Yesterday there were riots, and blood ran in Piazza Barberini and Via Veneto. We are told that Vincenzo and Lucie Florio [his second wife, Lucie Henry] have been released.[12]

TINA

*Rome, 26 March 1944*

A dreadful, monstrous affair. German soldiers were going through the town on bicycles and singing, and the infuriated people fired on them from the windows. 32 Germans killed, among them 2 officers, so the German police seized 320 people from those houses, and they have been shot [in the Fosse Ardeatine]. It seems women and children are also being carried off. Real tragedies. Old men marched away with arms above their heads. 600 young boys have been seized and sent off to the North. It was a miracle that Pace was not among those executed. He told us he had been on the very spot only a quarter of an hour earlier. Ration of bread officially reduced to 100 grams instead of 150 a day. We approach the end of another weary month.

Many of the 320 were in fact taken from the prison in Via Tasso. This was the prison from which the Florios had been released the day before.

DELIA

*Rome, 4 May 1944*

Going through awful days. On Tuesday Norina was very ill again. Then our servant Marchetti started his bronchial attack; he coughed incessantly, and in the morning was dead of heart failure. Meanwhile big bombs rained down all round Rome, the house shaking and windows rattling. Then the upsetting news that a German head-quarters to be moved from the Via Veneto into the Croatian Embassy opposite. This is so that the centre of Rome can be safeguarded from air attacks. We are in the 'environs', and it does not matter if we are bombed. . . . Butter now 600 *lire* the kilo, rice 280 *lire* and flour ditto. Effie has sent word asking for milk from our cow, but Mama says of course we must refuse her. Everyone learning English and trenches being dug in the Villa Borghese.

Friends, distressed by Norina's plight, rallied round as much as they could – when it was reasonably safe to do. Sometimes they were as many as six visitors at a time. Apart from the D'Alias, the Princess del Vivaro and Biagio Pace (who was helping to translate *Sicily and England* into Italian), they principally included Giovanni Caprì (a lawyer, Antonino's biographer), Princess Luisa Orsini, Donna Maria Felice Lequio (great-granddaughter of Corrado Valguarnera), Baroness Grenier (Roffredo's sister), Vittorio Emanuele Orlando and his wife, and Donna Diana Bordonaro (who as Diana Theodoli went with Norina to her first ball).

TINA

*Rome, 19 May 1944*

The battle rages south of Rome [Cassino was captured on the eighteenth]. Terrible loss of life on both sides. The Allies however continue, it would seem to advance, but from all accounts German troops and reinforcements still are pouring down to the Hitler Line [it was finally broken on the twenty-third]. Our German nurse met Graziani's A.D.C. [Graziani had been 'Minister for Defence' since 8 September] who told her he is taking his wife north. Soldiers as well as police are retiring to Viterbo, in preparation for making it the new headquarters should Rome fall.

The Allies must soon have got to hear of this plan, for Viterbo was thoroughly bombed on the twenty-fourth. The prison was partly destroyed, as a result of which all its inmates escaped, including Manfred who had been there for over a year. He joined some partisans, and in due course made his way to the British lines – where he was promptly (but only briefly) arrested, again as a suspected spy – for trying to help a sergeant with some German prisoners – and sent to a German P.O.W. camp, from which after two days he escaped.

On 23 May the Allies broke out of the Anzio beachhead.

DELIA

*Rome, 27 May 1944*

Are we really on the verge of being freed? Guns ever nearer. Not a drop of water in the house. The destruction at Tivoli has been terrible [Rome's water supply comes mostly from Tivoli]. Water pipes hit. The Allies are near the Via Casilina. Still we do not know whether the Germans are going to resist. Such bangs and crashes, sounds of machine-gunning in the roads. Luisa [Princess Ruffo di Calabria, mother of Paola Ruffo who married Prince Albert of Belgium] came up the back staircase. Poor dear, she broke down. She is in hiding, as the police are searching for her as she helped someone who has since been arrested. She had come to meet one of her sons here, Fabrizio, also in hiding, but she fears the other, aged 18, has lost his life.[13]

American troops from Cassino had already reached those from the Beachhead. The Germans hung on desperately, but on the night of 2 June their resistance broke.

DELIA

*Rome, 3 June 1944*

Still no water. Norina had a terrifying attack, and fainted. In despair

I telephoned Dr Rocco to ask him to come at once. He answered: 'Impossible, the Germans are leaving! Troops, cars, guns are all streaming past my house down Via Flaminia. I cannot move.' I then telephoned Randegger but received the same answer. His courtyard was packed with German guards and soldiers. Norina was so terribly ill we could not at the moment think of anything else. At last she got a little better, and about midnight I rushed to the radio and heard the great news confirmed: the Germans were really leaving. I went to bed at last about 2.30 a.m., but could not sleep. All night the sound of a distant roar – cars and tanks, and planes overhead. Once or twice I looked out of the window: flares and more flares in the sky, accompanied by explosions and noises of all sorts. A night never to be forgotten.

DELIA

*Rome, 5 June 1944*

All yesterday guns booming out, so near they seemed in our garden. It was at 9.30 that Pace telephoned to tell us that the Allies were *already* entering Rome – by the Porta Maggiore. Then Caprì rang and said they were passing under his windows, going towards Via Nomentana. But Norina was so terribly ill. It seemed unreal, that just as we should be rejoicing we should be made to suffer such anguish. . . . She had a horrible night, and we feel in a nightmare. All telephones have been cut off. No trams or other vehicles, no electricity, and of course no water. Cortini [Antonino's ex-batman] went out and says he found the town gone mad. Everybody in hysterics. The Americans throwing cigarettes, boxes of matches, chocolates, sweets as they go by in their cars. . . . In the early afternoon a visitor turned up. Cortini came in and announced gleefully: 'C'è un ufficiale inglese giù'. It was Captain Humphrey Brooke, a distant cousin [later Secretary of the Royal Academy, and a descendant of the heirs to Benjamin Ingham junior's estate]. He had just come from Cassino and two months ago had landed in Sicily on a special Allied commission for the protection of Italian art treasures. He gave us the first news of Malfitano that we had had for so long: it had been requisitioned since last July. First lot terrible – but they had managed to turn them out; now it is an American Headquarters, and all Palermo society is continually being entertained there. While Captain Brooke was in the house the deafening bangs went on; he told us he thought they must have been the anti-aircraft guns in the Villa Borghese going off as a 'celebration'. German guns are still supposed to be firing at Rome from Ponte Milvio.

So Rome was liberated once more, nearly seventy-four years after that other triumphant entry, by Victor Emmanuel's *bersaglieri*. The whole city came to life, the population was frenzied with relief and joy. But the three Whitaker ladies could not help having their own preoccupations.

DELIA

*Rome, 6 June 1944*

My birthday – aged 59. Another blow. Very early this morning we had an anonymous caller saying he must speak to us urgently. Dr Randegger had been arrested! The day before the Allied Police had taken him to the Regina Coeli. We were asked to send a letter to D'Arcy Osborne [British Minister to the Holy See, later Duke of Leeds] to implore his help. Norina suffering more than ever, and now we have lost medical attendance.

Randegger was in prison ten days and eventually managed to get his gaoler to release him, through sheer argumentative powers. It was true that he had been forced to attend both Goering and Ribbentrop at times, and this might have given the Allies reason for suspicion. However, one story[14] is that 'Taffy' Rodd, a son of Lord Rennell, had said to someone: 'Get hold of Randegger', meaning that he was the one man to advise on how to make the medical services run properly in Rome, and his words were misinterpreted. However Randegger was soon once more at Monti Parioli and attending Norina and Tina. British visitors were a bit taken aback by all the bowing and hand-kissing, which gave the house the aura of a court.

An Anglo-American commission set up a provisional Government in Rome. It was not quite freedom, as the Romans were to discover. Hotels and public buildings were requisitioned, drastic rationing was imposed, electricity was limited. Meanwhile the war went on. Perugia fell, then Arezzo. Florence was only cleared – after terrible destruction – on 30 August.

Other Whitaker relatives appeared at Monti Parioli. One, Major-General Jack Whitaker, son of Albert, was reprimanded for daring to wear shorts.[15] Sometimes Tina sang opera for them. Her fund of stories about the family usually sounded either mischievous or inaccurate. She would greet each new member with some high-flown phrase, such as: 'Here comes my nephew, straight from the burning sands of the Sahara.' When introducing Delia she used to say: 'This one is the least intelligent.' Other early visitors included Major Ian Greenlees, later to became Director of the British Institute in Florence, and Lord O'Neill (two weeks

before he was killed at Bologna), who brought the news that his brother
Terence, the future Prime Minister of Northern Ireland, had married
Jean Whitaker of Pylewell. Tina enjoyed these visits to Monti Parioli,
and the atmosphere of semi-veneration that had been engendered, and
would have enjoyed them more but for the worry over Norina, who was
getting very much worse, with an ulcerated mouth and tongue, and her
skin a mass of eruptions through constant perspiration.

Delia ended her diary with a postscript:

We are now of course in contact with Palermo. All our friends were
quite convinced we were no more, and all wrote much relieved at
finding that we had not been murdered at the Fosse Ardeatine. As for
Malfitano, the first lot there we hear behaved disgracefully – even girls
were brought into the house. Mama is very upset because her mother's
room was the scene of 'entertainments'. Dinner service, valuable
glasses smashed. Linen ruined, blankets stolen. The cellar almost
emptied, including 20 bottles of brandy of 1785 and 1821. Our smaller
car has been shipped to Naples. Oaks in the garden chopped down for
firewood. . . . Life here for many has been very gay, entertaining and
being entertained – chiefly by the Americans. The scandalous behaviour
of the latter is most unfortunate – money showered on good-for-
nothing women, all going to the bad. Thefts and murders happen
continually in the streets and in people's houses. Regular gangsterism.
Streets dirty, soldiers dead drunk everywhere, and then, as a contrast,
the awful misery of the poor who do not go in for selling themselves
or doing black market trade. At least I can now write without fearing
what trouble would occur if this sheet of paper flew out of the window.

For a month they were in constant and grave anxiety for Norina.
Humphrey Brooke managed to get them the telephone, but they were
limited to four calls a day. For the whole period they were without
electricity, and often there was no water. When Jack Whitaker asked:
'How did you fare under the Bosch, Aunt Tina?' he received the snappy
reply: 'Far better than we fare now.' By mid-July there were at last signs
that Norina was improving.

Audrey thought that Manfred had been transferred north, so his
arrival in Rome was an enormous shock for her. She was very wasted and
suffering from malnutrition. Effie, on the other hand, hardly seemed to
understand the difficulties in making ends meet and was constantly
demanding luxuries that were quite impossible to find. Her temper was

worse. As far as Tina was concerned, for the rest of her life she never forgave Manfred for the danger in which he had put the two families;[16] her dictum 'Remembering is to forgive' certainly did not apply to him, in spite of both her daughters' pleas. In due course she decided to transfer the blame to Audrey, for having been an 'accomplice' – it was Audrey who was supposed to have taken the incriminating letter to Padre Woolf. Finally she fell back on his heredity: the 'bad blood' of Effie's background in Malta.

D'Alia died, so Tina's work on her reminiscences had to end. She soon got well into the habit of diary-writing again:

> *Rome, 1 November 1944*
>
> From today Rome is supposed to be entirely in the Italian Government's hands, with Filippo Doria *Sindaco*. We have learnt of the horrid death of Dora Ruspoli, falling through a skylight [this was Dora Labouchere, who after her Odescalchi marriage had married Prince Eugenio Ruspoli, son of the Princess of Poggio Suasa]. Poor Dora, in her day she was one of the most beautiful women in Rome, though she had bad hands. Alessandra, her [Rudinì] sister-in-law, was far less dazzling, despite the legends that now seem to surround her memory. In 1892 we had Alessandra staying with us in London, and her father I recall warned us not to allow her near Hyde Park after dusk. I see she died, a penitent, with the charming name of *Madre Maria di Gesù* [Mother Mary of Jesus]. . . . I ramble on. Few people seem to realize that it was my cousin Martino Beltrani who saved Rudinì's life at the *Sette e Mezzo* rebellion of 1866. They were surrounded by an angry crowd in the Piazza Municipio; when Beltrani saw a man pointing a gun at Rudinì, he drew a revolver and shot him dead instantly. Beltrani had a gentle character and was very upset at having caused this death, but when Rudinì got into power one of his first thoughts was to make him a Senator.

> *Rome, 22 December 1944*
>
> The new, weak Bonomi ministry has been formed [Bonomi, Prime Minister 1921–2, was now thus the first post-fascist Prime Minister]. How long can it last? Oh, our beloved Italy, will you be able to pull yourself up once again? I remember in 1920 I wished the downfall of Nitti [then Prime Minister], but now I see salvation in him with a socialist state that remains a monarchy [he was a senator of the Right from 1948–53]; I have sent letters to G. M. Trevelyan and Lina Waterfield, urging both to return to Italy[17] and quoting d'Azeglio's words which

alas! have now even more to be remembered: 'Abbiamo fatto l'Italia. Resta da fare gli Italiani' [We have made Italy. Now it remains to make the Italians]. I feel the disgrace of this *borsa nera* [black market] which is turning abominable criminals into millionaires. We are quite unable to get money from England, and I am now reduced to about 185 *lire*! I asked Delia for a loan of 2000 *lire,* but she said she could only manage 1000. The maid insisted on showing me 3 good-sized onions wrapped in a dirty paper; they cost 23 *lire,* which she considered cheap. Salt still up to 500 *lire* a kilo. . . . Meanwhile British colonels and majors turning up constantly with letters of introduction, all expecting to be entertained. Yesterday an avalanche of people, including a very young American Di Giorgio, a soldier from Philadelphia; Delia went to find Christmas presents in Via Condotti [the 'Bond Street' of Rome] but came back empty-handed! Such is the state of Rome now. The new nurse for Norina irritates her in everything she does. I am reminded of that nurse sent by Janet Ross from Florence 48 years ago when my mother lay dying at Malfitano. Though trained by the English, she proved quite incapable and the girls called her Gawk.

The state of penury did not presumably last for long. In spite of difficulties in obtaining food, the teas provided were always copious. She lectured her guests on monarchism, the qualities of Field-Marshal Smuts, whom she greatly admired, the perils of state monopoly, and how France was the 'real enemy'. Harold Acton, 'worthy great-nephew of Laura Minghetti' has described one such tea-party.[18] Although Delia, he says, looked hardly younger than her mother, Tina ordered her about like an infant; Palmerston and Lord John Russell were her heroes, and she inveighed against the Bourbons. She was an 'exotic blend of Sicilian and Victorian English'.

The Germans in Italy surrendered on 2 May 1945. The war in Europe ended on 7 May. Such terrific events only merited short entries in Tina's diaries, though she continued to amass newspaper cuttings. On 11 June Albert died, the last of Pip's brothers; in a way this was even more traumatic for Tina. He had been created a baronet in 1936, which had always been a matter of pride. His widow Eileen, Effie and 'the impossible Berthe', wife of Ingham Whitaker, were the only surviving sisters-in-law, Berthe being impossible because in 1905 she had raffled her dog at a church bazaar. Tina never attempted to leave her villa and its garden. She got into the habit of signing her still very lively letters 'Your broken down old Tina', which upset friends such as Robert Hichens. Other people's problems, except Norina's, barely touched her – those of Pace, for instance, who was trying to live down his fascist past. She worried a bit about Cerretani, since his letters to Norina gave her relapses; he had been Antonino's A.D.C. and was supposedly due to be handed over to the Yugoslavs as a war criminal. At the smallest excuse her diary kept straying to the past.

*Rome, 3 November 1946*

I told Harold Acton that Sir James Lacaita would call Admiral Guglielmo Acton 'un erudito anzichè un marinaio' [a scholar rather than a sailor]. When the Admiral was over 70, Sir James came in one day and found him learning modern Greek. . . . The tragedy of these British soldiers at the end of their military service who wish to bring their dogs home with them and are faced with the absurd six months' quarantine. We are told of an American captain who, wishing to spend some time in England on his way to New York, drugged his Alsatian and then hid it in a roll of bedding. I, who never wished to own a dog again, for fear of having my heart broken a second time, recall our mongrel Tuffy-Too whom we found, covered with fleas and following a cart in Milan in 1889. We rescued him from an evil-looking owner and every year took him to London; when we reached the Customs at Dover we would hide him in a gladstone bag smeared with chocolate. Once we caught a stray dog on the docks, and – having been obliged to declare Tuffy in advance – presented it to the customs man in his place, and I remember H. M. Stanley strongly objecting that the creature had then been unjustly inflicted with the long quarantine. Hamilton Aïdé based a play on this incident.

The great event of early November 1946 was the blowing up of the British Embassy by Palestinian Jews. It shocked Tina deeply, just as much perhaps as the death of her sister-in-law.

*Rome, 26 February 1947*

Poor Effie gone on Monday and the funeral today. Almost to the last she was able to say her prayers, repeating constantly 'Lay me to rest O Lord with my son and my daughter [Gladys who had died in 1945] whom I did not appreciate in life.' She had some really good qualities in a cracky way. I always remember her loyalty to Pip. . . . Delia a great disappointment these days. When I wish to discuss the proposed requisition [for *sfollati,* refugees] of Malfitano she turns on me and says I cannot understand business matters at my age. Yesterday the *Sindaco* of Palermo came to discuss it, and Norina had a bad night in consequence. It is true I am going down hill rapidly. We are now in the midst of discussing with Pace about the translation of my *Sicily and England* for the centenary of the glorious 12th January, 1848, which started Sicily on her path to liberty.

Delia had the burden of checking the translation, which had been poorly done.[19] Then, suddenly, Norina announced that she wanted to see Malfitano again. Excitement grew. Tina also felt she could make the journey. Would that not solve the problem of stopping Malfitano being requisitioned? Delia volunteered to go to Naples to book rooms 'either for one night or the whole winter', in case it would all suddenly prove too much and they were stranded on the way. Then Tina heard that she would have to travel in a pre-war Wagon Lit, so Delia was sent to the station for an hour to test the beds. But Norina, when she knew that somebody would have slept in her bed the night before, refused absolutely to go by rail – a hired aeroplane, that was the only solution.

Such complications. Tuesdays and Fridays were unlucky, so were the thirteenth and seventeenth, and it would be dangerous to fly on holidays, as there would be too many other aircraft. The weather must be absolutely calm, and there must not be a single cloud between Rome and Palermo. Noise, what about noise? Randegger must supply ear-plugs. Oxygen? Cushions? Would it be cold? There were anxious telephone calls every day to the airport at Ciampino. Tina was fussing because she had not yet made a will. At last –

*Malfitano, 28 September 1947*

The miracle has been performed. We left Rome on the 13th [!] and arrived here safely. Whilst in the air I sang 'Agugghie e spingole' and 'U sacciu ccu n'sugnu bbedda ma c'è ccu mi talia' [Sicilian folk songs].

Not a word about the state of Malfitano, after ten years' absence, except that General Patton had written twice in the visitors' book. Indeed it seems that they found the house, all things considered, and thanks to the servants, in a pretty good state. During the journey Delia had frequently been compelled to go into the cockpit to prod the pilot with her parasol and tell him to fly lower. One of her first jobs on arrival was to visit the cemetery.

*Malfitano, 12 November 1947*

Entering into my ninetieth year from today. A long letter from Princess Marie Louise. Several kind friends have asked to come and see me, but I begged the girls to let me pass the day in perfect quiet.

I intend to spend what energies I have on looking through the last chapters of the translation of my blessed *Sicily and England*.

The book was not published until April.

Tina could not, naturally, be expected to comment now on such things as the horrifying resurgence of the *Mafia*, the new poverty as a result of the bombing, the contamination of the water supply, the fact that six out of every hundred persons in the province of Palermo were said to be living in makeshift shacks and shanties[20]. . . . Perhaps she was unaware of such things.

Delia meanwhile was having a thoroughly enjoyable time in the 'giddy world', away from the confines of the family – bridge parties, receptions, dog and flower shows. Tina received among other people the Cardinal of Palermo and Monsignor Pottino, acknowledged since the publication of *The Leopard* as the original of the young priest in that book's last chapter. Occasionally Norina was able to walk along the corridor to see her mother. She had a constant horror of germs and would never, for instance, touch a door handle with her bare hand – an old cardigan would be used for this purpose.

*Malfitano, 12 June 1948*

Norina asks if I am really willing to return to Rome. What can I answer? The friends who come here ask if I am happy to be once more in my home. Alas! it is for me full of the memories of happy days gone by, and of the ghosts of those who are gone, whom I have loved so dearly. The daughters have all the friends from childhood clamouring to see them; no one of my generation left, except Carolina Verdura and Titì [Caterina] Salvo, much younger than myself, to talk of past days, and no one actually of my girlhood. No one to help me to put my papers, letters, books, in order even! Norina brave, but always more or less suffering. Shall we both be fit for the air journey? Delia has returned in high spirits from Motya.

They flew on the thirtieth. Tina obviously still preferred Monti Parioli to Malfitano, but she felt restless and melancholy.

*Rome, 3 August 1948*

In this house, years ago, my very dear husband passed on to the great unknown. We had 50 years of perfect understanding and mutual love on all the chief points of life, and he went, with the conviction as he wrote, that we are to meet again. Alas! I have not that faith to lean on, as my son-in-law Antonino had not either. If only we could make a proper will and decide what is to become of Malfitano. Even my father's books not sure of a resting place! Choose an heir from the Whitakers or Di Giorgios? Turn the whole house into a museum, and the garden as a public benefit to the *Comune*? My dear Peppino loved the garden and planned it himself, and Norina and Delia love it, dearly, also.

Roman and Anglo-Roman visitors resumed their pilgrimage: ex-Prime Ministers, ambassadors, generals, princes, writers. For them Tina had almost become one of the sights of the city. Her manner was so grand and she had such dignity. With the gold-embroidered, damask train of her Worth presentation dress as a shawl over her knees, she spoke about politics and the past with extraordinary conviction. Delia was always 'the poor child', and people were distressed by the way Tina would talk of her daughter's 'limited' intelligence to her face. Her many prejudices were always expressed vehemently. 'The exploits of her Risorgimento ancestors thrilled her with actuality as she talked.'[21] When John Leslie came to see her before leaving for London, she asked: 'And will you be seeing dear Queen Mary?' Then of course there was always a chance she might break into an aria from *Cavalleria Rusticana* or *Traviata*.

*Rome, 3 November 1948*
As for Carlo Sforza, minister of foreign affairs, a renegade from the monarchy [i.e. he was a republican], and once a self-styled 'Count', one has to admit that he has the tradition of the *gentiluomo* [gentleman] of old diplomacy, with an able wife to help him. Yet I can only echo my patriotic old grandmother, Caterina Scalia, who with her sharp tongue knocked people off their seat by exclaiming '*è un riddicolo*', [He is ridiculous], putting in the second *d* to emphasize her despising someone. So I despise that man. De Nicola [President January–May 1948] must have a good place in history eventually; his only mistake having been to retire in order to make way for Sforza. . . . I have decided to accede to the girls' suggestion that I should fly back to Palermo for my 90th birthday.

It had been a short stay. A new routine was established. They flew backwards and forwards every year, spending only the late summer and autumn in Rome. When Tina was at Malfitano, she spent nearly all her day in her large upstairs sitting-room. Once she went for a drive with Delia to look at the ruins caused by the Allies' bombing. She disliked the experience, and this made her determined not to emerge again into the town if she could help it.

The question of the will became more pressing, so it was suggested that 'clever, amusing' Gwen Charlton, Arthur Whitaker's daughter, and her husband Claud should come to Palermo. Claud, now a General, had been a stockbroker since his retirement from the army and looked after their British investments; he surely would give sensible advice. Gwen and Claud were not however invited to stay at Malfitano. Perhaps they preferred their freedom, for the gates were locked every night at 7 p.m. and dogs loosed in the garden, for fear of the *Mafia*.[22] So they stayed at the 'ancestral home', the Hotel des Palmes. Claud's letter to his daughter gives a very real picture of life at Malfitano – one indeed that would have held good for some years to come.

*Hotel des Palmes, 22 January 1950*

We lunch most days at Malfitano. It is a palatial mansion with enormous lofty rooms and lovely furniture. They had a tea party in our honour there yesterday, and the double doors between four rooms were opened. The large drawing-room is Louis XV and the room next it is Louis XVI, both absolutely correct in every detail, including the antique damask and pinkish yellow silk curtains. There is a drive of about 200 yards up to the house, and the great wrought-iron entrance gates are opened for one's car, while an aristocratic-looking gentleman with bristling moustaches (the gate porter) who might be a retired Italian general stands hat in hand at attention as we glide past. Sometimes we walk from here and are received at the gates with the same ceremony. Generally as we walk up the drive there are 5 under-gardeners squatting on their hunkers weeding. They solemnly take off their hats (still on their hunkers) and remain bareheaded until we pass.

At the house we drive *under* the pillared portico, and the double front door is flung open and we are received with bows by 2 footmen. . . . A man comes with a cocktail which is almost too modern for the surroundings. After lunch we go up in a lift to see Aunt Tina seated in state in her boudoir surrounded by cushions. She is in her 92nd year and is an old dear and a regular marvel. She is hardly deaf and can read a newspaper without specs. Her mind is quite clear but she gets rather muddled when she is tired.

*24 January.* We are getting on very well with the Malfitanos and at the moment I am a golden-haired boy on a pedestal. . . . It has been an awful job getting Delia down to business. We are really sorry for poor Norina who is practically an invalid from first one thing and then another.

Gwen enclosed a letter in which she said:

Aunt Tina is a real old *'grande dame'*, 5 ft 11 and absolutely stiff and straight. She walks with a stick with which she waves directions to the manservant who follows her, carrying cushions and shawls, Delia hovering around and Dad and I in attendance. If it were not all rather pathetic, it would be like a comic opera. But Dad is a bit worried as he cannot get any of them to decide the business matters he has come out for. . . . They say *a domani* [tomorrow] and put everything off from day to day. They live in a byegone century. . . . She (Aunt Tina) treats us as if we were 20 and 30, instead of nearly 70 and 80, and tells me to keep Dad in the limelight and not let his good brain rust. Really for our age I do not feel we stagnate.

Stagnate was something the Charltons had never done. At home in Essex they were considered just about the most energetic people in the county; Claud had been High Sheriff the year before. When they first saw Tina, she was eating. They sat in silence while she munched, then a manservant brought a salver on which were her teeth wrapped in a white napkin.

Needless to say, the will was not discussed. And it was never made.

Tina was as diligent as ever with her diary, as though it were her only confidant. One quotes more or less at random:

*Malfitano, 20 April 1951*

'A sense of proportion, my dear Tina, please,' Hamilton Aïdé would say, when my Sicilian blood used to make me over-excited. Am going off my head for daily life and can only remember far-off days. Pip, when I would comment on his writings, used to say: 'Yes, my dear, but let me have what you have said in black and white.' Then Emily Medici's words: 'In all life's adversities keep your tail up, Was the dying advice of a pug to her pup.' My daughters do not realise the 'isolated' life I lead, This is quite different from complaining, as they think I do, of being 'lonely'.

*Malfitano, 17 January 1952*

Norina still with wonderful memory and clearness of perception, a true Anichini but without fixed interests. Delia, who keeps me on leading strings, takes more after Pip, so good for all the details of life and self-sacrificing, but *slow*. We are concocting an answer to Queen Mary's card of good wishes. My pulse perpetually being taken, which

is of no importance. Heart and lungs still sound, but no help for my
*materia grigia* [grey matter].

*Malfitano, 2 February 1953*

Yesterday afternoon by request I attended a confused female tea-party
arranged by Delia. Norina too suffering to see anybody and I could
not recognise one from the other. Norina and I can now only keep in
touch by writing one another letters. Late in life I am learning the
lesson to which all subordinates must submit: 'You must not speak
unless you are spoken to.'

*Rome, 20 May 1953*

Delia bursts in and seizes my pulse, and is quite satisfied! With her
permission and help I am to write a letter to John Leslie on my
recollections of Adelina Patti.

*Rome, 8 June 1953*

Yesterday great anxieties. Norina had no less than 22 small *polipi*
removed from her nose, necessary for her breathing. I was kept
upstairs with *Schwester* Weisskopf dashing backwards and forwards
with the latest news. Delia, so devoted to her sister, standing by during
the lengthy operation, which mercifully seems to have gone satisfactorily. I was shown the 22 little bright-red *polipi* afterwards.

*Rome, 28 January 1954*

Evening. Waiting, hoping to be able to see our beloved Norina, to
wave a kiss to her. Delia seems seriously worried. And I a drivelling
idiot, wanting to make a will and nobody heeding me. Is it Saturday
today? I am writing after my breakfast. Rosetta comes and says it is
Monday. I can barely even at this hour say whether two plus two
equals four.

This was virtually the final entry before Norina's death on 1 April.
From then onwards Tina was in the habit of writing odd thoughts on
scraps of paper. She never went back to Sicily. Norina's room was left
exactly as it had been when she died. Even her handkerchief was kept
folded on the bedside table.

Tina's life dwindled to its sad end.

*Rome, 2 August 1955*

7.20 a.m. Woke singing 'God Save the Queen'.

*Rome, 7 October 1955*

A *lonely* tea, anxiously waiting for Delia's return from Ostia. She
having gone with her cousins, I suppose, to 'paddle'. Nearly a century ago,

in October, 1855, in exile my Sicilian father and Tuscan mother were married in London.

*Rome, 10 September 1956*

Days pass, I know not how. I can say the words 'Our Father which art in heaven', but alas have not the comforting belief that my husband possessed.

*Rome, 12 November 1956*

*Nell'ombra silente cadon le foglie di sole.*
[In the silent shadow fall the leaves of the sun.]

*Undated*

*Je n'ai rien a faire avec le temps. J'ai mes brouillards et mes soleils au dedans de moi.* [I have nothing to do with the weather. I have my mists and my suns within me.]

*Rome, 2 February 1957*

Woke at 8.30, having dreamt of our coachman Don Santo and my very dear Appenine [her pet name for Pip, a diminutive of Peppino] going with our friend Lord Ronald Gower to the Corso dei Fiori.

*Rome, 10 April 1957*

In Italy we say that the sun is male and the moon is female, but we do not know whether they are brother and sister or husband and wife.

Perhaps this was her last piece of writing. Tina died of pneumonia on 22 July 1957, aged just over ninety-eight years and seven months. She was carried to Norina's room to die on her daughter's bed.

# *Epilogue*

MALFITANO today is almost as it was at the end of Tina's life. Delia, approaching her nineties, in a blonde wig, is there alone except for the servants, some also becoming aged. Space in the garden room – its blue-grey wall paintings of trellised garlands, one of the most attractive features of the house – has been cleared for a gigantic television set; otherwise the furniture must be within inches of its original positions. Music by Tosti lies open on the stands in the ballroom, but the grand piano has not been tuned for a decade perhaps. The polar bear skins are still on the floor. As you enter the house from the main portico your eyes are caught at once by two *cloisonné* elephants, originally from the summer palace at Peking and bought by Pip at Christie's in 1887 for £162 the pair. Nearby are two eight foot bronze cranes, also Chinese, holding lamps in their beaks and standing on tortoises, symbolising earth, air, fire and water. It is cool and dim in that grand central corridor, absolutely quiet except for the canaries chirping in the conservatory, with its marble statue of an 1880s girl in a bathing suit, the only piece of naughtiness in the house. The five great Gobelin tapestries from the Palazzo Colonna are still the prize treasures of the house, but only a palace such as Malfitano could house them. Hamilton Aïdé's water-colours, his bequest to Tina, are round the silent, rather sad and dusty billiard-room. In the Louis Seize room there are one or two fine examples of Trapani coral-work that somehow escaped Effie's collection. And there are signed photographs of Queen Mary, Princess Marie Louise, Prince Oskar and King Victor Emmanuel III, all in statutory silver frames with crowns on top. Late Victorian floral vases must in their day have provided that modern touch to the Louis Quinze drawing-room, where standard lamps are perhaps the only incongruity.

Upstairs you can still see General Scalia's collection of leather-bound books, and very professionally done they are too. In the same room are portraits of his heroic mother Caterina, Pompeo Anichini and Tina's Mama in a black poke bonnet. All Pip's papers dealing with his ornithological and archaeological interests are in neat piles behind locked glass doors in his little, modest study. Tina's photograph of herself in the Court dress made by Mr Worth hangs in her upstairs boudoir.

A picture of the beloved Tuffy-Too is in a place of honour on the stairs. At meals white-gloved waiters stand behind your chair, so that conversation is strictly of the *pas devant les domestiques* variety. With the dessert you are served with an ancient marsala that sends the blood rushing at once to your face. If you walk in the garden, you are aware that someone is always solicitously watching you (in case of the *Mafia?*). When you return up the marble steps, flanked by slumbering lions, doors open silently before you. The wistaria and the dracaena are vast now. Strelitzias, like purple and yellow water-fowl, are a great feature of the garden. Sometimes roses bloom on Christmas Day. There are so many varieties of palms, all well matured, and so many other rare trees and shrubs that Malfitano has become a place of pilgrimage for botanists. The greenhouses, however, are barely usable, as boys throw stones over the walls and break the glass. But the cane-work garden furniture is intact, pure Betjeman. One is conscious of the tall, inquisitive apartment blocks looming behind the eucalyptuses on the fringe of the garden. To obtain Ronny Gower's view of Monte Pellegrino one would have to climb now on to the roof of the house. The Villino is practically empty, Pip's collections of skins and stuffed birds having been presented to Edinburgh and Belfast museums – they were offered first to various Italian institutions but refused, as the Italians traditionally are not much interested in birds. The royal trophies, on the other hand, have been kept.

Delia, as she drifts through her drawing-rooms, does not have her mother's interest in literature and politics to sustain her. The visitors' book and her photograph album, which she kept until Norina's marriage in 1922, are her chief solace. She has given up going to London now. Generally in May she spends about three weeks on Motya. The *cuisine* at Malfitano is always first class, and she takes her chef to Motya. When she gives tea-parties at Malfitano you can see from the way she pours out and passes round the cups how scrupulously she was trained to be the perfect hostess.

On birthdays and feast-days a gardener gathers a posy and Delia is driven to the Vergine Maria cemetery. For a few minutes she will sit alone in the family tomb, one of the four niches – her own – being empty. Part of the late summer might be spent in the house in Rome, now known as the Villa Di Giorgio. The routine is always the same; down-stairs by midday, lunch, siesta, a hurried tea, followed by a snail's pace drive through the city in the rush-hour traffic. Antonino's faithful old batman, Cortini, acts as guide; they will visit the Hilton Hotel perhaps, and admire the hair-dressing salon and bar. Otherwise Delia scarcely ventures out of the villa grounds. If a guest wants to go shopping or visiting in Rome, consternation ensues and there are complicated arrangements in case times of meals are affected. Norina's room remains untouched.

She once offered to leave Malfitano to the British Consulate, but Her Majesty's Government decided that the upkeep would be too much of an extravagance. Nevertheless, for the gesture she was awarded the M.B.E. She has her worries, but as far as possible everyone tries to keep her insulated from the world's petty problems. Only once in recent years, in 1965, was she seriously troubled, by an affair that would seem ludicrous in most western countries but is worth chronicling here briefly, if only to show the pitiful lack of libel protection in Italy and the unscrupulous way in which the Italian popular press fosters such absurdities by giving them front page prominence.

A woman of nearly fifty named Giovanna Russo Molichella suddenly announced in Palermo that she was the daughter of 'Contessina Sofia Beatrice Whitaker' – and of the Duke of Windsor, none other. It was never clear whether this Sofia Beatrice was supposed to be Boots, Audrey or Norina, for she appeared to have lived at the Villa Sofia, Via Cavour and Malfitano all at once. No matter, Signora Molichella claimed that her own name was really Marie Louise Windsor, and that not only was she the rightful heir to the British throne but the owner of all Whitaker property in Sicily. As for Delia, she was an impostor; the real Delia had died in a concentration camp during the war and her place had been taken by a woman who was in appearance strikingly similar.

All this was reported with glee in the papers. The story became wilder and wilder. 'Marie Louise' had herself photographed with asparagus grass on her head to show how like she was to Queen Victoria with her crown on. Her sister then said that her own real name was 'Geltrud Oppenhaimer Hannover' and that she was heir to the Grand Duchy of Luxembourg. 'Marie Louise' told the Press that the Duke of York, later George VI, had fallen madly in love with her mother. He had become so jealous that he stabbed her many times; 'Marie Louise' had also been wounded (shades of Anastasia) but had been wafted away in a sack to safety in Sardinia. And so on. Eventually the woman became so clamorous that various representatives of princely houses in Palermo and Rome had to go through the gamut of appearing in court to testify that Delia was Delia and that they had known her all their lives.

What of other descendants of Joseph Whitaker? One has been a Labour M.P. and is a close friend of Danilo Dolci. Some still live in enviable comfort. Others include a parson, a doctor, a psychiatrist, an ex Arab Legion Colonel and two novelists. One has evolved his own religion based on spiritualism. There are some successful businessmen, but no giant of the Benjamin Ingham stature has emerged. The bombed part of the Via Cavour *palazzo* has been pulled down and rebuilt as the *Prefettura*. The Villa Sofia is a hospital. Blocks of flats cover Effie's tennis courts at Sperlinga. In England, however, a Whitaker is still at Pylewell, but Grayshott is a 'health farm' and Hesley a home for crippled children.

The Palazzo Butera is an ugly, gaping eyesore and has been thus since it was bombed over a quarter of a century ago. The Princess of Paternò, said to be the image of her beautiful mother, Giulia Trabia, has much of the famous Butera furniture at her villa in Bagheria. Perhaps it was as well, from a human point of view, that so many of the slums were destroyed by Allied bombs; there were terrible casualties but the stinking, narrow alleys were once the shame of Sicily. Some of the bombed areas have, surprisingly, been left untouched to this day. Meanwhile great, featureless blocks of flats, of no special architectural merit, spill out into the Conca d'Oro. Simond, Ensign Charlton, Ormonde, not to mention Brydone, would be appalled by what has happened to Palermo, which is turning itself into a very ordinary modern industrial town such as one might find the world over.

Some of the villas built by the nobility are in a state of romantic ruin, like the renowned Villa Palagonia of the monsters and the Villa Lampedusa with its faded festoons of the period of Louis XVI. The plaster is flaking off the Villa Pantelleria, but the elegant Villa Maletto, renovated by the ancestor of the Duchess of Santa Rosalia in 1730, is still a masterpiece, all the more beautiful for the patina of centuries. The Villa Orléans is the seat of the Regional Government of Sicily. The Valguarnera and Belmonte villas are still in good order and still superb. As for the owners, or descendants of the owners, there are some of the older generation who are determined to maintain their aristocratic standards. 'This kind of mellow decay has great enchantment, don't you think?' an Alliata princess said recently. Baron 'Lulù' Bordonaro has been described as the nobleman most resembling the hero of *The Leopard*; he is theatrical and exuberant and lives in a palace that is far from crumbling, filled with dogs, Louis XIV furniture, Sienese primitives and pictures by Canaletto, Breughel, Rubens and Van Dyck. He no longer owns any Radalì property, as it has all been removed from him by the *riforma agraria*. To visit the Princess of Lampedusa is quite a contrast. First you must enter an unlikely-looking courtyard, with children and chickens scattering before you. A tug at an outside bell reveals an ancient, almost doddering servant. The Princess receives you in a dim library. She is large and dressed in flowing black, with a black band round her hair, and offers vodka and chocolates. Her accent is unmistakably northern European. Far from being rooted in the eighteenth century, she is not only an intellectual, but a practising psychoanalyst. Patiently she reiterates the story about her husband's manuscript going the rounds of Italian publishers and being 'discovered' by Giorgio Bassani at the house of Elena Croce. She regrets the disappearance of Palermo's palaces, but does not like the impression that she feels has grown up abroad of her husband mixing solely with nobles and moving in drawing-rooms of the 'twirling pearls' sort. He was a very modest, quiet man, who latterly would spend many hours a day working on his book in a back room of the Café Mazara in off Via Maqueda; his best friend was a pastor's son on the Swiss border in Northern Italy.

Gioacchino Lanza Tomasi, Lampedusa's adopted son, is an expert on architecture, a music critic and a journalist on a Communist newspaper. He has inherited the title of Duke of Palma and is the grandson of Luisa Mazzarino. The widowed Princess of Niscemi, an American, a popular figure and friend of Delia, lives in the family villa near Maria Carolina's Chinese pavilion in the Favorita. One of her daughters until recently designed jewelry in New York, as does another descendant of Corrado Valguarnera, the Duke of Verdura. The daughter of Peppino and Valentine Scalea is a protagonist in the much-needed birth control movement in Italy. The Palazzo Scalea and the Villa Scalea's land have been sold. Gangis, however, retain their palace in the centre of Palermo, regarded as the true showpiece of really grand eighteenth century décor; they do not live in it, but use it for entertaining or letting out for social occasions. Here, in the ballroom scene of the film of *The Leopard*, Burt Lancaster and Claudia Cardinale waltzed under the ormolu and crystal chandeliers that hang from painted ceilings whose allegorical scenes would have made the room quite unsuitable for Consul Goodwin's church services. The walls of the ballroom are hung with yellow damask, and at the back you can see the little room where the men would have visited the spilling vats. And at the other end there is the *sala dei specchi*, with its double ceiling, rococo mirrors, majolica floor and the poufs on which the chattering monkeys would have sat; dominating all is the portrait of Maria Anna Valguarnera, 'hereditary princess', born in 1739 and married in 1749.

The always much more humble Palazzo Scalia, hardly a palace at all in fact, where Alfonso Scalia plotted with Pisani and Carini in 1848, is now a slum, its walls a network of sewage pipes from tenements. The Gardner and Rose houses are slums too. Descendants of the former family have retired for good to America. Forester Rose's son lives in Brazil. The Bridports still live at Maniace, gradually extending their vineyards and citrus plantations over the rough ground. Indeed the eastern side of Sicily, especially Taormina, is now the part of the island most favoured by expatriates.

A Whitaker descendant owns the Villa Ingham at Racalia outside Marsala, a house that is as cool and delightfully English as ever in that otherwise rather harsh landscape. It looks across to Motya, where the name of Whitaker – thanks to Pip's genius, energy and prodigal investment – will for a long time be remembered. Excavations recommenced here in 1961 under the aegis of Leeds University, and since 1964 they have been mostly conducted by Rome and Palermo Universities. Motya has now become for archaeologists perhaps the most important Phoenician site in the western Mediterranean. Indeed more can be learnt there about living conditions of the period than in the repeatedly destroyed and built over metropolitan cities of Tyre and Sidon. The *cothon* was drained in 1969 (by the Leeds contingent) to reveal a splendid piece of late sixth century B.C. architecture. Some of the most spectacular finds have been at the Cappiddazzu and the sanctuary or *tophet* – votive statuettes, urns, jewelry, grotesque masks – and are in Pip's museum, now much expanded.

The Florio, Woodhouse and Ingham, Whitaker firms are mostly housed in the old *Baglio* Florio – Benjamin Ingham might even gave been amused at this. The Palladian house built by Ingham is empty, and the gardens have disappeared. America is still easily the biggest field for export, followed by Germany, Australia, Britain, Finland, Switzerland, Sweden, Belgium, Venezuela, France and Vatican City in that order. No less than fifty-nine other firms are dealing in the wine, which again is competing with madeira. And the building that was once the British church in Marsala has been turned into a night club.

Of the place today of that degrading institution the *Mafia* the less said here no doubt the better, remembering the fierce emotions aroused by Gavin Maxwell's book. The situation in the country districts has in some ways improved since the death of the vain, incredible bandit Giuliano – heir to Leone – in 1950, partly thanks to denunciations such as those by Serafina Leale, in revenge after her *Mafioso* husband and son were shot dead in 1960 and 1962 respectively. Yet it will be a long time before the

*Mafia* mentality can be eradicated from western Sicily, where the Arab ancestry is strongest. In the eastern, or Greek, side of the island the *Mafia* is hardly regarded as a threat at all.

In the capital, Palermo, however, the situation has recently become much worse. The foreign Press sometimes compares the city to Chicago in the 1920s. There have been some terrible murders. Ruthlessness and intimidation are still to be reckoned with. Superstition and graft are still powerful. In May 1971 it was said publicly by an eminent citizen: 'Palermo is not a city in the hands of the *Mafia*. It is entirely a *Mafia* city and always has been.'[1]

Sicily has had a form of regional autonomy since May 1946 – an ambition fulfilled after a struggle that had lasted at least 126 years. The results have been criticised, and there has been disillusion, but again it is prudent to avoid a controversy which is no part of this book. Perhaps a quarter of the population, particularly in the west, is still illiterate. Ruthlessness and intimidation are still to be reckoned with. Superstition and graft are still powerful. Time and again one is made conscious of the fact that the Sicilian nature can only too easily be roused to emotion and violence. There are squalid streets still in Palermo, but consciences at home and abroad have been stirred so that many tenement rooms incongruously possess expensive washing machines and television sets, and well fed little girls in American party dresses can be seen chasing one another among the garbage piles, under dripping sheets slung in traditional manner from window to window. Dolci's centres at Partinico and Trappeto have become world-famous in their fight against poverty, waste, parasitism and obscurantist intimidation. He has earned hatred from some, but in the fight against the *Mafia* he will go down to history a hero.

It is a curious sensation to walk among the excavations at the Motya *tophet,* and to see the urns in their haphazard layers; and in the necropolis where graves still contain fragments of bones of forgotten, nameless people who struggled for survival, loved and hated, were themselves merchant princes. Their burial treasures are dug up with understandable excitement and put on display. But they were placed in the graves with reverence and expected to accompany the spirits to another world, even if – in Pip's words – the Phoenician religion was 'of a most revolting and degrading character, human sacrifice and licentiousness entering largely into it'. One has the same mixed feelings, the same sense of shock, on visiting the bombed site of what was once the Protestant cemetery at Marsala and finding old John Woodhouse's tombstone with its face propped against a wall. Or at the dispersal of the contents of a great Palermo palace, such as the Palazzo Mazzarino, when every tapestry, every scrap of furniture, every small ornament down to a miniature *bisquit* bust of Queen Victoria, were sold because of a quarrel between the numerous heirs.

I once went with Delia to tea at the Hotel des Palmes. First of all she said she would drive me to the Villa Sofia. It was a disastrous experience. The man at the lodge gates had never heard of the name of Whitaker and was not impressed by it. The garden was overgrown, the Moorish fountain, inspired by the Zisa, in collapse, the lily pond full of tomato purée tins and old bandages from the hospital. The hotel was a pleasant relief after such squalor. We passed through the opulent entrance hall, adorned with soapy statues placed there by Enrico Ragusa, and peered into the *salone* where Wagner had held court. Finally we settled in a small room that must have belonged to the original Ingham house. The piped music suddenly played a Beatles song. Delia at once cheered up and gently began to move her body in rhythm. 'You know', she said, 'I would rather enjoy that music if I were young.'

*London, June 1971*

# Envoi

Not long after this book was finished Delia died at Malfitano, at 1.15 a.m. on 21 July 1971. She had been failing for the past months, but her end was relatively sudden. She had just passed her eighty-sixth birthday.

The lying in state was in the ballroom. She was placed on her mother's bed. The piano was draped in dark red velvet and turned into an altar, with two candlesticks originally from the British church at Marsala on top of it. At the final mass her two faithful servants, Francesco and Raffaele, sat on either side of the altar; they had been with the family during Pip's lifetime. The Princesses of Niscemi and Paternò, with Prince Alexander Romanov, Marquis Ugo, the last of the 'pigeons', and the children of Peppino and Valentine Scalea, were nearby, as chief mourners. There were also representatives of the Scalia family, and Whitakers had flown out from England.

The procession moved down the drive, past the palm trees, past the giant *Ficus magnoloides*; the old princesses followed in the evening light. Another service was held in the English church, opposite the Hotel des Palmes, the house of Benjamin Ingham, to whom Delia owed her fortune and who was so very different in character from her. The body was laid in the fourth niche in the Malfitano vault at Vergine Maria, and two hundred years of Anglo-Sicilian history ended. Within three months Francesco and Colonel Lipari, who had looked after Motya for her, were also dead; they had nothing else to live for.

Delia's closing years appeared to have been unhappy. She was so lonely amid all her riches. Yet she had no enemies; indeed many people were fond of her, and did their best to help her. Her tragedy was that she had few interests. The last time the author of this book saw her was on her final trip to London when she lunched with him in the Post Office Tower. She was enchanted by the revolving restaurant – one felt she approved of the march of Science, that she took it all as a matter of course. In her will she left 68,000,000 *lire* (about £45,000) to charities, including 30,000,000 to the *Infanzia Abbandonata*. The house in Rome given to the Di Giorgio family. Her residuary estate in Italy, including Malfitano and Motya, went to form a non-profit-making organisation called the 'Joseph Whitaker Foundation', one of the main aims of which was to 'promote in general the study and knowledge of Punic-Phoenician culture in the Mediterranean.' Malfitano would be the headquarters, the character of its interior as far as possible left unchanged. Pip's museum on Motya would be kept intact, and gradually added to as the excavations proceeded. Delia also stressed that the Foundation should be used to further botanical studies, but, strangely, she did not mention ornithology, an even greater passion of her father's.

So Sicilians would still have cause to be grateful to the name of Whitaker, thanks ultimately – one has to admit it – to Benjamin Ingham's brand of genius.

# *Acknowledgements*

M Y gratitude must go first and foremost to the Joseph Whitaker Foundation and to Delia, who so generously made available to me her mother's diaries, papers and books, as well as some of her father's writings. It was very touching when she made me a present of her own wartime diary – she knew she would never look at it again. She was very patient, and one of the kindest of hostesses imaginable. I own that I sometimes felt that she thought I was simply writing about gorgeous balls and receptions in Rome and Palermo during the Belle Epoque.

Several people who provided me with information and anecdotes have also, alas, died. Baroness Giovanella Grenier, sister of Roffredo Caetani, was absolutely splendid, her memory bright in spite of over ninety years gone. My cousin John Leslie was a fund of uninhibited stories, about Rome in particular. I also gathered much material from Viscount Bridport, Giuseppina Cervello, 'Nozzy' (Sir Richard Nosworthy), Dr Giorgio Randegger and Jim Utley. Above all, I wish that Delia's first cousins, Gwen Charlton and Sissie Morrison, could have been alive to see my book published. Sissie was essential to me, and it was she who first introduced me to Benjamin Ingham's letter-books. Elizabeth Wiskemann, a good friend, read and advised me on the sections dealing with the Risorgimento and fascist periods.

The Whitaker family is so numerous that I cannot list all who have helped me. In particular I must mention William Whitaker of Pylewell Park, his late mother the Hon. Mrs William Ingham Whitaker, Mrs Cecil Whitaker, Wing Commander and Mrs Raymond Whitaker, Anthony Whitaker, Ben Whitaker, Penelope Whitaker and Mrs Paul Neal, who was born a Whitaker. Among their cousins who have been specially helpful are Colonel Wingate Charlton, for lending me his great-grandfather's diary, Mrs Kenneth Macleod, Bernard Richards and Dr and Mrs Mordaunt Richards. Humphrey Brooke and Sir Edward Brooke come more into the category of kinsmen; both have given me useful material.

I would also like to thank, for their help in various ways: Ronald Blythe, Marchesa Antonietta Bonaccorsi di Patti, Donna Diana Bordonaro,

Dr Roger Bullen, Dr Rosario Chiovaro, Edith Clay, Jeremy Dereham, Professor Gaetano Falzone, Yvonne ffrench, Vera Fog, Richard Garnett, Countess Bona Gigliucci, Anthea Hastings, Dr Mario Jung, Donna Rosita Lanza di Scalea, Don Gioacchino Lanza Tomasi Duke of Palma, Prince Ferdinando di Leporano Acton, Donna Maria Felice Lequio, Alan Maclean, Colonel Giulio Lipari, the Earl and Countess of Mount Edgcumbe, Margaret Princess of Niscemi, Carola Oman, Mrs Mary Prowse, Mrs Maude Reddie, John Forester Rose, Luisa Saporito Scalio, Professor Carmelo Trasselli, the Marquis Salvo Ugo, the Duke of Verdura, Baroness Alma Villa, John Willey and Mrs Sproat Williamson. Major R. P. Woodhouse kindly gave me access to his own history of the Woodhouse family and answered many letters. The works of Harold Acton and Denis Mack Smith have been quite invaluable, and Miss Irene Neu's thesis was the very spadework for the entire Benjamin Ingham section of the book. I should also here record three other essential sources: Tina Whitaker's *Sicily and England*, published in 1907, her monograph *Benjamin Ingham of Palermo*, published in 1936, and Robert Sanderson Whitaker's family history *Whitaker of Hesley and Palermo*, published in 1907.

Janet Venn-Brown gave up much time on my behalf in the early days. Raul Balin has helped me at every stage; to him I am especially grateful.

The letter from Princess Marie Louise is quoted with the kind permission of Prince Richard of Gloucester. I must also thank Dr Mary Moorman and Dr Tom Trevelyan for allowing me to quote the letters from G. M. Trevelyan; the Oxford University Press for extracts from *In Sicily 1851–1852* by Arthur Clayton Tidman; the Folio Society for extracts from John Parris's translation of *The Fight for Freedom: Palermo 1860* by F. Brancaccio di Carpino (edition for Society members only). The picture of 'The Leopard' is the property of Donna Carolina Tomasi Caro Traina dei principi di Lampedusa; I am most grateful to her, and to Margaret Princess of Niscemi for letting me reproduce the photographs of Corrado Valguarnera and Garibaldi, given to me by her late husband. The pictures of Franca Florio and the Kaiser, Ignazio Florio and Giulia Trabia are reproduced with the permission of S. F. Flaccovio Editore of Palermo.

# Bibliography

APART from the Whitaker papers, I have made use of documents in the Florio, Lojacono, Mount Edgcumbe and Rose archives. Some other works are also mentioned in Notes and Sources. In common with any student of the nineteenth century history of Sicily, I must acknowledge a debt to the bibliographies in the books by Harold Acton, Christopher Hibbert, Denis Mack Smith, George Martin, Christopher Seton-Watson and G. M. Trevelyan, who have done so much of the essential sifting.

ABBA, GIUSEPPE CESARE: *The Diary of One of Garibaldi's Thousand*, London and New York, 1962.

ABBA, GIUSEPPE CESARE: *La vita di Nino Bixio*, Turin, 1905.

ACTON, HAROLD: *The Bourbons of Naples*, London, 1956.

ACTON, HAROLD: *The Last Bourbons of Naples*, London, 1961.

ANONYMOUS [E. LOWE]: *Unprotected Females in Sicily, Calabria and on the top of Mount Etna*, London, 1859.

ANONYMOUS [J. FIELD]: *Things I Shouldn't Tell*, London, 1924.

*Annuario Generale del Commercio e dell'Industriale*, Palermo, 1854.

ARRIVABENE, COUNT CHARLES: *Life Under Victor Emmanuel*, London, 1863.

BAMFORD, FRANCIS and BANKES, VIOLA: *Vicious Circle*, London, 1965; New York, 1967.

BARRETT, WALTER: *The Old Merchants of New York*, New York, 1868.

BARZINI, LUIGI: *The Italians*, London and New York, 1964.

BELTRANI-SCALIA, MARTINO: *Memorie storiche della rivoluzione di Sicilia 1848–9*, Palermo, 1932, 1934.

BIANCO, GIUSEPPE: *La rivoluzione siciliana del 1820*, Florence, 1905.

BLESSINGTON, LADY: *The Idler in Italy*, London and Philadelphia, 1839.

BRANCACCIO DI CARPINO, F.: *The Fight for Freedom, Palermo, 1860*, Translated and edited by John Parris, published by the Folio Society for members, London, 1968 (original Italian version *Tre mesi nella Vicaria di Palermo nel 1860*, Milazzo, 1901).

BRYDONE, P.: *A Tour through Sicily and Malta in a series of letters to William Beckford Esq., of Somerley in Suffolk,* London, 1773; Boston, 1792.

BUCKINGHAM, DUKE OF: *The Private Diary of Richard, Duke of Buckingham and Chandos,* K.G., London, 1862.

CAPRI, GIOVANNI: *Antonino Di Giorgio,* privately printed from *Secolo Nostro* no. 10, Rome, 1938.

CHURCH, E. M.: *Sir Richard Church in Italy and Greece,* Edinburgh, 1895.

CLAY, EDITH: *Ramage in South Italy,* London, 1965.

COCKBURN, GENERAL SIR GEORGE: *A Voyage to Cadiz and Gibraltar, up the Mediterranean to Sicily and Malta, in 1810 and 11,* London, 1815.

COLLETTA, GENERAL PIETRO: *History of the Kingdom of Naples,* Edinburgh, 1858.

*Correspondence respecting the Affairs of Naples and Sicily 1848–1849, presented to both Houses of Parliament by Command of Her Majesty May 4th, 1849* (Parliamentary Blue-books), London, 1849.

*Correspondence respecting the Affairs of Italy, 1860, to be laid before the Houses of Parliament, parts i–x;*
*Correspondence respecting the affairs of Naples, 1860;*
*Dispatches relating to departure of expedition from Genoa, 1860;*
*Correspondence respecting Landing of Garibaldi etc.*
(Parliamentary Blue-books), London, 1860 – 1.

DE CESARE, RAFFAELE: *La fine di un regno,* Città di Castello, 1908.

DENNIS, GEORGE: *A Handbook for Travellers in Sicily* (Murray's Handbook), London, 1864.

DE RIZZOLI, TULLIO: *Il Corpo d'Armata Speciale (Di Giorgio),* Turin, 1933.

DICKINSON, WILLIAM: *Diario della rivoluzione Siciliana dalla notte del 9 al 10 gennaio 1848 sino al 2 giugno 1849* in *Memorie della rivoluzione Siciliana dell'anno MDCCCXLVIII pubblicate nel cinquantesimo anniversario,* Palermo, 1948.

DI GIORGIO, ANTONINO: *La Battaglia dell'Ortigara,* Rome, 1935.

DI GIORGIO, ANTONINO: *Scritti e discorsi vari (1899–1927),* Milan, 1938.

DOLCI, DANILO: *To Feed the Hungry,* London, 1959.

DRAGE, CHARLES: *Servants of the Dragon Throne,* London, 1966.

DU CAMP, MAXIME: *Expédition des Deux-Siciles,* Paris, 1861.

DUMAS, ALEXANDRE (*père*): *Journeys with Dumas in the Speronara,* London, 1902.

DUMAS, ALEXANDRE (*père*): *On Board the Emma,* London and New York, 1929.

ELLIOT, FRANCES (Mrs Minto): *The Diary of an Idle Woman in Sicily*, London, 1881.

ELLIOT, SIR HENRY G.: *Some Revolutions and other Diplomatic Experiences*, edited by his daughter, London, 1922.

ELLIOTT-DRAKE, LADY (ed.): *Lady Knight's Letters*, London, 1905.

EVANS, G. W. D.: *The Classic and Connoisseur in Italy and Sicily*, London, 1835.

EVOLA, N. D.: *Il Generale Alfonso Scalia nelle guerre per l'indipendenza*, Palermo, 1933.

FILIBERTO, IGNAZIO: *Sul viaggio del brigantino siciliano Elisa alle Indie Orientali*, Palermo, 1839.

FINCATI, ENRICO: *Un anno in Sicilia 1877–1878: ricordi di un bersagliere*, Rome, 1881.

FITZGIBBON, CONSTANTINE: *Miss Finnigan's Fault*, London, 1953.

FOOT, M. R. D. (ed.): *The Gladstone Diaries*, London and New York, 1968.

FORBES, COMMANDER C. S.: *The Campaign of Garibaldi in the Two Sicilies*, London, 1861.

FORSYTH, J.: *Remarks on Antiquities, Arts and Letters during an Excursion in Italy 1802 and 1803*, London, 1813; Boston, 1818.

GALLENGA, ANTONIO: *Italy Revisited*, London, 1875.

GALT, JOHN: *Voyages and Travels in the Years 1809, 1810 and 1811*, London, 1812.

GAULD, ALAN: *Founders of Psychical Research*, London, 1909.

GIACHERY, LUIGI: *Piazza Marina ed alberghi di Palermo nel secolo scorso*, Palermo, 1923.

GIACOLONE-MONACO, TOMASO: *La politica del vino Marsala*, Venice, 1938.

GIBBS, JOHN ARTHUR: *The History of Antony and Dorothea Gibbs*, London, 1922.

GIUFFRIDA, ROMUALDO: *I Rothschild e la finanza Siciliana (1849–1855)*, Caltanissetta, 1968.

GOODWIN, JOHN: *Progress of the Two Sicilies under the Bourbons, Journal of the Royal Statistical Society*, vol v, London, 1842.

GOWER, LORD RONALD: *Old Diaries*, London, 1902; selections from *Old Diaries (Records and Reminiscences)*, New York, 1903.

GREGOROVIUS, FERDINAND: *Siciliana*, London, 1914.

GRIMM, A. TH VON: *Alexandra Feodorovna Empress of Russia*, Edinburgh, 1870.

GROSSKURTH, PHYLLIS: *John Addington Symonds*, London, 1964.

HARE, AUGUSTUS J. C.: *Cities of Southern Italy and Sicily*, London, 1883; New York, 1881.

HIBBERT, CHRISTOPHER: *Benito Mussolini,* London, 1962.

HIBBERT, CHRISTOPHER: *Garibaldi and His Enemies,* London, 1965; New York, 1966.

HICHENS, ROBERT: *Yesterday,* London, 1947.

HILLARD, GEORGE STILLMAN: *Six Months in Italy (1847–8),* London and Boston, 1853.

HOBSON, BULMER: *Ireland Yesterday and Tomorrow,* Tralee, 1968.

HOLYOAKE, GEORGE JACOB: *Bygones Worth Remembering,* London, 1905.

HOOD, SIR ALEXANDER NELSON (Duke of Bronte): *The Duchy of Bronte,* privately printed, Weston-super-Mare, 1924.

KING, BOLTON: *A History of Italian Unity, 1814–1871,* London, 1898; Revised edition, New York, 1924.

KNIGHT, CORNELIA: *The Autobiography of Miss Cornelia Knight,* London, 1851.

LACAITA, CHARLES: *An Italian Englishman, Sir James Lacaita 1813–1895,* London 1937.

LAMPEDUSA, GIUSEPPE TOMASI DI: *The Leopard,* translated by Archibald Colquhoun, London and New York, 1960 (original Italian edition *Il Gattopardo,* Milan, 1958).

LAMPEDUSA, GIUSEPPE DI: *Two Stories and a Memory,* translated by Archibald Colquhoun, London and New York, 1962.

LANZA TOMASI, GIOACCHINO: *Le ville di Palermo,* Palermo, 1967.

LA PEGNA, ALBERTO: *La Rivoluzione Siciliana del 1848,* Naples, 1937.

LEAR, EDWARD: *Journals of a Landscape Painter in Southern Calabria etc.,* London, 1852.

LE DUC, VIOLLET: *Lettres sur la Sicile,* Paris, 1860.

LEVI, CARLO: *Words are Stones,* London, 1959; New York, 1958.

LEWIS, NORMAN: *The Honoured Society,* London and New York, 1964.

LUCAS, MATILDA: *Two Englishwomen in Rome,* London, 1938.

MACFARLANE, CHARLES: *A Glance at Revolutionized Italy,* London, 1849.

MACK SMITH, DENIS: *A History of Sicily: Modern Sicily after 1713,* London, 1968.

MALLET, VICTOR: *Life with Queen Victoria,* London, 1968.

MARIO, ALBERTO: *The Red Shirt,* London, 1865.

MARTIN, GEORGE: *The Red Shirt and the Cross of Savoy,* London, 1970; New York, 1969.

MASSOCH, RICHARD G.: *Italy from Within,* London, 1943.

MAXWELL, GAVIN: *The Ten Pains of Death,* London and New York, 1959.

MELENA, ELPIS: *Garibaldi, Recollections of his Public and Private Life,* London, 1887.

MELVILLE, HERMAN: *Journal of a Visit to Europe and the Levant,* edited by Howard C. Horsford, Princeton, 1955.

MOENS, W. J. C.: *English Travellers and Italian Brigands: A Narrative of Capture and Captivity,* London, 1866.

MORGAN, LADY: *Italy,* London, 1821.

MOSCATI, RUGGERO: *I Borboni in Italia,* Naples, 1970.

MOUNT EDGCUMBE, EARL OF: *Extracts from a Journal kept during the Commencement of the Revolution at Palermo in the Year 1848,* London, 1850.

MOZLEY, ANNE (ed.): *Letters and Correspondence of John Henry Newman during his Life in the English Church,* London, 1891.

MUNDY, REAR-ADMIRAL SIR RODNEY: *H.M.S. Hannibal at Palermo and Naples,* London, 1863.

MURRAY'S HANDBOOK: see Dennis, George.

NAMIER, L. B.: 1848: *The Revolution of the Intellectuals,* London, 1946; New York 1964.

NAPOLI, LUIGI: *Rivendicazioni attraverso le rivoluzioni siciliane nel 1848–60,* Treviso, 1927.

NEU, IRENE D.: *An English Businessman in Sicily 1806–61,* The Business History Review vol XXXI no 4, Cambridge, Mass., Winter 1957.

OMAN, CAROLA: *Nelson,* London, 1947; Hamden, Conn., 1968.

ORMONDE, MARQUESS OF: *An Autumn in Sicily,* Dublin, 1850.

PAGET, WALBURGA LADY: *Embassies of Other Days,* London, 1923.

PAGET, WALBURGA LADY: *In My Tower,* London, 1924.

PANTALEONE, MICHELE: *The Mafia and Politics,* London and New York, 1966.

PEARSE, MRS GODFREY: *The Enchanted Past,* London, 1926.

PEDICINI WHITAKER, MANFRED: *A Record of English Families in Sicily,* privately printed, 1970.

PEPE, LIEUT-GENERAL GUGLIELMO: *Narrative of Scenes and Events in Italy from 1847 to 1849,* London, 1850.

PIERCE, HARRY H.: *Railroads of New York,* Cambridge, Mass., 1953.

POWER, GIOVANNA: *Guide per la Sicilia,* Naples, 1842.

RADICE, BENEDETTO: *Memoriche storiche di Bronte,* 2 vols, Bronte 1906 and 1936 (part republished as *Nino Bixio a Bronte,* with introduction by Leonardo Sciascia, Caltanissetta, 1963).

RAUMER, FREDERIC VON: *Italy and the Italians,* London, 1840.

RAWSON, W. RAWSON: *On the Sulphur Trade of Sicily* in the *Journal of the Royal Statistical Society,* vol II, London, 1839.

RENDA, FRANCESCO: *Risorgimento e classi popolari in Sicilia 1820–1821,* Milan, 1968.

RHODES, ANTHONY: *The Poet as Superman,* London, 1959; New York, 1960.

RODD, SIR J. RENNELL: *Social and Diplomatic Memories 1902–1919,* London, 1925.

ROMEO, ROSARIO: *Il Risorgimento in Sicilia,* Bari, 1950.

ROSSELLI, JOHN: *Lord William Bentinck and the British Occupation of Sicily 1811–1814,* Cambridge, 1956.

RUMBOLD, SIR HORACE: *Further Recollections of a Diplomatist,* London, 1903.

SANSONE, ALFONSO: *La rivoluzione del 1820 in Sicilia 1820–1821,* Milan, 1968.

SAN TEODORO, TERESA DUCHESSA DI: *Memoirs,* London, 1929.

SCIASCIA, LEONARDO: *Nino Bixio a Bronte,* Caltanissetta, 1963.

SENIOR, NASSAU WILLIAM: *Journals Kept in France and Italy from 1848 to 1852,* edited by M. C. M. Simpson, vol 2, London and New York, 1871.

SERMONETA, VITTORIA DUCHESS OF: *The Locks of Norbury,* London, 1940.

SETON-WATSON, CHRISTOPHER: *Italy from Liberalism to Fascism 1870–1925,* London, 1967; New York, 1967.

SIMOND, L.: *A Tour Through Italy and Sicily,* London, 1828.

SLADEN, DOUGLAS: *In Sicily,* London, 1901.

SLADEN, DOUGLAS: *Segesta, Selinunte and the West of Sicily,* London, 1903.

SMYTH, CAPTAIN WILLIAM HENRY: *Sicily and its Islands,* London, 1824.

SONNINO, SIDNEY: *I contadini in Sicilia,* Florence, 1877.

STANLEY, ARTHUR PENRHYN: *The Life and Correspondence of Thomas Arnold, D.D.,* London, 1858.

STRUTT, ARTHUR JOHN: *A Pedestrian Tour in Calabria and Sicily,* London, 1842.

STUDI SEMITICI, CENTRO DI, Rome University: *Mozia I–VI,* Rome, 1964–70 (vols V–VI) Centro di Studi per la Civilita fenica e punica).

TACCARI, MARIO: *I Florio,* with introduction by C. Trasselli, Caltanissetta, 1967.

TACCARI, MARIO: *Palermo l'altro ieri,* Palermo, 1966.

THOMPSON, RICHARD WALKER: *Benjamin Ingham and the Inghamites,* Kendal, 1938.

THOMPSON, W. H.: *Sicily and its Inhabitants,* London, 1813.

TIDMAN, ARTHUR CLAYTON: *In Sicily 1851–1852,* Oxford, 1927.

TORREARSA, MARCHESE VINCENZO FARDELLA: *Ricordi della Rivoluzione Siciliana degli anni 1848 e 1849,* Palermo, 1887.

TREVELYAN, G. M.: *Garibaldi's Defence of the Roman Republic,* London and New York, 1907.

TREVELYAN, G. M.: *Garibaldi and the Thousand,* London, 1909; New York, 1948.

TREVELYAN, G. M.: *Garibaldi and the Making of Italy,* London, 1911; New York, 1948.

TROLLOPE, THOMAS ADOLPHUS: *What I Remember,* London, 1887; New York, 1888.

WATERFIELD, LINA: *Castle in Italy,* London, 1961.

WHITAKER, J. I. S.: *The Birds of Tunisia, being a history of the Birds found in the Regency of Tunis,* 2 vols, London, 1905.

WHITAKER, JOSEPH I. S.: *Motya,* London, 1921.

WHITAKER, ROBERT SANDERSON: *Whitaker of Hesley and Palermo,* London, 1907.

WHITAKER, TINA: *Sicily and England,* London, 1907.

WHITAKER SCALIA, TINA: *Benjamin Ingham of Palermo,* Palermo, 1936.

WHITE, MAUDE VALERIE: *Friends and Memories,* London, 1914.

WICKS, MARGARET: *The Italian Exiles in London 1816–1848,* Manchester and Freeport, N.Y., 1937.

WILLIS, N. P.: *Pencillings by the Way,* London, 1833; New York, 1852.

WINNINGTON-INGRAM, REAR-ADMIRAL H. F.: *Hearts of Oak,* London, 1889.

WISKEMANN, ELIZABETH: *Italy,* Oxford and New York, 1947.

WISKEMANN, ELIZABETH: *Fascism in Italy: Its Development and Influence,* London and New York, 1969.

# Notes and Sources

A single name refers to the author of a work listed in the bibliography.

CHAPTER ONE (pages 3–11)
1 William Dickinson. The diary was published by the municipality of Palermo in 1898 in honour of the fiftieth anniversary of the revolution.

2 Neu, quoted from Romeo.

3 *Baglio* derives from the Latin *vallum* or Low-Latin *ballium*, a yard enclosed by high buildings or walls. Cf. also 'bailey', a walled court, in Norman England.

4 In 1840 61,103 immigrants reached New York alone.

5 Florio archives.

6 Some of these titles were inherited after the death of the Duchess's brother in 1851.

7 According to Giuseppe di Lampedusa (*Two Stories and a Memory*) Via Bara was 'crawling with poverty and squalor'. One imagines that in Joseph Whitaker's day it must have been slightly more salubrious.

8 The Sicilian ounce or *onza* was probably the equivalent of sixty pence (twelve shillings); in 1852 it was worth three Neapolitan gold ducats.

CHAPTER TWO (pages 12–22)
1 This Ingham, son of a hatter, went to Georgia as a missionary with the Wesleys in 1735 and remained there thirteen months. Afterwards he attached himself to the Moravians, but having 'found their arrogance too much' he decided to found his own sect. He was 'amiable, jealous in all Christian work', according to some, and ultimately he associated himself with the hazy views of Robert Sanderson, of the family also now famous in the wine trade. In 1741 he had married Lady Margaret Hastings, twelve years older than himself; she was the youngest daughter of Theophilus, seventh Earl of Huntingdon, and sister-in-law of that eccentric campaigner for the Wesleys, Selina Lady Huntingdon. (R. W. Thompson)

2 The fiancée was a relative, a Miss Brooke of Healey Hall.

3 'In the beginning of the present century . . . Sicily became with Malta the depot of English trade. From those places the products of the British colonies as well as of British industry were smuggled into the blockaded ports and along the coasts of the Mediterranean.' (Julius C. Kretschmar, American Consul in Palermo, writing in April 1854)

4 In effect the pirates were only brought under control by the French after 1830.

5 The matter of the forged passport was discovered by Professor Carmelo Trasselli among the archives of Cardinal Ruffo: *Nuovi quaderni del Meridione*, Year VII (Palermo, 1969) no. 25.

[6] Edward Charlton, 1784–1852. Later Colonel and a Knight of Hanover. The quotations are from an unpublished diary in the possession of Colonel Wingate Charlton.

[7] The Cassero was the same as the street known as the Toledo, now the Corso Vittorio Emanuele; the lowest part, near the Marina, was known as the Cassero Morto. La Nuova was the present Via Ruggiero Settimo, i.e. the continuation of the Via Maqueda.

[8] 'How lamentable to see so fine an island so totally neglected! Frequently for twenty miles together I have not perceived any appearance of the country being inhabited, or cultivated' (W. H. Thompson). 'The present state of Sicily, I am inclined to think, resembles very much what I conceive to have been that of England in the reign of Henry VIII. The church is falling, the nobility are losing their feudal influence, and the pretensions of the Crown and the consequence of the commons are visibly extending.' (Galt)

[9] Goodwin, Royal Statistical Society.

[10] Trinacria was the ancient name for Sicily on account of its triangular shape. Lilybaeum had been founded in 396 B.C., peopled by refugees from the neighbouring island of Motya. Its modern name of Marsala comes from the Saracenic Mars-al-Allah, harbour of God.

[11] The harbour had silted up a great deal since ancient times and in any case there were some dangerous sunken rocks not far from land – *et vada dura lego saxis Lilybeia caecis* (Virgil, *Aeneid* iii, 706). 'Mr Woodhouse has weighed a sufficient number of the sunken stones [from Roman times] to form a very respectable mole, opposite to his establishment on the south side of the town. But large ships must lie to the south-west of the city, at a distance of nearly two miles off shore.' (Smyth)

[12] The temple of Venus Erycina on Mount Eryx was a great landmark for classical sailors. St Julian is said to have put Saracen attackers to flight; hence the name San Giuliano. The town is now known as Erice. Samuel Butler believed that the author of the *Odyssey* was a woman who lived at Trapani. Ithaca was the island of Marettimo, the Cyclops and Polyphemus lived on Mt Eryx, the Formiche rocks between Trapani and the Aegadean Islands were those hurled by Polyphemus at Ulysses. (Samuel Butler, *The Authoress of the Odyssey*, London 1897, Chicago 1967)

[13] Such was the Woodhouses' reputation for integrity that the family was never once molested by the *Mafia*, right up to their final departure in 1928. There being no stable currency in western Sicily during that period, payments had to be made in Maria Theresa silver dollars imported from Malta. John Woodhouse was even able to drive around the countryside, unarmed and unescorted, with a keg at the back of his cart containing the dollars.

[14] A pipe these days holds 105 gallons. A hogshead holds fifty-two and a half gallons, and an octave thirteen and a half gallons.

[15] Marsala is still sometimes drunk in naval wardrooms in the Mediterranean, depending usually on the taste of the officer looking after the wines and the wealth of the wardroom concerned. Normally it is drunk as an apéritif, but it is often available after dinner.

[16] Not at the Palazzo Palagonia (which is in Via Alloro) as is sometimes stated. How such a legend began has not been established. Tradition in Palermo has it that on arrival they went to the 'Casino Vega' in the garden of the Palazzo Cattolica at the south end of the Marina. The Palazzo was burnt down in 1820 and rebuilt as the Palazzo Baucina. They then moved to a larger house near the Mole, usually regarded as having been the Palazzo de Gregorio (Giachery). However the Palazzo de Gregorio was not built until 1850. The present Marquis de Gregorio has no documentary proof of there having been

in a house on the site of his palace, though he agrees that there is a possibility. The alternatives therefore would be the Quinta Casa dei Gesuiti, next to the Arsenal, or the Villa Montalbo.

17 Nelson had also been created a baron by the British Government after the Nile. His first agent at Bronte, on the suggestion of Sir William Hamilton, was the landscape gardener Graeffer, who had laid out an English garden at Caserta. Graeffer's extravagant ideas ate vastly into the expected income from the estate. The title and property of Bronte went after Nelson's death to his brother, the Rev. William Nelson. Maniace was named after the Byzantine General Maniaces, who in 1040 with the help of Norwegians and Normans defeated a large army of Saracens. Originally it had been a Benedictine monastery. The Borgia Pope, Alexander VI, was Abbot there from 1471–91.

18 'The miserable hotel . . . opposite to which was the principal gaol of the town. As the street was narrow [at the back of the hotel] we could hear the groans and lamentations of the wretched creatures all night' (Cornelia Knight). The gaol was the detested Vicaria Prison. Later Cornelia Knight and her mother moved to the Palazzo Benso, next to the Palazzo Butera and where Goethe had had an apartment in 1787. Brydone wrote a very libellous account of Madame de Montagne, a 'noisy troublesome Frenchwoman', that caused much amusement among his contemporaries and distress to his victim. 'Ah, mon Dieu! comme ces Anglais sont sauvages!' she could be heard muttering when he did not find her attractive.

19 Brydone noted 'the curious pastime of concerts in a sort of temple on the Marina, lasting until 2 a.m. The better to favour pleasure and intrigue, there is an order that no person, of whatever quality, shall presume to carry a light with him.' Thus one circulated in utter darkness, and ladies – to avoid being compromised – usually wore masks.

20 'That superficial, grasping and vulgar minded woman', as Charles Lock, the British Consul-General in Palermo, wrote of Lady Hamilton (Sermoneta). She was, he said, at the bottom of 'all the mischief which has rendered my stay so uncomfortable'. This discomfort was largely concerned with rows with Nelson over the victualling of the fleet, a sinecure which Lock had hoped to obtain for himself. No doubt he strongly disapproved of Nelson ordering wine direct from John Woodhouse.

21 The original of the contract was long considered lost, possibly in the bombing of Marsala in 1943. It was rediscovered in 1968 among some old business letters in Hove by Mr Peter Gerry, manager of Peter Dominic Ltd.

22 Later Nelson used the signature 'Bronte Nelson of the Nile' and 'Nelson and Bronte'.

23 The marriage was by Papal dispensation. A distant cousin of Gibbon, Sir John Acton had been invited to Naples by Maria Carolina at the suggestion of her brother, Leopold of Tuscany. Her infatuation for him (it is said simply because he was not interested in her) had led to his appointment as supreme commander on land and sea and Prime Minister of the Two Sicilies, which posts he held for twenty-nine years. He died on 12 August 1811; a sad and fulsome memorial tablet from his widow is to be seen at Santa Croce, Palermo. One son was a Cardinal, and the first Lord Acton his grandson.

24 A brand of madeira, originating from Cretan vines, is now known as Malmsey. The type of Malmsey in which the Duke of Clarence met his fate is still to be found on the Lipari, or Aeolian, Islands.

25 This highly coloured fragment of Ingham's 'romance' with Estina Fagan seems to have been part of a projected novel by Tina Whitaker in the 1880s.

[26] Robert Fagan, whose family came originally from Cork, was born in 1761 and died in Rome in 1816. He first became Consul-General for Sicily and Malta in 1809. Earlier he had been in Rome, where in 1795 he had been snubbed at a dance because of his liberal views and ungentlemanly background by Cornelia Knight, who had thus incurred the displeasure of Prince Augustus of England (Elliot-Drake). He had been born a Catholic, but changed his faith in England, and had changed again to marry the lovely daughter of C. Ritson's *valet de chambre*, Anna Maria Ferri, aged sixteen. He took advantage of the French invasion of Italy to acquire, for about £2,250, two famous landscapes by Claude from the Palazzo Altieri: 'The Landing of Aeneas' and 'The Father of Psyche sacrificing at the Temple of Apollo', now at Anglesey Abbey, Cambridgeshire. Fagan conducted excavations at Tindaris in 1808 and at Selinunte between the years 1809–10 (this latter without much success); systematic excavations at Selinunte were only begun in 1822–3 by Harris and Angell. Some Attic fragments from his archaeological collection are today on view at Palermo's National Museum. He was also a portraitist and painted Lady Acton and her children, Lady Holland, and Lady Amherst and her children. Estina (or Esther) eventually married Francis Acton, nephew-cum-brother-in-law of Sir John, in 1820; the marriage seems to have been considered socially a bad match by the Actons.

[27] Nobody could have been further removed in personality from Sir John Moore than the Queen, whom he variously described as violent, wicked, meddling, and incapable of discretion. Ensign Charlton's account of a dinner party at Noto on 16 April 1807 reveals this difference to perfection:

> The kind and amiable manners of Sir John impressed everyone strongly in his favour, indeed both these Generals [the other being General Oakes] were excellent specimens of the superior ranks of the Army. Sir John Moore appeared extremely diffident in female society, the *double entendres* so freely passed at the Prince's [the Prince of Villa Dorata] table before the ladies disconcerted him not a little and often heightened the colour of his handsome countenance. The Sicilian ladies present seemed no way abashed, indeed they rather seem to enjoy what no English lady would have sat to listen to. The chief promoter of these unrestrained conversations was, strange to say, the *Vicario*, or Bishop, a portly good-tempered old son of the Church. General Oakes appeared highly amused with Sir John's surprise and embarrassment.

[28] C. R. Cockerell wrote: 'Though a paradise compared to Greece, I find Sicily seething with discontent; and were it not for Lord W. Bentinck, to whom the people look up as the only honest man among the authorities, there would be an insurrection.' (*Travels in Southern Europe and the Levant 1810–1817*, London and New York, 1903)

[29] An eloquent and anonymous pamphlet, written in Palermo, was published and circulated in London in 1817; it was entitled *Address of the Sicilians to the British Nation, which guaranteed the Constitution violated by the King of Naples.* 'The yoke of the Moors', runs its peroration, 'appears to us preferable to the injustice of being accounted an enslaved province of Naples.' And this was a sentiment that was to remain with the Sicilians for over forty years.

[30] Other main Woodhouse *soleras* in the future were 1836, 1837, 1860 and 1870. Later ones were called Nelson, Vergine, Garibaldi, Trinacria, I.P. (Italian Particular) and Corona. The best Ingham *soleras* were 1834, 1835, 1836, 1837, 1850, 1870, 1871, 1872, 1873. The *solera* called Old Golden Syracuse, or O.G.S., was a particularly sweet marsala.

CHAPTER THREE (pages 23–35)

¹ Simond's comments on the roads were somewhat unfair. Such highways as there were had definitely been improved by the English.

² Gibbs (born in 1758) had, in the time of Nelson, been a partner in the banking firm of Gibbs, Falconet and Noble, later known as Gibbs and Co. He came from near Exeter and had first gone to Italy in 1775. In 1799 he and his family had shared the *palazzo* near the Mole with Nelson and the Hamiltons. In 1803 he visited Bronte for Nelson, as his agent, after the death of Graeffer. Since he was also banker to the court of Naples, he had served not only King Ferdinand, before and after his restoration, but Joseph Bonaparte and Murat. Henry Gibbs (Lord Aldenham), Governor of the Bank of England, was descended from Abraham Gibbs' uncle.

³ G. Leydings Heirs & Co., and Vallin, Routh and Valentine.

⁴ Mazara del Vallo was (and still is) the major fishing port of Sicily. Payne had been there since the end of the eighteenth century and dealt at first mostly in flax, almonds, oil, soda, barley and semolina. He later branched out into wine and was joined by John Hopps, whose descendants are now naturalised Sicilians and still involved with the wine trade. Mazara was not a particularly attractive place in which to live, 'abundantly showy at a distance, within a collection of relicks and rubbish', whilst the land outside was as 'desolate as Hounslow heath, and equally susceptible of cultivation.' (Galt)

⁵ In fact the phrase Two Sicilies had been in common use since the fifteenth century. Hitherto the King had been Ferdinand III of Sicily and Ferdinand IV of Naples. On 8 December 1816 he decreed that he would in future be known as Ferdinand I of the Two Sicilies.

⁶ Oates recovered in due course. Craufurd Tait Ramage knew him in Naples: 'I dine out that night [New Year's Day, 1827] with one of the principal merchants here, Mr Oates.' (Clay)

⁷ Mary Gibbs was five in 1799 when her family lived with Nelson and the Hamiltons in Palermo. Nelson gave her a passage home in a warship in 1803. In London she had been much under Lady Hamilton, from whose influence cousins had carefully removed her. Gossip must have circulated about this 'preference' on Abraham Gibbs' estate, for in a family letter Mary refers to the 'misapprehension in 1816' and says 'If you had known my husband you would never have credited them.' In fact the Colonel settled for about £10,000, after creditors had threatened to sue Abraham Gibbs' brother in Genoa.

⁸ *Benjamin Ingham of Palermo* (Whitaker). The late Sissie (Alexandrina) Morrison would say that her mother, *née* Ackie Whitaker, never liked to mention the matter of the tattoos.

⁹ Captain Smyth gave this description of travelling in Sicily:

The mode of proceeding being either on mules, or on horseback, but more generally in a *lettiga*, (a corruption of *lectica*), a kind of narrow chaise, with room for two persons to sit opposite to each other, mounted on two long poles, and carried by mules at the average rate of three miles and a half an hour. The tourist should be prepared to fare coarsely, in the cheerless inns of the island, where miserable beds, bad wine, dirty cookery, and inconveniences of every kind, are unavoidable. . . . People generally travel with one or two Campieri or guards, who are well armed.

Over forty years later Murray's *Handbook* elaborated on the *lettiga*, still just as uncomfortable:

The motion is very unsteady and unpleasant, resembling, from the centre of gravity being thrown too high, that of a boat at sea; besides which, the sloping position the vehicle assumes on ascending or descending throws the one passenger into the other's lap; and the ear is eternally deafened by the clang of innumerable bells with which the mules are decorated, and without it is said they will not travel. There is also considerable danger of upsetting on very rugged ground.

[10] 'In Palermo alone, the advocates, solicitors, notaries, clerks etc. are said to amount to four thousand, and . . . large fortunes are reaped by men of inferior talents. There is no person of the most moderate income, who does not find it necessary, regularly to pay an annual retaining fee to one or more solicitors.' (Smyth)

[11] Simond.

## CHAPTER FOUR (pages 36–51)

[1] The actual place called Santa Rosalia is in the province of Catania. The *festa* had become internationally famous ever since the publication, in many translations, of Brydone's book. Most people travelling to Palermo (including Goethe) would refer to the *festa* as a matter of course, admitting that Brydone's description could not be bettered. The celebrations in 1820 must have been much as they were in his day, when the streets were described as being decorated with some two thousand wooden, brightly painted arches and pyramids, all entwined with artificial flowers and aglow with small lamps. An enormous triumphal car, seventy feet long, was the show-piece. Later there would be a fireworks display out to sea, after which the grand families of Palermo, dressed in their jewels and 'greatest gala', made a procession in their coaches through the streets.

[2] Sansone. Aci was actually murdered in Via della Conceria, some 450 yards from Ingham's house in Via Bara. General Cockburn met him in 1811: 'He is what we call in Ireland a thorough-going supporter of whatever the court wishes.'

[3] Dumas *père* tells how the Prince of Cattolica had been pursued from room to room. The Prince eventually hid between two mattresses. Later he was betrayed by a child who spotted him creeping out when he thought the coast was clear.

[4] Richard Church, 1784–1873. The son of a Quaker merchant in Cork, his life was adventurous from the start. He ran away to join the army when he was sixteen and fought at Aboukir Bay in 1801. From 1806–8, as a captain in the Corsican Rangers, he was in command of the garrison at Anacapri. Then he raised a regiment of Greek light infantry in the Ionian Islands. After 1815 he was invited back to Naples by King Ferdinand, who made him a Major-General and Governor of Bari and Otranto. After the Palermo incident in 1820 he had to leave Naples, but he was back (knighted by George IV) in 1824, as we read that he dined with Lady Blessington: 'He is full of military ardour and has studied his profession *con amore*.' In 1827 he went to Greece at the outbreak of the War of Independence and became generalissimo of the armed forces. He lived in Greece for the rest of his life and in 1843 was made a Senator. Gladstone consulted him on the problem of the Ionian Islands.

[5] *Carbonari*, literally charcoal-burners. As Lady Morgan said, they 'grew to be a generic name for all that was enlightened and liberal in the kingdom; but it long represented rather an opinion than an organized society. In its original formation there were no mysteries to conceal, no forms to celebrate, no dogma, no secret. The league was that of intellect, of spirits ardent in the cause of liberty and of truth . . . and soon embraced all that desired or deserved to be free.' Carbonarism appeared originally during Murat's reign. After the restoration of the Bourbons it spread to northern Italy and thence to France. The 1820 revolution in Naples was the first to be promoted actively by *Carbonari*.

[6] The Hotel d'Angleterre was on the corner of the Via Pappagallo, on the east side of the Piazza Marina. Originally it had been known as Page's Hotel, having been once owned by an Anthony Page. It had been sold in 1818 to Guglielmo Tigone, who had changed the name to Hotel d'Angleterre. It ceased to be an hotel in 1846. Travellers have caused much confusion about Palermo's hotels. To clarify a little: In 1827 Page's daughter Anne married Antonio Gagliardo, the owner of the Prince of Wales and Great Britain Hotel, on the south side of the Piazza Marina; on their marriage they revived the name of Page's Hotel for their own establishment. J. H. Newman stayed in the second Page's Hotel in 1833. Originally it had been the Crown and Anchor, when the building was leased in 1808 to Francis Wolff by the Marquis of Sant'Onofrio. Wolff sold the lease to Gagliardo in 1810, and in 1838 the Palazzo was bought by the Giachery family who changed the name once again, to Hotel de France.

The other main hotels were the Albion, in the east side of the Piazza Marina, started by L. C. De Martino in 1838 and where Gladstone stayed in that same year, and eventually to become the Albergo d'Italia; and Madame de Montagne's. After Madame de Montagne's death her hotel was run by her sister and her husband; early in the 1800s it was sold to Antonio Marletta, who called it the Hotel de Londres. He died in 1838, and it then became the Albergo della Fortuna. The hotel closed in 1860.

The Palazzo Benso, where Goethe stayed and where Cornelia Knight eventually moved, was also sometimes known as Grande Albergo. On the northern corner of the Palazzo Butera, overlooking the Marina, it was sold to the Prince of Butera in 1801. The Albergo Trinacria, mentioned in the last chapter of *The Leopard*, was opened in July 1844 and was to the south of the Palazzo Butera proper, although part of the same building. This closed in 1911.

[7] E. M. Church.

[8] This Prince of Belmonte is more usually known in history as the Prince of Pandolfina. He was son of the prince who had been arrested in 1811 and had died in 1814.

[9] The agent for the Nelson estate, Philip Thovez, played an important part in the last stages, leading a deputation to Messina to prevent an army marching on Bronte.

[10] Colonel Pietro Orlando, who had taken Caltanissetta with the Prince of San Cataldo. When Colonel Costa advanced from Messina, Orlando had to appeal for a large quantity of reinforcements from Licata. He attacked and was beaten, so Caltanissetta returned to the Bourbons.

[11] Bianco.

[12] Renda.

[13] The Rev. Patrick Brontë, father of Emily, Charlotte and Anne, had been born with the name of Prunty. It is probable that his admiration for Nelson decided him to change it to Bronte; later he added an accent – first it was Bronté, then Brontè and finally Brontë with the famous diaeresis.

[14] Their real names were Joshua (needless to say) and Mary. The family consisted of five sons and five daughters. The fourth son, William Bairstow Ingham, born in 1849 and therefore after Anne Brontë's departure, went out to Queensland in 1872 with a reputed fortune of £60,000. He started a sugar plantation on the Herbert River, owned a paddle-wheeled steamer and ran the first sawmill. Later he was appointed a government resident in New Guinea. In 1878 he went to the Brooker Islands to make an inquiry about a murder. Some say that he was hustled overboard by natives and swam back laughing to his boat, others that he was wounded by a blow from a tomahawk and thrown out to sea.

At any rate when he grasped the gunwale, all his fingers were chopped off, and he was finished off with a spear as he struggled in the water. The rest of his crew were also massacred. Since the natives were cannibals, one can but draw conclusions about the fate of the corpses. The affair caused a great commotion in Queensland, where Ingham had been well esteemed. As a result a newly gazetted township on the Herbert River was named after him, a town which flourishes to this day.

There is also a theory that he went to the islands to sell iron tanks, and that when he had his back turned the cannibals hit him on the head. 'They soon had him roasting on the fire' (letter to *The Times* 4 September 1929). A search party was sent to find him, but only the indigestible soles of his feet were left.

15 No doubt Maria was the daughter of the Countess Lucchesi who had fled to Malta in 1820.

16 Sanderson's portrait shows that he had an agreeable whiskered face, with a long nose. His main office was in the famous Palazzata in Messina.

17 Romualdo Giuffrida in an article on 'La Cartiera Turrisi' in *Il Risorgimento in Sicilia* (Palermo, Jan–Dec 1969).

18 The *soleras* for 1834 and 1870 were to be regarded as among Ingham's best 'sherry type'. Those known as O.P. (Old Particular) and S.O.M. (Superior Old Marsala) were 'port type'.

19 Information Major R. P. Woodhouse.

## CHAPTER FIVE (pages 52–62)

1 *Boston Directory*, 1828.

2 A letter from Ingham on 18 October 1841 complains of the interference of temperance societies with the consumption of marsala in Boston.

3 Another uncle was Sir George Rose (1782–1873), master in chancery and a noted wit.

4 The Duke's tour was from 1827–8.

5 Lord Ossory's tour was in 1832.

6 Murray's *Handbook* gives a quotation from W. E. Gladstone's diary in 1838 on the subject:

The mule seems to have no sense of fatigue, of kindness or emulation; a light or a heavy load, a long or short distance, a good or a bad road, provided only the pace be not rapid, are all without the slightest effect on the physical composure of a mule . . . they really seem like Frankensteins of the animal creation. Sympathy, however they have; and with a faint yet wild and unnatural neighing they will sometimes recognise friendship.

7 The subsequent history of Bronte, involving some truly nightmarish episodes, has clouded memories of the post-Nelson and pre-Garibaldi period. So much so that the word 'hero' in connection with Nelson would always be used sarcastically by opponents of the Duchy (and invariably with an allusion to the execution of Caracciolo), and indeed the English in general came to be regarded as the prime cause for all Bronte's troubles. Benedetto Radice in his *Memorie storiche* was positively virulent against the poor Duchy: 'Due sono i più grandi mali che affliggono Bronte: L'Etna et la Ducea' [The two greatest evils that afflict Bronte are Etna and the Duchy]. Actually there was an anti-English bias long before Nelson. Brydone tells how peasants had talked of an English queen who had been condemned to burn for ever in Etna, as 'she was the wife of a king that had been a Christian and that she had made him a heretic'. This queen was none other than Anne

Boleyn. By the time that Radice got hold of the story, it had been twisted round so that Queen Elizabeth was the soul in torment.

[8] Mozley.

[9] *Sicily and England* (Whitaker).

[10] Cholera came originally from India. It appeared in Moscow and then throughout Russia in 1830 (the Tsarevitch Constantine was one of its victims), and in Paris and the British Isles for the first time in 1832.

Usually it is spread either from a polluted water-supply or from flies. The first stage in the illness consists of diarrhoea and vomiting, followed by severe stomach pains due to lack of salts; the temperature rises, but the flesh is cold and bluish, and there is a terrible thirst – drinking only making matters worse, because of a further dilution of the body salts. All this can happen within three to twelve hours. In the second stage the skin becomes dry and almost purple, the voice is husky and urine ceases. Death can now occur almost immediately, but sometimes a victim can linger on for two to three weeks. On occasion people have been seen literally to drop down dead in their tracks.

[11] *Sicily and England.*

[12] Goodwin, Royal Statistical Society.

[13] Routh, the son of a Chief Justice for Newfoundland, first sailed for Naples in September 1796, when he was seventeen. He enjoyed himself and was given a job in the counting house of his friend Vallin. Then the French came, and he had to escape back to England. He returned in 1805 and a partnership was formed with Vallin and another Englishman, Valentine. His wife Harriet was the sister of Sophia Sanderson's mother.

## CHAPTER SIX (pages 63–80)

[1] *Benjamin Ingham of Palermo.*

[2] 'The charm of an English villa is in cool seclusion; that of a Sicilian one must be in as much publicity and little shade as possible.' (*Unprotected Females* etc., Anon.)

[3] Temple led 'one of the easiest and pleasantest of diplomatic lives in the most beautiful country in Europe.' As Envoy Extraordinary in Naples 'he certainly had no extraordinary or hard work to complain of.' (MacFarlane)

[4] The American Government did not then have entire control of its own funds, which until 1836 were largely in the hands of a corporation known as the Bank of the United States. Jackson maintained that the existence of the Bank was unconstitutional, merely 'to make the rich richer and the potent more powerful'. In 1836 its charter was renewed, but the Bank was deprived of a great deal of its strength. The deposit of Government funds into various local 'pet' banks merely created new difficulties.

[5] Gladstone in his diary recorded (October 1838) that the people of Alcamo believed that the Cardinal Archbishop had been given cholera in a pinch of snuff from one of the King's generals. Gaetano Maria Trigona e Parisi became Archbishop of Palermo in 1832 and Cardinal in 1834.

[6] The Prince of Campofranco died in 1856.

[7] More specifically one would read of human livers having been roasted and eaten. See for instance Charles Lock's assertion (Sermoneta) that the inhabitants of Augusta had devoured the livers of blind French refugees from Alexandria in 1799. The charge of cannibalism had also been levelled against the Bourbon troops in the massacres following the execution of Caracciolo in 1799. As, for that matter, in the Irish revolution of 1798, when British troops were also accused of having eaten human flesh.

[8] The Governor of Malta was Major-General Sir Henry Bouverie, much respected by the Maltese for his courage during the cholera epidemic in Malta.

[9] William Wilton Barker, born in Cambridgeshire in 1769, came to Sicily during the time of Nelson. In 1801 he married Antonia di Giorgi; he had fallen in love with her through hearing her sing whilst she was still at a convent school – before he had even seen her face. Robert Fagan appointed him Vice-Consul in Messina in 1812. The Duke of Buckingham had been bored by stories of his financial problems, obviously chronic, during an hour's interview in 1827.

[10] Goodwin died *en poste* on 13 December 1869. The thoroughness of his study of Sicily and Naples is shown by the articles in the *Journal of the Royal Statistical Society*. He had a kindly manner but could also be brusque with people whom he thought were wasting his time. There is a story of a newly arrived stranger who came to his office and asked what he should see first in Palermo. Goodwin replied in a high-pitched voice: 'The outside of my door, if you please.' In 1828 he had been Consul in the Cape Verde Islands and in 1832 he had been in Naples.

[11] The great Roman bank of Torlonia had been founded in 1814 by Giovanni Torlonia (1755–1829), whose right to the title of Prince had been confirmed by Pio VII, in consequence of his acquiring the principality of Civitella Cesi. The family had been established in Rome since 1750. Giovanni's principality was inherited by his second son Alessandro (1800–1886).

[12] Sansone. Figures vary in different sources.    [13] Gregorovius.    [14] Stanley.

[15] The Duchess of Berry, the 'heroine of the Vendée', was still conspiring to make her son Henry V of France.

[16] *The Life and Letters of Lord Macaulay* by Sir G. O. Trevelyan, London, 1876.

[17] Consular papers, Public Records Office, London.

[18] Filiberto.

[19] *Benjamin Ingham of Palermo*. Barrels of madeira were often used as ballast in English ships going to the East Indies during the eighteenth century, as the rolling and heat were said to improve their quality.

[20] The formation of the steamship company was an immediate result of a new concession from the Bourbon Government, breaking a Neapolitan monopoly and allowing private steam vessels *cabotaggio*, the right to trade locally. The Neapolitans up to now, in a typically ostrichlike manner, had been concerned only with their mainland communications. Other distinguished shareholders were Ruggiero Settimo, the Marquis of Rudinì, the Princes of Campofranco, Scordia, Cutò and Palagonia, and the Dukes of Cumia, Serradifalco and Verdura. Among the foreigners were Messrs Gardner (Edward, the adopted son of Benjamin), Dickinson, Morrison, Thomas and Rose. Taix, Aycard also had a holding.

## CHAPTER SEVEN (pages 81–93)

[1] Vincenzo Florio had been born in Calabria in 1799 and brought as an infant to Palermo (though Taccari speculates whether the family originally came from Ragusa). His uncle Ignazio ran a 'herbalist's depot' or *drogheria* in Via Materassai not far from the Ingham office. This business was left in 1819 to Vincenzo, who would call on Ingham for advice 'in any commercial difficulty' (*Benjamin Ingham of Palermo*). Florio launched an insurance company in 1829, backed by Ingham and other British merchants. He built his

*baglio* in 1832, and a sugar refinery in 1833. By the end of the 1830s he was agent for the Rothschilds. He exported citrus fruit and in 1841 started the Oretea iron foundry in Palermo. His first *tonnara* had been bought at Arenella in 1829. Other *tonnare* were acquired mostly round Trapani and especially on the island of Favignana. Florio was responsible for radically changing and simplifying the method of catching tunny. In 1841, with the backing of the Pallavicini family of Genoa, he launched a company to expand the Favignana *tonnara*; understandably Ingham took several shares in it.

[2] Rawson.

[3] Goodwin, writing of course from the British point of view, made the point that the workers in the mines had hitherto been well treated: 'Every stranger must be forcibly struck by the hardy and healthy look of the miners and burners, to which the lean and sickly aspect of the southern population forms a thorough contrast.' Actually, to the modern way of thinking, the method of employment not only then but at least until the 1870s (see Sonnino) seems perilously near to slave labour, particularly in the use of small boys, between the ages of seven and eleven. These boys, because of lowness of the galleries, were employed for carrying the ore on their backs to the surface. The mining itself was also at times exceedingly dangerous, with a constant threat of fire.

[4] 'A few years ago a band of brigands took refuge for some time in a cavern very near here [the villa of the Prince of Partanna at the Zucco] and were actually dining in the Prince's house, when a party of soldiers, with an officer, arrived from Palermo to arrest them. The brigands seeing that they were not known, invited the soldiers to partake of the meal, whilst the lieutenant was hospitably entertained by the Princess.' (Strutt)

[5] The Prince of Radalì had come to Sicily during the British occupation as Lieutenant Georg Wilding, and in 1816 had married Stefania Branciforte e Branciforte, the mother of Prince Pietro Lanza of Trabia – she was the Princess of Butera in her own right, and thus the grandest person in Sicily. As she had kept seven *feudi*, each carrying titles, for herself after her first husband's death, she gave Wilding one of them: Radalì. Lady Blessington wrote: 'Prince Buttera [sic] dined with us yesterday. He is Hanoverian by birth, but speaks English perfectly well. He was a soldier of fortune, went with his regiment to Sicily, where he captivated the Princess Buttera, the heiress of a very large fortune, who bestowed her hand, wealth and title on him; and he is now among the most fashionable of the fashionables. Strange destiny! to become from a mere soldier of fortune the master of immense wealth, and from an obscure name, prince of one of the most ancient titles in Sicily.' After his death, his brother Ernst obtained the title (in 1842). Actually Georg came from Dresden. When Stefania died, he married a Russian, Princess Barbara Schahosky.

[6] Grimm.

[7] Colletta.

[8] King Ferdinand was very attentive to the Tzarina, putting his stables at her disposal and banishing beggars from the area. The Tzarina also caused something of a sensation by her daily drinking of ass's milk, which was supposed to be less fatty than that of a cow or goat. For this purpose a young peasant appeared every morning at the gates of the villa. When she left for St Petersburg, both peasant and donkey accompanied her.

[9] One Sicilian cantar was 80 kgs.

[10] The fire had happened as long ago as 20 July 1845. Three hundred buildings in the business section of New York had been burnt, and property losses had amounted to $7,500,000. Ingham was particularly involved in the destruction of a cargo of sugar which he had underwritten.

[11] Giovanna Power in her *Giuda per la Sicilia* (1842) had been full of praise for the *ottimo* Trifiletti and his 'pretty and swift vessel'.

[12] Gaetano Fiamingo (1795–1857) must have been unpopular for his Bourbon sympathies, since he took refuge in Naples during the revolution in 1848. He returned in 1850, when he relinquished the post of Russian Consul – which, needless to say, had carried some responsibility during the Tzarina's visit.

[13] By *Capella* Ingham meant *I Cappelli*, the people who wore hats; in other words the bigwigs or *notabili*, those who decided who should do what in Marsala – the equivalent of the heads of the *Mafia*. Being the owners of the vineyards it was in their interest to keep prices down. The *Berrette* were people of the lower classes.

[14] Barrett. '. . . the credit of his house, its standing at home and abroad – was dearer to him than all the national difficulties of Europe. He thoroughly understood the business. He never neglected it. He was careful, prudent and just; but the moment a merchant failed, then goodbye to any feeling of equality.' Livingston (1803–61) entered the firm of Henry and George Barclay in 1819 and became a partner in 1824. The name of the firm was altered to Barclay and Livingston in 1834. The Barclays were sons of the British Consul-General for the Eastern States, and another brother, Anthony, also became British Consul. The firm was the agent for Lloyds of London.

[15] Neu.

[16] Pierce.

[17] Very few Europeans held stock in the New York Central; among them was W. M. Thackeray, who had fifty shares. Corning (1794–1872) began his career as an ironmonger in Albany, his father having been a revolutionary soldier. By 1838 he was President of the New York State Bank and the Albany Pier Company. He also owned an extensive iron business, from which it is said he had collected a fortune of $3,000,000 by 1860. He was in Congress from 1857 to 1859 and 1861 to 1863.

[18] Ernest Augustus, third Earl of Mount Edgcumbe, was born in 1797 and died in 1861 on his yacht off Erith at the mouth of the Thames. 'A most lovable character' he was aide-de-camp to both William IV and Victoria, and Vice-Chamberlain to Queen Adelaide. His sister Caroline married Reginald Macdonald, twentieth captain and chief of Clanronald, father of Annie. Unfortunately the original journal was destroyed when Mount Edgcumbe house, on Plymouth Sound, was bombed in March 1941.

[19] 'Let but a hand of violence be laid upon an English subject, and the great British lion, which lies couchant in Downing Street, begins to utter menacing growls and shake his invincible locks. An English man-of-war seems to be always within one day's sail of everywhere. Let political agitation break out in any part of the globe, if there be even a roll of English broadcloth or a pound of English tea to be endangered thereby, within forty-eight hours an English steamer or frigate is pretty sure to drop anchor in the harbour with an air which seems to say "Here I am. Does anybody want anything of me?"' (Hillard, a Bostonian).

[20] *To Dobree, Maingay & Co., Naples*　　　　　　　　　　　*14 September 1846*
We quite agree with you that it would not be prudent to let the property go into Mr Dickinson's hands, without he can give a solid and undoubted guarantee. . . . He is a curious person to have anything to do with, but we have always been and are still willing to assist him when we can do so with safety. At the same time we cannot help saying that he is getting from bad to worse in circumstances, with not a farthing of real capital, but what amount of debts we have no means of knowing.

Dickinson was born in Ireland in 1808 and died in 1851. He came out to Sicily in 1833 and was one of the shareholders in Ingham's steamship company.

[21] When quoting from Dickinson's diary, some discreet editing has generally been necessary.

CHAPTER EIGHT (pages 97–117)

[1] Napier (1819–98) was in due course ambassador to the United States (in 1857). Whilst in Naples 1846–9 he was gathering material for his very slim volume called *Notes on Modern Painting at Naples*, published in London in 1855. 'He rejoiced openly when the revolutionary ferment began at Naples. . . . When the Sicilians rose in rebellion his sympathies were all with them. . . . Lord Napier made his house a place of rendezvous for all the fiery young men of the Neapolitan society, and himself the centre of a political faction.' (MacFarlane). Napier had taken over the previous year when William Temple (Palmerston's brother) had gone on his long holiday – a holiday which had started in 1847 and was to last until November 1848. Temple had, so MacFarlane said, taken his departure 'at the very moment when there was a prospect of difficult work to do'. It had been put around that he refused to return, because his house in Naples was being redecorated and 'the smell of fresh paint and plaster was very offensive to him'.

[2] Marston, American consul from October 1837 (following Benjamin Gardner's death) until 1850. [3] Torrearsa.

[4] The new Vicaria was built in 1840 by Giachery. The name Vicaria was retained, but it was also called the Ucciardone, a corruption from the French *au champs d'échardons*, at the field of thistles. The old Vicaria had degenerated not only into an eyesore, but a 'positive nuisance, literally and morally polluting the neighbourhood.' (Murray's *Handbook*)

[5] Later Admiral Sir Stephen Lushington. He commanded the naval brigade at the siege and capture of Sebastopol.

[6] Some people even now hold that the Neapolitans are simply craven by nature; others regard their unwarlike qualities as part of their *dolce far niente* attraction, matched by some of the most glorious scenery in the world. 'The soft climate of Naples has melted away the two great guardian virtues, in which the security for all the others resides: valour in man, chastity in woman. In their verb there is but one tense, and that is the present . . . childlike unconcern for the future.' (Hillard, writing of 1847)

[7] Later Admiral of the Fleet Sir Henry Codrington.

[8] There were two Palazzo Lampedusas: one in Via Bara, next to the Whitakers, the other on the Marina where the Consul lived. Giuseppe Lampedusa in *Two Stories and a Memory* tells how a shell in 1848 destroyed a fine painted ceiling and some frescoes in the Marina palace. [9] Pepe.

[10] James Colquhoun Morrison was born at Greenock in 1789. As a young man he had poor health, so in 1811 he was sent to Martinique, where he became a second lieutenant in the Royal Martinique Volunteers. When he came to Palermo, he went into partnership with a Mr Seager. He married Harriet, daughter of William Routh of Naples, in 1828. He often travelled back to Scotland and died in 1873.

[11] The Paris branch was run by Jacob Rothschild. Karl (1780–1855) was in Naples, always the least important branch. The other brothers were Nathan (London), Anselm (Frankfurt) and Solomon (Vienna). [12] Mount Edgecumbe archives.

[13] Baron Alfredo Porcelli di Sant'Andrea was born in 1824, the same year as Annie

Macdonald. He was descended from an old Provençial family and was later created a knight of the Crown of Italy by Victor Emmanuel II. He returned to Sicily after Garibaldi's landing. According to *Sicily and England*, the marriage was not happy. There were four children, the first being born on 16 January 1849, almost nine months exactly from their marriage. Porcelli died of a heart attack in 1884 in Florence and was given a military funeral. Annie returned to England where she married Major Edward Woolhouse. She died in 1897.

14 William Thovez was the nephew of the Philip Thovez who had been agent for the Duchy in 1820, having taken over in 1837. 'My family had left him [William] to his own devices too long and he came to regard himself as virtually master, resenting interference; and my father . . . had to retire him on a pension. He had married a disagreeable English-woman, governess to his daughter, and she helped and succeeded in making great un-pleasantness' (Hood). Thovez's first wife, Rosaria Fragalà, died in 1856. His disagreeable second wife was Hannah Arnold, sister of Jemima Sanderson, one of Sophia Whitaker's sisters-in-law. He was dismissed from Bronte in 1871 and died in 1873.

15 The National Guards were a form of civilian conscription at first chiefly bourgeois, established also in Sicily and soon to lead to abuse and corruption.

16 George Fagan, who was in any case half Italian and married to a Sicilian (Maria Carbone), was a useful attaché to have, with his sister married to an Acton. He was Commissioner for British claims in Naples in 1849 and in Messina in 1851. In 1856 he was appointed secretary to the legation of the Argentine confederation, where he again was involved with settling British claims. He became Chargé d'Affaires in Ecuador and later was Minister to Venezuela. He died of yellow fever in Caracas in 1869.

The correspondence regarding his quarrel with Barker is in the Public Records Office. In 1838 he wrote to the Foreign Office claiming consular fees that had been due from Barker to Robert Fagan way back in 1816. He must have known well enough that this claim was a fast one.

17 It is sometimes inaccurately stated that the delegation went in H.M.S. *Porcupine*. The *Porcupine* did in fact proceed separately to Genoa about the same time.

CHAPTER NINE (pages 118–133)

1 Lord Stanley was the future Earl of Derby, Prime Minister in 1852.

2 The rest of the £25,000 required seems to have come from Florio and Varvaro, another Sicilian financier. It has recently come to light that the Government gave all three some of the confiscated church plate as a guarantee for their loans. Ingham sent his share to Marseilles (but was made to return it when the Bourbons came back to Sicily).

3 General Antonini (1792–1854) had served with the Napoleonic armies from 1811–14, and in 1824 had been in the Polish army. He had been in Sicily in 1844, but had been arrested as an accomplice of the brothers Bandiera (both Mazzinians), who were shot by court martial after the Cosenza rising. Mieroslawsky (1814–78) was known to his contemporaries as the 'leader of lost causes'. His mother was French and as a youth he had fought in the Polish revolution of 1830–1. He had been in command of the revolutionary forces in Poznania from March–May 1843. In 1849 he was fighting in Baden, and he was again in Poland in 1863. A writer of 'baroque exuberance', he believed fervently in the principles of freedom but lacked the common touch (cf. Namier).

4 The outline of Forbes's later story is given in G. M. Trevelyan's *Garibaldi's Defence of the Roman Republic*. In April 1848 he had fought for the Venetian Republic. During the

retreat from Rome he was in command of the 900 men joined by Garibaldi at Terni. He and his son by his first marriage were also with Garibaldi at San Marino; later he was imprisoned at Pola for some months. He then went to America where he 'took up the cause of the negroes'. After quarrels there he returned to Europe, was in Sicily again in 1860. From 1861–3 he was fighting in Poland. He died in reduced circumstances in 1892.

[5] Bolton King.　[6] Bolton King.　[7] G. M. Trevelyan.

### CHAPTER TEN (pages 134–147)

[1] Tina Whitaker.

[2] Tidman was in Marsala in June 1852. He died three months later, aged twenty-seven.

[3] Richard Brown Cossins (1823–98), George Dennis, in Murray's *Handbook* wrote approvingly of the activity at the *Baglio*: 'the smiths, coopers and distillers, the application of steam, the division of labour, and the order and regularity observable throughout, are gratifying to the visitor, as offering the unwonted spectacle of British industry in a lazy land.'

[4] *Annuario Generale del Commercio e dell'Industriale* (Palermo, 1854).

[5] Among the largest of these firms were: Wedekind, bankers, also dealing in sponges and cloth; Langer, banking and glass; Hirzel (who was also Swiss Consul), sumac and nuts; Kayser and Kressner (the latter being Prussian Consul), banking, sulphur, manna, citrus fruit, cork, cloth. German and Swiss firms also became established in Messina. The Danish firm of Fog approximated most in size and importance to that of Fratelli Jung.

[6] *Two Letters to the Earl of Aberdeen on the State Prosecutions of the Neapolitan Government* (London, 1851). Forty-two people had been accused and the trial had lasted for seven months. George Fagan, as a friend of Poerio, had been responsible for arranging for Gladstone and Senior to visit the prisons. It was Gladstone's first visit to Naples since 1838; he had gone there in the hope that the climate would benefit his daughter's eyesight.

[7] The Prince of Scordia had turned the theatre into a hotel in 1844. 'One of the best regulated hotels south of the Alps' (Murray's *Handbook*), there were at first forty-four rooms, twenty facing the sea. Its first guest of importance had been the King of Bavaria who had gone there with his suite a month after its opening. It was run by Salvatore Ragusa, a Genoese, a model *hotelier* who knew the fads and dislikes of Anglo-Saxons. He never went out of the building, so did not possess a hat when his daughter was married. *Giornale 'La Cenere'*, nos. 54 and 60 (Palermo, 1844); *Giornale 'Il Precursore'* no. 101 (Palermo, 3 April 1877).

[8] *Sicily and England.*

[9] Goodwin told Senior: 'The sufferers from the sulphur monopoly were at first ready to accept in full £1500. But when the British Government took them up they asked £150,000, and actually got £30,000. These fradulent claims, supported by British cannon, are making us detested throughout the weaker states, against which we enforce them. To be at the same time cheated and bullied is very galling.'

[10] War had been declared on 27 March. Lucan had reached Scutari by the end of April and no doubt would have ordered his marsala on the way. He had enough trouble on his hands with his brother-in-law, Lord Cardigan, to bother about such small matters as payments.

Lucan's younger brother Richard Bingham had been a secretary at the Naples embassy. In 1848 Richard married Maria Thomas, a cousin of Edward Bevan Thomas of Prior,

Turner and Thomas. Thomas, from Carmarthen, was Edward Gardner's father-in-law. Apart from banking, Gardner had at first dealt in sumac, selling it in both Britain and the U.S.A. In about 1840 he turned to sulphur mining at Lercara. He married Martha Beaumont, also from Wales and noted for her violent temper. All his children were born in Palermo. Edward Gardner eventually took over the sulphur business in conjunction with the two Thomas sons, Beaumont and Wilson, and his own two sons-in-law, both in the Rose family.

[11] Sir Henry Ward, High Commissioner for Corfu 1849–55.

[12] Tina Whitaker.

[13] Herman Melville called at Messina that same year. After admiring the 'Salvator Rosa look' of the mountains across the Straits, he noted that a large tract of the town had been demolished expressly so that the rest could be commanded from the sea.

[14] Dumas *père* held a more sombre view: 'Who has not seen a Sicilian beggar knows nothing of poverty.'

[15] At least one assumes the *palazzo* was erected by Ingham. It is possible that he bought it already built from Radalì.

[16] The entrance to the Hotel is on the Via Roma, where the main alterations were made. Ingham's entrance was on the south side, opening on to what is now the Via Stabile. The name Via Ingham was abolished at the time of Sanctions in 1935.

[17] The *Handbook* was the result of four visits by Dennis to Sicily, in 1847, 1852, 1857 and 1863.

[18] *Sicily and England.*

[19] *Sicily and England.*


CHAPTER ELEVEN (pages 148–166)

[1] Brancaccio.

[2] Mundy.

[3] Elpis Melena.

[4] The description was by Maria Paternò di Castello. Rose archives.

[5] James Rose was then aged fifty-one.

[6] Lyla was the daughter of James Colquhoun Morrison. She was then twenty-six.

[7] *Hearts of Oak*, from which all quotations from Winnington-Ingram's diary are taken.

[8] Madame Celesti was the daughter of Thomas Child, who had died of cholera in Messina in 1854. In 1877, as a widow, she married Robert Sanderson, Sophia Whitaker's brother; he had already been married to her sister, Amelia Sarah Child (died 1863).

[9] The Commander was bad at spelling Italian names. When quoting him it has therefore been necessary to put these to rights.

[10] General Salzano: Commander-in-chief of the Neapolitan garrison.

[11] Lampedusa always said that the character of Tancredi was based on his own adopted son, Gioacchino Lanza Tomasi di Mazzarino, later Duke of Palma. One tradition is that Corrado was denounced to the Government by a great-aunt.

[12] There are many 'discrepancies' such as this between the real facts and the story told in *The Leopard*; as a result some of Corrado's descendants are said to be displeased. A novel, however, even a great one, is a novel, and not necessarily history. . . .

Presumably the objections are mostly to the marriage of Tancredi with Angelica, the daughter of the upstart Sedàra and grand-daughter of the filthy 'Peppe 'Mmerda', a character entirely invented by Lampedusa. Corrado did not in fact marry until 1866, his wife being Maria, daughter of Baron Favara. It must be confessed that Favara was only a 'cattle baron' and his exact status is obscure. He came from Partanna, where there were many Niscemi *feudi*. The *gabbelloti rifatti*, or enriched, used to assume the prefix 'Don' or even 'Baron'. There were cases when the *gabelloto* would give money to the owner of the land who in return would marry off his daughter to the *gabelloto*'s son, on condition that the latter would be given a title. Corrado's father used to say 'La mia casa stava crollando, ma il bastaso è il puntello.' This was a pun; literally it means 'My house was crumbling but the rafter is its support', *bastaso* meaning rafter. In Sicily *v* and *b* are often interchangeable, and *vastaso* means a vulgar man. It is worth noting that Partanna is only ten miles from Santa Margherita Belice, where the Palazzo Cutò, the Donnafugata of *The Leopard*, was destroyed in the earthquake of 1968.

[13] The word *Mafia*, although considered to have Arab origins, only really became current as a result of the play *I Mafiosi della Vicaria*, presumed to have been written by Giuseppe Rizzotto (1825–95) and first performed in 1863. To a western Sicilian there is a great difference between *Mafia* with a large M and *mafia* with a small one. The *tipo mafioso* is good-looking, to be admired, representing originally *omertà* (from *hombredad* in Spanish), the equivalent of manliness. *Mafia* with a large M is the world famous gangster secret society, and in its case *omertà* is twisted into arrogance, bullying, ostentation and cold-blooded cruelty; it also means 'league of silence', criminal solidarity. Indeed the society is considered to have some origin in the National Guard, which had been formed in 1848 and had degenerated merely into a corrupt body of self-seekers and embezzlers pretending to act in the name of law and order. For an excellent essay on the *Mafia* see Barzini.

[14] De Cesare. Barstow had been American Consul since 1856. He was replaced by Luigi Monte in August 1861.

[15] Another who saw the execution was one of the Whitaker children, Arthur, aged eight. As an elderly man he remembered being held up to watch from the nursery window at Via Bara, from which one could see the Square where the rebels were shot.

[16] Lampedusa.

[17] Goodwin.

[18] Cossins had said that Letizia could shoot him if he liked but he must face the consequences. Eventually the arms were removed by force. Luckily the wind was favourable, and within twenty hours the Woodhouse schooner *Lightning*, captained by John Leseur, was able to anchor at Valetta.

[19] Son of Frederick Marryat, author of *Mr Midshipman Easy*.

[20] 29 May 1860.

[21] Despatch of 14 May from Commander Marryat to Vice-Admiral Sir Arthur Fanshawe.

[22] Two of Acton's brothers were to become admirals in the Italian navy, one being Ferdinando also a Minister of Marine.

[23] The shot is still in the possession of the Woodhouse family.

[24] Marryat.

[25] Garibaldi was 'of middle height, square built and muscular, with a small, well-shaped head, light brown hair, hazel, penetrating eyes, and a singularly kind expression'. From the article 'Garibaldi's Englishman' by Frances M. Peard in *The Cornhill Magazine* (July–December 1903).

[26] Samuel Butler chose to spend much time at Calatafimi between 1893 and 1900. (An 'ugly modern town' – Murray's *Handbook*.)

[27] In 1928 the flag was given by the firm of Ingham, Whitaker to the *Società di Storia Patria* in Palermo.

[28] Abba (diary).

[29] Viollet Le Duc.

[30] After the battle Abba saw 'a little dwarfish monster', ferociously stabbing a dead Neapolitan. It was Bixio who gave chase with a raised sabre, shouting 'Kill the brute!', but the 'savage creature slid away among the rocks and disappeared.'

[31] Ferdinando Lanza, who was now eighty and very deaf. He had been in command of the Neapolitan troops defeated by Garibaldi in 1848.


CHAPTER TWELVE (pages 167–182)

[1] *H.M.S. Hannibal at Palermo and Naples*, from which Mundy's diary entries are taken.

[2] G. M. Trevelyan.

[3] 'War Journals of "Garibaldi's Englishman"' by G. M. Trevelyan in *Cornhill Magazine*, vol. xxiv (London, 1908). See also C. S. Forbes.

[4] Rose archives.

[5] Antonino Bertolini to the Duke of Serradifalco, published in *Gli avvenimenti del Maggio e del Giugno visti dall'Amministratore di una nobile casa* by Costantino Masaglia, Archivio Storico Siciliano Serie III, vol. XVII (1967).

[6] No record has come to light in Sicily of any Fiamingo having married an English-woman, so this reference by Mundy is something of a mystery, especially taken in conjunction with Winnington-Ingram's meeting with Marchesa P——. Gaetano Fiamingo had, it will be recalled, been a partner with Ingham, Florio and Bordonaro in the *Palermo* project.


CHAPTER THIRTEEN (pages 183–200)

[1] Viollet Le Duc, who had recently been in Marsala.

[2] There were now six leading firms: Gill and Corlett, Lipari, Wood, Woodhouse, Florio and Ingham, Stephens.

[3] Castellamare del Golfo is not of course to be confused with the fort of Castellamare in Palermo.

[4] Giacomo Medici, 1817–82. His father had been an exile in Portugal, and in 1840 Giacomo went to London where he came to know Mazzini. He met Garibaldi at Monte-video in 1845, and in 1848 returned to Italy. After a short period of exile in England, he went back to Italy to live in Genoa, where he remained until 1860.

[5] John Whitehouse Peard (1811–80) was the son of Vice-Admiral Shulman Peard, who had served under Nelson. He left the Inner Temple in May 1859 to take service as a private with Garibaldi in Lombardy. The news of the departure of the Thousand reached him too late. Garibaldi made him a Colonel after the battle of Milazzo and in 1864 stayed with him at his house on the river Fowey. By temperament he was cool and dis-passionate, though some of the British reacted against him most unfairly as a 'bloodthirsty man, who, unable to gratify his penchant for murders in his own country, comes out here and gloats over his victims' (C. S. Forbes). He was responsible for the surrender of the

Neapolitan troops at Soveria in Calabria and commanded the British Legion at the Battle of the Volturno.

⁶ G. M. Trevelyan. Jessie (1832–1906) had met Garibaldi in Nice in 1855. In prison she showed 'great firmness of character'. 'The Garibaldi *culte* has been with her truly and literally the object (apart from her devoted love for her husband, an equally ardent worshipper at the same shrine) for which she has lived, and for which she has again and again affronted death' (Trollope). She was sent to Rome in 1867 to treat over the exchange of wounded prisoners and was in France with Garibaldi in 1870. In her old age she was reduced to teaching English in Florence. Both she and her husband wrote several books. Alberto Mario was a 'man of large literary culture, a brave soldier, an acute politician, a formidable political adversary, and a man of perfect and incorruptible integrity' (Trollope). He edited a newspaper in Rome in his later years and was condemned to imprisonment for consistently calling the Pope 'Signor Pecci'.

⁷ Alberto Mario, *The Red Shirt* (London, 1865).

⁸ John William Dunne (1827–1906) came to Sicily with the Cavourian agent Scelzi before the capture of Palermo and together they organised a band of some hundreds of *squadre* in the mountains. After a very distinguished career throughout the campaign, he was shot in the back by one of his majors at the Battle of the Volturno, because he had refused to promote the man on grounds of cowardice. Later Dunne fought in Denmark and Poland. At the end of his life he spent much time on the Riviera, and he died in Nice. 'Era un uomo strano, credo un po alcolizzato, ma bravo e coraggioso, sino alla temerità' (letter to Joss Whitaker *c.* 1906 from a patriot of 1860, name illegible).

⁹ Daniel Dowling, born *c.* 1827. In March 1860 he was a captain in the British army, so he must have enlisted as a sergeant in Garibaldi's service. He was promoted to colonel in the artillery on 1 October 1860 and attached to Garibaldi's staff; at the Volturno he received the Cross of Savoy. He tried to enter the Italian army in December 1861, so it was suggested that he should be put *a disposizione* for six months in order to learn Italian and be able to take the necessary artillery exams. The War Office in Turin, however, decided against the idea, and he was 'exonerated from service' with six months' pay instead, on 5 January 1862.

¹⁰ Patterson provided much useful first-hand information for G. M. Trevelyan's *Garibaldi and the Making of Italy*.

¹¹ J. Dolmage told G. M. Trevelyan that Ragusa had said that for thirty days he would dine any of the Thousand for nothing, but 'there had not been a man of them but had insisted upon paying his bill'.

Dolmage was a regular officer in the British army and happened to be on leave in Sicily in the summer of 1860. He thus attached himself 'unofficially' to Türr's brigade and was able to take part in much of the fighting from June onwards.

¹² As *The Times* correspondent in Turin carefully put it: 'It was felt to be of the utmost importance that Garibaldi should have other advisers at his side than Sirtori, Bixio, and other daring young enthusiasts, who are so much more fit to upset a state than to set it up.' For the detailed story of the struggle with La Farina and the imbroglio over the question of annexation see Denis Mack Smith, *Cavour and Garibaldi 1860* (Cambridge 1954, New York 1968).

¹³ In the *Illustrated London News* of 23 June 1860 there is a dramatic picture by Frank Vizetelly of a *sorcio* being chased by the populace. The correspondent gives this account:
At their head was a man running at full speed with blood streaming from numerous

wounds about his head: one gash in particular was frightful; it extended from the temple to the chin, and gave an awful appearance to the wretched creature who was shrieking as he ran for mercy. But those who came behind had none for the spy who had been found lurking about the quarters of the 'committee', and as the fleetest of his pursuers came up with him, stab after stab was made with their gleaming knives till he sank exhausted in a doorway of a house near the American Consul's, into which he was dragged by some passing soldiers. (See plate 22.)

14 Narciso Cozzo was hit by a cannon ball just before the Battle of the Volturno and died of gangrene on 4 October. Ciccio and Corrado were by his side. The moving story of his death takes up the last pages of Brancaccio's book.

15 The articles formed the basis of Dumas's *Les Garibaldiens* (Paris, 1861). See also his *On Board the Emma*, translated by R. S. Garnett (London, 1929).

16 According to Brancaccio, they had been asked to a ball given by Baron Bordonaro, who was mayor of Caltanissetta. The other Garibaldini wanted to go as well, but had not been invited for reasons of class. There were cries of 'Down with the Aristocrats' and some jeering. After such an insult resignation was the only course.

17 Arrivabene.

18 G. M. Trevelyan.

19 Its members were also known as the Excursionists [see Holyoake]. Styles appeared in London as a captain and later promoted himself to major – Garibaldi had been free with conferring promotions after Milazzo, so his captaincy might well have been bona fide. Anyway, after a while Styles invented and sold commissions, keeping the proceeds for himself. The American De Rohan, who claimed the rank of Admiral, helped in the confusion, but at least he was honest. The Legion arrived in Naples on 15 October, numbering about 600, some being mere riffraff in search of adventure. The Battle of the Volturno was already over. Styles was arrested within the hour of arriving for misappropriation of funds, and Peard was put in charge – he wrote to Mrs Thomas Adolphus Trollope: 'Defend me from ever again commanding a brigade of English volunteers in a foreign country. As to the officers, many were most mutinous and some something worse.' A lot was due, it was said, to that old, old British complex of the East beginning at Calais. Then there was the cheap wine. To be fair, most members of the Legion fought quite bravely in the few small actions in which they were involved. Everyone was relieved to see them go on 15 December.

20 For his story see Drage. See also Maxime du Camp and Gallenga, who writes amusingly of his encounters with English volunteers.

21 Garibaldi's batteries at the Punta Faro were defended by some mediocre cannon taken from the *Tükory*, his only warship, originally the Bourbon *Veloce* which had deserted to him. On the night of 13/14 August some Garibaldini on the *Tükory* attacked the man of war *Monarca* at Castellamare di Stabia near Naples. It had been believed that her captain, Vacca, and the crew were all pro-Piedmontese and would at once surrender. Vacca, however, was away, and Guglielmo Acton was temporarily in command. Acton defended the *Monarca* bravely, although wounded in the stomach, and the *Tükory* was obliged to retreat.

22 The Countess della Torre, another of Garibaldi's flames. She had met him in London in 1854.

23 Sciascia's *Nino Bixio a Bronte* was taken from Benedetto Radice's *Memorie storiche di Bronte*. Radice, to whom the late Lord Bridport would refer as Mr Root, was born in

Bronte in 1854 and died in 1931. Levi's book contains a fierce indictment of the Duchy, which he says was given in the first place to Nelson for 'having saved the kingdom by getting rid of the liberals'.

24 A witness said that Bonina had in reality eaten salted tunny-fish but had boasted that he had eaten Cannata's liver.

25 Abba.

26 The letters are in the Public Record Office, London, as is that from Goodwin on 11 August 1860.

27 Romeo.

## CHAPTER FOURTEEN (pages 204–221)

1 The Ascensos married in 1882, when Lady Louisa – daughter of the third Earl of Clare and niece of Byron's 'eldest and dearest friend' – was fifty-eight. Carmelo was by then a General. There is a delightful story about Carmelo and Louisa by her great-grandson Constantine FitzGibbon in *Miss Finnigan's Fault* (London, 1953). After the marriage he gave her a cheque which bounced. As she had always understood that he was a wealthy Sicilian landowner, there was a tremendous row. 'It was as neat a trick as any writer of a French farce evolved for his second act.' Carmelo was always cold at Mount Shannon, his wife's home near Limerick, and even in mid-summer would be blowing on his fingers to warm them. He used to like to sit on the hot pipes in the greenhouse. After 1887 they went to live in Palermo, where they seem to have been supported to some extent by the Whitakers, who thereby acquired some of the FitzGibbon silver. Carmelo died in 1892.

2 Neu.

3 Pip's real name was Joseph (Joseph Isaac Spadafora Whitaker – Spadafora because the Duchess was his godmother). Peppino is the Italian diminutive of Giuseppe, i.e. Joseph.

4 Lampedusa's description of the ballroom is really a picture of that in the Palazzo Monteleone where Antonio Pignatelli lived. The palace was in the Piazza San Domenico and had its front cut off when the Via Roma was laid out. The ballroom used in Visconti's Twentieth Century Fox film was in the Palazzo Gangi, now the only 'old type' palace on the grand scale left in Palermo.

5 Mack Smith.

6 W. J. C. Moens, from whose book the rest of this account is taken.

7 Richard Cossins' first wife, died 1871. She was *née* Gill and must have been related to the Mr Gill (if not his daughter) of the Corlett and Gill *baglio*. Since her family came from the Isle of Man it seems reasonable to suppose that the Gills had been attracted to Marsala by the Woodhouses. The Concern had a *baglio* at Campobello, close to Selinunte, hence the reference to the temples.

8 Some blamed the cholera infection on the Italian troops, sent to suppress the revolt without undergoing the usual quarantine.

9 Raffaele Cadorna, 1815–97. The first in a line of three generations of distinguished soldiers.

10 From Lojacono's unpublished memoirs. 'This incomparable and mummified man who moved like a young man in spite of having completed 80 years.' Lojacono's dates were 1843–91.

11 The Ingham fleet appears to have been mostly sail: it included the *Lady Sale*,

*Porcupine, Vigneto, Rattler, Belle, Resolution, Racalia, Sofia* (after Sophia Whitaker), *Duchess, Emilia* (after Emily Ingham), *Elisa* and of course the *Sumatra*. The old *Sumatra* was sold in 1860 for about £750 and a new one was bought in 1868, but she seems not to have been a success. The *Rattler* was sold in 1866 for about £2040. The *Sofia* was certainly steam.

CHAPTER FIFTEEN (pages 222–236)

1 Emilio Kunzmann, the head gardener at the Villa Sofia, a refugee from Alsace after the 1870 Franco-Prussian war.

2 Lewis.

3 Presumably Medici's daughter died in June 1877. She was allowed to inherit the title on 5 June, but on 11 July there was a further royal decree granting succession to Luigi 'in mancanza di eredi' (literally, heirs being lacking).

4 Tommasi-Crudeli, 1834–1900. He studied medicine in Florence, Paris, Vienna and Berlin, and in 1859 was in the Cacciatori delle Alpi with Garibaldi. He came to Sicily on the second expedition, at the head of 800 Tuscans. Promoted to Major at Milazzo, he finished the campaign in command of the 77th Infantry Regiment. In 1864 he became a professor in Florence, and in 1866 was professor of anatomy at Palermo. He was the author of *La Sicilia nel 1871* (Florence, 1871) and wrote on malaria in the Pontine Marshes. In 1872 he was deputy for Cortona and twice re-elected. In 1892 he was made a senator, and he was made an honorary citizen of Palermo for his work there during the cholera epidemic of 1866. His marriage with Sophie was childless.

5 The financier Bordonaro had died in 1868.

6 11 November 1876.

7 Lewis.

8 Originally a traveller for a Palermo cloth-merchant, Leone had been a bandit since 1868. The gang had been headed first by Biagio Valvo, who died in 1873, and then by Di Pasquale whom Leone murdered in 1875. Other personalities whom he had captured included Baron Sgadari (£5200 ransom) and Sig. Saeli (£2600). *Episodi nella vita del masnadiere Leone*, Giornale di Sicilia (Palermo, 1877); see also Fincati.

9 *The Times*, 6 February 1877.

10 Rose archives. According to Fincati, Leone was far from looking like a Sicilian country gentleman when he was captured. His clothes stank and were covered with grime and blood. He was killed at Montemaggiore Belsito. The bodies were put on show in a chapel, and sightseers flocked to see them. Photographs were taken. When the father of Leone arrived, he pretended not to recognise his son, but the mother gave the show away by bursting into tears.

11 Cousin Joe died in 1883. His body was removed to Woodchurch, Yorkshire, in 1898. When the old British cemetery in Marsala was sold after the Second World War, all the bodies were transferred to a new area. Great was the consternation when Joe's tomb was found to be empty. Eventually the truth was discovered, but ever since he has been known in the Whitaker family as the 'missing corpse'. Effie had been going to Marsala since she was thirteen, as her mother was a Corlett, the granddaughter of Stuart Corlett, Benjamin Ingham's competitor after the Napoleonic Wars.

12 In fact the *Educatorio* was really founded by Sophia.

13 Maude's father, Alfred Bennett, had also been a marine engineer. He had died in 1863. Alice had gone to Palermo to be prepared for confirmation by Canon Burbidge.

She was met off the *postale* by Beau Gardner, who promptly fell for her. The marriage of his step-daughter to such a wealthy man brought William Rowdon Saunders with his family, including Maude, to Palermo. Mrs Burbidge used to claim that she had been a Mazzinian and that she brought messages in her shoes to and from Leghorn.

## CHAPTER SIXTEEN (pages 239–250)

[1] Loosely translatable as 'Memories of somebody who has outlived everybody else'.

[2] *A Few Remarks on the Present Laws of Marriage, Adultery and Seduction in England* (London, 1836).

[3] Sydney Morgan was born in Dublin about 1783 and died in 1859. Her books were nearly always controversial. In the 1840s her house at 11 William Street, Albert Gate, was known as the 'House of Peers' because of the distinguished company. At her gatherings she would wield a large green fan.

[4] Giulia once attended a dinner party given by Mrs Inwood Jones, who was also entertaining Mr Chorley of the *Athenaeum*. 'Mr Chorley was known to be eccentric, and was supposed to be rather erratic, owing to excessive drinking of absinthe.' During the meal he rose from the table, without causing any particular comment. Shortly afterwards, however, a servant came to Mrs Inwood Jones and whispered something to her. She became extremely agitated and 'in the greatest distress' announced to Giulia and her fellow-guests: 'Can you conceive anything so unpleasant happening to anyone? Mr Chorley, in a fit of absentmindedness, thinking himself in his own house, has gone into *my* room, has undressed, and has got into *my* bed!' Mr Chorley's valet, succeeded in getting him out of the bed. His master was 'very crestfallen' and 'actually returned to the table before dinner was over. But the good lady declared that her bed had been contaminated, and that she could never occupy it again.'

[5] Arrivabene was liberated as an act of courtesy to Queen Victoria, simply because he had written to Lady Ely who was 'known to be one of the Queen's ladies'.

[6] Vito Beltrani's dates were 1805–84. He founded the literary periodical *La Falce* in Palermo. In 1848 he was elected a deputy to the Camera with the specific job of reforming the 1812 Constitution. He was exiled in 1849 and went to Florence, where he had several articles on art published. He was made a Senator in 1874. His son Martino Beltrani (1829–1909) also was active in the 1848 revolution and subsequently exiled. After some time in London he returned to Palermo in 1852. His experiences in the Vicaria in 1860 were perhaps responsible for his interest in penal reform, on which he wrote several books. In 1879 he was Director-General of prisons, a post which he held on various subsequent occasions, and in 1896 he became a Senator. His reminiscences were published posthumously.

[7] Giacinto Carini, 1821–80. A cavalry colonel and member of the war committee in 1848–9, after which he emigrated to London. He was severely wounded at Calatafimi and later made a major-general. His son Monsignor Isidoro Carini (1843–95) became well-known as a historian at the Vatican.

[8] La Pegna. Giacomo Longo's dates were 1818–1906. He was liberated in 1860 and reached Palermo in July of that year, when Garibaldi made him Minister of War. He was wounded at the Volturno and fought at Custozza. In 1876 he was made a Senator.

[9] Literally 'All our arguments, spoken with blood in our eyes and our souls upon our lips, could not gain for us any better promises from the British government.' On 30 October 1848 Padre Ventura wrote from Rome quoting the French ambassador in

London who had said that members of the British Cabinet were out shooting in the country and thus unable to meet in order to discuss Scalia's proposals.

[10] George Fagan's son Louis was Panizzi's first biographer: *The Life of Sir Anthony Panizzi*, 2 vols (London and New York, 1880). The story of Panizzi's efforts as a rescuer are also told in *Prince of Librarians* by Edward Miller (London, 1967). Panizzi launched a fund in 1855 and received subscriptions from such people as Lord Holland and Mrs Gladstone totalling nearly £1500. Fagan's transfer to Argentina was a blow to the cause, but in 1859 the Neapolitan Government suddenly decreed that sixty-six of the prisoners might be sent to New York. During the voyage their ship was successfully hijacked and they disembarked instead at Cork, whence they made their way to London.

[11] Mrs Lynn Linton died in 1898. Her novels included *Azeth the Egyptian*, *Arrymore*, *Grasp Your Nettle*, *Lizzie Lorton of Greyrigs* and (most sensational perhaps) *The Girl of the Period* (1868), an onslaught on modern developments in feminine manners. *Joshua Davidson* (1872) was a best-seller and a 'daring adaptation of the gospel story' (D.N.B.). *The Autobiography of Christopher Kirkland* (1885) was really her own autobiography in male guise, and included portraits of Panizzi and others.

[12] Elizabeth Patterson, born in Baltimore, married Jérôme Bonaparte in 1802. Napoleon was furious and had the marriage annulled. In her old age she lived on milk and brandy and regretted that she had married 'a Corsican brigand instead of an English lord'. She died in 1879 aged ninety-two.

[13] Abraham Hayward, 1801–84. The author of *The Art of Dining* (London, 1852).

[14] Robert Percy ffrench (1832–96) came from Co. Galway. A Knight of Malta, he was in the diplomatic service from 1852–78. In 1863 he married a Russian, Sophie de Kindiakoff, but they seem soon to have separated. In the 1850s he was mostly at the embassy in Naples. He was in St Petersburg in 1872 and Vienna in 1873. Sir Horace Rumbold wrote how he met him frequently at Holland House in the 1870s; 'that Irish cosmopolite speaking all languages with equal volubility.'

[15] Sir John Harington, 1821–77.

## CHAPTER SEVENTEEN (pages 251–264)

[1] De Cesare.

[2] Brancaccio.

[3] Pilo, born in 1820, had been in constant touch with Alfonso over the question of raising funds. In September 1859 he had sent him a picture to sell, the proceeds to be given to Mazzini.

[4] Evola.

[5] Wife of Sir Edmund Filmer, at that time M.P. for West Kent.

[6] In the usual Sicilian manner titles were used according to the whim of the owner. The Prince of Pandolfina was also sometimes known as the Prince of Belmonte.

[7] Napoli.

[8] Brancaccio.

[9] Charles Hamilton Aïdé died in 1906, 'well over seventy' (*The Times* obituary), probably aged eighty. His father was reputed to have been a Greek diplomat. His novels *Rita*, *Confidences*, *Carr of Carlyon* etc., were typical mid-Victorian works. Henry Irving acted in his play *Philip* (1872), and he 'captured the town' in a farcical comedy *Dr Bill* in the 1890s. He was 'one of the people you "meet everywhere" and was always at wordly

or literary receptions, first nights, great receptions' (*The Times*). His drawings were said to be of the very best amateur standard.

¹⁰ 'Just before we reached Berlin the train went off the line, the carriage in which were my sisters, myself, our nurses and governesses rolling down the embankment. Nobody was hurt but naturally we were all severely shaken and greatly frightened. My father, none of us, realized what a terrible shock it was to my mother. . . . The day after he left [for St Petersburg] she took to her bed which she never left again. Within a month we were motherless' (Mrs Godfrey Pearse, *née* Cecilia de Candia). Mario was sent for and came by special train. On finding his wife's room empty, he fell to the floor in a faint. The children in the next room heard the noise of the fall; it was their first inkling that he had arrived.

¹¹ *Sicily and England.* The palazzo admittedly was not large, its feature being an inner courtyard with a flight of stairs leading up an attractive arcaded balcony.

¹² 'Who can doubt there are able men, like Scalia, the late Commanding General of Sicily, who if invested with the necessary powers, would before long sweep away this curse of brigandage – as I know he offered to do' (letter signed E.W.P., 13 November 1876). Medici of course had also been suggested.

¹³ 1876 was the year of the first production of *Aïda* at Covent Garden, Patti's greatest triumph to date. Nicolini took the part of Radames and was deemed 'magnificent'.

¹⁴ From the diary (in English) of the eleven-year-old Peppino Lanza of Scalea:

*Palermo, 11 January 1881*

You cannot imagine the fuss and preparations going on here, the whole town has been in a commotion. Tuesday the 4th January their Majesties arrived in Palermo. The wharf was decorated and covered with green and banners, and the ladies amongst whom was also Mamma (Princess of Scalea) went there to receive the court. . . . The Queen was dressed in a dark blue velvet dress, richly embroidered with gold. The King and the Duke of Aosta [Amedeo of Savoy] were in grey uniform, and the little prince [Prince of Naples, later Victor Emmanuel III] was dressed like a *torpediniere.* . . . Towards evening the fireworks were lighted. . . . Sunday: Aunt Belmonte asked us to Acquasanta (the Villa Belmonte). Not less than seven we were all in a heap, packed in a brougham, you may imagine how comfortable it was. Arrived at the Villa we went out on the terrace and saluted the King and Queen with our handkerchiefs when they were coming, and gathered ourselves together with Ignazino Florio and Giulia [children of Ignazio Florio; Giulia was the future Princess of Trabia], who were the only invited, and then greeted the royal family with profound and solemn bows. The Queen came to us and after asking all who we were and after kissing us she sat down and we went to play with the Prince of Naples. He is very nice and taught us a new play 'the ship' and was very familiar with us. . . . The Prince Pandolfina gave the arm to the Queen, the King to Aunt Belmonte, and Prince Amedeo to Lily Belmonte. Arrived at the end of the staircase, the Queen saluted all of us and entered into the open carriage, but found that the evening air was too damp. She wanted to have it closed, but the leather of the carriage was so very swollen with the rain that it could not be shut. The Queen laughed and said it was a ridiculous scene, and in the meantime the King put his hand upon my head and smelled some roses that he had in his hand. They had to wait about a quarter of an hour until the carriage could be shut, but it had passed so cosily and nicely that I was quite sorry when the real moment of departure came.

¹⁵ Renoir painted his portrait of Wagner at the Palmes two days later. Wagner

conceived the idea of *Parsifal* in 1858. The libretto was completed in 1877, and the orchestration had occupied three years. The first performance, at Bayreuth, was on 26 July 1882.

16 When Guy de Maupassant came to the Hotel many years later, he claimed that Wagner's wardrobe still smelt of roses. Wagner had kept his linen in there and liked to have it sprinkled with strong scent, his sense of smell having been impaired from taking snuff.

17 Blandine von Bülow and Biagio Gravina were married at Bayreuth on 25 August 1882.

18 The missing corpse, see note 11, Chapter Fifteen.

19 In actual fact the prototype of the Prince of Salina died in Florence in 1885. Augustus Hare did not think much of the Trinacria in 1883: 'A beautiful sea view, but cold rooms, with north aspect and very high ceilings: the hotel has greatly declined as to comfort and management, but is comparatively cool in summer.'

CHAPTER EIGHTEEN (pages 261–281)

1 Grayshott took five years to convert and must have ended by looking vastly different from what it was in Tennyson's day. Ingham, however, only put in two bathrooms, one being for the servants.

2 Giacomo Medici had died on 9 March 1882 at the Albergo Quirinale, Rome.

3 'On no other Phoenician site, perhaps, are so many ruins of an important fortified city still to be found standing in *situ* at the present day as at Motya. Once overcome and destroyed . . . Motya apparently ceased to exist as a town, and such of its ruins as were allowed to remain . . . were covered up by the protecting soil and débris, and have probably thus remained, untouched by the hand of man, until the present day. In this lies the great archaeological interest and importance of the site.

'San Pantaleo . . . has been visited from time to time by archaeologists and those interested in ancient history, but its ruins have never before been systematically excavated. The old name of Motya, which for so many centuries had lapsed into oblivion, is, however, gradually coming into use again.' (Joseph I. S. Whitaker)

4 'Sfoga la tua brutalità sul corpo mio, o bruto.'

5 London, 1887, translated from the Swedish by Maude Valérie White.

6 Sperlinga was acquired in 1883–4. It was here that Joss had intended to build his house, but on the death of his father and the opening up of the Via Cavour he instead built the *palazzo* with the Venetian front.

7 The Villa Favard is now the Facoltà di Scienze Economiche e Commerciale. It was built in 1857 by the architect Giuseppe Poggi. Described in *Italian Architecture 1750–1914* by Carroll L. V. Meeks (New Haven and London, 1966).

8 Tina kept a press cutting describing her Worth dress. She wore 'a skirt of satin Merveilleux rose crevette, draped with crêpe de Chine and tulle, and buillonnés of crêpe fastened here and there with bouquets of roses of various shades and ox-eyed daisies; the bodice and train, rose crevette, were damask silk broché, with raised bouquets of shaded roses and large daisies; the bodice was also trimmed with crêpe de Chine, with a bouquet of roses and daisies on one shoulder.' She also carried in her hand a bouquet of shaded roses and marguerites.

9 Ernest Augustus Perceval, grandson of Spencer Perceval, the Prime Minister assassinated in 1812.

10 Donna Laura's first husband, who had died in 1863, had been the Prince of Cam-

poreale. Minghetti died in 1886. Her dates were 1829–1915. She had once set her cap at Sir James Hudson, the British Minister in Turin, but he – then a bachelor – had rejected her. She described her marriage to Minghetti as 'un giorno di scirocco'.

[11] *Embassies of Other Days* (London, 1923). Donna Laura, who was unable to speak English, when excited would 'intoxicate herself with her own words'. For Lady Paget (1839–1929), the only thing in her favour seemed to be that she was a good musician and sang Neapolitan songs. Minghetti looked very much the professor, was generally dressed in black broadcloth from head to foot, his white face and hair a strange contrast. His eloquence was enchanting and, in contrast to his wife, he gave an impression of *naïveté* and innocence.

[12] Grosskurth.

[13] 'She was vulgar, earthy and addicted bad company'; valuable objects had a habit of disappearing during her séances (Gauld).

[14] 'So accurate and up to date were his writings at that time that this will for long remain the standard work on that country.' (David Bannerman writing in *The Ibis* January 1937)

[15] The phylloxera aphides, or plant-lice, came originally from America, but the French wine industry was in turn saved by the introduction of American vines.

[16] The Royal College of Surgeons had censured Mackenzie in January 1889 for writing *Frederick the Noble*, a justification for his hardly polished part in the violent and unseemly quarrel with jealous German doctors.

[17] *Old Diaries.*

[18] Gower's dates were 1845–1916. By 'one of those aristocratic arrangements common to Whigs and Tories' he was M.P. for Sutherlandshire from 1867–74, but he rarely opened his mouth in Parliament. He was a Trustee of the National Gallery and of Shakespeare's Birthplace.

[19] Information the late Mr Luke Fildes.

[20] *Things I Shouldn't Tell.* Perrin had been working on the American stand at the Universal Exhibition in Paris when Gower had induced him to desert from the army. After a while Gower had grown tired of him (admittedly, judging by the Prince Hal statue, Perrin did not look all that intelligent). People were sorry for the poor boy, including the Duke of Teck. Perrin had himself photographed in evening dress, put a big mourning band round the photograph and sent it to Gower at San Remo, with a note attached: 'When you receive this I shall be dead.' Then he swallowed some poison, put a slop pail by his bed, cut his wrist and bled himself to death.

[21] Patti's début was in *Lucia* in New York on 24 November 1859. The critics did not agree with Strakosch. 'She took the house by storm; she not only sang as only she can sing, but looked lovely and acted well. Though a little timid at first, she showed her great dramatic powers in the Mad Scene.' Melba had signed a ten years contract with Strakosch in 1887. The story of her breaking the contract in Brussels to sing in *Hamlet* and Strakosch's lucky (for her) death, is told in her memoirs, *Melodies and Memories* (London, 1925). She made her first appearance as Ophelia in *Hamlet* at the Paris Opera House on 8 May 1889. It was in 1890 that she met the Duke of Orléans, an encounter that led to her husband petitioning for divorce.

CHAPTER NINETEEN (pages 282–306)

[1] Pip published an article in *The Ibis* (1899) pp. 502–5, on the first breeding of Purple

Gallinules in captivity, at Malfitano. Purple Gallinules were often then to be seen, half tame, with the fowls in Sicilian backyards.

2 Tamagno had scored his first success in Palermo, in *Un Ballo in Maschera*. His tour of South America was a fabulous success and he appeared often at Covent Garden and the Scala. His greatest performance was in *Otello* at the Scala in 1887: a performance which has gone down to history as unsurpassable.

3 Franca's father had been one of the sparks in the Türr division.

4 Mrs William Hulton wrote on 15 November how she 'went to see Marchesa Spinola where we heard Mrs Whitaker sing a *Romanza* by a new Sicilian composer – very modern Italian style, rather vulgar. She also sang an aria from *Cavalleria Rusticana* – too dramatic for a drawing room!' (information Lady Berwick).

5 Notarbartalo was born in 1834. In 1860 he had been on the *Charles and Jane*. He was mayor of Palermo from 1873–5, when the Teatro Massimo was started. The following year he became Director General of Bank of Sicily but was dismissed when he tried to reform the corrupt *Comitato* of the Bank. In 1882 he had been kidnapped by five brigands and ransomed for 51,000 *lire*.

6 *The Ibis* 1894, pp. 78–100, and 1895, pp. 85–106.

7 1813–95. 'Lacaita looks and speaks like an English gentleman. For a man who has never been in England, his English is wonderful', Senior wrote in 1851, the year in which Lacaita was imprisoned by King Bomba. Napier wrote from Scotland to George Fagan in Naples: 'I heard of Lacaita's arrest and liberation the same week. You may conceive our distress and surprise. I have intelligence of my sister's confinement the same day, but of the two deliveries I must confess Lacaita's from the womb of jail was the most gratifying' (information Keith Fagan). Lacaita owed his knowledge of English to Enos Throop, the American Chargé d'Affaires at Naples whom he first met in 1838. He subsequently became legal adviser to the British embassy there; hence his friendship with Temple. He was with Minto in 1856–7, and Cavour tried to get him to stop Garibaldi going into Calabria in 1860.

8 Janet Ross (1842–1927) had been living in Florence since 1867. As a girl she had mixed with Tennyson, the Carlyles and Thackeray. Meredith was supposed to have been in love with her. In Egypt she had been *The Times* correspondent. By 1894 she had published four books, among the best known being *The Land of Manfred* (1889).

9 Mme Zola was *née* Alexandrine Melez (1839–1925). In the Goncourt Journals one reads how pleased Mme Zola was, on her return from Rome, to have been treated with a politeness accorded to society women, something to which she was not accustomed.

10 Crispi died in 1901. In 1896 he was already beginning to fail. Giolitti and the leader of the Leftists, under Cavalotti, had launched a virulent attack on his private life, reviving the charge of bigamy. He had also been accused of implication in the Banca Romana affair. When he took libel proceedings against Giolitti, the latter once more withdrew abroad for a 'rest'.

11 No confirmation of this dire suspicion of Carini being poisoned has ever been brought to light.

12 Pip went on a short trip along the coast to Sousse in the spring of 1897 (*The Ibis* 1898, pp. 125–132). He was mainly concerned with egg-collecting, though many birds were slaughtered. 'I secured the hen-bird [*saxicola moesta*] in each instance, after having seen her enter and leave her nest-hole, and in two of the cases I shot what was presumably

the cock-bird as well. I doubt the male parent taking much, if any, part in the incubation of the eggs.'

[13] Berenson was in the full flush of obtaining masterpieces from British collections for Isabella Stewart Gardner: Titian's *Europa* (£20,000); a Rembrandt self-portrait (£3000); a Botticelli (£3000).

[14] Symonds' daughter Madge was then the great friend of Mrs Ross's niece, Lina Duff Gordon, later Waterfield, and came to stay at the Rosses' house, Poggio Gherardo, after her father's death.

[15] When Ouida was thirty-two, her attention had been fixed on Mario de Candia. The fact that he was living with Grisi as husband and wife made no difference to her. Mario, however, did not return her advances.

[16] *In My Tower.*

[17] The Favignana villa was nearly as odd as their fashionable Palermo villino, finished by Basile in 1902: a mad Bluebeard's châlet.

[18] Mrs Minto Elliot was the author of *The Diary of an Idle Woman in Sicily* (which included an account of a visit to Maniace) and other sprightly works, under the name of Frances Elliot.

[19] Alick Yorke, 1847–1911.

[20] Alec Hood, 1854–1937.

[21] Frank Hird, 1873–1937.

[22] Frank Hird was known to the Anglo-American set in Rome as 'the post-boy', because of his youth (Lucas).

[23] Fassini eventually amassed a large fortune and was responsible for 'launching' Capri and Ischia. He also dabbled in cinemas.

[24] Wilde arrived in Palermo on 2 April.

[25] The planting of American vines continued 1921–4. As women did the picking of the grapes, production of wine was not appreciably reduced during the Great War years.

## CHAPTER TWENTY (pages 307–335)

[1] Hammerfield had belonged once to James Nasmyth (d. 1890), the inventor of the steam-hammer, hence the 'Hammer' in the name of the house.

[2] Farnborough Hill was built in the 1860s for Thomas Longman the publisher.

[3] During the expeditions to Tunisia Pip had also obtained specimens of the then rare Addox antelope which he presented to the Natural History Museum, South Kensington. He subsequently acquired Lord Lilford's collection of 5000 bird skins and added it to his own, bringing the total to 11,000 (*Rivista italiana di ornitologia*, year VII, series II, 1937, article by Carlo Orlando). Five sub-species of birds were named after him. Ronny Gower left an account of a dinner of 'bird-fanciers' with Pip: 'I sat between Pip and the Chairman, old Mr Philip Sclater [editor of *The Ibis*, erstwhile Secretary of the Zoological Society] who my host said had been responsible for making him take up ornithology as a "hobby", a pleasant old boy though very deaf. Much discussion after dinner, when some dead specimens were exhibited and passed round the table – an albatross among others. A poor little live finch, or some other small bird, was also exhibited, which one would have thought would have been none the better for the smoke of a score of cigars. We dined at 7 and left at 10.' The walls of the Villino were decorated with several trophies, including the heads of ibex shot by Umberto I and a fallow deer shot by Victor Emmanuel II.

[4] 'An arab on horseback appeared, warning us that we were to be attacked by the Wafella tribe. He tried to persuade our men to abandon us, and to leave the two Christians to their fate. . . . The next day, through field glasses, we saw numerous arabs hiding behind bushes in a valley through which we were about to pass. We immediately changed our route.' Dodson had also experienced danger when in Morocco for Pip in 1896, among the warring tribes of the Lower Atlas.

[5] Robert Hichens, 1864–1956.

[6] A Sicilian journalist wrote of Norina and Delia that very month in more flowery language as: 'Two tender, fair creatures, fragrant as corollas, evanescent as two shafts of light that might secretly have escaped from a dewy, Springlike canvas by Sandro Botticelli.'

[7] Franca had also given birth to a stillborn child. Two children, daughters, survived.

[8] Edward had suggested that he should visit Germany in March 1904 but had been told that the Kaiser had to go to the Mediterranean as he was recovering from an illness. In the end they met at Kiel in July, an encounter which was considered a great success.

[9] The senior member of this group was Otto Géleng, an artist who came to Taormina in 1863 and has ever since been regarded as its first tourist; it is not known whether he was in fact a real 'barone'. Wilhelm von Glöden and Karl Stempel were however bona fide barons. Von Glöden was a famous photographer, whose pictures of fauns and satyrs in Homeric dress, or undress, can still be bought as postcards in Taormina today. The Kaiser attempted to visit his studio in the spring of 1905 but was rebuffed, because of a quarrel many years previously with von Glöden's stepfather, Hammerstein. Edward VII was more fortunate and allowed access the following year. He even bought some nude photographs. All three 'baroni' lived to a great age. Other leading lights were Lord Stopford and 'King Carlo' Wood (American), also known as Woodo, a 'painter of the almond blossom type' (Tina). In 1910 Robert Hichens had the distinction of being the first to drive a motor car up to Taormina.

[10] Lady Currie was nicknamed *La violette fanée* by people in Tina's set.

[11] The Grand Hotel had opened in 1894. It still retains its aura of late Victorian luxury living, with 181 bedrooms.

[12] Lady Paget wrote the usual account of this visit. She soon realised that everybody was terrified lest she would mention the subject of birds to His Holiness. The audience room was packed, a 'regular Cook's tourist business'. She managed at least to kiss his ring, but immediately afterwards he 'galloped' away, with every sign of fear and agitation.

[13] See Teresa's *Memoirs*.

[14] The Duchess Massimo, according to Sir Rennell Rodd, was a 'living protest against social innovation'.

[15] Sharp was indeed the same as Fiona Macleod. He died and was buried at Maniace in December that year.

[16] Gina Lollobrigida starred in an idealised film of Cavalieri's life: *La Donna più Bella nel Mondo*.

[17] Josephine Curtis had been brought up in Paris by her much older sister who had married the Marquis de Talleyrand. It is said that she considered her Italian marriage quite a *mésalliance*.

[18] Seton-Watson.

[19] Mack Smith.

[20] Baron Rousseau was going as Minister to Bolivia. His title was a Napoleonic

creation. He ruled his family and his wife, who was twenty years younger than him, with maximum strictness, so much so that his son ran away from home.

²¹ *Contessone* = big fat countess. *Il* because of her masculine appearance.

²² Tina brought Gwen Whitaker, the twenty-two-year-old daughter of Pip's favourite brother Arthur, to the reception. In 1906 Gwen married Claude Charlton, grandson of the Ensign Charlton who had visited Palermo in 1807.

²³ Rhodes. As for the Casati, she was an amazing creature too, eccentric and beautiful. Robert Hichens thought she looked serpentine, and she certainly was interested in keeping snakes as pets. Once at the Grand Hotel a fellow-guest was startled to find his bath 'occupied by a large serpent', belonging to the Marchesa.

²⁴ The Duchess had married Michelangelo Caetani, Duke of Sermoneta in 1872, as his third wife. Born in 1804, he was a remarkable figure, both politically and in the arts, with a prodigious memory. He went blind in 1865, but in 1870 was elected President of the provisional Government in Rome; it was said that he could recite the whole of the *Inferno* by heart. He died in 1882. The third Duchess wrote his biography (*Alcuni ricordi di Michelangelo Caetani*, Milan 1904), in which she made some disparaging remarks about a certain Georgiana Bland, 'la brutta Miss Bland', the ugly Miss Bland, who was having a flirtation with Michelangelo in 1827. As that Miss Bland was the great-great-grandmother of the author of this book, he cannot help reading Tina's reference to the 'Ugly' Duchess with a certain amount of *Schadenfreude*.

²⁵ Lady Pirbight had a lobster-coloured wig, was plump and covered with masses of valuable jewellery.

²⁶ A version of this story appears in *The Glitter and the Gold* by Consuelo Vanderbilt Balsan (London, 1953), but —— appears as an 'alluring American girl'. Here the Crown Prince was infatuated with her, and the ring was one that had been given to him by his mother for first communion.

²⁷ Princess Marie Louise was the daughter of Princess Christian and granddaughter of Queen Victoria. Her marriage to Prince Aribert of Anhalt was dissolved in 1891.

²⁸ Later Prince Louis became Marquess of Milford Haven and assumed the surname of Mountbatten. He was grandson-in-law of Queen Victoria.

²⁹ The Prince of Camporeale was Laura Minghetti's son. In 1888 he had married a Bostonian, Florence Binney Kingsland.

³⁰ Dearest Madame Tina, *Capodimonte, 2 April 1906*

I wanted to write yesterday but from the moment I entered this house (at 8.30 a.m.) till the hour of bed (11.30 p.m.) I had not one quiet minute interim to call my soul and weary bones my own. And now that I have taken up my pen to try and send you some of all the grateful devotion in my heart, I feel how inadequate any words, etc. etc. . . . We tumbled and pitched from the very moment we left till we were nearly in Naples harbour. . . . At two o'clock we drove to the races, where we stood and walked from 2.30 to 6. More presentations to the inevitable Queen's Ladies. I wish that the Almighty had never created them. . . . It's so amusing hearing the Neapolitan view of Palermo and its society. Everyone here seems in love with Princess Trabia, and poor Donna Franca is only 'that *pauvre enfant*' – the two husbands in question are not viewed with favour, especially Florio. There have been many enquiries on the part of the Duke regarding you. Oh how happy Hélène and he are together. It does one good to see them and their delicious children. . . .

Your devoted friend Louie

[31] Most of the chief sporting events – the famous Targa Florio, the *Giro ciclistico di Sicilia*, the *gare aviatorie* [air displays] were due to the initiative of Vincenzo Florio. The Florios were behind the Automobile Club and the *Società Ippica*, and they also organised the *Corsi dei fiori* [parades of carriages covered with flowers in the Favorita].

[32] The firm of Fratelli Jung had been founded in 1867 and traded at first in sulphur. Later it dealt in liquorice, essential oils, nuts etc. Guido Jung, always a close friend of the Whitakers, died a bachelor in 1949.

[33] As Ackie's daughter remarked, if the Morrisons were merchants, what were the Whitakers? And wasn't Ackie's husband their second cousin?

[34] Tina had had a quarrel with Emmie, who 'stormed' at her for saying 'many cruel unkind things' about an unspecified person, presumably Maude.

[35] Marquis Giulio della Cerda, married to Carolina di Niscemi.

[36] Sandra had been operated on for cancer in May 1906 and left him in January 1907 when he started an affair with Giuseppina Mancini. In 1917 she became a Prioress. In 1930 she founded the Carmel du Reposoir. She died in 1931. Her story has been told in full by Lucy Napoli Prato in *Tre abiti bianchi per Alessandra* (Milan, 1954).

[37] Hamilton had introduced Henry James to George du Maurier and in 1879 James had taken Hamilton to meet Turgenev.

[38] Nevertheless Consuelo Vanderbilt obtained a divorce from the ninth Duke of Marlborough in 1920. Gladys Deacon married him in 1921; Bernard Berenson had a soft spot in his heart for Gladys (*Forty Years with Berenson* by Nicky Mariano, London and New York, 1966) and she was Proust's 'Miss Foster'.

[39] The table, laid for seventeen, was decorated with white roses and lilies, with silver plates and rose-tinted Baccarat glasses. The menu consisted of *croustades* of macaroni *à la Nantes*, cold fish *à la Ecossaise*, lamb cutlets *à la Villeroy*, roast turkey, Russian salad, *pêches Hélène*, strawberries, *fichi d'India*, melon, *cassata à la Sicilienne*.

## CHAPTER TWENTY-ONE (pages 336–368)

[1] Like Jan Kubelik, a pupil of Ševčik, Vivien Chartres had made her début in Prague at the age of nine.

[2] *Vicious Circle* by Francis Bamford and Viola Bankes. I am indebted to this book for many details about the case.

[3] Hobson. The story is repeated in *The Other Love: An Historical and Contemporary Survey of Homosexuality in Britain* by H. Montgomery Hyde (London, 1970; in America *The Love that Dared Not Speak Its Name*, Boston, 1970). Montgomery Hyde also outlined the story in his *Cases that Changed the Law* (London, 1951), but in this the name of Shackleton was not even mentioned. The jewels had originally been the property of Lady Conyngham, George IV's mistress. There had been a famous homosexual scandal at Dublin Castle in 1884. It possibly was responsible for Labouchere's last-minute interference in the Criminal Law Amendment Act, making male gross indecency in private punishable by hard labour and thus creating the climate of homosexual terror that later made it impossible to proceed in the Crown Jewels affair. It is ironical that Labouchere and his daughter, Dora Rudinì, should have been so friendly with men whose lives were distorted by this Act.

[4] Edward Legge, *More About King Edward* (London, 1913).

[5] A distinguished writer on Egypt and Russia, ex Director of the Foreign Department

of *The Times*, a future groom-in-waiting to both Edward VII and George V, and a bachelor.

[6] A reference to the Duke of Abruzzi's journey to the North Pole. He had climbed Mt Ruwenzori in 1906.

[7] Nasi died in 1939 at Erice, where a statue has been raised with a defiantly eulogistic inscription.

[8] *Castle in Italy.*

[9] A version of this story appears in *My Memories of Six Reigns* by Princess Marie Louise (London, 1956).

[10] Fabrizio Alliata of Pietratagliata. The late Archibald Colquhoun, translator of *The Leopard*, would say that the Alliatas claimed descent from the Sun God. Like the Settimos they were originally a Northern Italian merchant family (they came from Genoa, the Settimos from Pisa). They arrived in Palermo in the fifteenth century and in the sixteenth acquired land and were ennobled.

[11] When Robert Woodhouse came to Marsala, he found casks of wine standing in the *baglio* that had been there since 1818. They had never been 'bunged up', so the wine was still good.

[12] Maud Allan, a Canadian, was the unfortunate victim of the 'Black Book' Trial in May 1918, when she and her producer unsuccessfully sued Noel Pemberton Billing after his remarks concerning her plans to dance 'The Dance of the Seven Veils' from *Salomé*. Lord Alfred Douglas was one of the most vocal witnesses at the Trial.

[13] 'Poor Tina,' a relative said, 'a young man had only to smile at Norina and she would start saying: "Do you think he's interested? Should we stay on a little longer?" '

[14] 'A quarter of an hour after the earthquake there was a seaquake, and while those who could were trying to escape, with ruins falling about their heads, their feet entangled in wires, stumbling into holes, a huge wall of sea rushed up into the town with a roar. It was pitch dark. Just before people on the ships could hear hundreds of voices on the quay calling for boats. But now there was a dead silence, the most awful moment in that terrible half hour. Not a scream for help, the wave had sucked them all in and covered them with débris. Then fire broke out, the gas mains caught light, and heaps of broken furniture fed the flames.

'There was a famine of food and water, aqueducts of course being broken. Men were fighting and committing murder for a piece of bread. Many went mad. The looting and pillage! For which soldiers shot at sight.'
(A letter from the Rev. Canon Skeggs, British chaplain at Palermo.)

[15] Huleatt was 'One of those men of transparent goodness and abounding human brotherhood' – *Sicily* by Spencer C. Musson (London, 1911). For other descriptions of the disaster see *Sicily in Shadow and Sun* by Maude Howe (Boston 1910, London 1911); *Sicily Past and Present* by Ashley Brown (London and New York, 1928); *Messina prima e dopo il disastro*, anonymous (Messina, 1914).

[16] *My Recollections* by the Countess of Cardigan (London, 1909).

[17] Catherine Walters. She flourished in the 1860s. Her nickname came from the time when she had a drunken quarrel with some Guards officers and said she would knock them down like a 'row of bloody skittles'.

[18] Bamford and Bankes.

[19] Bamford and Bankes.

[20] *Cappiddazzu*, Sicilian word for a large hat. It was Delia who gave this name to the

spot, about a hundred yards from the north gate and probably the site of the principal and most recent buildings on Motya. The 'Cappiddazzu' was supposed to be the ghost of an old hermit, wearing a hat, who haunted the island. It has usually been assumed that excavations here did not seriously begin until April 1913.

[21] The third sister, Teresa, married Baron Piccolo and was the mother of Lucio Piccolo, the Sicilian poet and intimate of his cousin Giuseppe Lampedusa.

[22] We read elsewhere that Alick Yorke liked to wear buttonholes of 'large geraniums and yellow jasmine'.

[23] Marguerite Chapin, 1880–1958. She met Roffredo in Paris, where she had been studying music with Jean de Reske. Roffredo was also musical and a composer. *Botteghe Oscure* was founded in 1948, with Giorgio Bassani as literary director. The first extract from *Il Gattopardo* (*The Leopard*) appeared in its pages. She also published Alberto Moravia, Carson McCullers, Truman Capote, Tennessee Williams, Elizabeth Bowen, Bertolt Brecht, James Agee, Theodore Roethke and W. H. Auden, and the first version of *Under Milk Wood*.

[24] *Yesterday* (1947).

[25] A more recent theory is that the *cothon* might have been a sacred fishpond. When Pip came to Motya it was being used as a saltpan.

[26] The reorganisation of the Woodhouse firm was shortly to be delegated to Fred's two sons. This was under way when war broke out and both had to leave on active service.

[27] Salsomaggiore, in the foothills of the Appenines near Fidenza, had become fashionable because of its saline springs, full of iodine.

[28] Auletta died in 1943, unmarried.

[29] Hichens added:

It is a world struggling in its beginnings. The Russian ballet has turned smart London into a fancy ball. We dance furiously on the edge of – what? The King and Queen are working desperately hard, poor things. The Suffragettes are half demented now. But who cares? The picture papers contain nothing but pictures of girls with saucer eyes and nearly naked men. Carpentier [the boxer] is our only hero. I have never before seen England in such a curious condition.

[30] J. I. S. Whitaker, *La grande guerra: Inghilterra e Germania – L'Italia* (Palermo, December 1914).

## CHAPTER TWENTY-TWO (pages 371–395)

[1] Boots' nickname came from the Sicilian *Bibbuzza* (Baby).

[2] *Castle in Italy*.

[3] General Luigi Cadorna (1850–1928), son of General Raffaele Cadorna (1815–97).

[4] The Villa Sofia had a small ballroom. As Malfitano was laid out on the grand scale, entertainments there tended to be organised accordingly.

[5] Her letters were privately printed in Florence by her sister Countess Bona Gigliucci in 1965, under the title of *Nerina, un'antologia*.

[6] Giovanni Caprì.

[7] Giacomo De Martino, ambassador in London 1920–2, in Washington 1925–32.

[8] He was indeed Hungarian, a Serene Highness which made him much grander than his genuinely Italian Odescalchi relatives.

[9] The copyright in Wagner's operas had expired in 1913. The war years and ensuing

inflation had been diastrous for the family. Tina's statement is difficult now to verify, even at Bayreuth. The festivals started again in 1924. Siegfried Wagner, who was looking after his mother, received an 'honorary royalty' in 1925 and in 1927–30. The diary entry may also have been an oblique reference to Isolde von Bülow's unsuccessful, though obviously valid, claim that she was really Wagner's daughter (she died in 1921). Blandine, who was older, has usually been regarded as a genuine daughter of von Bülow.

[10] Filippo De Filippi, great friend of Mrs Ross, was inclined to be excitable and argumentative, especially when drunk. He had accompanied the Duke of Abruzzi on various expeditions. Although not fascist, he renounced his British knighthood during Sanctions.

[11] Queen Marie was the daughter of Prince Alfred, Duke of Edinburgh and Saxe-Coburg-Gotha, son of Queen Victoria.

[12] Pace's dates were 1889–1955. He became Undersecretary at the Ministry of Education. At various times he was professor at Palermo, Pisa, Naples and Rome Universities. His main work was *Arte e Civiltà della Sicilia* in several volumes.

[13] Carolina Lampedusa died in January 1924, aged eighty-two, and Concetta in September 1930, aged eighty-six. They lived in the pink-washed Villa Lampedusa near Terrerosse and tried to add to their income by selling titles.

[14] Son of the Nobel Prize-winning Emil Theodor Kocher, pioneer in the treatment of goitre by the removal of the thyroid gland.


## CHAPTER TWENTY-THREE (pages 396–418)

[1] Edith Somerville to her sister, when she visited Maniace with Ethel Smythe in February 1920; quoted in *Somerville and Ross* by Maurice Collis (London, 1968). Alec Hood's father had made the first carriage road to Maniace in 1873, and soon afterwards the alterations to the castle were begun; a garden was laid out and orange groves planted. Alec's many guests included Hamilton Aïdé, Mrs Lynn Linton, Lady Paget, Mrs Minto Elliot, Alfred Austin, Jessie White Mario (a 'tiresome Englishwoman who invited herself') and D. H. Lawrence. He divided his time in Sicily between Maniace and his villa in Taormina. His sister, Rosa Evans, 'in a gorgeous chestnut wig and pearls, as big as eggs' (Somerville), lived with him.

[2] Harold Nicolson, *King George V: His Life and Reign* (London, 1952).

[3] Her husband, Roberto, was the great-great-grandson of Ettore Lucchesi-Palli and the Duchess of Berry. Della Grazia was a Campofranco title.

[4] P. Morton Shand wrote of marsala in *A Book of Other Wines – than French* (London, 1929): '. . . To most people rather common, almost a caretaker's wine', sometimes with only 8° alcohol. But he did praise Florio's Gold Label '1850'.

[5] The inhabitants of Piana dei Greci were descended from Albanians, refugees from the Turks, and still belonged to the Greek Orthodox religion. Victor Emmanuel visited the village in 1922. On entering their church, the tiny king found himself suddenly lost in the crowd and hustled to a font. A baby was thrust into his arms and in a trice Victor Emmanuel was named godfather. The baby was Don Ciccio's.

[6] Ashley Brown, *Sicily Past and Present* (London, 1928).

[7] The 'corporative state' had been inaugurated by Rocco in April 1926. The 160 syndicates of workers and employers were the basis of this structure, and at the top was the Ministry of Corporations.

[8] Gualino transferred the Woodhouse firm to Cinzano. A new company, comprising

Ingham Whitaker, Florio and Woodhouse, was formed, called SAVI, *Società Anonima Vinicola Italiana.*

⁹ Senator Giuseppe Pitrè, 1841–1923, physician, the great writer on Siciliana and President of the Academy in Palermo.

¹⁰ 1935. A collection of his speeches and various writings, *Scritti e discorsi vari,* was published by Norina in 1938.

¹¹ Marquis Aldo Castellani (1877–1971), famous as a specialist in tropical medicine. His honorary KCMG was removed from him in 1940 but restored at the end of his life.

¹² Domenico Di Giorgio, known as Mimì, was indeed arrested for being an *amico degli amici,* i.e. a friend of the Mafia.

¹³ Gian Andrea Serrao (1883–1964). He was married to Giuseppina Sanderson, *née* Uffreduzzi, the singer; her first husband had been Willy Sanderson, Pip's first cousin. In 1924 Serrao had been knighted for his services to Britain before and during the Great War. Until 1940 he was legal adviser to the British Embassy (and so hardly discreet in this case).

¹⁴ Ashby died in May 1931. He had been Director of the British School in Rome from 1906–25.

¹⁵ The *Infanzia Abbandonata* still continues today (1972).

¹⁶ *The Ibis* 1910, pp. 331–353.

## CHAPTER TWENTY-FOUR (pages 421–453)

¹ Signora Cimino had been head of the *Unione delle Donne Italiane* in 1918.

² The Duke of Aosta died of T.B., a prisoner of war in Nairobi, on 3 March 1942.

³ Massoch.

⁴ Aprile's father was a Sicilian patriot, friend of Mazzini and five times Minister of Justice.

⁵ Colonel Fagà's sister-in-law was married to a Hopps of Mazara. The Hopps family was now Italian by nationality, but because of their English name their *baglio* and other property at Mazara were confiscated.

⁶ Norina's Di Giorgio niece was married to Sganga, the director-general of prisons.

⁷ General George S. Patton, *War as I Knew It* (Boston 1947; London, 1948).

⁸ John Leslie had been consulted by his friend Sir Orme Sargent, deputy Under Secretary at the Foreign Office in London, about a suitable place to bomb on the outskirts of Rome. He had recommended the Campo Verano cemetery – 'After all, you can't do any harm to people who are already dead, Moley.' Unfortunately the bombers were not very accurate and hit the basilica, which was just on the edge of the cemetery.

⁹ Giorgio Randegger, cousin of Guido Jung the Palermo merchant and great-nephew of Queen Victoria's master of music, Alberto Randegger, conductor and composer. He was the leading society doctor in Rome. In fact he had principally gone to the Villa Savoia to see Princess Mafalda, who had had a fall and was thought to have broken her knee. Until Sanctions he had been a British subject.

¹⁰ Prince Aimone had been made King of Croatia in 1941, but never went there.

¹¹ Filippo Doria had suffered much for his antifascism, ever since Sanctions; when he wrote to the then King, his heretical views were passed at once to Mussolini. Thus from the outbreak of war until the fall of Mussolini he had been in a concentration camp. On the night before the attempted arrest, a noise of knocking had been heard at the main door. Filippo, Princess Doria, their daughter Orietta and a friend hid in the archives room, whilst the butler opened the door. It was the Gestapo. After a peremptory search the

Germans left and – rather stupidly – said they would return the next morning, which provided plenty of time for an escape. Filippo, disguised as a priest, made for Trastevere, where he became one of the leading lights in helping escaped Allied prisoners. The Princess and Orietta hid elsewhere, dyeing their hair black. It was especially difficult to conceal Orietta, with her stately, fair, northern looks. An English-born Italian woman bravely went later to the palace to recover the Doria jewels, including the famous emeralds. The *palazzo* remained intact, but the contents of the Villa Doria on the Janiculum were looted or smashed.

[12] The Florios had been arrested in January and did not expect to return alive. Unable to get money out of Sicily, they had been selling valuables in order to live – something forbidden by the Germans. On her arrest Lucie tied up her jewels in a handkerchief and threw them into a courtyard outside. She then wrote a note to a friend to look for them; they were found and saved.

[13] Princess Ruffo had three sons, one of whom, Augusto, died at sea near Pescara in September 1943.

[14] As told to the author by Dr Randegger himself.

[15] Jack Whitaker was D.M.T. (Director of Military Training).

[16] On 27 May 1946 Manfred was totally exonerated by an Italian military tribunal.

[17] Tina wrote: 'A generation of sheep, now bitterly disillusioned, requires a firm hand and above all an united army. Do not give us up and trust us still.'

[18] *More Memories of an Aesthete* (London, 1970).

[19] 'The late Duchess' had been, for instance, translated as 'la tarda Duchessa', i.e. the tardy Duchess.

[20] Dolci.

[21] Acton.

[22] Since the arrival of the Allies the *Mafia* had had a new resurgence, the reason being that the Americans had put men of recent Sicilian extraction in positions of command – not realising that several were simply refugees from Mori's purge in the 1920s.

EPILOGUE (pages 455–462)

[1] Dr Virgilio Titone, after the murder of Pietro Scaglione, reported in *The Times*, 7 May 1971.

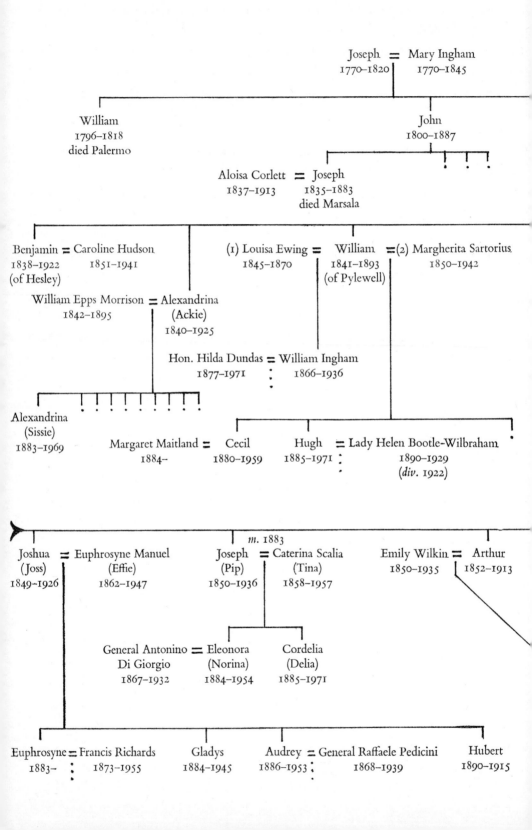

Joseph = Mary Ingham
1770–1820 | 1770–1845

William
1796–1818
died Palermo

John
1800–1887

Aloisa Corlett = Joseph
1837–1913    1835–1883
died Marsala

Benjamin = Caroline Hudson
1838–1922    1851–1941
(of Hesley)

(1) Louisa Ewing = William = (2) Margherita Sartorius
1845–1870    1841–1893    1850–1942
(of Pylewell)

William Epps Morrison = Alexandrina
1842–1895    (Ackie)
1840–1925

Hon. Hilda Dundas = William Ingham
1877–1971    1866–1936

Alexandrina
(Sissie)
1883–1969

Margaret Maitland = Cecil
1884–    1880–1959

Hugh = Lady Helen Bootle-Wilbraham
1885–1971    1890–1929
(div. 1922)

Joshua = Euphrosyne Manuel
(Joss)    (Effie)
1849–1926    1862–1947

m. 1883

Joseph = Caterina Scalia
(Pip)    (Tina)
1850–1936    1858–1957

Emily Wilkin = Arthur
1850–1935    1852–1913

General Antonino = Eleonora
Di Giorgio    (Norina)
1867–1932    1884–1954

Cordelia
(Delia)
1885–1971

Euphrosyne = Francis Richards
1883–    1873–1955

Gladys
1884–1945

Audrey = General Raffaele Pedicini
1886–1953    1868–1939

Hubert
1890–1915

# WHITAKER

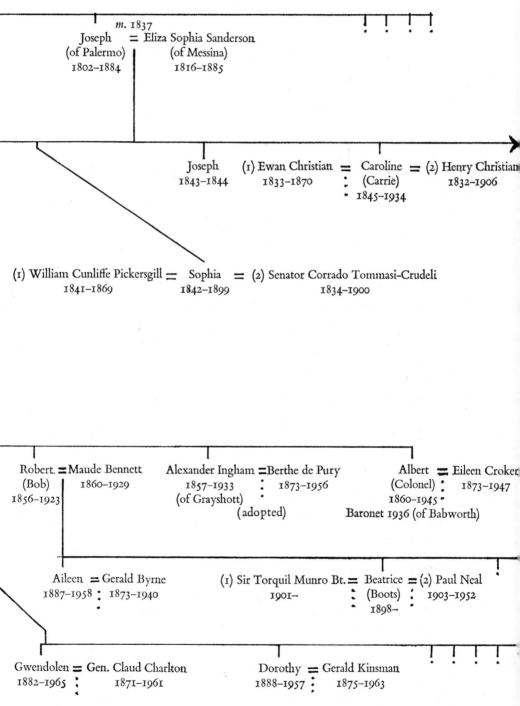

*m.* 1837

Joseph = Eliza Sophia Sanderson
(of Palermo)   (of Messina)
1802–1884   1816–1885

Joseph   (1) Ewan Christian = Caroline = (2) Henry Christian
1843–1844   1833–1870   (Carrie)   1832–1906
  1845–1934

(1) William Cunliffe Pickersgill = Sophia = (2) Senator Corrado Tommasi-Crudeli
1841–1869   1842–1899   1834–1900

Robert = Maude Bennett   Alexander Ingham = Berthe de Pury   Albert = Eileen Croker
(Bob)   1860–1929   1857–1933   1873–1956   (Colonel)   1873–1947
1856–1923   (of Grayshott)   1860–1945
  (adopted)   Baronet 1936 (of Babworth)

Aileen = Gerald Byrne   (1) Sir Torquil Munro Bt. = Beatrice = (2) Paul Neal
1887–1958   1873–1940   1901–   (Boots)   1903–1952
  1898–

Gwendolen = Gen. Claud Charlton   Dorothy = Gerald Kinsman
1882–1965   1871–1961   1888–1957   1875–1963

# TRABIA – BUTERA – SCALEA – MAZZARINO

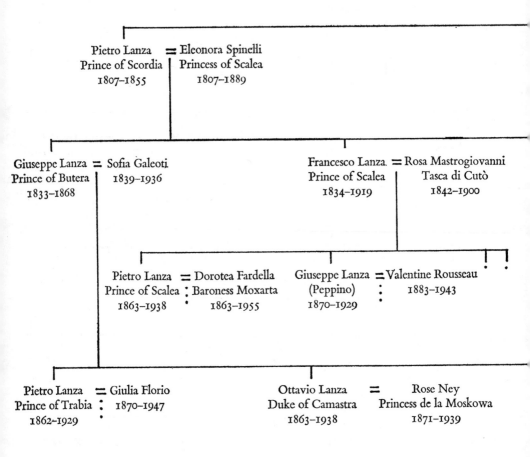

Pietro Lanza = Eleonora Spinelli
Prince of Scordia | Princess of Scalea
1807–1855 | 1807–1889

Giuseppe Lanza = Sofia Galeoti
Prince of Butera | 1839–1936
1833–1868

Francesco Lanza = Rosa Mastrogiovanni
Prince of Scalea | Tasca di Cutò
1834–1919 | 1842–1900

Pietro Lanza = Dorotea Fardella
Prince of Scalea : Baroness Moxarta
1863–1938 • 1863–1955

Giuseppe Lanza = Valentine Rousseau
(Peppino) : 1883–1943
1870–1929 •

Pietro Lanza = Giulia Florio
Prince of Trabia : 1870–1947
1862–1929 •

Ottavio Lanza = Rose Ney
Duke of Camastra | Princess de la Moskowa
1863–1938 | 1871–1939

*Author's Note on the Sicilian family trees*

I have consulted many books of reference in Sicily and have sometimes discovered small discrepancies in dates, particularly births, with those in the *Libro d'Oro* and the *Almanach de Gotha*. It has been suggested by a Sicilian friend that, in the past, certain persons as they got older advanced the dates of their births. The biggest mystery hangs over the two marriages of Stefania Branciforte in the Trabia-Butera tree; some books show her to be married to Wilding whilst Giuseppe Lanza was still alive, others show Wilding to be remarried whilst Stefania was still alive.

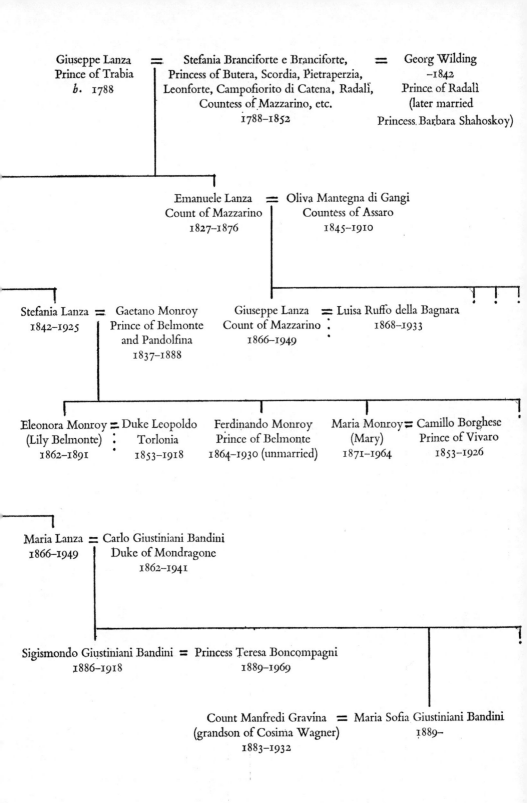

Giuseppe Lanza
Prince of Trabia
*b.* 1788
=
Stefania Branciforte e Branciforte,
Princess of Butera, Scordia, Pietraperzia,
Leonforte, Campofiorito di Catena, Radalì,
Countess of Mazzarino, etc.
1788–1852
=
Georg Wilding
–1842
Prince of Radalì
(later married
Princess Barbara Shahoskoy)

Emanuele Lanza
Count of Mazzarino
1827–1876
=
Oliva Mantegna di Gangi
Countess of Assaro
1845–1910

Stefania Lanza
1842–1925
=
Gaetano Monroy
Prince of Belmonte
and Pandolfina
1837–1888

Giuseppe Lanza
Count of Mazzarino
1866–1949
=
Luisa Ruffo della Bagnara
1868–1933

Eleonora Monroy
(Lily Belmonte)
1862–1891
=
Duke Leopoldo
Torlonia
1853–1918

Ferdinando Monroy
Prince of Belmonte
1864–1930 (unmarried)

Maria Monroy
(Mary)
1871–1964
=
Camillo Borghese
Prince of Vivaro
1853–1926

Maria Lanza
1866–1949
=
Carlo Giustiniani Bandini
Duke of Mondragone
1862–1941

Sigismondo Giustiniani Bandini
1886–1918
=
Princess Teresa Boncompagni
1889–1969

Count Manfredi Gravina
(grandson of Cosima Wagner)
1883–1932
=
Maria Sofia Giustiniani Bandini
1889–

# LAMPEDUSA – NISCEMI – FAVARA

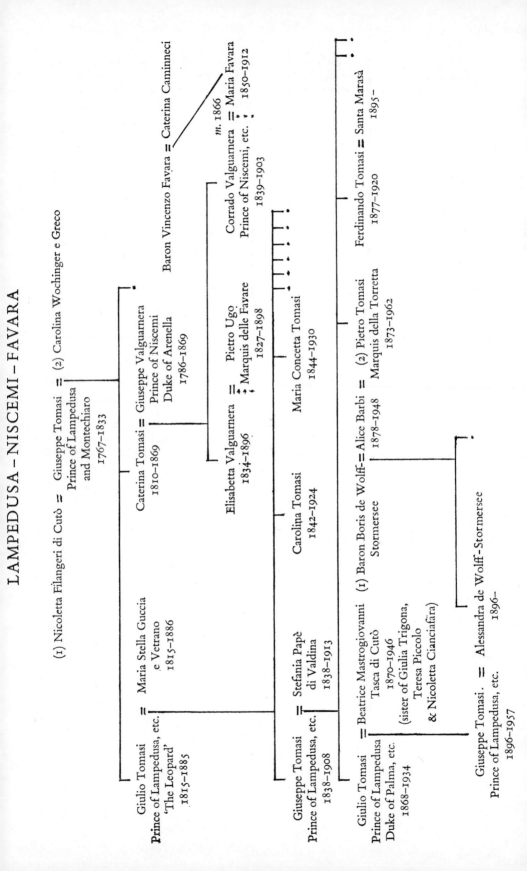

# Index

*Note:* Main references to women are usually under their married names, except in the case of the Whitaker family and where maiden names are more frequently used in the text. As regards Italian and Sicilian titles, one must plead mercy in the matter of disentangling correct form. Except in a few cases, surnames have been disregarded, and the individual has been indexed under the name most commonly used in the text, with appropriate cross references.